LATINO POLITICS IN AMERICA
Community, Culture, and Interests

FOURTH EDITION

John A. García
University of Michigan

Gabriel R. Sanchez
University of New Mexico

ROWMAN & LITTLEFIELD
Lanham • Boulder • New York • London

Acquisitions Editor: Jon Sisk
Editorial Assistant: Benjamin Knepp
Sales and Marketing Inquiries: textbooks@rowman.com

Credits and acknowledgments for material borrowed from other sources, and reproduced with permission, appear on the appropriate pages within the text.

Published by Rowman & Littlefield
An imprint of The Rowman & Littlefield Publishing Group, Inc.
4501 Forbes Boulevard, Suite 200, Lanham, Maryland 20706
www.rowman.com

6 Tinworth Street, London SE11 5AL, United Kingdom

Copyright © 2021 by The Rowman & Littlefield Publishing Group, Inc.
Third edition 2017. Second edition 2012. First edition 2003.

All rights reserved. No part of this book may be reproduced in any form or by any electronic or mechanical means, including information storage and retrieval systems, without written permission from the publisher, except by a reviewer who may quote passages in a review.

British Library Cataloguing in Publication Information Available

Library of Congress Cataloging-in-Publication Data
Names: García, John A., author. | Sanchez, Gabriel R., 1979- author.
Title: Latino politics in America : community, culture, and interests / John A. García, University of Michigan ; Gabriel R. Sanchez, University of New Mexico.
Description: Fourth edition. | Lanham : Rowman & Littlefield, [2022] | Includes bibliographical references and index.
Identifiers: LCCN 2020049485 (print) | LCCN 2020049486 (ebook) | ISBN 9781538144053 (hardcover) | ISBN 9781538144060 (paperback) | ISBN 9781538144077 (epub)
Subjects: LCSH: Hispanic Americans—Politics and government. | Political participation—United States. | Hispanic Americans—Social conditions. | Hispanic Americans—Ethnic identity. | Community life—United States.
Classification: LCC E184.S75 G367 2022 (print) | LCC E184.S75 (ebook) | DDC 973/.0468—dc23
LC record available at https://lccn.loc.gov/2020049485
LC ebook record available at https://lccn.loc.gov/2020049486

∞™ The paper used in this publication meets the minimum requirements of American National Standard for Information Sciences—Permanence of Paper for Printed Library Materials, ANSI/NISO Z39.48-1992.

Contents

List of Figures, Tables, and Boxes		v
Acknowledgments		ix
Acronyms		xiv
1	AN INTRODUCTION TO LATINO POLITICS	1
2	COMMUNITY BUILDING IN LATINO AMERICA	23
3	CULTURE AND DEMOGRAPHICS	41
4	LATINO SUBGROUPS IN THE UNITED STATES	63
5	THE POLITICS OF INTEREST AND CULTURE	87
6	LATINO POLITICAL PARTICIPATION	103
7	LATINOS IN THE ELECTORAL ARENA	129
8	LATINO ORGANIZATIONS AND LEADERSHIP	157
9	IMMIGRATION AND LATINO IMMIGRANTS	184
10	EDUCATION, HEALTH, AND VOTING RIGHTS POLICY	220
11	BUILDING POLITICAL ALLIANCES	252
12	THE LATINO COMMUNITY: GOING BEYOND RECOGNITION POLITICS	285
13	COVID PANDEMIC AND RACIAL JUSTICE MOVEMENTS	312

Glossary	319
References	330
Index	372

Figures, Tables, and Boxes

Figures

3.1	Forecast of the Latino Population of the United States, 2016–2060 (in millions)	44
3.2	Latinos in the United States by National Origin and Population Size	46
3.3	US Fertility Rate by Race and Origin of the Mother	49
3.4	Latinos' Foreign-Born Status over Time, 1970–2015	50
3.5	English Proficiency among Latinos, 1980–2015	52
3.6	High School Completion Rate among 18–24 Year Olds	55
3.7	Educational Attainment by Levels of Schooling, 1950–2016	55
3.8	Latino Household Income	57
3.9	Poverty Rates among Latino National-Origin Groups	59
3.10	Population of Millennials or Younger Represents 60 Percent of All Latinos	60
4.1	Largest Hispanic Origin Group by State, 2010	64
5.1	Label Choice among Five Major Latino Subgroups	90
5.2	How Hispanics Describe Themselves	91
5.3	Preference for "Latino" vs. "Hispanic"	91
6.1	Distribution of Generations as a Percentage of the Eligible Voters, 2000–2020	119
6.2	Proportion of Millennials' Share of the Major Racial and Ethnic Groups, 2016	120
7.1	Voter Turnout Rates of Naturalized Citizens	132
7.2	Percentage of US Latinos Eligible to Vote	133
7.3	Main Reasons Eligible Latinos Have Not Naturalized	134
7.4	Latino Midterm Turnouts	135
7.5	Voter Midterm Turnout Rate across Racial and Ethnic Groups, 1990–2018	137
8.1	Growing Racial and Ethnic Diversity in Congress	163
8.2	Unionization Rates among Mexican Immigrants and Other Foreign-Born Workers by Date of Arrival, 2004	174

8.3	Unionization Rates by Type of Worker: National Origin, Nativity, and Citizen Status, 2004	175
9.1	Growth of Immigrant Population, 1950–2010	195
9.2	Source Countries of Foreign-Born Immigrants, 2018 (in millions)	196
9.3	Resources Accessed by DACA Recipients	201
9.4	Saliency of Immigration as a Mobilizing Issue for Latinos	206
9.5	Annual Number of New US Citizens and Legal Permanent Residents, 1980–2016	209
10.1	Proportion of Latino Pre-K through 12th Grade and College Enrollment	224
10.2	Percentage of Latino Students Enrolled in 90 Percent+ Minority School	225
10.3	Most Important Issues Facing Latino Community That Politicians Should Address in the 2018 Election?	232
10.4	Proportion of Individuals Supporting Expansion of Health Care Coverage	233
10.5	Access to Affordable Health Care	234
10.6	Possession of State-Issued Photo ID by Race/Ethnicity Aggregation of All 20,000+ Respondents	248
11.1	Incidence of Discrimination and Support Experienced by Latinos by Generation	265
11.2	Incidence of Discrimination and Support Experienced by Latinos in the Past Year	268
11.3	Rate of Discrimination Based on Skin Tone	269
11.4	Has Trump Made You Feel Angry or Disrespected by Something He Has Said or Done?	283
12.1	Hispanic Population to Reach 111 Million by 2060	286
12.2	The South Has Seen the Nation's Biggest Latino Population Growth since 2008	287
12.3	States with Fastest-Growing Latino Populations, 2000-2014	289
12.4	Two-Thirds of Hispanic Adults Say Being Hispanic Is Part of Their Racial Background	291
12.5	Latino Share of US Electorate, 2020	295
12.6	Voter Turnout Rates, 1990–2018	295
12.7	Hispanic Voters' Disapproval of President Trump and Dissatisfaction with the Nation's Direction	299
12.8	Latino Registered Voters' Perception of Concern Shown by Democratic and Republican Parties, 2018	300
12.9	Identification among Americans with Hispanic Ancestry as Hispanic or Latino across Immigrant Generations	308
13.1	Most Important Educational Issues Government Should Address	315
13.2	Remedies Latino Parents and Grandparents Support for School Actions to Ensure a Safer Return	315
13.3	Latinos Who Have Experienced Incidents of Excessive Force by Law Enforcement	317

Tables

2.1	Latinos by Racial Selection in the 2010 Census	35
2.2	Race of Major Hispanic Ancestries	36
3.1	Hispanic and Latino Population by State, 2000–2017	43
3.2	Top Ten States with the Largest Percentage Latino Population Gains, 2000–2014	44
3.3	Foreign-Born Population from Latin America and the Caribbean by Country of Birth, 2010	51
6.1	Political Orientations among Minority Group Members in the CMPS	110
6.2	Arenas of Civic Engagement for CMPS Respondents by Race/Ethnicity	111
6.3	Number of Political Activities Engaged in by CMPS Respondents	112
6.4	CMPS Respondents' Assessment of the Importance of Different Political Activities	113
6.5	Range of Political Activities CMPS Respondents Engaged In by Gender and Nativity	115
6.6	Participation on Social Media and Civic and Political Engagement among CMPS Respondents in Percentages	117
6.7	Perceived Effectiveness by Percentages of CMPS Respondents of Different Political Tactics by Use of Social Media	117
6.8	How Social Media Influences More Political Involvement	121
6.9	Contacting Officials by Generation and Citizenship among Respondents to the Latino National Survey	121
7.1	Latino Vote Choice in the 2020, 2016, and 2012 Presidential Elections by Party ID, Gender, Nativity, and Dominant Language	140
8.1	Elected Latino Officials Serving in Congress by State, 1863–2021	159
8.2	Organizational Dimensions and Aspects of Latino Organizations	166
9.1	Immigration Policies for Reform by Support by Racial and Ethnic Groups	207
11.1	Extent of Affinity and Identification among Latinos in the CMPS	257
11.2	Sense of Feeling Positive or Not about One's Racial/Ethnic Group among CMPS Respondents	258
11.3	Extent of Agreement or Not among CMPS Respondents Regarding Spanish Language and Interests	259
11.4	Extent of Commonality (Affinity) among Latinos toward Immigrants, Minorities, and African Americans among CMPS Respondents	260
11.5	Extent of Connections with Immigrant and Minority Groups by Gender and Racial/Ethnic Group among CMPS Respondents	262
11.6	Connections with Immigrant and Minority Groups among CMPS Latinos, African Americans, and Asian Americans among CMPS Respondents	263

11.7	Perceived Extent of Discrimination for Racial and Ethnic Groups by CMPS Respondents	266
11.8	Latinos Respond to Factors Contributing to Discriminatory Treatment	267
11.9	Race/Ethnicity of Friendship Network by Generation and Citizenship	272
11.10	Race/Ethnicity of Coworkers by Generation and Citizenship	274
12.1	Age and Citizen Voting-Eligible Latinos, 2012–2030 (millions)	294

Boxes

1.1	Hostile Rhetoric, Hostile Climate, and the Latino Community	5
1.2	Citizenship Status on the 2020 US Census	8
4.1	The Changing Faces of Latino America	68
4.2	Puerto Rican Political Strategies: Changing Geography but Advocating Mainland and Island Issues	69
4.3	South American Latinos: Being Peruvians in the United States	80
4.4	The Colombian Community	84
5.1	Another Focus Group Vignette, 2006	97
6.1	Here Today We March, Tomorrow We Vote	107
7.1	Latinos and the 2014 Midterm Elections	137
7.2	A Latino's Cultural and Political World	152
8.1	Newer Latino Organizations Come Forward	178
8.2	Social Movements, Latinos, Immigration, and Organizational Elements	180
9.1	Immigration Policies and Developments, 2005–Present	185
9.2	Basis for Immigration Area Personal for Latinos	203
9.3	The Temporary Protected Status Story	204
9.4	Noncitizen Veterans and Trying to Realize Established Pathways toward Citizenship	212
11.1	The Collaborative Multiracial Post-Election Survey (CMPS)	254
11.2	Racial/Ethnic Coalitions in Los Angeles?	260
11.3	Latinos, across National Origin, Respond to Hurricane Maria and the 2020 Earthquakes	277
12.1	Immigrants and Latinos Bring Population Growth to Rural Communities	290

Acknowledgments

THROUGHOUT THE WRITING AND PRODUCTION of this rather unexpected fourth edition of *Latino Politics in America*, I began to acknowledge the meaning of the phrase "With age comes wisdom." The dynamism of Latinos has been ingrained in American life for a long time, and Latinos still exhibit a resilient energy and desire to improve the well-being and status of a complex set of communities. Latino/as' movement forward, even in times of polarization, fear, and negativism, can only improve America's social and political fabric. The inclusion of Gabriel Ramon Sanchez as my coauthor for this fourth edition is indicative of my evolving wisdom. While our connection spans nearly twenty years in a variety of personal and professional settings, it is Gabe's reputation as a significant contributor to Latino research and to the advancement of more generations of well-trained scholars that will keep this community moving forward. In addition, it is the strength and "rightness" of his character that brings to this fourth edition an enhanced, updated, and relevant perspective. There is a Tito Puente album titled *Una Combinacion Perfecta*; while this work is not perfect, it represents a combination of more than seventy years of research and teaching and brings together a great deal of attention, focus, interaction with, and involvement in the Latino community.

The challenge in writing a fourth edition of *Latino Politics in America* is that we must tackle dynamic communities in the middle of this new millennium in which strong political currents and changes are rapidly occurring. Changes made in the third edition were not modest; this version is no different. First, Latino politics epitomizes the interface of the internal dynamics of this vibrant set of national-origin and pan-ethnic communities with the American polity, which has a wider-ranging tone of rancor with governing as well as contested policy content than ever before. We must balance individual behaviors and attitudes with collective efforts and organizations when trying to understand a variety of social and partisan movements, loud and divisive public discourses, and political and economic institutions under siege, as well as when we're rethinking institutions and structural relationships. Secondly, the expansion and depth of knowledge production regarding Latinos and their political relationships has grown significantly.

Personally, I began my systematic analyses of the Mexican-origin community in 1967. Over the course of more than fifty years, I have accumulated direct research and experienced countless encounters with the Latino community in my efforts to pursue change and affect American society and its political system. Gabe and I have built a community of active and knowledgeable colleagues, friends, mentors, and practitioners along the way. Our in-depth discussions have resulted in new perspectives, reviewing key developments and new research approaches that help us understand and explain Latino experiences. Latino politics and Latino studies have continued to grow exponentially, theoretically, and empirically since the first edition of *Latino Politics in America*. As one of the senior members of this field, it is gratifying to see a new generation advancing the field and disseminating their results and interpretations in a wider array of publication outlets (both academic and popular). This more recent cohort of scholars has formed a dense social network in which members share, interact, and engage with one another's works and ideas. Our use of the Collaborative Multiracial Political Survey (CMPS) is an excellent example put forth by the current generation of scholars of Latino politics. As the senior member of this team, my longer perspective has included the belief that there is rarely anything *totally* new within our foundational knowledge base.

A broader scope and insightful understanding of Latino communities can affect the perception of the current American political system and confront prevailing myths. This would involve testing and extensions of prevalent models and theories as well as developing, challenging, and pursuing bolder ways to understand the complexities of politics, social identities, race/ethnicity, social change, and the expanding world of what is considered "political." For example, many Latinos are incorporating themselves into the American fabric while maintaining a sense of self with their own customs and traditions. While some observers and commentators have portrayed this as antithetical to the American ethos and culture, the Latino community has moved the discourse to include what it means to be an American and the distinctive manifestations of being Latino as part of the American fabric. This pattern raises questions as to the real bedrock of what being American means in terms of beliefs, values, and attachments.

A personal, but I think important, idea is in bridging the gaps of knowledge and communicating to all members of communities (i.e., academic, racial/ethnic, social groups, general publics, and globally). Knowledge, evidence, and discourse are valuable in opening lines of understanding and perspectives. As trained researchers, we have found that interactions with practitioners and various publics is a very integral part of linking knowledge with political and policy applications. In so doing, we can activate more participants in both public and intellectual discourses about the American political system and how Latinos are effecting change and visions. For many researchers of Latino politics, their passion lies in the pursuit of justice, equity, and effective civic and political engagement for Latino communities and the nation. This is done in combination with analytical rigor and standards of excellence in the projects in which we participate. A welcomed analytical and strategic advocacy on behalf of Latinos' experiences and conditions is evident in the works of contemporary scholars of Latino politics.

With Gabe Sanchez joining this effort, this "textbook" takes on a longer life (given that subsequent editions could follow) with the infusion of the growth and dynamism of his professional and personal development. We have included many of the post-2015 publications that have helped us present, analyze, and discuss the major and significant developments occurring. These are reflected in the text, figures, tables, boxes, and the expanded references section. I would encourage readers to explore in greater depth the articles and books listed in the references.

In a more traditional sense, the acknowledgments section cites individuals who had a bearing on the task of preparing such a publication. My exchanges at professional meetings and conferences with the scholars of Latino politics, whose works I have utilized, helped me to crystallize important themes and emphases. A big thanks to Luis Fraga, Rodney Hero, Matt Barreto, Valerie Martinez, Michael Jones-Correa, Alejandro Portes, Cecelia Menjivar, Michele Michaelson, Ruth Zambrana, Eduardo Bonilla-Silva, Gary Segura, and Clara Rodriquez. In acknowledging and thanking the contemporary Latino politics scholars, a partial list includes Efren Perez, Sophia Wallace, Heather Silber Mohamed, Chris Zepeda-Millan, Regina Branton, Edward Vargas, Betina Cutia Wilkinson, and Eric Juenke. There are so many graduate students I have worked with, formally and informally, who have also provided an invaluable infusion of ideas, challenges, and perspectives. We are grateful to the faculty who teach Latino Politics and provided Rowman & Littlefield such helpful insights about improving this edition. Professionally and personally, my experience in working with Rowman & Littlefield has been comfortable, supportive, and purposeful. In their resolve to promote works on race and ethnicity, we join other colleagues, such as Paula McClain and David Wilkins in their Spectrum series. A special note of appreciation goes out to Traci Crowell, who was editor of the third edition and instrumental in advocating for a fourth. While she was unable to see this effort to its completion, she was critical.

Moving more closely to my family, I wish to acknowledge my wife, Nancy Ellsworth García, who was reintroduced to the tedium of preparing the fourth edition. She read carefully all the revised chapters with a meticulous eye for clarity, consistent content, and basic understandability (for all kinds of readers). I was not only the beneficiary, but those who read this book will secure a better grasp of our efforts. It was yet more evidence of what a good partnership entails. My adult "children," Clarissa and Joel, and my grandchildren, Jackson Dylan and Ella Sophia, serve as living and loving reminders of a future full of promise and hope. Previously, I had expressed untold appreciation for my now-deceased ninety-nine-year-old mother, Dora G. García, whose strength, talent, and unwavering support were also reflected in her brother, "tocayo" Armando Torres (recently deceased at age ninety-five), who shared many of the same qualities. Hopefully, for all of us, the fabric and content of our respective families provide each of us resilience, hope, and self-improvement. For everyone whom I have not mentioned: Without consciously knowing it, we are influenced and impacted by the many we encounter in our lives. So, thank you all. I hope that readers are informed, broadened, and motivated to think about Latinos, American politics, and life in America today. Another personal insight lies with my experiences as past director of the Resource Center for Minority Data at the Inter-university Consortium for Political and Social Research (ICPSR), where I developed the habit of continually searching for the latest works, studies, and data on minority populations and social issues. Again, this afforded me the opportunity to discover important works and provided contact with a wider set of researchers to draw upon.

From Gabe Sanchez's Perspective

The completion of the fourth edition of *Latino Politics in America* has been an amazing experience and an opportunity to revisit a lot of the core theories and research questions that comprise the basis if Latino politics in 2020 and that we believe will continue to be relevant into the next decade. As noted in the introductory chapter of this book, these are challenging times for Latinos in the United States, with many Latino Americans feeling as though there is an anti-Latino and/or anti-immigrant climate in the country. Engaging the data and literature to write this book was challenging at times, given the gravity of the sociopolitical environment in the nation today, which provided the overall context for this book. However, by providing an honest assessment of how this context has impacted Latinos and the implications it is having for Latino political behavior, we believe that we have provided an outlet for students and other researchers to identify some paths to improve the situation and continue to expand our growing knowledge of "Latino politics."

As I reflect on the process John and I worked through to get this project completed, it is remarkable to me that we were able to get the revision done within the four-month timeline we set for ourselves. I believe our success was largely due to the great working relationship we have built over nearly twenty years. I first met John at the Ralph Bunche Summer Institute recruitment fair back in the summer of 2001; John was recruiting on behalf of the University of Arizona, and I was finishing up the summer program as a participant. It was clear after spending some time with John over lunch at that event that he was the ideal mentor for me, as I remember him reviewing my summer paper's statistical model focused on Latino group identity with me on several napkins, which was super helpful. With John's strong mentorship, I have had a wonderful career and have been able to mentor a wide range of Latino and other scholars of color, including three Latinas who earned PhDs this academic year. I believe John's willingness to welcome me as an author to a book that has been highly successful speaks to the strength of our relationship and of John's consistent willingness to open up opportunities for others to advance their careers. For undergraduate students reading this book, I emphasize the importance of having strong mentoring in place in whatever graduate program you may be considering, as, in my view, this is the most important factor in that decision-making process. Dr. John García has been the best mentor imaginable, and I want to thank him for the time and energy he has invested and continues to invest in my development.

One of the unfortunate outcomes associated with my job duties, which are increasingly administrative, is that I do not get the opportunity to teach undergraduate courses as often as I would like. However, I happened to be teaching a Latino politics course this semester while we were writing this book. This provided a great opportunity to put the draft chapters in front of the students for real-time feedback—ideal given that this is the primary audience for the textbook. The class also allowed John and me to develop lecture slides tied to the book that were able to be tested by the students and improved before being made available for instructors interested in using the book. I thank the class for their thoughtful input and for being willing to use the draft chapters that were often a bit rough for part of the assigned readings for the course. It has been a challenging semester interrupted by the coronavirus; thanks to this class of students who have been flexible and have helped my mental health by being some great folks to chat with over the phone, email, and Zoom about Latino politics.

As John has noted in his comments, the ability to put a book like this together, one that attempts to take a comprehensive approach to Latino politics, requires the support of a wide number of folks who contribute to the efforts behind the scenes. On my end, this included support from multiple graduate students from my team who provided time and energy reviewing drafts, adding relevant citations, sharing thoughts about any gaps we had in our coverage of each of the core topics in the book, and helping to update tables and figures. This includes Barbara Gómez-Aguiñaga, Mia Livaudais, Brooke Abrams, Melanie Sayuri-Dominguez, Aakrit Joshi, and Carlyn Pinkins. Thanks to all of you for your help; the book was much stronger as a result of your support. To avoid the risk of leaving any of my colleagues in the discipline off of a shout-out list, I want to provide a general thank-you to all of the wide range of coauthors and colleagues I have had over the years who have improved my knowledge of Latino politics, and social science more broadly. I am blessed to know many people who are not just colleagues but lifelong friends who have made me a stronger scholar, and consequently improved the quality of this book. I would also like to acknowledge Rowman & Littlefield, who were very supportive in allowing me to join John on this project. In particular, thanks to Traci Crowell for working with John and me on feedback the press received from the prior edition of the book and providing us with the freedom and flexibility to approach the new edition with some latitude to expand on certain chapters and take on some new content. I believe that this has led to a more comprehensive book that will hopefully be more useful to those who choose to read it.

Finally, and most importantly, I want to thank my family for their support and patience. The quick turnaround required for the project and the challenges of having a lot of other work on my plate required me to use early mornings, weekends, and evenings to focus on the book. Both my wife, Anna, and daughter, Gabriella, were great in giving me the time I needed to make progress, including during the Christmas holiday break. I am often asked how I can remain so positive despite having a really demanding set of work requirements spread across both the University of New Mexico and the political opinion research firm Latino Decisions. I always reply that it is because I have as close to a perfect home life as you can possibly have. No matter how stressful the workday is for me, I know that when I come home and see my wife and daughter all that stress goes away. We all support each other in our home, and the creation of this book could not have been successful without their support.

Both John and I worked hard on this project, which I believe has resulted in a great resource for anyone interested in learning more about Latino politics and the Latino community more broadly. We hope that those of you who purchase the book or check it out at your library will be better informed about the Latino population and use the book to push the collective research on this community forward. As we look at the next generation of scholars in the field, I am extremely optimistic about what the future holds for the study of Latino politics and look forward to seeing where that generation takes us with their work.

Acronyms

ACA	Affordable Care Act
ACDP	Asociación Comunal de Dominicanos Progresitas
ACLU	American Civil Liberties Union
ACS	American Community Survey
ASPIRA	Spanish word for "aspire"—Hispanic organization dedicated exclusively to developing the educational and leadership capacity of Hispanic youth
ATEDPA	Antiterrorism and Effective Death Penalty Act
CAFÉ	Cuban Americans for Engagement
CANC	Cuban American National Council
CANF	Cuban American National Foundation
CBDG	Community Block Development Grant
CBP	Customs and Border Protection
CCD	Committee for Cuban Democracy
CHC	Congressional Hispanic Caucus
CHCI	Congressional Hispanic Caucus Institute
CLILA	Coalition of Latino Leaders
CMPS	Collaborative Multiracial Post-Election Survey
CONGUATE	Coalition of Guatemalan Immigrants in the United States
COPS	Community Organized for Public Services
CSO	Community Services Organization
CVAP	Citizen Voting Age Population
DACA	Deferred Action for Childhood Arrivals
DANR	Dominican American National Roundtable
DAPA	Deferred Action for Parents of Americans and Lawful Permanent Residents
DHS	Department of Homeland Security
EEOA	Equal Employment Opportunity Act
GOP	Grand Old Party (Republican Party)
GOTV	Get Out the Vote

HACR	Hispanic Association for Corporate Responsibility
HACU	Hispanic Association of Colleges and Universities
HERE	Hotel Employees and Restaurant Employees Union
HNBA	Hispanic National Bar Association
IAF	Industrial Areas Foundation
ICE	Immigration and Customs Enforcement
IIRIRA	Illegal Immigration Reform and Immigrant Responsibility Act of 1996
INA	McCarran-Walter Act or Immigration and Nationality Act
INS	Immigration and Naturalization Service
IRCA	Immigration Reform and Control Act
LADO	Latin American Defense Organization
LCLAA	Labor Council for Latin American Advancement
LCRJS	Latino Coalition for Racial Justice for Salvadorans
LNPS	Latino National Political Survey
LNS	Latino National Survey
LPR	Legal Permanent Resident
LULAC	League of United Latin American Citizens
LUPA	Latinos United for Political Rights
MALDEF	Mexican American Legal Defense and Education Fund
MAPA	Mexican American Political Association
MAS	Mexican American Studies (Tucson Unified School District)
MENA	Middle Eastern and North Africans
MPP	Migration Protection Protocols
MWVREP	Midwest Voter Registration and Education Project
NABE	National Association of Bilingual Educators
NAHD	National Association of Hispanic Dentists
NAHJ	National Association of Hispanic Journalists
NALACC	National Alliance of Latin American and Caribbean Communities
NALEO	National Association of Latino Elected and Appointed Officials
NCLB	No Child Left Behind Act
NCLR	National Council of La Raza
NHCC	National Hispanic Corporate Council
NHLI	National Hispana Leadership Institute
OLAW	Organization of Los Angeles Workers
OMB	Office of Management and Budget
PHRC	Pew Hispanic Research Center
PRA	Permanent Resident Alien
PRCSEA	Puerto Rican Coalition of Service Employees Association
PRLDEF	Puerto Rican Legal Defense and Education Fund
PRMA	Puerto Rican Merchants Association
PRWORA	Personal Responsibility and Work Opportunity Reconciliation Act
PTA	Parents and Teachers Association
RNC	Republican National Committee
SEIU	Service Employees International Union

SES	Socioeconomic Status
SHPE	Society of Hispanic Professional Engineers
SFS	Sanctuary for Salvadorans
SIG	Special Interest Group
SNS	Social Network Services
SSI	Supplementary Security Income
SVREP	Southwest Voter Registration and Education Project
SWCLR	Southwest Council of La Raza
TFNA	Task Force for New Americans
TPS	Temporary Protected Status
TUSD	Tucson Unified School District
UAC	Unaccompanied Alien Children
UnidosUS	formerly known as National Council of La Raza
UNITE	Union of Needletrades, Industrial and Textile Employees
USCIS	United States Citizenship and Information Services
USHCC	US Hispanic Chamber of Commerce
USMCA	United States Mexico Canada Agreement
VAP	Voting Age Population
VEP	Voting Eligible Population
VRA	Voting Rights Act

An Introduction to Latino Politics

Emprendimos una peregrinación y nos preguntamos ¿Dónde están nuestras raíces, los hilos de la historia y las experiencias en estas tierras las conocidas tanto como las nuevas? Al hacer el reconocimiento, percibimos perspectivas de todas las direcciones y siempre miramos hacia el futuro con esperanza y dignidad.

Undertaking a pilgrimage to find our community, we ask ourselves, where are our roots, those strands of history and experiences in lands both known and new? As we search, our reconnaissance takes in views from many sources, and we are always looking to the future with hope and dignity.

Gilroy and El Paso: Latinos in the Crosshairs

It was near the closing of the Gilroy Garlic Festival on July 28, 2019, when Santino William Legan cut through fencing at the rear of the festival grounds. Armed with an AASR-10 semi-automatic rifle, Legan disposed of thirty-nine rounds in his seventy-five-round drum magazine. In a span of minutes, three persons were killed and an additional seventeen people were wounded. The combination of a self-inflicted gunshot wound to the head and police firing eighteen rounds at Legan ended this mass shooting episode.

The Gilroy Garlic Festival draws 80,000 to 100,000 festival gatherers in Gilroy, California, each year. Gilroy has a long-established Latino population that constitutes almost three-fifths of the city. At Santino Legan's home, evidence was found of his "exploring violent ideologies" (Kennedy 2019) and of potential targets, including the Gilroy Garlic Festival, religious organizations, courthouses, federal buildings, and political institutions. One of his online posts complained about the Garlic Festival congesting the countryside with "horses of mestizos" (Scutti 2019).

Less than a week later, Patrick Crusius drove 650 miles from Allen, Texas, to the El Cielo Mall in El Paso. He was armed with a WASR-10 rifle and opened fire in the Walmart parking lot before moving inside the store. Crusius made clear that his targets were Latinos of Mexican origin; twenty-two people were killed and twenty-four were injured, including a young married couple gunned down while covering their infant with their bodies. The Cielo Mall is a commercial center for El Pasoans and residents of Juarez, Mexico, and amid the terrified scrambling for shelter, acts of heroism were on display. It was noted, for example, that Gilbert Serna, a Walmart employee, ushered around 150 customers and employees through a fire exit.

Law enforcement officials arrived on scene in just six minutes, and Patrick Crusius surrendered outside the store. Of the murdered victims, nine were women and thirteen were men. Eight of those killed were Mexican citizens. After Crusius's arrest, investigators reported that he wanted to shoot as many Mexicans as he could. Crusius had posted a manifesto in which he detailed both white nationalist viewpoints and anti-immigrant rhetoric. A reading of his manifesto made direct references to a "Hispanic invasion" and endorsed the "great replacement" theory. Just before his cowardly and violent acts, he gave a clear political motivation for his actions by posting his desire to "remove the threat of the Hispanic voting bloc" and to stop the "invasion from taking control of local and state governments of my beloved Texas." There was also an indication that he did not expect to survive his attack but hoped it would inspire others to conduct like-minded assaults.

The El Paso mass shooting marked the 251st US mass shooting of 2019, which, unfortunately, could allow these events to be forgotten among the many others that took place across the country. However, the responses by public figures, activists, and members of the grassroots Latino communities made clear that these events were unique and had direct relevance to contemporary Latino politics. For example, the Mexican foreign minister acted to ensure the safety of Mexican nationals when they traveled north of their border. An interesting contrast in response to this mass shooting was evident between national leaders, Latino elected officials, and other Latinos. As reflected in the quotes below, many Latino leaders made a connection between the actions of these domestic terrorists and the underlying anti-Latino climate that has been perpetuated nationally since the last presidential election.

In response to the El Paso shooting, President Trump's comments focused upon the tragic nature of the mass shooting as an act of cowardice and condemned this hateful act, saying, "These barbaric slaughters are an assault upon our nation, and a crime against all humanity. We are a loving nation and our children are entitled to grow up in a just, peaceful, and loving society" (The White House 2019). Many other public officials also responded to these major mass shootings. For example, Texas governor Greg Abbott, Vice President Mike Pence, former vice president Joe Biden, Senator Corey Booker, and Senator Kamala Harris all expressed dismay, condolences to victims' families and the local community, and the need to end such violence and hatred. An examination of statements by Latino public officials and community activists throughout the nation focused more directly on the senseless taking of lives, roots of hatred, and the targeting of communities of color.

Julián Castro, an aspirant for the Democratic nomination for president, spoke of the government's need to protect American lives. Ted Cruz (R-Texas) was "deeply horrified by the hateful anti-Hispanic bigotry expressed by the shooter's 'manifesto'" (Ramirez 2019). Comments by other Latinos placed emphasis on a community under siege by the persons and organizations that exhibited anti-immigrant and anti-Hispanic views, as well as negative views about communities of color overall. The tone, rhetoric, and inciting characterizations by politicians (of which much criticism has been directed toward President Trump), media commentators, and organizations is seen as detrimental and harmful to the Latino community specifically. For example, the

Latino Policy Forum (Chicago) joined other leaders in Illinois and nationwide asserting the need to hold national leaders accountable for using divisive rhetoric.

Miguel Andrade, spokesperson for the Philadelphia activist group JUNTOS, placed emphasis on the effect of targeting Latinos in El Paso. "What happened in El Paso is a direct result of the racist language coming out of Trump's mouth . . . We should be outraged that it has gotten to this point, that the 'racist-in-chief' is perpetuating this kind of rhetoric and vitriol against marginalized communities" (Vourvoulias 2019). In Wisconsin, Christine Neumann-Ortiz noted the El Paso shootings resembled events in her own community, from hate crimes targeting immigrants to teachers from immigrant backgrounds being bullied at schools. As executive director of Voces de la Frontera (an immigrant advocacy organization), Neumann-Ortiz observed more fear from Latinos, who were expressing that their environment has been (or is being) overtaken with targeted hatred toward themselves and immigrants.

Rep. Joaquin Castro (D-TX) mirrored the previous comments about the rise of negative rhetoric toward Latinos and immigrants and the role President Trump has played in fostering fear and hatred. "This vile act of terrorism against Hispanic Americans was inspired by divisive racial and ethnic rhetoric and enabled by weapons of war," Castro said (Castro 2019). "Hispanic Americans and immigrants have been directly and violently attacked. This crime was intentional violence to strike fear in our communities, in our lives, and for our families."[1] Similarly, Rep. Veronica Escobar (D-TX), in an NPR radio interview, commented, "Not only an epidemic of guns, but also an epidemic of hate and the residents of the city and county that are about 83 percent Latino all feel targeted" ("Weekend Edition" 2019).

These reactions were repeated throughout the United States via newspapers interviewing Latinos about the underlying factors of the shooters' motivation. Emphasis was placed on Patrick Cursius's remarks to investigators that he had wanted to shoot as many Mexicans as he could. While many Latinos expressed an atmosphere of fear and feeling targeted due to their ethnicity and/or immigrant background, their responses did not stop there. Voicing a sense of defiance, resolve, and coming together as Latinos for change and stronger voices, Perla Y. Lara (WHYY-PBS, August 15, 2019) presented her perspective on the recent chain of events. Perla, a social psychologist who specializes in intercultural dialogue and criminology, talked about her evolving understanding of hostility "against my people." She stated that it comes from ignorance, which "feeds insecurity and fears, which turns into intolerance and later violence." She indicated that Latinos "cannot afford to be indifferent or desensitized to these criminal and violent acts . . . Our humanity is at stake and so are our lives." Her response, echoed by other Latinos and non-Latinos alike, is to resist such rhetoric and actions and continue to repel the anti-immigrant policies in the face of escalating violence and hatred. Lara ended her PBS interview by saying, "We don't need to wait until we are personally impacted in order to take action. Everyone can contribute to the fight . . . vote, call your representative, protest, protect the ones who need your solidarity and privilege, volunteer."

A statewide survey of Latinos in Texas conducted in September of 2019 by Latino Decisions, a political opinion research firm, revealed that the Latino electorate had reactions to the violence that were similar to those of their leaders and spokespeople. For example, 69 percent of respondents from the poll felt that the language President

Trump used in his speeches and on Twitter was part of the problem. A similarly high percentage believed that the shooter was influenced by Trump.

While more detailed accounts of the shootings in Gilroy and El Paso are available, our description of these shootings serves as the contemporary context in which we discuss and analyze Latino politics. In this edition, we have underscored the themes of community, interest, and culture. At the same time, we recognize that the umbrella term of "Latinos" represents a multilayered congruence of communities bonded together by national origin, nativity and immigrant status, sexual orientation, gender, and other significant social groupings. A larger "pan-ethnic" community is an ongoing reality that is reflected in local and national organizations, their leadership, and their strategies, as well as media characterizations. Discussions of Latinos in America often center on the "**Latinization**" of their engagement and presence in nearly every facet of American life as well as their growing voices in public life and US institutions.

Latino Politics and Contemporary Dynamics

So, how are we using the Gilroy and El Paso shootings to provide a panorama of Latinos and their intersections with America's public life? The level of public rhetoric has been such that communities of Latinos across the country feel targeted and under siege. This is reflected in the high percentage of Latinos across the country who already felt pessimistic and insecure about their place in the United States well before the attacks occurred. Indicative of the overall climate, a Latino Decisions poll conducted in April 2019 showed that 80 percent of Latino registered voters think racism against Latinos and immigrants is a problem, with 51 percent reporting it as a major problem.[2]

As indicated earlier, a visible response to this negative rhetoric is resistance, coming together to fight back, and increasing the avenues of social change and influence. In the last three years particularly, questions about Latinos' loyalties to this country, their character and morality, and the extent of their contributions in all facets of America's life have been portrayed negatively and with much hostility and distrust. This climate and the actual and real experiences of Latinos propagate self-reflection and reaching out to others with common backgrounds and experiences. Our exploration of these different layers of Latino communities helps us to see how political involvement occurs, through what mechanisms, and Latinos' target for engagement.

Another aspect of these past shootings lies with the basis for specifically targeting Latinos as "foreigners," not part of the real American fabric, and as contributing to the invasion on America's values and its makeup. The raised issues regarding immigration (the undocumented, asylum seekers, and mixed-status households) have a direct bearing on the everyday lives of many Latino households and communities. The concept of "six degrees of separation" has noteworthy application for Latinos and their politics. Who are the real Americans? How do they protect against violation of human rights and criminalization of persons seeking refuge and opportunity? What are "legitimate" bases for deportation, access to due process and representation, and policies that have the impact of emphasizing deterrence and punitive actions in opposition to a more welcoming nation and processes that provide full and fair treatment and participation? How do issues of gun violence, environmental concerns, and reproductive rights play into the Latino policy agenda?

We will be discussing and analyzing the intricacies of community, of overlapping and salient interests, and the changing cultural manifestation of Latinos living in the United States. In the midst of the 2020 election events, Latinos actively focused on voter registration and turnout, effective political knowledge, and efficacious attitudes, as well as expanding leadership with the organizational skills and infrastructure to have an even greater impact on socioeconomic and political life in America. As we move forward in this fourth edition, we are attempting to clarify our themes.

Our discussion of the Gilroy and El Paso mass shootings adds to the overall experiences of Latinos. Our earlier edition noted Latinos' electoral import in the election of Barack Obama in 2008 and his reelection in 2012. This impetus continues to expand with Latinos' participation in the 2018 midterm elections and the highly contentious election of 2020 (Latino Decisions 2019). The country's heightened political polarization, primarily along partisan divisions and issues like reproductive rights, immigration, health care access and costs, gun control, and police-community relations, places Latinos in the fray of American politics.

BOX 1.1 Hostile Rhetoric, Hostile Climate, and the Latino Community

Our introductory narratives about the shootings in Gilroy and El Paso carried an underlying theme about the current climate that Latinos are experiencing with fear, threats, and negative rhetoric. Many Latino leaders following the mass shootings pointed toward harmful and hateful language heightened by President Trump and other political leaders. What have been the responses and effects on the Latino community? A study by Latino Decisions (2020) found 51 percent of Latinos thought racism against Latinos and immigrants was a major problem. In addition, Pew Hispanic Research Center (PHRC) (Lopez et al. 2018) discovered that nearly one-half of Latinos indicated that their situation had worsened, a 32 percent increase since the 2016 election. Latinos' greater exposure to violent "metaphors can increase support for political violence among persons with aggressive personalities" (Kalmoe 2014). One consequence of such rhetoric is the dehumanization of the groups targeted and the portrayal of them as a threatening force.

Some aspects of this hostile climate can show their effects on a wide spectrum of Latino community members (i.e., class, gender, nativity, "legal" status, etc.). It can begin similar to the experience of Luis, an upper-class American Latino (Vallejo 2016). After working many hours restoring a classic Chevy truck (and therefore dressed in grease-stained clothes), he decided to test drive his truck in his affluent neighborhood. While parked to examine a mechanical problem, a police officer responded to a call from a neighbor. The neighbor reported that an "unauthorized" Mexican immigrant was casing the neighborhood. These stories have repeated themselves in other parts of the country where middle-class Latinos are perceived as criminals, likely to be illegal, and unassimilable.

A survey of patients (Carroll 2019) at three urban California emergency departments found one-half of Latino citizens and legal residents, as well as three-quarters of undocumented immigrants, feel unsafe because of comments made by members of the Trump administration. One-fourth of undocumented immigrants were so frightened they delayed going to the emergency room for

BOX 1.1 (continued)

days. Dr. Robert Rodriguez, professor of emergency medicine at the University of California, San Francisco, and a physician at San Francisco General Hospital, stated that "statements coming from the administration and the President really do have significant effects on Latino populations. Not only have they induced fear in undocumented immigrants, but they have also caused a substantial proportion of Latino citizens to have concerns about their safety" (Rodriguez et al. 2019). Similarly, Chavez et al. (2019) studied the effects of negative and positive rhetoric on Mexican American youth. Their overall conclusion was that negative emotional responses, in turn, were associated with participants' higher perceived stress, lower subjective health, and lower subjective well-being. Altogether, these findings suggest that political rhetoric matters for the targets of that rhetoric.

The pattern of a hostile climate and rhetoric is further illustrated in the study by Barajas-Gonzalez et al. (2018) of the impact of immigration enforcement threats on Latino children. Stress and emotional discomfort were found to be prevalent among those who belonged to mixed-status families, which have at least one citizen or legal immigrant child and at least one undocumented parent. At the same time, this hostility was harmful for Latinos, regardless of their immigration status. "Mixed-status families may change their daily activities in attempts to protect themselves, consequently becoming more socially isolated.... For some children, the stigma associated with being from an immigrant family, experiences with discrimination and increased consciousness of legal status is marked by fear, hyperawareness and hypervigilance" (Barajas-Gonzalez, Ayón, and Torres 2018). This almost PTSD condition affects children's ability to focus in school, making it difficult to succeed socially, academically, and emotionally. "Deportations and family separations at the border are incredibly disruptive and traumatic to youth and their families. The detrimental impacts of family separations on child development and family systems are serious and long-lasting.... Even for youth and families who are not directly threatened by these deportation or family separation policies, the policy climate is creating a more hostile and unsafe environment" (Wray-Lake et al. 2018).

A final example shows a hostile climate has a more direct political effect. In their analysis, Gabriel Sanchez and Barbara Gómez-Aguiñaga (2017) demonstrate that Latinos outperformed expectations as a cohesive voting bloc against Trump in 2016. The literature on the racialization of the Latino population through hostile campaign rhetoric and punitive immigration policy platforms suggests that Trump should not have done well among this electorate. The Latino Decisions Election Eve Poll data bears this out, finding that the GOP nominee had the lowest level of Latino support ever recorded for a presidential candidate. Will Latino political behavior be longer-lasting with this pattern? The answer will hinge largely on whether President Trump attempts to repair a clearly damaged relationship with the Latino electorate during his first term in office. If the Trump administration and the GOP more broadly continue to alienate Latinos, this could mobilize more eligible Latinos to register and vote and continue to push them toward the Democratic Party. Racist political rhetoric hinders social acceptance, creates a climate of fear, and legitimizes discrimination.

In the last edition, the spring of 2006 was depicted as a tumultuous time in which more than three million people, primarily immigrants and many originally from Mexico and other Latin American countries, demonstrated by taking to the streets of Chicago, Los Angeles, Phoenix, Milwaukee, Detroit, Denver, Dallas, and dozens of other US cities. They marched to protest proposed legislation (the "Sensenbrenner Bill," HR 4437) placing emphasis on more restrictive and punitive measures toward undocumented individuals. In effect, many components of the proposed law had the net impact of criminalizing (felony charges with harsher penalties) immigration-related infractions. As a counterpolicy response, Latino protestors advocated for comprehensive immigration reform legislation that would provide pathways for citizenship and normalizing their status (Bada, Fox, and Selee 2006; Cano 2004). The magnitude of the 2006 immigrant protest marches, with so many participants taking such a visible role in a national policy discussion, was unprecedented. Latino immigrants (along with immigrants from Asia and other parts of the globe) were voicing their displeasure with the hostile and negative anti-immigrant climate, the negative tenor of immigration reform in the area of border enforcement, and the heightened "criminalization" and negative stereotypes of **undocumented persons** and their family networks.

The Trump administration has pushed for policy initiatives like "Build That Wall," further militarization of the border, greater restrictive and punitive immigration policies for asylum seekers and DACA and DAPA registrants, and reducing basic human rights for all immigrants, regardless of status. Louder and more frequent xenophobic rhetoric has been part of "everyday" America's discourse, and Latinos continue to be the recipient of negative narratives concerning disloyalty, public charges, and impacting the economy adversely. As we begin preparations for the pivotal 2020 decennial census, Latinos, politics, and public policy are playing out in this arena as well.

"Da Forma a tu Futuro. ¡Comienza Aquí!" Shape Your Future

The Spanish-language version of the 2020 US census "slogan" is one of more than forty versions in which the decennial census campaigns try to reach out to a more diversified United States. Generally, the information collected produces population tabulations with counts and detailed descriptions of all persons, including Latinos/Hispanics.[3] So, how are people classified racially/ethnically, and what are the consequences and implications of the classification? In the summer of 2019, the Supreme Court overturned a Trump administration initiative to include a "citizenship question" in the 2020 decennial census. Such an initiative had serious implications for a full and open count and participation of Latinos and other marginalized communities. Latino organizations and leaders joined in the legal proceedings to overturn this action; however, the impact of speculation that the citizenship question would be included had a marked impact on Latinos' trust in filling out the census form.[4] We will discuss later how achieving a full and accurate count has consequences for reappointment and redistricting plans and actions.

BOX 1.2 Citizenship Status on the 2020 US Census

Although the adjudication of the US census every ten years is never free from politics, the run-up to the 2020 census became much more contentious than usual with the prospect of adding a citizenship status question on the form. It was not until the Supreme Court of the United States (SCOTUS) blocked the Trump administration from including citizenship that the administration dropped its fight to include that item on the census form and began printing forms without the controversial item. The decision of SCOTUS was viewed as a victory for critics who argued that the inclusion of citizenship was part of a larger effort to skew the census results in favor of Republican candidates.

At the heart of the fight was the social science question of whether having citizenship on the census form would negatively impact Latino participation. Federal court cases in California and New York provided some insights on this question, as an expert witness report conducted by Professor Matt Barreto included a national survey of Latinos that focused specifically on the impact of the citizenship status question on Latino participation in the census. Dr. Barreto's report made clear that having the citizenship status question on the census form would yield a high undercount of Latino and immigrant members of the US population.[a] This was not a major surprise, as officials at the Census Bureau itself have said that including the question would lead to an undercount of noncitizens and minority residents. As a result, areas with more immigrants, which tend to vote Democratic, would have lost both representation and federal funding.

Although the SCOTUS decision was applauded by many Latino leaders and organizations, even though the citizenship status question would not be included, the contentious debate about this issue had serious implications for Latino engagement in the census. For example, a survey conducted by Latino Decisions in New Mexico right after the SCOTUS decision found that while a large segment of the Hispanic population in the nation's highest Latino population state said that the decision to leave off the citizenship status question increased their desire to participate in the census, a large percentage noted that they remained very fearful of participating, particularly Spanish-speaking and immigrant Hispanics. This put a lot of emphasis on the need for community organizations, such as those discussed in this chapter, to work hard to increase trust in their communities in the process of participating in the census. It had to include education on why it was so important to the provision of resources and ensuring that Latinos would be properly represented in the political system.

[a] Barreto's report and associated tables are available at http://mattbarreto.com/research/census2020.html.

When the Trump administration, under Secretary of Commerce Wilbur Ross and Attorney General William Barr, attempted to include a citizenship question in the 2020 decennial, the stated rationale was to be able to get accurate counts of the citizen voting age population (CVAP) and to report the population counts to the states in time for redistricting. Information was desired at the block level, arguing that such additional information would strengthen Voting Rights Act activities. Many state attorney generals (especially Xavier Becerra–CA) took the lead to challenge this initiative. This litigation finally went to the Supreme Court for a decision. Chief Justice John G. Roberts Jr., in the majority opinion, stated that the explanation used by the Trump administration "appears to have been contrived" (Liptak 2019) and that the Trump administration would have the opportunity to submit another rationale, if they chose to do so. Judge Roberts went on to say that executive branch officials must "offer genuine justifications for important decisions, reasons that can be scrutinized by courts and the interested public." He added that "accepting contrived reasons would defeat the purpose of the enterprise. If judicial review is to be more than an empty ritual, it must demand something better than the explanation offered for the action taken in this case" (Epps 2019). Subsequently, the citizenship question remained off the census form, but the Trump administration, through Ross and Barr, ordered governmental agencies to extract from extant agency data sources information on citizenship status.

This controversy has a direct bearing on the political world of Latinos and other communities of color. Thomas Hofeller, a major Republican party consultant who died in 2019, had concluded in a 2015 unpublished study that adding a citizenship question to census forms would produce the detailed data needed to redraw state and local voting districts in a way that would be "advantageous to Republicans and non-Hispanic Whites." The shift to using CVAP, rather than total population counts, as the basis for redistricting would reduce the numbers of Latinos and other groups with significant foreign-born segments as well as noncitizens. A study by Baum et al. (2019) conducted a survey experiment in which the results indicated there would be a 12.03 percent reduction in Latino participation in the 2020 census. This was substantiated by an expert witness report conducted by Dr. Matt Barreto for the California lawsuit. Factors such as lack of trust in government, fear of confidentiality, and suspicion of motive for inclusion of the citizenship question would affect response rates, especially with reporting household members who are Hispanic.

Thinking about Race and Ethnicity: Separate but Related?

Questions about identity, socioeconomic status and mobility, population growth, and geographic distribution derived from the census can be interwoven to depict a political world of Latinos who are pursuing greater empowerment and equity. The Census Bureau, as in previous decennial censuses, explored the possibility of combining the race and Spanish-origin questions into a singular item. Latino leaders and organizations were, generally, not supportive of this change, concerned about the potential to undercount the Latino population. The Spanish-origin question was first included in the 1970 census as an ethnic self-identifier. The information elicited by this question has served as the basis for voting and civil rights legislation and policy implementation in a variety of service-delivery programs. In 1997, the Office of Management and Budget (OMB) revised how racial and ethnic data were collected.[5] After lengthy public input and feedback from federal statistical agencies, the OMB revised the race question format for Census 2000 so that multiple responses to the racial categories were allowed. Other suggestions over the past two decennials included the addition of a separate multiracial category, and more recently, the inclusion of a Middle East/North African (MENA) category.

The inclusion of two separate questions regarding race and ethnicity has undergone scrutiny and debate. But in compliance with current OMB standards, the 2018 End-to-End Census Test and the 2020 census will continue to use the two separate questions for collecting data on race and ethnicity.[6] Since the 1990 decennial census and subsequent decennials, the Census Bureau has researched combining the two questions with Hispanic/Latino added as a racial category. Some of these initiatives stemmed from the significant numbers of persons marking "some other race," of which around 95 percent of these responses were Latinos (García 2016; Liebler et al. 2014). An interpretation of this pattern indicated that perhaps Latinos saw themselves as a distinct racial group.

Recognizing the sociopolitical construct of race, population counts do vary based upon the question content and format. For Latinos, a combined question, and whether multiracial responses are allowed, will result in different population counts and differing impacts on Latino national-origin-group members. That is, the numbers of Latinos identified can fluctuate depending on choices of racial categories and on a multiple-response option. In addition, the concept and meaning of race can be "driven" by a host of different factors (prevalent racial schema, national origin, language, indigeneity, etc.). Latino advocacy organizations have generally opposed a combined race/ethnicity question due to lost information and projected lower population counts (Fontenot 2018). Significant changes for 2020 census questions regarding race and ethnicity included: collecting identification of multiple Hispanic ethnicities, such as Mexican, Colombian, Puerto Rican; adding a write-in area with examples for the white and black racial categories; removing the term "Negro"; and adding examples for the American Indian or Alaska Native racial category. The Census Bureau did not use a combined-question format for collecting race and ethnicity or a separate "Middle Eastern or North African" category on the 2020 census form.

A person has the option of marking more than one racial category (White, Black, Asian, Pacific Islander, Native American/Alaska Native, and other). In addition, the OMB separated Asians from native Hawaiians and Pacific Islanders to create five racial categories. The ability to mark more than one option enables people of multiracial backgrounds to self-identify from all of the various stated racial categories. With the multiple-response option remaining for the 2020 census, one persistent issue lies with the way in which the population tabulation method(s) are conducted and reported. In previous censuses, each person fell into only one racial category. For Census 2000 and beyond, the tabulation was more complicated as people could indicate multiple responses. For example, indigenous populations from Mexico and Central and South America were included in the American Indian/Alaska Native category. Yet this racial category generally represents legally recognized tribes in the United States rather than indicating whether the respondent is of indigenous origin, regardless of national origin.

What happens to the individual who marks herself as African American and white and checks off Spanish origin on the ethnic-origin question? How is this person counted and in how many different ways? The classification method selected has a direct bearing on civil and voting rights and program-participation monitoring, as well as on how the government determines who Hispanics/Latinos are. To further complicate the classification is to potentially merge the Spanish-origin and race questions into one item. For example, if an individual marks that he is of Spanish and non-Hispanic origin (i.e., of mixed Hispanic origin), how is that person counted? As the nation continues to be more diverse, the proper measurement of the population will become increasingly challenging.

The reverberation of the proposed addition of the citizenship question for Census 2020 will have additional political ramifications not only in 2020, but well beyond. We will amplify these links to census measurement approach in later chapters, especially talking about reapportionment. Our brief description of current governmental policy decisions and classification schemes is based on the concepts of race and ethnic origin, context needed to properly approach the important question, "Who are Latinos?"

While significant media attention has highlighted the continual growth of the Spanish-origin population, it is not always clear whom we are discussing, or why people whose ancestry is tied to Chile are associated with others whose ancestry is connected to Honduras. Our exploration of communities of interest and culture would suggest that the interconnecting ties across national origin and other ties (indigeneity, nativity, language, etc.) have relevance, at times, with pan-ethnic activities, while in other circumstance, national origin, sexual orientation, and/or gender play a more central role in political expressions and engagement.

Our perspective recognizes the dynamic and evolving nature of being Latino in America and how that is manifested both in terms of combinations and foci of political involvement. This book addresses the dialectics of diversity and similarity among people and communities of Spanish origin. In many ways, Latinos and their politics reflect a community that is being influenced by Latino elites and organizations, "mass" intergroup interactions, the mass media, and governmental policies and agencies. Regardless of the derivation of the Latino/Hispanic concept, the idea of a group of people tied together by language, cultural values and practices, similar histories in the United States, and public policies is clearly visible on the American landscape; its political ramifications are very dynamic.

Critical to our discussion of Latinos and the American political system is an examination of both the basis and construction of identity and its salience for group identification. This important dimension affects Latinos living in the United States and forms an important basis for community among a collection of people from twenty-plus national-origin groups. Most Latinos think of themselves in terms of their own national-origin group (Honduran, Cuban, Argentine, etc.), and this subgroup identification is an important component of the core definition of community (F. C. García 1997). At the same time, there is a sense of **pan-ethnicity**,[7] or seeing oneself not only in national-origin terms but also as part of a larger community. The "Hispanic" or "Latino" label has been serving as an important identifier in the formation of a Latino community, yet it is the meaning and attachment beyond the use of the label that establishes a sense of a working community and ways to identify common concerns, interests, and situations. We will focus, as well, on these commonalities between race/ethnic lines, sexual orientation, and other important social groupings, including arguments made by some that a pan-ethnic identity is decreasing among Spanish-origin Americans, particularly among those of the millennial generation.

The concept of **ethnicity** (and, to a lesser degree, race) represents social boundaries in which group identity exists, is created, and is redefined. The **social construct of race** usually refers to a group of people who define themselves as distinct due to perceived common physical characteristics (Cornell and Hartman 1998). This group is socially defined based on physical characteristics and fated by biological factors. Historical precedents and policies, such as the one-drop rule that was common in the South, constructed a racial category. The "one-drop rule" categorized a person with any African lineage as "Negro" or African American. In this case, the state defined anyone with one thirty-second Negro ancestry, or one drop of Negro blood, as being of black racial identity (Payne 1998). As a result, the Jim Crow laws in the region defined participation in social life based on one's race (Payne 1998).

The work of Omi and Winant (1994) further extends the development of race as a social product of human actions and decisions. The concept can be changed over time by members of the racial group and/or through "external" social actions, issues, and public attitudes. With census plans to tabulate multiple responses on the Spanish-origin question, and with identity including more national-origin groupings, these layers of communities can be more delineated to see how and when these "subgroups" come together or operate as more distinct communities. For example, the honoring of one's group could be manifested in annual parades and celebration of one's ancestry, culture, and music. In the case of Latinos, members can be categorized into racial as well as ethnic groups and targeted for specific policies or governmental actions.

Ethnic groups deal with group attachments connected to descent. In reality, direct "blood" ties to ancestry are less important than belief in descent. This reinforces the socially constructed basis of ethnicity. The "strands" that cultivate this belief in common descent can include physical attributes, cultural practices, and a shared historical experience (Cornell and Hartman 1998, 16–17). What makes ethnicity distinctive is that this shared affinity serves as the basis for community formation. The work of R. A. Schermerhorn (1970) reinforces this view of ethnicity by defining it as a "collectivity within the larger society having a real or putative common ancestry, memories of a shared historical past, and a cultural focus on one or more symbolic elements defined as the epitome of their peoplehood." Consistent with these definitions is the presence of self-consciousness among members of an ethnic group. Ethnicity lies within the core of one's identity. At the same time, the self-identification that a person "takes on" may be influenced by external factors such as public policies that provide punitive costs or possible benefits for ethnic group membership, or direct experiences with others that categorize a person as an ethnic even though the person has not identified her/himself as such. Thus, ethnicity operates among persons who identify with others of their descent and are also influenced by individuals outside their group's boundaries.

One way in which race and ethnicity can differ is that there may be more pervasive burdens and consequences on those carrying the racial and/or ethnic designation. Movement across racial boundaries is more restricted by social traditions and customs than across ethnic categories. For ethnic individuals, the demarcation by the larger society may be externally imposed; however, affiliation with the group is usually asserted by members of the ethnic group. Race becomes a way in which defining and assigning differential status is associated with power, control, inferiority, and majority-minority-group status and racial resentment.

A continual dilemma reflected in having a clear distinction between race and ethnicity can be seen with the decennial censuses. As previously stated, in the 2000 census, more than thirteen million Americans checked the "some other race" option, and Latinos/Hispanics constituted more than 95 percent of this category, showing that Latinos are checking off the ethnic question in the "Spanish origin item" as well as indicating a different "racial option" than the established OMB designations. Do we interpret this response as meaning that many Latinos consider themselves a distinctive racial as well as ethnic group in America? Are Latinos using the notions of race and ethnicity interchangeably? Or are Latinos trying to state that they are a distinctive group in the racial/ethnic scheme of America? For the most part, there is evidence that all three scenarios resonate with segments of the Latino community. Research by the Census Bureau (Jacob and Marks 2020) and Telles (2018) looked at the fill-ins for "some other race" response. The three major fill-ins are Hispanic, Latino, and a national-origin designation. The overlap of race and ethnicity (Garcia 2019) reflects the fluid, dynamic, and multidimensional nature of these two concepts, which challenges researchers to add clarity to the role of race and ethnicity for Latinos.

The persistence of ethnicity also has an external group designation. Ethnicity includes the element of self-concept and identification that is also associated when members of an ethnic group start to define their ethnic category. They fill in their own content and meaning, casting their own histories and experiences, to determine what it means to be "an ethnic." This process can be described as the social construction of ethnicity from within. At the same time, interactions with others and sociopolitical policies serve to influence how a person sees her/himself as well as how they're seen by others. In many ways, our book is an examination of the social construction of *latinidad* in the United States as a viable community and how it manifests politically. Clearly, race and ethnicity overlap regarding a sense of group identity and the nature of **power relations** that position a group's members in the larger society.

Our discussion understands that **ethnic identity** may be primarily a matter of individual choice or circumstance, but the development of such identities is influenced by sources external to the ethnic community, such as political institutions (the courts, political parties, policies, etc.) and agencies like the Equal Opportunity Commission, Civil Rights Commission, and Department of Justice, which deal with policies such as voting rights, civil rights protection, and entitlements specific to group categories like minorities, African Americans, Hispanics, and so forth. For example, the **Voting Rights Act of 1965** focused initially on institutional exclusionary voting practices directed toward African Americans in the South. The prohibitions against literacy tests, grandfather clauses,[8] **limited voting** registration location(s), and so on were policy interventions intended to open up the electoral process. The subsequent Voting Rights Act amendments incorporated the concept of linguistic minorities and implemented bi- or multilingual voting materials and assistance. As we will discuss in the chapter on voting, techniques of voter suppression, photo-ID laws, corresponding perspectives, and **partisan gerrymandering** are contemporary challenges that Latinos confront in their effort to expand their political influence.

Legislation, official governmental data gathering, and mass media characterizations that aggregate Hispanics/Latinos as a "singular" pan-ethnic community can serve to simplify complicated issues by reducing a large and potentially diverse collection of people to a simpler grouping. For example, an issue confronting many Latino subcommunities is the extent to which Latino subgroups (Guatemalans, people of Mexican origin, Argentineans, etc.) are connected to one another and whether an inclusive appeal can work to collaborate on common causes effectively. The use of the labels "Hispanic" and "Latino" give to the broader society a much simpler picture of who persons of "Spanish origin" are and what they are about. Rather than examining and assessing each national-origin group in terms of its own political needs and status, such labeling converts them from a diverse and complex mix of groups into a simplified and more manageable package as a new "ethnic group." This helps policy makers understand more easily their changing political world and expanded demands made on it. Our challenge in this book is to improve the understanding of a complex set of dynamics that shape Latino politics and who the participants are. Included will be a brief discussion of the emergence of the term "**Latinx**" to describe the Latino or Hispanic population that is gender and sexual-orientation neutral, which, as we note in the book, is very popular among a small segment of the Latino community.

One result of **pan-ethnicity** is the creation of concrete benefits to which organizations and members of this broader group category can now respond to and participate in. For example, bilingual educational programs are based on the existence of students who have limited English proficiency as well as the perception that bilingualism is primarily a Latino issue. Consequently, a pan-ethnic grouping, with a much larger population base, can emphasize its need and use its sizable constituency to maintain and expand bilingual education programs. An in-depth understanding of Latinos and community building should integrate the role of public policies and social institutions (mass media, governmental agencies, decision-making bodies, etc.) affecting Latino subgroups' activities and developments, as well as the links that connect the Latino subgroups, into collaborative efforts.

Another critical factor for examination of community building is the general climate and the broader public's attitudes toward and awareness of Latinos. Public concerns about cultural and linguistic balkanization, immigration swells, multilingualism, and the like portray Latinos as problematic and possibly a threat to the "American way of life." Sociopolitical issues carry an underlying theme in which segments of non-Latino communities see many Latinos as unwilling to Americanize and assimilate. Such concerns increase the possible costs of being Latino.

For example, the 1997 welfare reform legislation barred "permanent resident aliens" from participating in Social Security's Supplementary Security Income (SSI) and other federal entitlement programs. Congress did not choose to differentiate between undocumented immigrants and permanent resident aliens. Similarly, initiatives in California regarding immigrant access to social services and discontinuing bilingual education programs targeted Latinos. For many people of Spanish origin, this has resulted in defensiveness, even sending them into "survival mode." But the resultant Latino civic engagement can also increase in the form of protest activities, higher voter-registration and turnout levels, and greater political interest (Sierra et al. 2000; Hardy-Fanta et al. 2016). Throughout this book, we will place emphasis on the need to understand identity, its constructions and dynamic character, as well as its sources, in order to interpret and analyze Latino politics.

Context and the Development of Latino Politics

Latino politics can be found in many social contexts (García 1997; Bonilla and Morales 1998), including institutions such as schools and state and local city councils' actions, referenda and initiatives, and other public policies, as well as public opinion and political representation at all levels. Yet scholars focusing on the Latino community have not thoroughly researched the many areas where important political actions have direct impact on Latinos. For example, researchers have only recently begun to examine Latino community organizations and their political involvement with urban redevelopment, local school issues, and environmental "racism" (Pardo 1998; Pulído 1996). More research findings do exist for the Mexican-origin population than for Central and South Americans and Caribbean groups. Only in the past ten to fifteen years have researchers begun to examine the political domains and actions of Latinos in their own communities. At the same time, a limited number of national databases and subsequent analysis have become more readily available for the discussion of Latinos and their politics (Pew Hispanic Research Center, Latino Decisions).

Any examination of Latinos and their political spheres needs to start with an assessment of power relations among Latinos, Latino subgroups, and established power holders and institutions. This examination includes both historical and contemporary power relations and how Latinos have survived, adapted, and succeeded in terms of power-exchange terms. That is, have Latinos or Latino subgroups (Mexican Americans, Cubans, Puerto Ricans, Panamanians, etc.) successfully accessed political and economic institutions or placed key issues or concerns on the policy-making agenda?

Power relations focus on political resources, agenda setting, organizational development, leadership and **mobilization**, authority, influence, and legitimacy. Investigating governmental policies (at any governmental level) that have influenced Latino communities can lead to a greater understanding of the extent and use of power by all participants. In some respects, governmental initiatives and actions that classify persons by group terms or identities (i.e., race, ethnicity, and social class) can serve as indicators of political presence. Part of the political-empowerment process entails recognition of the group, even in symbolic ways. At the same time, the substance of such policies may have punitive, restrictive, and detrimental intent and implications.

Whether or not the political system is organized to be responsive to Latino communities, political institutions through their practices and/or benign neglect indicate that there is a clear need for Latinos to develop power bases to promote effective strategies. The 1980s were designated the "decade of the Hispanic." Projections of extraordinary population growth, with Latinos becoming the nation's largest minority group by 2003, heightened an expectation of Latinos basking in the "political sun." At the same time, Latinos' socioeconomic status (household income, families living below the poverty line, single-parent-headed households, and percentage of adults with a high school diploma, etc.) continued to lag even further behind that of whites. Recognition and responsiveness from governmental institutions was much slower than the rapid Latino growth rate. To a significant degree, Latinos were evolving in the US political system from a relatively obscure or invisible group into one that political institutions had some degree of political awareness about and familiarity with, especially at the national level.

In addition to the contextual elements that contribute to the basis and context of Latino politics, other important factors include sociodemographic status (such as occupational locations in the labor market), economic status, residential and regional concentrations, access to social institutions (their own or societal), and legal prohibitions (restricted immigrant rights and participation, reduced impact on **redistricting**, etc.). The sociodemographic maps identify the resource bases for Latinos as well as possible policy issues and concerns. Given the youthfulness of the overall Latino population and the significant proportion of Latinos who are foreign-born, issues such as educational quality, persistence in staying and completing their education, immigration reform, and increased militarization of the border are all likely policy extensions of Latinos' sociodemographic profile. Also, the relatively low percentage of high school and college graduates among Latinos, as well as their concentration in service-sector industries, has implications for political mobilization and resources. Lower levels of educational attainment, lower job status, and lesser income levels reduce the conventional type of personal resources that individuals can convert for political purposes such as voting or running for office.

Political participation and mobilization (Verba, Scholzman, and Brady 1995; Rosenstone and Hansen 1993) are closely connected to an individual's socioeconomic status, positive political predispositions (or attitudes), and available time to engage in political activities. Chapter 3 develops a sociodemographic "map" of Latinos to assist in the construction of the extent of their political resources and the range of issues that will compose our discussion. Our book focuses on the creation, maintenance, and redefinition of community and the role that external stereotypes and perceptions about Latinos and/or Latino subgroups play in framing Latino politics. Culture and its expression within the Latino communities through both mass and Spanish-language media, traditions and practices, and Spanish-language maintenance can define and sustain a sense of community. In addition, individual membership in and attachment to the Latino community is reinforced through social networks, living in Latino residential areas, experiences with discrimination, and shared experiences in the workplace. These "arenas" are at the core of creating bridges for a Latino community at the grassroots level.

Ethnicity and identity reflect self-choice in how an individual places himself or herself within a group affiliation. Latinos who continue to speak Spanish and participate in cultural events and whose practices maintain ethnically "dense" social contacts with other Latinos are seen as living their Latino-ness. The whole spectrum of being Latino or Cubano or Dominicano lies in their daily routines. How one communicates, the composition and content of one's interactions, lifestyle preferences, and behaviors, and the extent of affinity toward persons of similar ancestry contribute to one's self-definition and its relevance to one's life (Sanchez 2006a). Immersion as a Latino, or more likely, a Cuban, Puerto Rican, or member of another Latino subgroup, is related to social contexts and the involvement with activists and organizations that link their daily experiences as Latinos, and this can direct social and political actions. Numerical growth helps Latino communities assert their identity and command necessary resources. Awareness of the key distinctions between citizens (native-born and naturalized), permanent resident aliens, undocumented persons, and political refugees is critical to understanding the range of similarities and diversities within this dynamic community. Similarly, class differentiation among Latinos serves to create close-knit communities or, perhaps, accentuate class bifurcation.

The examination of class variation, or class bifurcation, in the African American community regarding its impact on mobilization, organizational growth and development, and maintaining consensus on public policies is minimal (West 1994; Dawson 1994). It shows that the connectedness between the African American underclass and the upwardly mobile and successful middle class may create some different policy agendas and alliances, but there is an underlying strong racial identity across social classes. This sense of **linked fate** among African Americans has been found to mobilize this community politically and lead to cohesive voting behavior and policy preferences (Dawson 1994). The existence or extent of class bifurcation among Latinos with possible cleavages between the foreign- and native-born has not been researched thoroughly. However, there has been a growth of research that demonstrates that Latinos maintain a meaningful sense of linked fate (Sanchez and Masuoka 2010) and that this form of identity has been partially driven by punitive immigration policies (Vargas, Sanchez, and Valdez 2017). Cultural maintenance and practices are critical for group identity and community building. At the same time, our theme of similarity and diversity suggests that the Latino community does not require unanimity or complete consensus in order for its members to engage as a political community. Like many political coalitions, Latino politics entails common bonds, experiences, conditions, and interests that can bridge Latino subgroups for collective action on various occasions.

So far, our introductory comments and ideas serve as an overview for an examination of Latino politics. The rest of our commentary in this introduction delineates specific dimensions of community building and politics for the more than fifty-six million Latinos in the United States. The basis for a Latino community will be shared interests, with culture serving as the vital connection. It is important to establish definitions of ethnicity, identity, and community, as well as to analyze how political institutions, processes, policies, and political actors help shape the nature and substance of Latino politics. An "inside and outside" set of processes and actions is at play. Latino activists, organizations (local and national), political parties, and national "events" (such as **English-only initiatives**, SB 1070, fatalities along the border, and restrictive and punitive immigration executive orders, etc.) weave a set of contributing factors that can bring people together for common purposes. One of the challenges for us lies in achieving enough breadth and depth in covering the many different Latino subgroups; in many cases, sparse literature is available.

Chapter 3 provides a demographic profile of Latinos in the United States by incorporating the characteristics of shared interests, social status, cultural indicators, geographic concentrations, and educational and economic status within the Latino subcommunities. The demographic profiles are then linked to community building and agenda setting. The themes of diversity and similarity are interwoven throughout this book. We will explore two particular bases for community: a **community of common or similar cultures** (García and Pedraza-Bailey 1990) and a **community of interests**. A community of common cultures exists when individuals are linked closely by their participation in a common system of meaning with concomitant patterns of customary interactions of culture. Shared cultural practices, celebrations, and traditions serve to bridge Latino subgroup boundaries and potentially provide common bases and resources for effective mobilization. Other writers (Espiritu 1992; Hayes-Bautista 1980) refer to these dynamics as elements of a pan-ethnicity in which several national-origin groups coalesce under a broader identity and community reference.

A community of interests represents the conditions, statuses, and experiences that Latinos share with members of other Latino subgroups. With the exception of Puerto Ricans, a significant proportion of each Latino subgroup consists of foreign-born persons and immigrants. At the same time, the commonwealth status of Puerto Rico and continual efforts of self-determination and full rights can parallel themes of foreignness and marginalization. The current national climate is filled with serious concerns about immigration policies and perceived negative consequences of continued immigration. Latinos are seen as the dominant source of immigrants. Therefore, the immigration issue impacts many Latino communities and can serve as a contributing factor in developing a broader community of interests. Also, the concept of Latinization raises flags of nativism, who belongs, and whether Latinos should be falling under the "American umbrella."

Chapter 4 attempts to provide a substantive understanding of the many Latino subcommunities and includes focused discussions of the subgroups and their historical and power relations in the United States. In addition, we present an overview of how communities may exist in relative isolation from other Latino communities and conversely be linked in various ways to other Latino subgroups. An interesting aspect of intergroup dynamics is discernible in the Census 2010 findings. Not only have Latinos increased in number during the past decade, but their migration patterns have become more regionally diverse, extending into areas less traditionally identified as Latino. For example, increases among Mexican-origin individuals have exceeded an 80 percent growth in southern states such as Arkansas, Georgia, North Carolina, and Tennessee, with major gains in both rural and urban communities. This migration of Mexican-origin persons to the Northeast and the South is substantial in terms of population and growing political activities. Central Americans have become geographically dispersed throughout America.

Since the mid-1980s, the number of Central Americans, especially asylees and refugees, has not only increased, but they have migrated in significant numbers to both traditional areas of Latino concentrations as well as newer areas of Latino influx. One result has been a reconfiguration of Latino issues, a more diverse organizational milieu, and some intergroup competition. An analysis of Latino politics must address the dynamic nature of the composition of the Latino communities and their evolving political networks. Analyzing power relations and particular public policies is one way to explore the nature and character of Latino subcommunity politics and their connections to broader collective Latino politics.

Ethnicity, group identity, and pan-ethnicity involve the social construction of identity, which occurs within the respective groups and is influenced externally. The contributing factors of culture, daily experiences, social contexts, and public policies are introduced to assess the extent and "permanence" of Latino subcommunities and the broader Latino national community. Pan-ethnicity is explored in terms of both its political utility for Latinos and the interplay of mass and elite "forces" involved in its social construction. Authors such as Peter Skerry (1993) have suggested that many Latino leaders perpetuate a sense of ethnicity or "Latino-ness" to maintain their power bases. In this vein, the social construction of ethnicity and resulting community is an artificial one or, at best, one contrived for the benefit of a limited number of activists. On the other hand, our basis for community indicates that Latino identity and affiliation must include dimensions of self-choice and conscious acceptance of belonging to a community defined as Latino or a specific Latino subgroup. Again, the basis for community will be related to the viability of pan-ethnicity.

We will discuss Latino political participation in a number of chapters that break down the contributing factors of participation into individual, organizational, social, attitudinal, and **structural factors** for Latino subgroup members. We attempt to differentiate between the crucial factors of being foreign-born versus native-born, gender, class, and regional location in analyzing political participation while also incorporating the dimensions of time, money, and skills (Verba, Scholzman, and Brady 1995). The participation chapters will focus on the many modes of participation: voting, electoral activities, organizational involvement, protest, individualized contact, and office holding. Using the extant research on specific Latino subgroups, we will portray the variations and similarities that exist across the Latino community as well as how the use of social media has influenced the ways in which Latinos engage in the political system.

Aspects of political mobilization in Latino politics are interwoven across multiple chapters. Queries as to when Latinos are asked to become politically involved, by whom (organizational leaders or neighbors), and who tends to get involved and who does not, will be discussed. Political involvement is not solely a function of an individual's decision. People can be approached and asked in different ways to get involved and, as we discuss in this book, many Latinos are not approached at all by parties, candidates, or organizations. Very simply, this is a way to define political mobilization as the "outside" force that influences individual political involvement. Characterizing mobilization in this manner serves as a mechanism to introduce organizations and leadership into the Latino politics equation. Using specific Latino-focused organizations, we illustrate the range and scope of organizational goals, arenas of involvement, membership and resource bases, and their political impact in a variety of policy areas. We will examine the extent of involvement in Latino organizations and how those organizations are involved with the Latino community and its needs.

We will also address Latinos' leadership styles, communication skills, and linkages with the "masses."[9] Leadership is studied in terms of the articulation of goals that are conveyed to Latinos and its coherency, which can influence specific political activities. Some have suggested that Latino political empowerment would be greatly enhanced if there were one or even two national Latino leaders who had followings in all of the Latino subcommunities. Others have argued that the core of Latino interests and needs resides in local communities where leadership activities and development are situated. They suggest that a singular leader, or even two or three, would be a difficult challenge for any community of size and diversity to achieve.

The role of Latino leadership serves to crystallize issues, strategies, and "targets." The issue of gender bias, which is inherent in our discussion of leadership, is examined. Viable national leaders are more likely to be males, whereas leaders at the grass roots are often women. Characterizing leadership in this manner serves to introduce the concept of vertical and horizontal leadership. Again, we introduce specific examples to illustrate the issues and impact associated with various leaders. The work by Hardy-Fanta et al. (2016) enables us to know more about Latina elected officials, including their motivation to seek office and policy priorities.

Public Policies, Arenas, and Latinos

Many times, greater attention is focused at the national and state levels; however, Latino politics at the local level is a very active arena. It has been suggested that the intensity and soul of Latino politics deals with local struggles (location decisions regarding toxic waste sites, delivery of services, educational equity and quality, residential gentrification, etc.). Several locally focused community organizations have arisen over the past two decades in many Latino subcommunities, and many cities have elected Latino mayors. Organizing principles, efforts, strategies, and outcomes are important dimensions of Latino politics. They are often overlooked and underanalyzed. Therefore, we have attempted to characterize and analyze local Latino politics in the context of Latino empowerment and political development.

An understanding of Latino politics involves a focus on the ongoing political dynamics occurring across the Latino communities, as well as external forces and actions in the larger society. In this context, legislative initiatives and policies such as the civil rights and voting rights acts have played an important role in generating electoral representation, equal opportunities, and fuller civic participation. In the latter chapters of this book, we examine the origin of voting and civil rights legislation and policies that have impacted Latinos. Other legislative changes (Titles VI, VII, and IX of the Higher Education Act, the Equal Employment Opportunity Act [EEOA], etc.), lobbying efforts, and major court decisions will be analyzed as part of the political assessment of Latinos and the political system. Such organizations as the Mexican American Legal Defense and Education Fund, the Puerto Rican Legal Defense and Education Fund, and Unidos are key groups considered in these sections.

Our discussion of Latinos focuses on specific public policy areas to maintain consistency with the theme of community, shared interests, culture, and conditions that help shape why these are critical issue areas for Latinos. The politics of culture is connected with language, cultural distinctiveness, English-only initiatives, and xenophobic movements directed toward Latinos. First-generation immigrants and international migration bring immigration policies, border enforcement, immigrant and noncitizen rights, political integration, and avenues for participation into our discussion of Latino politics. To some extent, the immigration question is a test of political loyalty, with many Latinos forced to decide whether to risk discrimination and alienation by showing support for immigrants, including members of their own extended families.

Equality-of-opportunity issues deal with educational quality and resources, labor market participation (i.e., access to jobs and opportunities for advancement, preparation for employment with job mobility, protection from discrimination, and equal and competitive pay), economic participation and income mobility, access to higher education, and social service participation. Within this context, the debate over, and the impact of, affirmative action is important. To some extent, foreign policy concerns (Cuba and the Castro regime, the economic embargo of Cuba, Puerto Rican statehood/independence, the USMCA–U.S. Mexico and Canada Agreement, US economic investments in Latin America, drug interdiction, etc.) are aspects of the public policy discussions with particular relevance to Latinos. We have also seen greater evidence of Latinos' interest in environmental policy, including a growing concern for global warming. Integral to this section is attention to an understanding of the American policy-making process. An understanding of agenda setting, monitoring policy implementation, and reviewing policy consequences form an integral part of analyzing specific policy areas.

Finally, our analyses point to the future of Latino politics and revisit the concepts of community, shared interests, culture and organizations, and identity construction, as well as current and trending external factors and actions in the political system. Chapters 11 and 12 look at coalition formation within the Latino communities and with other minority communities. Our discussion of trends for the next decades will complete our discourse, but the future of Latino politics remains dynamic and ever developing. Where will the Latino community be in the next twenty years? Will its identity be thinner and more externally assigned rather than heavier and more assertive? Given the changing demography of the Latino community (growing numbers of Latinos from Central America, South America, and the Caribbean, greater geographic dispersion and intermixing of Latino subcommunities, etc.), will the agenda and its leadership structure also undergo some major changes? We have developed four possible scenarios based on different directions of community building and their political outlooks.

Conclusion

In our introduction of this new edition, we have tried to lay out important concepts with which to describe and analyze Latino politics. The challenge is to discuss the politics of Latino subcommunities without necessarily assuming that Latino politics (in the pan-ethnic sense) is the pervasive form of identity relevant for this community. That is, we define politics at the national-origin community level (Cuban, Salvadoran, Mexican-origin, etc.) for both national and local arenas. At the same time, a Latino political force exists that, at times, more closely resembles a single group than a collection of multiple independent Latino subgroups. An important question regarding the position of Latinos in American society is the extent to which they impact political arenas and agendas as a pan-ethnic community as opposed to a loose consortium of semi-independent interests. The task has begun and the chapters that follow try to analyze Latino politics with the vitality and personality that constitute the Latino peoples.

Discussion Questions

1. What defines a Latino? Do Latinos comprise an ethnic group, a racial group, or some other differently characterized social grouping?
2. How well does the concept of ethnicity fit the Latino community in the United States?
3. Recently, the "label" of "Latinx" has been used in a variety of settings and promoted as a broader way to capture *latinidad* (sexual orientation, gender, race, and class). What are the benefits and areas of debate for greater incorporation of Latinx as a better descriptor?
4. This book tries to establish a sense of community among Latinos. How well does the framework of communities of common culture and interests help in understanding Latinos?
5. We introduce the concept of pan-ethnicity and suggest its utility for understanding Latino politics. Discuss this concept and how applicable it is to contemporary American politics.
6. Latino politics can be characterized as defensive politics, defending itself from "attacks" against fitting in and really belonging to American society. Is this a good way to look at Latino politics, or are there other more appropriate characterizations?
7. Ethnic and racial identity can share some things in common as well as have some differences. Discuss how that works for each of you as to how you see yourself and which groups you identify with.

8. Specifically, what community of interest situations and issues can bring together the Latino national-origin communities?
9. What would you identify as important policy issues for Latinos and why? Does it make a difference to think of issues in national versus state and local terms?

Notes

1. Castro, "Congressional Hispanic Caucus Statement on Shooting in El Paso."
2. https://fivethirtyeight.com/features/the-share-of-latinos-who-say-its-gotten-worse-in-the-u-s-has-skyrocketed.
3. The title of our book uses the descriptor "Latinos" to represent persons of Spanish/Indigenous heritage from the Americas and the Iberian Peninsula. Our selection of the identifier "Latino" as a general descriptor of persons of Hispanic origin/ancestry provides us a "vehicle" to explore the many facets of their lives in the United States. We recognize continual discussions of other descriptors, especially the newer term of "Latinx." While we acknowledge the use of multiple descriptors for this population, our use of "Latino" (and its feminine counterpart) affords us a recognized "label" without attaching necessarily ideological meanings.
4. A Latino Decisions poll conducted in New Mexico in the summer of 2019 found that 20 percent of Hispanics stated a lack of trust in the current administration as a reason why they did not plan to participate in the 2020 census.
5. OMB directive 15 contents.
6. The concepts of race and ethnicity warrant additional clarification. The census recognizes five racial categories: white, black, American Indian/Alaska Native, Asian/Pacific Islander, and other. The last category, "other," represents persons who identify themselves racially in ways that differ from the other four categories. In the case of ethnicity, ancestry or country forms the basis on which origin is categorized. Persons who identify themselves as of Spanish origin are asked a follow-up question seeking their particular ancestral group (i.e., Mexican, Cuban, Puerto Rican, Central/South American, or other [to be specified]). In essence, ethnicity in the census is limited to "Spanish origin."
7. Pan-ethnicity refers to a sense of group affinity and identification that transcends one's own national-origin group. A pan-ethnic identity does not necessarily replace national-origin affinity, but it includes a broader configuration in defining the group. The labels "Latino" and "Hispanic" encompass several national origins.
8. The grandfather clause requires a potential registrant to show that his grandfather was a registered voter before he can register to vote. For African Americans, the grandfather clause hearkened back to the period of slavery, when blacks had no rights, especially not voting rights.
9. By "mass interactions," we mean inter-Latino interactions at the grassroots level. What is the extent of contact between persons of a specific Latino subgroup origin with other Latinos? These interactions could be social, familial, employment based, or related to any one of a variety of social interactions within the local community.

CHAPTER 2

Community Building in Latino America

Píntame un cuadro donde se representan imagenes de nuestra comunidad. El/la artista pinta de acuerdo su propio punto de vista. Todas las perspectivas, la abundancia de rostros y figuras forman el carácter de lo que significa ser parte de una comunidad que es evolucíon.

Paint me a picture in which images of our community are represented. The artist paints according to his or her own point of view. With so many perspectives, a multitude of faces and personalities make up the character of our changing community.

OUR EXAMINATION SHOWS LATINO POLITICS in the United States to be the dynamic formulation of community incorporating all the diversities and similarities among its members. Our discussion of politics centers on power, influences, resources, and interest articulation. Thus, Latino politics represents an aggregation of persons whose origins and/or ancestry can be connected across more than twenty countries in Latin America and the Iberian Peninsula. While we explore the rich and important variations across the book, in this chapter we focus on the common or collective experiences that help define "Latino" politics. Our underlying perspective is the assumption that persons with a common ancestry and culture can come together to achieve common objectives and address common concerns through civic and political engagement. Our perspective is therefore in contrast to the assertion that Latinos of different national-origin groups cannot be expected to share a sense of commonality, given that they originate from different countries and have different immigration histories.

Our discussion of pan-ethnic identity in this chapter and in chapter 5 is organized largely around the research focused on linked fate among Latinos, a concept we noted in chapter 1, which has been found to mobilize African Americans politically and lead to cohesive voting behavior and policy preferences (Dawson 1994). Dawson's classic book, *Behind the Mule* (1994), on linked-fate acquisition among African Americans noted that this politicized sense of identity was driven largely by a common historical connection to slavery and shared experiences of racial discrimination. Dawson also found that linked fate among African Americans was not impacted by variation in socioeconomic status. We reference the research focused on factors that drive linked fate among Latinos (Sanchez and Masuoka 2010; Sanchez, Masuoka, and Abrams 2019) to organize our discussion of pan-ethnic Latino identity. Sanchez and Masuoka's attempt to identify sources of this specific form of identity over two periods of time (2006 and 2016) provides a backdrop for a more comprehensive discussion of the foundation for Latino pan-ethnic community-building in this chapter.

The sources of Latino identity must include a review of the similar historical experiences, cultural values, nativity, and shared connection to the Spanish language that bind many Latinos (Gómez-Quiñones 1990; Stavans 1996; Fox 1997). This discussion begins with a brief summary of the historical context of this community, which provides the backdrop for our discourse. We then move to the powerful role of language and nativity that has been well documented as a source of pan-ethnic identity across the Latino community but that has also been noted as a source of important internal variation that can, at times, set boundaries for a sense of collective identity that spans generational status and a connection to the immigration experience. Finally, we summarize the discrimination experiences and exposure to public policies that target or racialize Latinos that have been found to be a source of linked fate for Latinos, particularly in the current era of punitive immigration politics and policy (Vargas, Sanchez, and Valdez 2017; Sanchez, Masuoka, and Abrams 2019).

Similar Historical Context

A strong factor in the development of a pan-ethnic community is based in the Latino community's historical experiences with the US government. The combination of the swelling growth rates among Latino subgroups and the creation of "situational ethnicity" by Latino activists served as a key element in the promotion of a Latino community. The significant influx of Latinos into the United States began in the mid-1970s, with the fastest-growing elements within the Latino community being people from Central and South America and the Spanish-speaking Caribbean.

While each group was growing faster than the national average, their respective size and regional concentration was limiting their national presence. Mexican Americans were seen as a regional minority, primarily concentrated in the Southwest and oriented toward regional issues. Puerto Ricans were a New York City metropolitan phenomenon, coping with a declining manufacturing economy and living on the mean streets of "El Barrio." Cubans, on the other hand, were seen as active entrepreneurs living in concentrated ethnic enclaves and promoting anticommunist policies in Congress. These oversimplifications summarize dominant perceptions of the situation relevance and policy domains of the three larger subgroups. The development of a pan-ethnic grouping and identity became a means to expand group size, scope, and national visibility. Thus, the outgrowth of "**Hispanicity**" or "Latino-ness" represented a strategic decision among activists to enlarge the community and, potentially, its political capital and resource base.

The changing internal Latino demography and the strategic development of an expanding Latino population base are not mutually exclusive evolutions. Some writers on Latino politics have characterized the political actions of Latino activists as perpetuating ethnicity or pan-ethnicity in order to ensure a political base and a following. Thus, these leaders may not reflect the assimilation and upward mobility that many Latinos are achieving. This perspective goes to the very heart of community and community building. The realities of daily living among Latino subgroup members include contact and awareness of not only fellow national-origin members but also other Latinos in their community and elsewhere. While we recognize some symbolic utility of using a pan-ethnic identity, our reference to community is based upon the reality of a daily life in which being Latino is relevant and ongoing.

Prior to the 1980s, Latinos were characterized as specific national-origin groups in particular regions of the United States, not as a pan-ethnic community or ethnic group. The Chicanos/Mexican Americans in the Southwest traced their ancestry to the sixteenth century, as did the newly arrived "Mexicanos" from Mexico's central plateau. Puerto Ricans lived predominately in the Northeast, especially in the New York City metropolitan area. There was a significant post–World War II out-migration from "La Isla" to the industrial centers of the Rust Belt as well as to the agricultural sectors in the Northeast and the South. After Fidel Castro came to power in 1959, several waves of Cuban political refugees and exiles descended on the southern United States. Even though Cuban refugees participated in refugee-placement programs that included resettlement throughout the United States, most Cubans preferred to reside in Florida. Subsequent waves of Cuban refugees in the 1980s and 1990s augmented an entrepreneurial and better-educated community in southern Florida.

Mexicans, Puerto Ricans, and Cubans, then comprising the three largest Latino communities, became more established and visible to the larger American public. However, the significant influx of Latinos into the United States began in the mid-1970s, and the fastest-growing elements within the Latino community were persons from Central and South America and the Spanish-speaking Caribbean. Movement by Central American and Caribbean Latinos was initially followed by their migration to the Northeast and Midwest and then to California and Texas and the South. Chapter 3 provides more specific discussions of these demographic profiles over time. One result of greater Latino migration throughout the United States was a more diverse mix of Latino subgroups, a pattern that challenged the established Mexican American, Puerto Rican, and Cuban communities' dominance of Latino politics. The "big three" began to have more contact with individuals from Central and South America. Such a confluence of persons with linkages to the Spanish language, Spanish colonial histories, and US hegemony assisted with possible cultural and political connections. It also created some competition for housing, neighborhoods, and political recognition.

The liberation struggles in El Salvador, Nicaragua, and Guatemala, together with high birthrates, political instability and violence, and inadequate economic growth and opportunity, have fueled out-migration of Central Americans into almost every region of the United States. For the most part, Central Americans have been designated as economic migrants rather than political refugees. Public policy distinctions between economic and political migrants reflect national foreign policy commitments rather than individuals' conditions or situations. Regardless of differences in motivation to migrate to the United States, we contend that commonalities in experiences upon arrival have led to a collective sense of community.

The word "**community**" refers here to the connections between persons that formulate a sense of place, being, and membership in a larger whole. The origins of Hispanics or Latinos can be traced to various strands of US history and events. For example, federal legislation in the mid-1970s, initiated by Congressman Edward Roybal, required all federal agencies to maintain records and designations of persons of Spanish origin, generally defined as individuals from Spanish-speaking countries and the Iberian Peninsula. One challenge of implementing this policy entailed formulating a uniform "standard" for identifying persons of Spanish origin. The range of standards included Spanish surname, ancestry, birthplace, foreign-born parentage, self-identification, and language used when growing up.

The 1970 census also reflected a different method for identifying persons of Spanish origin. On both the short and long census forms,[1] ancestry and self-identification determined Hispanicity. That is, an individual who deemed herself a person of Spanish origin would self-identify as such. There were no prescribed criteria, such as Spanish-language use or foreign-born status, to direct a person to declare himself or herself as being of Spanish origin. The self-identifier introduced in the 1970 census has been the consistent Hispanic "marker" ever since. Technically, it is referred to as the ethnicity item or Spanish-origin identifier. This distinction might be helpful to distinguish between race and ethnicity.

Much scholarly and popular literature has discussed race in terms of phenotype, skin color, biology, social structure, and ancestry. Public policies such as the one-drop rule have reinforced the concept of race as more directly connected to skin color and a defined racial categorization. On the other hand, ethnicity is commonly associated with ancestry or national origin. To be an ethnic is to be, for example, Irish American, Italian American, or Cuban American, with ties to cultural practices and traditions. Although we have discussed the conceptual and theoretical underpinnings of race and ethnicity, the social and historical context of these terms is also an important dimension of politics, power, and influence in American society. For these purposes, we will operate on the notion that ethnicity and race are interrelated concepts that establish group boundaries, behaviors, and inter- and intragroup relations.

Following the census distinction between race and ethnicity, a Spanish-origin person can be of any race.[2] While the American understanding of race is strongly related to skin color and other phenotypical attributes, these serve as an external influence on group identification. Ethnicity is viewed more as one's national origin and ancestry and is influenced greatly by assimilation and acculturation processes. Therefore, an important factor that has contributed to the configuration of "Hispanic" or "Latino" as an umbrella term has been the formulation of public policy establishing the collection and operationalization protocol in categorizing Spanish-origin people.

Latino Pan-Ethnicity Motivated by Latino Elites and the Mass Media

Mass media is another important factor contributing to the development of the umbrella term "Latino/Hispanic." The development of pan-ethnic grouping and identity becomes a means to expand group size, scope, and national visibility. Thus, the outgrowth of "Hispanicity" or "Latino-ness" represents a strategic decision among activists to enlarge the community and, potentially, its political capital and resource base.

The changing internal Latino demography and the strategic development of an expanding Latino population base are not mutually exclusive evolutions. Some writers of Latino politics have characterized the political actions of Latino activists as perpetuating ethnicity or pan-ethnicity in order to ensure a political base and a following. Thus, these leaders may not reflect the assimilation and upward mobility that many Latinos are achieving. This perspective goes to the very heart of community and community-building. The realities of daily living among Latino subgroup members include contact and awareness of not only fellow national-origin members but also other Latinos in their community and elsewhere. While we recognize some symbolic utility of using a pan-ethnic identity, our reference to community is based upon the reality of a daily life in which being Latino is relevant and ongoing.

The mass media response to the changing demography of the United States evolved from reporting on specific national-origin Latino subgroups (Puerto Ricans, Mexicans, Dominicans, etc.) to using the more pan-ethnic label of "Hispanic." Toward the end of the 1970s, the media began reporting and discussing both established and recently arrived Latino national-origin groups as solely Latinos. Many major news magazines and newspapers started referring to the 1980s as the decade of the Hispanic. Sound bites like "Hispanics' day in the sun," "fastest-growing minority," and "soon to be the largest minority group" became typical characterizations of this aggregation of people from twenty-two Spanish-speaking countries.

Ironically, descriptors such as "an awakening sleeping giant," "the invisible minority," and "bronze/brown power" were used in the early 1960s to depict Mexican Americans in the Southwest. One parallel theme for both periods was potentiality and promise. The focus on significant population growth and its continuation in the future projected Latinos as a "new" political and economic force in American society. Mass media centers in the eastern part of the United States conducted exploration and fact-finding projects on the relatively unknown Hispanics. There was utility in the media's assigning one label and identity to varied national-origin group members. Such clustering of the many national-origin groups into one ethnic status[3] simplified discussions of public policy and news regarding Latinos. This illustrates how factors outside the Latino community play an important role in shaping understanding and characterization of these communities. Clearly, some subgroup differentiation does take place, but the "Hispanic/Latino" descriptor is used more often.

Spanish Language Use and Nativity Are Key to Community Building

Language and nativity (country of birth) are critical cultural dimensions that help define the Latino community of common cultures. The coexistence of native-born and "immigrant" Latinos in the same or proximate neighborhoods, sharing familial social networks, common work environments, and business interactions provides a regular basis for cultural exchanges and experiences. These interactions can reinforce cultural expressions and values or, perhaps, create cultural tensions over assimilation, acculturation, or even cultural authenticity. Cultural dynamics would be less likely to exist without the persistence of Spanish-language use and the steady influx of immigrants. In addition, the sizable percentage of foreign-born members in Latino communities helps bring forth the extended and complex set of issues and policies related to immigration rights, legal standing, and access to services. In fact, Sanchez and Masuoka (2010) found linked fate to be strongest among Spanish-language-dominant Latinos in their analysis utilizing the Latino National Survey, and they found foreign-born Latinos to have a greater sense of linked fate not only in 2006, but 2016 as well (Sanchez, Masuoka, and Abrams 2019).

Latino communities are composed largely of those born in Spanish-origin countries, making the large presence of foreign-born Latinos now living in the United States a bridge that brings the customs and traditions of the home country to those who are further removed from the immigrant experience. Most notable among these cultural factors is the Spanish language, which can be a strong foundation for a sense of pan-ethnic identity.

In many ways, Latinos' relationship to Spanish is complex. Latinos are a bilingual group, with a significant first-generation (or foreign-born) population who are predominately Spanish-speaking and a growing segment who are more English dominant and who have increasingly distant connections to their countries of origin. Many Latinos have been discriminated against for speaking Spanish, yet those in New Mexico have lived in a state that has recognized Spanish as an official language for multiple generations.

The Pew Hispanic Center has identified several important trends in Spanish-language use through analysis of US census data. First is the sheer size of the Spanish-speaking population in the United States, with roughly forty million people in the country indicating that they speak Spanish at home. This makes Spanish the second-most-spoken language in the United States. However, Pew noted there has been a reduction recently in the number of Latinos who speak Spanish and an increase, over the same time, of predominantly English-speaking Latinos.

The authors of this research believe that a decrease in parents who indicate they speak Spanish to their children, particularly among the second generation and beyond, as well as an increase of Latinos not married to another Latino, attributes to the increase in English-dominant Latinos (see Lopes et al. 2018 Pew Report in the "Links to Suggested Readings" section).

Even with the rise in Latinos who are not fluent in Spanish over time, the continued Spanish-language use among many Latinos lends a perception of loyalty or familiarity to Spanish, and the rise in English-only laws and other policies that attack Spanish-language use leads to a strong attachment among virtually all Latinos to the Spanish language. The strong relationship between Spanish and ethnic identity among Latinos has been at least partially driven by the growth of Spanish-speaking media, particularly networks Univision and Telemundo, who along with Spanish-language radio help to connect many Latinos not only to their language, but to Latino-focused news and political information that cues a sense of pan-ethnic community (Gómez-Aguiñaga 2020; Kerevel 2011). The role and impact of Spanish-language media will be discussed in more detail in chapter 7, especially in relation to campaigns and elections.

Nativity goes hand in hand with Spanish language in helping to drive a sense of pan-ethnicity among Latinos. The composition of US immigration changed dramatically in the latter half of the twentieth century as Latin American and Asian immigrants came to dominate the migration stream. There are almost twenty-eight million foreign-born people in the United States, of whom 41 percent are Hispanics. Furthermore, almost two-fifths of all Latinos residing in the United States are foreign-born. Overall, the percentage of foreign-born Latinos is 38 percent, compared to foreign-born non-Hispanics at 12.5 percent. While the percentage of American permanent resident aliens overall is slightly greater than 10 percent,[4] the overall percentage for Latinos is 40 percent (6.1 percent for non-Hispanics).

The number of foreign-born Latinos and experience with immigration laws varies across the different Latino subgroups. More than 60 percent (60.8 percent) of Cubans are foreign-born, as are 77.5 percent of Central Americans and 69.5 percent of South Americans. The Cuban community's foreign-born members have refugee status with access to specific governmental assistance programs, while the rest of Latinos are viewed as economic migrants (there have been initiatives by Salvadorans and Guatemalans to obtain refugee status). Finally, the distinction of Puerto Ricans born in the United States or on the island is associated with their citizenship status. Puerto Rico is a commonwealth, and Puerto Ricans are US citizens. At the same time, their perspectives and experiences as Puerto Ricans may be affected by their place of birth.

Discrimination Faced by Latinos: A Strong Foundation for Ethnic Identity

Our delineation of Latinos or Hispanics has focused on notions of a group of people linked by a common language, interrelated cultural traditions and values, and similar experiences in the United States. Since the 1990s, social scientists have added that common experiences with discrimination and relegation to minority status in many facets of American life have motivated a strong sense of racial or ethnic identity among Latinos.

Latinos have been subject to a long history of brutal discrimination, such as having separate and unequal schools, restaurants, theaters, swimming pools, and even cemeteries (Kamasaki 1988; Massey 1989). Like African Americans, they have also been excluded from being able to vote and seeking public office through intimidation (Gutierrez et al. 1999; Smith 1990; García 1986a). Further, Latinos, particularly in the Southwest, were subjected to lynching and violence in response to their calls for political inclusion and overall empowerment (Nelson and Lavariega 2006). These state-sanctioned discriminatory policies worked together to keep Latinos largely concentrated in certain industries and occupational sectors and in residential enclaves (Denton and Massey 1988; Croucher 1997).

Although Latinos overall have clearly faced exclusion and discrimination throughout their history, they unfortunately continue to deal with discriminatory practices in the United States today. According to Latino Decisions Election Eve Survey, 10 percent of all Latino voters in 2016 reported that discrimination against Latinos or immigrants was the most important issue that the federal government should address. Roughly 93 percent of Latino respondents to the 2016 Collaborative Multiracial Post-Election Survey (CMPS) reported that there is at least some discrimination directed at Latinos in society, with 40 percent noting that they face "a lot" of discrimination.

Scholars of Latino politics have found discrimination experiences and perceptions that Latinos face discrimination in society are major drivers of pan-ethnic identity among Latinos. For example, Sanchez and Vargas (2016) found that discrimination experiences were the primary driver of both group consciousness and linked fate for Latinos. Similarly, Sanchez and Rodriguez Espinosa (2016) found that discrimination from outside groups yielded higher rates of linked fate among Latinos.

We contend that a sense of pan-ethnic identity can emerge from a reaction to threatening or racialized public policies. Numerous scholars observed heightened feelings of politicized group identity in response to anti-immigrant policies across various national-, state-, and local-level contexts (Zepeda-Millán 2017; Ramírez 2013; Barreto et al. 2008; Vargas, Sanchez, and Valdez 2017; Vargas, Sanchez, and Juárez 2017). These scholars note that exposure to punitive immigration policies generate an underlying sense of ethnic attachment, regardless of one's own nativity or immigration status.

In this section, we have identified several factors that motivate a sense of pan-ethnic identity by building a sense of community that moves beyond one's specific national-origin group. These are factors that we return to across each successive chapter, as they serve as informal organizing themes that construct our thoughts and theories regarding the state of Latino politics.

In the next section, we provide greater clarity and direction on the:

- common historical context in the United States that bonds Latinos' experiences,
- mass media and Latino politics elites who cue a sense of pan-ethnicity,
- attachments to the Spanish language and nativity that provide a bridge to cultural norms and practices,
- discrimination experiences and perceptions that Latinos, as a group, face in society, and
- laws and policies that are perceived as a threat to Latinos, their culture, and their overall well-being.

Is There a Latino Community, and What Does That Mean?

As discussed in the prior section, each Latino subgroup has a unique history in the United States, experiences of contact with, and migration to, this country, social class distribution, and legal status (political refugee, legal permanent resident alien, or undocumented migrant). The two bases of community are associated with the concepts of commonality of culture and commonality of interests (García and Pedraza-Bailey 1990; Cornell and Hartman 1998). Communities of common or similar cultures endure when persons are tied together naturally by their involvement in a "common system of purpose with accompanying patterns of traditional interactions and behaviors rooted in a common heritage" (Cornell 1985). This common heritage or tradition includes national ancestry, language, religion and religious customs, observance of holidays and festivals, and familial networks. For the Mexican-origin population, Keefe and Padilla (1989) explore Chicano ethnicity and identify several dimensions of culture. When familial interactions are primary and serve as conduits of cultural transmission, the "products" are customs, folklore, linguistic loyalty, ethnic loyalty, and group identity. Thus, a person can be enveloped by a sense of ethnicity, usually within a national-origin context (Mexican American, Salvadoran, Dominican, etc.). However, this sense of ethnicity may not automatically lead to community actions.

The result of perceived and accepted common interests may lead to the development of a new or reinforced identity. For example, the "official usage" of pan-ethnic terms such as *Hispanic* may reorient a person to incorporate that label and strategically use that identity to maximize political effects. A Mexican American activist in Arizona might oppose a referendum effort to remove bilingual education programs because such programs do not ensure educational excellence and equity for all Hispanic children. The Latino subcommunity is the reality experienced by Mexican-origin children; yet, the broader identifier "Hispanic" is used to contextualize the issue nationally as well as locally.

The concept of a community of interests works to examine and construct new boundaries of group affiliation; it also aids analysis of comparable conditions among other social groups and understanding structural relations between the group and social and political institutions. As we emphasized in our discussion of drivers to linked fate, a central element within these analytical insights is the role played by discriminatory practices and prejudicial attitudes on the part of the larger society and manifested in public policies. For example, the Immigration and Naturalization Service may conduct sweeps only or primarily in Latino residential neighborhoods. If only individuals who appear Latino are detained to show proof of legal status, then that policy action has a disparate impact on Latino communities. In 2010, the state of Arizona passed a law enabling local and state law enforcement officers to detain persons until they provide proof of legal status. (We discuss this issue and resulting litigation battles in chapter 9.) For our purposes, **minority status** is a relational concept in which minority-group members have limited access, opportunity, power, and influence. Minority status is associated with differential treatment and power, being an identifiable group, and group awareness. For Latinos, language, customs, phenotype (to some extent), and social networks help promote that identifiability. In addition, stereotypes and prejudicial attitudes toward Latinos, as well as unfair treatment, serve to perpetuate this identifiability. The issues of empowerment, representation, equity, power, access, and participation become a major part of defining a community and its interests.

The dimension of commonality (community linkages, bonds, affinities, interactions, and individual affiliations) is important in our discussion of Latino community. This collectivity is a set of ties of various associations but, at the same time, does not require uniformity or complete consensus among all the Latino subcommunities. The theme of diversity and similarity emphasizes that conformity and unanimity are not realistic expectations for community membership and operations. While the analogy is not perfect, variations in character, lifestyle, personality, and so on can be found within most families and can challenge the maintenance of a family entity, but the family structure remains.

If Latino subcommunities can share commonalities of culture and interest, each can work interactively with the other. That is, cultural cues and symbols can encourage persons of Spanish origin to work toward specific goals and objectives. At the same time, cultural maintenance and practices can serve as the political content of a Latino political agenda. For example, the use of, or at least exposure to, the Spanish language while growing up serves as a common cultural experience. It also serves as a point of political conflict with respect to English as the official language of the United States, structuring and maintaining bilingual educational programs, and loyalty to and assimilation into American society. The persistence of Latino culture fuels the politics of culture. In our broadest sense, commonality of culture and interests can be seen as perceptions and experiences among Latinos that reflect positive affinities and substantial interactions and awareness of Latinos in the various subcommunities.

Latino/Hispanic as a Viable Identity

In the past thirty years, a growing body of literature has developed the concept of pan-ethnicity (Espiritu 1992; Cornell and Hartman 1998). The work by Padilla (1986) explores this concept in the context of the Latino population in Chicago. Padilla espouses the idea of Latino consciousness, which includes both an ideological and a pragmatic sense of group identity. The ideological aspect conceives of the interrelatedness among persons of Spanish origin in terms of their communal cultural values and routines in addition to political, economic, and social conditions and consequences. The latter connection ties in structural biases and policies that disadvantage persons who are Mexican, Guatemalan, Colombian, and so on. Thus, there is a cost to being Latino, in terms of opportunities, equity, access, and rights that transcends any specific Latino subgroup.

The pragmatic dimension of Padilla's Latino consciousness contemplates the potential benefits of expanding community beyond national-origin boundaries. In this way, a group is significantly empowered through the notion of strength in numbers, so that rather than speaking of one million Cubans in the United States, a Cuban American leader can reference fifty million Latinos. The larger population base and greater national geographic dispersion serve to enhance greater political effectiveness and visibility. At the same time, larger numbers do not necessarily translate to guaranteed political power. In some ways, the pragmatic nature of creating a Latino community is a strategic move to expand the potential political resource base by accenting both commonalities of culture and interests.

The Pan-Ethnic Dimension, Racial Identity, and the "Latino-Hispanic" Label

Pan-ethnicity, as discussed so far, refers to the process of group formation due to common conditions and bases for community. The other critical component lies with the situational nature of pan-ethnicity (Lopez and Espiritu 1990). That is, individuals can consciously choose a group identity that serves a specific utility—political, for our purposes. Since Latinos can be viewed as covering more than twenty national-origin groups, we posit that there need not be a "natural" clustering based on that connection alone. We have suggested that practical and strategic purposes are served by using a pan-ethnic identity.

Group consciousness and social identity constitute significant forms of pan-ethnic community or identity. Group consciousness refers to the cognitive elements of group attachment; a person incorporates group identity(ies) as part of his or her social identity. In addition, group consciousness includes an evaluative assessment of the group's relative position in society. This identity represents an attachment and affinity to particular social groupings. For our purposes, people of Mexican, Dominican, and Colombian origin, for example, can include a sense of pan-ethnic group attachment and affiliation, while, at the same time, maintaining their own national origin or ancestry. In addition, many other social identities (parental roles, work groups, etc.) can constitute a person's social identity constellation.

This idea captures the idea of multiple social identities that have relevance to each person (Barvosa 1999). Therefore, we can have coexisting multiple identities that reflect our daily lives and situations in which we find ourselves. For example, research scholars (Segura 1984; Cordova 1993) discuss and analyze what is referred to as "triple oppression," that is, the intersection of class, ethnicity/race, and gender compounding circumstances and experiences. For instance, the "stigma" of a female person of color occupying a lower socioeconomic class may have a cumulative negative effect on opportunities and ambitions. This example has a direct bearing on many Latinos' life chances; the intersection of these three identities can affect their daily lives. Add to the "triple oppression" identities the possibility that the individual may also be coming from a particular country of origin or region of the world, an immigrant, undocumented, or a non-English speaker, and you can imagine an entire Latino/a's "constellation" of social identities. So, in our political discussion of pan-ethnic identity, being a Latino/Hispanic person is real and relevant, but a singular identity for any individual would be rare.

The literature on social identity and group consciousness focuses on the individual dynamics of identity (Sanchez 2006b); clearly the social context can establish or reinforce the basis for group affiliation and affinity. Works by Padilla (1986), Espiritu (1992), Nagel (1996), and Nelson and Tienda (1985) have used, to varying degrees, the concepts of group identity and group consciousness to construct pan-ethnicity.

The "Latinization" of the United States (Fox 1997; Cuello 1996; Benitez 2007) over the last three decades has been accompanied by the transformation of immigrant and indigenous groups into minority groups (Wilson 1977). Miami is now recognized as a "Latino city" in which Cubans have important political and economic influence. Los Angeles, with its sizable Mexican-origin and growing Central American communities, rivals cities in Latin America in terms of population concentrations. More than one out of every five persons in Chicago is Latino, with a mix of Mexican, Puerto Rican, and Central American origins. New York has not only a large Puerto Rican population, but also fast-growing Dominican, Colombian, and Peruvian communities. Three national Spanish-language television networks broadcast daily throughout the United States and Latin America. In sections of many US cities, most residents speak English infrequently, and streets are lined with Latino-based and Latino-oriented businesses. As Cuello (1996) points out, this nation has undergone dramatic cultural changes in a very Latino sort of way (Benitez 2007).

For our purposes, the Latinization of the United States has a direct impact on the US political system and processes. Our focus on pan-ethnicity reflects the cognitive and psychological dimensions of group identity and consciousness. Such group identity represents an affinity with, and sense of attachment to, a broader social category than national origin alone. Building on the concept of group consciousness (Verba and Nie 1972; Miller et al. 1981; García 1982; Sanchez 2006b), we focus on two key dimensions: an evaluation of one's group status politically in American society and a collective orientation toward social and political action.

For Latinos, individuals with a group consciousness have a positive affinity for being Latino; they assess their group as experiencing lower levels of socioeconomic and political status and opportunities, and they are inclined to participate in some collective activity to change the situation. It is this desire to change one's social position through collective action as politicized identities that leads many to refer to group consciousness and the related concept of linked fate.

By exploring the extent of "Latino-ness" or "Hispanicity" in the context of community building and bridging the twenty-plus Latino national-origin groups, we can establish the basis for a political community. In addition, we examine the relevance and impact of such community formation on the larger political system. The latter point encompasses the identification of issues and public policy preferences, organizational and leadership development, political mobilization, electoral politics and representation, and policy implementation. While much attention has been directed toward the phenomenal population growth of Latinos over the past several decades, our perspective does not revolve around growth alone. Population size and geographic location and concentration do serve as a resource base, but converting numbers of people into an effective political base requires additional elements.

The process of constructing or developing a Latino identity and affinity can stem from situations and conditions within the Latino subcommunities as well as general societal developments. For example, work by Padilla (1986) in Chicago highlights the conscious efforts by leadership in the various Latino communities (Mexican, Puerto Rican, Cuban, etc.) to promote a pan-ethnic identity. The use and social meaning of the word "Latino" to reflect a community of Spanish-speaking and culturally and politically similar groups was evident in the early 1970s. Now in contemporary America, the prevalence of the terms "Latino" or "Hispanic" is much less an issue of presence, but for some, a question of relevance (Beltrán 2010). That is, do familiarity and exposure to these terms result in actual internalizing of this identity in "everyday life"?

One of the focus groups conducted as part of the **Latino National Survey** (LNS) in 2005 was held in Chicago. A central area of exploration was identity and labeling. A group of fifteen to twenty Latinos (of varied national origins and ages) participated in a discussion of how each saw himself or herself. For the most part, each person included being Latino as part of his or her social identity. In fact, without any cues from the focus facilitator, the use of "Latino" and/or "Hispanic" was very commonplace in most everyone's conversation. In addition, participants' characterization of what the use of those terms meant reflected a sense of community among all persons of Latino background. For our purposes, self-description as Latino or Hispanic indicates the integral role of that identity without it being the only identity a person internalizes.

Are Latinos a Racial or an Ethnic Group?

An example from the 1989 **Latino National Political Survey** (LNPS) Chicago focus groups is the set of responses from one young adult Latina. Her parents were of "mixed" Latino background; one was Puerto Rican and the other Mexican. She had married an Italian and lived in a South Side Polish Catholic neighborhood. Her parents were divorced. She described a series of situations in which her four-year-old daughter was already attuned to her sense of identity. When visiting her grandmother, the granddaughter referred to her Mexican-ness, and when visiting her grandfather, she accented her Puerto Rican identity. At the same time, while living in her South Side neighborhood, the young girl placed greater emphasis on her father's Italian ancestry. In school, the young girl was more likely to refer to her European or white ethnic background. When traveling on the bus from the far South Side to the Loop (downtown commercial area), she was quick to identify herself as a minority or person of color. Finally, with her mother and her uncle (mother's brother), she referred to herself as a Latina.

These two foundational bases for the creation and maintenance of the Latino community (i.e., culture and interest) are viewed as clusters of both perceptions and experiences that can produce positive affinities and meaningful interactions between activists in the various Latino subcommunities.

Given our discussion about group identity and affinity, an ongoing issue is whether to categorize Latinos as a racial group or an ethnic group. This discussion has been prevalent among federal statistical agencies, especially the US Census Bureau. With the inclusion of the Spanish-origin question in the short form of the census, Latinos/Hispanics were characterized in the ethnic question, and the race question was a separate item. It is fairly common to have a statistical presentation about Latinos to indicate that Latinos can be of any race. One outcome of this policy has been the concern about clarity among the citizenry, demographers, and other social and political scientists as to whether one can differentiate race from ethnicity.

In table 2.1, we present the results of the 2010 census and the race question. For Latinos, a majority place themselves in the white category (53 percent), but a significant percentage (36.7 percent) marked some other race. Latinos who respond as some other race have been the overwhelming majority (90 percent plus) over the past three censuses. In table 2.2, we can see the extent that different Latino national-origin groups respond to the race question. Except for the Cubans, all the other Latino subgroups respond at nearly 40 percent or greater, with the Central Americans in the mid-50 percent. One interpretation is than many Latinos do not see themselves "fitting into" the prevailing American racial categories.

In the 1995 Current Population Series study, persons were asked about race, ethnicity, national origin, and group label preference (Tucker and Kojetin 1996). Most people do not perceive a real difference between race, national origin, and ethnicity. In several instances, these terms were used interchangeably. Compounding the general ambiguity among the populace about race and ethnicity was the option to indicate "some other race" rather than one of the established racial categories.

TABLE 2.1 Latinos by Racial Selection in the 2010 Census

Census Racial Categories	Population	% of All Hispanics and Latinos
White	26,735,713	53.0
Some other race (Mestizo, Mulatto, etc.)	18,503,103	36.7
Two or more races	3,042,592	6.0
African American	1,243,471	2.5
American Indian and Alaska Native	685,150	1.4
Asian	209,128	0.4
Native Hawaiian and Pacific Islander	58,437	0.1

Source: US Bureau of the Census, 2010 Census.

TABLE 2.2 Race of Major Hispanic Ancestries

Latino Ancestry	Total	White	African American	American Indian/Alaskan Native	Asian	Other[a]
Mexican	31,798,258	16,794,111 (52.8%)	296,778 (.9%)	460,098 (1.5%)	101,654 (.3%)	14,145,617 (44.5%)
Puerto Rican	4,623,716	2,455,534 (53.1%)	403,372 (8.7%)	42,504 (.9%)	24,312 (.5%)	1,697,994 (36.7%)
Cuban	1,785,547	1,525,521 (85.4%)	82,398 (4.6%)	3,002 (.2%)	4,391 (.3%)	170,235 (9.5%)
Salvadoran	1,648,968	663,224 (40.2%)	16,150 (1.0%)	17,682 (1.1%)	4,737 (.3)	947,175 (57.4%)
Dominican	1,414,703	419,016 (29.6%)	182,005 (12.9%)	19,183 (1.4%)	4,056 (.3%)	790,443 (55.9%)
Guatemalan	1,044,209	401,763 (38.5%)	11,471 (1.1%)	31,197 (3.0%)	2,386 (.2%)	597,392 (57.2%)
All Others	4,087,476	2,018,397 (49.4%)	112,521 (2.8%)	75,796 (1.9%)	50,299 (1.2%)	1,830,463 (44.8%)
Totals	50,477,594	26,735,713 (53.0%)	1,243,471 (2.5%)	685,150 (1.4%)	209,128 (.4%)	21,604,132 (42.8%)

Source: US Bureau of the Census, 2010 Census, Self-Identified Race, Hispanic or Latino Origin Population by Type, Table 1, https://www.census.gov/prod/cen2010/briefs/c2010br-04.pdf.

[a] "Other" indicates some other race, two or more races, Native Hawaiian, other Pacific Islander.

With subsequent censuses, the number of persons marking "some other race" has increased to more than nineteen million. One way to interpret this number is that "some other race" would constitute the third-largest racial category in this country. At the same time, those who opt for this choice have a variety of reasons; their responses might include such alternatives as national origin, ancestry, or being part of the entire human race on the 2010 census.

This development has had relevance for Latinos. Of all the persons who marked "some other race," 96.8 percent were people who indicated they are of Hispanic background. Among Latinos, almost two out of five respondents marked "some other race," and another 12.2 percent gave a "no race" response. Since the 1990 census planning efforts, the bureau has investigated and researched alternative ways to gather information about racial groups, including combining the race and Spanish-origin question into one item (del Pinal et al. 2007; Humes, Jones, and Ramirez 2011). They have also tried to analyze the write-ins for those who marked "some other race" to understand what that other race would be. The four largest response categories for Latinos were Mexican origin (44.3 percent), Hispanic (22.7 percent), Latin American (10 percent), and Puerto Rican (3.7 percent). Should one interpret these Latino race responses to mean that Latinos see themselves as a distinctive racial group?

The Census Bureau, along with many of its advisory committees and researchers, has not reached a firm conclusion. The separate race and ethnicity continued in the 2000 and 2010 censuses, and the situation was still undergoing review as to what course to take for the 2020 census at the time of this writing. The challenges have been that the nature of race as a **social construct** does not lend itself to any uniform understanding or basis upon which persons could agree. A racial response is affected not only by people's own notions about themselves, but by their experiences and interactions with others and societal institutions.

What is clear is the development of the concept of "otherness." As we have discussed, people take on a variety of social identities, and these identities have meaning and consequences. By "otherness" we mean that people have a sense of who they are, and if they do not find acknowledgment of their existence, they feel like an "other."

For most of America's history, race has been viewed as a "binary system" represented by "black versus white" distinctions. Other than American Indians (Native Americans), no other social/ethnic groups were categorized into America's racial system. Since the latter half of the twentieth century—and more so during this millennium—American society has become even more diverse (racially and ethnically), especially with the growth of the foreign-born populations. As a result, notions about race and additional "racial categories" have moved us away from a "black-white" racial paradigm.

An additional consideration in this discussion is the racialization of Latinos, especially Latino immigrants. In sociology, racialization is a process of ascribing or assigning racial connotations to the activities of minority group members. This social process is one by which certain groups of people are singled out for distinct treatment based upon real or imagined physical and/or cultural characteristics. As we have said, Latino group status involves power relations and social status. Racialization is often born out of the interaction of a group with a group that it dominates and ascribes identity for the purpose of continued domination.

The changing breadth and understanding of what race is in America has Latinos in the middle of a societal transition. Our examination of Latinos and the American political system is predicated on the distinctiveness of Latinos as a racial/ethnic group (comprised of many cultural, linguistic, and phenotypical attributes) and the dynamics of attaining power, influence, and political representation and responsiveness. The nature of Latinos' political development and impact makes an "official" declaration of a separate racial group less necessary.

As we move into the various aspects of Latinos and the political system, let us briefly frame a concern about the appropriate pan-ethnic label—"Latino" or "Hispanic." In the popular media and governmental circles, the use of "Hispanic" is much more prevalent than "Latino." At the same time, there is slightly greater use of "Latino" among activists, academics, and some advocacy organizations. More importantly, "Hispanic" is the preferred pan-ethnic term among the population itself. The survey firm Latino Decisions begins each of its surveys with a question that directly asks respondents which term they prefer to be called, both as an indicator of preferred terminology as well as to reference this term throughout the rest of the survey, as a means of establishing cultural credibility with respondents. National samples in Latino Decisions's surveys consistently choose "Hispanic" over "Latino." This question has recently included the identification term "Latinx," a term that its proponents contend is neutral in regard to gender or sexual orientation (Juárez 2018). While not pervasive enough to rival "Latino" or "Hispanic" across the full Latino population, this term is gaining traction with Latino youth and may become more prominent over time.

While some works (Oboler 1995; Sanchez 2012) have placed emphasis on the political meaning and ideology associated with each label, an overriding fact is the presence and relevance of a pan-ethnic identity. We contend that this is a foundational basis for group formation, interactions, and collective actions. The proof is in the importance of political life for these communities and the American political system. The remainder of this book can validate, or at least give credence to, the realities of Latino politics. Labels provide some common reference and connections, and we would not diminish those functions. Essentially, we will use "Hispanic" and "Latino/a" interchangeably to connote a group of people who share a common culture and set of interests and experiences in the United States.

Conclusion

Our discussion of pan-ethnicity, linked fate, group consciousness, and an underlying sense of community is the product of the intersection of individual Latino/a lives and the society in which they live, which serves as the dynamic that will contextualize Latino politics. It also illustrates how within-group socialization and external cues influence the identification process. For our purposes, the development of a sense of being Latino can be a "product" of shared cultural values and practices (language, origins, traditions, etc.), intergroup interactions, and societal constructs (positive, but usually negative) of persons of Spanish origin. The latter is the result of stereotypes, prejudices, discriminatory behaviors, and punitive public policies. As we examine the development and existence of community among persons of Latino origin in the United States, our primary purpose is to explore the linkages of community to the political realms of agenda setting, political mobilization, political resource development, and public policy outcomes and implementation.

The next chapter presents more demographic information that illustrates how socioeconomic status, immigration (nativity) status, age, and cultural practices can link Latino national-origin group members together under a pan-ethnic label that has meaning and political relevance. These aspects serve to indicate common experiences and policy concerns and priorities. Some data presented in the next chapter will include Spanish-language use among Latinos, age structure, household composition and income, nativity, educational attainment and occupational status, and religious affiliation and religiosity. As documented in this chapter, Spanish language has consistently been identified as one of the cultural glues for Latinos, being found as one of the strongest predictors of both group consciousness and linked fate. Another example of the impact of Spanish-language use that will be discussed in more detail later is the growth of Spanish-language media, especially on television (Telemundo, Galavision, and Univision), which confirms the existence of Spanish-language markets and mass media transmission of culture and Spanish language. The number-one radio station in the Los Angeles metropolitan area is KLVE, whose programming includes Latin pop, urban hip-hop, and traditional music.

Over the course of our analysis, the distinctions of language use, nativity, and generational status in the United States are key elements in assessing the cross-cutting connections among Latinos. Hopefully, the demographic characterization of Latinos, especially Latino subgroups, helps to paint a partial portrait of the connections among Latino/as that have political relevance to this community and the nation.

Discussion Questions

1. Communities of interests and common or similar cultures have been identified as building blocks for Latino communities. Given a significant foreign-born segment, how much do such persons' experiences connect with those of their native-born counterparts?
2. It is common for the media, individuals, and public officials to use the terms "Latino" and "Hispanic." What is in a label? That is, how are these terms used, and what difference does it make to use one descriptor or the other?
3. A significant part of this chapter examines socioeconomic characteristics among Latinos as a basis for identifying common interests. How else might you approach this connection and what indicators would you use?
4. This chapter introduced the concept of linked fate. What is this term and what are the main factors that help motivate a sense of linked fate among Latinos?
5. Latinos include persons from many different countries of origin living in different parts of the United States. How do these aspects affect the development of Latino common interests?
6. Over the past forty years, the term "Hispanic" has been used in a variety of settings and by different institutions and leaders. Some have posited that this pan-ethnic term is artificially created and has little meaning in the lives of persons of Latino origin. How does the concept of multiple identities and situational identity come into play in the discussion of use of labels?

7. Group consciousness is one of the dominant concepts introduced in this chapter. What is this form of group identity and what are the dimensions of group consciousness that are used to measure the concept by social scientists?
8. The long-standing pattern of Latinos being the predominant group that marks some other race on the census raises questions about how people see and understand race in the United States. What do you think are the factors and/or reasons that a sizable number of Latinos choose "some other race"?

Links to Suggested Readings

https://www.pewresearch.org/fact-tank/2018/04/02/most-hispanic-parents-speak-spanish-to-their-children-but-this-is-less-the-case-in-later-immigrant-generations

https://www.tandfonline.com/doi/full/10.1080/21565503.2019.1638803

Notes

1. The US decennial census is an attempt to enumerate all persons living in the United States on April 1 in the first year of each decade. The short form includes basic information such as number of persons in the household, as well as their ages, races, genders, and relationships to one another. The short form is distributed to all households. The long form is sent randomly to one in six households and asks for much more detail (labor market, migration, ancestry, language use, etc.).

2. Racial categories in the census include the following: white, black, Asian/Pacific Islander, American Indian/Alaska Native, and other. For the 2000 census, race included the same categories but separated Asian populations from the Pacific Islanders, making five racial categories. In addition, individuals were instructed to mark all applicable racial categories.

3. The depiction of cross-national groups as a more singular ethnic group happened not only for Latinos but also for Asian Americans, Arab Americans, and American Indians. The basis for group aggregation is perceived cultural similarities, which are usually couched in cultural, linguistic, and religious terms.

4. In 1997, the percentage of foreign-born persons in the US population reached a record high since the previous record levels of the early 1900s.

Culture and Demographics

¿Somos parte de la amplia comunidad de latinos o principalmente parte de una comunidad específica y bien definida? Los valores, el idioma, las tradiciones y estilos de vivir son aspectos del carácter de cada uno de nosotros. ¿Las dimensiones de las culturas comunes y las circunstancias diarias son nuestra realidad o dudamos eso?

Are we part of an extended Latino community or primarily a part of a specific, well-defined community? Values, language, traditions, and lifestyles are aspects of the character of each one of us. Are these dimensions of our common cultures and our daily circumstances part of our reality, or do we doubt that?

THIS CHAPTER WILL INTRODUCE OTHER vantage points to amplify the bases for community among Latinos. The greater awareness about the presence of Latinos by the larger public provides an opportunity to evaluate how they are viewed by non-Latinos. Continued releases by the US Census Bureau, polling firms, political campaigns, and the news media are placing greater focus on racial and Spanish-origin populations. Earlier attention assigned much emphasis on the sustained and significant levels of growth for Latinos. Projections were being advanced about Latinos' growing roles in partisan and electoral politics. Currently, these visible "impressions" about Latinos' significant population growth (to which immigration was a major contributor) and their cultural persistence (manifested mostly through Spanish-language use) in the face of unprecedented hostility from a president whose campaign racialized Latinos like none other (Sanchez and Gómez-Aguiñaga 2017) have reinvigorated public interest in these communities.

Our basic theme of community building is grounded in the understanding that Latinos are ancestrally linked to a variety of countries, giving them historic and cultural ties as well as common circumstances and conditions while living in the United States. The labels "Latino" and "Hispanic" have been used to identify persons of Spanish origin, and established Latino communities in the United States date from the seventeenth century. Other Latinos are more recent residents of the United States, while still others have been here for some intermediate length of time. Characteristically, Latinos are among the oldest groups in America as well as the most recent newcomers.

Pan-ethnicity is neither endemic nor viewed positively by national-origin Latinos who are potential "members." We understand the term "Latino" or "Hispanic" represents a *social construct* in which the idea is created and generally accepted by members of society. In this way, the concept of pan-ethnicity connects people in and through social institutions and leadership that give the idea meaning. A good contrast is the notion of primordial or fundamental characteristics of people that have been present since the beginning. For our purposes, the basic elements of national origin, language, and familial patterns represent the primordial nature. We see pan-ethnicity as incorporating a sense of group consciousness as the result of deliberative efforts, societal policies and experiences, and socialization.

The tables and figures that we provide will offer a demographic "road map" about Latino communities and what they share in terms of nativity, socioeconomic status, and cultural practices. The demographic profile of a community is directly linked with their political power and behavior. Developing a clear understanding of the underlying demographics of the Latino population will help you make connections to the theories and concepts that we introduce in the later chapters of the book. For example, table 3.1 provides a summary view of the distribution and population growth of the Latino population size across the top ten states from 2000 to 2017. We utilized a mixture of overall or aggregate statistics alongside those of key subgroups of the Latino population, including the largest national-origin groups. This helps to visualize the identification of Latino communities.

The Continued Increase and Dispersion of Latino Population across the United States

By 2019, the Hispanic or Latino population in the United States numbered 59.9 million people, representing approximately 18.3 percent of the total population. There are now ten states with one million or more Latino residents. The sheer size of the Latino population has led to an enhanced presence not only in politics, but in all other aspects of American life. The power of the Latino market is a direct result of these underlying numbers.

In the 1970 US census, the Spanish-origin population (Hernandez, Estrada, and Alvirez 1973) was only 9.6 million and constituted some 4.7 percent of the total population. The population exploded between the 1990 and 2000 decennial censuses, when the Latino population increased by more than 57 percent to reach 35.3 million people (the total US population increased by 11.5 percent). The population growth of Latinos within several individual states has been appreciable. For example, while Latinos represent one-third of the state population of California, their 29.1 percent increase has occurred since 1990. Similarly, in Texas and Florida, the Latino population has increased since 1990 by more than 30 percent. In the first decade of the new millennium, Latino growth continued to outpace that of the general non-Hispanic population (32.9 versus 4.7 percent). Population projections into 2060 place Latinos at 111.22 million, which is almost a 70 percent increase from 1920 (see figure 3.1). The continued growth of the population well into the future suggests that Latino influence will grow as well.

TABLE 3.1 Hispanic and Latino Population by State, 2000–2017

State	2000 Population	% 2000 Population	2010 Population	% 2010 Population	% Growth 2000–2010	% 2012 Population	% 2015 Population	% 2016 Population	% 2017 Population
Arizona	1,295,671	25.3	1,895,149	29.6	46.3	30.2	30.7	30.9	31.4
California	10,966,556	32.4	14,013,719	37.6	27.8	38.2	38.8	38.9	39.1
Colorado	735,801	17.1	1,038,687	20.7	41.2	21.0	21.3	21.3	21.5
Florida	2,682,715	16.8	4,223,806	22.5	57.4	23.2	24.5	24.9	25.6
Illinois	1,530,262	12.3	2,027,578	15.8	32.5	16.3	16.9	17.0	17.2
Nevada	293,370	19.7	716,501	26.5	81.9	27.3	28.1	28.5	25.8
New Jersey	1,117,191	13.3	1,555,144	17.7	39.2	18.5	19.7	20.0	20.4
New Mexico	765,386	42.1	953,403	46.3	24.6	47.0	48.0	48.5	48.8
New York	2,867,583	15.1	3,416,922	17.6	19.2	18.2	18.8	19.0	19.2
Texas	6,669,666	32.0	9,460,921	37.6	41.8	38.2	38.8	39.1	39.4

Sources: US Census Bureau, "Census 2010 News," Census.gov, retrieved January 16, 2018; US Census Bureau, "Population by Race and Hispanic or Latino Origin for the United States: 1990 and 2000 (PHC-T-1)," Census.gov, retrieved January 16, 2018; World Population Review, "Hispanic Population by State 2020," https://worldpopulationreview.com/state-rankings/hispanic-population-by-state, retrieved June 11, 2020.

FIGURE 3.1 Forecast of the Latino Population of the United States, 2016–2060 (in millions)

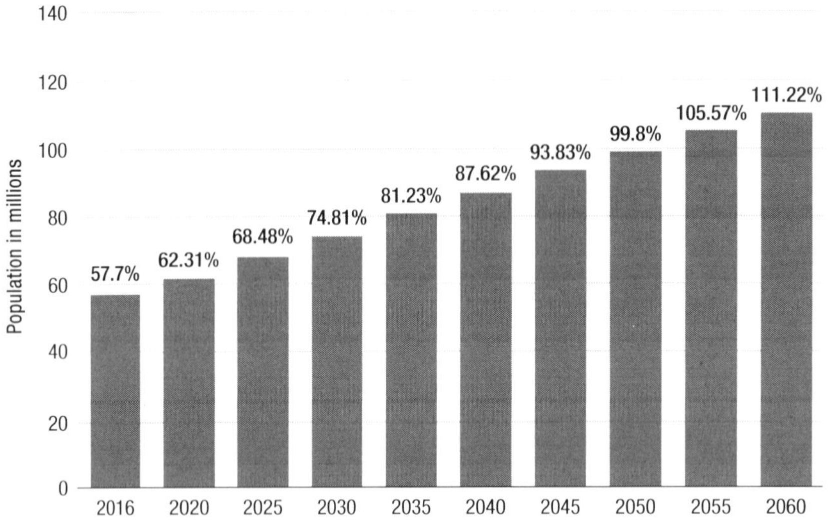

[Bar chart showing Population in millions from 2016 to 2060:
2016: 57.7%
2020: 62.31%
2025: 68.48%
2030: 74.81%
2035: 81.23%
2040: 87.62%
2045: 93.83%
2050: 99.8%
2055: 105.57%
2060: 111.22%]

Source: © Statista 2021.

TABLE 3.2 Top Ten States with the Largest Percentage Latino Population Gains, 2000–2014

States	2014 Latino Population	2000 Latino Population	% Change, 2000–2014
South Dakota	29,000	10,000	190.0
Tennessee	322,000	117,000	175.2
South Carolina	258,000	95,000	171.6
Alabama	190,000	72,000	163.9
North Dakota	18,000	7,000	157.1
Kentucky	145,000	57,000	154.4
Maryland	556,000	231,000	140.7
Arkansas	205,000	86,000	138.4
North Carolina	890,000	377,000	136.1
Virginia	732,000	333,000	119.8

Source: Pew Research Center tabulations of the 2000 decennial census and the 2014 American Community Survey (PUMS).

In table 3.2, we list the top ten states with the highest percentage population gains from 2000 to 2014, allowing us to show the geographical dispersion and migration patterns throughout the United States.

Latinos therefore continue to reside in large, populous states with substantial electoral votes and expanding service economies and in industrial-based states. However, Latino populations are the largest minority group in twenty-seven states, and, in an increasing number of states, they comprise more than 5 percent of the state's population. This development illustrates that a Latino political presence has been established in most areas of the country at a level of critical mass.[1] With continued dispersion the number of states that are considered politically relevant to Latino politics will increase.

In addition to the continued population growth of the Latino communities, it is important to note that there has been significant Latino migration (both internal and international) into the South and Midwest (Iowa, Nebraska, Wisconsin, etc.). This trend reinforces the geographic dispersion away from the traditional locations (Southwest, Northeast, and Florida) referenced in the last edition of the book, with a significant portion of that regional migration moving to rural and suburban communities.

Politically, another noteworthy consequence of Latinos' spreading geographical distribution is their influence in more electoral college states as well as those that have grown through reapportionment. The decennial census for 2010 resulted in additional congressional seats for Arizona, Nevada, Texas, and Florida, which are among the top ten Hispanic population states. Even in states that may lose some congressional seats (New York, New Jersey, Massachusetts), Latinos can position themselves to compete actively for the redrawn congressional districts or to serve as a critical voting bloc.

The states showing overwhelming gains are in the deep South (Alabama, Mississippi, the Carolinas, etc.) with the lure of an active economy (i.e., agriculturally related, service, and construction sectors) and growing connections with families and friends. An example of this southern migration can be seen in Dalton, Georgia, a town in the northwestern part of the state known as the "carpet capital of the world." In a span of ten to fifteen years, the percentage of Latinos in the town's population has increased from 5 percent to more than 30 percent. The economy of the South, particularly in traditional areas of agriculture, along with the expansion in food processing, manufacturing, and a generally lower cost of living, has served as an attractor to Latino migration. As a region, the South has experienced a significant population growth of residents migrating from the Northeast and Midwest. As a result, the South is undergoing some major adjustments in terms of intergroup relations and cultural clashes. As noted at the beginning of this chapter, these changing demographic patterns have direct political and policy repercussions for the Latino community. Our contention is that a pan-ethnic community creates a broader-based community more inclusive to all Latino national-origin subgroups.

The results presented in the population-related figures in this chapter reinforce and amplify the theme of substantial population growth for Latinos over the past three decades. We will summarize the Latino impact on the 2018 congressional and state and local elections. We believe the next election cycles will be critical for Latinos in converting their population growth, geo-spatial location, and pressing policy issues into greater and more effective electoral "muscle."

Demographic Profiles of Major National-Origin Groups

Figure 3.2 provides a more detailed breakdown of the size of each of the Latino subgroups. In the next chapter, we will provide a bit more of a historical and contextual account of many of the Latino subgroups (i.e., their historical presence and unique experiences in the United States) to expand on this demographic profile. The Mexican-origin population has been and continues to be the largest subgroup, approaching almost two-thirds of the total Latino community. This represents a slight increase from 2000, at which time they occupied approximately three-fifths of the Latino community. Of note, the residents of this subgroup are not only continuing to

FIGURE 3.2 Latinos in the United States by National Origin and Population Size

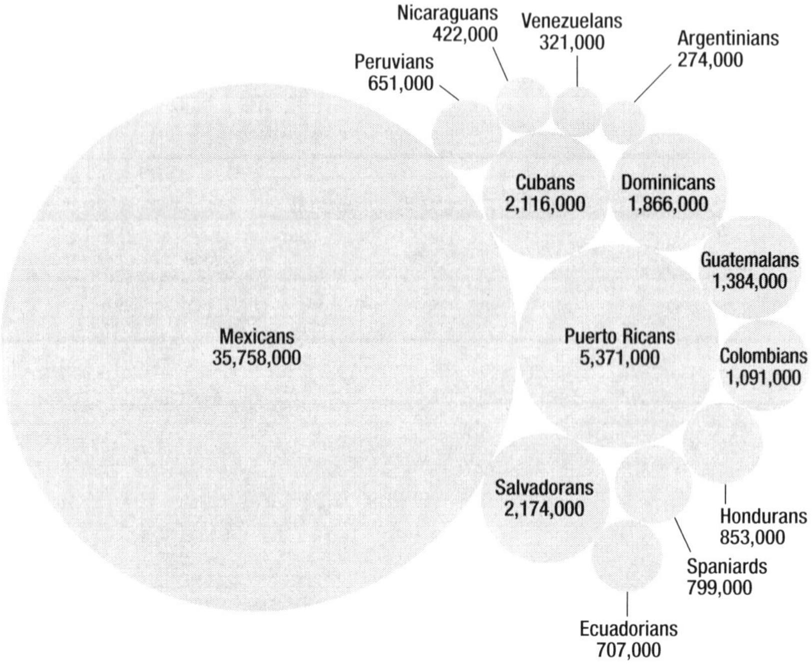

- Mexicans 35,758,000
- Puerto Ricans 5,371,000
- Salvadorans 2,174,000
- Cubans 2,116,000
- Dominicans 1,866,000
- Guatemalans 1,384,000
- Colombians 1,091,000
- Hondurans 853,000
- Spaniards 799,000
- Ecuadorians 707,000
- Peruvians 651,000
- Nicaraguans 422,000
- Venezuelans 321,000
- Argentinians 274,000

Source: PEW Research Center.

migrate to the traditional areas of Mexican residence but are also expanding to newer destinations in the South, Northeast (such as the New York metro region), and central Midwest.

Puerto Ricans continue to be the second-largest Latino subgroup. It is estimated that the Puerto Rican population in the United States is nearing 6 million (with another 3.4 million on the island), accounting for roughly 10 percent of the total Hispanic population (Noe-Bustamante, Flores, and Shah 2017). Although Puerto Rican Americans continue to be highly concentrated in the Northeast (20 percent of Puerto Ricans live in New York, 8 percent in New Jersey), they have expanded into other areas, particularly Florida, where one in five Puerto Rican Americans now lives. The impact of Hurricane Maria on the Puerto Rican population is hard to overstate. The number of Puerto Ricans leaving the island for the mainland increased by 26.9 percent in 2018, a year after the hurricane. Roughly half of this post-Maria population settled in the South, with the West also receiving a higher number of migrants than the year before (Glassman 2019).

The biggest change for the remainder of the Latino subgroups has been the substantial growth among several national-origin groups beyond the "big three" of Mexican, Cuban, and Puerto Rican. For the most part, these subgroups are comprised of persons from Central and South American countries. Latinos from El Salvador are the next-largest group outside of the big three, comprising 4 percent of the overall Latino population, with 2.3 million residing in the United States in 2017 (Neo-Bustamante, Flores, and Shah 2017). Salvadorans are tied with Cubans as the third-largest population of all Latinos in the United States, fueled by a sharp 225 percent increase in population since 2000. Salvadorans are more likely to be foreign-born than Latinos overall, and roughly 44 percent of Salvadoran immigrants have lived in the United States for more than twenty years.

According to the 2017 American Community Survey (ACS), an estimated 421,000 Hispanics of Venezuelan origin reside in the United States, just less than 1 percent of the overall Latino population. Though still relatively small, the Venezuelan-origin population has increased 353 percent since 2000, growing from 93,000 to 421,000. For Venezuelans, political instability, protests, and a collapsing economy have resulted in major out-migration to Colombia, other parts of South America, and the United States. Nearly thirty thousand Venezuelans applied for asylum with US Citizenship and Immigration Services in 2018, which is roughly one-third of all claims filed that year (O'Toole 2019). Increased migration from Central America, especially Honduras, Guatemala, and El Salvador, has raised focus on US asylum polices, which have become more restrictive under the Trump administration and border enforcement.

Most Venezuelans seeking asylum in the United States arrive via the Miami airport, tend to be highly educated, and have the means to afford legal counsel, helping them to have much better success than asylum seekers from Central American countries (Faiola and Miroff 2018). The Venezuelan population also benefits from a relatively welcoming city, as many Cuban Americans in Miami are empathetic to their plight.

The US populations of El Salvadorans, Dominicans, Guatemalans, and South Americans from Peru and Colombia are also growing at a fast rate. As of 2017, Colombians were the seventh-largest population of Hispanic origin living in the United States, accounting for 2 percent of the entire US Hispanic population. Reflecting a larger trend in population growth among South Americans since 2000, the Colombian-origin population increased 139 percent, growing from 502,000 to 1.2 million. The Colombian population is more likely to be foreign-born (61 percent) than Latinos overall and is concentrated in the states of Florida (31 percent), New York (14 percent), and New Jersey (12 percent) (Neo-Bustamante, Flores, and Shah 2017). New York and Miami are the two cities with the largest Colombian communities.

Also, as of 2017 there were nearly 680,000 Latinos of Peruvian origin living in the United States, accounting for about 1 percent of the total US Latino population. Since 2000, the Peruvian-origin population has increased 174 percent, growing from 248,000 to 679,000. Peruvians are just under twice as likely to be foreign-born than Latinos overall, and 58 percent of foreign-born Peruvians have gone through the naturalization process to become US citizens. The migration of Peruvians to the United States has had a marked impact on many cities, most notably Patterson, New Jersey, which has become an unofficial home to Peruvian culture. It's estimated that there are forty-five Peruvian-owned restaurants in the city, and the city council recently voted to name a section of the downtown "Peru Square" (Negro-Chin 2016).

Until recently, Cubans had constituted the third-largest Latino subgroup, but partially due to an older median age (the Cuban population is eight to twelve years older than the other subgroups), El Salvadorans and Dominicans have surpassed the Cuban population totals, and Guatemalans are approaching the size of the Cuban community (Humes et al. 2011).

According to a Pew Research Center analysis of the US Census Bureau's American Community Survey (Neo-Bustamante, Flores, and Shah 2017), the Dominican-origin population has increased 163 percent, growing from 797,000 to 2.1 million since 1990 and comprising 4 percent of the total Hispanic population. The Dominican population is concentrated in the Northeast, with 42 percent of Dominican Americans living in New York and another 15 percent in New Jersey; 41 percent of all Dominicans live in just four counties in the state of New York (Zong and Batalova 2018). However, like other Latino groups, a sizable share of Dominicans reside in Florida (13 percent).

Demographically, the remainder of the Latino community is consolidated into three general categories: Central Americans, mainly from El Salvador, Guatemala, Honduras, Panama, and Nicaragua; people from Spanish-speaking South American countries such as Colombia, Peru, Venezuela, and Argentina; and those from the other Spanish-speaking areas of the Caribbean, particularly the Dominican Republic. Since the 1990s, these three segments have represented the fastest-growing sectors of the Latino community. They include more immigrants and refugees[2] than native-born persons, and settlement is occurring in both longer-established Latino communities and newer destinations in the South, Midwest, and New England. Part of the settlement pattern includes certain Eastern suburban communities, such as Long Island, New York.

The influx of Latinos into areas previously of lower concentration became more noticeable during the 1990s. For example, Central Americans have become the largest Latino group in Washington, DC; Dominican and Colombian populations are rivaling the Puerto Ricans in New York City; and Puerto Ricans and Central Americans are the fastest-growing Latino subgroups in Florida. Both the Salvadoran and Dominican communities had exceeded the size of the Cuban community by the mid-2010s (Lopez, Gonzalez-Barrera, and Cuddington 2013). According to 2010 census figures, Salvadoran Americans are now the fourth-largest Latino group in the United States. Those whose roots extend to El Salvador, one of the smallest and densest countries in the Western Hemisphere, now number more than 2.3 million in the United States, with about 35 percent residing in California. The latest tally means that Salvadoran Americans have surpassed Dominican Americans in number and are swiftly gaining on Cuban Americans (O'Brien 2011).

Underlying Trends in Latino Demographics Fuel Continued Population Growth

This trend of continued significant growth rate among Latinos is reflected further by population projections well into the mid-twenty-first century. As indicated in figure 3.1 and the latest Census Bureau population figures, Latinos are projected to exceed one hundred million people and comprise nearly one-fourth of the total US population by 2050. According to the 2050 projection, the base population of 12.5 million (in 2000) will have doubled in the span of forty years. This substantial growth rate is attributed to three primary factors associated with most population increases: (1) significant portions of the female population in the fertility age range, (2) higher birthrates than the general population, and (3) international migration. The spike in international migration evidenced in the mid-1990s has remained significant well into the early twenty-first century.

The combination of higher fertility rates than the general population and youthfulness of Latinos indicates that the native-born segment is outpacing new Latino migrants and the non-Latino populations. The overall youthfulness of the Latino

FIGURE 3.3 US Fertility Rate by Race and Origin of the Mother

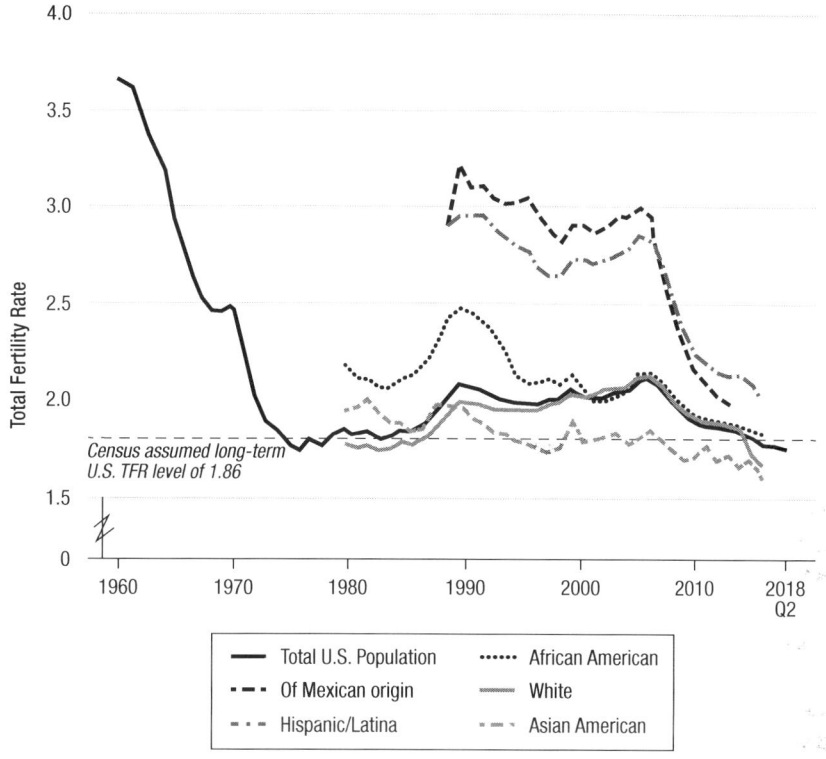

Source: US Centers for Disease Control and Prevention (CDC); National Center for Health Statistics; National Vital Statistics System (NVSS) Rapid Release.

population and greater percentage of Latinas of child-bearing age would indicate that birthrate rather than migration will serve as the major contributor of growth well into the future. Changes in fertility patterns in the United States by race and origin of the mother are shown in figure 3.3. Like all industrialized nations, the US population has been declining significantly since 1960, and the United States essentially experienced "zero population growth" in 2018. While Latinas reflect that declining fertility rate, their rate is still about 25 percent higher than other minority groups (African Americans and Asians primarily have fertility rates closer to those of whites).

That Latinos are primarily an immigrant population is a common belief held in the United States. National immigration debates and restrictive immigration policies concerning the foreign-born segment have kept immigration reform a highly salient policy arena for Latinos. In figure 3.4, we see the declining share of the foreign-born segment across all the Latino subgroups. This pattern is even more pronounced when you examine the under-eighteen age group in which the ratio of native- to foreign-born is nearly 3 to 1. From 2000 to 2013, there was a 5 percent decline overall with even more significant declines in specific Latino subgroups. For example, the foreign-born share of Nicaraguans declined by 18 percent, Dominicans and El Salvadorans dropped 13 percent and 16 percent, respectively, and Guatemalans declined by 15 percent. Cubans, Ecuadorans, Venezuelans, and Peruvians all recorded declines in the

FIGURE 3.4 Latinos' Foreign-Born Status over Time, 1970–2015

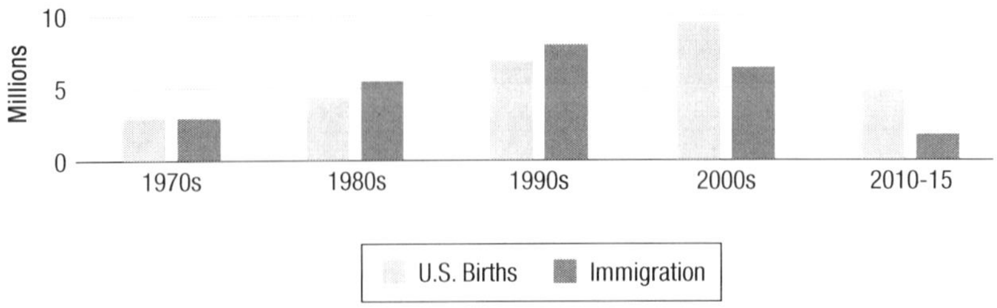

Source: PEW Research Center.

10 to 12 percent range. The results in table 3.3 provide the actual numbers of foreign-born persons from Latin America and the Caribbean.

In the same period, 2000–2013, the decline of the foreign-born share for those of Mexican origin was closer to 6 percent, mirroring the average for the overall Latino population. The larger portion of native-born Latinos has direct political consequences, such as an expanding electoral base and greater socialization into the American social and political system. Even when Latinos constitute a significant segment of a state's populace, the actions of governors and political parties can be quite different.

For example, in 1998, then Texas governor George W. Bush incorporated a targeted effort to seek Hispanic support through public policies such as bilingual education reform and funding and opposition to anti-immigrant and English-only initiatives. On the other hand, between 1994 and 1998, then California governor Pete Wilson supported several statewide propositions (e.g., against immigration, affirmative action, and bilingual education) that resulted in increased Latino political participation and declining support for the Republican Party. Since 2003, the rise in anti-immigrant state initiatives (e.g., Arizona Senate Bill 1070) has had a partisan effect. For the most part, these initiatives have been proposed and passed by Republican elected officials with substantial Latino protests. In chapter 6, we will discuss in more detail political engagement and related developments considering the significant Latino immigrant segments of the population.

Culture, Latinos, and Demographics

So far, the demographic profile we have presented has focused on the size and national-origin makeup of the Latino communities in the United States. We have provided details about the foreign-born segment, reasons for their declining numbers, and the significance of the growing native-born Latino population. We have also suggested than an important element of the community of common cultures would include language since a common perception is that the Spanish language unifies Latinos. We highlight some demographic information regarding Spanish-language use to provide some context for the earlier discussion regarding Spanish and pan-ethnic identity.

In 1990, about 14 percent of the US population spoke a language other than English at home; in 2016, the percentage jumped to 20.7 percent. Spanish was the most common non-English language, spoken by more than 62.3 percent of all non-English

TABLE 3.3 Foreign-Born Population from Latin America and the Caribbean by Country of Birth, 2010

Region and Country of Birth	Number		Percent of Total		Percent of Region	
	Estimate	Margin of Error (%)	Estimate	Margin of Error (%)	Estimate	Margin of Error (%)
Caribbean	3,371	42	17.6	0.2	100	N/A
Cuba	1,105	27	5.2	0.1	29.6	0.6
Dominican Republic	879	24	4.1	0.1	23.6	0.6
Haiti	587	21	2.8	0.1	15.7	0.6
Jamaica	660	20	3.1	0.1	17.7	0.5
Other Caribbean[a]	500	17	2.4	0.1	13.4	0.4
Central America	14,764	90	69.6	0.2	100	N/A
Mexico	11,711	83	55.2	0.3	79.3	0.3
El Salvador	1,214	34	5.7	0.2	8.2	0.2
Guatemala	831	29	3.9	0.1	5.6	0.2
Honduras	523	24	2.5	0.1	3.5	0.2
Other Central America[b]	485	17	2.3	0.1	3.3	0.1
Total	21,224	90	100	N/A	N/A	N/A

Source: US Census, American Community Survey.
Note: Numbers in thousands. Data are based on a sample and are subject to sampling variability. A margin of error is a measure of an estimate's variability. The larger the margin of error is in relation to the size of the estimate, the less reliable the estimate. The number when added to and subtracted from the estimate forms the 90 percent confidence interval. For information on confidentiality protection, sampling error, non-sampling error, and definitions, see https://www.census.gov/programs-surveys/acs.
N/A = not applicable
[a] "Other Caribbean" includes Anguilla, Antigua and Barbuda, Aruba, Bahamas, Barbados, British Virgin Islands, Cayman Islands, Dominica, Grenada, the former country of Guadeloupe including St. Barthelemy and St. Martin, Martinique, Montserrat, and the former country of the Netherlands Antigua including Bonaire, Curaçao, Saba, St. Kitts and Nevis, St. Lucia, St. Vincent and the Grenadines, Trinidad and Tobago, Sint Eustatius, Sint Maarten, and Turks and Caicos.
[b] "Other Central America" includes: Costa Rica, Belize, Nicaragua, and Panama.

speakers. This represents more than 38.3 million people. Overall, nearly 76 percent of Latinos reported growing up in Spanish-speaking homes, while slightly more—one-half of Latinos—also indicated they spoke English well (see figure 3.5). In contrast to the percentage of Spanish-speaking Latinos, the second-largest non-English language group was Chinese (5.7 percent).

Proficiency in the English language is considered an asset when maneuvering through the US political system and other social institutions that are primarily in English. The data in figure 3.5 is derived from a three-part question on the census as well as from other statistical agencies. Individuals were asked if they spoke a language other than English, what that language was, and, finally, how well they spoke or understood

FIGURE 3.5 English Proficiency among Latinos, 1980–2015

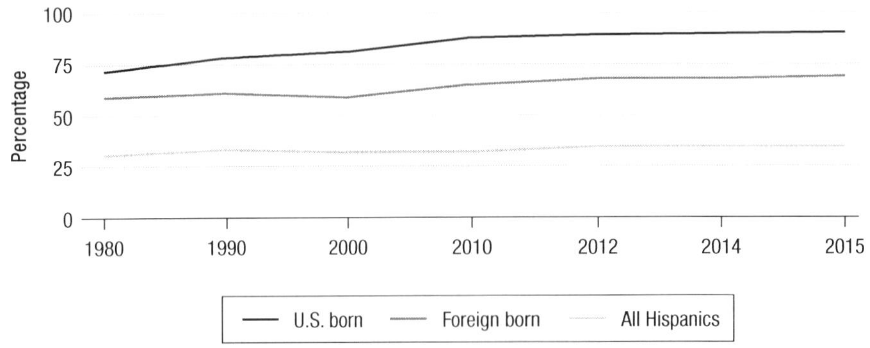

Source: Pew Research Center tabulations of 1980, 1990, and 2000 censuses (IPUMS) and 2010, 2013, 2014, and 2018 American Community Surveys (IPUMS).

English. Responses ranged from excellent to not well.[3] For Latinos age five and older, an average of 68 percent reported being proficient in English. The Latino subgroups who exceeded that average were Puerto Ricans, Argentineans, and Venezuelans. The Mexican-origin population mirrored the overall percentage of Latino Spanish use. Those subgroups reporting below the 68 percent average included Guatemalans, El Salvadorans, Hondurans, and Dominicans. In many cases, there is a close association between English-language proficiency and the proportion of the population that is foreign-born. As we can see from figure 3.5, foreign-born Latinos have the overall lowest percentage of being English proficient (approximately 23 percent).

As we discussed in the last chapter, speaking Spanish is still a nearly universal experience for most Latinos, which makes it a driving force for pan-ethnic identity formation. Research suggests that there has been a slight decline in Latino households that speak Spanish at home, as the rate has dropped to 66.3 percent (Ortman and Shin 2011). The role of Spanish-language use, the extent of language loyalty, and the degree to which the public arena reinforces or discourages bilingualism are aspects of Spanish-language persistence for Latinos. In addition, the growth of Spanish-speaking media, particularly the Univision and Telemundo networks, and Spanish-language radio helps to meet the service needs of Latinos. Spanish-language media also provides a vehicle for Spanish-language maintenance and acquisition among primarily younger and native-born Latinos. The role and impact of Spanish-language media will be discussed in chapter 7, especially in relation to campaigns and elections.

Nativity and generational distance from the immigration experience are important factors to explore across the Latino population. The significant presence of foreign-born Latinos in the country perpetuates Spanish-language use, customs, and traditions, all key contributors to ethnic identity. Since the 1970s, more Latinos have immigrated into the United States than members of any other group. The composition of US immigration changed dramatically in the latter half of the twentieth century as Latin American and Asian immigrants came to dominate the migration stream. Almost two-fifths of all Latinos residing in the United States are foreign-born. While the percentage of American permanent resident aliens overall is slightly greater than 10 percent,[4] the overall percentage for Latinos is 40 percent (6.1 percent for non-Hispanics), and the proportion of immigrants from Cuba is the highest of any group.

The number of foreign-born Latinos varies across the different subgroups. More than 60 percent (60.8 percent) of Cubans are foreign-born, as are 77.5 percent of Central Americans and 69.5 percent of South Americans. The Cuban community's foreign-born members have refugee status with access to specific governmental assistance programs, while the rest of Latinos are viewed as economic migrants (there have been initiatives by Salvadorans and Guatemalans to obtain refugee status). Overall, the percentage of foreign-born Latinos is 38 percent compared to foreign-born non-Hispanics at 12.5 percent. Finally, the distinction of Puerto Ricans born in the United States or on the island is associated with their citizenship status. Puerto Rico is a commonwealth, and Puerto Ricans are US citizens. At the same time, their perspectives and experiences as Puerto Ricans may be affected by their place of birth, as 29 percent of Puerto Ricans were born on the island of Puerto Rico.

Language and nativity (country of birth) are critical cultural dimensions that help define the Latino community of common cultures. The coexistence of native-born and "immigrant" Latinos in the same or proximate neighborhoods, sharing familial social networks, common work environments, and business interactions, provides a regular basis for cultural exchanges and experiences. These interactions can reinforce cultural expressions and values or, perhaps, create cultural tensions over assimilation, acculturation, or even cultural authenticity. Cultural dynamics would be less likely to exist without the persistence of Spanish-language use and the steady influx of immigrants. In addition, the sizable percentage of foreign-born members in Latino communities helps bring forth the extended and complex set of issues and policies related to immigration rights, legal standing, and access to services.

A clear political connection for Latino communities with a significant foreign-born segment is either the extent of or the lack of naturalization. Citizenship status links directly with electoral participation, which tends to offset the rapid growth rate that Latinos have experienced. That is, while Latino population growth is very high, the youthfulness and significant noncitizen segment of the Latino community undercuts its corresponding electoral base. A legal permanent resident alien can pursue US citizenship after five years of residence. Naturalization requires demonstrating good moral character, knowledge of US government and history, respect for the law, and competence in the English language, as well as completion of a personal interview process and payment of the naturalization filing fees.

There are almost twenty-eight million foreign-born people in the United States, of whom 41 percent are Hispanics. Of all foreign-born people in this country, 62 percent naturalize, whereas on average, 45 percent of Hispanics have become citizens (the rate is 74 percent for non-Hispanics). For example, only 42 percent of immigrants of Mexican origin are naturalized, in contrast to 57.3 percent of Cuban immigrants. The rising segment of immigrants (Central Americans) averages about 23 percent. Examining those rates by specific Latino subgroups reveals some variation as well as the proportion of foreign-born within each Latino national group. According to the National Association of Latino Elected and Appointed Officials **(NALEO) Educational Fund** analysis, 461,317 Latino permanent residents became US citizens in Fiscal Year (FY) 2008. From FY 2007 to FY 2008, Latino naturalizations increased by 95 percent compared to a 58 percent increase for all naturalizations. Mexico was the leading country of birth for persons naturalizing in 2008 (231,815), representing 22 percent of all new citizens. The other Latino subgroups that experienced significant increases in naturalization in Fiscal Year 2008 were Cubans (160 percent), Salvadorans (109 percent), Nicaraguans (120 percent), and Guatemalans (109 percent). The naturalization percentage for Central and South Americans has been increasing since the turn of the new millennium.

Even with these gains, millions of eligible Latinos still have not applied for citizenship, and the increased financial costs have been identified as an impediment. The consequences of lower numbers of foreign-born Latino citizens are connected to electoral impact, job opportunities, immigration petitions, and scholarship opportunities. This demographic sketch serves to establish the size and extent of the group of foreign-born Latinos. Its implications will be analyzed in several chapters across the book, as immigration policy continues to be the most salient policy to Latinos.

Communities of Interests

Language and immigrant status are two markers of culture and linkages to one's country of origin. In sociological terms, Latinos' social networks can be very dense ethnically, with interactions that incorporate Spanish language, cultural practices, and familial contacts with recent arrivals. Those same common conditions and situations also contribute to a sense of community. Differential treatment, societal stereotypes, and similar socioeconomic status, for example, can serve to connect elements of the Latino community. One such area lies with educational attainment and Latinos. Lower levels of educational attainment, living in poorer school districts, lack of available bilingual programs, and attending "lower-quality" schools are common experiences among a major segment of the Latino community. Educational attainment is highly correlated with income and political participation, two key outcomes that are influenced by inequalities in educational resources for Latino students.

Figures 3.6 and 3.7 provide information on the levels of schooling for Latino/as, showing that in 2016, more than 90 percent graduated from high school and more than 25 percent graduated from college. In comparison, for the general adult population age twenty-five and older, only 11 percent of Latino males and 13 percent of Latinas are college graduates, and almost 80 percent are high school graduates. There are indications that the younger generation of Latinos is completing more schooling than their older counterparts; however, the gap between non-Latinos and Latinos is lessening, with 87 percent attaining high school graduation (see figure 3.6). Looking at educational advancement over time, there is a steep incline for Latinos since 2000, especially since 2008.

Another important consideration is the differential in the educational attainment between US-born and foreign-born Latinos (78 percent versus 45 percent, respectively, are high school graduates). Again, we see how immigrant status influences socioeconomic status and standing, certain institutions, and policy areas. In addition to Latino subgroup status, the age structure for each group is relevant. In 2014, Latino schoolchildren constituted 29 percent of the children in the US school systems. Today, Latino, African American, and Asian minority students comprise most of all schoolchildren. The gamut of relevant educational issues includes bilingual education, quality of educational facilities and programs, access for immigrant children, school retention rates, and discipline policies (Meier and Stewart 1991; San Miguel 1987; Gandara and Contreras 2010), as well as participation in school decision making.

FIGURE 3.6 High School Completion Rate among 18–24-Year-Olds

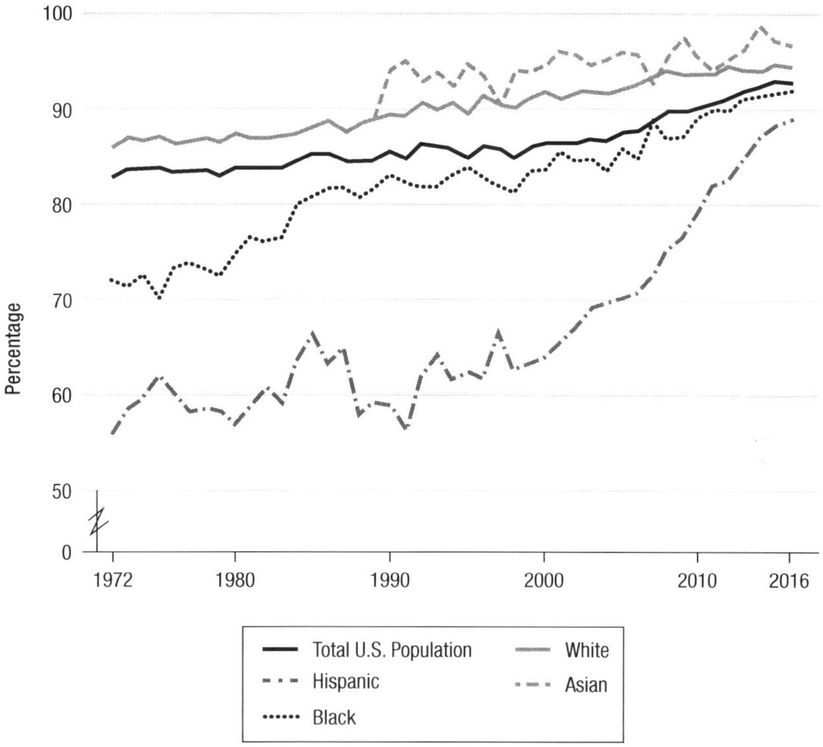

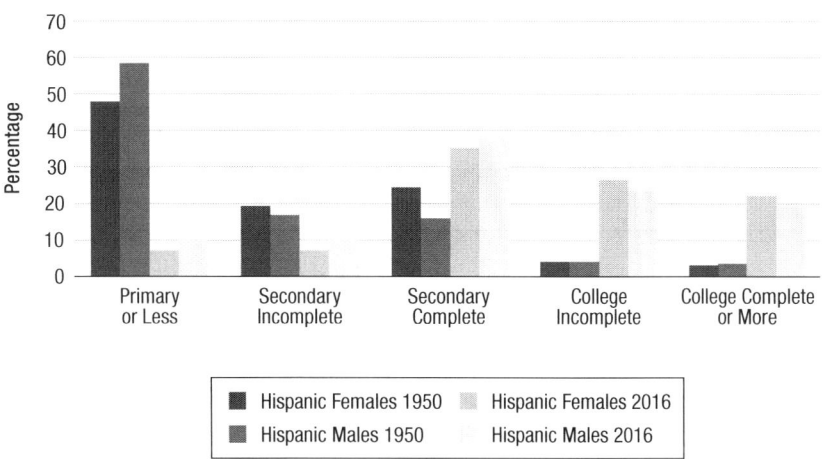

Source: US Department of Commerce, Census Bureau, Current Population Survey, October 1972–2016.

FIGURE 3.7 Educational Attainment by Levels of Schooling, 1950–2016

Source: Pew Hispanic Research Center.

For example, in 2014 the average Latino student in California likely attended a school that was 84 percent non-white with high rates of concentrated poverty (Leal and Meier 2011). Chapters 8 and 9 on public policy will explore how these issues relate to the Latino community.

Along with educational attainment, the labor market presents another aspect of socioeconomic life for Latinos. Participation rates in the labor force, particularly among Latino males, have been higher than those of non-Latino populations. Since the 1950s, gains in educational attainment have been more positive for Latinas, especially for participation in post-secondary education and college completion. This change among Latinos/as poses some interesting queries as to contributing factors and what the implications are for leadership roles, policy issues, and mobilization.

Latinos are more concentrated in blue-collar jobs and in the service, manufacturing, and construction industries. Thus, if more Latinos tend to be occupationally "stratified" and employed in particular industry sectors, then their issues, problems, and union or organizational connections serve as common bases for mobilization and action. Additional occupational information for Latino/as shows significant unemployment rates for both Latino males and females are 50 to 100 percent greater than for their non-Latino counterparts. Figure 3.7 illustrates educational attainment among Latina and Latino workers; the trend is that more Latinas are attending college with higher numbers graduating.

Two general occupational clusters serve to highlight a common foundation among Latinos. The first is professional, administrative, and sales and service; the second is skilled, production, and transportation. Whereas non-Latino males are evenly divided between the professional and administrative and skilled/semi-skilled occupations, the distribution among Latino males is more skewed toward the service and skilled/unskilled workforce. Similarly, for Latinas, the disparity exists but is not as extreme (74 and 26 percent for non-Latina females versus 56 and 46 percent for Latinas). Latinas are more commonly found in the sales and office sectors as well as in production and transportation. There are measurable differences between most of the Latino subgroups and Cubans. While the percentage of Cuban males employed in professional/administrative work falls below that of non-Latino males (44 percent versus 50 percent), the other Latino subgroups range from a low of 23 to 37 percent. A similar pattern exists for Cuban women in comparison to other Latinas.

Occupational location of Latinos is also influenced by nativity; US-born Latinos fare better occupationally than their foreign-born counterparts. As labor force participation rates continue to increase, especially for Latinas, all Latinos in the labor market will play a greater role in the composition of the workforce and thereby contribute more to the Social Security system, and they could have more human resource labor force mobility (Morales and Bonilla 1993).[5] Thus, such issues as job mobility, job training and educational preparation, labor market discrimination, and entrepreneurship become salient issues for Latino communities. Latinos' occupational participation in all three sectors shows an upward trend, with the professional and technical sectors having the steepest incline. Chapters 9 and 10 on public policy and Latinos will further explore these dimensions of community interest.

Figure 3.8 provides a graphic representation of Latino household incomes from 2000 to 2014. An examination of the five quintiles shows that 56 percent of all with a household income between $0 and $49,000 occupy the lower two. In 2014, the

FIGURE 3.8 Latino Household Income

	2000	2004	2009	2014
$100,000+	6%	8%	12%	14%
$75,000–$99,999	7%	8%	10%	11%
$50,000–$74,999	17%	17%	18%	18%
$25,000–$49,999	33%	33%	30%	28%
$0–$29,999	38%	33%	30%	28%

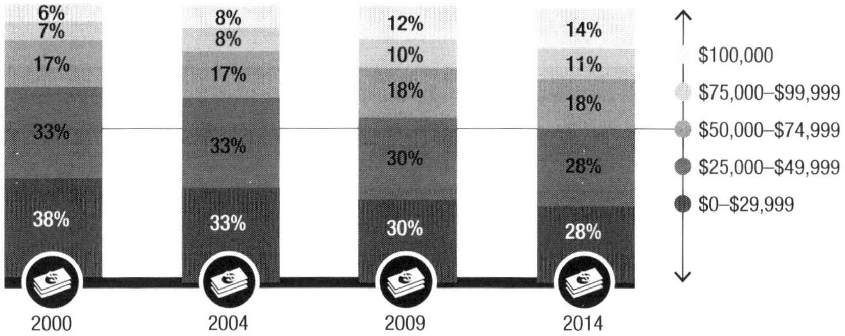

Source: US Census Bureau 2000, 2004, 2009, and 2014 American Community Survey, 1-Year Estimates, © 2016 The Nielsen Company.

national median household income was $53,657, compared to $45,520 for Latinos. In 2018, those income levels were $61,937 and $51,404, respectively (Guzman 2019). While the Latino household income has increased by almost 25 percent since 1990, there remains a significant gap with non-Hispanic whites that is not reflected in their aggregate income gains. Dominican Americans have a relatively low income level, with a median income of $37,000 in 2016 and 24 percent of Dominican families living below the poverty level (Zong and Batalova 2018).

Data from the 2015 US census shows that in comparison to white men, Hispanic women earned just 58 cents on the dollar. The pay gap among Latinas reflects the greatest disparity among all women of color. Even more alarming, while other women of color (African American, American Indian, and Asian women in particular) made major progress toward closing this pay gap over time, Hispanic women only narrowed the gap by five cents from 1980 to 2015. Scholars have used an intersectional framework to identify and try to explain this gender pay gap. This framework suggests that the pay disparity is the product of group discrimination toward both women and Latinos, in addition to other stereotypes affecting Hispanic women specifically. The report provided as a link for recommended reading for this chapter summarizes the economic research attempting to explain this pay gap, noting that discrimination and structural barriers facing Latinas in the workplace are two of the strongest factors that have led to the persistence of this important inequality.

Another aspect to assess the income levels of Latino households is the size of the households to use this income. This disparity of household income for Latinos and non-Latinos, and subsequent lack of resources, has implications in terms of socioeconomic mobility, political engagement, health care, and organizational activities.

Our examination of the Latino family includes information on family income status, Latino families living below the poverty line, and family type. Substantial literature, both social scientific and literary, portrays the central value of Latino family life as a source of social and financial support as well as cultural reinforcement. Values such as respecting elders, maintaining extended families, supporting familial social and cultural rituals, and the centrality of family for identity and well-being have been identified as core for Latinos (Zambrana 2011). This demographic information embodies a mix of both cultural and common dimensions.

Latinos represented more than 12 percent of the total families in the United States in 2018, constituting 13.3 million families. The larger size of Latino families is an important factor, with two-fifths of Latino households including children younger than age eighteen. Also relevant is the percentage of individuals born outside the United States (60.8 percent). There is a substantial difference among Latino households based upon nativity, especially with the significant percentage of foreign-born Latinos. As mentioned earlier, the ratio of native- to foreign-born Latino/as is almost 16 to 1; it is the adult population that makes the foreign-born population noteworthy.

Also indicative of the economic disparities between Latinos and non-Latinos is the percentage of families living below the poverty level. Among all family types (two-parent, female-headed, etc.), three times as many Latino families live below the poverty level as non-Latino families. The poverty rate among Latinos in 2017 was 18.3 percent, down from 19.4 percent in 2016. Almost two-fifths of all Latina-headed families live below the poverty level. The rate is considerably higher for Puerto Rican female-headed households (64 percent). The interrelated factors of a youthful age structure (especially for Mexican-origin and Puerto Rican populations), residential locations in central cities, and declining urban economies contribute to struggling financial situations for many Latino families.

With the centrality of family being a positive value for many Latinos, the economic condition of a substantial segment of Latino families warrants concern and attention. Thus, the linkage of family economic status as a common interest is quite likely. Figure 3.9 highlights the relative poverty percentages by Latino national origin. With the overall Latino poverty rate at slightly more than 18 percent, those above the average are Hondurans, Dominicans, Guatemalans, Puerto Ricans, and Mexican-origin Latinos. Factors such as human capital resources, family structure, language proficiency, local economic opportunity structures, legal status, and discrimination have independent and interactive effects (Hartman et al. 2016).

Data on family type and size presents a complementary profile of Latino families, confirming that Latino families have a greater number of members than non-Latino households. In 1997, the percentage of Mexican-origin and Cuban "couple" families was similar to that of non-Latino "couple" families (72.2 percent, 76.9 percent, and 77.2 percent, respectively). On the other hand, female-headed households were much more prevalent among Mexican-origin, Puerto Rican, and "other Hispanic" demographics. The more telling information lies with the size of families. Latinos are three-fifths less likely to fall into the category of two-person families; Latino households are 2.2 times more likely than non-Latino families to include five or more members. Mexican-origin households are 2.6 times more likely to have five or more members. Central and South American families exhibit similar larger-family tendencies than the other Latino subgroups. Larger families, lower levels of family income, and corresponding higher rates of family poverty place Latino families at risk in terms of quality of life (e.g., housing conditions, educational isolation,[6] limited employment opportunities, economic segregation, and vulnerability to violent crime), which suggests both common ground and limited political resources to mobilize for effective change.

The age component is the final demographic factor to consider before closing this chapter, and age can be somewhat of a double-edged sword for Latinos. The youthfulness of the Latino population is what is fueling steady and continuous population

FIGURE 3.9 Poverty Rates among Latino National-Origin Groups

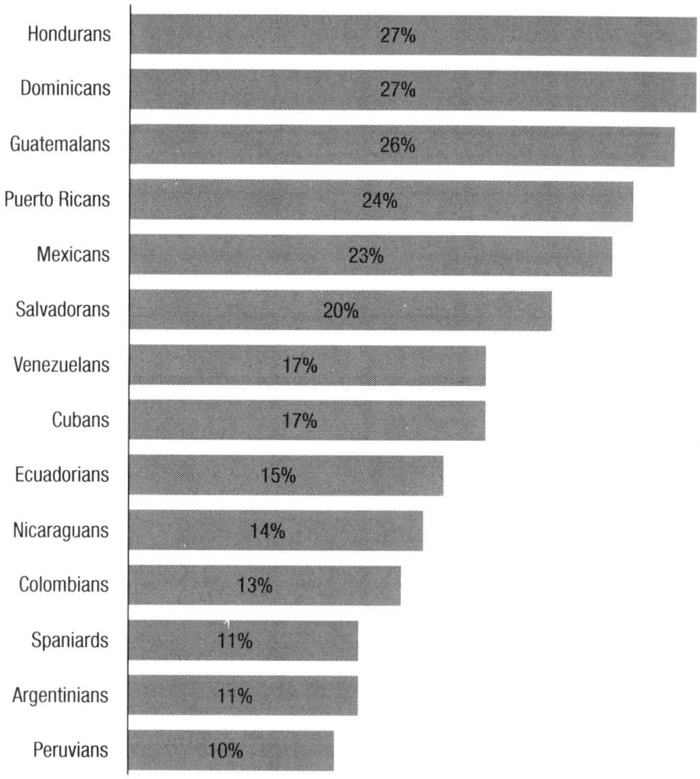

Group	Poverty Rate
Hondurans	27%
Dominicans	27%
Guatemalans	26%
Puerto Ricans	24%
Mexicans	23%
Salvadorans	20%
Venezuelans	17%
Cubans	17%
Ecuadorians	15%
Nicaraguans	14%
Colombians	13%
Spaniards	11%
Argentinians	11%
Peruvians	10%

Source: Pew Hispanic Research Center.

increases over time, but it is also suppressing Latino political influence. As we noted earlier, a large segment of the Latino population is younger than age eighteen, making them ineligible to vote. Latinos who are eligible to vote are disproportionately of the millennial generation, a cohort of Americans that has generated attention from political scientists who have noted their distinctive political behavior from older generations (see figure 3.10). We discuss the ideology and voting trends of Latino millennials in future chapters. The age disparity between Latinos and the rest of the general population in figure 3.10 illustrates just how much younger Latinos are than the rest of the general population, as nearly 60 percent of all Latinos are of the millennial generation or younger, compared to 39 percent among non-Hispanic whites.

Conclusion: Communities of Interests and Common Cultures

In this chapter, we have developed some demographic indicators supporting the concepts of the community of common or similar cultures and the community of interests based on similar socioeconomic conditions. Latinos of various national origins do share some commonalities central to life's experiences and situations that can serve as bases for common and collective actions. The following chapters examine and discuss developments within the Latino community in a variety of political arenas and activities.

FIGURE 3.10 Population of Millennials or Younger Represents 60 Percent of All Latinos

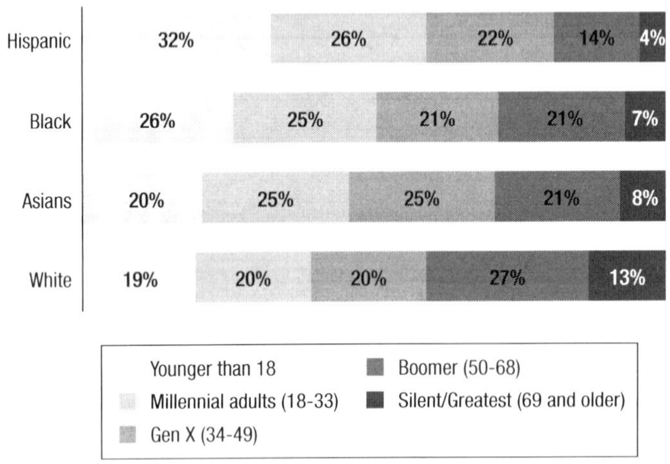

Group	Younger than 18	Millennial adults (18–33)	Gen X (34–49)	Boomer (50–68)	Silent/Greatest (69 and older)
Hispanic	32%	26%	22%	14%	4%
Black	26%	25%	21%	21%	7%
Asians	20%	25%	25%	21%	8%
White	19%	20%	20%	27%	13%

Source: Pew Research Center.

In our "community of culture" segment, the dimensions of Spanish language and nativity (or the extent of foreign-born status) constitute a significant constellation of cultural connections. Spanish-language persistence, reinforced to a large degree by continuous Latino migration, establishes and expands Latino enclaves, maintains "ethnically and culturally" dense social networks, contributes to a sustained Latino presence and visibility in the United States, and creates demands for business and media services.[7] The net effect is that culture is dynamic and extends beyond the traditional boundaries of Latino national-origin communities. Another aspect of a visible maintenance of "Latino culture" is that segments of the "host" society are raising concerns about integration, incorporation, assimilation, loyalty, and a general notion of whether Latinos belong in America.

A community of interests consists of similar socioeconomic conditions and statuses. We have presented information on occupational status, educational attainment, and family type among different Latino groups. There are more similarities, or clusters of attributes, among Latino subgroups than there are substantially different statuses. The one national subgroup that is somewhat less similar, Cubans, have bridged with other Latino subgroups on social welfare issues and, to some extent, immigration reform. The basis for a pan-ethnic community is evident and open to even greater community-building efforts.

This demographic profile provides the context for our later discussions of Latino political attitudes and engagement with the US political system. As we have noted in this chapter, the sheer size of the Latino population provides tremendous potential political influence and power. However, the relatively high percentage of Latinos who cannot vote, due to either being younger than age eighteen or not being citizens, limits the ability of Latinos to capitalize on this potential. This is further complicated by lower income and educational attainment levels among Latinos. It is our hope that by the end of this book you will have a more complete picture of why Latinos face some of the economic inequalities identified in this chapter and a better understanding of how policy reform could help address them.

Discussion Questions

1. A pan-ethnicity is viewed as a socially constructed category or identity. As a result, there is debate as to whether the Latino/Hispanic identity has real meaning and any real-world applications to an individual's daily life. Discuss whether this identity is "real" for persons of Latino origin and their daily lives and why.
2. At least twenty-two national-origin subgroups can be placed under the Latino group umbrella. Some of these groups are linked to other Latino national-origin groups, while others seem not to have much in common. Discuss how a person's national-origin background and experiences impact a sense of pan-ethnicity in the United States.
3. A major segment of the Latino community are foreign-born immigrants. Discuss the uniqueness within this subcommunity as identified by their demographic profile and its impact on the Latino native-born population. Also discuss how the present climate about immigrants, a well-defined image of America, and rhetoric affect the native-born Latinos and pan-ethnicity.
4. This chapter focuses on culture and demographics. How much does being further removed from the immigration experience (i.e., multigenerational status in the United States) affect the cultural dimensions of a Latino community?
5. Using demographics as one way to explore links and commonalities across Latino national origin groups, what other "measures" would you suggest?
6. We have hinted at the relationship that exists between this demographic profile of Latinos in the United States and Latino politics. Identify three examples of how the underlying demography discussed in this chapter influences the political power of the Latino community.

Links to Suggested Readings

https://www.pewresearch.org/fact-tank/2016/07/01/racial-gender-wage-gaps-persist-in-u-s-despite-some-progress

https://www.pewresearch.org/hispanic/2016/04/20/the-nations-latino-population-is-defined-by-its-youth

https://equitablegrowth.org/the-intersectional-wage-gaps-faced-by-latina-women-in-the-united-states

Notes

1. In this context, the idea of critical mass would suggest that Latinos now comprise a major community of presence and possibly have the political and economic impact to influence their state's decision-making process.
2. In terms of US policy, "refugee" refers to political status and official designation—a person who is fleeing a totalitarian regime, experiencing political persecution and a threat to life. Seeking political asylum in the United States is a formal process. The State Department is primarily responsible for determining which regimes are totalitarian. This has been a particular point of contention, especially for Central Americans, whose countries have experienced significant political turmoil and violence.
3. The items from the census used to determine English-language proficiency are a self-reported three-item sequence. The first question asks the person if he or she speaks a language

other than English. The person who answers affirmatively is then asked what that other language is. Finally, the respondent is asked how well (or not) he or she speaks English.

4. In 1997, the percentage of foreign-born persons in the US population reached a record high since the previous record levels of the early 1900s.

5. It has been documented that the traditional American workforce is aging, and the newest and most expansive segments of the workforce are women and minorities. Given the youthfulness of Latinos, they should continue to increase their proportion of the workforce, as well as contribute significantly to the Social Security system.

6. The idea of educational isolation refers to students who attend racially and/or ethnically segregated schools, with lower-quality school facilities and less-qualified instructional staff, as well as poorer educational outcomes (higher dropout rates, less high school completion, more disciplinary actions, lower standardized test scores, etc.).

7. This point illustrates the demand structure that can result with a critical mass of culturally similar persons, so that ethnic enterprises will cater to Latino customers and serve as potential employers. In addition, the mass media (print, radio, television), especially Spanish-language outlets, serve to highlight and inform the public about Latinos, as well as help to establish Latinos' economic impact as consumers.

Latino Subgroups in the United States

Los latinos somos de muchas nacionalidades distintas. Pero, dime que nombre prefiere, y yo puedo calibrar nuestra afinidad como una familia más grande. Pues, quizás no pueda. El proceso de extenderse más alla de familia, de patria, depende en las experiencias que compartimos y como nos entendermos y nuestras interacciónes. Pero, primero necesito definir a cual grupo pertenezco.

Latinos are of many distinct nationalities. But tell me which name you prefer, and I can gauge our relationship in the larger family. Well, perhaps I cannot. The process of extending one's identity beyond family and country depends on the experiences that we share, how we understand one another, and our interactions. But first, I need to decide to which group I belong.

CRITICAL TO OUR UNDERSTANDING OF Latinos and their political involvement is the analysis of the formation of a community and their intra- and intergroup linkages. Even though the mass media and governmental policies often group all Latinos together, the extensiveness of community across the Latino subgroups has tended to be more nuanced. National social surveys (Latino National Survey, Washington Post–Pew Hispanic Surveys, CBS News, CNN–All Politics Polls, Latino Decisions, etc.) and regional surveys (Florida International University, Texas A&M University, UCLA) focusing on Latinos have portrayed many Latinos as more familiar and interactive within their own national-origin group than with other Latino subgroups. This characterization prevailed until there was a sustained set of systematic surveys of Latinos after 2000 (Pew Hispanic Surveys, Latino National Survey, Latino Decisions, Bendixen & Amandi Surveys, etc.). The pattern of subgroups' regional concentration (80 percent of the Mexican-origin population concentrated in the Southwest, 60 percent of Cubans in Dade County, Florida, and 80 percent of Puerto Ricans in the Northeast) is no longer the case. New destinations in the South and the Midwest and increased international migration since the 1990s have produced greater geographic dispersion among Latinos. But the opportunity to interact across Latino groups is not limited by geography alone; it is also related to family, historical, and homeland connections, as well as common experiences.

FIGURE 4.1 Largest Hispanic Origin Group by State, 2010

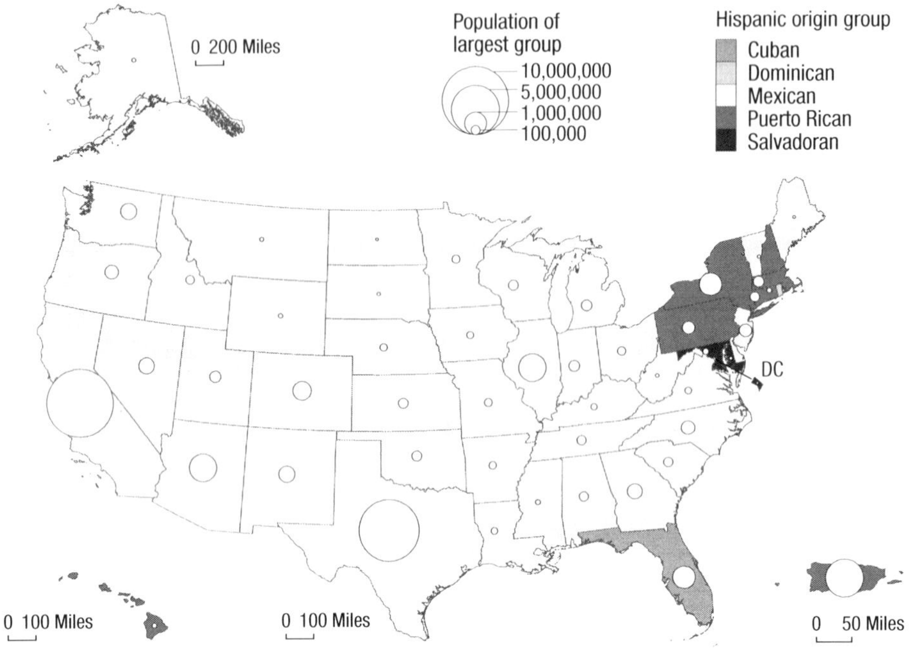

Source: US Census Bureau, 2010 Census Summary File 1.

The map in figure 4.1 illustrates the geographic distribution of Latino subgroups throughout the United States in 2010. An examination of the map's legend indicates where the major Latino subgroups reside in significant numbers. For example, the Mexican-origin population is now found throughout the United States, especially in newer communities in the South and even the New England and northeastern regions. However, the map makes clear that the Mexican-origin population continues to be most highly concentrated in California and Texas. While Florida remains an area of major concentration for Cubans, there has been a significant influx of Puerto Ricans in central Florida as well as continued migration of Central and South Americans to South Florida. Cubans are the plurality Latino subgroup in that state but no longer the majority of all Latinos in Florida.

This chapter provides some characterization of Latino subgroups to complement the demographic profiles discussed in chapter 3. Following a short synopsis of several Latino subgroups, we will highlight their settlement and historical development in the United States. There is a wealth of historical and interpretative accounts of Latino subgroup experiences over an extended period of their history in the United States. Hopefully this brief introduction might encourage you to explore in greater depth the diversity of all national-origin Latino groups. The greater influx of Latino immigrants since the 1990s has led to a significant increase in the Latino population, a contributing factor affecting the process of how these dynamic communities are being shaped. These brief sketches will hopefully serve to give a fuller picture of the many subcommunities that make up what we call Latinos or Hispanics.

More than half of all the Latinos in the United States reside in the states of California (28 percent), Texas (19 percent), and Florida (8 percent). These states are not only populous states; they are still experiencing population growth. They exemplify electoral significance, either as a key for an electoral college base *or* as a prize for winning a competitive state's electoral college votes. As the residents of these key states become more diversified, including multiple Latino subgroups, the political capital of pursuing a "pan-ethnic" community becomes more important.

Mexican-Origin Communities: Growing throughout the United States

Historically, the Mexican-origin population has been the largest and oldest of the Latino subgroups. In 2019, the Mexican-origin population exceeded 36.5 million. About 50 percent of foreign-born Mexicans have been in the United States for more than twenty years and 32 percent are US citizens. Consistently, they represent more than three-fifths of the total Latino population. They predate the English settlements in the eastern section of the United States, with Spanish expeditions to what is now the American Southwest that began in the early sixteenth century. Mission settlements lined much of the region, particularly in the current states of California, New Mexico, Arizona, and Texas. The presence of Spaniards, Mexicans, and mestizos (i.e., descendants of Spanish and Indian or indigenous cultures) is also reflected in the names of many southwestern states (e.g., Nevada, Montana, Colorado, New Mexico) and countless cities and towns. At the same time, Mexican-origin people include recent migrants (both legal permanent resident aliens and undocumented persons). Migratory patterns to the agricultural regions and industrial sections of the United States were established in the latter 1800s and early 1900s. Now, the service sectors of the American economy serve as destination areas for the more recently arrived Mexicanos.

For much of the period since the **Treaty of Guadalupe Hidalgo** (1848), Mexicanos have been concentrated in the five southwestern states (California, Arizona, Texas, New Mexico, and Colorado). Then, heavy manufacturing in steel, auto, and railroads largely influenced the noticeable migratory stream to the Midwest. In the second decade of the new millennium, Mexican people settled throughout other regions of the country (the Northwest, Northeast, and South). For example, meat-processing plants, textile manufacturers, and service industries in the states of Arkansas, Florida, and North Carolina have become destinations for Mexican immigrants. Similar patterns are still developing in the other regions, as mentioned in chapter 3. Obviously, Mexico's physical proximity and its economic dependence on the American economy serve as major contributors to the flow of goods and people across the border. Similarly, US immigration policy has provided impetus for alternately freer and more restricted movement across the border. We will discuss the current immigration developments in chapter 9. Mexico's proximity and continuous migration have also served to maintain cultural contact and economic exchanges with family, relatives, and other social networks.[1]

In this brief accounting of the Mexican-origin population, the themes of long-standing residence and continuous international migration coexist as the context for Mexican American/Chicano political life and issues. The demographics of this group, as well as its cultural maintenance (largely in terms of social affinity and identification, bilingualism, and familialism), contribute to the people's experiences in the United States and their political integration. Regions of the Southwest (southern Texas, northern New Mexico, and southern California) provide examples of power and economic relations for Mexican Americans. The preponderance of Mexicanos in South Texas (El Valle del Rio Grande) serves as evidence that population size alone does not automatically translate to political and economic power and influence. At the same time, the continued growth of this group in both traditional and newer destinations has raised issues of negative stereotypes (Vargas et al. 2021), discrimination, and punitive legislation (primarily regarding documented status and access to services, housing, and jobs) (Ybarra, Sanchez, and Sanchez 2016). Current rancorous debates about immigration and the undocumented carry the "face of the Mexican immigrant" as the symbol of "unwelcome immigrants."

Mexicanos have served as a labor force and flexible labor pool for the agricultural economy without controlling ownership or production. It was once as if two separate societies existed, the owners and the others, with worker status and ethnicity being the dividing line (Montejano 1987). The 1960s saw the advent of Chicano power and major efforts by Mexican Americans to achieve political control. The rise of a third-party movement (La Raza Unida) in primarily rural South Texas saw several city councils, school boards, and county offices secured by Chicano candidates. Although short-lived, this "electoral takeover" set the foundation for subsequent political efforts and organizational development. Middle-class organizational efforts among workers and targeted educational reforms assisted ensuing political advances and mobilization (Shockley 1974; Foley 1988). The upcoming chapters, particularly chapters 6 through 8, focus on political resource development (socioeconomic and psychological predispositions and political attitudes) and organizational development (strategies, skills, leadership, and the utilization of greater resources), which are primary components of Latino political involvement.

The Hispano experience in New Mexico differs from that of rural South Texas, where economic and political subjugation has been a long-standing reality (Montejano 1987). The unique historical context of New Mexico has been described well by legal scholar Dr. Laura Gómez, whose book contends that the racialization of Mexicans in New Mexico has led to the Hispano population distancing themselves from Mexicans in favor of Spanish identification (Gómez 2018). Even before the Mexican-American War of 1848, the Hispanos encompassed a propertied and business class. Although the advent of territorial government and resulting statehood saw Hispanos' economic and political power diminish, they maintained political leverage. Ironically, contemporary New Mexico has experienced significant interregional migration of non-Latinos into the state, particularly in the north. Hispanos, with almost one-half (48 percent) of the state's population, continue to serve as "players" yet engage in continuous political struggles to maintain their political position. The 2000 elections in New Mexico saw the statewide election of Hispanos as attorney general, secretary of state, state treasurer, and state auditor. In 2002, Bill Richardson, a Latino, was elected governor, and he was followed shortly thereafter by Republican Susana Martinez in 2010. Then in 2018, Michelle Lujan Grisham (Dem.) was elected governor, establishing New Mexico as the leader in Hispanic political representation.

Southern California represents the legacy of the "Californios" (Pitt 1966), but even more so, the rise of extensive Mexican migration to this state. After World War II, noticeable numbers of Mexican Americans migrated from Texas to California in search of better opportunities and less discrimination. After the 1960s, California became the major destination state for international migration, especially from Mexico. The combination of push-pull factors (lack of job opportunities in Mexico, peso devaluations, proximity to the US border, economic pull of jobs, and an established Mexican-origin community) contributed significantly to the growing Mexican-origin population. The expansive California economy (in the service sectors, traditional agriculture, high-tech manufacturing operations, etc.) made it the major port of entry for immigrants. The translation to appreciable political and economic influence did not become evident until the 1990s.

During the previous decade, redistricting, activism by Mexican American organizations (Mexican American Legal Defense and Education Fund, Southwest Conference of la Raza, Southwest Voter and Education Project, etc.), and anti-immigrant and nativism movements set the stage for increased Mexican American political group awareness and activity. In the mid-1990s, state initiatives such as Propositions 187, 209, and 237 stimulated Mexican Americans and their organizations to mobilize and register to vote. One result of this increased activism has been the greater numbers of Latino elected officials at the state and federal levels. For more than four decades, the Mexican-origin community was portrayed as "the sleeping giant," "an awakening minority," and "a group whose time for a place in the sun has arrived" (García 1996). There are clear indications that Mexican Americans and other Latinos are exerting their political impact now.

The Mexican-origin population holds a national presence with expanding political involvement of Mexican American organizations who are diversifying their goals and objectives, as well as their constituency base, by incorporating other Latino subgroups into their membership with a broader range of issues and policies (de la Garza, Kruszewski, and Arciniega 1973). For example, the National Council of La Raza (NCLR) was called the Southwest Council of La Raza in the late 1960s and is today known as **UnidosUS**. Its primary goals were economic development, social services, and advocacy on behalf of Mexican Americans, but since the inception of UnidosUS, the organization has adopted a national orientation, with its headquarters in Washington, DC. Its constituency base includes all Latinos, with membership and board members representing most segments of the diverse Latino community. It has developed a film production company, supplies venture capital for small businesses, provides resource development for community-based organizations, and engages in applied research, policy analysis, and advocacy. UnidosUS illustrates the evolution of Mexican American organizations in the latter half of the twentieth century.

The dispersion of Mexican Americans throughout the United States has broadened their contact with other Latino subgroups and expanded their identity beyond purely national origin. For example, the concept and label use of "Latino" in Chicago is widespread among Latinos of Mexican, Puerto Rican, Cuban, Salvadoran, and Central and South American ancestry. While conducting field research with several Latino community-based organizations in the early 1970s, John García encountered a conscious effort by Latino leaders to construct a Latino identity. The activist elements instilled a sense of identifying as Latinos to help broaden the population base of the emerging Latino community. Almost twenty years later, when the Latino National Political Survey was conducting focus groups in Chicago, the presence of a Latino identity was evident. Focus participants had integrated a sense of national-origin awareness and identity, as well as broader group identification as Latinos. Again, fifteen years later (spring 2005), as part of the Latino National Survey research group, focus groups were conducted in more than ten communities. Whether they were Spanish speakers, English monolinguals, immigrants, or native-born citizens, those referring to persons of Spanish origin consistently used the "Latino" and "Hispanic" labels. For Mexican Americans, broadening intergroup contacts and incorporating a pan-ethnic[2] identity serve as building blocks for a Latino community.

Long-standing Mexican American communities have established social networks, traditions, and cultural practices that contribute to the definition and maintenance of community. In addition, the evolution of Mexican American organizations (e.g., mutual aid societies, labor movements, cultural organizations, civil rights and professional groups, and advocacy/litigation organizations) represents a substantial history of organizational activities and definable agendas. In general, the core of those agendas has focused on civil rights, access to and participation in economic and political arenas, educational quality, and increased political empowerment. In addition, a wider mix of Latino subgroups has moved into established Mexican-origin communities.

BOX 4.1 The Changing Faces of Latino America

The historically Mexican face of the Texas Latino community has changed in the past decade. Lori Rodríguez (2001) of the *Houston Chronicle* put real faces to stories about this diverse mix. She described the Chanax family (from Guatemala), which migrated to Texas in the 1990s. The seven nephews of Don Esteban worked, started families, and settled in Houston. He speaks minimal English, but one daughter speaks with a "Latin lilt," and his son Giovanni, a college-bound marine veteran, speaks English with a Texas accent. They represent a non-Mexican influx into Houston, whose proportion of the state's Latinos has more than doubled since 2000 (from 10.3 to 24 percent). The proportion of Mexican-origin immigrants shrank from 80 to 73 percent in Harris County. Similarly, in Brazoria County (part of the Houston metropolitan area), the proportion of non-Mexican population grew from less than 10 percent to 23 percent, with similar jumps in the other counties in the metro area. Whereas Mexican Americans have accounted for around 90 percent of all Latinos in Texas, the abrupt shift to other Latinos now residing in the state is quite striking. The same patterns are evident in Austin (12.7 to 23.3 percent), El Paso (4.7 to 16.7 percent), Dallas (12 to 17 percent), and San Antonio (8 to 30 percent).

In Houston, Guatemalan immigrants have secured employment in one of the city's largest supermarkets, Randall's, now estimated to employ more than a thousand Guatemalans. Other indicators of an ethnic mix are found in the Randall's bakery, which offers coronas, roscas, and other traditional Guatemalan breads next to bolillos, pan de huevo, and other Mexican pastries. Nestor Rodríquez (University of Houston), who has examined migration to the Houston area, notes the significant migration from Central and South America with a "sprinkling" of Puerto Ricans and Cubans. While this is documented in Houston and other parts of Texas, similar additions of other Latinos to traditional concentrations of Mexicans, Puerto Ricans, or Cubans are evident in Florida, New York, California, and other regions with established Latino communities.

The community's leadership has expanded from grassroots and labor leaders to include others with corporate skills. Their continuous migration from Mexico contributes to population growth and their geographic dispersion. The broadening of a pan-ethnic community, by linking themselves with other Latino subgroups at both the elite and grassroots levels, affects the scope of the public policy agenda. After the 2006 immigrant protest marches and the continued advocacy aftermath, accompanied by more intense opposition to any immigration reform, including pathways to citizenship and "normalization," the need for Latinos to integrate more recent immigrants into the body politic is even more evident. As the largest subgroup, the Mexican-origin community plays an important role in facilitating the coalescing of all Latino subgroups.

Puerto Ricans: Manhattan or La Isla Borinquen (Puerto Rico)?

Historically, a significant number of island transplants from Puerto Rico migrated after World War II to the New York City metropolitan area. However, the current population of slightly more than four million has a longer history in the United States. Attracted by agricultural labor and cigar-making in the late nineteenth century, a number of Puerto Ricans began migrating to the Southeast. As a result of the Spanish-American War, Puerto Rico became a US possession. The Jones Act of 1917 established Puerto Ricans as US citizens and allowed them the right of being a congressional "observer" without a vote. In 1947 the act was amended to enable Puerto Ricans to elect their own governor and other officials, except for members of the Supreme Court.

Puerto Rico's status has been a long-standing concern. As a commonwealth, it enjoys a degree of autonomy while participating in entitlement programs and citizenship benefits. The independence movement in Puerto Rico reached an apex on July 25, 1952, with a push for the island to become a free-associated state. Alternatives to commonwealth status include free-associated state status, statehood, and independence.

BOX 4.2 Puerto Rican Political Strategies: Changing Geography but Advocating Mainland and Island Issues

The long-established residency of most of the Puerto Ricans in the United States has been concentrated in the New York City metropolitan area. In autumn 2015, members of Congress of Puerto Rican background, activists, and other Puerto Rican leaders organized a two-day conference in Orlando, Florida, to prioritize a national policy agenda. What made this action noteworthy was the staging of the conference in central Florida rather than New York City. Secondly, the scope of the working policy agenda focused on issues in the mainland (i.e., the United States) and the Commonwealth of Puerto Rico. A key element of this organizing strategy was conducting the meeting in the "swing" state of Florida with the hopes of accenting a political spotlight in which both political parties and candidates would be more aware of the political policy agenda of the national Puerto Rican community.

One of the central issues involved seeking congressional action on restructuring Puerto Rico's debt obligations ($72 billion debt and a looming health

BOX 4.2 (continued)

crisis). The issue has been before Congress for some time, with Latino members submitting legislation to restructure its debt through chapter 9, like Detroit. Another issue discussed at the conference dealt with the repeal of the 1920 Jones Act, which requires US mainland vessels built by US workers to be used to ship goods in and out of Puerto Rico. This has made island shipping costs much higher. According to Edwin Melendez, director of the Center for Puerto Rican Studies at Hunter College, "The whole point of the national agenda is to tell the American public and elected officials and candidates for elected office . . . even though we care about local issues, we also are concerned about what is going on in Puerto Rico." Puerto Rico has been experiencing population loss since 2006, including many health-care professionals, while the mainland Puerto Rican population has reached 5.2 million (in comparison to the island's 3.4 million).

The strategic objective of this conference was to situate the Puerto Rican community into a national policy agenda. Congresswoman Nydia Velasquez stated that "given that Florida is a battleground state with over a million Puerto Ricans living there, the message is clear that you ignore the Puerto Rican community." In addition, the conference attendees worked on voter registration and mobilization plans to register Puerto Ricans to vote not only in Florida, but also in Pennsylvania, Cleveland, North Carolina, and cities throughout the South.

Conference participants have taken the position that Puerto Rican voters, while leaning toward the Democratic party, are conservative, especially the current migrants, and warrant attention from both parties to gain their support and affiliation. The only Republican Puerto Rican member of Congress is Representative Raúl Labrador of Idaho, who did not attend the conference. A final policy issue dealt with the Puerto Rican population in the United States and its increasing division over the issue of whether the island should become a state, remain a commonwealth, or be independent, according to Angelo Falcon, director of the Institute for Puerto Rican Policy.

In this chapter, we highlight activities and developments within the specific Latino subcommunities this development within the Puerto Rican community represents: more recent concentration of Puerto Ricans outside metro New York City; a policy agenda that focuses on both local and national American politics and issues on the island; and integrating their concerns both into a broader Latino policy agenda as well as the overall national agenda.

Source: Adaption of the news story "Island Fiscal Crisis Shifts Puerto Rican Power from NY to Florida," by Suzanne Gamboa, *NBC News* (October 8, 2015).

There have been several plebiscites—in 1967, 1993, and 1998 (HR 856, United States–Puerto Rico Political Status Act). In those cases, maintaining the status quo, commonwealth status, received the greatest number of votes. The statehood option has been the second most preferred, with independence running a distant third. There are some variations among supporters for these options; the more conservative Puerto Ricans favor statehood, with liberals favoring independence.

On November 6, 2012, another referendum was held on the political status of Puerto Rico. It was the fourth referendum on status to be held in Puerto Rico and the first time in which a majority voted for statehood. Puerto Rican voters were asked two questions: (1) whether they concurred with the position to continue with Puerto Rico's territorial status; and (2) to indicate their preferred political status from a set of three possibilities: statehood, independence, or a sovereign nation in free association with the United States. The results to the first question indicated that the majority, 970,910 (54 percent) vs. 828,077 (46 percent), were opposed to maintaining the current political status. The vote distribution on the three options in question number two were 834,191 (61.11 percent) choosing statehood, 454,768 (33.34 percent) choosing free association, and 74,895 (6.00 percent) choosing independence.

The status of Puerto Rico remains an issue among many Puerto Ricans living on the US mainland. Intertwined in these debates are themes associated with autonomy, trade options, cultural maintenance, identity, and the costs and benefits of each option. Since the last plebiscite, the results have been challenged as to whether there was a clear-cut sentiment toward statehood, citing a significant percentage of invalid ballots and the closeness of the preferences. As a result, several initiatives were taken by Puerto Rican officials, President Obama's administration, and Congress, ranging from a congressional law to initiate movement toward statehood with another plebiscite to going before the United Nations assembly to argue for self-determination for Puerto Rico. Presently, no formal actions have been taken, but the better prognostication focuses on another plebiscite with some commitment to implement the "will of the Puerto Rican" as evidenced in the election results.

For Puerto Ricans living on the mainland, there are a number of dimensions related to the political-status question. The first is an interest in being directly involved in the discussion and vote. With the framing of House Bill 866, one of the points of contention was whether Puerto Ricans living on the mainland would be allowed to vote in the plebiscite. The close cultural and familial contact and affinity between Puerto Ricans living in the United States and in Puerto Rico stirs both interest and support from Puerto Rican organizations to ensure mainland participation in the plebiscite. Second, cultural and group identity among **Boricuas** in the United States interprets the political-status question as activating issues of cultural identity, economic opportunity, and pride, which are important in both locations. (The terms "Boricua" and "Newyorican" refer to Puerto Rican populations in the United States.) Third, the question of political status can serve as a focal point for the political status of Puerto Ricans in the United States.

For example, numerous Puerto Rican leaders advocate for the inclusion of the population of Puerto Rico in the total count of Latinos in the United States (an additional 3.9 million). Empowerment, active political engagement, cultural maintenance, and targeted policy advocacy from their own perspective (Jennings and Rivera 1984; Jennings 1994; Cruz 1998) motivate the Puerto Rican community. A more recent action of Puerto Rican leadership on the mainland involves the island's financial crisis and its massive $72 billion public debt (Gamboa 2015; Gamboa and Khalid 2015). The legal protections and federal assistance available to states and communities do not exist for Puerto Rico. A meeting was held in Orlando, Florida, in October 2015 to advocate for action from Congress to empower Puerto Rico to have the opportunity to access bankruptcy laws for debt restructuring (see box 4.2). Representatives Velasquez (NY) and Gutierrez (IL), along with city council members and state legislators, primarily from the Northeast, participated in this meeting. The meeting served to illustrate not only the intertwined nature of the Puerto Rican community's political life, both on the mainland and the island, but also the significance of the meeting's Florida location, highlighting the one million Latinos living in that state.

The historical concentration of Puerto Ricans in the Northeast has changed since 1995. While 55.6 percent of Puerto Ricans live in the Northeast, 27.2 percent live in the South (with 17.8 percent of all Puerto Ricans in Florida); communities are in Holyoke, Hartford, Chicago, Miami, Bridgeport, and Los Angeles. The status and condition of Puerto Rican communities can be compared with those of many of the other Latino subgroups. With a median group age of twenty-nine years, the younger Puerto Rican population faces problems with inadequate housing, lesser educational resources, and higher rates of unemployment, single-headed households, poverty, and residential segregation. Their long-standing location in the New York City metropolitan area highlights these problems. The elimination of low-skilled central-city manufacturing jobs, economic globalization, and relocation have contributed to higher rates of joblessness, social welfare participation, inferior schools, and limited and substandard housing (Kasarda 1985, 1989; Sanchez Korrol 1994).

Work by Denton and Massey (1988) on residential segregation highlights the formation and perpetuation of subcultural practices and social networks that have impeded the incorporation of Puerto Ricans into mainstream economic and social life. Torres-Saillant and Hernández (1998) and Moore and Pinderhughes (1993) suggest that the distinctive Puerto Rican island culture and language, along with targeted labor recruitment by certain industries (e.g., agriculture and manufacturing) and racial discrimination, have contributed to economic disparities and barriers in the housing market.

Clara Rodríguez (1998, 2000) discusses the American basis of race and how it constitutes a different racial order from that found in Puerto Rico. Whereas Rodríguez characterizes race in America as white and other (primarily black), Puerto Rico has a multiplicity of "racial categories" or distinctions: black, indigo, trigueno, negro, moreno, and white or Spanish. Thus, the US schema, which categorizes people as white, black, possibly white, not white, and not black, leaves Puerto Ricans outside the racial order. Rodríguez contends that race, ethnicity, and culture are interconnected in the Puerto Rican experience and inconsistent with the American view of race. For Puerto Ricans, the phenotypical variations form an integrated system. Yet, America and its institutions may differentiate between Puerto Ricans by different racial categories when they identify themselves in cultural terms with race as a subset. The introduction of race and ethnicity also brings forth discriminatory theories that can bar Latinos from equal opportunities and access to many realms of life in the United States.

Overall, issues confronting Puerto Rican communities center on housing costs and access, urban relocation due to gentrification and urban renewal, educational quality and curriculum (including the dropout problem, language and bilingual education, and participation in higher education), unemployment, female-headed households, poverty and children living in poverty, and crime and public safety. Especially since the 1960s, Puerto Rican organizations have targeted community improvement, adaptation, and empowerment goals. For example, from the origins of the Puerto Rican

Forum came ASPIRA and the Puerto Rican Community Development Program (Fitzgerald 1971).

Organizations like the Puerto Rican Merchants Association (PRMA) and the Puerto Rican Civil Service Employees Association (PRCSEA) address the economic dimensions of life in the United States. The theme of continued connection with the Commonwealth of Puerto Rico is further reinforced by the presence of its office in New York City to assist Puerto Ricans with referrals. In the 1980s, the commonwealth office also participated in a voter-registration campaign in the city. Finally, organizations such as the Puerto Rican Legal Defense and Education Fund and the Institute for Puerto Rican Policy deal directly with issues of political empowerment and policy advocacy. Limited studies on Puerto Rican political behavior indicate lower rates of political participation, especially in the electoral process (Nelson 1979; Falcón and Santiago 1993) on the mainland as opposed to the island.

Puerto Rican communities have broadened their geographical presence and are actively engaged in local politics and policies, especially in central Florida (Orlando). The social and economic issues mentioned in the demographic profile constitute much of the political agenda for Puerto Ricans. Continued close ties with Puerto Rico and well-established neighborhoods on the mainland have served to maintain a strong sense of cultural identity, Spanish-language use, and pride (J. Cruz 1998; C. Rodríguez 1998; Jennings 1994; Jennings and Rivera 1984). Immigration has been characterized as a lesser concern for Puerto Ricans because of their status as US citizens. In 2010, Ohio turned down Puerto Rican birth certificates as acceptable documents for a US driver's license, arguing the greater possibility of fraud. Puerto Rican leaders, however, see this policy change as part of the anti-Latino/anti-immigrant climate embroiling many state and local policies. We will discuss in a later chapter Latino/as as a pan-ethnic group of immigrants and subsequent policy issues and impacts on local communities.

Cubanos: Still an Exile Community?

Cubans in the United States have been characterized as living primarily in southern Florida, hostile toward the Fidel/Raul Castro regime, ardent anticommunists, listeners to *el son y boleros* (forms of Cuban music and rhythms), and active politically. Cubans are the third-largest population (tied with Salvadorans) of Hispanic origin living in the United States, accounting for 4 percent of the US Hispanic population in 2017. Since 2000, the Cuban-origin population has increased 92 percent, growing from 1.2 million to 2.3 million over the period. At the same time, the Cuban foreign-born population living in the United States grew by 53 percent, from 853,000 in 2000 to 1.3 million in 2017. The Cuban population is concentrated in Florida (66 percent), California (5 percent), and New Jersey (4 percent).

While the broader public knowledge about Cubans usually begins with the political demise of Fulgencio Batista in 1957, Cubans in the United States have an earlier presence. Historically, Cubans have lived in Florida since the 1850s along the Gulf of Mexico. Major numbers, largely involved in the cigar industry, populated the Key West area. Trade, labor, and commerce connected Cuban workers and entrepreneurs during the expansion of cigar production for much of the latter part of the nineteenth century. The Spanish-American War and subsequent US control of Cuba established both political and economic ties. American investments, export partnerships, and extended foreign relations almost made Cuba a US satellite.

In a more contemporary context, the rise of Fidel Castro and his communist regime helped create an exile community for many Cubans. Accounts since the late 1950s have referred to Cuban migration as the "golden exile," the flight of Cuban elites and professionals from the Castro regime. These exiles were primarily white, well-educated professionals, entrepreneurs, and urban residents. Between 1963 and 1972, 296,000 Cubans resettled into 2,400 communities. Because they immigrated as political refugees, American policy helped in the areas of job training, English instruction, college loans, free certification for health professionals, housing subsidies, food stamps and food surpluses, and citizen exemption from certain jobs. Between 1961 and 1971, federal allocations for Cuban refugee assistance equaled $739 million. In addition, federal funds went to Dade County schools ($120 million) to assist with refugee children and youth. When the federal immigration law changed in 1965, the Cuban Adjustment Act of 1966 exempted Cubans from the newly imposed 120,000-immigrant ceiling for persons from Western Hemisphere countries.

The status of political refugee and the corresponding federal legislation differentiate Cubanos from other Latinos. The contrast lies in the program and financial assistance received to facilitate adjustment to life in the United States and in their political motivation to leave Cuba, which conveys a strong commitment to political issues and concerns. Anti-Castro-ism and anti-communism are central elements of many Cubans' politics and activities. Organizations like the Cuban American National Foundation (CANF) (previously led by Jorge Mas Canosa) and movements such as Brigade 2506, Alpha 66, and Omega 7 focus their activities on efforts to wrest control of Cuba from the communist regime. Military efforts, economic sanctions and embargoes, and Radio-TV Martí show why Cubans have been referred to as an exile community. For the most part, exile communities address their concerns to the political regime in control and seek policies in their "new" home to affect regime-change pressures.

Cuban migration underwent significant socioeconomic, racial, and political changes with the Mariel boatlifts. Unlike their pre-1980 counterparts, these refugees were more likely to be single adults, service and semiskilled workers, "social misfits," rural people, and less-educated individuals. Racially, this wave of Cubans included more Afro-Cubans compared to the predominantly white, elite refugees of earlier years. Politically, Cuban refugees had enjoyed a receptive climate as exiles leaving a communist regime and producing economic and social successes in America (e.g., bringing major entrepreneurial ventures, educational advances, stable and supportive family structures, economic revitalization of urban centers).

Yet, the nature and timing of the Mariel flotilla was interpreted as Fidel Castro's "dumping" of social misfits and criminals, and a growing anti-immigrant hostility began to develop in the United States. The unsuccessful efforts of Haitian émigrés to gain a favorable entry status, with their boatlifts being turned back, angered African Americans and heightened the sense of intergroup conflict in South Florida. For example, the Dade County Commission passed an English-only ordinance despite the positive contributions that the Cuban community had made to the revitalization of the South Florida economy.

The politics of an exile community has focused on policies that would achieve the "demise" of Cuba's communist regime, assist with continued family reunification in the United States, and provide long-term resettlement assistance. For example, the CANF lobbied the Clinton administration to support the Cuban Democracy Act, which tightened trade embargoes with tougher sanctions for firms involved with Cuba and established Radio-TV Martí. Radio Martí, situated in South Florida, conducts news and informational broadcasts targeted at Cuba, much like the Radio Free Europe model for communist Eastern European countries. Yet, by the late 1990s, Cuba and its leadership comprised only one of a broader range of domestic agenda issues for the Cuban American community. Some have described this development as a transition from exile politics to American ethnic politics. Limitations on travel and remittances by Cubans to family members in Cuba have been viewed as too restrictive and as failing to inflict political instability on the regime as intended.

Since 2000, there have been more directed policies to limit travel and remittances while allowing for trade of agricultural and medical products. In 2009, a poll conducted by Bendixen & Amandi indicated that 67 percent of Cuban Americans wanted the restrictions removed (an 18 percent increase from the second George W. Bush administration). There are indications of some impatience with the old policies. The Obama administration began easing such restrictions and supported legislation such as enabling Cubans to receive Social Security checks in Cuba.

A historic 2014 decision by President Barack Obama and Cuban president Raúl Castro to normalize relations opened a new era for Cuban migration. Anticipating an end to their special immigration treatment, Cuban arrivals more than doubled from fewer than 24,300 in fiscal year (FY) 2014 to 56,400 in FY 2016. During the final days of his presidency in January 2017, President Obama ended the "dry-foot" aspect of the policy, which had resulted in thousands of Cubans making their way through Central America and Mexico to reach the US border. Since then, Cubans who have attempted to enter the United States without a visa have been deemed inadmissible and subject to deportation like other foreign nationals. However, those who enter on a visa remain eligible for a green card after one year in the country.

When Donald Trump came into office, he dramatically expanded deportations. While President Obama prioritized deporting undocumented immigrants who committed violent crimes, the Trump administration said it would deport any immigrant in the country illegally, including Cubans. In fiscal year 2016, 64 Cuban nationals were deported back to the island, according to Immigration and Customs Enforcement. Two years later, in 2018, that number shot up to 463, more than a sevenfold increase. "There are now more Cubans in detention facilities than any other time that I remember of," said Santiago Alpizar, a Cuban American immigration attorney in Miami. "Cubans are treated as any other migrant from any other part of the world" (Rivero 2019; Sheridan 2019).

Interestingly, second-generation Cubans display some political attitudes that differ from those of their parents. This generation, representing 37 percent of the Cuban population, consists of individuals who have lived all their lives in US society (Hill and Moreno 1996). They express lower levels of trust in the US government, show greater diversity in partisan preference (less Republican domination), identify less with the Cuban community only, and favor decreased governmental spending (Moreno and Warren 1992; Hill and Moreno 1996). In addition, second-generation Cubans are more likely than their parents to use a pan-ethnic identity (i.e., Latino or Hispanic) by a percentage of 27.7 to 5.8 percent. This generation speaks Spanish less frequently, and whereas 58.9 percent of their parents perceive no discrimination, 23.5 percent of the second generation responded that they do.

There are other indications of a more moderate orientation toward Cuba. Organizations such as Cambio Cubano and the Committee for Cuban Democracy (CCD) describe themselves as moderate and support a willingness to negotiate with the Cuban regime. Eloy Gutierrez-Menoyo's return to Cuba (Elliston 1995) was marked by the government's show of tolerance and respect. Marcelino Miyares of CCD advocates dialogue, reconciliation, and respect for Cuban sovereignty. At the same time, a desire for democratization is a central element among moderate Cuban Americans. The election of Alex Perales as Dade County executive mayor in 1996 marked the rise of second-generation Cubans to elective office.

President Obama's action to normalize relations with Cuba in December 2014 also illustrated some shifts within the Cuban American community. The Cuban Americans for Engagement (CAFÉ) held a conference in March 2015 to discuss greater expansion of normalization activities such as individuals' ability to invest in Cuban businesses, less stringent travel restrictions, and more open trade opportunities. A poll by Bendixen & Amandi International (April 2015) showed that 54 percent of Cuban Americans supported normalized relations with Cuba while 40 percent were opposed. A higher percentage (56 percent) endorsed easing travel restrictions and more open trade. The supporters for normalization tended to be younger, US-born, and recent immigrants. Clearly, the demographic changes this community is undergoing have direct political consequences.

Newspaper articles (Preston and Alvarez 2016) note not only the changing demography of Florida but its manifestations in party affiliation. The significant influx of Puerto Ricans in central Florida as well as from Central and South America, and population gains in second- and third-generation Cuban Americans have contributed to Cubans lessening their affiliation with the Republican Party. In 2006, 37 percent of Florida's Latinos registered as Republicans, with 33 percent registering as Democrats and 28 percent as Independents. By 2016, those figures shifted, with 26 percent registered as Republicans, 37 percent as Democrats, and 35 percent as Independents (Preston and Alvarez 2016). Factors such as being more supportive of Democrats' stand on social issues, Trump's negative comments about Latinos, including about Miss Universe from Venezuela, and shifts in current immigration policies indicate the Cuban community's reassessment of partisan support and affiliation as well as the partisan mix of other Latinos in Florida.

A central characteristic of Cubanos is their affinity toward entrepreneurship. The number of Cuban entrepreneurs and the growth of firm receipts and new firms far surpass figures for any other Latino subgroup or other minority. It has been suggested that this changing exile community's elite background and geographic concentration in southern Florida contributed significantly to the development of ethnic enclaves and enterprises (Portes and Mozo 1985; Portes and Stepnick 1993). Personal resources and attitudinal dimensions such as motivations tied to family ambitions, entrepreneurial role models, and family norms for independent business formation influenced the rise of the Cuban business class (Petersen 1995). In addition, a large Spanish-speaking social network provided consumer demand and access to a Cuban labor force. Loans were available, if necessary, and when resources were lacking, a rise in partnerships occurred. The opportunity structure, market conditions, resource mobilization, and access to ownership propelled the Cuban community to experience a faster rate of upward economic mobility than any other Latino group. At the same time, their entrepreneurial successes helped revitalize the southern Florida economy; the region now serves as a major US gateway to Latin American trade.

While the Cuban community maintains demonstrated exile fervor in this new millennium, it has expanded its focus to include domestic issues (economic development, civil rights, immigration policy, etc.). Cuban leadership was instrumental in the passage of the Cuban Liberty and Solidarity Act,[3] which includes expropriations after 1959. At the same time, the exit polls in the 2008 and 2012 presidential elections indicated more support for Barack Obama than during previous presidential races. In 2008, Barack Obama garnered almost half of the Cuban votes in Florida; in 2012, he received about 60 percent of the overall Latino vote. The Cuban community has exhibited the character of a resource-affluent group, with active leadership and a focused agenda emphasizing US relations with Cuba. It is generally well organized, geographically concentrated, culturally immersed, and politically active. Within our theme of examining the various Latino subgroups as dynamic communities, the Cuban community exhibits common ground with other Latinos (e.g., social welfare policies, civil rights, language and immigration, economic mobility), as well as distinct policy perspectives and priorities regarding economic sanctions and restrictive policies for the current Cuban regime, lower levels of support for affirmative action, lower perceptions of discrimination directed toward Latinos, greater support for political refugee status, and arguments for "pro-democratization" initiatives. The Cuban community has remained politically and economically active into the first decade of the twenty-first century even as its population base has been surpassed by Dominicans and Salvadorans as the third-largest subgroup.

The Northern Triangle of Central America

The **Northern Triangle** of Central America refers to the three Central American countries of Guatemala, Honduras, and El Salvador, especially in regard to immigration, asylum, and temporary protected status. Nearly half of the approximately 3.5 million Central American immigrants residing in the United States as of 2017 came to the United States before 2000. Immigrants from the Northern Triangle comprised 86 percent of the Central Americans in the United States. In 2017, Central American immigrants represented 8 percent of the United States' 44.5 million immigrants.

There were an estimated 1.4 million people of Honduran origin living in the United States in 2017. Hondurans are the eighth-largest Latino population, accounting for 2 percent of the US Hispanic population in 2017. Since 2000, the number of Hondurans in the United States has increased 297 percent, growing from 237,000 to 940,000. During the same time, the Honduran foreign-born population grew by 215 percent, from 184,000 in 2000 to 579,000 in 2017. Guatemalans are the sixth-largest Latino group, accounting for 2 percent of the US Hispanic population in 2017. Since 2000, the US Guatemalan population has increased 245 percent, growing from 406,000 to 1.4 million over the period. At the same time, the Guatemalan foreign-born population grew by 171 percent, from 319,000 in 2000 to 864,000 in 2017.

An estimated 2.3 million Salvadorans resided in the United States in 2017, making Salvadorans the third-largest population (tied with Cubans) of Latinos, 4 percent of the US Latino population in 2017. Since 2000, the Salvadoran population has increased

225 percent, growing from 711,000 to 2.3 million over the period. During this time, the Salvadoran foreign-born population grew 141 percent, from 539,000 to 1.3 million.

Under the rubric of Central and South Americans, we have grouped Latinos from these countries as the "other Latinos." Latinos from Central America constitute the fastest-growing Latino national-origin groups and now comprise one of every twelve Latinos. We highlight several South American countries in the next section of this chapter. Among Latinos, the Central and South American groupings have the highest proportion of foreign-born persons, with the majority of those more recently entering the United States.

We should note that labor migration among Central and South Americans occurred in the late 1800s and early 1900s. Industries such as cigar and munitions factories, sugarcane and other agricultural product processing, and shipyards, for example, were venues for earlier labor market relations between Central and South Americans and the United States (Figueroa 1996). More significant migration has occurred since the mid-1970s and continues at a high rate. Whereas the three largest Latino subgroups tend to concentrate in certain regions of the United States, Central and South Americans are more widely distributed. Hondurans are concentrated in Texas (17 percent), Florida (16 percent), and California (9 percent); Guatemalans are concentrated in California (29 percent), Florida (8 percent), and Texas (7 percent); and Salvadorans are concentrated in California (32 percent), Texas (15 percent), and New York (9 percent).

Major factors for Northern Triangle migrants have been civil wars in El Salvador, Guatemala, and Nicaragua during the 1980s. Displacement, economic instability, and insecurity followed, and even though peace accords brought a formal end to civil conflict in all three countries the following decade, political and economic instability continued, as did migration northward, many arriving illegally. From 1980 to 1990, the Central American immigrant population in the United States tripled. Several natural disasters, notably Hurricane Mitch in Honduras and Nicaragua in 1998 and a series of earthquakes in El Salvador in early 2001, led the United States to designate Hondurans, Nicaraguans, and Salvadorans eligible for Temporary Protected Status (TPS) (O'Connor et al. 2019). This designation grants nationals of designated countries, who already reside in the United States, work authorization and provisional relief from deportation. In 2017 and early 2018, the Trump administration sought termination of TPS status to some 425,00 persons; El Salvadorans and Hondurans (approximately 300,000 of the total TPS population) would have eighteen months to leave the United States. However, the Trump administration's actions have been challenged in federal court, and TPS remains in effect pending court decisions (Kopan 2018; Raphelson 2017).

Today, Central Americans continue to flee insecurity as well as poverty that has been exacerbated by drought and significant crop failure. The Northern Triangle countries are especially affected by high homicide rates (though these have been falling in recent years), gang activity, extortion, and corrupt public institutions. According to US laws and international refugee policies, Northern Triangle migrants may come to the United States petitioning for asylum. However, the Trump administration imposed executive actions and policies that are meant to act as deterrents but have punitive effects. We will discuss the currently changing immigration policies and the very harmful effects on asylee petitioners in chapter 9 on immigration.

While Latinos continue to be described as the fastest-growing minority, this characterization is most appropriate for the Central American communities. The two largest segments come from El Salvador and Guatemala. Salvadorans now represent the fourth-largest Latino subgroup (1.6 million), slightly larger than the Dominicans. They are a heavily foreign-born group (64.7 percent), with 58.4 percent having arrived in the United States since 1990. Political unrest and US intervention in the region served as major impetus to emigrate. Geographically, a majority of Salvadorans are found in California (40 percent) and Texas (14 percent), with the rest scattered throughout the United States. As a largely "immigrant" group, Salvadorans place the highest priority on issues of social and economic well-being, securing asylum as political refugees, and US immigration policies in general.

Guatemalans are now the sixth-largest Latino subgroup (986,000), and 69.4 percent are foreign-born or among the first generation born in the United States. Like Salvadorans, 70 percent of Guatemalans have arrived in the United States since 1990. California (33.9 percent) and the southern region of the United States (32.4 percent) are the major areas of settlement. The Coalition of Guatemalan Immigrants in the United States (CONGUATE) advocates for Guatemalan interests (i.e., political and economic rights and opportunities). CONGUATE represents some twenty-five organizations in Los Angeles, Chicago, New York, Houston, and Washington, DC. Guatemalans' policy agenda reflects their interests in the United States and their home country. Matters of educational opportunity and health care access (more than 40 percent are without health insurance) and maintaining an active role in Guatemalan politics (Guatemala approved expatriate voting in national elections) serve as good examples. In addition, Guatemalans have initiated more than a million petitions for political asylum, with some receiving temporary asylum status, granting work authorization and no deportation. Most Central Americans experience the same challenges as other Latinos, such as adapting to life in the United States, navigating the opportunity structures they encounter and the obstacles they face, and maintaining continued ties to their home country.

In the summer of 2014, unaccompanied minors, largely from El Salvador and Guatemala, were crossing into the United States in significant numbers. Many of these young people had crossed through Mexico riding the trains and were subjected to harassment, robbery, rape, drugs, extortion, and the like (Amnesty International 2010). As a result, they are psychologically fragile, and those who successfully reached the United States faced apprehension, detention, and, at times, incarceration with adults. Political instability and prevalence of gangs have been major motivators for the departure of Salvadorans and Guatemalans from their countries. It has been documented that parents risk sending their children alone in the hope that the children will have a better future (Resnick 2014). There has been much debate concerning the appropriate actions regarding the young people, from immediate deportation or prosecution and incarceration to governmental assistance as refugees. Latino immigrant rights advocates are actively involved with these groups of young, unaccompanied immigrants as part of the larger sets of issues dealing with immigrant rights, border enforcement and treatment by law enforcement, and legal protection and representation for these youths. Fortunately, more news coverage is being directed toward the "other Latinos," with systematic research being conducted as well.

As the fastest-growing segment of Latinos, Central and South Americans are establishing their presence and impact in the United States as well as altering the mix and chemistry of Latinos and their primary interests. The relatively broad geographic distribution of Central and South Americans throughout the United States and their proximity to the three larger Latino subgroups demonstrates a pattern of maintaining their own community identity but extending the range of interactions with other Latino groups. The Latinization of a national community can be assisted by the presence of diverse Latino subgroups living in the same residential areas. The nature and extent of intergroup contact are established. For example, a second-generation Salvadoran woman, in response to an article outlining the historical presence of Salvadorans in America, commented, "I was born and raised in the U.S. and therefore feel American. Spanish was taught to me and I will certainly do my best to pass it on . . . Interestingly enough, I rarely identify myself as a Salvadoran-American preferring the term Latin-American. This is in great part to my feelings of connectedness to all Latino people living in the U.S. I feel the Latino-American population here is unique and diverse; a population whose strength lies in its shared immigrant experiences rather than their countries of origin. To that end, I also feel connected to all children of immigrants, as we face similar challenges" (Fraga et al. 2010).

BOX 4.3 South American Latinos: Being Peruvians in the United States

In 2017, South American immigrants represented 7 percent (or 3.2 million) of the 44.5 million foreign-born people in the United States (up from 1 percent in 1960). The five largest countries of origin are Colombia (783,000, or 25 percent of all South American immigrants), Peru (459,000, 14 percent), Ecuador (454,000, 14 percent), Brazil (451,000, 14 percent), and Venezuela (351,000, 11 percent). Together, they accounted for 78 percent of the total South American immigrant population in the United States.

While providing some more details about Colombian and Venezuelan communities, our focus will be on Peruvians. Approximately 52 percent came to the United States prior to 2000. At the same time, since 2000, the Peruvian-origin population has increased 174 percent, growing from 248,000 to 679,000 over that period. In addition, the Peruvian foreign-born population living in the United States grew by 119 percent, from 193,000 in 2000 to 423,000 in 2017. The Peruvian population is predominantly found in three states—Florida (19 percent), California (16 percent), and New Jersey (14 percent).

In an article in the *Atlantic* magazine (Negro-Chin 2016), accounts of early Peruvian migration in the first years of the 1960s to the city of Paterson, New Jersey, are given. One such story relayed is that of Guillermo Callegari-Balarezo, who arrived in August 1962 carrying only one bag. At that time, he says, "there were about 11 Peruvians in Paterson." Even though one of the Peruvians was supposed to pick him up, his wait was long. After some time passed, he went into a Puerto Rican restaurant to ask if there were any Peruvians around. Within forty-eight hours a nephew took him to an auto shop, where Guillermo was employed the next day.

Callegari-Balarezo started to notice that weekly another four Peruvian men arrived. "Then every week after that there would be 20 or 30 coming." At first, most of them came from Surquillo, a district in Lima, but new arrivals started coming from other districts and cities as well. It is not uncommon for Latino migrant "settlers" to come from the same areas or communities and move to the same destination communities in the United States.

The influx of Peruvians to Paterson persisted and grew such that it is now home to 10,000 Peruvians, although community members estimate the number to be closer to 30,000. Market Street, a major street in the city, is lined with Peruvian-owned restaurants, hair salons, bakeries, and travel agencies. Local newspapers indicate that in 2009, Peruvians owned half of the city's 2,800 Hispanic-owned businesses, including 45 restaurants. It is not uncommon for the red and white *rojiblanca* flag to fly over stores that are not obviously Peruvian.

The political turmoil involving Sendero Luminoso (which translates to "Shining Path") and the Túpac Amaru Revolutionary Movement caused many Peruvians to migrate to the United States and other South American countries. Paterson was known as "Silk City" due to its textile production and industrial jobs, which attracted Peruvians as well as previous waves of European emigrants before them. When those factory jobs declined in the 1980s, many Peruvians shifted to entrepreneurship, re-creating a microcosm of their home country, now known as "Little Lima."

In 1986, local Peruvians initiated Paterson's Peruvian Parade to honor the city's connections to Peru. In a way, Paterson became the unofficial capital of the Peruvian diaspora. Every July, tens of thousands of people celebrate at the Passaic County Peruvian Day Parade, passing along Market Street. One consequence of the parade's success was the opening of a Peruvian consulate, which serves the more than 75,000 Peruvians living in the state of New Jersey. Paterson's city council renamed a central plaza "Peru Square." The continued engagement of Peruvians in their local community represents the integration of this community with the socioeconomic and cultural life of living in America, yet with lasting connections to Peru.

Alfredo Garcia, adjunct professor in the department of languages and culture at William Paterson University, commented that the newly named square "is a slice of Peru and this will be more evident once it is known as Peru Square." Garcia stated that he is fond of his adopted home country but has not forgotten where he comes from. "Sometimes, people in Peru think that once we leave, we become gringos, but we are still Peruvians and we continue to fight for our country," he says. Our brief account of Peruvians and Paterson, New Jersey, tells a narrative of lively culture developed in the past few decades, and that even though Paterson is a city of just 150,000, it's become a household name in Peru.

The difficulty of achieving political refugee status for Central Americans has had a direct bearing on undocumented migration since the 1990s. One of the accompanying results of many Central Americans' plights was the advent of the "sanctuary movement" in which religious organizations and other groups established an underground network to help them enter the United States. In addition, these organizational efforts focused on obtaining official political refugee status for Central Americans. Providing proof of clear danger of persecution and personal harm upon returning home due to political beliefs and activities has been difficult. Individuals caught in the crossfire between government and rebel forces were considered victims of a civil war or political instability rather than political dissidents. While immigration policy and rights are central issues for Central Americans, it is a focus of all Latino subgroups.

In addition to the question of political refugee status, specific areas of concern include equal protection, actions of the Immigration and Naturalization Service, access to entitlement programs, and discriminatory practices in the labor market and housing. The actions of organizations like the Task Force for New Americans, the Latino Coalition for Racial Justice, and Sanctuary for Salvadorans (Jordan 1995) represent efforts to protect and advocate on behalf of Central American immigrants and their families. The Central American communities have now developed better organizational skills and resources with more stable organizational structures and maturing leadership. In 1996, more than 2.9 million Central Americans resided predominantly in nine states. Since 2009, federal policies that require a formal "judicial process" for people apprehended as illegal entrants have heightened critical responses to extant immigration policies. We will explore this policy area in greater detail in chapter 9.

For Central and South American "Latinos," their increasing demands and issues may start with a strong focus on immigration and immigrant rights, but access to social programs, civic and political engagement, and inclusion in the Latino leadership carries them into the broader Latino pan-ethnic community and politics. There are national group-specific organizations as well as indicators of cooperative ventures among Puerto Ricans, Dominicans, and Colombians. Overall, the expanding presence of Central and South Americans in the Latino landscape defines the changing parameters of evolving Latino politics.

Los Dominicanos

The Dominican population in the United States has been experiencing continuous growth, particularly since the mid-1960s. This predominantly immigrant community is slightly more than 60 percent foreign-born. In 2008, its population numbered almost 1.2 million, with primary residences in the New York City metropolitan area. As reflected in figure 4.1, other areas of concentration include New Jersey (11 percent), Florida (less than 3 percent), and Massachusetts (less than 1.5 percent) (Waldinger 1989; Torres-Saillant and Hernández 1998). The Washington Heights area on the Upper West Side of Manhattan represents the largest concentration of Dominicans (41.1 percent). More recently, groups like Domincanos USA have concentrated their efforts to increase voter registration and education among Dominicans living in New York City and Providence, Rhode Island. In 2013, the mayor of Providence, Angel Tavares, decided to run for governor and, in New York City, Adriano Esparillat challenged the congressional seat held by Rep. Charles Rangel. As of 2014, more than 26,000 Dominicans have been registered with the organization, specifically identifying Dominicans among the eligible electorate (NBC News 2015). New York has been the site of many other organizations (Centro Cívico Cultural Dominicano, Alianza Dominicana, Asociación Communal de Dominicanos Progresistas, etc.) and police-community conflicts. Because of their population growth, Dominicans (along with Salvadorans) are rivaling the Cuban community as the third-largest Latino subgroup.

The notable migration of Dominicans has been most evident since 1966. During the twelve-year regime of President Joaquín Balaguer (1966–1978),[4] family planning policies and economic forces stimulated the migration of Dominicanos to the United States and Puerto Rico. Economic policy, high unemployment, external debt crisis, high international interest rates, and the deterioration of commodity prices motivated them to go to the urban areas of the East Coast. Even though the Dominican Republic altered its economic policy to establish free trade zones, expand tourism, and export nontraditional products, the economic push factors remained strong. Dominican migrants are primarily people from rural areas who are less educated, unskilled, and of lower socioeconomic status. Disproportionate numbers of women, as well as persons between the ages of twenty-five and forty-four, are in the migration stream.

The initial waves of Dominican migration to the New York City metropolitan area occurred during the economic restructuring from a manufacturing to a service economy. Many Dominican workers were employed as operatives in manufacturing or in wholesale segments of the service and manufacturing sectors. The demographic profile of Dominicans in New York City reflects slightly lower rates of labor participation: 60.7 percent vs. 67.9 percent for Latinos and 68.3 percent for all workers (Torres-Saillant and Hernández 1998). Their **human capital** resources, or lack of them, have contributed to their depreciated socioeconomic status. For example, the Dominican poverty rate is 45.7 percent, compared to 37.2 percent for all Latinos or 23.8 percent citywide. In addition, the percentage of Dominican female-headed households exceeds that for other Latinos (49.7 percent vs. 44.1 percent) as well as the citywide rate (25.6 percent).

With the growth of the Dominican community came the formation of a variety of organizations, especially in the Northeast. Initially, many organizations reflected the cultural and immigrant-related adjustments of newcomers to the United States. Their focus centered on immigration, the educational system, and employment and social counseling (Sassen-Koob 1985; Guarnizo 1994). Groups such as the Centro Cívico Cultural Dominicano, Asociación Dominicanas, and Club de San Juan Pablo Duarte represent efforts of voluntary organizations to facilitate the transition to life in a new country. Some of these organizations date from the early 1960s, with a movement toward advocacy and political empowerment taking shape in the late 1980s. For example, the Asociación Communal de Dominicanos Progresistas incorporated activities dealing with employment, empowerment, financial support, and advocacy for more responsive social institutions. In addition, gender-specific organizations (Collectivo de Mujeres Provincianas) have emerged that advocate for services and opportunities for women. Similarly, there are increasing numbers of professional or work-related organizations for travel agents, accountants, and so on. The Dominican American National Roundtable (DANR) serves as a forum for planning, action, and analysis of the Dominican community's status and position in US society. Political and economic rights, educational quality and relevant programs, and immigration policies remain primary concerns. Many Dominican organizations have ties with other Latino organizations (e.g., LULAC, NCLR, NALEO, ASPIRA, etc.).

Until recently, Dominicans have been portrayed as almost invisible politically. Given the community's high foreign-born percentage, they rank ninth in naturalization rates. Since 2008, the DANR and other Dominican organizations have focused attention on aggressive voter registration and promotion of naturalization. Currently Dominicans represent 13 percent of Latino voters and 3.5 percent of all New York City voters (Falcón and Santiago 1993; Lopez 2015). To some extent, anti-immigrant sentiment and policies have activated greater political interest and activity among Dominicans. For example, immigration-reform legislation potentially eliminated participation in some entitlement programs by permanent resident aliens. Even though much of policy makers' attention has been directed toward the southwestern US border and Mexican and Central American immigrants, the broader sweep of "restrictive" immigration reforms has had a direct impact on most Latino immigrants. Issues such as immigrant rights, policy backlash that targets the foreign-born, crime and drugs, and representation are part of the political agenda for Dominicans. For example, between 2000 and 2008, 33,000 Dominicans were deported, and 70 percent of the incarcerated foreign-born prison population are Dominican (Hernández and Stevens-Acevedo 2011).

Dominicans, like many other Latino subgroups, are confronting issues of cultural and political identity and political orientation focused on the United States. Recent gains in electoral representation at the city and state levels serve as indicators of political development in the Dominican community. Yet, there is support for a state of mind in which individuals remain engaged with their native country while becoming acclimated to the norms and activities of US society. Some researchers have referred to this as "political duality." A person has dual loyalties and interests in both the home and "host" countries. Political duality became an option for Dominicans in 1996 as the Dominican Republic provided for dual citizenship. The impact of this policy reflects the development of both a domestic policy agenda and homeland engagement in US foreign policy (Portes, Escobar, and Radford 2007).

The advent of Dominican studies at City University of New York and continued organizational growth and activity should advance Dominicans' political development as a community in the United States. Greater activity and involvement will open more interactions within the New York City metropolitan area with other Latino subgroups. The growth of the Dominican and Colombian communities in the Northeast is already reconfiguring the larger Latino community in this region (see box 4.4). For example, there is some indication of competitiveness between Dominicans and Puerto Ricans for political visibility, advantage, and systemic attention from the major institutions. The future of Latino political activity lies not only with community formation across national-origin boundaries but also with the bases for independent and interdependent agendas and strategies across all Latino subgroups.

BOX 4.4 The Colombian Community

Semana highlighted an example of the growth and involvement of the Colombian community. In early May 2001, Colombian Americans held their first Convention of Colombian Organizations in the United States in Atlanta, Georgia. The *Semana* story emphasized that a half million "legal" Colombians reside in the United States (primarily in Miami and New York), representing a 60 percent increase since 1990. The story also mentioned that an estimated 1.5 million undocumented Colombians could be living in the United States. In addition, estimated remittances of $2.5 billion annually are sent to Colombia. Concerns about political clout and representation constituted much of the convention discussions.

For the Colombian community, issues of health-care coverage and improving their children's educational opportunities have affected the formation of political and social clubs. Geographically, Colombians are found in the Northeast (New York, 22 percent; New Jersey, 14 percent) and Florida (31 percent), with Texas and California newer areas of growth. Many Colombians' belief that they will eventually return to their homeland makes them a center of attention for Colombian political parties and presidential candidates. It is not uncommon for Colombian presidential candidates to visit Colombians in New York City and elsewhere to secure votes and campaign contributions. Now, Colombians living abroad can elect a senator to represent their interests in Bogotá, solidifying their link with their homeland. This brief example demonstrates the growth of "other Latino" communities, their efforts to engage the US political system and the challenges they face, and their active involvement in transnational politics.

Similar experiences serve to distinguish the differences between Dominicans, Cubans, Peruvians, and so on. The immigrant strand prevalent among the Latino subgroups helps define much of the Latino experience in relation to continued ties with one's home country, adjustment to most phases of life in the United States, focus on cultural maintenance, and societal responses to immigrant communities by non-Latinos and other Americans.

The socioeconomic status of many Latino subgroups (education levels, labor market participation, income levels, family structures, household size, etc.) is quite similar and presents opportunities for cooperative ventures. The overlap of residential location in areas with significant concentrations of Puerto Ricans, Cubans, and Mexican-origin people affords opportunities for different kinds of interactions, particularly for Central and South Americans. These interactions can be beneficial, conflictual, or very infrequent. Yet, common cultural orientations and customs and situational conditions that warrant action can stimulate the bases for contact and interactions. The nature and existence of common cultural and socioeconomic situations have a fundamental linkage to political resources and involvement. In chapter 5, we will explore the political connections associated with these sociodemographic and cultural underpinnings of community for Latinos.

Conclusion: Latino America—Rich in Diversity and Commonalities

Our brief portrait of the histories and experiences of several specific Latino subgroups in the United States is intended to provide some insight into the nature and content of the national-origin groups that make up the Latino political community. The demographic profiles in the previous chapter provided a picture of the size, socioeconomic status, and residential location of each group. These portrayals take into consideration the themes of common interests and common cultures. The factors of language, Spanish-language influences on cultural practices, institutions, religion, and the like cut across all the Latino subgroups, yet unique experiences and variations also exist.

Discussion Questions

1. The Mexican-origin community continues to be the largest Latino subgroup, comprising more than three-fifths of all Latinos. What are the implications of being so much larger than the other subgroups in terms of leadership, agenda, and intergroup relations?
2. Until the mid-1990s, in thinking about Latinos in the United States, the big three (i.e., the Mexican-origin, Puerto Rican, and Cuban subgroups) dominated the Latino community. Presently Dominicans and Salvadorans are the third- and fourth-largest Latino subgroups, respectively. What changes have occurred within the Latino community with the significant increases among Central and South Americans?
3. While the foreign-born segment in the Cuban subgroup remains the majority, how has the increase in the native-born segment affected the nature of the Cuban community's political agenda and partisan politics?
4. Even though the location of specific national-origin Latino subgroups is geographically concentrated, there is evidence of greater Latino residential diversity. What are the implications of more contact among different Latino subgroups in building a pan-ethnic community?
5. In nontraditional areas of Latino settlement (i.e., the South and Midwest), we have witnessed the rapid growth in Latino in-migration. How have these migratory patterns affected intergroup relations with the Latino national-origin groups, as well as with non-Latinos?
6. In regions and metropolitan areas like New York City or Atlanta or rural Nebraska, what would you expect the kinds of experiences of recently arrived Latinos to include?

Notes

1. This latter point has been an area of some discussion and debate regarding the lower levels of Mexican American political participation. Close attachment to Mexico and the supportive system of political involvement in that country seem to suppress political involvement and interest in the American political system.

2. The term "pan-ethnic" refers to a socially constructed group identity that extends beyond traditional national-origin groupings like Irish, Mexican, Panamanian, and so on. The pan-ethnic movements represent an "umbrella" cluster of similar but distinctive group members. The labels "American Indian," "Asian American," and "Latino" serve as good examples of pan-ethnicity.

3. This legislation allows lawsuits in US courts against traffickers who seize property belonging to Cubans living in the United States.

4. Joaquín Balaguer was president of the Dominican Republic on three different occasions: 1960 to 1962, 1966 to 1978, and 1986 to 1996. He held posts under the dictator Rafaél Trujillo, serving as vice president just prior to Trujillo's demise. He was ousted by the military in 1962 and returned in 1965 at the time of the US military intervention. He won the presidency in 1966 and again in 1970 and 1974. His election in 1994 was so marred by fraud that opposition protests and international pressures forced Balaguer to agree to resign after an abbreviated two-year term.

CHAPTER 5

The Politics of Interest and Culture

Nuestro pueblo, la comunidad, nuestra gente, todos son expresiónes de haber entendido que somos una familia con una voz fuerte y unida. Sin embargo, igual que muchas comunidades, nuestras vidas son diferentes con relación a la comunidad, la cultura, la política y la familia. El gran desafío para la comunidad latina es de utilizar esos elementos de nuestra cultura y experiencias para tener verdadero poder político.

Our towns, our community, our people—all are expressions of having understood that we are a family with a strong, united voice. Nevertheless, like many communities, our lives vary in relationship to the community, the culture, the politics, and the family. The great challenge for the Latino community is to use these common elements of our culture and experiences in order to obtain real political power.

THUS FAR, OUR DISCUSSION OF Latinos has explored the various elements of community, identifying many of the contributing factors for cultivating a sense of commonality and group affiliation. In chapter 2, we used the concepts of group consciousness and linked fate to motivate our primary theme of Latinos being a community of common or similar cultures and a community of interests. In the previous two chapters, we also attempted to identify and describe aspects of the various Latino subgroups that can serve to build a broader community, including a summary of the underlying demographics of the Latino community. Implicit in this discussion is the idea that the construction of a Latino community is the combination of external forces (structural factors, social movements, and public policies and campaigns) as well as activities within the Latino community and organizational efforts to connect across subgroup boundaries.

We have identified the ways in which Latinos can share common cultural traditions and practices, as well as similar situations in the workplace, education, and the like. Yet, identification with and emotive attachment to this community is essential in building and maintaining an organic community that works on behalf of its known interests. Since Latinos come from a number of national-origin ancestries, our discussion uses the concept of pan-ethnicity, a sociopolitical collectivity made up of people of several different national origins (Espiritu 1992). In identifying with others of different national origins, individuals undergo a shift in their level of identification from smaller boundaries to broader affiliations. These individuals augment, but do not necessarily replace, their national-origin identity by including a broader identity of Latino/Hispanic. In this chapter, we will broaden this discussion by providing a summary of how identities are formed psychologically and how identities can be fluid and situational. By that we mean that Latinos can possess attachments to their national-origin group (Mexican, Cuban etc.) while having a meaningful and powerful pan-ethnic identity. We will discuss the complexity that race and racial identity create for the Latino community who have not been defined as a racial group by the federal government, but who have been racialized by recent political campaigns.

Internal group definitions and experiences do not solely define the nature and origin of ethnicity; structural conditions and treatment also create and reinforce ethnic groups. Legislative policies that categorize individuals by groups and define them by national origin, ancestry, race, and so on control both benefits and enforcement in the areas of civil rights and increasing access to educational opportunities, labor markets (job training, language classes, etc.), and health services. Yet, this type of policy categorization has other costs, including stigmatization and victimization, in addition to creating benefits for group membership. How political and economic institutions treat and interact with people from different ethnic groups can help impose and affect identity formation. In this sense, ethnicity has dimensions of voluntary status as well as imposed group affiliation.

Expanding our discussion from chapter 2, we will examine ways in which public policies can heighten a sense of pan-ethnic identity, including how political campaigns and candidates can cue a sense of ethnic identity by either emphasizing ethnic pride (as is often the case with Latino candidates) or generating a sense of fear or threat. Connecting these external factors can motivate ethnic identity with mobilization and mobilization theory, one of the more dominant concepts referenced often in the second half of this book. In this chapter we will also emphasize how political parties, candidates, interest groups, and community organizations all work to mobilize or engage Latinos in the electoral process using cues that activate pan-ethnic identity among Latinos. Before we can engage in the relationship between mobilization and ethnic identity, we must first tackle one of the most commonly asked questions in Latino politics: What ethnic terminology is most appropriate when referencing the Latino community?

Changes in Identification Terminology Preferences and Usage over Time

We have introduced how the use of labels such as "Hispanic" or "Latino" can be politicized when applied to communities. However, we have limited that discussion to these two pan-ethnic terms, which leaves the need to identify the many ways in which Latinos have defined themselves over time. This is an important discussion to have given that survey data has consistently found that Latinos prefer to identify themselves with national-origin terms rather than pan-ethnic ones, including "Latino" or "Hispanic."

We must begin our discussion with racial identification among Latinos. As we have highlighted already, because Latinos are an ethnic group and have not been defined as a separate racial group, they have the option of choosing any race among the six racial group categories on the US census. The 2010 census revealed that just over half (53.0 percent) of the Hispanic population chose white as their racial group, while about one-third (36.7 percent) provided responses that were classified as "some other race" alone when responding to this question (Ennis et al. 2011). Only 2.5 percent of Hispanics identified as black or African American, with 1.4 percent as American Indian and Alaska Native alone, and even smaller percentages as Asian American (0.4 percent) and Native Hawaiian and Other Pacific Islanders alone (0.1 percent). Finally, roughly three million Hispanics (6 percent) indicated they were of multiple races, with a large proportion reporting a race combination involving "some other race" (Ennis et al. 2011).

The high proportion of Latinos who identify as "some other race" on the census have motivated some discussion by the US Census Bureau and social scientists about whether respondents who choose this category are implying that they consider Latino a separate racial group. The Pew Hispanic Research Center has surveyed Latinos who chose these specific identification options on the census follow-up questions to dive deeper into this concept (Parker et al. 2015). The authors find that a large number (67 percent) of Latinos believe that their racial and ethnic identities are linked, providing strong evidence that Latinos do, in fact, consider Hispanic or Latino a separate racial category. We will explore potential differences in political behavior based on these racial categories in future chapters.

For our purposes, ethnic identity is dynamic and multidimensional and has both symbolic and instrumental political functions. While Mexican-origin political activists used "Mexican American" and "Chicano" during the 1960s and 1970s to make a statement about their dual identities as Americans who had distinct cultures based on their Mexican origin, the use of labels has been broadened and altered, but many remain politicized for members of the communities that use them. Mexican Americans, like other individuals, have multiple and, at times, changing ethnic and social identities (Saperstein 2013; Barvosa 2008). Broader inclusiveness and multiple layers of affinity and loyalty reflect the contemporary nature of identity. Thus, Mexican Americans can have a variety of specific identities that connect them with local situational factors and in larger social contexts. For example, a Mexican-origin woman may identify herself as a minority, a Hispanic, a Mexican American, a person of Mexican ancestry, a Spanish speaker, a woman of color, and a Latina. Each identity can serve to extend a person in a variety of networks and frames of reference. Modern ethnicity, Latinos included, results from a dynamic, fluid, and contextual process (Barvosa 2008).

"Hispanic" can define who is not Hispanic as much as who is part of the community. Padilla (1986) outlines the Latinization of groups in Chicago in which a pan-ethnic label ("Latino" in this case) expanded the size of the local community and forged an added identity for greater political mobilization. The dynamics related to ethnicity, national origin, and race are changing over time. The advent of pan-ethnicity and the broadening of its scope beyond national origin have redefined group parameters, but it remains a loose coupling concept since it is difficult to explain precisely what determines who is a Hispanic, at all times and in all situations. The Latino pan-ethnic community has developed into a perceived and actual interest group that shares cultural traditions, situations, and practices. At the same time, the involvement of Latino elites and activists has affected the evolution and development of an identifiable Latino community.

FIGURE 5.1 Label Choice among Five Major Latino Subgroups

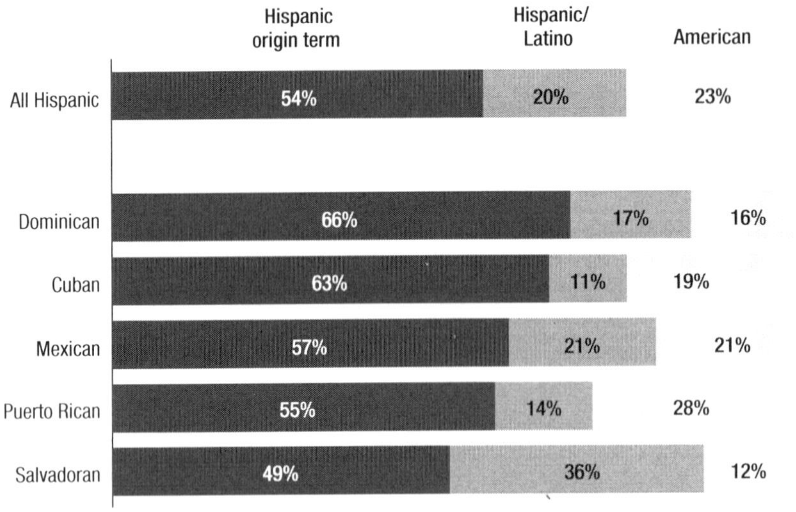

	Hispanic origin term	Hispanic/Latino	American
All Hispanic	54%	20%	23%
Dominican	66%	17%	16%
Cuban	63%	11%	19%
Mexican	57%	21%	21%
Puerto Rican	55%	14%	28%
Salvadoran	49%	36%	12%

Source: Adapted from Pew Research Survey of Hispanic Adults, May 24–July 28, 2013 (*N* = 5,103).

In 2012, a study of Latino identity conducted by Taylor with the Pew Hispanic Center asked about terms most used (Latino/Hispanic, national origin, or American) and found differences based on nativity, generational status, socioeconomic class, and language use (see figure 5.1). Overall, one in four used the term "Latino" or "Hispanic" while the national-origin usage was slightly over one-half (54 percent). The smallest categorical choice was "American" (23 percent). Among the foreign-born, almost three in ten used "Latino" or "Hispanic," mostly among Spanish-dominant speakers, the less educated, and those of Mexican origin. The usage of the term "American" rose for second- and third-generation Latinos (see figures 5.2 and 5.3).

Works by Hurtado and Gurin (2004) and Portes and MacLeod (1996) look at ethnic identities among Latinos and Mexican-origin respondents in two surveys. Hurtado and Gurin (2004) found that mastery of the English language and one's reference group (i.e., who the respondents compare themselves with—fellow immigrants, countrypersons still in their country of origin, or other Americans) influenced whether one selected "Mexican" or "Chicano." The Portes and MacLeod survey (1996) found that those who were least assimilated, less English-proficient, low in self-esteem, and living in poverty used the term "Hispanic." In 2015, a study by Mohamed (2013) examined gender differences among Latino/as and found that Latinas are less likely to identify as Americans and more inclined to want to maintain their cultural traditions than their Latino counterparts. Also found was that Latinas had higher participation in terms of voting, naturalization, and seeking citizenship.

A central basis for our discussion of Latino politics is a sense of community and important connecting strands. The pervasiveness of the reference to pan-ethnic groups (i.e., Latinos, Asian and Native Americans, Muslims, etc.) has become an ever-present reality of American life. Research that taps people's label preference(s) and identities

FIGURE 5.2 How Hispanics Describe Themselves

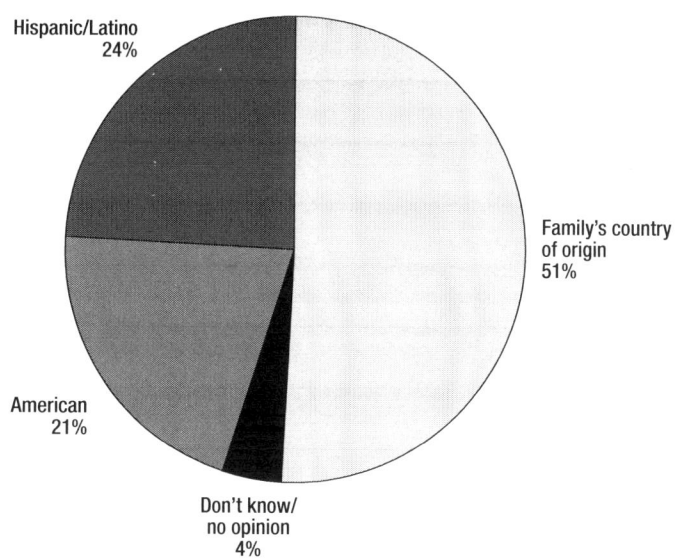

Source: Adapted from "A Conversation about Identity," May 29, 2012, Pew Research Center.

FIGURE 5.3 Preference for "Latino" vs. "Hispanic"

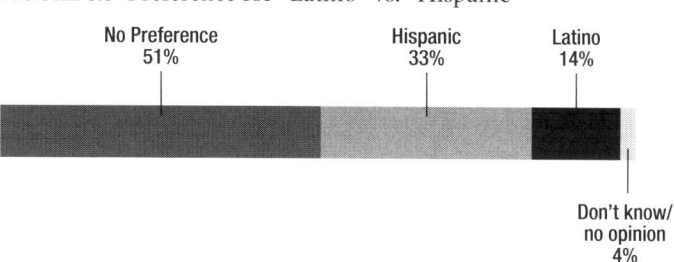

Source: Adapted from "A Conversation about Identity," May 29, 2012, Pew Research Center.

tends to focus on a singular identity. Our perspective is grounded on a "constellation" of multiple identities and activation by a variety of situations and intervening circumstances.

An interesting result from the Taylor et al. (2012b) study mentioned earlier indicated that only one in four Latinos responded that they share a common culture. More recently, the Pew Hispanic Research Center found that identification with either pan-ethnic term is lower among Americans with Spanish-origin ancestry four generations or more removed from the immigration experience (Lopez, Gonzalez-Barrera, and Lopez 2017). According to a Pew Research Center survey of this group, the vast majority who confirm they have Hispanic ancestors (a parent, grandparent, great-grandparent or earlier ancestor) but do not self-identify as Hispanic say they have never thought of themselves as Hispanic. When asked why this is the case in an open-ended follow-up question, the single most common response (27 percent) was that their Hispanic ancestry was too far back or their background is mixed. This report raises an important question of how pervasive Latino identity will be in the future as the Latino population continues to evolve through both intermarriage and slowed external migration.

In helping to understand Latino politics, we will continue to explore and examine these kinds of developments as well as analyze and critique the approaches used in making these assessments.

Our discourse about identification among Latinos would not be complete without a brief discussion of the newest identification term, "Latinx." "Latinx" (pronounced "La-teen-ex") is a gender-neutral alternative to the other pan-ethnic terms of "Hispanic" and "Latino." Referenced mostly by academics, activists, and journalists, "Latinx" has become more popular among some circles of the Latino community. Advocates of the term contend that it is the most inclusive of pan-ethnic identification terms, as in addition to men and women from all racial backgrounds, "Latinx" also makes room for people who are transgender, queer, and others who do not find themselves with traditional binary sexual orientation or gender norms (see Juárez 2018). While limited survey data comparing "Latinx" to other pan-ethnic terms suggests that this term has not yet permeated the overall Latino community, future editions of this book will need to revisit this discussion to see if this changes over time.

The Role of Latino Political Elites and Activists in Identity Formation

Political elites and activists translate and interpret political and social necessities and realities. They frame critical meanings and contexts for the Latino community to advance political agendas and increase their empowerment. Latino leaders inform, educate, and motivate members of the Latino community to relate their own circumstances, as well as opportunities and obstacles, regarding governmental institutions, policies, and actions. Thus, the Latino community is further defined and identified, increasing its involvement with American political life. The use of the pan-ethnic terms "Hispanic" and "Latino" broadens the size of these subcommunities and creates greater visibility in national arenas like Congress, the national media, and federal agencies. Many leaders of national Mexican American organizations participate in discussions focusing on clarifying some common denominators for this loose aggregation of Latino national-origin subgroups.

The 1980 census incorporated the ethnic term "Spanish origin," which applied to persons in more than twenty Spanish-origin countries, and the category represents the ethnicity question in the census. As a result, this ethnic category has expanded the size and geographic base of the Latino community vis-à-vis non-Hispanic political elites and has won some support at the grassroots level. This new ethnic group has a national presence as a significantly larger and more geographically dispersed group than a single Latino subgroup like Mexican or Puerto Rican Americans.

The potential of a pan-ethnic Latino/Hispanic community was further shaped by Latino political elites who projected both potential and actual power and influence. These leaders realized that this collective identity could create more opportunities for political mobilization, broaden the scope of awareness for group affinity and membership, and expand the resource base for Latino interests. All of these factors represent central elements of Latino community building.

Key components for a Latino community include some degree of group identification, affinity, and attachment between people of Spanish origin. Consensus, solidarity, and cohesion are objectives of community building, but they are not absolutely essential to it. Elements of community (group identity and affinity, common interests and circumstances) provide pragmatic opportunities to engage in collective efforts. The presence and perception of a national community serves as political capital for Latino leaders. It becomes the primary responsibility of leadership to capitalize on the various strands of Latino community life and to direct members toward specific actions and connections regarding the policies in the public and private sectors.

An example of this is the Mexican Americans' experience since the 1960s and the development of the pan-ethnic term "Hispanic." Critics like Gómez (1992) suggested that the term was a product of Madison Avenue public relations firms, Capitol Hill press corps, major media outlets, and government bureaucrats. This analysis saw the rise in marketing efforts (Mattel's Hispanic Barbie, Coors's Decade of the Hispanic, etc.) as reinforcing the evolution of identifying Mexican Americans and other Latinos as Hispanics primarily to simplify the selling of products to this growing market. Consequently, both print and visual media and governmental reporting promoted usage of the term, which has now exploded throughout the country. "Hispanic" has become the primary descriptor both for specific Latino national-origin groups like Mexican Americans or Chicanos and for all clusters of groups of Spanish origin.

The term "Hispanic" has been the product of external forces trying to simplify and homogenize a diverse aggregation of Latino subgroups. A data-gathering agency, the US Census Bureau, is credited with institutionalizing the label "Hispanic" by including it in the 1980 census. Yet Edward Fernandez of the Census Bureau's Ethnic and Spanish Division (Del Olmo 1998) indicates that the impetus for the Spanish-origin category came from Mexican American policy groups that were trying to respond to undercounts of Mexican Americans and other Latinos. The adoption of this broader term was one way to ensure a fuller portrayal of Latinos, as well as nationalization or pan-ethnic labeling of all the various Latino subgroups.

For the Mexican American community, there has been a long evolution of labels differentiating this population, from "Mexicanos" to "Spanish Americans" to "Latino Americans" to "Mexican Americans" and "Chicanos" (Acuña 1988; Gómez-Quiñones 1990). Distinguishing in-group and out-group contexts were an important factor in the derivation and use of specific labels. There were in-group preferences for specific labels, which varied by class, region, and generational distance from Mexico (García 1982). Different segments of the Mexican-origin community used such labels as "pocho," "Mexicano," "Raza," "Chicano," "Manito," and "mestizo," among others. The various ethnic labels usually reflected class, national origin, nativity, racial identification, cultural traditions, and language use (García et al. 1994; Patterson 1975). In addition, during the 1960s, labels also indicated political orientations and ideologies. For example, the Chicano label (Gutierrez and Hirsch 1973; Hirsch 1974; Gómez-Quiñones 1990) incorporated a more radical political ideology and approach for social change and justice. In a contemporary sense, the endorsement of "Hispanic" by some Mexican American political elites recognizes a modern form of ethnic identity.

Communities of common cultures and interests and the resulting networks established across the Latino subcommunities serve as connections from which communication, interactions, and collaborative opportunities are created. Latino organizations and leadership have made direct efforts that recognize these connections and build on them. Dialogue about the development of pan-ethnicity is an example of the community-building process among Latinos.

Seminal work by sociologist Felix Padilla (1986) argues that Mexican American and Puerto Rican elites adopted a political strategy to unite individuals around a common group identity. These efforts were responding to similarities across national origin based on limited political power, stagnant socioeconomic opportunities, and few institutional resources (Beltrán 2010). One important outcome of this pan-ethnic effort is a network of elite Latino professionals and group-based organizations such as the National Council of La Raza, the Congressional Hispanic Caucus, the National Association of Latino Elected and Appointed Officials, and other such pan-ethnic umbrella organizations (Mora 2009). These organizations have advanced pan-ethnic identification among Latinos as a means of establishing a national presence.

The Latino community's political capital is enhanced with the appearance of coherency and unity. This is an important resource because, on many occasions, political leaders, officials, and institutions (Congress, state legislatures, etc.) place the onus on Latino leaders to present their issues, positions, demands, and so on, as *one voice*. Such an "umbrella" concept encompassing a wide range of Latino subgroups has a more pragmatic and broader issue orientation than a specific subgroup's agenda. It also promotes the formation of intergroup political coalitions among Latino subgroups not limited to purely national-origin and regionally driven groups and issues. Consequently, the use of the terms "Latino" and "Hispanic" shifts the emphasis of community-based activities from primarily local-level electoral and policy advocacy to the state and national level as well.

A larger Latino configuration, which has been influenced internally by the Latino subcommunities themselves and externally by political institutions, officials, and the national media, is a realistic characterization of Latino development in the early twenty-first century. Regardless of the origin of "Hispanic" or "Latino," the role of Latino leaders is to define the labels' meaning and relevance. The movement to redefine the boundaries of communities complements strategies of Latino political elites to promote and add specific meaning to pan-ethnic terms.

Three specific developments have contributed to the movement toward a broader definition of ethnicity for Latino subgroups: (1) the transition to modern ethnicity that further interconnects race, ethnicity, culture, class, and gender[1] into broader categorizations; (2) the contextual nature of ethnic labels and identity; and (3) the coexistence of multiple identities (Barvosa 1999, 2008), with salient ones influenced by utility and context.

Puerto Rican, Cuban, and Central and South American political elites have followed a similar evolution and development. The broader distinction of the Latino umbrella has enabled different Latino subgroups to advance their issues and concerns in both local and national arenas. For example, the Salvadoran and Guatemalan communities have focused significant efforts on obtaining political refugee status in order to facilitate attaining legal status for many Salvadoran and Guatemalan immigrants. In addition to enabling pursuit of policy changes within their own organizations, the broader inclusion of Central Americans with other Latinos, especially immigrants, helps expand the constituency base, political visibility, and potential clout to effect immigration reform and policy adjustments. The Central American segment represents the most recent influx of Latino subgroups and the fastest-growing Latino segment. The utility of this group's adopting the Latino identity and its members' labeling themselves as such fuels the well-established image of a fast-growing population.

Community building among Latino subgroups does not preclude the persistence of Latino subgroup organizations or targeted efforts for their respective community needs and interests. The recognition that an individual has multiple identities has a parallel politically. Thus, political involvement on behalf of Latinos may be salient at times, while on other occasions Latino subgroup interests (Dominican, Cuban, etc.) may be more prominent. This differentiation is also relevant in terms of the arenas in which Latinos' political actions take place. This exploration of community among individuals and Latino subgroups reveals a network of connectors in which some degree of affinity and attachment occurs. It manifests itself politically with enough frequency to sustain a sense of community and, perhaps more important, to deepen a sense of community.

Latino Identity: Two Vignettes

The utility of Latino identity and its promotion by Latino activists and leaders are illustrated through two incidents that took place in Chicago some sixteen years apart. The first involved cross-communication between two local Latino community organizations, and the latter was a focus group's discussion of identity.

In 1971 and 1972, John García engaged in fieldwork with several progressive neighborhood-based community organizations—the Brown Berets, Latin American Defense Organization (LADO), Young Patriots, Black Panthers, and Young Lords, among others—involving free health clinics. All of these organizations were very politicized and viewed community control and radical reform as central to their mission. During this time, the city of Chicago was determined to close these clinics by requiring physician ownership. Each clinic was independent, and between the various organizations, there was very little contact and communication. Since they faced similar problems, there was potential for cooperative and coalitional efforts. The Brown Beret clinic (Benito Juarez) and the LADO clinic (Pedro Albizu Campos) arranged a joint meeting to discuss possible cooperative activities to deal with pressure coming from the Richard J. Daley political machine.

The meeting was held in the Brown Beret neighborhood (Pilsen), with many members of each organization attending. The youthful Brown Beret membership had a militaristic style of dress and demeanor. Entering the meeting, they marched in formation into the room with their leaders at the head of the line. LADO was based in West Town in an area with a mix of Latino subgroups, primarily of Puerto Rican and Mexican origin. Its organizational membership was a combination of families, young people, and seniors. Its members were diverse in terms of age and family status and entered the meeting in a less structured way.

The Brown Berets perceived the LADO organization as primarily a Puerto Rican group and less tied to the US mainland. The Brown Berets saw themselves as cultural nationalists concerned about liberation politics. As a result, the meeting highlighted national origin, cultural nationalism, and cultural differences rather than similarities of ideology, organizational goals, and culture. The meeting became tense and little progress was made in finding common ground and proposing joint initiatives. Some of the LADO members, lacking child care, had to bring their young children. The divisiveness of the two organizations centered on their respective national origins and perceived cultural differences.

At one point, a Brown Beret leader pointed to a couple in LADO; the male was Puerto Rican and the female, Mexican American. Their three-year-old daughter was also present. He reminded the parents that their daughter would one day have to decide whether she was Puerto Rican or Mexican American/Chicana. The LADO parents, without consulting each other or hesitating, simultaneously responded, "She does not have to decide that; she is a *Latina*!"

Some sixteen years earlier, I was a co–principal investigator for the Latino National Political Survey (the first probability sampling of Cuban, Mexican-origin, and Puerto Rican adults living in the contiguous United States). As part of the preparation of the survey instrument, a series of ten focus groups in five cities was conducted in 1988. Chicago was the site of two focus groups. One of the primary topics of discussion was how individuals see themselves and their social identity. A group of fifteen to twenty Latinos (bilingual or primarily English-speaking) agreed to talk for a couple of hours. As the conversation on identity progressed, many of the participants comfortably identified themselves as Latino/a. Over the previous fifteen to twenty years, Latino activists had made concerted efforts to promote Latino identification. At the same time, each participant assumed several other identities, such as Puerto Rican, Salvadoran, Mexican(o), immigrant, and so on.

As previously illustrated in chapter 2, this scenario (or example) involved a brother and sister with one Puerto Rican parent and one of Mexican origin. The sister was married to a man of Italian ancestry living on the South Side of Chicago in a primarily white ethnic neighborhood. The Latina mother had a daughter who attended a parochial school in the neighborhood. A discussion followed in which the Latina described a series of identities and situations for her daughter. When visiting her grandmother, the daughter emphasized and identified herself as a Mexican American. While visiting her grandfather (the grandparents were divorced), she considered herself a Puerto Rican. At home, the daughter's identity was Latina. At school, the daughter took the ethnicity of her father. Finally, the mother described trips they took together on the Chicago Transit Authority bus. While traveling toward the Loop (the central retail and business section of the city), the daughter was aware of her minority status and identity. Many of the other bus passengers were African Americans, and the daughter recognized the broader concept of people of color.

It was clear from the focus group setting that these people were cognizant of their multiple identities and that different situations triggered a different identity and label. An individual's multiplicity of identities can be transferred or taught to children. The socialization process has been researched in terms of the development of identities (gender, racial, ethnic, etc.) and how early that process begins (Bernal and Martinelli 1993; Barvosa 2008). Box 5.1 reveals how pan-ethnicity manifested itself in focus groups associated with the Latino National Survey in 2005.

> **BOX 5.1 Another Focus Group Vignette, 2006**
>
> I was fortunate to be part of the team of principal investigators of the Latino National Survey (LNS) in 2005 and 2006. We conducted eighteen focus group sessions in large urban areas as well as rural communities in the Midwest and the South. Participants included recent immigrants, noncitizens, and second-generation and beyond Latinos, as well as a range of ages and near-even distribution by gender. This chapter has directed particular attention toward a sense of being part of a pan-ethnic community of persons of "Spanish origin."
>
> One interesting outcome of the numerous focus groups was an almost universal use of the terms "Latino" and "Hispanic." Whether participants were newly arrived to the United States, long-term residents, or native-born, they seemed to incorporate the use of these terms naturally to talk about themselves, friends, neighbors, and coworkers. Contributing to this sense of pan-ethnicity was the composition of their social networks, which included persons from other Latino subgroups, other racial and ethnic groups, and both immigrants and native-born persons. Key connectors were social networks that began with their family members, circle of friends, and coworkers.
>
> Our focus group respondents also demonstrated a greater sense of ease and comfort with other Latinos as opposed to non-Latinos around certain activities (e.g., **tamaladas**, dancing venues and genres, cultural events). There was clear evidence that the 2006 LNS focus group participants lived in a much more interactive world in which knowledge of and experiences in the United States were widespread regardless of geographic location, yet their Latino world was an integral part of their daily lives.

How have foreign-born "Latinos" developed or "taken on" their senses of self and identification? In *Latino Lives in America* (Fraga et al. 2010), researchers contend that the labels of "Latino" and "Hispanic" are American identities and that their meaning and significance rest within the boundaries of the United States. However, the characterization in box 5.1 shows that many of the foreign-born participants were already referring to themselves and other family members and friends as "Latinos." More work has been conducted on the identity process among Latino immigrants.

This entire study of social identities, racial and ethnic identity, immigrants, gender, and other significant characteristics and experiences that Latinos confront is the basis of long and multifaceted relationships and research literatures. Within this context, we have introduced, and will continue to introduce, important elements and findings applicable to the themes of Latinos, politics, and group efforts for policy development and political impact with the hope of generating more discussion among readers.

Latino Community Building and Mobilization: The Critical Political Link

The examination of Latinos and their politics does not assume that political dynamics occur only because some basis for community exists. Another essential element is the mobilization of individuals and group members to act collectively. Mobilization is the process by which political candidates and parties, activists, and groups try to entice other people to participate. Effective mobilization occurs when efforts by these individuals or groups increase the likelihood of involvement by others (Tilly 1978; Rosenstone and Hansen 1993). Political mobilization includes both direct and indirect forms of inducement and persuasion. The direct form lies in opportunities to participate, such as signing petitions, posting campaign signs, registering to vote, or attending rallies.

By creating participatory venues, the mobilizers subsidize political information and the personal costs of involvement. Mobilization usually does not take the form of a "general" blanket call for involvement, but is more strategic in nature. **Targeted mobilization** involves identifying persons who, when contacted, are more likely to respond to the calls for involvement. Recent political science research has suggested that elites, including political candidates, often use cues to heighten a sense of pan-ethnic identity among Latinos to make their mobilization efforts more effective.

This approach is most obvious in the case of Latino political candidates whose very presence in the race can cue or motivate a pan-ethnic identity and increase turnout among Latino constituents (Barreto 2010). Political science research has found that Latino voters prefer to support Latino candidates when given the chance, particularly Latinos with a high sense of group identity or ethnic attachment (Manzano and Sanchez 2010). As we will discuss in future chapters, the relationship between Latino voting behavior and political representation has increased with a rise in the number of Latino candidates and representatives over time.

Our goal here is more focused on the ways in which political elites strategically mobilize Latinos with pan-ethnic cues. Our experience testing ethnically focused campaign messages through surveys has included the use of phrases that promote a sense of empowerment among Latinos or Hispanics or suggest that collective Latino political engagement can address racism directed at Latinos. We have already established that pan-ethnic identity can be motivated by the Spanish language, so it is not surprising that the use of Spanish by candidates and parties is a highly utilized mobilization tool when attempting to court Latino voters. This has included translating campaign materials into Spanish, utilizing Spanish media for targeted outreach, and even having candidates running for political office (including presidential races) speaking Spanish themselves during political debates or speeches.

Scholars have found that these ethnic cues are often employed in geographical areas that have a highly concentrated Latino population (Abrajano 2010b); there is less concern with these messages potentially having a negative effect among non-Latinos who might see the advertisements on billboards and such. Finally, Valenzuela and Michelson (2016) implemented a Get Out the Vote (GOTV) experiment featuring ethnic cues to illustrate that the effects of ethnic identity are greater in areas where Latino ethnic identity is already high. Their research made clear that ethnic identity is at least partially driven by external actors who attempt to cue a sense of pan-ethnicity for their electoral benefit.

Another set of external forces that have been increasingly linked with the formation of racial and ethnic identity are public policies and negative political campaigns. Since 1990, there have been many national debates, actions, policies, and public perceptions about immigration, especially undocumented migration. However, the last two presidential cycles have made immigration politics more contentious and harmful to immigrants and their families than arguably any other time in modern history. This included President Obama's two terms in office, which were a mixture of positive campaign messaging to Latinos and very aggressive deportation policies that had significant consequences for many Latino families. However, although President Obama's record with Latinos was decidedly mixed, the anti-immigrant rhetoric and discrimination were taken to new levels with the emergence of President Donald Trump.

Donald Trump set the tone for his campaign when he announced his candidacy for the nomination of the Republican Party with the following statement: "When Mexico sends its people, they're not sending their best . . . They're bringing drugs. They're bringing crime. They're rapists . . . It's coming from all over South and Latin America" (Ye He Lee 2015). The Trump campaign extended the racialization of Latinos for political gain when Trump openly criticized other GOP candidates based on their direct and indirect connections to Latinos and particularly Latino immigrants. This included personalized jabs at Jeb Bush, whose wife is a Mexican immigrant and has since become a naturalized citizen, and Ted Cruz, for having a Cuban-born father (Schleifer 2015; Smith 2015).

Another comment, widely discussed in the national media, was made by candidate Trump regarding federal judge Gonzalo Curiel, a US-born son of Mexican immigrants who oversaw the lawsuit against Trump University, which emerged in the middle of the Trump campaign. In short, Trump suggested that Judge Curiel could not be unbiased in his decision regarding Trump University due to his "Mexican heritage," given Trump's policy views regarding immigration, which he assumed would be disliked by the Mexican judge (Steinhauer, Martin, and Herszenhorn 2016). These actions generated concern among GOP leadership who recognized the implications for engaging the Latino electorate with the party beyond the 2016 election. Speaker of the House Paul Ryan even distanced himself from Trump's comments against Judge Curiel, stating that they were "the textbook definition of a racist comment" (Steinhauer, Martin, and Herszenhorn 2016).

Social science research has made clear that the Latino community is well aware of the current policies and circumstances related to immigration (Ybarra, Sanchez, and Sanchez 2016), which have had heavy impacts on labor and housing markets, law enforcement, educational access, and overall adjustment to life in the United States. This high level of consciousness about the toxic climate regarding immigration and immigrants has been a strong mobilizing agent for Latinos over this period, as the climate of fear created by these policies and rhetoric has led many to engage in the political process. This included the high Latino turnout against candidate Trump in 2016, resulting in a record low level of support for a candidate among Latinos (Sanchez and Gómez-Aguiñaga 2017); a higher-than-expected Latino turnout in the 2018 election was undoubtedly a referendum on President Trump's first two years in office.

Immigration policy activity has not been limited to the federal government, as the individual American states have also been passing and implementing record numbers of immigration laws over the past two decades (see Ybarra, Sanchez, and Sanchez 2016), many of which were punitive toward immigrants. Arizona Senate Bill (SB) 1070 is representative of this latest wave of state-initiated legislation in the immigration policy area. In the late spring of 2010, the Arizona State Legislature passed SB 1070, which gave new powers to state and local police to detain and arrest suspected undocumented immigrants. This legislation produced greater polarization between proponents of more restrictive immigration policies and those advocating more "humane" and "immigrant-friendly" reforms. In addition, SB 1070 represented more active efforts by state and local governments to act due to increased impatience and frustration with the federal government. SB 1070 raised Latino-specific issues of profiling and scapegoating (Menjívar and Bejarano 2004; Magaña and Lee 2013).

Public protests, organizational responses, and litigation followed, but other state legislatures have enacted similar legislation. The immigration reform area is a good example of how mobilization efforts by leaders, activists, and Latino-based organizations inspired Latinos to get involved through a number of different venues and forms of political interest (Bloemraad and Trost 2008; Mohamed 2013).

Scholars of Latino politics have found that immigration politics and policy have mobilized Latinos through increasing perceptions of linked fate or group consciousness (Vargas, Sanchez, and Valdez 2017), two concepts we introduced in chapter 2 but that require more in-depth development. McClain et al. (2009) provide an extensive discussion of the concepts of group membership, group identity, racial identity, linked fate, and group consciousness. Group membership and group identity focus on a sense of attachment and belonging, on establishing a more general sense of identity. How these connections develop among different minority groups can vary based upon culture, language, residential situation, phenotypes, and so on. The latter three concepts—racial identity, linked fate, and group consciousness—include a person's sense of group affinity but also consider how being a member of that group is impacted by the behaviors and attitudes of "outsiders." Sanchez (2006a, 2006b) focuses on group consciousness, which is comprised of three components: group identification as a Latino, an assessment of Latinos' group status in American society, and orientation toward collective action on behalf of the Latino community. Latinos who possess these "components" of group consciousness are more likely to be engaged, politically and civically.

This connection is more evident if the issues or circumstances are directly impacting and/or targeting the Latino community (Sanchez 2006b). For example, the current anti-immigrant and "nativistic" climate against undocumented immigrants has been presented as Latinos being the "face" of the "immigration problem." The high connection to immigrants across all segments of the Latino community has meant that the effects of immigration policy have been felt even among US citizens who are well assimilated into US culture. Latino Decisions polls (2013; Pedraza and Vargas 2015) showed that many Latinos, irrespective of nativity, legal status, or socioeconomic status, know or are connected to a relative or friend who is an undocumented person. The salience of immigration as a major policy issue cuts across the breadth of the Latino community, and the policy preference includes more "immigrant-friendly" reforms, not more punitive measures (i.e., incarceration, formal deportation, and further criminalization of immigrants).

The concepts of group identity, consciousness, and a sense of linked fate serve as key aspects of Latinos' investments and motivation for political involvement. Masuoka's (2006) research on Asian Americans and Latinos shows that political interest is a key element to predicting presence and levels of group consciousness. Linked fate is therefore heightened through exposure to political information, including campaign rhetoric. Mohamed (2013) reinforces the role of group consciousness by demonstrating how Latinas exhibit higher levels of group consciousness than their Latino counterparts. Latinas are more likely to be advocates for maintaining "Latino cultural practices," particularly regarding issues of voting, seeking naturalization, and not describing themselves as Americans. The potential for cross-mobilization to occur among Latinas, who may be responsive to gender and ethnic cues from candidates and political messaging more generally, will be discussed in more detail in future chapters.

Clearly, the role of Latino group consciousness, perhaps in conjunction with ethnic group-specific consciousness (such as Mexican, Salvadoran, etc.), strengthens a sense of community and motivates people to act collectively to address the needs, concerns, and conditions of Latinos. The discussion of Latino politics would not be relevant if there were not a set of linkages (real and everyday) that "bind" individuals together.

Conclusion

This chapter's discussion has centered on the bases for community among Latinos, adding the important "ingredient" of group identity and the resulting linkages with political involvement. It is, therefore, somewhat of a bridge between the first section of the book, which focuses on historical context, demographics, and the foundations of pan-ethnic identity, and the second half, which focuses more squarely on political participation and the policy preferences and outcomes that are important to the Latino community.

There is a clear link between individual motivation, resources to participate, and mobilization efforts by organizations and activists to assist in that process. The individual component provides insight into the motivations and capacities that a person develops as well as her or his cumulative experiences in different political arenas. As we have discussed in some detail in this chapter, external forces such as public policies or campaign messages can provide cues to Latinos that can mobilize them into political action. For Latinos, limited resources, language barriers, a historic lack of political engagement in the United States, and lack of contact with recruitment networks have all contributed to a previous pattern of lower levels of political involvement. The power of group identity in its many formats is a resource that may be able to help Latinos overcome these limitations to actualize their political potential. The chapters on elections, organizations, and other forms of political participation will further develop these connections and processes.

The remaining chapters examine the individual and mobilization aspects of Latino participation in a variety of different venues (voting, campaigning, organizational involvement, partisan activities, school-related activities, letter writing, etc.). For the most part, our knowledge about participation levels for specific Latino subgroups (primarily Mexican Americans, Cubans, and Puerto Ricans) has been limited. Although more recent research tends to group all Latinos together, there has been more specific analysis of some subgroups (i.e., Dominicans, Salvadorans, and Guatemalans). In addition, the data is pertinent only to particular participatory modes (primarily voting and election returns).

This discussion would not be complete without expanding on the mobilization dynamics in which individual political behavior and attitudes intersect with the targeted actions of organizations and activists that have been introduced in this chapter. With the development of a stronger Latino community, how do Latino-based organizations and Latino leaders and activists motivate and influence fellow Latinos to get more involved in the American political process? Does organizational affiliation and engagement, whether the group is specifically political or not, provide interest, knowledge, and networks from which to mobilize? Does greater attention to and visibility of Latinos on the American landscape become an extra incentive to be more political? How does issue salience serve to activate Latinos and/or give mobilizers the substance to encourage and reduce the costs of Latino participation?

Finally, the role of Latino group consciousness serves to place more Latinos into the political arena. The primary research questions deal with the development of a Latino group consciousness (i.e., contributing factors) and the direct link of having a Latino group consciousness with political behaviors. Embedded in this discussion of Latino group consciousness is the dynamic of pan-ethnicity and how that translates into connections that cross national origin to incorporate a complementary social identity. The nature and form of political engagement are also affected by the context in which Latinos reside. The cliché "place matters" helps to complete the political landscape in which Latinos live.

Discussion Questions

1. How people label themselves usually indicates an identity to which they have a strong attachment. What interpretations can be made about persons who label themselves as Latino or Hispanic? What about those who choose to identify themselves as white racially, as we have seen a large segment of the Latino community do?
2. Even when a person identifies with a specific label, other identities may also be important. Discuss the concepts of multiple and situational identity and how they relate to the development of a Latino community.
3. There has been discussion that "Latino" and/or "Hispanic" is a socially constructed category promoted by Latino elites to develop a base from which they can operate and benefit. Discuss the "realness" of being Latino or Hispanic in "everyday life" for many Latinos and their political engagement.
4. The link between mobilization and political participation has been illustrated through discussions of ethnic appeals of candidates to Latinos and through policy threat driven mostly by immigration policy. Can you think of any other incidences that demonstrated the mobilization-politics link?

Links to Suggested Readings

https://www.pewresearch.org/hispanic/2017/12/20/hispanic-identity-fades-across-generations-as-immigrant-connections-fall-away

https://www.census.gov/content/dam/Census/library/working-papers/2014/demo/shedding-light-on-race-reporting-among-hispanics/POP-twps0102.pdf

https://www.pewsocialtrends.org/2015/06/11/chapter-7-the-many-dimensions-of-hispanic-racial-identity

Note

1. Although we do not elaborate on gender consciousness and its ideological aspects related to pan-ethnicity here, chapter 3 on political community for Latinos discusses and analyzes its impact.

CHAPTER 6

Latino Political Participation

¿Y que tal tu vida cívica? ¿Aprendiste de tus padres? ¿Qué talentos desarrollaste para trabajar en la comunidad? Si se te pide que trabajes en la comunidad ¿Cómo vas a responder?

And how is your civic life? Did you learn from your parents? What talents have you developed to serve our community better? If someone asks you to join in the effort with other members of our community, how will you respond?

THE PRESIDENTIAL ELECTION OF 2020 marks an election cycle driven by informational and mis-informational campaigns through a variety of social media outlets with an unprecedented amount of financial resources to be spent to mobilize the electorate, including a sizable investment in the Latino electorate. This country and its electorate continue to be increasingly polarized, and fervent emotions predominate attitudes and behaviors. All forms of political expressions and activities cover the political landscape. We have noted the expanding role of Latinos in the American political system and the challenges they still face to heighten their political influence. Barreto et al. (2010) moves away from single indicators such as turnout and voter choice to a more multifaceted set of factors of in-group population traits, electoral volatility, and mobilization. So, our focus in this chapter examines the linkage between the in-group traits of Latinos with demonstration of civic and political engagement. Engagement can be defined by "having an interest in, or paying attention to, or having knowledge, beliefs, opinions, attitudes, or feelings about either political or civic matters" (Barrett and Brunton-Smith 2014).

On the other hand, we can view participation as expressions of politically and civically involved behaviors. Both concepts involve working to make a difference in the **civic life** of one's community and developing the combination of knowledge, skills, values, and motivation to make that difference. This means promoting the quality of life in a community, through both political and nonpolitical processes. The different forms of political and civic engagement and participation are revealed by different patterns and contributing factors that operate at different levels, and they include contextual factors, demographic factors, proximal social factors, and endogenous psychological factors. Our discussion of engagement and participation shows any variations as a function of complex interactions between macro, demographic, and psychological factors.

Over the course of previous chapters, we have posited that Latinos have expanding engagement and influence in America. This chapter examines the nature and character of Latino civic and political engagement (and participation) at all levels of our society, as well as what factors can enhance and expand their influence and impact. Latinos not only want to make a difference for their families and local communities but also to ensure the responsiveness of American political institutions and leadership to all segments of its populace. We could characterize earlier periods of Latino politics as times when recognition of their existence and seeking an active role in the political system were the major themes. While political legitimacy and being part of that political arena have improved, the continued progress of Latinos can, in large part, rest with the development of a more active Latino "constituency," with an organizational base and resources and leadership and effective mobilizing strategies in the policy arenas making a difference. We have outlined the scope of political participation and exploration of what needs to be done for Latinos to be effectively engaged in the US political system.

In the twenty-first century, will the rising trajectory of Latino political involvement be redesigned, modified, or tailored to the current political climate of polarization? Are there any possibilities that Latinos will backtrack to earlier low levels of collective involvement? Or will their political involvement surge and have an even greater impact and visibility on the American political landscape? Will relationships with the major political parties incorporate this community's leadership and policy agenda for upward mobility and sociopolitical equity? For Latinos, the objective of converting a growing adult population into an even more politically oriented and immersed population remains a central goal. This chapter examines current patterns of Latino political participation, the critical contributing factors, and areas in which there is a need for systematic information. It is important to note that our focus in this chapter will place greater emphasis on civic and nonelectoral forms of participation. We have a comprehensive discussion of Latino involvement in elections and electoral politics in the next chapter, with some natural overlap in our discussion based on some factors that are relevant in both arenas.

American political culture envisions political participation as a fundamental right, obliging each person to play a role in political processes and institutions. Having access, pursuing political interests, knowing the rules of the game,[1] developing effective political resources, having responsive representatives, and influencing the policy-making process are central dimensions of political participation. Political participation focuses on individuals or groups whose central objective is to influence the policy-making process and the substance of policies themselves. This involves accumulating and utilizing resources, developing efficacious participatory orientations, and recruiting others to get involved. Political resources include time, money, and communication and organizational skills. Resources equip a person to engage in the political arena with knowledge, available time, and the pertinent skills to articulate their objectives and effect change. Participatory orientations develop political attitudes conducive to involvement, such as political and personal efficacy, political trust and interest, and a sense of group consciousness. Another side of the participation is recruitment. A person may initiate his or her own actions as a result of being encouraged by other people or organizations to get involved in particular ways. In other words, a person may become active because he or she was asked to do so (Verba et al. 1995). When we discuss political mobilization of Latinos, the extant research demonstrates the importance of "**co-ethnics**" (i.e., persons of same racial/ethnic background) as effective contacts with other Latinos and explains that the presence of Latino candidates serves as an important motivator to participate.

Evolution of the Participatory Process

Early socialization plays a critical role in the development of an individual's participatory future. Family discussion of things political and exposure to political events such as rallies and campaigns can make a lasting impression on a young person. Similarly, early pre-adult experiences such as involvement in extracurricular activities, participation in religious organizations, and having politically active parents make a strong imprint on children and help to teach them about civic and political life. Such background characteristics as gender, race, and ethnicity also play an important role in early socialization. For instance, familial expectations that girls will be less involved, or not involved at all, can affect female political participation. Being subjected to discriminatory treatment can cause a person to become politically involved to combat such treatment in the future (de la Garza and Vaughn 1984; Umaña-Taylor and Fine 2004). The cycle of life experiences and early socialization establishes the foundation from which an individual chooses whether to get involved.

However, early socialization does not completely predetermine any individual's participatory life. One important note about the role of political socialization: Among Latino immigrants, the children (both the US-born and those who migrated to the United States at an early age) often become socializers of their parents (García-Castañon 2010; Cruz 2010). For example, the heightened mass protest in 2006 regarding immigrant rights and social justice marked the increased involvement of Latino youth and their spillover effects on parents (Hayduk and García-Castañon 2018; Barreto et al. 2009; Pantoja et al. 2008). This has carried over into the social movement surrounding DACA, with a large group of "**DREAMers**" mobilizing to push for the deferred action policy to allow undocumented immigrants who came to America as young children to have an easier path to citizenship.

Extensive literature on political participation (Verba and Nie 1972; Verba, Scholzman, and Brady 1995; Milbrath and Hoel 1977; Rosenstone and Hansen 1993) identifies who the participants are as well as when, where, and how they participate. According to Verba, Scholzman, and Brady (1995), participation involves (1) resources, (2) psychological orientations, and (3) recruitment. Resources include the accumulation of time, money, and skills—all factors we covered extensively in the demographic chapter of the book. Time refers to having both opportunities to participate and the time available to do so. Money provides a valuable resource for engaging in political activities as well as being identified in networks. Skills include the ability and confidence to engage in political activities, and in some cases the basic research skills to acquire information on political issues and the political system. Education plays a major role in skill acquisition. Educational attainment provides greater political knowledge and information, as well as communication skills (writing, public speaking, organization and expression of thoughts and ideas, etc.). Higher educational attainment generally positions a person in higher-status jobs and income levels. In addition, positive participatory orientations, like personal and political efficacy, political trust, and sense of civic duty, are associated with greater educational attainment. Finally, higher levels of education are generally associated with organizational affiliation and involvement.

All these ingredients for political participation center on an individual's abilities and acquired skills,[2] position in a job setting, and resource base from which to engage in political matters. As already noted in the demographic profiles presented earlier in the book, many Latinos, as a group, do not as often possess the necessary time, money, and skills to be engaged civically at the same rate as non-Latinos. In addition, factors such as language (English-language proficiency, nativity, legal status, etc.) pose additional consideration in terms of their participation. As we have noted, participation must include recruitment and mobilization as people become politically engaged when asked to do so. Political mobilization entails efforts by political parties, organizations, candidates, and leaders to persuade individuals to participate. Mobilization efforts can be direct, by contacting and encouraging persons to carry out specific actions and responses, or indirect by using social networks to communicate the message. Use of primary networks is usually based in the workplace or in the neighborhood.

So far, we have identified political participation as originating with the individual or in targeted efforts by third parties to persuade individuals to get involved in a specific activity or issue. The results of targeted mobilization include creating opportunities to participate and subsidizing the costs of both gathering political information and conducting political activism. The latter point refers to providing materials, rides to the election polls, individuals to assist, and so forth, so that the targeted individual does not have to expend as much time and energy as he or she would if participating alone (Valenzuela and Michelson 2016; García Bedolla and Michelson 2012; Michelson 2003b).

Thus, the act of mobilizing entails identifying people who can efficiently identify, contact, and persuade individuals to participate. In the identification process, mobilizers have a good sense that the people they recruit will likely respond to the call for action. Research by Rosenstone and Hansen (1993) indicates that those most likely to be targeted are employed, belong to and serve as leaders in organizations, are more educated, have higher income levels, and have some partisan (political party) history. Mobilization efforts tend to be more successful if the contact is made between people who know each other. Personal connections establish a more receptive setting for the message and request. It is also important that once contacted, the individual will be effective and well positioned to solicit the help of others in his or her networks. Mobilization research on Latinos places emphasis on the effectiveness of a co-ethnic being the one who is contacting a fellow Latino/a. Timing becomes an essential ingredient when asking individuals to participate, since the issue (e.g., a city ordinance) or event (e.g., hearing or election date) is usually very near and/or highly visible. That is, the outcome is hanging in the balance and identifiable consequences will be affected.

Most Americans' political participation is very limited and sporadic. Given the costs of participation, many different options and distractions can get "in the way" of becoming politically involved. Nonparticipants are individuals who either cannot participate, do not want to, or have not been asked to get involved. People who cannot participate are excluded by such restrictions as age requirements, noncitizen or felon status, language barriers, and the like. People who do not want to participate are usually not interested, deem other things more important, do not have enough time, find politics too complicated or boring, or feel distrustful of and cynical about politics. The last category of nonparticipants consists of those who have never been asked by anyone or any organization to get politically involved, usually because the mobilizers do not perceive such individuals as likely participants or as positioned in useful networks. The size of the nonparticipant group varies by the type of political activity available.

How and where do Americans participate politically? The most common form of political participation centers on elections, the central focus of the next chapter (Tienda and Mitchell 2006; del Real 2018). The United States holds the greatest number of elections each year of any country in the world. As a result, political participation is seen as election-dominated, and voter registration and turnout become the primary indicators of political engagement. In addition to voting, political campaigning involves making campaign contributions, doing volunteer work, posting campaign signs or wearing campaign buttons, and attending rallies (see box 6.1).

BOX 6.1 Here Today We March, Tomorrow We Vote

In the spring of 2006, millions of persons took to the streets in virtually every major city and many others throughout the United States to protest the Sensenbrenner immigration bill and advocate for a more "humane" and comprehensive immigration policy. A substantial proportion of the participants and organizers were immigrants (mostly Latino) of both documented and undocumented status. It was estimated that more than three million people in 130 cities participated in pro-immigrant marches (Cano 2008). This highlights some major patterns of mobilization among Latino immigrants who had been considered either apolitical or politically uninformed and uninterested in American politics (García and Sanchez 2004; García and de la Garza 1985). Traditional forms of mobilization formed part of the efforts to organize and direct participants toward collective action (i.e., developing strategy, accessing resources through unions and other sources). In many regards the object of the protest marches was to put a public and personal face on the objects of punitive and restrictive policies, including the scapegoating of immigrants for many societal ills (e.g., unfair job competition, drains on social and health programs, lost taxes, increased criminal activity), and to develop policy discussions and initiatives that were both more comprehensive in scope (away from the emphasis on border enforcement and criminalization) and responsive to immigrant and Latino interests and concerns.

From a mobilization perspective, the less-expected techniques included utilizing modern technology and the mass media to publicize and stir up support for this cause. More specifically, Spanish-language media (especially radio and radio personalities), websites (e.g., www.march25coalition.org), text messaging, and social networking sites (e.g., Facebook and Instagram) played a role by providing the necessary information for participation as well as the "rules of engagement" and the rationale for the protest marches (Reyes 2006). The size of these marches and degree of organizational effectiveness challenge perceptions of immigrants as apolitical and politically unsophisticated.

In addition, the participation of Latino "citizens" reflects the extensive ties the undocumented have with US citizens. A Latino Decisions poll (2013) found that 85 percent of Latino undocumented immigrants had family ties with US citizens. Within Latino undocumented households, 62 percent had a US-born child, and 13 percent had a spouse who was a US citizen. These connections and a broader characterization of undocumented immigrants will be discussed in chapter 9. The analysis of immigration policy provides more information about the Latino immigrant sector and its political engagement.

The ultimate form of participation is seeking political office, but a very small fraction of people campaign and ultimately obtain those positions. However, political participation extends far beyond the electoral arena in both individual and collective ways. People can make direct contact with public and/or bureaucratic officials regarding an individual problem or on behalf of their neighborhood or group. Another dimension of political participation includes belonging to organized groups that may or may not be explicitly political. Involvement with an organization as a member, financial contributor, or leader gives one access to information and knowledge, policy preferences, organizational skills, and experience with collective efforts. Other forms of political participation include protest activities, engagement in discussions about politics, attempting to persuade individuals to support given candidates or propositions, and involvement in partisan activities. The opportunities for political participation are substantial, and many people do choose to become politically engaged.

While active political participation is an integral part of a viable democracy with laws, practices, and traditions in place to try to reinforce an individual's regular political engagement, the actual practice of participation is very uneven. At the same time, institutional practices and laws can also serve to inhibit participation. We will discuss this aspect briefly in this chapter and more extensively in chapter 10. We will now try to construct a systematic picture of Latino political participation and examine why the current picture exists. This portrait will have some blank spots because social scientists, marketers, and journalists have only recently chronicled Latinos in the political system.

Latino Political Participation

Early works on Latino political participation (Tirado 1970; García and Arce 1988) focus almost exclusively on Mexican-origin people. From 1970 to 2000, systematic examination of Mexican American and other Latino political behavior has been restricted to specific communities or limited forms of political participation (e.g., voting or organizational activities) (Briegal 1970; Márquez 1985; Allsup 1982; García 1986a, 1997; Chapa 1995). General conclusions regarding Latino political participation may be summarized as follows: (1) overall rates of participation are lower than those for the general population; (2) there is evidence of incorporating participatory orientations, but participation does not necessarily follow; (3) rates of organizational involvement and activities are lower; (4) rates of voter registration and turnout are lower; (5) a significant proportion of the Latino subcommunities is comprised of foreign-born noncitizens and a higher proportion of young people (under age thirty) than the general population; and (6) there is a feeling of distance from and disinterest in the political world (García 1997; Falcón 1992; Moreno and Warren 1992; García and Sanchez 2004).

In earlier editions of this book, we relied on three primary sources for the portrayal of Latino political participation. They included the Participation in the America II study by Sidney Verba, Kay Scholzman, and Henry Brady (1995), the Latino National Survey (Fraga et al. 2006a), and the Pew Hispanic Research Center surveys (prior to 2009). Since that time, there has been a significant increase in surveys and Latino-oriented research centers that focus on Latinos or include purposively more Latinos in the national sample (i.e., American National Election Survey). Even with more data on Latinos, there is a skewed focus on elections and voting behaviors. As a result, it is more difficult to present a national profile of Latinos' political engagement in organizations, or a wide range of civic engagements, levels of political discussions, and local involvement. Nevertheless, we can provide a fuller picture than earlier editions.

In this edition, we rely more on the 2016 Collaborative Multiracial Post-Election Survey (CMPS).[3] A total of 10,145 completed interviews were collected online in a respondent self-administered format from December 3, 2016, to February 15, 2017. The survey (and invitation) was available to respondents in English, Spanish, Chinese (simplified), Chinese (traditional), Korean, and Vietnamese. Because of the 2016 election, the CMPS started with a large sample of registered voters in order to provide a large sample size for analyses, but nonvoters are also included. In general, five forms of civic participation, excluding voting, can be identified in which Latinos can engage. They involve campaigns or electoral-related activities, contacting a public official, belonging to civic/political organizations, participation in direct actions or protest activities, and being involved as a political partisan (i.e., involved in a political party). The CMPS study also allows for the inclusion of engagement in politics through social media, an activity that has become much more discussed in the political science literature and is a useful tool for mobilization, particularly among young Latinos.

In the next paragraphs, we will briefly summarize the patterns of Latino participation. Latino participants who are registered voters are more likely to be involved in all five of the different activities. While voting is a core activity, it can have spillover effects on other kinds of political engagements. At the same time, there are "political domains" or activities in which nonregistered voters may be the key background characteristic. For example, protests for and advocates of immigration reform include significant numbers of Latinos who may not be voters, may be noncitizens, and may come from the younger segments of the community.

Using the CMPS, we present in table 6.1 an important prelude to Latinos' civic and political engagement. That is, does an individual express any interest in politics? Political interest and knowledge serve as critical antecedents to motivate someone to participate in a variety of activities. Our political orientations include politics as too complicated, level of interest in politics, having a say in what government does, and public officials acting on their behalf. In table 6.1, we can compare Latinos' responses to those of whites, African Americans, and Asian Americans. Combining the two categories of "very" and "somewhat interested," almost three-quarters of Latinos answered affirmatively. Interestingly, Latinos were slightly lower than their white and African American counterparts but higher in the "somewhat interested category." For example, the percentage of Latinos (23.2 percent) who reported that they were "very interested" in politics in the 2016 CMPS survey was lower than non-Hispanic white respondents (26.0 percent) and black respondents (23.4 percent). Our earlier discussion on the role of mobilization would suggest that effective and efficient mobilization efforts in the Latino community could serve as a catalyst to increase civic and political involvement. More noticeable differences between Latinos and particularly non-Hispanic whites was found in government responsiveness, such that Latinos were more pessimistic about being heard and having issues addressed.

When asked how one becomes interested in politics, the overwhelming response was presidential elections. Thus, the presidential election cycles represent excellent opportunities not only to expand the Latino base but also to build a long-term

TABLE 6.1 Political Orientations among Minority Group Members in the CMPS

Political Orientations Affecting Participation	White Non-Hispanics	Latinos	African Americans	Asian Americans
How much interest do you have in politics?				
Very Interested	269 (26.0%)	695 (23.2%)	727 (23.4%)	443 (14.7%)
Somewhat Interested	484 (46.8%)	1,400 (46.6%)	1,392 (44.9%)	1,465 (48.7%)
Not That Interested	163 (15.8%)	545 (18.2%)	609 (19.6%)	750 (25.0%)
Not at All Interested	118 (11.4%)	362 (12.1%)	374 (12.1%)	348 (11.6%)
How often does your group have a say in how government handles problems?				
All of the Time	127 (12.3%)	111 (3.7%)	135 (4.4%)	90 (3.0%)
Most of the Time	309 (30.0%)	358 (11.9%)	299 (9.6%)	373 (12.4%)
About Half the Time	371 (36.1%)	1,083 (36.1%)	888 (28.6%)	828 (27.5%)
Rarely	180 (17.5%)	1,192 (39.7%)	1,373 (44.3%)	1,464 (48.7%)
Never	42 (4.1%)	258 (8.6%)	407 (13.1%)	251 (8.4%)
How often do public officials work hard on behalf of your group?				
All of the Time	93 (9.0%)	109 (3.6%)	113 (3.6%)	85 (2.9%)
Most of the Time	301 (29.1%)	413 (13.8%)	297 (9.6%)	443 (14.9%)
About Half the Time	353 (34.1%)	1,253 (41.7%)	1,090 (35.1%)	817 (27.5%)
Rarely	229 (22.2%)	1,045 (34.8%)	1,288 (41.5%)	1,417 (47.6%)
Never	58 (5.6%)	182 (6.1%)	314 (10.1%)	214 (7.2%)
Sometimes politics and government seem so complicated.				
Strongly Agree	123 (11.9%)	352 (11.7%)	387 (12.5%)	303 (10.1%)
Agree	322 (31.1%)	953 (31.7%)	849 (27.4%)	1,131 (37.6%)
Neither Agree nor Disagree	271 (26.2%)	888 (29.6%)	861 (27.8%)	945 (31.4%)
Disagree	214 (20.7%)	516 (17.2%)	609 (19.6%)	437 (14.5%)
Strongly Disagree	104 (10.1%)	293 (9.8%)	396 (12.8%)	190 (6.3%)

Source: Data for this table was derived from analysis of the 2016 CMPS.

Note: The Collaborative Multiracial Post-Election Survey (CMPS) is a national survey of voters and nonvoters on political and social issues conducted post-election. Since 2016, the CMPS is conducted via the internet, and it is one of the few surveys that includes enough respondents to do across racial group analysis. The CMPS is currently housed at UCLA.

foundation for sustained involvement. By contrast, when asked why people are not interested in politics, the modal response was a basic distrust, followed by viewing politics as too complicated. As a result, mobilization efforts need to promote greater political efficacy and, perhaps, stronger collective identity to link the value of involvement with more relevant social policies and equity.

Historically, Latino political participation in nonelectoral areas has been lower than for other racial and ethnic groups. Individuals can engage in direct contact with public officials to present grievances or present to persons who have some authority over the matter at hand. Within the CMPS, respondents were asked if they participated in the undertakings of a wide range of civic and political activities. These activities included: participating in a civic, social, or political group, regularly attending meetings of their group, discussing politics with family and friends, contacting governmental officials, working with others to solve a community problem, attending community meetings to discuss local problems, and using social media to engage in politics.

TABLE 6.2 Arenas of Civic Engagement for CMPS Respondents by Race/Ethnicity

Types of Civic Engagement	White[a]	Latino	African American	Asian American
Participate in social, cultural, political group or union				
One	13	9	14	11
More than one	12	8	9	8
None	75	82	77	81
Regularly attend meetings and engage in activities				
Yes	61	50	53	43
No	39	50	47	57
Do these organizations take stands on public issues?				
Yes	68	59	64	50
No	26	33	26	35
Don't Know	7	8	10	15
In past twelve months have you discussed politics with family and friends?				
Yes	88	80	82	77
No	12	20	18	23
Last twelve months, attended protest, demonstrations, rally				
Yes	8	10	11	6
No	92	90	89	94
Last twelve months, have boycotted product or company for political reasons				
Yes	23	13	14	14
No	77	87	86	86
Contacted elected representative or govt. official about policy issue				
Yes	30	13	18	11
No	70	87	82	89
Contacted representative or government official about problem you have				
Yes	20	13	16	12
No	80	87	84	88
Have you worked with others to solve local community problem?				
Yes	23	18	21	15
No	77	82	79	85

Source: Data for this table was derived from analysis of the 2016 CMPS.
Note: The Collaborative Multiracial Post-Election Survey (CMPS) is a national survey of voters and nonvoters on political and social issues conducted post-election. Since 2016, the CMPS is conducted via the internet, and it is one of the few surveys that includes enough respondents to do across racial group analysis. The CMPS is currently housed at UCLA.
[a] Represents the percentage answered for each response.

In table 6.2, we present the range of participation across the major racial and ethnic groups. Overall, we find that Latinos are very similar to the other groups in their participation. That is, comparable levels exist when discussing politics with family and friends and participating in rallies or demonstrations. On the other hand, Latinos have lower levels of participation when it comes to regular attendance at meetings, boycotting products, and contacting elected and administrative officials but will attend a community meeting designed to solve a local problem. The intersection of group identity/consciousness with political interest and with issues and problems can allow

Latino leadership and organizations to encourage conversion of political discussions within Latinos' personal network of family and friends to more collective arenas of participation. Previous research shows that if a Latino has an organizational affiliation, it is more likely to be membership in a church or religious group. Noncitizens form the second-highest group in terms of levels of organizational involvement in church and school-related activities.

Another vantage point from which to view Latino political participation is to assess the accumulation of Latino political areas on engagement. We counted across the seven different types of activities for each of the racial and ethnic groups we identified in table 6.2. In table 6.3, we sum the activities identified in table 6.2 to see how many actions each CMPS respondent engaged in.

The disparities are much less evident for respondents that do not participate in any activity. The numbers in the parentheses represent the percentages within each group. For example, no activity ranges from 11.4 percent for whites to 17.6 percent for Asian Americans. For the three racial and ethnic groups, a greater percentage is noted than for their white counterparts for participating in one activity (38.2 percent vs. 45.9 percent, 43.4 percent, and 47.1 percent for each group, respectively). At the higher levels (five or more activities), there is a slightly higher percentage among white respondents. Again, earlier discussions regarding socioeconomic resources,

TABLE 6.3 Number of Political Activities Engaged in by CMPS Respondents

Political Activities Engaged In[a]	Race and Ethnic Groups				
	White	Latino	African American	Asian American	Grand Total (%)
None	118 (11.4)[b]	427 (14.2)	422 (13.6)	528 (17.6)	1,495 (14.7)
One	395 (38.2)	1,379 (45.9)	1,346 (43.4)	1,416 (47.1)	4,536 (44.7)
Two	167 (16.2)	450 (15.0)	454 (14.6)	411 (13.7)	1,482 (14.6)
Three	131 (12.7)	345 (11.5)	368 (11.9)	304 (10.1)	1,148 (11.3)
Four	84 (8.1)	161 (5.4)	212 (6.8)	176 (5.9)	633 (6.2)
Five	80 (7.7)	132 (4.4)	168 (5.4)	79 (2.6)	459 (4.5)
Six	41 (4.0)	64 (2.1)	89 (2.9)	60 (2.0)	254 (2.5)
Seven	18 (1.7)	44 (1.5)	43 (1.4)	32 (1.1)	137 (1.4)

Source: Data for this table was derived from analysis of the 2016 CMPS.

Note: The Collaborative Multiracial Post-Election Survey is a national survey of voters and nonvoters on political and social issues conducted post-election. Since 2016, the CMPS is conducted via the internet, and it is one of the few surveys that includes enough respondents to do across racial group analysis. The CMPS is currently housed at UCLA.

[a] The activities that each respondent was asked to answer either yes or no to were: take some action on an issue or in an election; participate in social, cultural, or civic organization; regularly attend meetings; discuss politics with family and friends; contacted an elected representative or governmental official; contacted an official in any way about a problem; and worked or cooperated with others to solve a local problem.

[b] The numbers in the columns are the actual number of respondents, and the number in the parentheses represents the percentage of respondents.

social status, and opportunity structures continue to be quite relevant to understand Latino political participation.

While results from the Latino National Survey (LNS) (Fraga et al. 2006a) indicated that persons responding are moving from problem identification to collective action, a noticeable percentage (18 to 28 percent) would do nothing. On the other hand, more than three-fifths would work collectively either in a formal organization or on an ad hoc basis. The results of the CMPS, some ten years later, reflect the persistent challenge of activating more Latinos to engage in collective endeavors. Part of the explanation for less engagement could be an evaluation of the utility and effectiveness of different political activities. Within the CMPS, respondents were asked the importance of engaging in certain political activities. The response categories ranged from very important to not at all important. In table 6.4, we look at five specific activities. They range from electorally related activities to working together to pursue community concerns. There is almost near unanimity among Latinos (82 percent) that voting is very important.

Interestingly, the second-highest effective activity is getting together to work on community problems. While the national "stage" received greater visibility regarding collective efforts, an important consideration for Latino political mobilization is to

TABLE 6.4 CMPS Respondents' Assessment of the Importance of Different Political Activities

	Racial/Ethnic Groups (%)			
Types of Political Activities[a]	White	Latino	African American	Asian American
Importance of voting in elections				
Very/Somewhat Important	88	82	84	82
Not That Important/Not at All[b]	6	9	9	10
Important to donate money to campaign/causes				
Very/Somewhat Important	32	34	42	34
Not That Important/Not at All	52	46	40	51
Important to work together on community problems				
Very/Somewhat Important	72	74	78	73
Not That Important/Not at All	15	14	11	16
Important to attend protests on salient issues				
Very/Somewhat Important	29	45	52	38
Not That Important/Not at All	56	39	32	48
Important to contact public officials about salient issues				
Very/Somewhat Important	60	57	64	56
Not That Important/Not at All	24	26	21	28

Source: Data for this table was derived from analysis of the 2016 CMPS.

Note: The Collaborative Multiracial Post-Election Survey is a national survey of voters and nonvoters on political and social issues conducted post-election. Since 2016, the CMPS is conducted via the internet, and it is one of the few surveys that includes enough respondents to do across racial group analysis. The CMPS is currently housed at UCLA.

[a] The stem of this question battery asks, "Do people you care about, like friends and family, think that each of the following political activities are important to do: _____."

[b] The percentage of "Don't Know" responses are not shown but when combined with other responses will total 100.

pursue a "bottom-up" approach to generate greater interest and involvement. Continued discussions about Latino political participation need to look over time in order to assess progress as well as the rate of progress relative to other Americans.

Among the remaining activities, the lowest regarded activity is donating to campaigns and "causes" (34 percent for Latinos). Comparable to African Americans, Latinos see more of a benefit in participating in protest-related activities (52 percent and 45 percent, respectively), which is much higher than whites and Asian Americans. Intergroup comparisons also become significant when we discuss, in a later chapter, coalition building both with the Latino pan-ethnic communities and other racial and ethnic groups. An integral part of our discussion about Latino political participation would require looking at internal variations within the Latino community. In table 6.5, we break out the numbers of political activities Latinos engage in by both gender and nativity. It has been demonstrated that Latinas are voting at higher levels than their Latino counterparts, serve as community activists, and are organizationally critical for Latinos' successes. The dimension of nativity within the political worlds of Latino noncitizens has been receiving more systematic attention and analysis in the past ten to fifteen years (Barreto and Muñoz 2003; Pantoja and Gershon 2006; Leal 2002). The heightened saliency and punitive governmental actions on immigration and immigrants have had a broad-ranging impact on this community (Gonzales 2008; Bada et al. 2006). While the immigration-related marches receive the greater notoriety of noncitizens' political engagement, their actions have not been limited to just protests.

Recent research by Carey, Branton, and Martinez-Ebers (2014) examined the impact of the 2006 immigration protest demonstrations on making this area of interest more salient among Latinos. They found that these protests did increase Latinos' perception of undocumented immigrants as a very important problem facing the broader Latino community, particularly if the Latino knew someone or had family members of undocumented status (Latino Decisions polls on issues). Similarly, Barreto et al. (2009) found that support for these marches cut across class, generational status, language use, and various other factors among members of the Latino community.

Latinos' response to working together to solve local issues reinforces the salience of informal community activities and usually revolves around neighborhood issues, school-related matters, or other locally based activities. Overall, the level of Latino informal activity is comparable to that for whites, Asian Americans, and African Americans. In table 6.5 we examine some possible internal variation across two important aspects of the Latino community: gender and nativity. An understanding of Latino political participation needs to go beyond an overall summary of activities to explore specific inner-group characteristics. Again, we look across the four racial and ethnic groups. The extent of political activity engagement for Latinas and Latinos reveals that a greater percentage of Latinas do not have any involvement in the seven political activities (16 percent vs. 10.4 percent). On the other hand, slightly more Latinas participate in at least one activity (47.7 percent) compared to 42.4 percent of Latinos. As we move to those with more activities, a slight gender gap does appear. Obviously, it would be important to qualitatively distinguish the specific types of activities that might differentiate higher levels of engagement by gender for Latinas versus Latinos. Our comparisons between native-born Latinos and foreign-born Latinos find more similarity than difference.

TABLE 6.5 Range of Political Activities CMPS Respondents Engaged In by Gender and Nativity

Race and Ethnic Groups

Civic/Political Activities Engaged In[a]	White Female	White Male	Latino Female	Latino Male	African American Female	African American Male	Asian American Female	Asian American Male
None	81[b] (12.7)	37 (9.5)	325 (16.0)	100 (10.4)	309 (14.4)	113 (11.8)	316 (17.6)	209 (17.3)
One	270 (42.2)	124 (31.7)	971 (47.7)	407 (42.4)	953 (44.5)	392 (41.0)	907 (50.6)	509 (42.2)
Two	92 (14.4)	75 (19.2)	296 (14.5)	154 (16.0)	319 (14.9)	134 (14.0)	244 (13.6)	166 (13.8)
Three	78 (12.2)	53 (13.6)	220 (10.8)	124 (12.9)	244 (11.4)	124 (13.0)	158 (8.8)	144 (11.9)
Four	46 (7.2)	38 (9.7)	91 (4.5)	70 (7.3)	135 (6.3)	77 (8.1)	87 (4.9)	88 (7.3)
Five or more	73 (11.4)	64 (16.3)	133 (6.5)	106 (11.0)	183 (8.5)	116 (12.1)	81 (4.5)	90 (7.5)
	US Born	Born Outside US	US Born	Born Outside US	US Born	Born Outside US	US Born	Born Outside US
None	112 (11.4)	6 (8.8)	302 (14.2)	98 (13.6)	397 (14.2)	25 (12.7)	300 (18.3)	228 (16.6)
One	380 (38.6)	15 (22.1)	954 (44.8)	358 (49.7)	1,246 (44.4)	100 (50.8)	734 (44.9)	682 (49.7)
Two	156 (15.9)	11 (16.2)	314 (14.7)	114 (15.8)	426 (15.2)	28 (14.2)	218 (13.3)	193 (14.1)
Three	123 (12.5)	8 (11.8)	250 (11.7)	78 (10.8)	348 (12.4)	20 (10.2)	163 (10.0)	141 (10.3)
Four	80 (8.1)	4 (5.9)	127 (6.0)	27 (3.7)	203 (7.2)	9 (4.6)	107 (6.5)	69 (5.0)
Five or more	133 (13.5)	24 (35.3)	184 (8.6)	46 (6.4)	185 (6.6)	15 (7.6)	113 (6.9)	58 (4.2)

Source: Data for this table was derived from analysis of the 2016 CMPS.

Note: The Collaborative Multiracial Post-Election Survey is a national survey of voters and nonvoters on political and social issues conducted post-election. Since 2016, the CMPS is conducted via the internet, and it is one of the few surveys that includes enough respondents to do across racial group analysis. The CMPS is currently housed at UCLA.

[a] The activities that each respondent was asked to answer either yes or no to were: take some action on an issue or in an election; participate in social, cultural, or civic organization; regularly attend meetings; discuss politics with family and friends; contacted an elected representative or governmental official; contacted an official in any way about a problem; and worked or cooperated with others to solve a local problem.

[b] The numbers in the columns are the actual number of respondents, and the numbers in the parentheses represent the percentage of respondents.

Comparable levels of both nonparticipation as well as involvement in political activities is evident. Native-born Latinos have higher numbers of activities than foreign-born Latinos. Unfamiliarity with the US political system, lower English-language proficiency, and, perhaps, lower political efficacy have been posited as important factors for less political engagement by foreign-born (García and de la Garza 1985; Barreto and Muñoz 2003; de la Garza and Yang 2015). In a period of strong polarization regarding immigration, "fitting into the American fabric, and perceived negative economic impact are stimuli for greater political involvement that cut across gender and nativity 'lines'" (Pastor, Scoggins, and López 2016).

A newer development in Latino political engagement and mobilization is the role of the internet and social-networking venues. In the previous edition, we relied on the Pew Research Center Internet and American Life project (2015). This study examined both online and offline political engagement and the role of social networking in people's political activities. A similar survey was conducted in 2008 in which the percentage of social-network users had grown from 33 percent to 69 percent. Currently, we make use of the 2016 CMPS that includes several items on internet/social media use as well as perceived effectiveness of social media for specific political activities.

As seen in table 6.6, the CMPS recorded the responses of participants who had engaged in civic/political activities with the use of social media. The three areas were discussion of politics with family and friends, signing petitions, and general use of social media to express concerns. Over one-third of Latino respondents (35 percent) use social media to discuss politics, which is comparable to white and African American counterparts. Not surprising given the literature suggesting that social media use for politics is heightened among millennials (Macias Mejia 2019; Livaudais, Vargas, and Sanchez 2020), we see higher use of social media to discuss politics among younger Latinos in the CMPS data. The general experience with petition circulation is more of a face-to-face interaction, but wider reach and facility to collect signatures now makes use of signing online. Two-thirds of Latinos who do sign a petition do so online, which seems to be the trend. Interestingly, more than four-fifths of Asian Americans sign online.

Finally, respondents were asked if use of social media is an effective way to express concerns about issues. When combining the "very important" and "somewhat important" responses, almost one-half of Latinos answered affirmatively. This combined total is higher than white and Asian American responses. Clearly, there is evidence that the creation and use of social media reflects the existence of social networks in which personal connections can have impact and influence over others' attitudes and behaviors. On a parallel body of research, political mobilization is more effective when there is a personal tie and when one is a fellow co-ethnic (Michelson, García Bedolla, and McConnell 2009; Michelson 2003b). Over the past three or four election cycles, campaigns have made greater use of social media and identifying social networks to get their message out there.

Table 6.7 goes a bit further with use of social media. CMPS respondents were asked to assess the importance of social media across a range of political activities. They included: contacting a public official, voice heard by rioting, voice heard by voting, and voice heard by nonviolent protest. For all these activities, except for rioting, Latinos expressed that social media is an important use for change. Especially in the case of voting, almost three-fourths of Latinos responded affirmatively. In the next chapter we will discuss the electoral arenas and the vote. Similarly, contacting public officials

TABLE 6.6 Participation on Social Media and Civic and Political Engagement among CMPS Respondents in Percentages

	Racial and Ethnic Groups			
Social Media Activities	White	Latino	African American	Asian American
Do you discuss candidates or issues on social media?				
Yes	32	35	34	25
No	68	65	66	75
Signed a petition on issue of concern[a]				
Online	66	66	67	81
Hardcopy	34	34	33	19
Perceived importance of using social media to express concerns about issues				
Very Important	9	17	22	9
Somewhat Important	29	32	30	31
Not That Important	25	21	19	31
Not at All[b]	24	14	14	15

Source: Data for this table was derived from analysis of the 2016 CMPS.
Note: The Collaborative Multiracial Post-Election Survey is a national survey of voters and nonvoters on political and social issues conducted post-election. Since 2016, the CMPS is conducted via the internet, and it is one of the few surveys that includes enough respondents to do across racial group analysis. The CMPS is currently housed at UCLA.
[a] The respondents are those who previously answered affirmatively to having signed a petition in the last twelve months.
[b] The percentages for "Don't Know" are not present but in combination with other responses will total to 100 percent.

TABLE 6.7 Perceived Effectiveness by Percentages of CMPS Respondents of Different Political Tactics by Use of Social Media

	Racial and Ethnic Groups			
Different Political Tactics	White	Latinos	African Americans	Asian Americans
Contacting public officials through social media				
Very/Somewhat Important	63	62	70	63
Not That Important/Not at All	36[a]	38	30	37
Important to get voice heard by rioting				
Very/Somewhat Important	7	23	28	18
Not That Important/Not at All	90	77	72	82
Important to get voice heard by voting				
Very/Somewhat Important	76	72	78	74
Not That Important/Not at All	24	29	22	25
Important to get voice heard by nonviolent protests				
Very/Somewhat Important	56	66	75	65
Not That Important/Not at All	45	34	24	35

Source: Data for this table was derived from analysis of the 2016 CMPS.
Note: The Collaborative Multiracial Post-Election Survey is a national survey of voters and nonvoters on political and social issues conducted post-election. Since 2016, the CMPS is conducted via the internet, and it is one of the few surveys that includes enough respondents to do across racial group analysis. The CMPS is currently housed at UCLA.
[a] Some groups' additive respondents add up to less than 100 percent due to rounding.

and using social media with nonviolent protest can reflect the changing mediums for communication. One other question regarding this rising use of social media, in so many facets of our lives, is who are the primary users of the social media? From table 6.7, we can see that Latinos are not the only group that uses social media, and their use has become a major vehicle for politics and campaigns. While there is still an internet divide (Brown et al. 2016), technological development, especially the smartphone, has enabled access to the internet without use of traditional desktops and/or laptops. The earlier Pew study of the internet and social media reveals that the use of online or internet media is generally lower among older respondents. The eighteen- to twenty-four-year-old age group is more active and engaged online.

We found from the earlier mentioned Pew study on internet and social media (2015) that interpersonal engagement among the survey respondents represents opportunities to express one's views/opinions, as well as to persuade others to rethink their views and take some action. Overall, more people engage in political discussions "offline" (76 percent vs. 44 percent), cutting uniformly across gender, age groupings, and, to some extent, racial/ethnic groups. In the case of the latter, Latinos rank 9–10 percent lower in engaging in political discussions. When it comes to online political discussions, younger respondents are the segment primarily involved. The fact that there is such a difference between online and media-driven engagement and more direct, personal exchange has implications for Latinos. More recent mobilization studies (Ramírez 2005; Michelson 2003b) have demonstrated that face-to-face contact, as opposed to robo-calls or mailings, is more effective in getting Latinos to vote or engage in other forms of participation. In addition, having a co-ethnic connection makes for a more effective mobilizing impact.

Latino Millennials: Distinctive and Growing Political Power

When discussing Latinos and American politics, the changing demography of this nation comes into play. Whether it is the changing racial-ethnic diversity, increases in foreign-born populations, or the aging of this society, these changes have political ramifications. We now define generations in the United States by marking cutoff birthdates and associated names. They are: Gen Z, iGen, or Centennials—born after 1996; Millennials or Gen Y—born 1981–96; Generation X—born 1965–1980; Baby Boomers—born 1946–1964; and Traditionalists or Silent Generation—born before 1946. Latinos continue to be about ten years younger (median age) than non-Hispanics. As a result, it is not unexpected that Latino millennials are the largest subgroup, representing 26 percent of all Latinos. If we include Generation Z, they make up 32 percent of all Latinos (Krogstad et al. 2016). Another important statistic is that approximately 900,000 to 1,000,000 Latinos turn age eighteen annually. We highlight this demographic trend to link it to the continued political development of Latino civic and political engagement.

As we have discussed in more detail in chapter 3, millennials comprise a larger share of the voting-eligible Latino population than other racial and ethnic groups in the United States. We are learning more about Latino millennials, particularly about their political orientations, behaviors (i.e. voting, policy areas of interest, other forms of engagement, etc.). For example, the Mi Familia Voto organization (2018) reports that, in general, Latino millennials are interested in matters of education, the economy,

FIGURE 6.1 Distribution of Generations as a Percentage of the Eligible Voters, 2000–2020

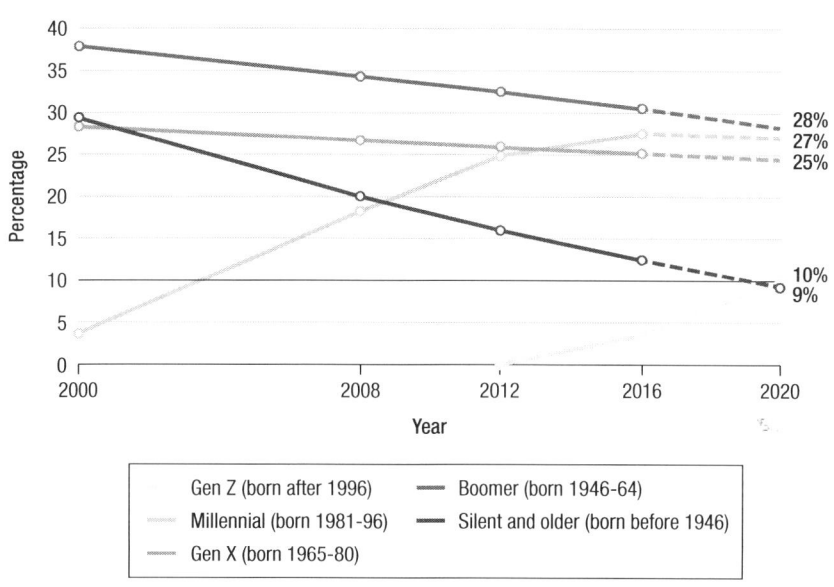

Source: Data from 2000 to 2016 from Pew Research Center analysis of 2000 decennial census and 2008, 2012, and 2016 American Community Survey (IPUMS). Data for 2020 from Pew Research Center projections of the electorate based on US Census Bureau 2017 population projections.

the health system, national security, climate change, and immigration. In the case of the latter area (immigration) the Hispanic Heritage Foundation (Yanez 2018) points to the Latino millennials' "intrinsic ties to the immigrant narrative." Works on the DACA registrants (Gonzales et al. 2014; Ellis et al. 2019) show how relevant politics and public policies are regarding normalizing their status in the United States, in addition to basic issues of equity and social justice.

In figure 6.1, we present a graphic of the composition of the Latino community by generation. Their trend lines reinforce our earlier narrative as to the sizable proportion Gen X and Z comprise of the total Latino community. Politically, Latino millennials make up 44 percent of the eligible voters (see figure 6.2). Relative to other racial and ethnic groups, no others have near the percentage of millennials. While a higher percentage of millennials are English proficient, they exhibit a pride in being Latino/a. On the other hand, only 20 percent of Latino millennials voted in the last midterm election. In addition, Latino millennials show distrust toward institutions and the two major political parties (Mi Familia Voto 2018). Despite the two youngest generations being the growth sectors for Latinos, there are challenges of lower voter registration and turnout and being "civically alienated" (Pew Research Center 2016).

We will discuss the electoral arenas and participation more specifically in the next chapter. Ideologically, Latino millennials are more self-identified liberals than the other generations (almost by one-third more). It should be noted that our data source is a poll of likely voters,[4] which will exclude noncitizens, less-frequent voters, and persons with low interest in the coming election. Millennials also are more supportive of

FIGURE 6.2 Proportion of Millennials' Share of the Major Racial and Ethnic Groups, 2016

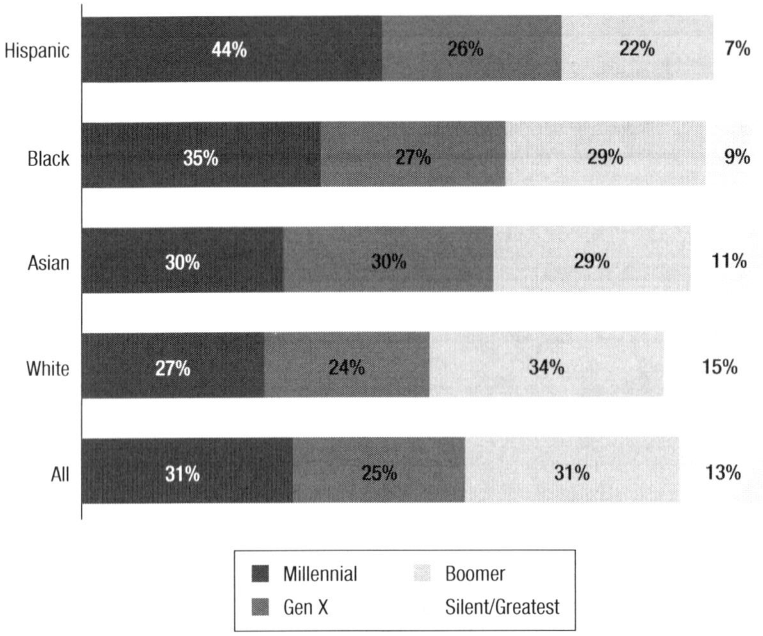

Group	Millennial	Gen X	Boomer	Silent/Greatest
Hispanic	44%	26%	22%	7%
Black	35%	27%	29%	9%
Asian	30%	30%	29%	11%
White	27%	24%	34%	15%
All	31%	25%	31%	13%

Source: Pew Research Center; see "Methodology" for details on 2016 projection.

progressive public policies addressing climate change, to the extent of the state going its own way to pass legislation independent of federal actions (72 percent).

Other Dimensions of Latino Political Participation

The role of political knowledge serves as a base for pursuing political interest, determining political assessment, and pursuing possible political actions (Galston 2001; Eveland and Hively 2009; Tolbert, McNeal, and Smith 2003). While the traditional sources for political information have been newspapers, television, and friends, the pervasiveness of the internet has changed that pattern. That is, finding directions, consumer goods, medical information, and many other areas of interest brings large numbers of people to the internet. Table 6.8 shows that among SNS (social networking service) respondents, 43 percent decided to learn more about a political/social issue because of what they read on social networks, particularly those younger than forty-nine. So how did that additional increase of information translate to the next step of acting? In this case, only one in five SNS respondents took any form of action; it was slightly greater for younger people and whites. For Latinos, it was only approximately one in nine. Because there is generally a drop-off between the gathering of information and acting, interactions with others can serve as an important catalyst.

The Latino National Survey provided information about a range of political activities. The act of contacting a political official is a relatively less common action. Considerations such as social status, levels of educational attainment, political knowledge, and political interest serve as resources and motivation to contact a public official. In table 6.9, the LNS respondents were asked if they had contacted a public

TABLE 6.8 How Social Media Influences More Political Involvement

	Percentage of SNS Users Who Have	
	Decided to Learn More about a Political/Social Issue Because of What They Read on SNS	Decided to Take Action on a Political/Social Issue Because of What They Read on SNS
Total for SNS Users ($N = 1209$)	43%	18%
Gender		
Men ($N = 525$)	44%	17%
Women ($N = 684$)	43%	18%
Age		
18–29 ($N = 323$)	48%	19%
30–49 ($N = 388$)	47%	17%
50–64 ($N = 323$)	35%	18%
65+ ($N = 167$)	30%	15%
Race/Ethnicity		
White, Non-Hispanic ($N = 847$)	46%	20%
Black, Non-Hispanic ($N = 143$)	38%	12%
Hispanic ($N = 136$)	34%	11%

Source: Adapted from Pew Research Center's Internet and American Life Project, July 16–August 7, 2012 Tracking Survey.
Note: SNS stands for social networking service.

TABLE 6.9 Contacting Officials by Generation and Citizenship among Respondents to the Latino National Survey

Response	Freq.	First Generation			Second+ Generation Citizen	Grand Total
		Noncitizen	Citizen	Total		
Yes	Freq.	657	750	1,407	1,122	2,529
	Row %	46.70	53.30	55.64	44.36	100.00
	Col %	17.21	38.36	24.37	41.48	29.83
No	Freq.	3,161	1,205	4,366	1,583	5,949
	Row %	72.40	27.60	73.39	26.61	100.00
	Col %	82.79	61.64	75.63	58.52	70.17
Total	Freq.	3,818	1,955	5,773	2,705	8,478
	Row %	66.14	33.86	68.09	31.91	100.00
	Col %	100.00	100.00	100.00	100.00	100.00

Question wording: "Have you ever tried to get government officials to pay attention to something that concerned you, either by calling, writing a letter, or going to a meeting?"
Table Tests of Independence: First and second+ generations: Chi-square (2 d.f.) 257.376 (P = 0.000). Citizen/noncitizen (first generation only): Chi-square (2 d.f.) 461.307 (P = 0.000).
Source: Fraga et al. 2006a.
Note: Island-born Puerto Ricans are coded as first generation.

official regarding a concern or issue. The categories in this table break down the Latino respondents into generational status and citizen status. Latino citizen and first generation are more likely to contact a public official. It might be expected that noncitizens would contact public officials less often than citizens; being a voter (or prospective voter) can be perceived as having more weight with a public official. Age and social status are key factors. In any event, this aspect of political behavior has political significance in that more motivation and knowledge are required, but such contact may involve more that the individual's circumstances. He or she may be approaching a public official for matters impacting the community, other Latinos, immigrants, and the like.

As more than half of Latino adults are foreign-born, factors such as assimilation, acculturation, and longer exposure to American society would suggest an upward participatory slope across generations (Segura and Santoro 2004). We examined contact with elected officials for the first and second generation and beyond. Also, we differentiated the foreign-born into noncitizens and naturalized citizens. Second-generation and beyond Latinos are two and a half times more likely to contact a public official than noncitizens. Naturalized citizens almost mirror the level of contact of second-generation and beyond individuals. These differentials can be the result of lesser familiarity with American politics among the foreign-born, a lower sense of the efficacy of and less trust in agents of US political institutions, a hostile climate directed toward immigrants, and lower levels of English-language proficiency than their native-born counterparts. The distinction of generation has become an important area of research on Latinos (García 2009) and can further define the political map of Latino political participation.

A participatory set of attitudes or orientations can serve to enhance involvement. People who are more interested in and informed about politics, political actors, and public policies tend to be more politically engaged. Our discussion regarding table 6.1 presented the extent of interest in politics and public affairs among Latinos in the CMPS. The small difference between US-born and foreign-born Latinos' interest could be due to the more contemporary hostile climate directed toward Latinos and foreigners. In this regard, there is an overlap of perceptions that Latinos are an immigrant group, whereas demographics indicate the majority of Latinos are US-born and that percentage will increase over time. Those Latinos showing some interest in politics represent opportune targets for leaders and organized interests in connecting their concerns and awareness with concrete political actions and issues. The general literature concerning levels of political interest indicates that higher socioeconomic status and greater educational attainment, personal and political efficacy, and economic resources are major contributors (Verba, Scholzman, and Brady 1995). In the case of Latinos, the added dimension of ethnic group consciousness, as well as the political climate, can be contributors to becoming more politically aware and being more inclined to get involved. This distinction between native and foreign-born persons may be less dividing with the rise of mixed-status households, geographic proximity across nativity status, and the general public image of Latinos as undifferentiated by nativity. At the same time, mobilization messaging might be tailored to different segments of the Latino community (i.e., gender, region, nativity, generation, etc.).

The attitudes of efficacy, trust, and cynicism/alienation are quite relevant in our participation discussion. People who are psychologically oriented toward participation and its relevance to their lives are more likely to be politically involved. Knowledge, interest, and personal and political efficacy all contribute to active involvement. Our presentation in table 6.2 indicates a lessening of a participatory gap for Latinos relative to other racial and ethnic groups and summarizes participatory scores for all respondents, males and females. Interestingly, the disparities by nativity and gender do reflect the need to expand Latinas' engagement across a wider range of political activities by the different indicators. While Latinas have a higher percentage of at least one political activity, a higher percentage of Latinos tend to have a greater number of cumulated political activities. Political efficacy in this chapter is reflective by CMPS respondents evaluating the effectiveness of different political activities. Voting, contacting officials, and engaging in nonviolent protest are viewed as important and effective. Thus, the participation model that includes personal resources, participatory orientations, and mobilization is quite applicable and, over time, marks progress for Latinos.

In chapter 7, we will give more attention to the electoral arena (i.e., voter turnout and registration, partisanship, electoral activities) while, in this chapter, we are looking at nonelectoral activities. We also note that the political arenas for Latino political participation range from the neighborhood, town/city, state, and national. It is the local arena that is characterized more by case studies and local peculiarities to each community. Nonetheless, local communities represent the "on ground" experiences of Latinos addressing their political and policy concerns (i.e., from representation, unmet policy needs, service delivery and responsiveness, etc.). In this work on Latino politics, it is difficult to deal specifically with local political dynamics in substantial detail.

We provide some insights into the local educational arena and Latinos' participation. Education has ranked consistently as an important policy concern for Latinos, especially parents who hold high educational aspirations and attainment to enhance their children's futures (Martinez-Ebers et al. 2000).

The LNS educational battery of questions asked Latino parents whom they had contact with in the schools. A summary of the LNS findings found that 90.3 percent of Latino parents had met with their children's teacher, though this was truer for Latinas (63 percent) than for their Latino counterparts (37 percent). A very high level of contact at the "ground floor" of the school system does challenge some common notions about Latinos' values for their children's educational attainment and quality, such as the notion of Latino parents not valuing education and being less involved in school matters. Similar questions were also asked pertaining to contact with the school principal, attending school board meetings, and attending PTA meetings. The extent of PTA meeting attendance by generation and citizenship status revealed that Latino attendance is high. In fact, first-generation or foreign-born parents are more likely to attend PTA meetings than second-generation and beyond parents. Naturalized and non-naturalized Latinos show no difference in this regard. Examination of meeting attendance by marital status with children in the household shows that foreign-born Latinos are more likely to be married with school-age children.

Latino parents' involvement as volunteers at their child's school indicated that a majority (52.9 percent) responded affirmatively. Second-generation and beyond parents had the highest incidence of volunteering (66.7 percent), followed by naturalized citizens (56.7 percent), with noncitizen parents at 47.8 percent. This would suggest that given the level of Latino parental involvement in education, with some variations based upon gender and generational status, changes in institutional conditions and situations (i.e., access, language capacities to deal with non-English-speaking parents and students) warrant inclusion into a broader picture of the political world of Latinos.

A final tier of parental involvement deals with parents' interactions with school officials. A relatively small percentage had had no contact with school officials (6.2 percent). On the other hand, those parents who rated the interaction with school officials as very good differed little by gender (53.01 percent for males versus 55.71 percent for females). Similar percentages of men and women (6.62 percent versus 5.85 percent, respectively) indicated not good contact or not too good. Continued research regarding the Latino community's concerns about the quality of education and access to decision making is necessary and reflects the educational arena as one of civic and political engagement.

In a later chapter, we will discuss educational policies and their importance for Latinos. Some studies (Meier and Stewart 1991) cite low socioeconomic status, immigrant background, and cultural barriers to explain low Latino involvement. Other studies (Carter and Segura 1979; San Miguel 1987) see levels of aspirations and commitment to children's educational attainment, significant percentages of Latinos in the school-age ranges, and a base of immigrants who seek to improve their children's future as indicators of Latino support and interest in education. Yet, recent research by Leal and Meier (2011) has indicated how increased representation of Latinos as elected school board officials, administrators, and teachers has a positive effect on Latino involvement in the schools and higher levels of perceived responsiveness. They also present the parallel challenges of achieving educational quality with an expanding Latino immigrant population, greater degrees of racial/ethnic school segregation, and "second generation" disciplinary policies (Murillo et al. 2009; Portes et al. 2014). Zambrana and Hurtado (2015) also reinforce the challenges facing Latino students in the K–12 grades, as well as Latinos in higher education (i.e., institutional climate, preparedness, support services, etc.). Finally, educational reform, particularly with educational standards and accountability (i.e., **No Child Left Behind Act** [NCLB] and Common Core), pushes this policy area into the national arena (San Miguel and Donato 2009).

Our discussion of Latino political participation portrays a population that has, in the last decade, demonstrated increasing levels of civic and political engagement, although it is somewhat less active than its non-Latino counterparts. These developments have been quite evident in the electoral area and direct actions like protests and demonstrations.

Analyzing the Contributors to Latino Political Participation

Our discussion of political participation has drawn from the general research literature on political participation, with some "wrinkles" of factors more specific to Latinos' backgrounds and experiences. Political participation centers on both individuals and groups who try to influence the policy-making process. In the political arena, political resources are critical for active involvement. While Latinos have been characterized as less politically involved than other segments of the American body politic, contemporary research results both challenge that pattern and identify the factors that can either facilitate greater involvement or impair it.

Clearly the demographic profile of Latinos reveals a mixture of liabilities and potentials. Liabilities include a youthful population, a significant foreign-born subcommunity, relatively lower levels of educational attainment, a greater proportion of non-English or limited-English speakers, lower rates of organizational affiliation and involvement, lower income levels and higher rates of poverty, and low rates of naturalization. Assets include a rapidly growing population that will also increase its proportion of the adult population, population concentrations in populous states and metropolitan areas, the rise of organizational capacities and experienced leadership, effective mobilization strategies, a hostile climate directed toward Latinos, and a slowly improving socioeconomic status. The contemporary "external" factor is the national climate that ties nativist animosities, in which Latinos as a community have been stigmatized as not really American and resistant to becoming part of the American mainstream. This rhetoric and corresponding "punitive policies" (i.e., militarization of the border, restricting access to social services, **denaturalization** efforts, etc.) can serve to activate more Latinos for political engagement.

The liabilities identified have a direct effect on the extent of political resources that come with being youthful, having a lower socioeconomic status, and having a significant immigrant segment. The youthfulness of Latinos tends to be negatively associated with high rates of political participation. Younger persons are less oriented to organizational and community involvement and less interested in politics. At the same time, more research is being directed toward the political socialization process among young Latinos (both native and foreign-born) and their impact on the political socialization of foreign-born parents (García-Castañon 2010). The participation of Latino youths in immigrant protest marches indicates that mobilization efforts can have success with this segment, as can the use of social media as evidenced in the presidential campaign of Barack Obama, which resonated well with younger voters (García 2014). Also, the means of communicating with younger Latinos has opened newer avenues of outreach for groups and movements (Krogstad et al. 2016; Zepeda-Millán 2017).

The relatively lower levels of education and income afford Latinos fewer opportunities and resources of time, knowledge, information, and money to get involved. The significant proportion of foreign-born Latinos presents several potential liabilities. For one thing, the legal status of "resident alien"[5] places limitations on electoral involvement because permanent resident aliens cannot register or vote. Naturalization requirements (including higher fees), as well as continued connections to the mother country, may keep naturalization rates lower for Latino immigrants than the overall average for all immigrants. In addition, some research (García 1981a; DeSipio and de la Garza 1998) indicates that levels of political integration, involvement, and knowledge are lower for immigrant populations. Similarly, they have lower rates of organizational affiliation and participation. Again, recent work on transnationalism and its political "effects" (Segura 2007; Portes, Escobar, and Arana 2008; García 2013b) on political and civic engagement indicates a complementary effect of being transnationally engaged and investing more in US civic life. Obviously, we must move away from popular notions of "the myth dream of return" (Jones-Correa 2009) and the lack of political knowledge and sophistication of immigrants (Renshon 2009) to develop a deeper and more complex examination of the political world of the Latino foreign-born.

The assets related to this Latino profile are manyfold. The Latino community's continued high growth creates a substantial political base from which to mobilize and exercise political influence. Since 2010, at least one-half million Latinos turned age eighteen, adding to the electoral base (Bendixen 2011). In addition, the concentration of Latinos in nine states (more than 90 percent of all Latinos are found in California, Texas, New York, and Florida)[6] has 10 percent residing in highly urban areas and more populous states. Recently, Latinos began to transform this population potential into political activity in California, with gains in the state legislature and municipalities. Also, several ballot propositions (Propositions 187, 209, and 227)[7] heightened Latino interest and involvement in elections. Recent increases in Latinos migrating to the South and the Midwest are reshaping the racial-ethnic makeup of those regions (Popke 2011; McConnell 2008).

In 2009, Arizona Senate Bill 1070 empowered state and local enforcement personnel to question the legal status of individuals in the process of conducting their law enforcement functions. Latinos were the main (if not the exclusive) targets of this legislation. Additional states also passed numerous laws that targeted undocumented immigrants and affected the larger Latino community (Ybarra, Sanchez, and Sanchez 2016). These more restrictive and punitive laws directed toward undocumented immigrants have been passed in southern states, which have seen a significant influx of Latinos (Ybarra, Sanchez, and Sanchez 2016; Jones-Correa and de Graauw 2013). Latinos have responded by mobilizing locally and across the nation to protect their rights and seek greater policy responsiveness from political institutions and parties (Barreto et al. 2009; Cano 2004). The mobilization process and its political effects are becoming more evident in the Latino community. This is due in part to an ever-evolving, higher level of political development and external factors (i.e., negative governmental actions, hostile public opinions, polarizing viewpoints, scapegoating) that serve to heighten Latinos' political interest, awareness, and motivation to engage in collective political behaviors.

Other developments affecting Latino political participation include the concentration of Latinos in residential areas of cities and towns throughout the United States (Rocha and Espino 2010). It is found that a sense of group solidarity is enhanced by greater residential segregation (Viruell-Fuentes et al. 2013; Schwartz et al. 2006). At the same time, study results indicated that higher levels of segregation between Anglos and Latinos can dampen the positive relationship between Latino group size and participation in ethnic political causes (Pearson-Merkowitz 2012; Price et al. 2011; Wilcox-Archuleta 2018). Schildkraut (2005) explored the relationship between perceived levels of discrimination directed toward Latinos and the group they identify with socially (American, national-origin or pan-ethnic), and how they affect levels of political engagement. Perception of discrimination toward Latinos who identify themselves as Americans does stimulate both behavioral and attitudinal alienation (i.e., nonvoting and low trust) (Krogstad and Lopez 2016).

On the other hand, political alienation can be overcome with the presence of a pan-ethnic or national-origin identity. Schildkraut's results point to the motivating effects discrimination can have for individual and collective engagement. In addition, work by Fraga et al. (2012) that examines these three identity "options" makes a strong case that pan-ethnicity, Hispanic or Latino, is an American identity. It is born out of the experiences of Latinos in the United States and in response to conditions and interests in the US political system. Ironically, Michelson (2003a) shows how Mexican-origin people become more distrustful/cynical about American government as they further incorporate (i.e., acculturate) into and are exposed to mainstream American culture. Her explanation is that greater exposure results in becoming more aware or concerned about racism and discrimination.

Conclusion

This chapter has laid out the basis for political participation in America and how the Latino community does or does not conform to those patterns. For the past forty-five years, Latino political participation has been characterized as limited or marginal. At the same time, the social science knowledge base pertaining to Latinos has existed for only forty years, and the primary focus has been the Mexican-origin community. Only since the mid-1990s has research into Latino political participation been conducted and published more extensively (Hritzuk and Park 2000). Now we know more about the patterns of involvement for other Latino subgroups, primarily Puerto Ricans and Cubans, and to a greater degree, Central and South Americans. The added dimensions of Latinos' backgrounds (language, nativity, generational status, acculturation, and integration) and the external climate in which they live and are subjected to negative characterizations are also contributors to understanding Latino political engagement. The ongoing developments and continually changing situations for Latinos in the United States are dynamics that need attention when trying to understand Latino politics. The next chapter examines the electoral arena to explore Latino political participation further, looking at past and present voter-registration and turnout patterns, partisan candidate choices, partisan affiliation and ideology, and the development and role of Latino organizations. At the same time, the election of Latinos to office is a function of political interests, organizational density, political base, leadership, and opportunity structures.

This presents a challenging set of analytical questions. Does the political assertiveness of Latinos to ensure equal status and representation produce a more positive orientation toward governmental responsiveness? Or do individual efforts by Latinos to seek and win elected office increase the Latino community's perception of governmental nonresponsiveness? What level of support do Latinos have for co-ethnic candidates and officeholders? Obviously, these factors are very much interrelated, and understanding their relationship is critical to understanding what Latino politics involves.

Discussion Questions

1. Socialization effects, especially for children, have been found to be critical in shaping political attitudes, behaviors, and knowledge. For Latinos, a major segment of the population is foreign-born. What are the socialization effects on this segment of the Latino community?
2. In general, the overall levels of political participation for Latinos are lower than for non-Latinos. Discuss the factors involved and why Latinos do not participate in American politics.

3. While more attention is given to the electoral arena, nonelectoral political engagement is an important mode of participation. Explore ways in which Latinos engage in nonvoting behaviors and why they choose to do so.
4. Targeted mobilization can be quite effective in awakening Latinos to political engagement and directing them to specific kinds of actions. What are the key ingredients for effective political mobilization?
5. Millennials represent the largest generation among Latinos and appear to be socially aware and more critical of the US sociopolitical system relative to other generations. What can we can expect from this segment in the 2020s, and what are effective ways to mobilize them?

Notes

1. The principle of "the rules of the game" entails the requisites for political involvement (by a citizen or permanent resident alien), including knowledge of the political system, registered status, knowledge of access points to the political system, information about procedures and decision making, and so on.

2. The specific nonpolitical job skills asked about in the Verba, Scholzman, and Brady (1995) study are as follows: writing a letter, attending a meeting and participating in deciding, planning or chairing a meeting, and giving a presentation or speech.

3. The Collaborative Multiracial Post-Election Survey (CMPS) is a national survey of voters and nonvoters on political and social issues conducted post-election. Since 2016, the CMPS is conducted via the Internet, and it is one of the few surveys that includes enough respondents to do racial group analysis. The CMPS is currently housed at UCLA.

4. One of the values in American political culture is that "good citizens vote." But, as with many ideals, more people claim to vote than cast ballots. So, one problem election pollsters face is that not all respondents who tell them they plan to vote will do so. Actual turnout (known only after the election) is generally lower than respondents' self-reports of voting intentions in pre-election polls. Therefore, the pollster's challenge is to try to identify those who will really vote on Election Day and which ones will stay home (AAPOR, https://www.aapor.org/Education-Resources/Election-Polling-Resources/Likely-Voters.aspx).

5. Foreign-born persons living in the United States can be permanent resident aliens, can hold a temporary visa as a student or businessperson, or can be undocumented. The latter category includes individuals who come into this country illegally without formally petitioning the Immigration and Naturalization Service.

6. The nine states with the most Latinos are California, Texas, New York, Florida, New Jersey, Arizona, New Mexico, Illinois, and Massachusetts (in descending order of population size).

7. The propositions were state initiatives to enact policy in areas that directly impacted Latinos and made them the subject of targeted blame and/or perpetrators of the problem area. Proposition 187 would limit access to social services (medical, welfare) and public education to undocumented populations in California. Proposition 209 would remove state affirmative action provisions for employment and higher education in California. Finally, Proposition 227 would end bilingual programs as currently constituted in California and create transitional immersion programs for a one-year period.

CHAPTER 7

Latinos in the Electoral Arena

Su voto es su voz. Ya conozco este llamado desde mucho antes del comienzo de este siglo. Las decisiones, los candidatos, los temas, los derechos, las campañas y hasta adquirir más atencíon. ¿Y qué hago? ¿Con quién consulto, y sobre que? Ya basta. Me tengo que mover tengo que actuar.

Your vote is your voice. I know that call from long before the beginning of this century. Decisions, candidates, issues, rights, and campaigns—they all require attention. And what do I do? With whom do I consult and about what? Enough! I have to get going and act.

WITH OUR DISCUSSION AND ANALYSIS of political participation among Latinos, two themes are noted: (1) a pattern of generally lower rates of political participation with significant increases since 2004 in most arenas[1] of political involvement; and (2) this rise in civic engagement appears to be the result of immigration and perceived discrimination among Latinos becoming mobilizing factors. Since 2000, the Pew Hispanic Center, university research centers, the Latino National Survey,[2] and polling firms specializing in Latino populations have provided detailed and expansive profiles to help us understand Latino political and civic engagement. More recently, Latino Decisions was formed by a team of Latino politics experts to focus upon policy areas and political engagement of Latinos. These data sources have served to not only inform us about Latino politics but also to enable researchers and other interested parties to explore analytically the contributing and/or explanatory factors that define the dynamics of Latino politics.

In addition to social science research data sources, governmental reports (especially the Bureau of the Census), commercial polls, and media accounts have covered Latinos in the electoral arena (candidates, campaigns, fundraising, issues, partisanship, and elections). This chapter builds upon the last by taking a more focused look at Latino engagement in electoral politics, including their voter registration and voting rates, involvement in campaigns as volunteers or donors, or as candidates for elected office. As stated in the opening paragraph, the general characterization of Latinos in the national media has been that they are less active in politics than other groups in the United States. Lower voter-registration and voter-turnout rates are used as evidence of their less-than-active role. A major contributing factor to this historic pattern lies in the demographics of the Latino community, with a significant segment of the Latino population being unable to vote because they are either under the age of eighteen or immigrants who have yet to go through the naturalization process. In addition, data cited in chapter 6 indicates that Latinos participate less in campaigns and tend to donate less money to parties and candidates. As we will discuss in the following chapter, this may be the result of fewer Latinos running for office as candidates who could directly engage Latino constituents in this part of the political process.

We will also touch on how discrimination and policy climates can accent political alienation and cynicism that can depress participation yet can also be a mobilizing force when candidates and campaigns use them to cue a sense of ethnic identity. Finally, structural factors such as partisan redistricting, voter identification laws, and voter intimidation also affect Latinos' political engagement. This chapter examines the electoral participation of Latinos, focusing on emerging patterns that deviate from general notions of limited Latino electoral participation.

Setting the Electoral Scenario

Are Latinos a significant force in national elections, and what factors might influence how influential the Latino electorate is to electoral politics? How critical is Latino electoral support for winning elections? Do the major political parties seek out and respond to Latino interests and concerns? Our discussion of Latino electoral participation will focus largely on the national level and will explore the extent of bloc voting among Latinos for candidates and political parties. Effective Latino bloc voting has been seen as motivating Latinos to vote in unison for the same candidates and political party to provide one or the other with a winning margin. An effective Latino voting strategy is converting the community's large population base into a sizable registered and voting electorate, and, perhaps, directing their vote to benefit a specific political party and policy agenda. The potential political, economic, and cultural significance of continued population growth among Latinos hinges on conversion into a stronger voting force. This remains a high priority for Latino organizations and leadership.

The importance and coherence of identifiable policies and issues motivate Latinos to vote as well as become important constituencies for political parties and candidates. We will focus on this constellation of critical factors as we examine in detail the patterns and dynamics of Latino electoral participation. Yet, the universe of Latino political participation does not revolve exclusively around national elections and voting. An old axiom about politics is that all politics are local. In many respects, the proximity of local concerns and issues has initiated significant mobilization of Latino communities with carryover effects for other local, state, and national issues and movements. A good example of the effects of local and state governmental action is the advent of immigration-based laws (e.g., denial of driver's licenses, penalties for hiring or renting housing, detaining undocumented persons, etc.), which has galvanized Latinos (across legal status, class, language use, etc.) to challenge these laws through voting to counter more punitive immigration legislation. In a direct way, these local and state actions have elevated immigration as a central issue for the entire Latino community.

Latinos: Critical Determinant of Election Outcomes?

Historically, discussion of Latinos and presidential elections focused on close outcomes and which factors, voters, or both would influence the results. To some degree, with such close voting totals in many states, different voting blocs (e.g., the religious Right, labor, Latinos, African Americans) could indicate that their votes made the difference. A League of United Latin American Citizens (LULAC) white paper outlined a scenario in which the concentration of Latinos in Illinois, Texas, California, and New York could affect the outcome of the 1960 election. The basic premise revolved around Latino partisan bloc voting, and moderate turnout levels would make Democratic candidates the primary benefactors of the Latino vote. If the election were close, then the states with significant numbers of Electoral College votes would determine the outcome. States with a large number of electoral votes and high Latino concentrations were key ingredients in the LULAC white paper. The Kennedy-Nixon race produced one of the closest votes in American presidential history. Analysis of the Texas returns indicated that the Latino vote (primarily Mexican American) was a critical factor in John F. Kennedy's victory. Since that white paper, the "critical swing vote" thesis has been a major theme in discussions of Latino electoral participation at the national level.

Latinos number more than fifty-three million persons and constitute about 16 percent of the US population. The US Census Bureau population estimate projects that Latino growth will continue so that by 2050, Latinos will comprise one-fourth of the nation's population. The image of the community as largely immigrant is only partially true. While international migration from Latin America was significant during the 1980s and 1990s, the larger growth segment is among the native-born, especially the segment younger than age eighteen. Since 2000, native-born Latinos have outnumbered their foreign-born counterparts. The proportion of foreign-born is higher among Latino adults. The requirement that people born outside of the United States become naturalized in order to vote makes this an important distinction.

The data on naturalization and areas of population growth among Latinos tells a mixed story. Rates of naturalization for Latino immigrants have been increasing since the late 1990s (due in part to a more hostile anti-immigrant climate and policy initiatives, as well as promotion by Latino advocacy to encourage naturalization). The overall Latino electoral base is increasing at a faster rate than any other group's, largely due to significant increases among the youthful segment turning age eighteen. However, a very large segment of Latinos is unable to vote due to not being old enough or not having gone through the naturalization process.

During the last two election cycles, many political pundits have noted that every thirty seconds a US-born Latino turns age eighteen and becomes eligible to vote. In fact, roughly three million Latinos turned age eighteen from 2014 to 2018 (Flores and Lopez 2018a). This reflects the huge potential of Latinos' population growth due to being relatively young compared to non-Latinos. Although the relatively young age of the Latino electorate is a tremendous resource, Latinos still have lower voter turnout and registration than other youths.

The growth of the Latino electorate has also been fueled by naturalization. There were more than 420,000 Mexican-origin Latinos alone who became citizens and became eligible to vote between 2014 and 2017. Furthermore, and contrary to

FIGURE 7.1 Voter Turnout Rates of Naturalized Citizens

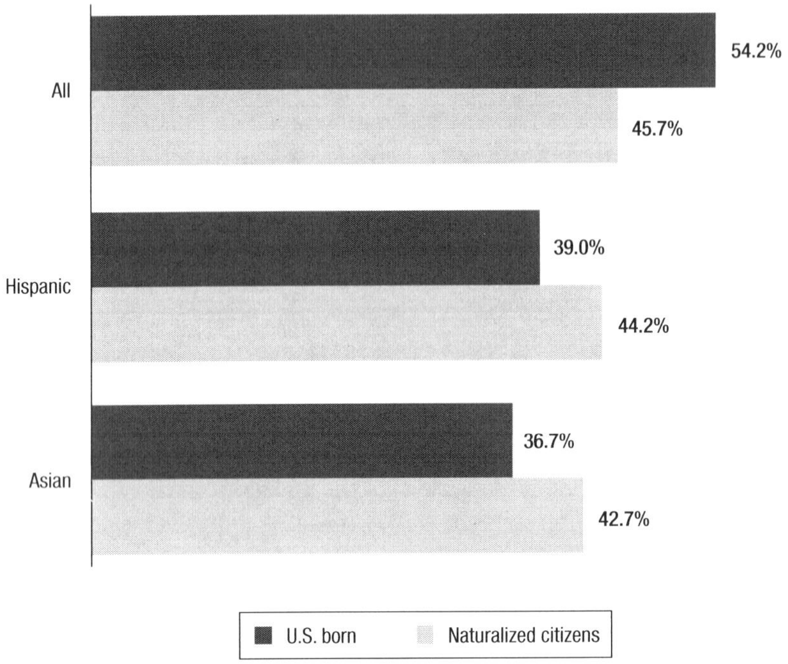

Group	U.S. born	Naturalized citizens
All	54.2%	45.7%
Hispanic	39.0%	44.2%
Asian	36.7%	42.7%

Source: Pew Research Center analysis of the 2018 Current Population Survey, November Supplement.

stereotypes about nativity and voter participation, naturalized Latino and Asian citizens register and vote at a rate about 8 to 10 percent higher than their native-born counterparts. As reflected in figure 7.1, foreign-born Hispanics had a 5 percent higher turnout rate in 2018 than their US-born counterparts. This trajectory is slowly closing the long-standing gap in voter turnout relative to other racial/ethnic groups, although the registration and particularly the turnout gap as compared to white and African American voters remains significant (see figure 7.1).

Naturalization is clearly an opportunity for increased growth in the Latino electorate. Of the 9 million immigrants eligible to naturalize, 4.95 million are Latinos. Rising costs and fewer English-language and naturalization classes have deterred some Latino immigrants from becoming citizens. Currently, there is an eighteen-month waiting period, so the foreign-born segment has faced a real challenge in moving through the citizenship pipeline. Research indicates that the hostile external climate and punitive policies directed toward Latinos have resulted in an important motivation to become more politically engaged. There is clear evidence of a greater number of organizational initiatives (e.g., NALEO) and support for the foreign-born segment. The heightened anti-immigrant climate has also accented unity across the Latino community, having a direct effect on higher rates of naturalization.

In 2016 a record-setting 27.3 million Latinos were eligible voters, a 4 million increase from 2012, which was the largest increase of any racial/ethnic group over the period (Bejarano 2016). This significant gap in Latino voter registration and voting speaks to the huge and unrealized potential of the Latino population to increase their

FIGURE 7.2 Percentage of US Latinos Eligible to Vote

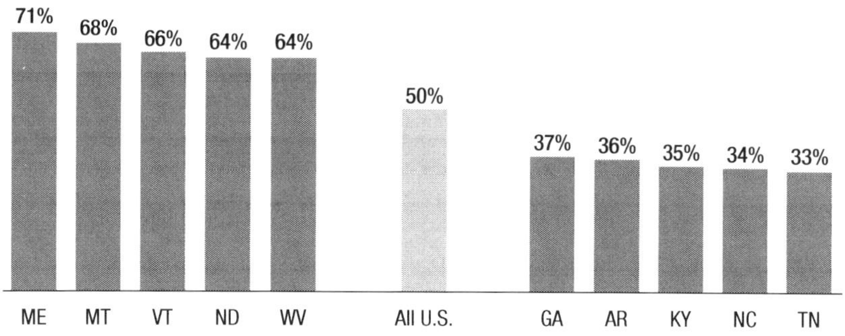

ME	MT	VT	ND	WV	All U.S.	GA	AR	KY	NC	TN
71%	68%	66%	64%	64%	50%	37%	36%	35%	34%	33%

Source: Pew Research Center.

political influence into the future. Latino Decisions analysis indicated that there were roughly 13 million Latinos who were eligible for voter registration but who did not register to vote, and if Latinos registered to vote at similar rates as whites and blacks, there would have been an additional 5 million Latinos on the voter rolls. This includes almost 990,000 eligible but not registered in the key battleground of Florida in 2016, and 458,000 in Arizona. This highlights the importance of voter registration efforts for Latino communities.

As we finish this book, the 2020 election is projected to continue this overall pattern. In 2020 it is expected that a record 32 million Latinos will be eligible to vote, making Latinos the largest racial and ethnic minority community in a US presidential election for the first time. This will equate to Latinos comprising roughly 13.3 percent of all eligible voters. While impressive, the number of Latino eligible voters is projected to remain much lower than the 60 million Latinos who are residents of the United States. As reflected in figure 7.2, only half of Latinos who live in the nation are eligible to vote, with much lower ratios across the southern states, including Georgia (37 percent), Arkansas (36 percent), and North Carolina (34 percent).

The two variables that work together to help assess Latinos' overall influence on presidential elections are their concentration in states and how politically competitive each state is. In short, if removing the Latino votes from a state's voting outcome would yield a different outcome, we generally can assume that Latinos were an influential voting bloc. For example, in 2020, Latinos were consequential to the presidential and US senate races in both Colorado and Arizona, two battleground states where Latinos have grown significantly over the past decade. Residence in key battleground states enhances their value to candidates and political parties, making Latinos who live in states like North Carolina and Virginia very important, despite relatively low Latino population numbers. Gross and Cuevas-Molina (2020) use a complex algorithm that includes the relative media attention Latinos garnered in 2016 to determine that Latinos had more overall influence in that election than they did in 2012. However, this growth in influence from 2012 was very modest, and definitely not as large as was projected given the presence of candidate Trump on the ballot after a significant growth in Latino eligible voters over the same period.

An evident theme for the future development of Latino political capital will be the conversion of political resources (i.e., growing adult populations and organizational development) into more concrete political gains. Such progress occurs when rates of voter registration and turnout improve from election to election. This motivates a discussion of the factors or interventions that could be engaged to improve Latino electoral participation. We draw from the literature focused on Latino electoral participation, some of which was also referenced in chapter 6.

Latino Voter Registration and Turnout: Patterns and Explanations

To register to vote in American elections, people must meet age and citizenship requirements. The Latino youth segment will produce more voter-eligible registrants, and additional mobilization efforts would aid their conversion into active voters. Recent gains in the naturalization rates among Latino immigrants are affected by a variety of factors: motivation and practical knowledge to pursue naturalization; the sociopolitical climate (both hostile, punitive, and structurally encouraging); the role of Latino organizations in facilitating the naturalization decision and process; and connections made between civic and political engagement and Latinos' collective interests. In the latter case, we are talking about a politicization process wherein Latino immigrants become more politically engaged and assess the value of becoming electorally eligible. As we will see in chapters 9 and 10, external factors such as anti-immigrant attitudes and referenda directed toward limiting Latino and immigrants' access and participation to social services, commerce, and employment have played a major role in motivating Latinos to become electorally involved, as well as to engage in other forms of political expression.

In figure 7.3, we see in greater detail the factors that influence permanent resident aliens (i.e., individuals who have sought and been approved for legal residence by the

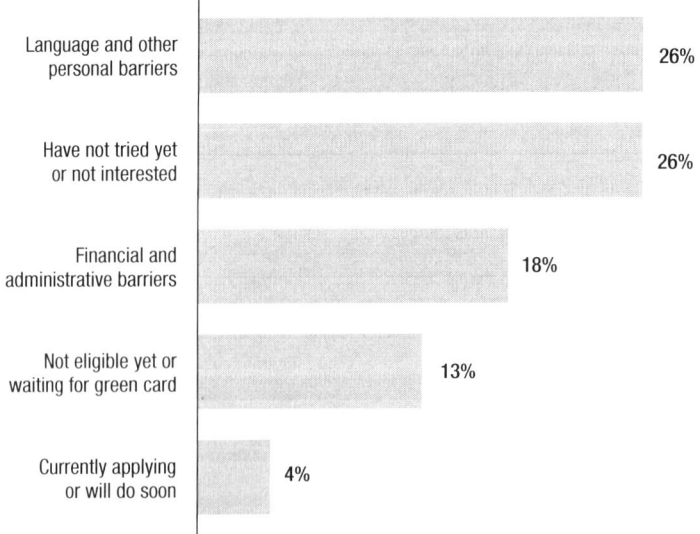

FIGURE 7.3 Main Reasons Eligible Latinos Have Not Naturalized

Source: Adapted from Pew Hispanic Center, 2012 National Survey of Latinos, Pew Research Center.

Immigration and Naturalization Service) to pursue or not pursue citizenship. If one combines language, personal, and financial/administrative reasons, that covers more than two-fifths of the main reasons. Personal reasons could include distrust of governmental agencies/officials, perceptions that the naturalization ceremony requires repudiation of all aspects of one's mother country, or negative experiences of other family members or friends. Conversely, another item on the Pew Survey of Latinos (Pew Hispanic Center 2014) asked those who pursued naturalization what their main reason was. While no single reason prevailed (all less than 20 percent), the top three reasons were to secure civil and legal rights, access to benefits and opportunities, and family reasons. Embedded in these rationales is a desire to integrate themselves more securely in the sociopolitical and economic arenas of life in America.

Overall, the percentage of voter registrants during this period has been relatively stable over time. It was once the case that there was a significant difference in voter registration by gender. However, the gender gap for male and female registration has disappeared over the past twenty years, and in 2011 women had higher registration rates. The differential between Hispanics and non-Hispanics remains significant. A comparison of Hispanic registration with that of Anglo registrants reveals a consistent fifteen-point or greater difference. Historically (i.e., going back to the period from 1960 through the 1990s) the gap was closer to an eighteen-point difference.

In figure 7.4, we can see a longer-term pattern among Latino registered voters, especially turnout. While the estimated numbers of Latino voters have risen considerably up to 2020, the number of eligible voters who did not vote still exceeds the number of Latino voters. The 2016 election outcome is symbolic of this larger trend. It is estimated that 14.8 million Latinos cast a vote in the 2020 election, an increase of 2.1 million relative to the 12.7 million Latino voters in 2016. However, the number

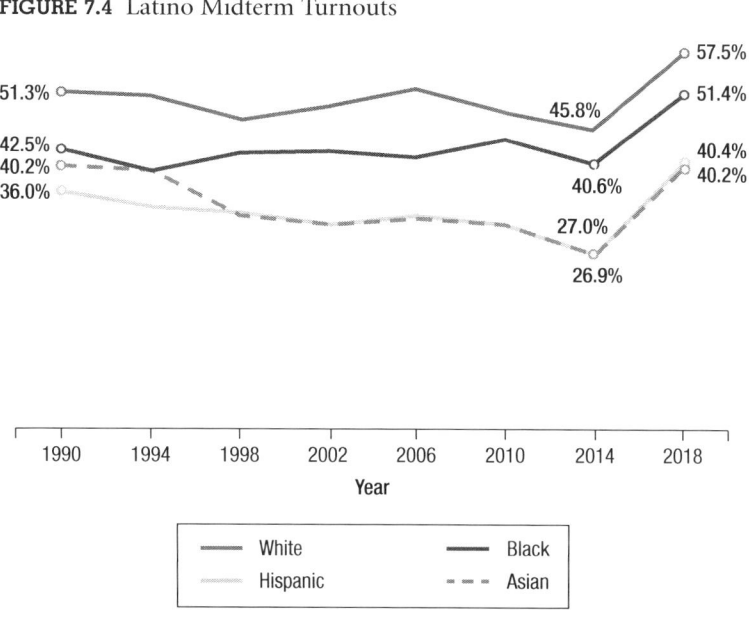

FIGURE 7.4 Latino Midterm Turnouts

Source: Pew Research Center/© Los Angeles Times.

of Latino eligible voters who decided to sit out the election exceeded the number of Latino voters by a wide margin in both 2016 and 2018, as reflected in the figure below (Krogstad et al. 2019). It appears as though 2020 followed the same pattern, with 14.8 million Latinos estimated to have voted relative to 32 million who were eligible.

While the gap has not decreased dramatically, the proportion of Latinos as a share of the total electorate has increased noticeably. As we indicated earlier, a combination of factors comes into play in assessing Latinos' electoral clout (i.e., growth as share of electorate, location in key states or central cities, conversion of the youth segment into active participants, expanded and effective mobilization efforts, and salient issues serving to provide concerted political capital for Latinos and elections).

It is important in examining voter-registration figures to determine how the base population is calculated. For example, voting age population (VAP) takes eighteen as the age baseline; from this, one can determine the registration rate based on all persons who are eighteen and older (VAP = population 18+). For Latinos, this would produce a lower percentage due to a higher percentage of foreign-born adults. The alternative base is the voting eligible population (VEP), which takes into consideration both age and citizenship status. If we remove noneligible Latinos (i.e., noncitizens), the gap is closed by half. Similarly, if we compare the percentage vote based on the registered voters only, then the gap between Latinos and non-Latino whites is 10 to 12 percent. From 2000 to 2018, the percentage of Latino registered voters ranged from 57.3 to 59.4 percent. The earlier registration figures (i.e., 1992 and 1996) reflect a VAP baseline (thus a lower percentage) for those election years. Nevertheless, the registration gap is closing, albeit slowly.

American voter turnout overall has been variable over this period (ranging from 47.8 to 63.8 percent). The 1996 election marked the lowest presidential turnout in the latter part of the twentieth century. That decline in voter turnout cuts across all racial and Hispanic-origin groups and all age groupings. The figures for Latino voters are significantly lower than for any other grouping (fifteen to twenty points lower). Turnout figures are also low for the eighteen- to twenty-four-year-old group, which can compound the challenges for the Latino community to be more competitive electorally.

Again, the low percentage of Latinos voting is partially attributed to the inclusion of all Latino adults, including noncitizens, except in the 2000 Current Population Report. The turnout gap is greater during nonpresidential election years, which is usually the case for all voters. Even in election years like 2018 when we saw a major increase in Latino turnout relative to 2014, the higher rate of turnout among other groups led to a major inequality (see figure 7.5 for the 1990–2018 midterm elections). Nevertheless, the challenge for Latinos is to demonstrate an upward electoral trajectory for all national elections. At the same time, if we consider the high population growth rate among Latinos, even unchanged registration and turnout rates can have an impact. For example, Latinos in California have increased in population by 42.6 percent since 1990. Their growth rate is five times that of the non-Hispanic population. Even though their voter-registration and voter-turnout rates have not changed appreciably, their proportion of the electorate has increased by "natural growth." In 1990 Latinos constituted 2 percent of the state's electorate, and in 1996, 7 percent (see box 7.1).

FIGURE 7.5 Voter Midterm Turnout Rate across Racial and Ethnic Groups, 1990–2018

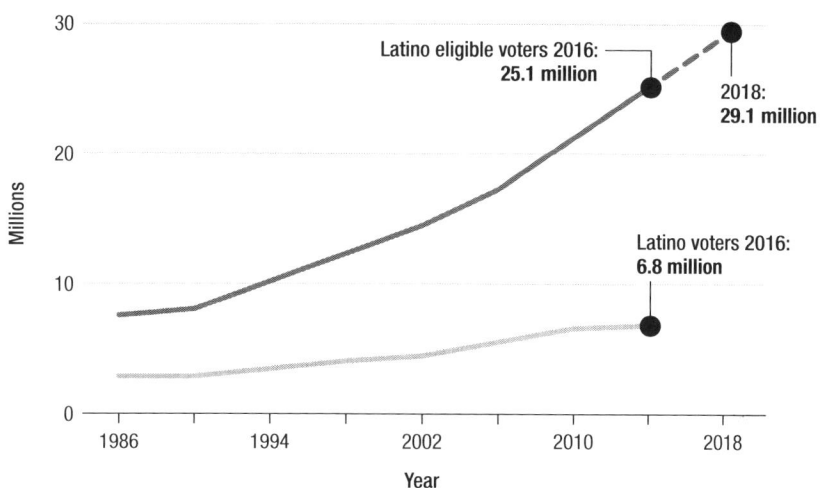

Source: Krogstad, Noe-Bustamante, and Flores 2019.

BOX 7.1 Latinos and the 2014 Midterm Elections

In the aftermath of the 2012 election, political observers and pundits of all political stripes contended that the support of Latino voters was pivotal to President Obama's victory over Mitt Romney.

During an appearance on NBC's *Meet the Press* in June 2013, Sen. Lindsey Graham (R-SC) declared that the Republican Party is "in a demographic death spiral as a party and the only way we can get back in good graces with the Hispanic community in my view is pass comprehensive immigration reform. If you don't do that, it really doesn't matter who we run [in 2016] in my view."

The Republican National Committee's (RNC) "Growth and Opportunity Project" noted that, "if Hispanics think that we do not want them here, they will close their ears to our policies.... Hispanic voters tell us our Party's position on immigration has become a litmus test."

In June of 2013 the US Senate—with the support of fourteen Republicans—passed comprehensive immigration reform (S.744) that included a pathway to citizenship for unauthorized immigrants. However, ... the focus shifted to the Republican-controlled House of Representatives.

... House Republicans acting on immigration reform is tantamount to political suicide as any legislation including a pathway to citizenship would create more Democratic voters and expedite changes to the country's political demography undercutting the party's electoral prospects ... with few Republican representing districts with significant shares of Latino voters, there are limited contexts where Republicans can be punished electorally for inaction on immigration reform.

For both the Democrats and the Republicans, short-term political considerations trumped the policy preferences of the Latino community and provided

BOX 7.1 (continued)

grist to America's Voice founder Frank Sharry's observation that "It's never convenient to help out Latinos."

I draw on the 2014 Latino Decisions Election Eve Poll to provide an overview of the linkages between immigration reform, voter participation, and partisan support. These data suggest four key takeaways.

1. Immigration remains a gateway issue. First, although political expedience may cause candidates of both parties to tread lightly on the immigration issue, for most Latino voters, immigration is a deterministic issue. Specifically, 67 percent of Latino voters responded in the Election Eve Poll that immigration was either the most important or one of the most important factors in shaping their vote choice. . . .
2. Turnout and immigration are linked, . . . how the parties address the issue not only affects how Latinos vote, but also whether they vote at all. Among Latinos registered to vote but who did not turn out in 2014, 60 percent reported that the decision by President Obama to delay executive action on immigration made them less enthusiastic about the president and the Democratic Party.[a] Yet an even larger share (68 percent) of these nonvoting Latinos responded that they would be more enthusiastic about the Democratic Party in the future if President Obama were to enact an executive order limiting deportations as he did in late November.
3. Democratic support is fragile. . . . Not only were there declines in Latino support for Democratic House and Senate candidates in 2014 as compared to 2012, but our poll also suggests that the Democrats are viewed by many Latinos as not being overly concerned with the Latino community.
4. *2014 party affect.* Latino political participation is not necessarily tied to partisanship . . . more Latinos indicated that they were voting to support the Latino community (37 percent) as opposed to supporting the Democratic Party (34 percent). . . . This represents a shift as compared to 2012 when 39 percent of Latino voters responded that they were voting to support the Democratic Party and 36 percent stated that their vote was motivated to support the Latino community.

In sum, participation . . . for many Latinos requires responsiveness, inspiration, and mobilization. . . . Latinos feel ignored by the Democrats and under attack by the Republicans. As a consequence, while the Democrats continue to receive the benefit of the doubt among many Latino voters, the party did little to consolidate Latino support in 2014.

Source: The above are excerpts from David F. Damore's "An Overview of Latino Influence in the 2014 Elections," *Latino Decisions,* January 26, 2015. David Damore is a senior analyst at Latino Decisions. He is associate professor of political science at the University of Nevada, Las Vegas, and a senior nonresident fellow in the Brookings Institution's Governance Studies Program.

[a] The 2014 Latino Decisions Election Eve Poll included a national sample of two hundred registered Latino voters who did not vote in 2014. Latino Victory Project, NCLR, and America's Voice sponsored the poll.

These kinds of gains can enhance the Latino electoral base but represent slow progress toward greater electoral empowerment. Dramatic gains can be accomplished by adding more native-born Latinos who are not currently registered. These additions can enhance Latinos' gains with relatively constant or declining registration and turnout levels for most other voters. As a result, the percentage of Latinos both registered and voting should increase, since all other groups are voting and registering at lower levels.

Latino Voting Behavior: Movement toward Democratic Candidates

The last three election cycles have seen Latinos move significantly toward Democratic candidates. As reflected in table 7.1, Latino Decisions data from the 2008 election had 72 percent of Latinos voting for President Obama in a historic election resulting in the first nonwhite president in American history. Latinos were once again part of the electoral coalition supporting President Obama in 2012, with a slight increase to 75 percent for Obama in his reelection campaign. This was a record level of support from the Latino electorate for any candidate. The record did not last long, however, as the emergence of candidate Trump and his anti-Latino and immigrant campaign rhetoric garnered only 18 percent of Latino voting support, a record low for any candidate in American history. Conversely, 79 percent of Latinos voted for Hillary Clinton. The nearly 80 percent support for Democratic candidate Clinton is more impressive when these numbers are put into a historical context. After all, it was not that long ago that Latinos were widely viewed as a swing-voting electorate, largely due to moderate views of many Latinos on social issues (Sanchez 2016). In 2004, President George W. Bush captured close to 40 percent of the Latino vote in his successful reelection campaign. Democratic support among Latinos in 2020 was 70 percent according to the Latino Decisions Election Eve Survey, down from 2016 and closer to the 72 percent in 2008.

Although there has been a significant movement toward Democratic candidates over the past four election cycles, there is some important variation within the Latino community. As reflected in table 7.1, partisanship is a major factor, as it is for the general population, in explaining vote choice. A robust 95 percent of Latino Democrats voted for Biden in 2020, with 84 percent of Latino Republicans voting for Trump. There was also a 6 percent gender gap among Latinos, with greater support among Latinas. This was down considerably from the 15 percent gender gap in 2016. Finally, support for Biden was greater among foreign-born and Spanish-speaking Latino voters in 2020.

In regard to state-level differences, Latino support for Biden ranged from a low of 59 percent in Florida to a high of 77 percent in Wisconsin. The low support in Florida is largely due to the relatively high support of GOP candidates among Cuban American voters, who only supported at 42 percent in the state relative to 71 percent among Puerto Ricans. Although it is true that Cuban voters tend to support Republican candidates largely due to the GOP's anti-Castro stance, they are in the midst of a significant partisan shift, as younger Cubans are more likely to say they feel closer to the Democratic Party (Krogstad 2014). We discuss the role of national origin and other factors that motivate Latino voting behavior in the section that follows.

TABLE 7.1 Latino Vote Choice in the 2020, 2016, and 2012 Presidential Elections by Party ID, Gender, Nativity, and Dominant Language

	2020		2016		2012	
	Joe Biden (%)	Donald Trump (%)	Hillary Clinton (%)	Donald Trump (%)	Barack Obama (%)	Mitt Romney (%)
All respondents	70	27	79	18	75	23
Party identification						
Democrat	95	4	97	2	97	2
Republican	14	84	22	75	9	90
Other	64	25	65	26	60	34
Gender						
Female	73	23	86	12	77	21
Male	67	31	71	24	73	25
Nativity						
Naturalized immigrant	84	13	84	13	80	18
US born	71	26	72	19	71	27
Language of interview						
English	70	27	75	21	67	25
Spanish	71	25	89	9	69	19

Sources: Latino Decisions 2020 and 2016 Election Eve Poll, impreMedia/Latino Decisions 2012 Election Eve Poll, and Latino Decisions/NALEO/impreMedia National Post-Election Survey—November 2008.

Critical Factors Affecting Latinos' Electoral Participation

What factors affect the level of Latino electoral involvement? The possibilities can be discussed based on two different data sources: (1) the current population reports for the Voting Rights Act provisions, and (2) the extant social science research literature on voting and elections. After the November 2016 elections, the Current Population Survey included a battery of items among voting-age respondents and asked their reasons for not voting in the election. One in four Latinos who did not vote in 2016 indicated it was due to the candidates who were running, up from 9 percent of eligible nonvoters in 2012. Thirty-two percent of Latinos stated it was because they were either too busy or not interested in voting (16 percent for each reason). This predisposition is often associated with political cynicism, apathy, and inefficacy (García 1997; DeSipio 1996). If you compare these responses with those of nonvoters in 1980, a much greater percentage of eligible nonvoters (7.6 percent in 1980 versus 32 percent in 2012) indicated that they had no time or were too busy to vote. Finally, the other noteworthy reasons given by nonvoters in 2016 were being ill or disabled (7.3 percent), being out of town (7.6 percent), inconvenient polling places (3.2 percent), and problems registering to vote (5.4 percent) (File 2018). The 2016 CMPS survey asked a similar question of respondents who did not vote in the 2016 election, and although some of the results were similar there was a greater percentage of Latinos who reported that the candidates were not to their liking (36 percent), and 22 percent reported that they did not feel informed about the issues.

In a general sense, the factors affecting nonvoting seem to center on voter apathy, disinterest, and some degree of cynicism. Given the rising "hostile" climate toward immigrants and Latinos and voter ID laws and other voting protocol changes, monitoring the reasons for not voting becomes even more critical. The impact of voter mobilization campaigns, part of the Latino electoral strategy, can be evaluated in terms of overcoming these nonvoting factors.

The effect of collapsing the various Latino subgroups into one general group can overstate the case and misdirect researchers, policy makers, and journalists into thinking of Latinos as a monolithic group with little internal variation. Latinos' voting patterns are not uniform, and we know little about the electoral patterns of many of the Latino subgroups. Our knowledge base of Latino electoral participation is rooted primarily in studies of the Mexican-origin community, so dealing with the Latino communities as primarily one large electoral group can mute the distinctiveness and specific history of each subgroup. Nevertheless, one theme of this book is the extent of community and connectedness across the various Latino subgroups. Thus, our reporting of Latino voting patterns below will include discussions of variation in Latino voting patterns to the extent possible with available data.

Mobilization

In general, connecting this growing Latino voting base with greater mobilization efforts will result in enhanced electoral participation and, consequently, political influence. Scholars of Latino politics have found convincing evidence that mobilization can increase Latino electoral participation (García Bedolla and Michelson 2012; Ramírez 2007; Ramírez 2005; Ramírez 2013), as the cultivation of a sense of civic identity with fellow co-ethnics activates Latinos as registered and active voters (García Bedolla and Michelson 2012). This makes mobilization one of the key mechanisms associated with increased civic engagement. However, due to the finite resources all mobilization agents (candidates, parties, organizations, etc.) have to work with to get out the vote each cycle, these entities may often strategically focus their efforts on segments of the electorate they view to be likely to vote. Consequently, Latinos are often neglected in the mobilization process due to having lower electoral participation rates (Ramírez 2013; Stevens and Bishin et al. 2005). This is a vicious cycle, as the low voting trends of Latinos are undoubtedly driven at least in part by lower rates of contact from mobilization agents, but because of the lower voting rates Latinos are not contacted to the same extent as other communities.

The 2016 election provides an opportunity to explore how multiple forms of mobilization influenced Latino electoral participation. This includes direct contact from candidates and the dominant parties. The 2016 Latino Decisions Election Eve Poll provides self-reported measures of contact among Latinos who voted in the election that reveal only 35 percent of Latinos in the survey had been contacted by a campaign, party, community organization, or anyone else asking them to register or vote. This is a particularly low number given that the sample of the survey were voters, people who should have been more likely to be contacted. Pantoja and Matos (2015), with a Latino Decisions survey of Dominicans, found respondents felt that candidates and community-based organizations can draw out Dominican voters by highlighting the importance of politics in addressing the policy issues (i.e., jobs, educations, housing, and immigration reform). They found that there was a need for more Dominican-focused community organizations to inspire civic participation. Among Latinos who reported that they were contacted, twice as many reported that they were contacted by a Democrat rather than a Republican, and Latino Republicans were less likely to report that they had been contacted.

The 2020 election showed similar patterns, with Latinos being less likely than both white and African American voters to be contacted by any candidates, party, or organizations. Similar to 2016, Latinos were more likely to be contacted by a Democrat, though the gap was much smaller in 2020. Latinos "self-mobilized" at a high rate in 2020, with 62 percent of Latino voters encouraging other friends and family members to participate in the election.

Another form of mobilization is reactive in nature, with 2016 providing a great example due to Latinos' potential reaction to the Trump campaign's racialization of Latinos. In the run-up to the election it was generally assumed that the hostile comments about Mexican immigrants in the Trump campaign would pose a threat to Latinos or anger them, which could lead to reactive mobilization among Latino voters nationally, similar to the reaction to California's **Proposition 187** a generation ago (Pantoja et al. 2001; Ramírez 2013). At the end of the millennium, a set of statewide propositions in California, beginning with Proposition 187 (limiting immigrants' access to health and social welfare services), were couched in terms of the negative impacts of undocumented and legal immigrants. This proposition targeted primarily Mexicans and other Latinos as the source of a range of economic and social problems in the state. These factors included designating all immigrants as a burden, characterizing the "culprits" as Latinos who negatively impact the economy, increase social service expenditures, and overcrowd health facilities.

This kind of targeted rhetoric stirred heightened political involvement by Latinos and Latino-based organizations. Voter registration campaigns, mass demonstrations, ad hoc organizations in opposition to Proposition 187, statements by the Mexican consul, and so on were directly associated with the dynamics of Proposition 187 (Pantoja, Ramirez, and Segura 2001; Tolbert and Hero 1996). Scholars have suggested that the current anti-immigrant climate and passage of several punitive immigration laws at the state and local level have generated a Proposition 187 effect (Barreto 2013).

Research suggests that Trump's statements on the campaign trail and policy platform that included the promise to build a wall along the southern border of the United States did engage Latinos in the campaign. Surveys conducted by Latino Decisions and others throughout the election season indicated that the high level of enthusiasm among Latinos was driven largely by a desire to keep Trump from winning the election, something scholars referred to as the "Trump Bump" (Mascaro 2016; Sanchez 2016). Not only did turnout increase in several key states from 2012, but candidate Trump earned the lowest support from Latinos of any candidate on record at only 18 percent (Sanchez and Gómez-Aguiñaga 2017).

Latinos, like all racial and ethnic groups, tend to vote at lower rates in off-year congressional elections when there is not a presidential candidate on the ballot. However, the 2018 election saw a sharp increase of 174 percent turnout among Latinos relative to 2014, which helped lead to a blue wave of Democratic victories across the country. Latinos supported Democratic congressional candidates at 74 percent, including 73 percent of Latinos who live in battleground states. This was a result of a combination of factors, including a reaction to President Trump's first two years in office. However, it is critical to note that having Latino representation in key roles that influence mobilization strategies for Latino voters was key. The leadership of Congressman Ben

Ray Lujan as head of the Democratic Congressional Caucus (the first Latino to hold that post), research from Latino Decisions to inform GOTV messaging, and the influence of political action committees like Latino Victory Fund helped fuel the impressive turnout among Latinos across the country (Gambino 2018). The 2018 campaign provided evidence that with substantial investment Latinos will engage in electoral politics; time will tell if this was a unique election or if it was a watershed moment of a shift toward higher levels of turnout for Latinos.

The Power of Descriptive Representation—Latino Support for Co-Ethnic Candidates

Having the opportunity to vote for a co-ethnic candidate is another important factor that has been linked to Latino participation in electoral politics (Barreto 2010). Latino candidates can mobilize their constituents through promoting a sense of ethnic identity, promoting policies that are in line with Latino voters' interests, and, in many cases, being the first candidate to actively court many Latino voters, including asking them to engage in the campaign or to donate money to a campaign. Academic research has also found that Latino voters will often support Latino candidates at high rates when they have an opportunity to do so. Manzano and Sanchez (2010) found that voting for a co-ethnic who is as qualified as the other candidate is preferred by a high percentage of Latino voters, and supporting a Latino candidate even when they are less qualified is chosen among Latinos with a strong ethnic identity. This has been supported by experimental research that has suggested Latino candidates cue a sense of linked fate among Latino voters through their shared ethnicity (McConnaughy et al. 2010).

Even though we provide much more information regarding Latino elected officials in chapter 8, the important role of Latino engagement in electoral politics as candidates is needed here as well. Among all mechanisms to engage in electoral politics, running for office is arguably the most direct mechanism to influence public policy outcomes.

Although we have yet to see a Latino at the top of the presidential ticket for either major party, several Latinos have made some noise in the primaries. Former New Mexico governor Bill Richardson ran for the Democratic nomination in 2008 and was often referenced as the most qualified for the office due to his wide range of experience in state and federal government. More recently, two Latino Republicans were represented in a crowded 2016 GOP primary that eventually nominated Donald Trump. Ted Cruz and Marco Rubio were both targets of candidate Trump's aggressive campaign style that racialized the Latino population throughout the run to the presidency. This included shots at Ted Cruz for having a Cuban-born father (Schleifer 2015; Smith 2015) and the odd exchanges between Marco Rubio and Donald Trump during debates and through social media regarding Rubio's height, which were emphasized by Trump's moniker of "little Rubio." Former San Antonio mayor Julián Castro ran for the Democratic nomination for the 2020 election but pulled out of the race weeks before the Iowa Caucus. Castro emphasized immigration policy and racial inequalities in his campaign, which ended early due to lack of funding.

The 2018 election was truly historic, as the success of Latino and other minority candidates resulted in several important outcomes, including the most diverse US

House membership in history. Latinos had more candidates for federal races and statewide offices than ever before. Although race and ethnicity were important themes, 2018 will be known in history as the election of gender representation. The intersectionality of ethnicity and gender makes women of color who run for electoral office unique from other subgroups (Gershon et al. 2019). Latinas have seen tremendous success as candidates in recent years, across several levels of government. The election of Michelle Lujan-Grisham (Democrat) as governor of New Mexico in 2018 followed the two terms of fellow Latina Susana Martinez (Republican), making New Mexico not only the only state to elect a Latina governor, but a state with successive Latinas overseeing the state's government. The 2018 election also saw the emergence of several new Latina members of Congress, none more prominent than Alexandria Ocasio-Cortez (D-NY), the youngest woman elected to Congress, often referred to as "AOC." Finally, and most recently, at the local level Regina Romero was elected in November 2019 as the first female mayor of Tucson, Arizona, making her the only Latina mayor in any of the fifty largest cities in the United States.

Partisanship

Party identification, or the political party that a voter is attached to and identifies with, arguably has the greatest influence on voting behavior among other factors identified in the literature (Campbell et al. 1960). In fact, partisanship has often been called the "unmoved mover" because it tends to remain pretty stable across the electorate but influences most political attitudes and decisions made by voters. Although partisanship does not have as strong of an impact on the voting behavior of Latinos as it does for African Americans, it is highly correlated with vote choice for Latino voters, particularly those with low levels of political knowledge or information (Nicholson, Pantoja, and Segura 2006).

The 2020 election more than any in recent memory demonstrated the degree of polarization based on partisanship there is in the United States, as 95 percent of self-identified Latino Democrats reported voting for Joe Biden and 84 percent of self-identified Republicans voted for Donald Trump. There is a growing percentage of Latinos who identify as independent, and in 2020 64 percent of that segment of Latinos supported Joe Biden. The movement of many Latinos toward independent status is reflected in the drop in Democratic identifiers over the past two election cycles. The Pew Hispanic Center found that 70 percent of Latinos identified as Democratic in 2012 with a slight drop to 64 percent in 2016, with more than 60 percent in both years believing that the Democratic party has more concern for Latinos than the Republican party (Lopez et al. 2016a).

The relationship between partisanship and vote choice among Latinos is unique for Latinos, largely because the process to formulate an attachment to one of the dominant parties is often different for Latinos, particularly those who are immigrants or whose parents are immigrants. Many Americans begin formulating opinions about the parties early in their lives, often as a result of being socialized to party politics by their parents. However, for Latinos who themselves may not have grown up in the United States due to being foreign-born, or whose parents are immigrants, this process is much different. This has been substantiated in the academic literature, which has found that Latino immigrants often have weak attachments to either party, but as their time lived in the United States increases, they become more strongly attached to the Democratic Party (Cain, Kiewiet, and Uhlaner 1991).

The combination of a soft attachment to either party and a rise in anti-Latino discrimination across the country has led to ethnic identity rivaling the role of partisanship in Latino voting behavior. One indicator of this shift is the question that comes from the Latino Decisions Election Eve Surveys, which ask Latino voters what their primary motivation was to vote in that election. In 2012, 36 percent of respondents said they voted to support the Latino community, compared to 54 percent who stated they were motivated by their partisan attachments. In 2016, the percentage of Latino voters who stated they voted to support or represent the Latino community jumped to 43 percent, 8 percentage points greater than Latinos who said they voted to support the Democratic candidate and 31 percentage points greater than those who said they voted to support Republicans and other candidates. In 2020, 23 percent of Latino voters indicated they voted to support/represent the Latino community, compared to 50 percent to support the Democratic candidate and 22 percent to support Republicans.

It appears as though Latinos are becoming increasingly motivated by their ethnic attachments in comparison to support for the two political parties. Morin, Macias-Mejía, and Sanchez (forthcoming) find evidence to support their theory that Latino voters are increasingly motivated more by their sense of linked fate to other Latinos and desire to support the Latino community than to support their party of choice. The authors also find that the power of ethnic identity can lead some Latinos to vote against their party to support the candidate they feel is more supportive of the Latino community.

This finding supports a broader literature that has demonstrated that group identity among Latinos influences both Latino electoral participation and voting behavior. Group consciousness was originally applied to voting behavior as a political resource (see Socioeconomic Status [SES]/Resource model discussed below) that could help explain how African Americans participated in elections at roughly the same level as whites despite lower SES levels (Verba, Scholzman, and Brady 1995). Scholars have found that group consciousness also increases political participation for Latinos (Stokes-Brown 2006), particularly when that activity is directly tied to the Latino community (Sanchez 2006b).

Socioeconomic Status, Resources, and Voting

The existing research literature offers other insights and findings to explain voting and nonvoting. In many cases, when research examines the electoral arena, the question of who votes and who they vote for is answered in terms of important sociodemographic characteristics, psychological orientations, and situational and structural factors associated with the individual. The socioeconomic model (Verba and Nie 1972; Wolfinger and Rosenstone 1980) identifies educational attainment, income, and occupational status as the key factors that differentiate voters from nonvoters. Persons with higher levels of educational attainment, income, and occupational status (professionals, entrepreneurs, etc.) are much more likely to vote than individuals with less human capital.[3] The concept of human capital, found in the economics and political science literatures, holds that as individuals invest in their human resource "portfolio," gaining more education, training, experience, and motivation, they are advantaged with greater returns in the job market via earnings. The acquisition of greater human resources is advantageous economically. In a sense, the idea of human capital can be thought of as political capital, for individuals with greater skills, knowledge, and interest in the political process can be more effective in their actions (Putnam 2000).

Acquiring these resources will give a person the relevant political information and a better understanding of the political process. With higher levels of educational attainment, the person has not only pertinent knowledge, but also communication and organizational skills and social status, which serve as beneficial assets for electoral participation. Similarly, higher levels of income afford an individual the economic resources to get involved in electoral activities and contribute to campaigns. Possessing a high-status job and money does enhance a person's available time and ability to see the direct benefits of political involvement.

Although the socioeconomic status model is at the heart of the electoral participation model, it does not fit Latinos in exactly the same way it does other populations. Educational attainment makes a difference for Latinos (García and Sanchez 2004) in terms of making them more likely to be registered and to vote regularly. As greater numbers of Latinos obtain high school diplomas and higher education, gains in Latino registration and turnout will continue. On the other hand, the strength of higher income attainment and occupational status does not have the same significant and positive effect for Latinos that it does for non-Latinos. That is, there is not the strong, explicit association for Latinos in higher income levels to be significantly more electorally active than those at lower economic levels (across studies that examine Latino electoral participation).

Similarly, Latinos in higher-status occupations are not significantly (statistically) more electorally active than Latinos in lower-status occupations. Part of the explanation might lie with the relative concentration of Latinos in lower occupational positions and lower income categories. The emerging Latino middle class is a recent phenomenon, and its impact electorally is a matter of more current examination. As more Latinos experience greater socioeconomic mobility, and as a greater percentage of the community reaches the age of eighteen, we may see stronger relationships between socioeconomic status and Latino voter registration and turnout.

The demographic factors that appear to perform similarly for Latinos and non-Latinos alike are age and gender. In the case of the former, researchers use the idea of a life cycle. As a person becomes more "settled" in her work and household, she has a more direct stake in what happens politically. An older person is likely to be a homeowner, to be situated in a higher tax bracket, to have children in school, and so on, which motivates her to be more aware of public policy and policy impacts. Research has consistently found that age is positively correlated with Latino electoral participation, with young Latinos voting at much lower rates than those who are older.

Prior to 2000, much attention and discussion focused on the idea of a gender gap. With women historically excluded from the political process, there were noticeable differences between women's and men's political participation. The relative absence of women as political and organizational leaders, active voters, campaign contributors, and partisan activists reinforced the stereotype of politics being a "man's game." The gender gap was highlighted in the electoral arena, as historically fewer women were registered than men, and they voted less. However, this has changed substantially over time. The gender gap has closed electorally, and the voting gap no longer exists in regard to turnout, and as we noted earlier, Latinas were highly active as candidates in 2018. In fact, analysis of the 2016 election suggested that Latinas turned out to vote at a higher rate than their male counterparts (Romero 2018). Our discussion of the effect of sociodemographic factors on voting has application to other forms of political involvement. Chapter 8 explores other aspects of political involvement, specifically organizational involvement and local community activities.

We use the results of the 2020 presidential election to highlight the socioeconomic characteristics of Latinos to examine vote choices (Trump versus Biden). Gender was significant, with Latinas being more inclined to vote for Joe Biden (+6 percent) than their Latino male counterparts. Latinos older than age sixty were the most likely to support Biden compared to their younger counterparts (+6 percent); Latinos earning less than $50,000 (14 percent) and non–college degree Latinos (+7 percent) supported Biden to a greater extent than their higher SES counterparts.

Psychological Factors and Political Attitudes

Other contributing factors that influence voters include psychological orientations, situational factors, and structural factors. The political orientations of efficacy, trust, and interest generate greater awareness and motivation to get involved in the political process and public policy making. The sense of political and personal efficacy empowers an individual to get involved and feel that he can make a difference. Researchers Verba and Nie (1972) and Rosenstone and Hansen (1993) point to socialization experiences as major factors in the development of these participatory attitudes, with family and schools being the primary agents.

Latinos tend to be less politically interested and less aware of political events and information (García and Sanchez 2004; Barreto 2010). For example, the percentage of Latinos (21 percent) who reported that they were "very interested" in politics in the 2016 CMPS survey was lower than non-Hispanic white respondents (27 percent) and black respondents (25 percent). With lower levels of political awareness and interest, there is usually less electoral involvement. On the other hand, Latinos exhibit levels of political trust (i.e., basic confidence in the fairness and evenness of governmental actions and actors) comparable to those of other voting segments of the population, and in some cases even higher than non-Latinos (Abrajano and Alvarez 2009). This political orientation should reinforce people's belief in the political system and motivate them to exercise their vote. For Latinos, this association is a weak one, and some studies find an inverse relationship (García and Sanchez 2004; García and Arce 1988; DeSipio 1996; Hero 1992).

This is somewhat ironic in that Latinos respond with a positive orientation toward the US political system (indicating confidence in how it works) yet do not register or vote to a degree comparable with non-Latinos. There is clearly a linkage problem or inconsistency in that evidence of Latinos' political support for the American political system does not translate into their taking a more active role as a voting public. Some researchers (DeSipio 1996; García 1988) have used the concept of **political incorporation** to assess the extent of involvement people have with the political system (Gerstle and Mollenkopf 2001; Bloemraad, Korteweg, and Yurdakul 2008). Individuals are politically incorporated via a socialization process that instills the core values and beliefs of the American political system (de la Garza, Falcón, and García 1996; Schildkraut 2005), and they assume the various roles of a participatory "citizen." Moving beyond socioeconomic status can lead us to another series of explanations for the lower rates of political participation, especially electoral behavior.

Social Structures and Participatory Roles

Given the adjustments that have been discussed, are Latinos assured of comparable levels of participation with non-Latinos and of being effective at policy making? To construct a fuller picture of the variety of factors that can influence participatory roles, we need to introduce the role of social structures. The structural factors have to do with the rules of the game and how political institutions function, especially focusing on access, an individual's or group's legal standing, rights and protections, and the formal requirements for participation. Such practices as the poll tax, the white primary, literacy tests, limited registration locations, and economic and physical intimidation (Grofman, Handley, and Niemi 1992) serve as examples of structural impediments for racial, ethnic, gender, and social classes in the United States.

This strand of participation explanations involves structural conditions and institutional practices and customs (Barrera, Ornelas, and Muñoz 1972; Barrera 1979). Concepts such as equality, fairness, discrimination, institutional racism, ethnocentrism, and subordination are used to describe power relations between the dominant society and minority populations. This perspective examines factors other than merely individual characteristics, orientations, and behaviors that can lead to specific levels of participation. Laws that exclude persons from voting, registering, participating in political parties, and so on serve as examples of social structures and institutional practices. As a result, Latinos are viewed as marginalized—economically, socially, and politically.

This line of analysis sees low rates of participation as purposive actions by the political system and its representatives to have minorities serve as subjects rather than active participants. In the electoral arena, restrictive policies such as poll taxes, literacy tests, limited registration places and times, hostile polling locations, physical intimidation, and so on (García 1986a) are structural examples that have negatively affected Latinos and other minority voters. The net effect ranges from the outright prohibition of participation to the active discouragement of Latino political involvement. Similarly, political institutions such as legislatures, city councils, and school boards can operate under election systems and rules (e.g., off-year, nonpartisan, or at-large elections) that can disadvantage Latino communities (Grofman and Davidson 2011) in terms of representation and productive participation.

The consequences of such structural conditions can be passivity, acquiescence, or withdrawal. To apply this perspective to Latinos, we will examine the provisions of the Voting Rights Act and its subsequent amendments, focusing on linguistic protections in the form of bilingual ballots, more facilitative registration systems, preclearance of election law changes prior to their implementation, and specified protective status for the purposes of Latinos' civil and voting rights.[4] These provisions identify some of the existing structural conditions and systematic responses that have been used to limit Latino electoral participation (Hopkins 2011). The legal remedies listed represent policies to remove these obstacles.

Active civil rights leadership and organizations, in combination with a number of other social liberation movements, have applied both political and economic pressure for the removal of biased practices that inhibit political participation (Tarrow 1998; Piven and Cloward 1988, 2000). Continuous advocacy and monitoring are still required to ensure protection from structural barriers. As a result, organizations like the Mexican American Legal Defense and Education Fund (MALDEF), the Puerto Rican Legal Defense and Education Fund (PRLDEF), and the Southwest Voter Registration and Education Project (SVREP) serve as vigilant Latino interest groups to ensure a fair and equitable electoral system and process. Since the early 2000s, there have been more active and sustained political mobilizations by Latino organizations and labor unions. The anti-immigrant sentiments and actions, as well as the push from the 2000 general elections, have resulted in the devotion of greater human and economic resources to such efforts (Michelson 2003b, 2006; Michelson, García Bedolla, and McConnell 2009).

Chapter 10 on voting rights discusses the specific efforts by MALDEF and PRLDEF for voting rights protection. The primary target in this litigation was at-large elections (Brischetto and de la Garza 1983; García 1986a), which made electing minority candidates very difficult. As a result of successful class-action suits and favorable interpretation of the Voting Rights Act and its amendments, the use of district or ward elections has become more the norm. Subsequent redistricting efforts after the decennial censuses sought to create competitive and favorable districts in which Latino candidates had a higher probability of success. Work by Barreto, Segura, and Woods (2004) has now demonstrated that Latino candidates have a direct effect on higher turnout among Latino voters, as well as stronger levels of Latino candidates' support. That is, when Latino candidates are on the ballot, Latino voters are more likely to take an interest in the elections and vote at higher levels than usual. Finally, in chapter 10 we discuss the recent Supreme Court rulings (Shelby County 2013; Arizona State Legislature 2015) and more frequent redistricting strategies that have had major impacts on Latino communities and electoral participation.

The most contentious obstacle to voting in the contemporary discussion of voting rights has been the rapid growth of states implementing photo-identification requirements to vote, many that require your name and address to match what is listed on the voter file of your state. During the early 2000s, there were state initiatives to require prospective voters to show proof of citizenship (legal status) in addition to a voter registration card. Recently, there has been a push for higher thresholds of identification required to register and cast one's ballot (voter identification laws) and other changes like periods for early voting, accepting challenged ballots, and so on, that have differential effects on racial and ethnic and low-income populations (Barreto et al. 2009; Matsubayashi and Rocha 2012). These laws disproportionately impact Latino voters, who often lack the required identification as well as the documents such as birth certificates to obtain the driver's license or other acceptable IDs (Barreto et al. 2018).

The Civil Rights Act of 1964 and the Voting Rights Act of 1965 were intended to eliminate many of these structural barriers. The situational factors revolve around salient issues, controversies, charismatic candidates, and the like, which stir interest in specific elections, office races, and propositions. Measures such as Proposition 187 in California or Arizona's Proposition 200 (limiting immigrants' access to social services and education) or **Proposition 227** (ending bilingual education) in California serve as situational factors to stimulate Latino voters' interest and involvement. In chapter 10 we will further discuss the recent Supreme Court decision that altered the coverage and **preclearance** sections so that states under Voting Rights Act (VRA) jurisdiction can be removed from the VRA's federal reporting and scrutiny. Other expanding structurally related developments have been initiatives, under the rationale of ensuring against fraudulent voting practices, requiring photo identification, altering early election practices, and challenging decisions at polling places.

Culture, National Origin, and Latinos

The concept of political incorporation, although it focuses on how persons learn and involve themselves with the American political system, is generally directed toward newcomers to the political system (either as young people assuming adult status or as immigrants) and toward marginalized populations such as minority-group members. For our purposes, political incorporation is the process by which group interests are represented in the policy-making process (Browning, Marshall, and Tabb 1990). Obviously, a central focus of this book is the efforts of the Latino community to become a more active and effective interest group in the American political system. We have been examining indicators and factors affecting Latino electoral behavior. In addition to socioeconomic status, mobilization by Latino organizations and leaders and situational circumstances (anti-Latino backlash, Latino-targeted referenda, partisan outreach, etc.) contribute to the political incorporation of Latinos. The use of political incorporation has also centered on the systemic factors (discrimination, segregated institutions, exclusionary practices, etc.) that minimize or severely restrict the extent of incorporation as individuals and group members.

A critical element of the Latino community, in terms of political incorporation, is the immigrant segment. Latino immigrants are exposed to a different culture (socially, politically, and civically) and require adjustment time to integrate into the American way. In J. García's work on political adaptation of immigrants (1986b), he outlines a three-step process involving political incorporation (integration). The first is the adaptive process, in which adjustments are made in terms of social relations, language, societal roles, and familiarity with institutions, norms, and values. After some degree of socialization has occurred, the second step deals with integration. The development and growth of organizations serves as the vehicle for contact with social and political institutions, informational networks, and communication. This organizational development establishes the presence of the migrant community and its interests within the host society and pursues societal responses (Portes, Escobar, and Arana 2008). The last stage of incorporation is societal absorption, in which immigrants' political and economic participation is regularized (or falls within the conventional realm of political involvement), and they are recognized as an active interest group engaged in the American policy-making process. Thus, one of the challenges for Latino communities is the integration of the Latino immigrant segment into all of the other dimensions that connect Latinos (national-origin subgroup, class, regional location, varying histories in the United States, etc.). Nicholson, Pantoja, and Segura (2006) found that Spanish-language usage by candidates was an important factor in Latino vote choice, especially among low-information voters.

In the case of the immigrant Mexican-origin community and other Latino immigrant subgroups, there is considerable debate about how to view Latinos. Do they make up a series of major waves of incoming immigrants from different political cultures, or are they part of a stream of indigenous populations? Historians Rodolfo Acuña (1976, 1981, 1998) and Mario García (1989) and political scientist Mario Barrera (1979) have analyzed the experience of Mexican-origin people in the Southwest as a politically and economically subjugated indigenous population. Since the 1970s, the influx of Mexican migrants into the United States has served to augment the Mexican-origin community, which has entered the adaptation phase. As a result, this community can simultaneously represent both an indigenous and a migrant population. Analysis of other Latino immigrant subgroups (Dominicans, Puerto Ricans, Cubans, etc.) by Sassen-Koob (1988) and Morales and Bonilla (1993) focuses on the global economy and how Latino migration is "manipulated" so that there is movement from less developed countries to more industrialized ones. The perspective suggests that an individual's migration decision is not determined solely by their desires and motivations, but also by structural conditions (especially economic opportunities or the lack of them in the country of origin). These factors serve as the backdrop for understanding the Latino political incorporation process and the varied experiences that can either unite or divide the Latino communities. Our discussion of Latino political incorporation focuses on the adjustments and the congruence (or lack thereof) with American political culture.

Thus, the concept of political incorporation entails full and articulated political involvement and activity, as well as adjusting to core American values and political practices (de la Garza, Falcón, and García 1996; Bishin and Klofstad 2012; Bloemraad, Korteweg, and Yurdakul 2008). For Latinos, politics coalesces as a community of interests and a community of common or similar cultures. We have numerous accounts about the political incorporation of European immigrants such as the Irish, Italians, and Jews (Fuchs 1990; Gerstle and Mollenkopf 2001). Part of that discussion lies in the analysis of how cultural values and practices (self-help associations, residential clustering, closed social networks, etc.) played a central role in the adjustment to living in America. Cultural factors such as language, values, the political culture of the country of origin, familialism, the extent of ties with the mother country, and the presence or absence of organizational life, for example, can be key determinants of the extent of political incorporation among Latinos (Almond and Verba 1963; Wilson 1977; Esman 1995; Flores 2003; Enchautegui 2013).

A partial explanation of Latinos' "limited" political incorporation (DeSipio 1996) lies with the persistence of Spanish-language use and their coming from more autocratic, less democratic, and elitist political systems that produce a legacy of limited participatory experiences, a sense of fatalism, a lack of organizational experience, and cultural and linguistic isolation (Skerry 1993; DeSipio and de la Garza 1998).

Latinos come from nonparticipatory political cultures; ethnic group cultural maintenance is seen as a deterrent to active participation in the American political system. For example, a strong sense of familialism would tend to deter Latinos (Tirado 1970; Márquez 1993) from joining secondary groups or formal organizations. As a result, primary social networks and knowledge gathering about the social and political system come primarily from family and other Latino community members.

This discussion of political involvement shows that organizational affiliation and involvement are directly connected to heightened political participation (Verba,

Scholzman, and Brady 1995; García and de la Garza 1985). Thus, being a Latino can be a liability in terms of political incorporation due to lesser organizational affiliation and involvement. Cultural values and traditions can serve as obstacles to integration into the American political system and group effectiveness. At the same time, maintaining Latino identification can serve as a basis for group mobilization around particular concerns or issues. These perspectives are not mutually exclusive but represent realities that exist within the Latino community and make up part of the challenges for Latino political participation.

Proponents of these explanations can take two different routes. The first suggests that unless assimilation (Gordon 1964) takes place (political, cultural, social, associational, identificational, and marital), Latinos will be in a marginal position both in society and as political participants. The assimilation process would involve departing from traditional cultural practices and values to become Americanized. Any distinctiveness as Latinos or attachment as part of a Latino subgroup would be, at best, symbolic (Barrera 1988). The second route suggests that although assimilation is a necessary precondition for greater political involvement, the process of acculturation is a more realistic characterization of what happens in American society. That is, assimilation does take place, but it is not a one-way process that by necessity includes complete loss of group identity, affiliation, practices, and social networks (see box 7.2). This latter perspective portrays the American political system in culturally and politically pluralistic terms. It should be noted that alternative explanations of immigration incorporation shift away from primarily an individual source of adaptation to one in which social structures, institutions, public policies, and societal attitudes and practices can facilitate or impede immigrant incorporation (Bloemraad 2006; Ramakrishnan and Espenshade 2001).

BOX 7.2 A Latino's Cultural and Political World

A Salvadoran living in Washington, DC, might be employed as a computer engineer with very good English-language proficiency and a non-Latina spouse. At the same time, he might belong to a Salvadoran social club and live in the Mount Pleasant neighborhood; most of his friends would be Salvadorans or Guatemalans. Thus, acculturation entails maintaining degrees and aspects of cultural values and practices during the acquisition of "American" customs and practices. The acculturation scenario leads to a pluralist model of American politics. That is, Latinos are an organized interest group for whom ethnicity and identity provide a primary basis for membership, resources, and issues.

Whether Latinos choose assimilation or acculturation, participation in American politics involves major adjustments and critical strategies in order for the Latino community to be effective. This explanation focuses on how the individual adjusts to life in American society and makes a variety of choices. The role and impact of culture and language are central elements from this perspective, as is an understanding of how they operate in the American political system. Structural analysis offers another basis for examining and explaining levels of political participation for Latinos.

Latino Electoral Participation, Key Factors, and the Future

This chapter has provided basic information about the level of Latino electoral participation as voters and the various explanatory factors that contribute to Latino voting patterns. Historically, Latinos have had lower voter-registration and voter-turnout rates. Part of the difficulty lies with the significant foreign-born proportion of the Latino population. In addition, the youthfulness of Latinos overall (on average, they are more than ten years younger than the general population) reduces potential voting strength. From these two starting points, we also see the effects of socioeconomic status, participatory orientations, structural factors (e.g., biased or targeted public policies, discrimination), and cultural factors (e.g., nativity, language, and homeland political culture). Finally, Latino voting behavior and choices are also affected by given situations and issues that arise, such as statewide propositions directly impacting Latinos.

With our focus in this chapter on elections, voting behavior, and Latinos, we have tried to paint a contemporary portrait of Latino registration and turnout. Despite some periodic improvements such as the 2018 election, there has also been some backsliding, and the electoral gap remains a challenge preventing Latinos from actualizing their potential influence. In terms of Latino voter-participation trends, gains have been made, assisted by Latino organizations and leaders, in stimulating more Latinos to become involved in the American electoral system. Part of that attention has been directed toward increasing the number of foreign-born Latinos who become citizens. In addition, more targeted and sophisticated voter education and registration drives have been more prominent since the late 1990s and showed promise in mobilizing Latino voters in 2018. The early part of this new millennium saw greater evidence that conversion of potential Latino voting clout is being realized more significantly. Gains have been made in the absolute number of Latinos registered and voting as well as in their percentage of the total electorate. Given the greater percentage of Latinos older than age eighteen and the increase in the number of legalized Latino immigrants, naturalized citizens should add to recent Latino electoral gains.

Conclusion

We conclude this chapter with recent indicators of significant changes among the Latino electorate that have carried over into this millennium. Some very specific developments and activities since the mid-1990s (active Latino organizations conducting voter registration drives, the number of Latinos turning age eighteen annually, and more focused mobilization activities, etc.) could well indicate upsurges in the electoral liveliness of Latino communities. These developments appear to have long-term implications and will alter the current electoral profile for Latinos in the future. In a real sense, both the 2014 and 2016 elections provide additional confirming evidence.

Recent electoral developments and activities can be viewed as positive indicators that Latino electoral participation is realizing more of its potential. Specific trends involved rising voter-registration rates among Latinos. Although many of the specific examples are set in California, there is evidence of increased voter registration throughout "Latino America." This increase is even more noteworthy in light of declining voter participation among other Americans. Two key segments within the

Latino community that are becoming more involved in the electoral arena are those younger than age thirty and those who are foreign-born.

The youthfulness of the Latino community contributes to its overall growth; yet, a large proportion remains too young to vote. The eighteen-to-thirty age group will be the fastest-growing segment into the next decade, potentially bringing more new voters. The micro-mobilization efforts utilized by Latino organizations such as UnidosUS and Voto Latino in 2018 and 2020 to target young Latinos proved to be effective, as the percentage of voters aged eighteen to twenty-nine among the full voting population was higher than in the past seven midyear elections. Results from the 2018 Latino Decisions Election Eve survey revealed that Latinos younger than age thirty were more enthusiastic participants in the election than older Latinos, including being more likely to contact others and encourage them to vote, donate or volunteer for a campaign, and attend a protest or demonstration. This suggests that Latino youth can be effectively mobilized and that when this happens, they can have a strong influence on political outcomes.

The data on increased naturalization petitions reflects a major shift that started in the 1990s and is projected to continue into the next decade. To some extent, the anti-immigrant climate and restrictive state and local policy initiatives following September 11, 2001, have served as catalysts for permanent resident aliens to pursue naturalization and more ardent Latino political engagement. In addition, Mexico joined the ranks of other Latin American nations that recognize dual citizenship (Jones-Correa 2001a), which has reduced the stress of maintaining Mexican citizenship or that of other Latin American countries at the expense of pursuing American citizenship. Thus, the continued development of Latino communities into a more significant electoral actor has become increasingly evident since the mid-1990s.

Latinos' increased electoral competition for political offices is seeing more success at local levels and enjoying relative stability at the state level. There is some recent evidence of newly elected Latino officials in areas where Latinos are not the dominant demographic. The added dimensions of partisan affiliation (i.e., Latinos running as Republican candidates) and salient issue clusters (i.e., immigration reform, the economy) will affect Latinos' interest, enthusiasm, and candidate preferences (Sanchez and Morin 2011; Rocha et al. 2010). Part of the gain in representation is the result of an expanding and increasingly active Latino electorate; yet, more energetic and effective Latino organizations and leadership are expanding the Latino political realm.

External factors such as a negative climate directed toward Latinos, public policies and initiatives that directly impact Latino communities, the nature and content of partisan appeals by both major parties, and broader public networks of information and connection among the diverse Latino communities are important sources of increased Latino electoral participation. The role of Latino organizations and leadership and their concomitant mobilization efforts are the subject of the following chapter. The intersection of Latinos with leaders and organizations soliciting, directing, and encouraging participation and involvement will convert political potential into concrete action.

Finally, the 2020 election identified a unique set of challenges and opportunities for Latinos. With a health pandemic that created high fear of spreading the virus through in-person voting, many states expanded access to mail-based voting and voting early. Many Latinos consequently voted early and/or through absentee ballots for the first time ever. With greater familiarity with this process we might see these trends persist into the future. However, there were also high levels of voter suppression directed at Latinos. For example, in Texas, voters who did not have a medical justification were not able to vote by mail, and voters were not required to wear a mask at the polls.

Link to Suggested Readings

https://latinodecisions.com/blog/lies-damn-lies-and-exit-polls

https://www.pewresearch.org/hispanic/2016/10/11/the-latino-vote-in-the-2016-presidential-election

https://latinodecisions.com/blog/new-data-shows-latino-electorate-continues-to-experience-wide-variety-of-voting-problems-at-polling-place

https://www.washingtonpost.com/news/monkey-cage/wp/2016/11/11/in-record-numbers-latinos-voted-overwhelmingly-against-trump-we-did-the-research

Discussion Questions

1. Recently, Latinos have been characterized as a critical force in national and state elections. What is the basis for making such a claim?
2. Despite gains in voter registrations and regular voting, there are noticeable variations among different Latino national-origin groups regarding electoral politics. What are possible explanations for Latino subgroup differences?
3. When an individual decides to become involved electorally, structural factors can affect the extent and nature of electoral engagement. In the second decade of the new millennium, what are these structural factors? Do they differ from those of the 1960s and 1970s?
4. Latinos appear to be mobilized by anti-Latino and anti-immigrant policies and climate. What evidence is there to support this statement and what are the mechanisms that explain the link between reactive mobilization and Latino political participation?
5. An expanding segment of the Latino electorate has consisted of immigrants who have become naturalized citizens. Discuss the motivations, requisites, and benefits of naturalization for Latinos and their communities.
6. While Latinos have been primarily Democrats, there has been a rise of Independents, and some difference on the Democratic Party's vigorous support for Latino policy preferences. What strategies should Latinos pursue to be more effective in America's two-party system?

Notes

1. We use the term "arenas of political involvement" to identify electoral activities, in addition to organizational, protest, and individualized involvement at various levels of government and affecting the policy-making process.

2. In the case of the LNS (both the initial survey and the New England supplement), the richness of a large and diverse group of national-origin respondents provides information on the full array of Latino subgroups, especially Central and South Americans. In addition, more systematic information has been collected about Latino political participation, its antecedent influences, and the mobilization process.

3. The concept of human capital is found in the economics literature. The idea is that as strongly motivated individuals invest in their human resource "portfolio" by obtaining more education, greater degrees of training, and more experience, they become poised to reap greater returns in the job market via earnings. The acquisition of greater human resources is advantageous for economic returns. Human capital can also be political capital in that those individuals with greater skills, knowledge, and interest in the political process can act more effectively.

4. The specification of which racial, national-origin, or linguistic groups are covered by the Civil Rights and Voting Rights Acts constitutes a clarification and delineation of constitutionally protected rights for members of certain groups.

CHAPTER 8

Latino Organizations and Leadership

La maquinaría de la edad moderna, estas estructuras sociales que pretenden representar nuestros sentimientos, nuestros puntos de vista pero realmente son personas de carne y hueso que dirigen estas máquinas sociales y estas son el vínculo con el pueblo.

The machinery of this modern age, these social structures that seek to represent our feelings, our points of view, are directed by real people—and they are the connections with our community.

OUR EXAMINATION OF VOTING AND elections has centered upon the changing numbers of Latinos who register and vote in US elections. We have outlined and discussed the major contributing factors that affect Latino electoral participation: socioeconomic status, participatory orientations, structural conditions and practices, and cultural dimensions. Progress has been made in terms of increasing Latino electoral and other modes of political involvement, but progress has been slow and uneven. In the past two decades, Latinos have shown gains in educational attainment, household income, and rates of naturalization. Mobilization and leadership do play positive roles in increasing Latino political involvement and can take the form of continuous efforts to activate the Latino community as well as actively responding to external movements like anti-immigration initiatives that curtail voting registration and redistricting measures that undermine Latino political impact (Ayala 2015).

This chapter focuses on the role of organizations and leaders in Latino political life. While organizations and leaders have been discussed elsewhere in the book, in this chapter we provide overviews of several specific organizations that have been vital to Latinos and will also examine these elements as linkages or bridges between Latinos and American political processes and institutions. Our earlier discussions of political involvement and participation revealed how increased individual political capital can position a person to join and be active in organizations, develop communication skills, and become part of social networks that reinforce becoming and staying active. Therefore, the political resources that a Latino can develop and obtain have payoffs for organizational involvement as well as leadership enhancement.

How do organizations serve the Latino political community? What role do leaders play in linking Latino community interests and experiences to focused activities in political arenas? How does having representation from your own community influence your views about government and politics? Being asked to participate, especially by someone who plays a visible and familiar role, serves as a key ingredient in activating Latino participants. Organizations are part of the mobilizing force that can subsidize political involvement (i.e., reduce the costs of participation) for individuals by providing information, access to decision makers, forums for discussion, and potential benefits (employment, services, tax benefits, etc.). Just as the Latino population has grown dramatically over the past three decades, the rise of newer and revitalized organizations (expanding the scope of long-standing Latino organizations) is quite evident. We will begin by examining the presence of Latino elected officials at multiple layers of government as well as the dominant theories of political representation that provide some context to the current status of Latino elected officials. Our attention will then turn to the purposes and bases for the existence of several Latino-based organizations.

Latino Political Representation

In the American political system, virtually all governmental decisions are made by representatives and not directly by the public. The American system is not a direct democracy, but a representative democracy, or a *republic*. Except for some town hall meetings and some referenda, the public's role in governmental decision making is not to make those decisions directly but to elect representatives who will make decisions for us and to attempt to influence them and their decisions on our behalf. This section of the book focuses on the concept of **descriptive representation,** or for Latino constituents, having a fellow Latino represent them in elected office. According to Dovi, "descriptive representatives are those who look like, or at least have experiences and interests similar to, the people they represent" (2007, 27).

We have already noted the strong relationship between having Latino candidates on the ballot and political participation. However, political scientists have argued that the presence of descriptive representatives who have the same race or ethnicity as their constituents promotes feelings of inclusion and efficacy, which yield improved levels of political involvement and establishing overall democratic legitimacy (Mansbridge 1999). Scholars of Latino politics have found evidence to advance this theory, including establishing a link between descriptive representation at the mayoral level and Latino ethnic identity and attitudes toward government (efficacy and alienation) (Sanchez and Morin 2011). However, the authors find that the power of descriptive representation among Latinos is more pronounced when there is a match in national origin, such as being of Mexican origin and having a Mexican-origin mayor, than having a pan-ethnic match.

Scholars interested in tracking descriptive representation will point to the rise of Latino elected officials at the federal, state, and local levels. In California alone, Latinos now occupy 762 elective offices, 20 percent of assembly and senate positions, and 6 seats on the state's congressional delegation. Nationwide, as of 2018 there were 6,749 Latino elected officials, an increase of nearly 700 since 2014[1] (see table 8.1). The four states with the largest number of Latino elected officials are Texas, California, New Mexico, and Arizona. In addition, changes in voter registration and turnout, as well

TABLE 8.1 Elected Latino Officials Serving in Congress by State, 1863–2021

State or Territory	Name	First Took Office	Service
Arizona			
AZ	PASTOR, Ed	102nd (1991–1993)	House
AZ	GRIJALVA, Raúl M.	108th (2003–2005)	House
AZ	GALLEGO, Ruben	114th (2015–2017)	House
California			
CA	PACHECO, Romualdo	45th (1877–1879)	House
CA	ROYBAL, Edward R.	88th (1963–1965)	House
CA	COELHO, Tony	96th (1979–1981)	House
CA	MARTÍNEZ, Matthew G.	97th (1981–1983)	House
CA	TORRES, Esteban Edward	98th (1983–1985)	House
CA	BECERRA, Xavier	103rd (1993–1995)	House
CA	ROYBAL-ALLARD, Lucille	103rd (1993–1995)	House
CA	SANCHEZ, Loretta	105th (1997–1999)	House
CA	BACA, Joe	106th (1999–2001)	House
CA	NAPOLITANO, Grace Flores	106th (1999–2001)	House
CA	SOLIS, Hilda L.	107th (2001–2003)	House
CA	CARDOZA, Dennis A.	108th (2003–2005)	House
CA	NUNES, Devin	108th (2003–2005)	House
CA	SÁNCHEZ, Linda T.	108th (2003–2005)	House
CA	COSTA, Jim	109th (2005–2007)	House
CA	CÁRDENAS, Tony	113th (2013–2015)	House
CA	NEGRETE MCLEOD, Gloria	113th (2013–2015)	House
CA	RUIZ, Raul	113th (2013–2015)	House
CA	VALADAO, David G.	113th (2013–2015)	House
CA	VARGAS, Juan	113th (2013–2015)	House
CA	AGUILAR, Peter Rey	114th (2015–2017)	House
CA	TORRES, Norma Judith	114th (2015–2017)	House
CA	BARRAGÁN, Nanette Diaz	115th (2017–2019)	House
CA	CARBAJAL, Salud	115th (2017–2019)	House
CA	CORREA, Jose Luis	115th (2017–2019)	House
CA	GOMEZ, Jimmy	115th (2017–2019)	House
CA	CISNEROS, Gil	116th (2019–2021)	House
Colorado			
CO	SALAZAR, John	109th (2005–2007)	House
CO	SALAZAR, Kenneth Lee	109th (2005–2007)	Senate
Florida			
FL	HERNÁNDEZ, Joseph Marion	17th (1821–1823)	House
FL	ROS-LEHTINEN, Ileana	101st (1989–1991)	House
FL	DIAZ-BALART, Lincoln	103rd (1993–1995)	House
FL	DIAZ-BALART, Mario	108th (2003–2005)	House
FL	MARTINEZ, Melquiades R. (Mel)	109th (2005–2007)	Senate
FL	RIVERA, David	112th (2011–2013)	House
FL	RUBIO, Marco	112th (2011–2013)	Senate
FL	GARCIA, Joe	113th (2013–2015)	House
FL	CURBELO, Carlos	114th (2015–2017)	House

(Continued)

TABLE 8.1 (Continued)

State or Territory	Name	First Took Office	Service
FL	SOTO, Darren Michael	115th (2017–2019)	House
FL	MUCARSEL-POWELL, Debbie	116th (2019–2021)	House
Guam			
GU	BLAZ, Ben Garrido	99th (1985–1987)	House
GU	UNDERWOOD, Robert A.	103rd (1993–1995)	House
GU	SAN NICOLAS, Michael	116th (2019–2021)	House
Idaho			
ID	LABRADOR, Raúl R.	112th (2011–2013)	House
Illinois			
IL	GUTIÉRREZ, Luis V.	103rd (1993–1995)	House
IL	GARCÍA, Jesús G. (Chuy)	116th (2019–2021)	House
Louisiana			
LA	LAZARO, Ladislas	63rd (1913–1915)	House
LA	FERNÁNDEZ, Joachim Octave	72nd (1931–1933)	House
Massachusetts			
MA	TRAHAN, Lori	116th (2019–2021)	House
Nevada			
NV	CORTEZ MASTO, Catherine Marie	115th (2017–2019)	Senate
NV	KIHUEN, Ruben J.	115th (2017–2019)	House
New Jersey			
NJ	MENENDEZ, Robert	103rd (1993–1995)	House
NJ	SIRES, Albio	109th (2005–2007)	House
New Mexico			
NM	GALLEGOS, José Manuel	33rd (1853–1855)	House
NM	OTERO, Miguel Antonio	34th (1855–1857)	House
NM	PEREA, Francisco	38th (1863–1865)	House
NM	CHAVES, José Francisco	39th (1865–1867)	House
NM	ROMERO, Trinidad	45th (1877–1879)	House
NM	OTERO, Mariano Sabino	46th (1879–1881)	House
NM	LUNA, Tranquilino	47th (1881–1883)	House
NM	MANZANARES, Francisco Antonio	48th (1883–1885)	House
NM	PEREA, Pedro	56th (1899–1901)	House
NM	HERNÁNDEZ, Benigno Cárdenas	64th (1915–1917)	House
NM	MONTOYA, Néstor	67th (1921–1923)	House
NM	LARRAZOLO, Octaviano Ambrosio	70th (1927–1929)	Senate
NM	CHAVEZ, Dennis	72nd (1931–1933)	House
NM	FERNÁNDEZ, Antonio M.	78th (1943–1945)	House
NM	MONTOYA, Joseph Manuel	85th (1957–1959)	House
NM	LUJÁN, Manuel Jr.	91st (1969–1971)	House
NM	RICHARDSON, Bill	98th (1983–1985)	House
NM	LUJÁN, Ben Ray	111th (2009–2011)	House
NM	LUJAN GRISHAM, Michelle	113th (2013–2015)	House
NM	TORRES SMALL, Xochitl	116th (2019–2021)	House
New York			
NY	BADILLO, Herman	92nd (1971–1973)	House
NY	GARCIA, Robert	95th (1977–1979)	House

(*Continued*)

TABLE 8.1 (Continued)

State or Territory	Name	First Took Office	Service
NY	SERRANO, José E.	101st (1989–1991)	House
NY	VELÁZQUEZ, Nydia M.	103rd (1993–1995)	House
NY	ESPAILLAT, Adriano J.	115th (2017–2019)	House
NY	DELGADO, Antonio	116th (2019–2021)	House
NY	OCASIO-CORTEZ, Alexandria	116th (2019–2021)	House
Northern Mariana Islands			
MP	SABLAN, Gregorio Kilili Camacho	111th (2009–2011)	House
Ohio			
OH	GONZALEZ, Anthony	116th (2019–2021)	House
Puerto Rico			
PR	DEGETAU, Federico	57th (1901–1903)	House
PR	LARRÍNAGA, Tulio	59th (1905–1907)	House
PR	MUÑOZ RIVERA, Luis	62nd (1911–1913)	House
PR	DÁVILA, Félix Córdova	65th (1917–1919)	House
PR	PESQUERA, José Lorenzo	72nd (1931–1933)	House
PR	IGLESIAS, Santiago	73rd (1933–1935)	House
PR	PAGÁN, Bolívar	76th (1939–1941)	House
PR	FERNÓS-ISERN, Antonio	79th (1945–1947)	House
PR	PIÑERO, Jesús T.	79th (1945–1947)	House
PR	POLANCO-ABREU, Santiago	89th (1965–1967)	House
PR	CÓRDOVA-DÍAZ, Jorge Luis	91st (1969–1971)	House
PR	BENÍTEZ, Jaime	93rd (1973–1975)	House
PR	CORRADA-DEL RÍO, Baltasar	95th (1977–1979)	House
PR	FUSTER, Jaime B.	99th (1985–1987)	House
PR	COLORADO, Antonio J.	102nd (1991–1993)	House
PR	ROMERO-BARCELÓ, Carlos A.	103rd (1993–1995)	House
PR	ACEVEDO-VILÁ, Aníbal	107th (2001–2003)	House
PR	FORTUÑO, Luis G.	109th (2005–2007)	House
PR	PIERLUISI, Pedro	111th (2009–2011)	House
PR	GONZÁLEZ-CÓLON, Jenniffer	115th (2017–2019)	House
Texas			
TX	GONZÁLEZ, Henry B.	87th (1961–1963)	House
TX	DE LA GARZA, Eligio, II (Kika)	89th (1965–1967)	House
TX	ORTIZ, Solomon P.	98th (1983–1985)	House
TX	BUSTAMANTE, Albert G.	99th (1985–1987)	House
TX	BONILLA, Henry	103rd (1993–1995)	House
TX	TEJEDA, Frank	103rd (1993–1995)	House
TX	HINOJOSA, Rubén	105th (1997–1999)	House
TX	REYES, Silvestre	105th (1997–1999)	House
TX	RODRIGUEZ, Ciro D.	105th (1997–1999)	House
TX	GONZALEZ, Charles A.	106th (1999–2001)	House
TX	CUELLAR, Henry	109th (2005–2007)	House
TX	CANSECO, Francisco Raul (Quico)	112th (2011–2013)	House
TX	FLORES, Bill	112th (2011–2013)	House
TX	CASTRO, Joaquin	113th (2013–2015)	House
TX	CRUZ, Rafael Edward (Ted)	113th (2013–2015)	Senate

(Continued)

TABLE 8.1 (Continued)

State or Territory	Name	First Took Office	Service
TX	GALLEGO, Pete P.	113th (2013–2015)	House
TX	VELA, Filemon	113th (2013–2015)	House
TX	GONZALEZ, Vicente Jr.	115th (2017–2019)	House
TX	ESCOBAR, Veronica	116th (2019–2021)	House
TX	GARCIA, Sylvia R.	116th (2019–2021)	House
Virgin Islands			
VI	DE LUGO, Ron	93rd (1973–1975)	House
Washington			
WA	HERRERA BEUTLER, Jaime	112th (2011–2013)	House
West Virginia			
WV	MOONEY, Alex X.	114th (2015–2017)	House

Sources: Office of the Historian: history@mail.house.gov; Office of Art & Archives, Office of the Clerk: art@mail.house.gov, archives@mail.house.gov.

as increased naturalization among foreign-born Latinos, describe a more active Latino electorate.

Scholars interested in descriptive representation often focus their research on the presence of minority representatives in the US Congress, the branch of the federal government that is in theory intended to provide the public with representation given the relative connection voters have with their member of Congress. As reflected in figure 8.1, there has been a steady increase in the number of nonwhite members of Congress (MCs) over time. More than 20 percent of voting members (22 percent) of the US House of Representatives and Senate are racial or ethnic minorities, making the 116th Congress the most racially and ethnically diverse in history (Bialik 2019).

Although the growing diversity in Congress over time should be celebrated (see figure 8.1), many groups remain highly under-represented in federal representation based on the concept of descriptive representation. When we compare the percentage of members of Congress of each racial and ethnic group to their share of the overall US population, some racial and ethnic groups are now on par with their share of the total population—thus having descriptive representation when measured this way. For example, roughly 12 percent of US House members are African American and 1 percent are Native American, which is close to these groups' share of the US population. Latinos, however, remain highly underrepresented, with the share of Hispanics in the US population (18 percent) being twice as high as it is in the House (9 percent). Similarly, Asians account for 6 percent of the national population but 3 percent of House members. The common factor among Latinos and Asians that may help explain their relatively low levels of descriptive representation is the high ratio of both groups who are foreign-born and who are ineligible to vote, due to either being younger than age eighteen or undocumented. Conversely, whites are overrepresented in the House, with their share of MCs being significantly higher than their ratio of the overall US population.

State and Local Levels and Latinos

Latinos have also made a significant impact in representation at state and local levels. Although Latinos have in the past been absent at the gubernatorial level, they have targeted governors' mansions and state legislatures to increase their representational

FIGURE 8.1 Growing Racial and Ethnic Diversity in Congress

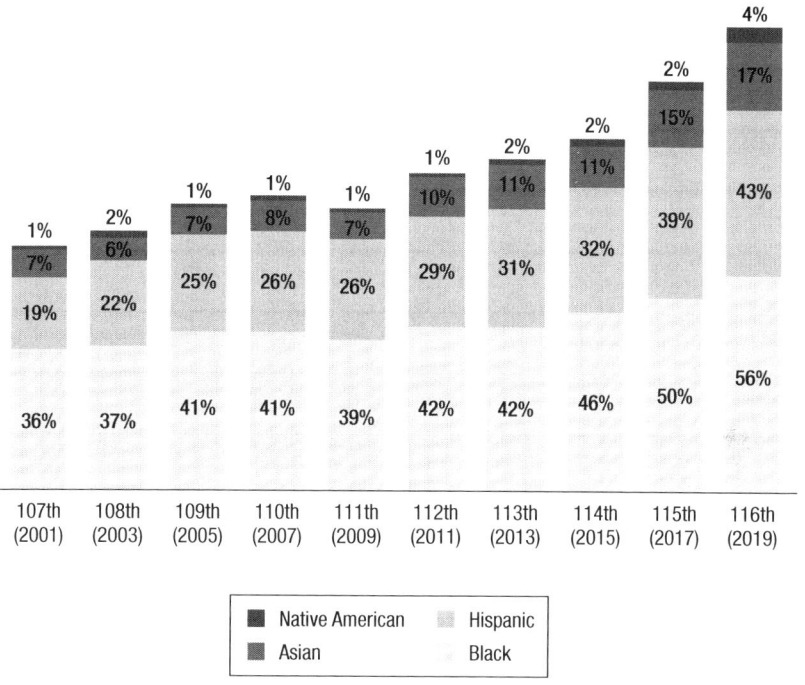

Source: Pew Research Center; Congressional Research Service, CQ Roll Call, Brookings Institution.

levels. In 2010, gubernatorial gains among Latinos increased by two with the election of Republicans Brian Sandoval in Nevada and Susana Martinez in New Mexico (both were reelected in subsequent elections). New Mexico has continued its leadership in descriptive representation with the election of another Latina to governor in 2018, Democrat Michelle Lujan-Grisham. Hispanic Americans have also had a large presence in state legislatures across the country. According to NALEO's analysis of Latino representation following the 2016 election, that election year was a watershed election for Latino state-level representation, where Latino legislators grew from 307 to 321. This included having 77 (up from 73) Latinos in the senate and 244 Latinos in the houses of their state (up 10 from 234). Among the 244 Latinos in state houses, 194 are Democrats and 50 are Republicans, reflecting a more historic trend of greater representation of Latinos within the Democratic party. The following quote from NALEO president Arturo Vargas reflects how 2016 marked an election where Latinos' presence as candidates was incredibly diverse:

> Latino candidates successfully ran for state legislative office in 33 states, winning bids in areas with both Latino population centers and without. There is no such thing as a Latino or non-Latino designated district anymore, with Latinos once again demonstrating the ability and expertise needed to build support from a broad coalition of Americans in Election 2016. (NALEO 2016)

It is not clear if the 2016 election was a sign of bigger things to come for Latino state-level representation or a high-water mark for Latinos, but the 2018 election was not as successful for Latino candidates. Latinos lost ground in both the senate and lower houses across the country. Although 2018 did not continue the overall growth in Latino representation over time, the strong increase in Latinas elected at the state level was very visible and reflective of the powerful role of gender across elections for office. After 2018 there were 103 Latinas serving in their state (up 5), and 36 Latins serving in their state's senate (up 4).

Virtually all the Latinos in Congress began their political careers holding local offices, which makes analysis of local-level offices such as mayor and city council important to discuss. In 2001 and 2002, Latinos sought the mayoralty in the major cities of Los Angeles, New York, Houston, San Antonio, and San Jose. They were successful only in the latter two cities. Despite the unsuccessful efforts of Fernando Ferrer (New York City), Orlando Sanchez (Houston), and Antonio Villaraigosa (Los Angeles—he later won the mayoral election in 2005 and left that office in 2013), their strong campaigns demonstrated the accumulation of political experience, which carries over to subsequent elections. Latinos have been elected mayor of several major cities, including Albuquerque, Miami, El Paso, Denver, Los Angeles, and San Jose, among others. Most recently, Regina Romero was elected in early November 2019 as the first female mayor of Tucson, Arizona. Mayor Romero is the only Latina mayor in the fifty largest cities in the United States.

Increasing mayoral competition has not been limited to the largest American cities; gains among Latino officeholders are increasing for communities of all sizes and for other local offices (Orr and Morel 2018). The presence of Latino candidates from subgroups other than the Mexican-origin, Puerto Rican, and Cuban communities is becoming more evident. In the second decade of the new millennium, a larger pool of candidates will come from these Latino subgroups. For example, Ana Maria Sol Gutiérrez, former school board member in Prince George's County, was the first Salvadoran to run for the Maryland state legislature. She was elected to the Maryland General Assembly in November 2002. In California, Norma Torres (Guatemalan) was elected to represent the thirty-fifth district in 2014. The pool of Latino candidates holding local offices becomes the next wave of Latinos vying for state and federal offices.

We now introduce another form of representation that many consider to be the most important type, substantive **representation**. This form of representation focuses on the outcomes of the policy-making process to determine if those outcomes advance the collective interest of the Latino community. There have been mixed findings in research focused on whether Latino elected officials are more likely to provide Latinos with substantive representation than non-Latino officials. Some scholars find that Latino MCs are more likely to vote on issues defined as important to Latino constituents (e.g., Welch and Hibbing 1984; Kerr and Miller 1997; Wilson 2010), while others do not (e.g., Hero and Tolbert 1995; Casellas 2007; Wallace 2014). There has also been some research that finds that Latinos in office provide support for Latinos under certain circumstances, such as in districts where there are high percentages of Latinos (Lublin 1997; Minta 2011; Casellas 2011; Casellas and Leal 2013). It therefore remains somewhat unclear if Latinos have benefited from gains in descriptive representation or if they have yet to reach a point of critical mass that may result in a great relationship with substantive representation.

Latinos and Organizations: Historical Origins

One of the benefits of sustained and directed research about Latinos, particularly since the late 1960s, is the extent of gained knowledge about Latino organizations, past and present. We know that organizations are an aggregation of individuals with common interests. For Latinos in the United States, the existence of Latino-based organizations serves a number of purposes and/or objectives. We know much more about Mexican-origin organizations than any other Latino subgroup due to the extensive research literature and their longevity in the United States. For the most part, Mexican American or Chicano organizations can be grouped by major purposes or goals (Tirado 1970): mutual aid societies/*mutualistas*, cultural/home-community clubs (largely immigrant-based groups), adaptation-/adjustment-focused organizations, civil rights and advocacy organizations, social service providers or facilitators, political organizations, professional (occupation-related) organizations, and community (or grassroots-based) organizations.

It is important to understand the different objectives of Latino organizations. Each basis for organizational existence impacts the organizational base (grassroots membership, immigrants, local residents, elites or professionals, etc.) and the primary strategies employed. At the same time, there are other important dimensions to identify and understand in examining organizations and their links to Latino political involvement. In addition to their membership bases, organizational size and resources, multiple goals and objectives, and modes of political action link Latino organizations with specific political arenas. Is the organization a mass-based group or is it composed of elites?

For example, the Mexican American Legal Defense and Education Fund (MALDEF) is composed primarily of attorneys and other professionals, but they act on behalf of a broader Latino constituency. Is the organization primarily local or national in scope? For a Latino-based group, what is the role of culture, group identity, and national origin in attracting members and influencing the organization's agenda or mission? Does class or gender come into play regarding the group's mission, membership base, and major organizational issues? Has assimilation or cultural pluralism, cultural nationalism, or political integration affected the formation of the Latino organization, its strategies, and its membership base?

Since the mid-1980s and beyond, the development of pan-ethnicity has broadened the organizational base to include more Latino subgroups. This places different organizational pressures and expectations on longer-standing Latino organizations and entails many challenges for newer organizations. Latino organizations are trying to represent a wider spectrum of all Latinos in national arenas as the demographics we discussed earlier in the book continue to evolve. This can motivate organizations to change where they house their offices and even what they are called. For example, the National Council of La Raza (NCLR) was originally the Southwest Council of La Raza (SWCLR), with its primary constituency being comprised of Mexican Americans or Chicanos. More recently, this organization again changed its name, taking on the brand of UnidosUS. The organization has noted that they made this decision after conducting focus groups and a national survey that suggested that the NCLR name did not resonate with many of their constituents and was providing an obstacle to increased engagement with members of the Latino community.[2] While its goal of reducing poverty and discrimination, as well as improving opportunities for Mexican Americans,

TABLE 8.2 Organizational Dimensions and Aspects of Latino Organizations

Organizational Dimensions	Organizational Aspects
Membership base	Mass or elite base (professionals), class based, gender based
Goals/objectives	Specific (material benefits, services, job placement, etc.) or general (assimilation, pluralism, equality, etc.), cultural maintenance, social, civil rights
Strategies	Electoral, voting, lobbying, direct actions/protests, coalitions, etc.
Organizational structure	Decentralized, local chapters, regional, centralized, permanent professional staff
Geographic base	Local or citywide, neighborhood base, national policy making, regional
Organizational resources	Membership dues, foundation grants, federal grants/funds, litigation judgments
Leadership	Autocratic, charismatic, popularly elected, bureaucratic, institutionalized, regularized

Source: Tirado 1970.

has not changed, its activities now target all Hispanics/Latinos. Similarly, the arena is more focused on Washington, DC, and national issues. It has extended its chapters into the Northeast, Midwest, and South. The research and advocacy unit of UnidosUS focuses much of its activities on national policies such as immigration reform, social welfare reform, reapportionment and redistricting, and affirmative action policies. This example illustrates the need for organizations that intend to represent the Latino community to evolve and grow to best reflect the population they serve.

The goal of this chapter is to weave the critical components of the origins and life cycles of Latino organizations through organizing principles that emerge from the questions raised above and through specific Latino organizations. Table 8.2 presents a general description of the central elements found in Latino organizations, as well as in most organizations in American political life. The key components include the following: (1) membership base, (2) primary organizational objectives or goals, (3) geographic base and focus of operation, (4) organizational structure and its leadership, (5) organizational strategies and approaches, (6) role of culture, class, and gender in organizational development, and (7) organizational resource base and adaptations to pan-ethnic developments.

The existence and activity of Latino-based organizations have been evident as long as Latinos have inhabited the United States. As mentioned earlier, there is significant documentation of Mexican-origin communities and their organizations. The organizations Orden de los Hijos de America and La Alianza HispanoAmericano (Briegal 1970) operated in the nineteenth century largely to assist Mexicanos to survive in the United States (providing burial insurance, rotating credit associations, cultural maintenance, etc.). The Alianza established chapters throughout the Southwest and even into Mexico. Its adaptability over the years of its operation has involved social service delivery programs directed to the Mexican-origin community, especially its immigrant segment. These organizations reflected the segregated and marginalized position that Mexicanos held in American society. Day-to-day survival and adaptation were the focus of early Mexican American organizations.

The turn of the nineteenth century saw a major influx of Mexicanos into the Southwest, partially due to political turmoil and the Mexican Revolution. As a result, migration continued to the Southwest and industrial, manufacturing sites in the Midwest (J. R. García 1980, 1995). The steel, automobile, railroad, and tanning industries, among others, served as employment magnets for many Mexican workers. In the Southwest, Mexican American organizations formed around labor groups and unions, mutual-aid societies, social clubs based on community of origin, and groups that promoted assimilation into mainstream American society.

League of United Latin American Citizens

A good example of the latter type of Latino organization is the League of United Latin American Citizens (LULAC), the oldest organization that operates on behalf of the Latino community. Formed in Texas in 1927, this group consisted of Mexican American citizens who sought to acquire the rights and privileges of American citizenship, as well as to honor the duties and responsibilities of being American. Membership was restricted to Mexican-origin citizens, and loyalty to the United States and assimilation to achieve economic mobility were a central aspect of the organization's creed. Nevertheless, LULAC (Márquez 1988) engaged in activities that dealt with Mexican culture and pride. Initially the group focused on promoting the use of English, educational achievement and opportunities, economic opportunities (jobs and job training), and political participation and access. Thus, the LULAC community did not include all Mexican-origin persons, although social service activities were not limited to citizens. For example, in the 1950s it founded the Little Schools of the 400, a preschool program to equip Mexican-origin children with a four-hundred-word core English vocabulary prior to entering public school.

Politically, this group saw itself as a nonpartisan policy advocacy organization. In the late 1940s and early 1950s, it sought to eliminate segregation of Mexican students (San Miguel 1987) in both California and Texas through litigation. Education has been a central issue for LULAC, which, since the late 1990s, has concerned itself with access to higher education and school financing for Latinos, as well as continuing its efforts to generate scholarship awards. It located its central offices in Washington, DC, and gave its executive director considerable latitude, with appropriate staffing to engage in national lobbying on Latino issues. In the mid-1980s, LULAC joined organizational forces with the NCLR, MALDEF, and the Congressional Hispanic Caucus (CHC) to defeat and then significantly modify the **Immigration Reform and Control Act of 1986** (IRCA) (Sierra 1991). LULAC has been a continuous proponent of comprehensive immigration reform since 2004.

While it had not excluded other Latinos, as a southwestern organization its core base was the Mexican-origin population. LULAC characterizes itself as a national organization, but it has been "fully entrenched" in Washington, DC, with federal policy makers since the 1970s. A national office with enough staffing, sustained lobbying efforts, and national media attention are the elements of LULAC. It maintains a decentralized organizational structure with localized chapters and officers and holds an annual national convention at which national officers and policy decisions are determined. LULAC has also had a significant presence at colleges and universities across the country, providing Latino college students with leadership opportunities.[3]

Civil Rights, Litigation, and Latino Organizations

While LULAC can be seen as a Latino organization that has evolved into a national advocacy organization, its strategies have been largely constructed around a large, "mass-based" membership that provides its leadership with a loud and sizable voice to exert pressure regarding issues important to the Latino community. Other Latino organizations have a different membership base and pursue different strategies for Latino sociopolitical advancement. Two such organizations are Latino Justice (formerly known as the Puerto Rican Legal Defense and Education Fund—PRLDEF) and Mexican American Legal Defense and Education Fund (MALDEF). The decision to change the name to Latino Justice was driven to some extent by the desire to recognize a common struggle facing Latinos based on immigration politics and policy.

Civil rights and equal opportunities for Latinos have been the focus of both groups. Founded in the early 1970s, their central objectives have been protection under law and civil rights for Puerto Ricans and Mexican-origin populations. Over time, the scope has expanded to be more inclusive of all Latinos. Each group's membership base consists primarily of attorneys, and funding is derived from foundation grants, legal fees and judgments, and fundraising (private and corporate gifts). For the most part, their areas of focus include educational equity, equal employment, voting rights, equal housing opportunity, and leadership development. MALDEF includes the policy area of immigrant rights as part of its central mission. Latino Justice has become a national leader in criminal justice reform, providing documentaries and research to inform and advocate on behalf of the Latino community. This has included a national survey with Latino Decisions that identified that Latinos overwhelmingly support increased funding to support rehabilitation and mental health services to address crime.[4]

These Latino litigation organizations identify specific practices, locations, and plaintiffs to pursue changes in current policies or seek the full implementation of the law. For example, in *Aspira v. New York Board of Education*, PRLDEF raised the area of language rights and access to bilingual education services and resources. MALDEF in *Tyler v. Phloe* challenged the area of free educational access by undocumented school-age children. The local school district required proof of legal status for school-age children to receive a "free" public education. As a result, the court ruled that access to education is a "basic right" accorded to all persons residing in a school district's jurisdiction. In the area of voting rights, PRLDEF and MALDEF have challenged the election structure of at-large districts since the 1970s (i.e., seeking district rather than at-large elections) and focused on redistricting plans in order to increase Latino representation (promoting the creation of **majority-minority districts**).

Both organizations have a board of directors and a general counsel to lead them. Representation comes primarily from the legal and corporate sectors, and they are less connected to a geographic or mass population base. The nature and policy arenas of PRLDEF and MALDEF render them unsuitable for being mass-based or grassroots-driven organizations. Even though their organizational bases are not directly linked to a mass-based Latino constituency, both organizations have ongoing ties with other Latino organizations and leadership that enable them to be effective and strategic in determining which areas, issues, and plaintiffs to work with. These organizations have served as policy protectors and initiators of policy expansion for the Latino communities. Challenging existing election systems (i.e., voter ID laws, limiting early voting, etc.) that are detrimental to Latino representation; contesting funding and program inequities in both K–12 and higher education in terms of educational quality, access, and opportunities; and fighting employment discrimination against Latinos due to phenotype, accent, or negative stereotypes represent policy-expansion initiatives.

Exile Organizations: The Cuban Community?

In many respects, several Latino subgroups can be viewed as incorporating an exile orientation and organizational vehicles for influence and action. For Latinos from Nicaragua, El Salvador, Guatemala, Argentina, and Uruguay (to name a few), political factors affect their decision to come to the United States. Yet, political refugee immigration status is not automatically accorded to persons from any Latin American country except Cuba. For the most part, on a case-by-case basis, proof of imminent danger due to political beliefs and activities serves as the primary criterion for achieving political refugee status. As noted in chapter 4, the growing Cuban community in the United States has been characterized as an exile group (Pérez 1985, 1986). In this manner, much of the community's attention and energy has focused on US foreign policy toward Cuba and the Castro regime. Goals have included trade embargoes, establishment of Radio-TV Martí, continued admission of Cuban émigrés as political refugees, democratization of Cuba via the growth of civil society, and the demise of Fidel Castro and his socialist state.

Thus, several major organizations in the Cuban community have the emphasis of an exile community oriented toward Cuba. At the same time, Cuban organizations assist the adaptation and adjustment of Cubans in the economic and political arenas of the United States. An example of an exile-oriented organization is the Cuban American National Foundation (CANF), until recently led by Jorge Mas Canosa and now headed by José Mas Santos. CANF actively promotes the self-determination of the Cuban people and the dismantling of the communist regime. It stands against a centralized, government-controlled economy and a one-party state. Founded in 1981, CANF has lobbied in Washington, DC, for political refugee asylum for Cubans, trade embargoes on and isolation of Cuba, aid for refugees, and media broadcasts (radio and television) as part of Radio-TV Martí. CANF has offices in Miami; Washington, DC; and Union City, New Jersey; as well as chapters in Texas, Georgia, Illinois, California, Spain, and Puerto Rico. Since 2003, CANF has placed greater emphasis on programs that promote expansion of an active civil society and democratic values, or what can be described as a "bottom-up" strategy.

This active organization has been quite effective in influencing US foreign policy toward Cuba. Programmatically, CANF supports the Cuban Exodus Relief Fund, informational and policy reports serving clearinghouse functions, Mission Martí, the Foundation for Human Rights in Cuba, the Endowment for Cuban American Studies, and the Commission for Economic Reconstruction of Cuba. In 1988, CANF was able to get legislation passed allowing fifteen hundred Cubans in other countries to come to the United States, with fifteen hundred more Cuban "exiles" admitted annually thereafter. By 1995, ten thousand Cubans had been brought to the United States under this program. Their primary focus on removing Fidel Castro and dismantling the communist system reinforces the image of Cuban organizations as exile oriented. Since 1994, the "wet foot, dry foot" policy has been in effect, which enables Cuban émigrés who try to enter the United States to receive asylum if they are able to physically reach American shores.

There is strong evidence of broad-based support within the Cuban community for CANF; seven out of ten Cuban households have contributed to the foundation, and a Univision poll found that it was considered trustworthy and effective. Given its Cuba-centered focus, it has had strong ties to national Republican leadership, especially during the Reagan administration, and to Sen. Jesse Helms (R-NC). This was evident with the passage of the Helms-Burton Act, the 1992 Cuban Democracy Act tightening the trade embargo on Cuba, and the 1996 Cuban Liberation and Democratic Solidarity Act. Policies by the William Jefferson Clinton and George W. Bush administrations have placed greater restrictions on remittances, travel, and humanitarian aid, to which CANF has raised objections. With President Obama's initiative to normalize relations with Cuba, CANF has remained consistent with its emphasis on a transition to a democratic state. That is, there is resistance to a lift of the trade embargo until significant democratic reforms are in place by the Cuban government. At the same time, CANF has set up a Blue-Ribbon Commission to assist in the economic revival of Cuba's economy under an open market economy.

CANF's pervasive character within the Cuban community may suggest to some both uniformity and singularity of vision among the Cuban population in the United States. Yet, other Cuban-based organizations take alternative positions regarding Cuba, and still others work on the domestic front. The Cuban American National Council (CANC) is active in the areas of education, housing, and economic and development services. As a nonprofit organization, it receives funding from numerous levels of government, private corporations, and foundations. Founded in 1972, this organization has Latinos and other minorities as its primary "service" clientele. Its service projects include coordination and supportive services for thirty thousand Cubans and Haitians in Guantánamo, Cuba, building new housing units, providing direct job placements and at-risk-student intervention programs, founding and managing alternative schools, and supporting more than sixty policy publications and annual national conferences. CANC has dealt with interminority relations (especially between Cubans and African Americans), Cubanization effects in Miami, redistricting and bloc voting, and educational attainment and language. Overall, CANC directs its energies toward issues impacting Cubans and other Latinos once they reside in the United States.

Other organizations focusing on US-Cuban policies are the Cuban Committee for Democracy and Cambio Cubano. Both are moderate in their orientation toward Cuba. Perhaps characterized as socially democratic ideologically, these organizations see a more involved role for government in providing jobs, housing, and bilingual education. The board members include several Cuban academics, and its policy directions lean toward reconciliation and dialogue with the Cuban regime and open travel to Cuba. The increasing proportion of Cubans born in the United States (Moreno and Warren 1992) is partially at play, with a more diverse set of attitudes and policy preferences within the Cuban community.

For example, in 2014, a Florida International University (FIU) poll of Cubans surveyed opinion about the trade embargo, diplomatic relations, and greater apertures for movement of people and goods. A slight majority (52 percent) opposed continuing the trade embargo; support in continuation of the embargo was strongest among registered Republicans. A large majority (69 percent) favored diplomatic relations with Cuba, and 69 percent favored the lifting of travel restrictions impeding Americans from traveling to Cuba. Continuation of current US policies like the "wet/dry foot" immigration policy and the Cuban Adjustment Act are widely supported (63 percent and 86 percent, respectively). With an eye to future elections, candidates who support reestablishment of diplomatic relations and replacing a trade embargo with "open market" initiatives would garner a majority of Cuban voters.

Another aspect of the FIU Cuban Poll revealed a marked "generational divide" with regard to these policy areas. The eighteen- to twenty-nine-year-olds are more supportive of establishing diplomatic relations (+22 percent), lifting travel restrictions (+20 percent), supporting those candidates in favor of reinforcing diplomatic relations (+22 percent), and the lifting of trade embargoes (+16 percent) (Grenier and Gladwin 2014). As Cuban American organizational life develops in this new millennium, the continual focus upon exile-related issues (in addition to a wider range of policy responses toward Cuba) will evidence more variations among policy options, especially among the second-generation Cubans. The focus of a broad range of domestic issues and minority-based concerns common to Latinos and other minority groups, as well as some partisan shifts, will also become more established.

Professional Organizations and Latinos

Any description of Latino organizations must include mention of the hundreds of groups that focus on specific public policy issues and whose memberships largely consist of professionals. The range of policy interests includes bilingual education, mental health, small business development, immigration, job training, foreign trade policies, and access to and participation in most of the professional associations and societies. There are Latino groups in the health care/medical, legal, academic, and business-related fields, the religious denominations, social welfare professions, unions, and education.

Most of these Latino-based organizations center on a specific policy or occupational arena, such as education, health care, social services, and so on. Their membership consists of Latinos active in these arenas as professionals, activists, and concerned citizens. For example, professional organizations of Latino attorneys (HNBA), dentists (NAHD), engineers (SHPE), journalists (NAHJ), and bilingual educators (NABE) have access to Latino-related professional organizations. Organizations like the National Hispanic Medical Association and National Hispanic Media Association can have significant influence in their areas of specialization.

On the policy front, these organizations seek changes within their respective professional organizations; they also conduct research and advocate policy at all levels of government. For example, the **National Association of Bilingual Educators** (NABE) describes itself as both a professional and an advocacy association. Through its research, professional development, public education, and legislative advocacy, it strives to implement educational policies and practices to ensure equal educational opportunity for diverse students. As is consistent with its organizational objectives, NABE pursues its activities on behalf of language-minority students with an added dimension of multiculturalism. NABE pursues its goals through special interest groups

(SIGs),[5] which enable its membership to pursue more salient interests in greater depth, as well as benefit the organization with thoughtful ideas, policy positions, and analysis. The SIGs serve as working policy subgroups that enable members who specialize in subfields of bilingual education to focus their expertise on developing policy analysis and recommendations to present to the general membership.

Another cluster of Latino organizations exists in the business and economic realms of public policy. These organizations emphasize the contributions of Latinos to economic growth and development, as well as to promoting greater participation by Latinos as entrepreneurs. Organizations such as the US Hispanic Chamber of Commerce (USHCC) assist the economic development of Hispanic firms with the corporate sector and governmental initiatives and programs. Many large cities have Hispanic Chamber of Commerce organizations that provide similar functions as the USHCC for their cities. Similar Latino organizations include the Hispanic Association for Corporate Responsibility (HACR), the National Hispanic Corporate Council (NHCC), and the US-Mexican Chamber of Commerce. The USHCC defines its mission as "actively promoting the economic growth and development of Hispanic entrepreneurs."[6] Its activities include strengthening national programs to assist Hispanic economic development, increasing business relationships and partnerships between the corporate sector and Hispanic-owned businesses, providing technical assistance to Hispanic business associations and entrepreneurs, and monitoring legislation, policies, and programs that affect the Hispanic business community.

While there exist business-oriented Latino organizations that focus on the employers' side of Latinos in the economy, others focus on the workers' side of economic issues. For example, the Labor Council for Latin American Advancement (LCLAA) is a trade union association that represents 1.4 million Latino workers in forty-three international unions. It serves as a Latino constituency group within the AFL-CIO and engages in advocacy and political work. The high concentration of Latinos in the workforce in the service industry makes the **Service Employees International Union** (SEIU) an important labor union to Latinos. While open to all racial and ethnic groups, the organization of two million or so members focuses on improving the lives of workers in these areas of the workforce and targets racial and ethnic discrimination in the workplace. Both labor unions address issues such as low wages, employment-related discrimination, union recognition, and socioeconomic mobility. Another workers' organization is the United Farm Workers of America (UFW; affiliated with the AFL-CIO), founded by César Chávez, Dolores Huerta, and Larry Itlong in the early 1960s (Griswold del Castillo and Garcia 1995). Focusing on agricultural workers, initially in the Southwest, it directed its efforts toward union recognition, wages, working conditions, health and safety issues, and employment-related benefits. Early struggles entailed organizing native-born and immigrant agricultural workers to seek collective bargaining status and legislation enabling federal and state coverage for these workers. Over the years, the United Farm Workers has had its share of victories and setbacks. After the death of César Chávez in 1993, the union was led by Arturo Rodriguez (president) and Dolores Huerta (secretary-treasurer). In 2018, Teresa Romero became the first Latina to become president of UFW, taking over for Arturo Rodriguez.

Since 2000, the United Service Workers Union has been more aggressively involved in organizing the immigrant segment of the workforce. Strikes in Los Angeles and Chicago illustrated the organizational force of office service workers and the extensive involvement of Latino immigrants (both undocumented and permanent resident aliens). During the 1990s, labor reassessed its position on immigration reform and the undocumented segment of the labor force. In contrast, the AFL-CIO leadership stated it would press Congress to grant amnesty to the nation's six to eight million undocumented immigrants (L. Rodriguez 2000). Also, during the 1990s, labor looked around the country to identify unorganized workers and found them in agriculture, meatpacking, hotels, and restaurants. For Latino immigrants and other undocumented workers, an alliance with the labor movement represented an opportunity to press for legalization and improved wage levels and working conditions. The UFW is currently focusing on addressing the extreme heat in many areas where immigrants work through legislation that would set national heat regulations for farm workers and establish greater paths to citizenship for agricultural workers.

Internal changes are also evident in the AFL-CIO, with Latino gains as labor organizers and officials (e.g., the election of Linda Chavez-Thompson as executive vice president of the AFL-CIO in 1995) within unions in the manufacturing, service, farming, and food-service sectors. Union organizers have worked within their states to ensure that adequate labor laws such as agricultural labor laws enable the formation of formal unions. In addition, many unions with foreign-born workers have initiated producing material in Spanish, bilingual union meetings, and access to leadership training (Bada, Fox, and Selee 2006). The immigrant protest marches of 2006 also witnessed significant labor involvement in the organization and leadership of these events (Milkman 2011; Barreto et al. 2009). At the same time, the extent of unionization among immigrant workers is affected by existing unions and their leadership in the economic sectors most populated by these workers. Both figures 8.2 and 8.3 provide some information as to these developments.

Although many of the organizations discussed so far have funded polling and research as they have modernized their operations, another sector of organizations is more policy and research oriented. For instance, the Pew Hispanic Center began as a joint enterprise by the *Washington Post*, the Kaiser Family Foundation, and the Pew Research Centers to conduct a 1999 national survey of Latinos in the United States. This was an important survey for researchers and scholars at a time when national data reflecting opinions of Latinos was much rarer than it is today.[7] This program has been conducting surveys ever since, covering a wide range of topics affecting the Latino community (immigration, political participation, education). Since 2000, the Pew Hispanic Center has made available its survey data for further analysis by researchers, the media, and advocacy organizations. In addition, a number of Latino/Hispanic research centers at several colleges and universities (e.g., the Latino Politics and Policy Institute at UCLA, Center for Latinos and American Politics Research at Arizona State University, the Mexican American and Latino Research Center at Texas A&M, and Institute for Latino Studies at Notre Dame) are conducting major research projects that serve to effect a Latino policy agenda and public knowledge base for the Latino community and its organizations.

More recently Latino Decisions was formed representing a combination of political scientists experienced with Latino populations and an understanding of how demographics, identity, public opinion, participation, and research methodology intersect. What makes Latino Decisions unique among other research entities is the direct link between academic research and applied electoral and policy research conducted by

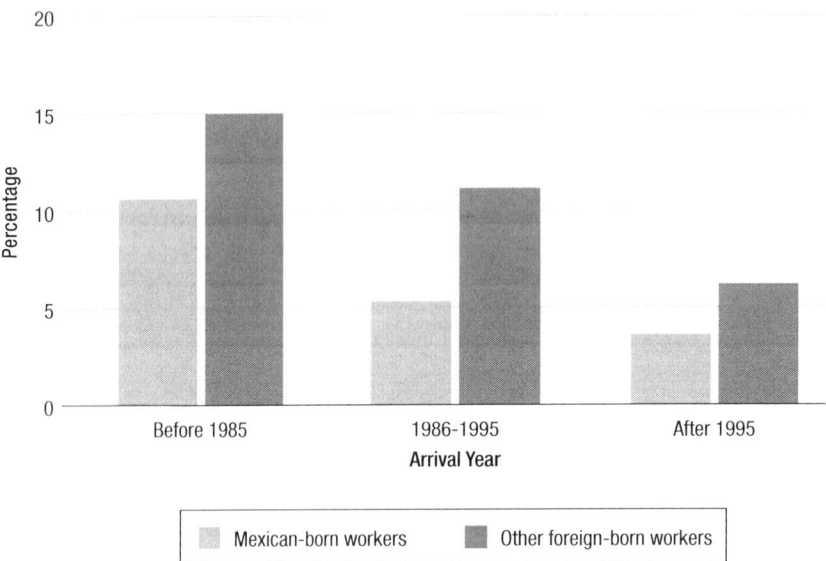

FIGURE 8.2 Unionization Rates among Mexican Immigrants and Other Foreign-Born Workers by Date of Arrival, 2004

Source: Adapted from US Current Population Survey, Merged Outgoing Rotation Group Files, and paper presented by Ruth Milkman, "Labor Organizing among Mexican-Born Workers in the United States: Recent Trends and Future Prospects," at the Race, Gender and Labor in the New Global Economy Conference in honor of Edna Bonacich, University of California, Riverside, June 2006.

the firm. This has included providing social scientists interested in Latino politics with cutting-edge data, such as the CMPS survey organized by Latino Decisions referenced prominently in this volume. However, the firm's cofounders, Gary Segura and Matt Barreto, also served as the Latino pollsters for the Hillary Clinton campaign in 2016, while principals Sylvia Manzano and Gabriel Sanchez led research efforts for several national Latino GOTV campaigns in 2016 and 2018. The effort of Latino Decisions to make most of the toplines and crosstabs of their surveys available to scholars of Latino politics through their webpage and blog has advanced our collective knowledge of Latino political behavior.

These research centers and similarly oriented organizations also influence students of Latino politics and their ability to analyze and test key relationships and trends for this community. The growth of such research centers and the increasing base of researchers provide opportunities for greater understanding and use of versatile skill sets to analyze and solve problems and formulate long-term strategies, media coverage, and content dealing with Latinos and the American sociopolitical system.

Latino Organizations within Political Institutions

The end of the second millennium brought a major shift for Latino organizations from a more regional and local scope to a greater national presence and involvement. Bridging the various Latino subcommunities to embrace a pan-ethnic focus has been a challenge as well as an opportunity to expand the Latino resource base and agenda.

FIGURE 8.3 Unionization Rates by Type of Worker: National Origin, Nativity, and Citizen Status, 2004

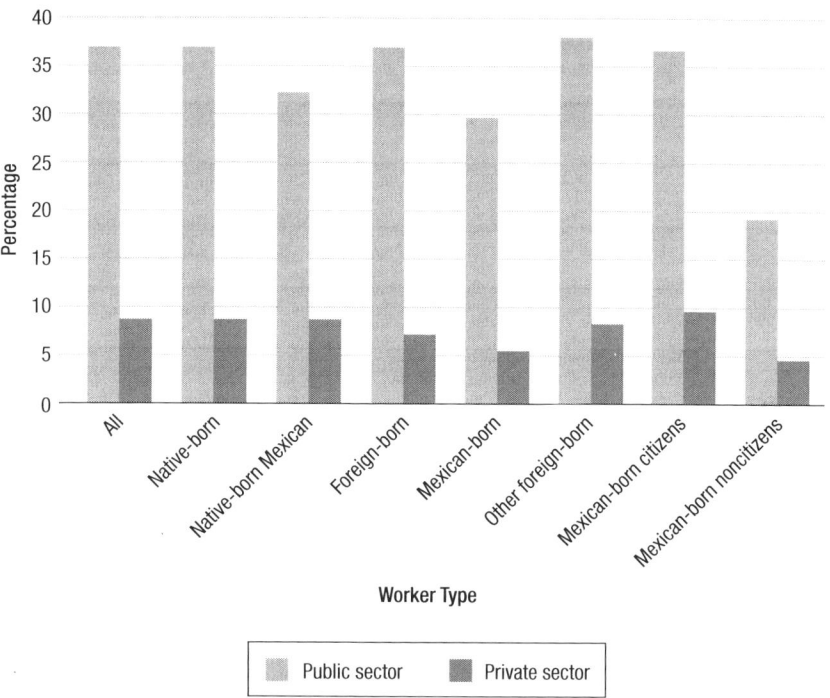

Source: Adapted from US Current Population Survey, Merged Outgoing Rotation Group Files, and paper presented by Ruth Milkman, "Labor Organizing among Mexican-Born Workers in the United States: Recent Trends and Future Prospects," at the Race, Gender and Labor in the New Global Economy Conference in honor of Edna Bonacich, University of California, Riverside, June 2006.

The Latino organizational leadership in political organizations has become more institutionalized in the sense that organizational skills, networks, and institutional positioning have supplanted charismatic appeal. The creation of the Congressional Hispanic Caucus and its institute, the CHCI, in 1976 marked the creation of a legislative organization within the US Congress comprised of members themselves. With only five Hispanic congresspersons at that time, the founders' goals were to work with other groups both inside and outside Congress to intensify federal commitment to Latinos, as well as to increase Latinos' awareness of the execution and purpose of the American political system.[8] By 1978, the CHCI had formed a 501(c)(3) nonprofit organization to add an educational component for leadership development and educational stipends and internships. Its board of directors has been expanded to include representatives from other Hispanic organizations and the corporate sector.

One of CHCI's primary functions is to unite its members around a collective legislative agenda for Latino interests, as well as to monitor executive and judicial policies that affect Hispanics. For example, for many years, the CHCI had been advocating to fill Supreme Court vacancies from a pool of several Latino federal judges. In May 2009, President Barack Obama nominated Sonia Sotomayor for appointment to the US Supreme Court to replace retired justice David Souter. The US Senate confirmed her nomination in August 2009 by a vote of sixty-eight to thirty-one. Previously, Sotomayor had been nominated to the US District Court for the Southern District of New York by President George H. W. Bush in 1991, and her nomination was confirmed in 1992. In 1995, she issued a preliminary injunction against Major League Baseball, which ended the 1994 baseball strike. Sotomayor made a ruling allowing the *Wall Street Journal* to publish Deputy White House Counsel Vince Foster's final suicide note. In 1997, President Bill Clinton nominated her to the US Court of Appeals for the Second Circuit. Her nomination was slowed by the Republican majority in the Senate, but she was eventually confirmed in 1998. On the Second Circuit, Sotomayor heard appeals in more than three thousand cases and wrote about 380 opinions. Sotomayor has taught at the New York University School of Law and Columbia Law School.

The CHCI's task force structure focuses on a wide variety of policy areas in addition to the more readily identifiable ones: education, immigration, civil rights, and economic development. The "less traditional" policy areas include arts and entertainment, health, telecommunications, and social security. Although the number of Latino congresspersons has increased to thirty-six (and four in the Senate), not all are members of the CHC. Some of the Hispanic Republican representatives (including those elected in the 2010 midterm elections) have been part of the CHC in the past, but none are currently. To some degree, the partisan dominance in the CHC and foreign policy differences regarding Cuba have contributed to the nonaffiliation of Hispanic Republicans. Reflecting the growing partisan polarization in Congress, in 2003, the Hispanic Republican members of the House formed their own group, the Congressional Hispanic Conference.

The other "insider" organization is the National Association of Latino Elected and Appointed Officials (NALEO), a nonprofit, nonpartisan organization founded in 1976 as a vehicle for political empowerment for the growing number of Latinos in public office. As of 2018, there were 6,749 Latino elected officials, an increase of nearly 700 since 2014.[9]

NALEO provides a wide number of important functions, including training and policy education for Latino elected officials and providing official counts of Latino elected officials referenced in the research of Latino political scientists interested in descriptive representation. Its annual conference serves as a focal point for establishing policy priorities and cementing working networks among fellow public officials.

A major NALEO initiative begun in the late 1980s was a proactive effort to promote naturalization among Latino immigrants. Its analysis regarding further political empowerment revealed the significant percentage of the Latino community that was unable to participate electorally because of non-citizenship. In the American tradition, immigrants make the naturalization decision on an individual basis without active encouragement from "the government" or civic organizations. NALEO undertook a major campaign to inform Latino immigrants and encourage them to pursue naturalization. Part of the plan entailed research to understand the dynamics of that decision-making process, the amount of information regarding the naturalization process, the myths or misinformation about naturalization, and improving the bureaucratic structures that deal with naturalization applications and approval.

NALEO's efforts were directed to ensure that naturalization is accessible to and affordable for permanent resident aliens. Their policy priorities include reducing the barriers to US citizenship, including the high cost of the application process. In addition, they advocate for more equitable English and civics naturalization requirements for older legal permanent residents and the fair administration of the naturalization exam. As a result, citizenship information lines and public relations programs were initiated. NALEO conducted a study of the Immigration and Naturalization Service (INS) regarding the processing of applications and the organization's accessibility to Latinos. This study, conducted by David North, documented extensive backlogs and wait periods of up to twenty-four months for a mandatory interview in some INS offices.

NALEO has also become the national leader in research and advocacy for Latino census participation outreach, including conducting important research to inform messaging to Latinos during census enrollment periods. NALEO was involved in the Census 2000 planning as well as subsequent decennial planning activities, and it supported the Census Bureau's plan to include sampling as part of the decennial enumeration process.[10] NALEO has also been active in promoting the full count of all Latinos with support for complete confidentiality, advertising targeted to Latinos, Spanish-language forms and information, and the hiring of bilingual and bicultural enumerators (citizens and permanent resident aliens). In the run-up to the 2020 census, NALEO conducted research to identify how the inclusion of a citizenship question on the US Census questionnaire would impact Latino participation and lead to significant undercounts of the Latino population across the country. These actions are examples of strategies for Latino political empowerment. NALEO sees the connection between pursuing the expansion of the Latino political base (i.e., converting more Latino immigrants into citizens and making a full count of resident Latinos) and increasing the number of Latino elected and appointed officials. An active constituency and greater political representation serve the general purposes of NALEO.

Two more organizations focusing on the political process are the Southwest Voter Registration and Education Project (SVREP) and the Midwest Voter Registration and Education Project (MWVREP). Both organizations have conducted voter-registration campaigns and have linked voting with policy preferences and outcomes. Over the past thirty-five years, they have honed their planning and timing to produce better voter-registration results. For example, SVREP used to plan its voter-registration campaigns many months prior to a local election or in years when no elections were scheduled. Later registration efforts in the same community would include reregistering several of the same persons who had been purged for nonvoting. Subsequent registration campaigns were timed closer to upcoming elections and involved one-on-one conversations about Latinos' views on politics, the government, public officials, and political participation.

This educational process connects Latinos' interests, elections, and representatives with higher rates of voting and more Latino candidates running for office. As a result, the voter-education dimension of these two organizations has enhanced the effectiveness of their voter-registration campaigns. Clearly, part of the political-empowerment goal for Latinos is to expand their electoral base to more closely approach the community's overall growth rate. While this book has focused on Latino organizations that are national in scope and tend to be pan-ethnic in representing Latino interests, a multitude of Latino organizations (often Latino subgroup only) exist throughout most communities in which Latinos live.

Latinos at the Grass Roots: Community-Based Groups

By their very nature, grassroots organizations are locally based and cover a wide range of electoral and nonelectoral political activities targeted to local institutions and issues. Many of their activities involve noncitizens as well. The history of Latino grassroots organizations in the United States is both long and dynamic. Latino organizations date back to the nineteenth century and are found in many communities where Latinos reside. Because grassroots groups are local in orientation, their longevity depends on specific issues and situations. Since the post–World War II era, a distinctive brand of community organizations has had a major impact in many cities and subregions, especially in the Southwest (see box 8.1).

BOX 8.1 Newer Latino Organizations Come Forward

The Dominican American National Roundtable (DANR) is a civic organization trying to bring together the voices of Dominicans residing in the United States. It focuses on issues pertinent to the Dominican community that cut across the existing organized sectors, such as grassroots groups, nonprofit organizations, and religious, social, and business entities. Since a significant segment of the Dominican community includes immigrants or first-generation residents in the United States, there is an emphasis on recognizing and maintaining the "rich culture" of the Dominican Republic.

The theme of the fall 2001 annual conference (held in Washington, DC) was "Empowerment through Education: The Way for Dominican Americans." The DANR provides a national forum for analysis, planning, and actions to advance the educational, economic, legal, social, cultural, and political interests of Dominicans. Over sixty organizations and supporters are affiliated with the DANR, and their locations extend beyond New York City to Rhode Island, Florida, New Jersey, and Washington, DC. Latino umbrella organizations will become more prevalent and inclusive of existing locally based Latino subgroups.

The Industrial Areas Foundation (IAF), founded by Saul Alinsky (1971), developed an approach, structure, and general philosophy of organizing have-nots for purposes of securing political and economic power. Alinsky was active in African American neighborhoods, particularly in the Midwest and the East, and played a pivotal role in the local areas. Integral to any Alinsky-based organization were the components of a professional, full-time organizer, an umbrella organization to incorporate already existing groups in the neighborhood, the ability to direct action and confrontation tactics, the development of multipurpose and concrete goals, and an active membership base. The Community Services Organization (CSO) in Southern California was the first Alinsky-style organization in which Latinos were involved as organizers and neighborhood activists. Latino leaders such as Edward Roybal, César Chávez, and Dolores Huerta were organizers trained by Fred Ross (the full-time Alinsky organizer assigned to the CSO). Issues such as voter registration, housing and landlord problems, and poor schools were the focus of CSO political actions.

In the late 1960s and 1970s, Community Organized for Public Services (COPS) surfaced in San Antonio, Texas, due to rising utility rates and inadequate drainage infrastructure on the heavily Mexican American west side of the city. COPS successfully involved previously less active West siders with positive, tangible outcomes (Márquez 1993). Subsequently, COPS continued its local involvement and became a significant political force in San Antonio. Other COPS community organizations were formed in Houston, Corpus Christi, Fort Worth, and Austin, as well as in the Rio Grande Valley (Valley Interfaith), El Paso (El Paso Inter-Faith Service Organization), and Los Angeles (United Neighborhood Organizations).

The philosophy of the IAF and Saul Alinsky incorporates the key concepts of empowerment, motivating self-interest, direct action, targeting political and economic institutions, and negotiating concrete services and resources. Over time, the IAF expanded effectively into the Latino community. Ernesto Cortés Jr. (currently IAF southwest regional supervisor) was the community organizer for COPS and subsequently for other IAF-based groups throughout the state of Texas (e.g., El Paso, Rio Grande Valley, Houston, Fort Worth). His influence has modified Alinsky's principles regarding institutional change. Cortés sees politics as engaging in public discourse and initiating collective action guided by that dialogue, including disagreements, arguments, confrontations, negotiations, and open conversation, making it possible for people to act. As a result, most of the professional organizer's early organizing efforts involved conducting numerous individual meetings for the purpose of identifying potential leaders. Then successive one-on-one meetings served to direct networks for agenda building and identifying specific areas and arenas for action.

A significant component of the contemporary IAF approach is to work through religious congregations in a federation structure. Congregations of faith serve as institutions built on personal networks of family and neighborhood and generally affirm meaningful goals in life (Cortés 1996). This context reinforces congregations' struggles to understand and to act. The action component is central to the IAF philosophy. Delivering concrete goods to build and sustain communities has been a benchmark for Alinsky community organizations' longevity. More recently, the IAF strategy has been to use the federal government's Community Block Development Grant (CBDG) program as a process for eligible neighborhoods to meet and discuss potential projects with costs attached. As more projects and total costs exceed CBDG allocation, the IAF members must bargain, trim some projects, and delay others to acquire mutual support (Cortés 1996). This process of negotiating and facilitating the bargaining among neighborhoods is intended to produce a more collective culture.

Finally, the IAF orientation emphasizes leadership development by training its organizers to act as teachers, mentors, and agitators who cultivate leadership for the community organization. This process allows persons to develop a broadened vision of their own self-interest, a key concept that enables motivation and agenda setting and makes possible the ability to recognize individuals' connections and responsibilities to others and communities. The IAF has adapted over the past forty years in both its strategies and community bases, which have become broader, more diverse, and less geographically defined to specific neighborhoods. Since the 1960s, the IAF has initiated community-based organizations, initially in the African American community and then in the Latino community.

This discussion of Alinsky and the IAF is meant to provide some insight into the IAF's significance, at the grassroots level, for a number of Latino communities, especially in the Southwest. While the membership of the organizations is overwhelmingly Latino and ethnicity and culture serve as the means of connecting with others and their experiences, the IAF approach does not want to define issues racially or ethnically. Their theme of a community of interest (or circumstances), using the cultural components of being Latino to attract and maintain membership, is a good representation of this Alinsky tenet. In a similar manner, organizing efforts by the United Farmworkers use religious symbols of Catholicism and uniquely Mexican-related symbols (i.e., la Virgen Guadalupe, Catholic priests, etc.) as part of the union's organizational milieu. While the Alinsky philosophy focuses more on the self-interest of the community involved, and the IAF does not see itself as a minority-oriented organization, it seeks to empower the have-nots. There is a considerable overlap between the have-nots and communities of color. The character of IAF community organizations is also influenced by the background and experiences of their professional organizers. Many Alinsky organizations reflect the character and Latino-ness of their Latino-trained IAF organizers. At the same time, the existence of Latino grassroots groups extends beyond the long-standing presence of Alinsky-based organizations.

In any community with a Latino population, there are local organizations that focus on their concerns and lives. As mentioned at the beginning of this chapter, the organizational goals encompass important facets of daily living (work, religion, social networks, family, education, immigration, etc.). For example, Latinos United for Political Rights (LUPA) advocates for immigrant rights. ASPIRA, a long-standing, primarily Puerto Rican organization, focuses on educational issues, usually in the Northeast. Many local areas have social and mutual self-help groups that are largely organized around immigrants' hometown origins in the Caribbean, Mexico, and Central and South America. Historically, groups like the Alianza Hispano-Americana and Orden de los Hijos de America served as mutual-aid societies to assist immigrants economically (rotating credit loans, burial insurance, etc.) and as social and cultural support systems. In a contemporary sense, many local Latino organizations assist the lives of Latinos in the United States. There is clearly a rise in grassroots organizations within the more recent Latino subgroups (Salvadorans, Dominicans, Colombians, etc.) as their communities grow in size and establish both presence and concerns (see box 8.2).

BOX 8.2 Social Movements, Latinos, Immigration, and Organizational Elements

The foreign-born segment had long been characterized as either apolitical or not equipped to be active participants in the American political system. Yet, in the spring of 2006, a significant number of American communities witnessed the mass protests of millions of immigrants, other Latinos, and proponents of comprehensive and more humanitarian immigration reform. More specifically, the House passage of HR 4437, or the Sensenbrenner Bill, placed further emphasis on border "fortification" and enforcement, and it expanded the criminal "nature" of being an unauthorized immigrant in America. For example, on May 1, 2006, an estimated 1.2 to 2 million persons participated in organized rallies associated with an economic boycott in sixty-three cities (Cano 2008). This series of demonstrations over several months marked an unprecedented social protest largely by a segment that had been mostly faceless and voiceless. In this chapter, I have discussed organizations, mobilization, and contributing factors that influence some Latinos to be more politically and civically engaged.

Yet, the magnitude and coordination of this social movement also provides some other insight into the organizational and mobilization processes that warrant some attention. Established organizations, ad hoc groups, activists, and youthful segments of the Latino community created a synergy that resulted in an underlying organizational dynamic. That is, established organizations such as the Catholic Church, labor unions (e.g., the Service Employees International Union), immigration advocacy groups, and local activists initiated actions interdependently in response to HR 4437 and the restrictive and hostile narratives surrounding immigrants and immigration policies (Cano 2008). The next effect was an organic process in which galvanization in this policy domain served to expand mobilization efforts and approaches, as well as to develop greater organizational skills and reach through a series of events and actions. For example, Cardinal Roger Mahoney of the Los Angeles diocese wrote to President George W. Bush in opposition to HR 4437. Labor organizers, especially those with significant immigrant membership, began to organize members and their families to voice opposition to the legislation and provide a more human face and narrative to the lives and positive impacts of immigrants on American society.

A noteworthy aspect of this social movement is the use of traditional forms of political mobilization in addition to modern technology and ethnic media (Reyes 2006). In the case of the latter, three elements were critical to the success of this movement: Spanish-language media and especially radio personalities, the internet, and text messaging. Spanish-language radio's clientele consists mostly of Spanish speakers and immigrant households. This medium provided information about the protest events as well as the "rules of engagement" and basis for the protests. For example, participants in the early protest marches displayed flags of their countries of origin, which raised questions about their affection for and ties to America. Subsequent marches included the carrying of the American flag. Popular DJs would inform, motivate, and shape the nature of the pro-immigrant social movement, targeting a previously less politically engaged segment of the Latino community.

The use of the internet as a tool to organize and promote civic engagement had been viewed as having a class bias (i.e., targeting middle- and upper-income segments); yet, evidence indicated that the internet and text messaging were used to communicate and network for political purposes and represented a "low-cost" mechanism for Latino participants (Reyes 2006). There was a connection between the use of "newer" technologies and age segments in this social movement. That is, Latino youths took active roles in this movement as identifiable allied groups in addition to being integrated into the overall social movement (Manzano et al. 2009). While the public display of political and civic engagement of these mass protests has subsided, both the contentiousness involved in immigration policy making and the debates about "appropriate" content of immigration and needed actions persist. More systematic attention has been directed toward the expanded range of mobilization strategies and techniques and toward previously under-researched segments of the Latino community (the foreign-born, undocumented, etc.). As a result, future discussions of Latino organizations and mobilization will have a broader scope and knowledge base.

Conclusion

Students of Latino organizational life in the United States need to keep in mind the various dimensions of organizations and follow up by looking at Latino activities in specific cities and metropolitan areas. The key aspects related to organizations include goals and their breadth or range; constituents and their characteristics; resources and sources of assets; strategies and methods; leadership styles, selection, and accountability; and arenas for action. This chapter has focused on the major aspects of Latino organizations and some of their activities without going into great detail regarding specific organizational and other types of leadership. Since leadership is primarily organizationally based, identifying and profiling specific Latino activists and leaders would require a much longer narrative.

While there has been some discussion about the need for a major Latino leader(s) at the national level, there has been little consensus on who that individual(s) is. Over the years, public figures, mostly elected officials, have been on a prospective list of Latino leaders, but levels of the general Latino community awareness of and recognition of that leadership status rarely exceed mid-twenties percentage for any one individual. As seen in the results of a poll taken in 2015 asking who the most politically influential Latinos were, 28.1 percent replied "None" while Supreme Court Justice Sonia Sotomayor headed the list with 21.2 percent. Those respondents who were answering "Who is a known Latino leader?" may be tapping name recognition and equating the Latino's institutional position (i.e., congressperson or senator, etc.) with political influence. Although the subject of leadership, including one's political base, effectiveness, and skill, represents a discussion and analysis beyond the scope of this book, political leadership is critical for the future development of Latinos in politics.

Organizational life for Latinos is active and has become more evident at the national level. Many of these groups use a broader pan-ethnic configuration to increase their constituent and resource base as well as to achieve greater legitimacy as national players in policy arenas. While we have not extensively profiled specific Latino leaders, the role of organizational leadership is central to effective Latino political involvement. This cadre of leaders, at both the national and local levels, contributes to the definition and clarification of group goals and issues, identification and planning of strategies, provision of motivating incentives and rationale for individual involvement, and negotiation of institutional responses on issues, demands, requests, and so on. The use of personal networks and a thorough understanding of cultural and personal experiences of Latinos in the United States enable Latino leaders to enlist Latinos' involvement, especially politically. Chapter 9 explores some of the key substantive policy areas and issues that are part of the Latino policy agenda and will illustrate the role of organizations and leadership, explaining why particular areas are salient for Latinos.

Discussion Questions

1. With greater national exposure and active Latino organizations, it has been suggested that a nationally recognized Latino leader would lead to greater political enhancement. Is this possible, desirable, and necessary for the Latino community to achieve greater political importance?

2. We have more Latino pan-ethnic organizations advocating on behalf of all Latinos at the national and state levels. What challenges do these organizations face in being effective for all Latinos?
3. Labor unions have long been active in the political realm. How has the rise of service unions, such as the Service Employees International Union and the **Hotel Employees and Restaurant Employees Union** (HERE), as well as the rise of Latino union leaders and members, affected Latino politics?
4. The Congressional Hispanic Caucus has been a long-standing interest and advocacy group in Congress. For the most part, Democratic representatives have been the major players in the CHC. With the numbers of Latino Republicans newly elected to the House, how do you think the CHC will be affected?
5. We have introduced the concepts of descriptive and substantive representation. What is each form of representation and how are they related to each other? After reading this chapter, do you believe that Latino elected officials provide more substantive representation to their constituents than non-Latinos?

Notes

1. https://naleo.org/wp-content/uploads/2019/10/2018_National_Directory_of_Latino_Elected_Officials-1.pdf#page=1.

2. See full explanation here: https://www.unidosus.org/about-us/faqs/.

3. Professor Sanchez served as the president of his LULAC Council at St. Mary's University in San Antonio, a council that included public policy expert Dr. Edward Vargas, who was also a student at the university.

4. https://www.latinojustice.org/es/news/national-poll-shows-latinos-are-concerned-about-police-violence-feel-less-safe-under-trump.

5. There are eighteen SIGs that focus on such topics as special education, early childhood education, higher education, research and evaluation, and so on. All members can select any of the SIGs with another member of the National Association of Bilingual Educators serving as the chair.

6. See http://ushcc.com/mission-statement.

7. For example, Dr. Sanchez used this dataset to complete his dissertation focused on Latino group identity and political behavior.

8. See http://www.chci.org/about.

9. https://naleo.org/wp-content/uploads/2019/10/2018_National_Directory_of_Latino_Elected_Officials-1.pdf#page=1.

10. The congressional oversight committee and the Republican congressional leadership felt that including a sampling component as part of Census 2000 would provide partisan advantage to the Democrats because the previously undercounted minorities and lower-income groups would be larger with the adjusted totals. Eventually, the sampling component was challenged in two federal district courts and then reviewed by the US Supreme Court. The court held that, for purposes of reapportionment, results from a "full enumeration" would be the sole basis for this decennial census. At that time, the court did not address directly the use of adjusted population totals (via integration of sampling results) for purposes of federal allocation of funds or redistricting.

CHAPTER 9

Immigration and Latino Immigrants

Ah, los pobres inmigrantes, los forasteros, los refugiados, los nativos americanos, con su larga historia en este país—formamos el mosaico de la comunidad hispana. Llevamos dentro muchas vivencias que han sido nuestro desafío para sobrevivir esta jornada a los Estados Unidos. Y a cado uno nos debe interesar oir todas las historias de cada persona en nuestras comunidades.

Ah, the poor immigrants, the foreigners, the refugees, the native-born sons and daughters with their long history in this country—we form a mosaic of the Latino community. We come with many different stories and challenges of survival from our journey to America, and we should listen to all the stories of all our community members.

THE UNITED STATES HAS ALWAYS proudly portrayed itself as a nation of immigrants. This fabric of America has forged a spirit of adventure, challenges, unforeseen accomplishments, and a community blended from many cultures and religions and a common vision of hope, opportunity, and freedoms. The ideologies that have made America distinguishable are now being seriously challenged by a rise of nativism and placing value selectively on which people and parts of the world are worthy to join this nation of immigrants. Fears about the compatibility of new floods of people seeking their dreams and escaping the fear and uncertainty in their home countries challenge America's capacity to sustain itself as a country that is a great and prosperous nation. Public and political rhetoric cites more recent newcomers as undermining America's values and basic democratic traditions, questioning whether they hold such values and traditions. As a result, there is a perceived need to be more selective about who this nation receives. "A vast number of 'newcomers' are not really Americans in heart and belief, so an open welcome is not in America's best interest." "Immigrants who come to America still come because of a belief in the American dream and a free and democratic society." These statements reflect both contemporary and longer-standing views in the United States about immigrants and international migration.

This chapter will attempt to merge, analytically, an examination of US immigration policies, the underlying values and goals of such policies, characterization and motivations of Latino and other immigrants, the contemporary climate and its impact on Latinos and their communities, and public sentiments and policy preferences regarding immigration and immigrants. This is a vastly expansive and complex area, and hopefully our examination will inspire our readers to explore in more and broader depth the whole range of personal, institutional, and societal worlds of immigration, immigrants, and public policies. Hopefully, our discussion of the subject can serve as an opening for even more conversation and analyses.

Latinos: A Panorama of Immigration in the United States

This nation has operated in cycles of interest, concerns, and policy reforms with regard to immigration (primarily punitive and restrictive) since its inception. Toward the end of the Obama administration, focus on securing our borders (essentially the southern border) and subsequent emphases on militarizing the border region, as well as more aggressively removing those here without documents, became more prevalent. Since the Trump administration took office, more militarization of the border (including the building of a 2,000-mile-plus wall), more border agents, and stricter enforcement of undocumented persons has occurred, and even those with legal status can be at risk. Latinos have become the face of what is "wrong" with this nation's immigration policy, of countries not sending the best of what they have to offer. Since the infamous Trump characterization of Mexican immigrants as rapists, criminals, and being morally unfit, the siege on Latinos has been even more present.

Over one-half of Latinos have someone in their personal network who has been deported or under ICE custody, an alarming statistic that speaks to the high volume of deportation and the close connection Latinos have to this highly vulnerable community (Latino Decisions 2018). As indicated in box 9.1, the Trump administration initiated more than fifty executive orders and other policy moves that are believed to enhance the deterrence, punitive, and restrictive effects to both incoming migrants and residential, foreign-born persons. For Latinos, the presence of mixed-status households (i.e., members who are US-born, legal residents, and/or undocumented) has placed them and their communities under increased risk of contact and fear. Researchers (Vargas et al. 2018; Martinez et al. 2015) have found detrimental effects, especially concerning children's mental health and behavioral issues at school and home, as well as reticence by Latinos to have contact with public services and officials.

BOX 9.1 Immigration Policies and Developments, 2005–Present

Immigration-Police Collaboration Programs

Secure Communities: The Department of Homeland Security (DHS), Immigration and Customs Enforcement (ICE) implemented Secure Communities in 2008, allowing local police to send the fingerprints of persons arrested to DHS to match them with immigration records to expedite deportations.[a]

The **287(g) Program**: Named after a section of the 1996 immigration law, the 287(g) Program allows ICE to train and deputize law enforcement officers to assist with federal immigration policing to detect and deport persons with immigration-status violations.[b]

BOX 9.1 (continued)

Arizona Senate Bill (SB) 1070: Arizona's racial-profiling, anti-immigrant law, passed by the Arizona state legislature and signed by the governor in April 2010, requires police to verify the status of suspected undocumented persons. Now no individual arrested in Arizona can be released until the police have verified his or her immigration status with ICE.[c]

US Border Militarization

The United States spent more than $800 million, or $15.1 million per mile, for fifty-three miles of "virtual fence" on the Arizona-Mexico border.[d] This includes cameras, heat and motion sensors, and other deterrents and detection mechanisms. Another $20.9 million has been spent on the US border with Canada. By early 2010, the United States had built over six hundred miles of border wall along the southwest border, affecting natural habitat and wildlife migration, expropriating traditional indigenous lands,[e] and putting border communities under heightened scrutiny.[f]

Operation Streamline

Operation Streamline criminalizes status violations and unauthorized entry and denies, or "waives," the due process rights of migrants, significantly jeopardizing the constitutional criminal justice system.[g] Under Streamline, US district courts along the border prosecute and convict persons of illegal entry prior to their formal deportation. In Tucson, Arizona, the US district court processes an average of seventy migrants daily, prosecuting, convicting, and sentencing them en masse, Monday through Friday, all within less than two hours per session. The convicted migrant prisoners are then usually turned over to a Corrections Corporation of America private, for-profit prison to serve their sentences.

There seemed to be public sentiment to continue and expand Operation Streamline.[h] Yet, in December 2009, the Ninth Circuit Court of Appeals found that the en-masse plea hearings in Tucson violate federal law. As a result, the Obama administration and Congress had to restore due process rights everywhere, for all, and modify or end Operation Streamline.

Spillover onto Ethnic Studies Opposition: Repeal Arizona SB 2281

SB 2281, dubbed an "ethnic studies cleansing" law, was passed by the Arizona legislature and signed by the governor in the same year that SB 1070 was passed. SB 2281 attempts to eliminate ethnic studies programs, specifically targeting the Mexican American Studies (MAS) program in the Tucson Unified School District (TUSD). Tom Horne, the former superintendent of public instruction and former state attorney general, was the prime operator for this legislation. Horne claimed that ethnic studies promoted divisions and hatred of the United States, despite evidence to the contrary. The Tucson community launched the organizing campaign Defend Ethnic Studies to preserve the MAS program. The TUSD's MAS program has conducted programmatic assessments that show MAS has helped students increase their interest in education and achieve higher grades and improved Arizona Instrument to Measures Standards (AIMS) test results. MAS is also credited with reducing dropout rates and producing a higher number of college entrants.

Denial of Birth Certificates and Public Education

The same Arizona legislature headed by SB 1070–proponent Arizona state senator Russell Pearce worked with Kris Kobach to draft legislation to prohibit granting birth certificates to children of undocumented parents. Kobach authored SB 1070 and is associated with the national group Federation for American Immigration Reform (FAIR) and other anti-immigrant organizations. This proposal challenges the US Constitution's Fourteenth Amendment, which declares all persons equal before the law and grants automatic citizenship to anyone born in the United States.

Provisions of Arizona's SB 1070

US federal law requires aliens age fourteen or older who are in the country for longer than thirty days to register with the US government and to have registration documents in their possession. SB 1070 makes it a state misdemeanor for an alien to be in Arizona without carrying the required documents and mandates that police make an attempt, when practicable during a "lawful stop, detention or arrest," to determine a person's immigration status if there is reasonable suspicion that the person is not in the United States legally. Any person arrested cannot be released without confirmation of his or her legal immigration status by the federal government pursuant to §1373(c) of Title 8 of the United States Code. The first offense under SB 1070 requires a *minimum* fine of $500 for a first violation, and for a second violation, a minimum $1,000 fine and a maximum jail sentence of six months. A person is "presumed to not be an alien who is unlawfully present in the United States" if he or she presents any of the following four forms of identification: a valid Arizona driver's license, a valid Arizona non-operating identification license, a valid tribal enrollment card or other tribal identification, or any valid federal, state, or local government-issued identification.

The act also prohibits state, county, or local officials from limiting or restricting "the enforcement of federal immigration laws to less than the full extent permitted by federal law" and provides that any legal Arizona resident can sue such agencies or officials to compel such full enforcement. If the person who sues prevails, that person may be entitled to reimbursement of court costs and reasonable attorney fees.

The act also targets the practice of hiring day laborers who wait at street corners. It is a crime for any person, regardless of citizenship or immigration

BOX 9.1 (continued)

status, to hire persons congregating at street corners for the purpose of performing day labor. Hiring from a vehicle that "blocks or impedes the normal movement of traffic is unlawful." Vehicles used in such manner are subject to mandatory immobilization or impoundment. Moreover, for a person in violation of a criminal law, it is an additional offense to transport an alien "in furtherance" of the alien's illegal presence in the United States, to "conceal, harbor or shield" an alien, or to encourage or induce an alien to immigrate to the state, if the person "knows or recklessly disregards the fact" that the alien is in the United States illegally or that immigration would be illegal. Violation is a class 1 misdemeanor if fewer than ten "illegal aliens" are involved and a class 6 felony if ten or more are involved. The offender is subject to a fine of at least $1,000 for each "illegal alien" involved. The transportation provision includes exceptions for child protective services workers, ambulance attendants, and emergency medical technicians.

State and Local Immigration Legislation

Laws enacted in the states of Arizona and Alabama were symbolic of a bigger trend nationally, as state immigration policy activity increased from 300 proposed bills and 39 enacted laws in 2005 to more than 900 proposed bills and 156 enacted laws in 2012 (Ybarra et al. 2016; National Conference of State Legislatures [NCSL] 2013). In 2012, states enacted a total of 156 such laws (NCSL 2013). Major contributing factors have been identified as influencing such passage of primarily restrictive immigration laws. These identified factors include a notion of state ideology (Chavez and Provine 2009; Monogan 2013; Zingher 2014); demographics (Boushey and Luedtke 2011; Marquez and Schraufnagel 2013); state wealth (Marquez and Schraufnagel 2013); the role of special interests (Nicholson-Crotty and Nicholson-Crotty 2011); unionization levels (Marquez and Schraufnagel 2013); and presence of undocumented populations (Nicholson-Crotty and Nicholson-Crotty 2011; Ybarra et al. 2015).

[a] See "Secure Communities: A Factsheet," Immigration Policy Center, http://www.immigrati onpolicy.org/just-facts/secure-communities-fact-sheet; "Secure Communities," US Immigration and Customs Enforcement, http://www.ice.gov/about/offices/enforcement-removal-op erations/securecommunities/index.htm.
[b] Eviatar 2009; fact sheets on "Section 287(g) of the Immigration and Nationality Act," Gorena Blog, http://www.gorena.org/287g.htm.
[c] Padilla 2010; also see text of the State of Arizona Senate, 49th Legislature, Second Regular Session, 2010, "SB 1070," at http://www.azleg.gov/legtext/49leg/2r/bills/sb1070s.pdf.
[d] See Gamboa 2010.
[e] See "Operation Streamline: Drowning Justice and Draining Dollars along the Rio Grande," Grassroots Leadership, http://grassrootsleadership.org/OperationStreamline/2010/07/19/op eration-streamline-drowning-justice-and-draining-dollars-along-the-rio-grande.
[f] See resource pages hosted by the School of Law, University of Texas, Austin, on affected communities, at http://www.utexas.edu/law/centers/humanrights/borderwall.

gSee "US-Mexico Border Fence/Great Wall of Mexico Secure Fence," GlobalSecurity.com, http://www.globalsecurity.org/security/systems/mexico-wall.htm.
hFoley 2010; also see the Chief Justice Earl Warren Institute on Race, Ethnicity, and Diversity report: Lydgate 2010.

The consequences of current immigrant policies and administrative actions have affected every sector of the Latino community. Latin American asylees seeking refuge have had to face greater aggression, not only from US immigration officials (and at times, private militia groups), but also from Mexican military and police, while traveling through Mexico. Physical risks, extortion, physical abuse, kidnapping and ransoms, and greater reliance on paid "coyotes" to reach the US border are all perils they have encountered in their efforts to reach the United States.

Asylum protocols are continually changing, with the underlying objectives of deterrence, intimidation, discouragement, and a hostile reception meant to discourage efforts to apply for and seek asylum in the first place. Family separations, requirements to stay in Mexican border towns (i.e., Migration Protection Protocols), delayed court hearings, rising numbers of rejections of asylum petitions, and extended periods of time in poorly equipped and "inhumanely" operated facilities are some of the hardships and hurdles faced by migrants. Being primarily from Central America and Mexico, but also including others from Venezuela, Cuba, India, the Middle East, and Russia, all are trying to escape conflicts, governmental regime instability, abject poverty, and other hardships of basic survival. Also to be considered are those children and young adult Latinos who were brought to this country by their parents without "authorization" and who received some protection through the **Deferred Action for Childhood Arrivals** (DACA) as well as the **Deferred Action for Parents of Americans and Lawful Permanent Residents** (DAPA). Unfortunately, and indicative of the changing political environment, both programs are now in jeopardy as both are targeted for termination, pending court appeals.

Linking Public Policy with Community Life

Our brief overview of immigration policies and their consequences for Latinos represents a living "snapshot" of the realities within the Latino community; the dynamics of public opinions, society's climate, and the political and policy perspectives and intentions by different segments of our sociopolitical system. In the next three chapters, we place emphasis on the effects of public policy, Latinos' issue priorities, and the organizational activities possible to alter the current policy directions. What are the impacts for Latinos based on the content of legislation? Do the consequences of public policies uniformly affect all Latinos or are they different for the various Latino subgroups? Are there institutional arrangements and political processes that limit access and influence to Latino concerns and actions? Do Latinos attempt to advance public policies and exhibit specific preferences through political action?

The nature of community among Latinos includes cultural practices and values as well as common experiences and interests, serving as a bridge between Mexicans or Salvadorans or Puerto Ricans. Spanish-language use and loyalty can contribute to public policies that both impact and concern Latinos. For example, the poverty rate among Latinos increased substantially during the 1990s, so social welfare reform became an associated policy area for Latinos. These bases for community are important in our examination of Latino politics as they represent the content and direction for Latino political participation and influence. We will link our previous discussions of organizations, leadership, and participatory patterns and resources to the issues of immigration, education, and voting rights, which are central to most Latino subcommunities.

The area of policy studies includes the causes and consequences of legislation, as well as the development of a policy agenda from which governments move in certain directions and with explicit purposes. Latinos are not only responding to existing public policies but are trying to formulate new policies or reformulate current ones. García (1996) examined the elements and goals of the 1960s and 1970s Chicano movement to see how they impacted the resultant politics and public policy. In doing so, he used five conditions Milton Esman (1985) set out as necessary and sufficient for the politicization of ethnic groups: (1) group identities based on objective social distinctions and feelings of solidarity that they generate; (2) grievances based on perceived social, economic, or cultural deprivation or discrimination; (3) rising expectations for improvement; (4) declining authority and effectiveness of the political center; and (5) effective political organization. These components formulate preconditions for Latinos and public policy. The combined elements of shared community, common issues, and interconnected organizations work to influence political institutions. The policy-making process deals with agenda setting and accessing decision makers.

What makes an issue, a concern, or a situation a Latino policy issue? The first guideline is whether governmental actions have a different, often negative, impact on Latinos. Are there situations or policies that affect Latinos in concrete and tangible ways? Given the cultural patterns of Spanish-language persistence and use, the educational attainment levels of many Latinos continue to lag. Questions of language use, bilingualism, cultural values, and curriculum serve to influence Latino involvement in the educational arena. Concerns held by policy makers and some of the general public about too many immigrants coming to the United States and their perceived negative impact can target Latinos as the perpetuators of many societal ills.

The second key factor is the awareness and understanding among Latinos that a specific issue and the subsequent policies differentially affect many Latinos. It is not enough that some policies have an impact on Latinos; Latinos must identify and portray the issue or policy as targeting them specifically. When Congress considers immigration reform and other related legislation, do Latinos see themselves as the catalyst for such changes as well as the targets of such proposals? Clearly, the first two factors are interrelated. Both the objective and subjective dimensions of policy impact for Latino communities are the experiences and perceptions of public policies that magnify Latinos' interest and motivation to become involved in the political process. Our current focus on immigration is a very good illustration of how public and policy discourse places Latinos at the center of "who" immigrants are and the "problems" they create. Scholars have used public opinion data or policy agenda scorecards created by Latino advocacy organizations to define "Latino salient policies" that are argued to differentially impact Latinos, and immigration has consistently been included in these sets of policies (Sanchez 2006b).

The third essential factor is the involvement of Latino organizations and leaders in policy arenas. It is through Latino organizations and activists that Latino issues and concerns get framed and directed toward specific policy arenas and policy makers. In some cases, Latino initiatives act to prevent the passage of proposed legislation, referenda, or initiatives. The long, involved immigration debate that resulted in the passage of the 1986 Immigration Reform and Control Act (IRCA) included extensive lobbying by Latino organizations to minimize the impact of or eliminate entirely the bill's proposed employee verification system (or national identification card). At the same time, lobbying by Latino organizations and efforts by members of the Congressional Hispanic Caucus (CHC) pushed to include a wide-reaching amnesty provision within IRCA, as well as civil rights protections.

Finally, public policy involves what governments (at all levels) choose to do. The relationship between governments and Latinos reflects the federal system and decentralization of authority and decision making in American politics. There are many levels of government that affect Latinos and the ways they can contest the policy-making process. For example, since the early 2000s, several states and local jurisdictions have enacted legislation and ordinances that sanction undocumented immigrants from obtaining employment, housing, social services, and so on. In Arizona, SB 1070 targeted undocumented immigrants and the foreign-born so that any encounter with local law enforcement required additional scrutiny to verify legal status in the United States. As a result, all Latinos ran the risk of falling into a suspect or "profiled" category for law enforcement personnel. Much of Latino politics takes place at the local level with grassroots organizations and localized issues. However, the policy-making process everywhere incorporates policy-making arenas; various political processes that Latinos learn and strategically use are generally applicable and can be utilized in changing the political landscape. Latinos who get involved in the policy-making process find opportunities to influence, bargain for, and translate concerns and issues into concrete proposals. However, survey data from Latino Decisions has revealed that many Latinos do not believe that policy makers consider the interests of the Latino community when making immigration policy.

We will explore the immigration policy area that has generated increased political activities, organizational involvement, and protests by Latinos, as well as counter protests from nativists. Immigration policy is no longer the exclusive domain of the national government; state governments and municipalities have entered this arena through referenda and other actions to define and limit immigrants' participation in governmental programs. This intergovernmental intersection is found in the Support Our Law Enforcement and Safe Neighborhoods Act, which requires police officers "when practicable" to detain people they reasonably suspect are in the country without authorization and to verify their status with federal officials, unless doing so would hinder an investigation or emergency medical treatment.

US Immigration Policies: A Historical Overview

Overall, US immigration policy has undergone several changes since the founding of this nation. The period from 1790 to 1875 could be characterized as one of open immigration. Few restrictions were placed on those who wished to enter the United States. Toward the end of this period, an organized anti-immigrant group, the Native

American Party (forerunner of the Know-Nothing Party), sought to extend the wait period for citizenship from five to twenty-one years. Another noteworthy change during this time period was the inclusion of the Fourteenth Amendment to the US Constitution, making the "law of the soil" (Landis 2018) the basis for citizenship.

The years 1876 to 1924 saw US immigration policy impose a series of qualitative controls on admittance into the United States; for example, prostitutes and convicts were banned from entering. Geographically and culturally, the exclusion of Chinese and Japanese immigrants resulted from formal treaty agreements. The American Protective Association was formed in 1887 as an anti-immigrant group advocating that persons should never vote for a Catholic candidate, never hire a Catholic worker over a Protestant one, and never join in a strike with Catholics. The anti-immigrant, anti-foreigner, and pro-Protestant policies have been a recurring element in US immigration history. Congress enacted a law declaring that any American woman marrying a foreign man would take on the citizenship of her husband and lose her US citizenship.[1] Literacy tests were finally included in immigration law in 1917, after several previous presidential vetoes. Fears of anarchists and seditionists also inspired restrictions.

The period from 1924 to the present can be characterized as one of both qualitative and quantitative restrictions for immigrants. The landmark **National Origins Act of 1924** set a ceiling on the number of immigrants admitted annually. A formula was based on the percentage of the national-origin group registered in the 1890 census, which heavily favored natives of northern and western Europe. Japanese and citizens of the Asiatic zone were excluded. By 1938, the National Origins Act was fully operative and 82 percent of those eligible to be admitted came from northern and western Europe, 16 percent from southern and eastern Europe, and 2 percent from the remainder of the world. Given these changes in immigration laws, countries from the Western Hemisphere (Mexico, Central and South America) were excluded from quotas. As a result, the US-Mexican border became an "open border" with freer migration flows.

The key governmental agency involved with federal immigration policies is the Immigration and Naturalization Service (INS). An agency in the Department of Justice, the INS is responsible for enforcing laws regulating the admission of foreign-born persons to the United States as well as administering immigration benefits, including the naturalization of qualified applicants for US citizenship. The INS works with other federal agencies in the admission and resettlement of refugees. In 1864, the INS was housed in the State Department with a commissioner of immigration. The problem of divided authority between the federal statutes being enforced at the state level and authorization at the federal level created the Immigration Act of 1891, which solidified federal control over immigration through a superintendent of immigration under the Treasury Department. INS was given authority over naturalization through the Naturalization Act of 1906. The 1906 legislation shifted naturalization from the courts to the Bureau of Immigration and Naturalization to administer and enforce US immigration laws and supervise the naturalization of aliens. These combined functions lasted for seven years as naturalization became a separate bureau in 1913, with the Departments of Commerce and Labor splitting the two functions. By executive order in 1933, the functions were consolidated again in the Labor Department. In 1940, the INS was transferred to the Department of Justice.

The **Border Patrol** was not established until 1924, and in 1933 the Bureaus of Immigration and Naturalization were merged with the Department of Labor. The primary mission of this agency has been to detect and prevent the smuggling and unlawful entry of undocumented aliens into the United States and to apprehend individuals in violation of US immigration laws; the agency also added drug interdiction along the land borders. A more important activity of the Border Patrol is referred to as "line watch." It involves the detection, prevention, and apprehension of undocumented migrants and their smugglers at or near the border by maintaining surveillance from covert positions. These operations follow up on leads, respond to electronic sensor alarms, and use infrared scopes during night operations, as well as employing low-light-level television systems, aircraft sightings, and the interpretation and following of tracks, marks, and other physical evidence. Examples of such activities include farm and ranch checks, traffic checks, traffic observation, city patrols, transportation checks, and administrative, intelligence, and anti-smuggling activities.

The extent of heightened patrolling and surveillance has varied, driven largely by the state of the US economy. For example, stricter enforcement by the Border Patrol of Mexican immigrants was more evident during the Great Depression of the 1930s. Mexican nationals and native-born residents felt the backlash between 1930 and 1932 as 330,000 were repatriated to Mexico (Hoffman 1979), with an estimated 500,000 Mexican people leaving under the "voluntary" program. The throes of the Depression, a negative view of foreigners, and a fear of too many immigrants on the welfare rolls were major factors contributing to this Mexican repatriation.

Another development during the 1930s was the American response worldwide to political upheavals and war. Refugees from the Spanish Civil War and Hitler's invasion of France, as well as Jews fleeing persecution in Germany and Eastern Europe, could emigrate. This pattern held during World War II and subsequent military conflicts. Finally, a major overhaul was evident by the 1952 passage of the McCarran-Walter Act (also known as the Immigration and Nationality Act, or INA), as the quota system was made even more rigid with annual per-country caps. In 1965, amendments to the INA established an annual ceiling for Eastern and Western Hemisphere immigrants of 170,000 and 120,000, respectively. In 1979, the US Refugee Act of 1980 (Public Law 96-212) was an amendment to the Immigration and Nationality Act and the Migration and Refugee Assistance Act. It was created to provide a permanent and systematic procedure for the admission to the United States of refugees of special humanitarian concern and to provide comprehensive and uniform provisions for the effective resettlement and absorption of those refugees admitted. During the 1960s and 1970s, immigrants from communist regimes were generally designated as political refugees.

A system of preference categories for close relatives and other family members was instituted for citizens and permanent resident aliens. Two categories of occupational preferences with specified skills, especially in the health professions, were also established. In addition, a seventh preference category was created for 10,200 refugees per year with attention paid to those individuals fleeing communist regimes or the Middle East, fearing persecution on account of race, religion, or political opinion, or people uprooted by catastrophic natural calamity. The per-country caps were applied to Western Hemisphere countries in 1976 (20,000 annually). Mexico's cap, originally expanded to 40,000, was eventually subjected to the same cap for all countries in the 1976 amendment to the act. The major basis for legal admission (family reunification) has been subject to criticism, with pressure to either remove this preference category or severely restrict which family members (spouses, dependent children, etc.) would qualify for family reunification.

US immigration policy can be depicted as the process of determining who is admitted, under what circumstances, the number who will be allowed, and from what areas of the world. Historically, the borders of the United States have changed. The Southwest was once part of Mexico, and both Cuba and Puerto Rico were formerly US possessions. The United States has been involved in Central and South America from the early 1800s (from the Monroe Doctrine and beyond), and all these associations have linked Latinos and US immigration policy, especially for Mexicans. Immigration policies received an abundance of attention during the 1970s, with much of the national discussion of immigration and policy initiatives being directed toward Latinos. As we will discuss in more detail in the sections that follow, immigration has remained a policy priority for not only the federal government, but state and local governments as well, from the 1970s until today. Given that migrants from Latin America have been the target of most immigration policies over this period, immigration policy and the political debates that surround it have been particularly salient to the Latino population.

9/11 and Dramatic Shifts in US Immigration Policies

During the 1990s, immigration-reform legislation allocated additional funding to the Border Patrol for added personnel and sophisticated equipment. The September 11, 2001, terrorist attacks in New York City and Washington, DC, added even greater concern for future terrorist attacks and other national security issues. It has been estimated that between the year 2000 and 2010, US taxpayers spent $90 billion on securing the already heightened border-control scrutiny of the US-Mexican border. This included such expenses as deploying 1,200 National Guard troops to the border at $110 million per year, with the average salary, in 2010, of a US Customs and Border Protection (CBP) agent being $75,000. Twenty thousand CBP agents were deployed to the US-Mexico border, 165 X-ray machines were purchased to peer into cargo trains and trucks (at $1.75 million each), along with the cost of building fences, employing drug-sniffing dogs, and paying for the use of predator drones and various other incendiaries (Office of Immigration Statistics 2014). Overall, life in the United States changed due to governmental policies that not only have affected national security but also a range of social and economic policies (Enders and Sandler 2005; Kaplan and Mukand 2011; Coleman and Kocher 2011; Makinen 2002).

Customs and Border Protection (CBP) reported that in 2000, they caught 1.6 million undocumented migrants, and in 2010 had apprehended approximately 463,000. Interestingly, the decline in apprehensions was attributed to a sluggish US economy. However, unemployment figures were up and consequently fewer immigrants took the risk of attempting entry with fewer available jobs. This decline in apprehensions has raised some policy questions, especially among Latinos, that such heavy expenses in border security are less a factor in the flow of undocumented migrants than the fluctuations in the US economy. The effectiveness of drug interdiction represents only a drop in the bucket in the revenues generated by drug cartels. Global Financial Integrity, a Washington think tank studying illicit flows of money, reported in a 2017 study that an estimated $426 billion to $652 billion is the retail value of transnational drug-trafficking crime (May 2017). CBP estimates that only 44 percent of the US-Mexico border is under "operational control." They also estimate that for every illegal immigrant they apprehend, three migrate successfully. Interestingly, what US taxpayers spend in ten years on border security is less than the dollar amount for one year of the war in Afghanistan.

The increased "militarization" (i.e., patrols and personnel, deterrence equipment and technology, etc.) of the US-Mexico border has framed undocumented immigration almost exclusively in criminal terms. A popular anti-undocumented migrant slogan, "What is it about illegal do you not get?" typifies that perspective. At the same time, the volatility and emotion related to the immigration policy arena invokes themes of patriotism, loyalty, the definition of who is really an American, and national security. The following discussion on contemporary immigration policies highlights the embedded themes of anti-nativism, anti-foreigners, "white nationalism," and conspiracy theories linking terrorist threats to border crossings. The image of Latinos as the "poster children" of "illegal immigration and immigrants" has elevated this policy issue to even greater salience for the Latino community. Increased and more formalized deportations, family separation of mixed-status households,[2] more restrictive state and local laws and ordinances, and polarizing rhetoric among politicians and President Trump are more present. Current policy proposals range from "normalizing" DREAMers' status and mixed-status families with eventual pathways to citizenship to termination of DACA and DAPA, more restrictive legal immigration regulations, and moving to a "merit-based" system.

Contemporary Immigration Patterns

Figure 9.1 provides a historical representation of the growth of the immigrant population in the United States since 1850. Immigration information from 1990 to 2010 shows more than a doubling of the immigration population, from 19.8 million to 40 million, with the percentage of the total US population increasing from 7.9 percent to 12.9 percent (Radford 2019; Singer 2014). A review of the years 2007 to 2009

FIGURE 9.1 Growth of Immigrant Population, 1950–2010

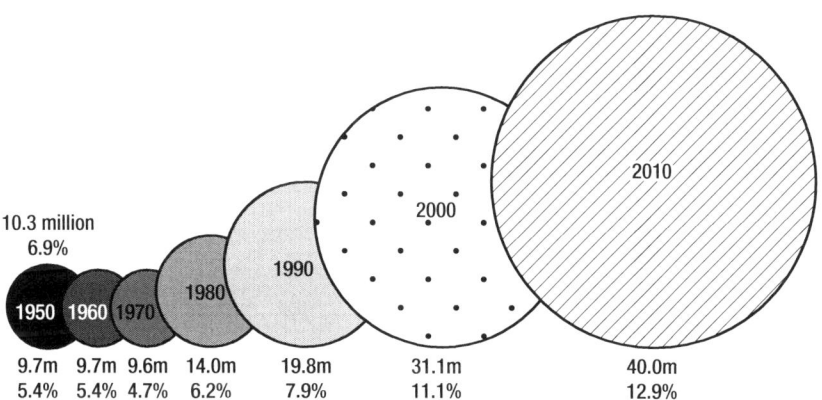

Source: Adapted from Gibson and Jung 2006, 2010 American Community Survey one-year estimates.

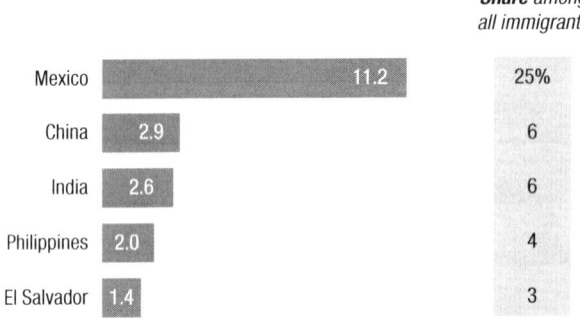

FIGURE 9.2 Source Countries of Foreign-Born Immigrants, 2018 (in millions)

Source: Budiman 2020 and Pew Research Center tabulations of 2018 American Community Survey (IPUMS). *Note*: China includes Macau, Hong Kong, Taiwan, and Mongolia.

demonstrates a steady but substantial flow of more than one million immigrants per year. While there are fixed hemispheric quotas, the family-reunification category, consisting of immediate family members, fluctuates annually, mostly due to processing and clearance functions. Most immigrants to the United States come from Latin America and Asia (12.6 million from Mexico and El Salvador and 7.3 million from China, India, and the Philippines) (Radford 2019). The immigration flows from Mexico and Central and South America are quite noteworthy. When combined with Asian immigrants, Central Americans and Mexicans make up four-fifths of all immigrants for the 1990s and early 2000s.

In figure 9.2, we see the numbers and share of immigrant populations for the top five countries in 2018. Mexican-origin immigrants far exceed any other national-origin group (11.2 million), representing about 25 percent of all foreign-born residents; Chinese (6 percent), East Asian Indians (6 percent), and Filipinos (4 percent) occupy the next-largest immigrant population categories. Clearly, since the mid-1950s, the geographical areas of international migration have shifted from Europe. Also, the higher percentage of foreign-born is not only a function of continued immigrant flow, but also the declining birth and fertility rates among American-born residents.

Since the 1965 Hart-Cellar Immigration Act of 1965, subsequent amendments have placed fixed caps for immigrants on each country, including Mexico. Before 1965, immigration from Mexico and other Latin American countries was largely unrestricted. This has created a backlog of applications for permanent residency and a lengthy waiting period for processing (exceeding seven years). The slowdown in seeking legal admission to the United States has resulted in an increasing effect on push factors (i.e., lack of jobs, family economic pressure, system instability, etc.). The motivation to migrate to the United States has not dissipated, but because the "legal" manner of immigrating is more difficult, undocumented migration becomes a more realistic option. The economic interrelationship between the United States and Latin America, in terms of both its formal and informal economies, plays a direct role in the ebb and flow of international migration. Since the latest global economic recession, migration flows have tended to increase. In the case of the Northern Triangle countries, violence and political corruption and instability have increased the inflow of Central Americans to the US border, primarily seeking asylum. This has been countered with heightened border fortification and more intense surveillance to "stem the tide" (see box 9.1 for an outline of recent immigration policies).

The categories of consideration for the admission of immigrants fall into either family reunification or occupational/special skills. Persons having close family relationships with a US citizen or legal permanent resident, those with needed job skills, and those who qualify as refugees account for the majority of the admissions. Policy impact on the legal status of many Latino immigrants comes from the 2.6 million former "illegal aliens" from 1982 to 1992 who gained permanent resident status through the legalization provisions of the IRCA. More than 70 percent of the legalized IRCA immigrants were Mexican, with another 10 to 14 percent coming from other Latin American countries (Baker 1997), adding significantly to the growing immigrant segments within the Latino community. Whereas the "pipeline" metaphor has been used for family reunification, the growing number of legal permanent resident aliens will enable more Latinos to pursue naturalization in the years to come. As of 2011, one-half of the eligible permanent resident aliens pursuing naturalization were from Latin America.

Recently, more attention has been paid to employment-based preference categories. There are five categories for which people can be admitted based on skills critical to the American labor market: (1) priority workers; (2) professionals with advanced degrees; (3) skilled workers, professionals without advanced degrees, and needed unskilled workers; (4) special immigrants; and (5) creative immigrants or investors. Policy discussions have considered reducing the emphasis on family reunification as opposed to labor market skills. Earlier, economist George Borjas (2001) argued for a more skill-oriented and economically driven immigration policy. That system would award points to prospective immigrants based on various characteristics and establish a passing grade to help the American government select among the applicants. Characteristics of the point system would include consideration of education, English-language proficiency, prioritized occupational/job skills, and age at time of entry (Borjas 2001, 194–99). Country of origin would be considered to ensure that no nation, culture, or language would dominate the immigrant flow. Finally, point consideration would be given to persons seeking employment in immigrant-dependent industries.

Other nations, like Australia, have instituted these "skills" selection criteria (Antecol, Cobb-Clark, and Trejo 2003) and found more positive labor market outcomes for male immigrants than females. The Trump administration policy, as part of its legal immigration proposals announced on May 16, 2016, was a more merit-based point system. At its core, the point system proposal developed by Trump senior advisor Jared Kushner sought to move the United States away from a family reunification system and toward one that favored applicants with desirable labor-market attributes. The proposal of a point system both looks to the mechanisms adopted by other high-income countries for selecting economic migrants and revives some elements of prior US legislative proposals.

While a full discussion of the merits and policy impact of such proposals is not the subject of this chapter, it is one of several examples of policy shifts of the Trump administration that have direct consequences on Latinos. The greater emphasis on an economic/labor market model for immigrant admission was reflected in the US Commission on Immigration Reform report and testimony (1995, 1997). Chair Shirley Hufstedler addressed the House of Representatives about the policy directions of the commission. She noted concerns about immigrants with poor English-speaking skills being confined to the lowest "rungs" of the American job market. "The national interest could be served by moderating entry of unskilled immigrants, except when other values prevail, notably nuclear family reunification, and by increasing the skills of those who have arrived" (Hufstedler 1999, 8–9). Continued reexamination of the quota limits based on family reunification and employment-based preferences will affect immigration reform in the future.

Increased State and Local Immigration Activity

Although much of the discussion regarding immigration policy focuses narrowly on federal policy, since 2004, many state and local governments have initiated legislation, ordinances, and initiatives that focus on immigration policy. Much of these policies target undocumented persons' access to social services, housing, and employment and limit legal recourse coverage (i.e., civil suits for injury, eligibility for punitive damages, etc.). Many of these laws have also led to more stringent regulations against loitering, smuggling, and harboring illegal immigrants and deny **birthright citizenship** to children born of undocumented parents (Stumpf 2007; Ybarra, Sanchez, and Sanchez 2015; Morse 2016).

In 2011 Alabama enacted what many believe to be the most severe anti-immigrant state law on the books. Among other things, Alabama's HB (House Bill) 56 requires police officers in the state to ascertain the immigration status of people stopped, detained, or arrested; it prohibits undocumented immigrants from receiving any public benefits at the state or local level; it bars undocumented immigrant students from attending public institutions of higher education; and it requires public elementary and secondary school officials to ascertain whether students are undocumented. The Alabama law is more extreme than the more visible Arizona SB (Senate Bill) 1070, which has generated international attention due to its extremity. The laws enacted in these two states are symbolic of a larger trend across the country, as state immigration policy activity has exploded from just 300 proposed bills and 39 enacted laws in 2005 to more than 900 proposed bills and 156 enacted laws in 2012 (National Conference of State Legislatures 2013). While state- and local-level policy action is not new, the severity and sheer volume of the legislation being proposed and passed has been unique to this environment where the federal government has increased attention to immigration but failed to pass any major legislation to address what many feel is a growing problem or challenge.

One of the major questions associated with the rise in state-level immigration policies has been what is motivating US states to engage more heavily in a policy issue often perceived to be a federal priority. Given that this explosion of laws took place during the recent economic recession that had a huge impact on states' financial realities across the country, it was somewhat natural to perceive that many states may have been motivated to pass punitive immigration policies as a means of restricting state-funded resources to a smaller segment of the population as a means of saving money.

At the same time, the role of race could not be overlooked given that the immigrants who were coming in large numbers to the United States during this period were predominately Hispanic or Asian. In fact, when combined, the Hispanic and Asian population grew more than 43 percent from 2000 to 2010, making up 23.2 percent of the total US population in 2010 (Humes et al. 2011). One research team attempted to identify whether economic or population shifts were stronger in influencing state-level punitive immigration policy activity, finding that despite the backdrop of the economic recession, growth in Hispanic population over time was just as powerful in explaining this outcome (Ybarra, Sanchez, and Sanchez 2015).

While much of these state and local policies is punitive in nature, many states and local communities have responded to the punitive immigration environment by passing positive or protective laws. These laws have included state- or city-level DACA policies, with provision of resources including health-care benefits to the undocumented. The most high-profile policy activity on this more positive front has been the growing number of local communities that have declared themselves to be "sanctuary" cities (Chen 2016). The term generally pertains to cities that do not allow municipal funds or resources to be used to enforce federal immigration laws—for instance, not allowing police or municipal employees to inquire about an individual's immigration status.

The policy was first initiated in 1979 in Los Angeles to prevent police from inquiring about the immigration status of arrestees, and more than thirty-one cities have followed suit. Officers are not supposed to arrest or book persons for violation of Title 8, Section 1325 of the US Immigration code. It is fairly common for Latino and labor advocacy groups to advocate for sanctuary city recognition and for more laws and ordinances that assist and stabilize undocumented households living in the United States. Recent initiatives by the Trump administration have been to remove most federal funding to local governments declared as sanctuary cites, as well as litigation against sanctuary cities to comply with **detainer orders** by ICE. This threat to cut or restrict federal funding from jurisdictions that declare themselves as being sanctuary has had a real impact on local-level decisions, including being the dominant explanation for why several locales have backed off becoming sanctuaries. For example, newly elected Latina mayor Regina Romero and other Democrats in Tucson did not support a ballot initiative put to voters in 2019 to declare Tucson a sanctuary due to fears of losing valuable federal funding. The initiative failed by large numbers.

Sanctuary state and city laws were contrasted with crime by President Trump and his administration, who consistently argued that jurisdictions that did not participate with federal ICE programs had elevated crime levels. However, researchers who have investigated the relationship between immigration population and crime, as well as sanctuary state or city policy, have come to much different conclusions. For example, crime is actually lower in sanctuary counties when they are contrasted with comparable nonsanctuary counties.[3] This is reinforced by the work of Gonzalez O'Brien, Collingwood, and El-Khatib (2017), who find no statistical difference in violent crime, rape, or even property crime rates when they compare sanctuary cities to nonsanctuary cities that are comparable across other factors that could influence crime rates. In contrast, social science research has consistently found that having local police forces cooperate with and enforce federal immigration policy interferes with the ability of police forces to do their jobs. This is often a result of immigrant communities, and Latino communities more broadly, not reporting crimes or cooperating with police due to concern over being asked for their documentation (See Wong et al. 2019). For example, a 2015 Latino Decisions/UNM RWJF Center for Health Policy Survey reported that 13 percent of a national sample of Latinos do not report crimes or talk to police because they do not want to be asked about their documentation status.[4]

The focus upon the Latino "undocumented" as the face of immigration debates and intense rhetoric has served to activate a broad spectrum of Latinos (i.e., class, nativity, legal status, citizens/noncitizens) and continues to elevate immigration to a very salient policy domain. Consequences, not only to the undocumented households, but to the larger Latino community, have revealed increased experiences of anxiety, fear, declining health status, and issues of daily survival (Vargas et al. 2018; Vargas et al. 2017). A set of tracking polls conducted by Latino Decisions (2018) during the 2018 midterm election period has confirmed four major patterns: (1) a salient concern about restrictive and punitive immigration policies that cuts across virtually any sociodemographic distinction among Latinos; (2) a feeling that all Latinos are being targeted within the context of nativist, racist orientations; (3) a dissatisfaction with both major political parties, especially the Democratic Party, for not advocating or pursuing more humane, Latino-supported immigration reform; and (4) a heightened interest in elections and candidates' positions on key Latino issues. The externalities of divided public opinions, negative stereotyping of Latinos, and targeting have resulted in increased fervor for greater political engagement and empowerment.

Two other issues affecting segments of the Latino community are the DREAMers and their families and unaccompanied minors crossing the US border primarily from Mexico and Central American countries. Although the Obama administration had a terrible record on deportation policy, the administration did issue two executive orders, Deferred Action for Parents of Americans (DAPA) and Deferred Action for Childhood Arrivals (DACA). DACA was initiated in 2012 so that young adults who entered the country illegally as children could be granted temporary deferred action status in order to apply for employment authorization and have "legal" status to remain in the United States. This applies to all people under thirty-one years of age who came to the United States before the age of sixteen, have lived continuously in United States since June 2007, are currently in school or have graduated, were honorably discharged from the military, and who have not been convicted of a felony offense or significant misdemeanor.

A study by Gonzalez et al. (2014) found that this policy opened access to new jobs, higher earnings, driver's licenses, health care, and banking. Using data from a national sample of DACA beneficiaries ($N = 2,381$), this article investigates variations in how undocumented young adults benefit from DACA. Their findings suggest that, at least in the short term, DACA has reduced some of the challenges that undocumented young adults must overcome to achieve economic and social incorporation. However, those with higher levels of education and access to greater family and community resources appear to have benefited the most. This study provides insights into how social policy interacts with other stratification processes to shape diverging pathways

FIGURE 9.3 Resources Accessed by DACA Recipients

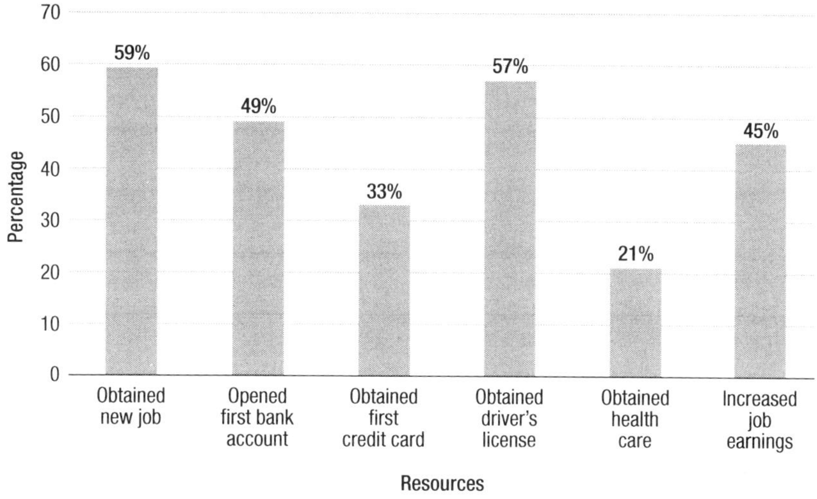

- Obtained new job: 59%
- Opened first bank account: 49%
- Obtained first credit card: 33%
- Obtained driver's license: 57%
- Obtained health care: 21%
- Increased job earnings: 45%

Source: Gonzales and Bautista-Chaves 2014.

of incorporation among the general pool of undocumented immigrants. Similar studies, such as Gonzales and Chavez (2012), show similar results of DACA registrants obtaining social security cards, finding new jobs, receiving internships, opening bank accounts and credit cards, receiving health care coverage, and volunteering for advocacy community organizations (see figure 9.3).

In September 2017, the Trump administration terminated the DACA program, indicating that President Obama's executive orders were unconstitutional and that Congress should be the institution to resolve DACA recipients' status. While the Supreme Court heard arguments in 2019, the court is not expected to render an opinion until the end of the Court's calendar in 2020. Mixed messages were being transmitted by Trump's administration with comments that characterize some DACA recipients, or DREAMers, as being criminals and "not very good people" (Forgey 2019). At the same time, President Trump indicated he was willing to support a pathway to citizenship (potentially including DAPA and Temporary Protected Status registrants), as a condition of a comprehensive immigration bill that would limit legal immigration, incorporate a merit system for admission, and allocate more funds for the border wall. Congress has been unable to pass any legislation to "normalize" DACA recipients' immigration status, and prospects are still unlikely.

Asylum and Deportations

An increased number of unaccompanied minors entering the United States has been the other recently highlighted development. In 2008, 8,048 unaccompanied minors were apprehended trying to enter the country; by 2012, the apprehensions increased to 24,481. One-half of the young people were from Mexico (most were repatriated to Mexico); the other half were from Central America. The Central American youths were turned over to the Office of Refugee Settlement, who placed them with relatives living in the United States until their deportation hearings were conducted. The motivation for these unaccompanied minors was to escape dangerous situations with gangs and personal threats to themselves and family members. The Central American youths had to travel through Mexico on their way to the United States and were subjected to violence, exploitation, inadequate supplies, sexual assaults, and environmental hazards. Although media and governmental spokespersons have characterized the movement of unaccompanied minors as a recent "surge," this pattern is a long-standing one given the political instability and violence in many Central American countries. This trend reflects the harsh reality that despite the rhetoric associated with immigrants being nowhere near as volatile as what comes from Republican politicians, deportations reached all-time highs during the Obama administration's two terms in office. This led to the president often being referenced as "Deporter in Chief" among many Latino activists and interest groups.

The number of unaccompanied alien children (UAC) apprehended entering the United States illegally along the Southwest border had bottomed out in April 2017. Following the inauguration of Donald Trump, a surge of nearly 685 percent by February 2019 was recorded. Similarly, the number of UACs deemed inadmissible at the ports of entry along that border surged 385 percent between March 2017 and February 2019. Doctors Without Borders (2020) reported that more than two-thirds of the migrant and refugee populations entering Mexico disclosed being victims of violence during their transit toward the United States and that almost one-third of women surveyed had been sexually abused during that trip. In FY 2009, children from Mexico accounted for 82 percent of the 19,688 UAC apprehensions at the Southwest border, while those from the "Northern Triangle" countries of El Salvador, Guatemala, and Honduras accounted for 17 percent. Within the first ten months of FY 2019, the proportions had reversed, with Mexican nationals comprising 12 percent of the 69,157 UAC apprehensions at the border and the three Central American countries comprising 85 percent. The United Nations also reported that the smuggling of aliens is big business for criminal organizations, valued at $3.7 to $4.2 billion a year (UNODC 2018). The processing of these migrants has placed a huge burden on the Border Patrol, both in terms of manpower and in financial costs for humanitarian aid and the expansion of more detention facilities, many with inadequate infrastructure and services.

Litigation from immigration advocacy civil rights organizations has focused on the conditions at detention centers, incidents of abuse and neglect, minimal information about the immigration process and proceedings, and fair and informed hearings regarding their asylum petitions. These asylees are facing not only the danger in making it to the American southwestern border, but also in encountering tougher US asylum policies. These policies and practices have included: (1) mass illegal pushbacks of asylum-seekers at the US-Mexico border; (2) thousands of illegal family separations, meant as a form of deterrence for asylum seekers, placing them in detention centers rather than being released to family members living in the United States; and (3) increasingly arbitrary and indefinite detention of asylum seekers without parole and instituting the Migration Protection Protocols (MPP), which has resulted in precarious living situations in Mexican border towns for those awaiting their hearing dates (Human Rights Watch 2020).

Simultaneously, the Trump administration policies have sought to dismantle the US asylum system by narrowing definitions of who qualifies for protection, in direct violation of international law. Actions like establishing third-country "safe zones," bilateral agreements of the United States with Guatemala, El Salvador, and Mexico that allow asylum seekers to be sent back to these countries while awaiting hearings and/or after asylum petitions have been denied. In several instances, these "petitioners" have been sent back to a country that is not their country of origin. Setting a dangerous precedent, the US government's abrogation of its obligations under human rights and refugee law is undermining the international framework for refugee protection, grossly violating the right to seek asylum and inviting a race to the bottom by other countries. The development of policies that serve more as deterrents and are punitive in nature are intended to discourage current and prospective migrants from attempting to come to the United States.

Deportations have been used to expand attention to border security with increased apprehensions and informal "voluntary" deportation. Those migrants who are formally deported are not allowed to enter the country for ten years. The Obama administration deported 409,849 people in 2012 alone, while the Trump administration has yet to deport more than 260,000 people in a year (Budryk 2018). US Immigration and Customs Enforcement (ICE) attributed the lower numbers to "an increased deterrent effect from ICE's stronger interior enforcement efforts," but administration officials have also noted an increased proportion of immigrants from Central America, who are legally more difficult to deport than those faced by the Obama administration. The agency has also increased the length of time it detains people, holding noncriminals an average of sixty days in detention, eleven days longer than convicted criminals, and nearly doubling the average in 2009 (Feriss 2019). In two of the box insets in this chapter, we highlight changes in asylum policies and deportation practices, especially for noncitizen veterans.

BOX 9.2 Basis for Immigration Area Personal for Latinos

Immigration reform is a deeply personal issue for Latino voters. When asked, "Do you know anyone who is an undocumented immigrant?"

- 64 percent of Latino registered voters said yes
- Among those who said yes:
  - 51 percent said they know a family member who is an undocumented immigrant
  - 84 percent said they know a personal friend who is an undocumented immigrant
- 51 percent of 64 percent = 32.6 percent
- Therefore, one in three Latino registered voters is related to an undocumented immigrant.

Source: Adapted from Latino Decisions National Poll on Executive Action, sponsored by Presente/NALACC/Mi Familia Vote.

BOX 9.3 The Temporary Protected Status Story

In October 2018 President Trump announced through an executive order that the Temporary Protected Status (TPS) policy would be terminated. A series of lawsuits challenging the administration's decision have blocked those orders from taking effect, and the Department of Homeland Security has extended TPS through January 4, 2021, for immigrants from El Salvador, Haiti, Honduras, Nepal, Nicaragua, and Sudan, the six countries that account for 98 percent of all current TPS recipients.

So, what is TPS and how are Latinos affected? Roughly, 317,000 people from ten countries currently have protected status after fleeing their home nations because of war, hurricanes, earthquakes, or other extraordinary conditions that could make it dangerous for them to live there.

Temporary Protected Status is temporary immigration status (passed in 1990) provided to nationals of certain countries experiencing problems that make it difficult or unsafe for their nationals to be deported there. It provides a work permit and stay of deportation for TPS recipients from those countries who are in the United States at the time. The Secretary of Homeland Security has discretion to decide when a country merits a TPS designation, but it must consult with other government agencies prior to deciding to designate a country—or part of a country—for TPS. For the most part, the consulted agencies are usually the Department of State, the National Security Council, and occasionally the Department of Justice (DOJ). The secretary's decision as to whether or not to designate a country for TPS is not subject to judicial review, according to immigration law. A TPS designation can be made for six, twelve, or eighteen months at a time. At least sixty days prior to the expiration of TPS, the secretary must decide whether to extend or terminate a designation based on the conditions in the foreign country. Decisions to begin, extend, or terminate a TPS designation must be published in the Federal Register. If an extension or termination decision is not published at least sixty days in advance of expiration, the designation is automatically extended for six months.

By 2016, a quarter (27 percent) of the 725,000 unauthorized immigrants from El Salvador in the United States had TPS coverage (Cohn, Passel, and Bialik 2019). These 195,750 Salvadorans have lived in the United States since February 13, 2001. There are also 57,000 Hondurans and roughly 2,550 Nicaraguans with TPS coverage. The termination of TPS leaves thousands of Central American immigrants living in heightened fear of deportation.

Some of the consequences of this termination involve TPS recipients who are removed from communities in which they have been integrated. They represent nearly 273,000 children who were born in the United States. They provide emotional and financial support to loved ones and shoulder responsibilities in schools, churches, and civic organizations. Thousands more work as nannies, caregivers for seniors or people with disabilities, and in other professions critical to the health and well-being of our communities. Most TPS recipients have been in the United States for decades, and TPS allowed them to integrate into and contribute to the US economy. The vast majority—88.5 percent—of TPS recipients participate in the labor force (higher than the national average). As a result, termination of TPS would have a major impact on the social and economic fabric of cities and towns across the country.

When TPS is terminated, TPS recipients can be deported. It is estimated that these individuals would cost taxpayers more than $3 billion in lost revenues. Over a decade, the inability of these individuals to work would result in more than $45 billion in lost GDP and $6.9 billion in lost Social Security and Medicare contributions (Ibe and Johnson 2020). Moreover, employers could incur close to $1 billion in turnover costs for the comprehensive termination of this population. The loss in GDP and turnover costs would be felt most acutely in the locations where Salvadorans, Hondurans, and Haitians are primarily located, which includes major metropolitan areas in Florida, New York, California, Texas, Maryland, and Virginia. Countries recovering from catastrophic events will not have the capacity to reabsorb tens of thousands of people; and the money that TPS holders send home has served as a lifeline to family and friends in devastated countries.

TPS does not make individuals automatically eligible for permanent residence or US citizenship, but some may apply for permanent lawful status. TPS does not provide beneficiaries with a separate path to lawful permanent residence (a green card) or citizenship. Two federal appellate circuits (the Ninth and Sixth Circuits) ruled that a person with valid TPS status could adjust status to lawful permanent resident if otherwise eligible through a family-based or employment-based petition, even if he or she entered the United States without inspection. In order to gain permanent resident status, a TPS recipient must instead depart the country to have a visa processed at a consular post (which means making re-entry almost ten years).

We would encourage our readers to explore in depth the TPS situation as our general discussion of changes in immigration policies under the Trump administration includes cuts in humanitarian programs and is having the greatest impact on Latinos from Central American and Caribbean African–descent nations. Bills have been introduced in Congress that would protect TPS holders. In June 2019, the House of Representatives passed the Dream and Promise Act, a bill that would offer a pathway to citizenship for people with TPS, Deferred Enforced Departure (DED), or Deferred Action for Childhood Arrivals (DACA). The Senate is still considering similar legislation.

Sources: Cohn et al. 2019; Ibe and Johnson 2020.

The increase of immigration-related practices by the Trump administration goes beyond what we have discussed so far. Additional policy changes include: listing of social media accounts on immigration forms;[5] increased denaturalization efforts (if there are inconsistencies in application or activity, citizenship can be stripped); expansion of the "public charge" protocol, reducing the use of public benefits to no more than twelve months out of thirty-six; domestic violence no longer being considered grounds for asylum; limits to Temporary Protected Status recipients; and revising the "credible fear interviews" that had been conducted by asylum experts. It is clear that contemporary immigration policies have been driven by a fundamental shift toward more restrictive criteria for admission (legal, refugee, asylum, etc.) and "narrower" definitions of which individuals are preferred over others. Our discussion, so far, illustrates the multifaceted strands associated with immigration policies, historical patterns on migration to the United States, and the economic benefits to businesses and migrants. Immigration policies have differential effects on particular countries, economic and trade relations, national security, and family reunification. We are experiencing a backlogged legal immigration process and a volatile public that is greatly polarized about the flow and characteristics of incoming immigrants.

One important result for Latinos is the increased saliency of immigration policy and greater support for reform that emphasizes immigrant rights and normalizing status with a pathway toward legal status/citizenship (Latino Decisions 2014). Figure 9.4 illustrates the issue saliency of immigration and how it figures into Latinos' vote participation and choice. Also, support for immigration reform regarding the content reform proposals is almost uniform across variants (national origin, nativity, language use, economic class, etc.) within the Latino community. In the Latino Decisions poll (Latino Decisions 2014), 89 percent of all Latino voters supported President Obama's executive action regarding DACA and DAPA, while 94 percent of Spanish speakers, 76 percent of Republicans, 95 percent of Democrats, 85 percent of non-Mexicans, and 83 percent of evangelicals also supported those actions. It is important to note that one of the main arguments made by Latino Decisions researchers is that DACA is popular

FIGURE 9.4 Saliency of Immigration as a Mobilizing Issue for Latinos

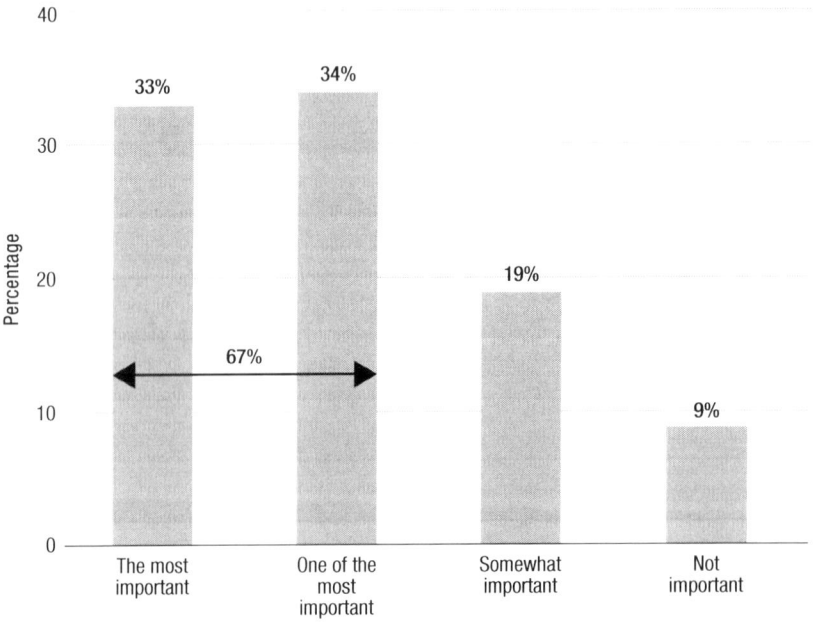

Source: Adapted from Latino Decisions Election Eve 2014 Poll, sponsored by LVP/NCLR/AV.

among virtually all subgroups of the electorate, including a majority of even white Republicans who are favorable toward the policy.

The Latino Decisions July 2018 poll on immigration presented several options to respondents regarding immigration policy direction to assess the opinions of Americans. They included: the Dream Act; pathway to citizenship; support for a border wall; removing domestic violence as basis for asylum; political "actor" responsible for family separation; and rejecting attacks on immigrants. As seen in table 9.1, virtually all Latinos were most supportive of policies that were responsive to immigrants and normalizing their status. They also demonstrated the lowest support for construction of a southern border wall. For the most part, Latinos placed blame on the Trump administration and fellow Republicans for a series of punitive and restrictive immigration policies. Asian and African Americans exhibited similar immigration reform positions as Latinos on the Dream Act, rejecting attacks on immigrants and in favor

TABLE 9.1 Immigration Policies for Reform by Support by Racial and Ethnic Groups

Immigration Policy Options	Racial and Ethnic Groups					
	Total (%)	Latino (%)	Asian (%)	African American (%)	Native American (%)	White (%)
Pass the Dream Act (Totally Good)[a]	79	86	77	82	74	77
Comprehensive immigration with path to citizenship	73	87	74	75	71	70
Support border wall	36	29	27	23	35	41
End domestic violence as basis for asylum	32	32	34	24	31	34
Who is responsible for family separation at border?						
Trump adminstration	74	79	80	80	68	71
Congressional Democrats	54	52	53	40	59	57
Congressional Republicans	73	75	79	80	71	71
How angry about child separation policy[b] (Totally Angry)	73	86	79	83	72	69
Voters support welcoming immigrants	66	79	75	77	63	61
Voters reject attack on immigrants (Totally Important)	84	86	86	87	82	82

Source: Matt A. Barreto, "Immigration and the 2018 Midterms: A View from Competitive Districts," July 2016 Imigration Poll. Latino Decisions.

[a] The remaining percentage (from 100 percent) from the Totally Good response represents the Totally Bad response.

[b] Responses are Very Angry, Somewhat Angry, Not Too Angry, and Not at All Angry.

of a pathway to citizenship. White respondents also shared those positions on the Dream Act and pathway to citizenship but were less critical of family separations and tended to place blame across the political spectrum. Clearly, immigration, and its many implications, has been on the Latino policy agenda, and the general political and public climate has only exacerbated its importance. The extensive personal connections among Latinos and undocumented immigrants reinforces the saliency of immigration and, potentially, the motivation for Latino permanent residents to pursue naturalization. Next, we will examine another aspect of the Latino immigrant's civic life: naturalization.

Immigration and Naturalization

One clear consequence of the increasing number of immigrants in the United States is the growing pool of those eligible for citizenship. Naturalization confers citizenship on foreign nationals with legal permanent resident (LPR) status in the United States, granting immigrants the same important privileges and responsibilities as US-born citizens, which includes the right to vote. For Latinos, the overall pattern of naturalization has been lower than that of other immigrants worldwide, especially for Mexican immigrants (García 1981c). The general naturalization requirements include being at least eighteen years of age, having lived as a legal permanent resident alien for five years in the United States, having good moral character, being able to read, write, speak, and understand commonly used words in the English language, and being able to demonstrate knowledge of US history and government.

In the 1990s, there was a marked rise in the number of immigrants becoming US citizens. Overall, slightly less than half of all permanent resident aliens have naturalized (Office of Immigration Statistics 2014). The proportion of naturalized immigrants varies substantially by their country of origin. For example, most of the immigrants admitted in 1977 became eligible to naturalize in 1982, and by 1995 about 46 percent had become citizens. Generally, the leading countries of origin are China, the former Soviet Union, and the Philippines, while immigrants from Mexico and Canada are the least likely to naturalize. The research literature on Latino naturalization has focused on Mexicans. For the most part, the key factors motivating Mexicanos to naturalize have been English-language proficiency, length of residence in the United States, higher levels of educational attainment, age of migration, and income (García 1981c; Pachón and DeSipio 1994; Smith and Edmondston 1998). While patriotism, allegiance, and cultural similarity with America have been key determinants for naturalization, becoming a citizen tends to be a more pragmatic decision. People become citizens to ensure access to governmental program participation (Supplemental Security Income, food stamps, Medicaid, etc.), employment, educational financial aid and scholarships, and improved positioning for family reunification preferences in immigration.

While naturalization rates for Latino immigrants have been lower than for immigrants from other regions of the world, they rose during the 1990s. With proximity to their mother country, especially Mexico, the Caribbean, and parts of Central America, a strong expectation for them to return to their country of origin had served as a disincentive to pursue American citizenship. For example, Mexicans would lose the right to own and inherit property in Mexico if they became US citizens. However, since the

FIGURE 9.5 Annual Number of New US Citizens and Legal Permanent Residents, 1980–2016

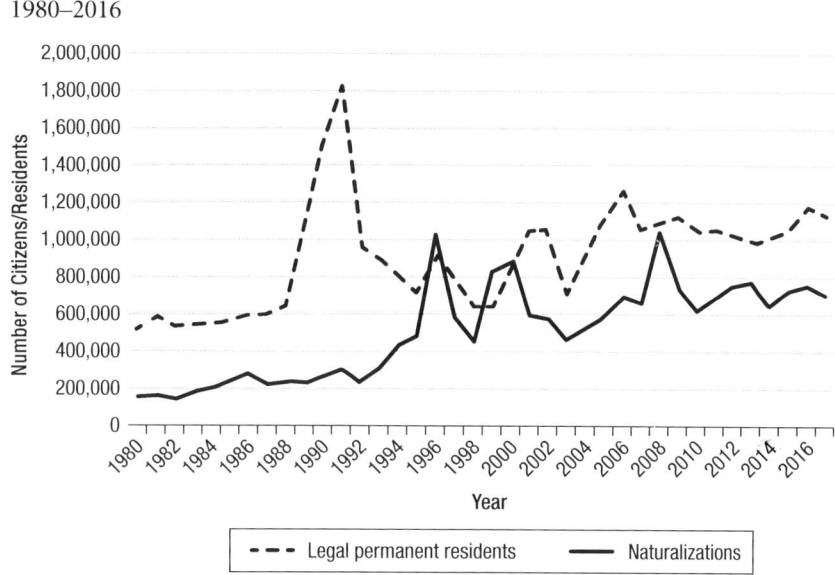

Source: Department of Homeland Security, Office of Immigration Statistics, *Yearbook of Immigration Statistics, 2017*.

early 1990s, more Latin American nations have implemented dual citizenship standing, which has removed one of the obstacles in seeking US citizenship for some Latino immigrants (Jones-Correa 2001a; Pantoja and Gershon 2006).

The surge in naturalization in the 1990s was rooted in individual motivation, general circumstances, and sociopolitical developments. There were several policy changes and new legislation that also impacted naturalizations. The INS Green Replacement Program, launched in 1993, the approval of Proposition 187, rising levels of immigration in the 1980s, the enactment of the Personal Responsibility and Work Responsibility Act, and Mexico's approval of dual citizenship all contributed to increased naturalization[6] (Barreto et al. 2005; Gershon and Pantoja 2008). Figure 9.5 shows the dramatic rise of immigrants in the 1990s and of the eligible population for naturalization from 2007 to 2011. People from Asia and North America (which includes Mexico) represented almost three-fourths of all naturalizations. Perhaps offsetting some of the impetus for increased naturalizations has been the increase in fees ($680 per individual in 2011 to $1,170 by 2020), a more extensive review process, and longer wait periods between the filing and actual interview and approval notifications.

The annual number of naturalization applications filed has increased in recent years. They rose by nearly 200,000 between FY 2015 and 2016 (783,062 to 972,151), and FY 2017 saw a small additional increase to 986,851. President Donald Trump's anti-immigration rhetoric during the 2016 presidential campaign and his administration's restrictive immigration policies have been credited with motivating immigrants to seek citizenship. The number of pending cases also increased substantially, from 518,707 at the end of FY 2016 to 728,301 at the end of FY 2017. In FY 2017, the most recent year for which data was available, US Citizenship and Immigration Services (USCIS) received 986,851 applications for citizenship and naturalized 707,265 individuals. The number of individuals who naturalized in FY 2017 represented a decrease of 6 percent from FY 2016 (753,060). USCIS denied 83,176 naturalization petitions in FY 2017, a decrease from the year before (86,033). Applicants can be denied citizenship if they cannot prove the required length of permanent residence, are found to lack allegiance to the United States, are determined to have bad moral character, and/or fail the required English-language or American civics test.

By the end of FY 2017, a large majority of USCIS field offices averaged wait times longer than seven months for a naturalization application to be processed, with some offices averaging as high as fourteen to fifteen months. The recent increase in applications has contributed to this backlog, but advocates have also accused the Trump administration, as part of its efforts to limit immigration and the benefits available to noncitizens, of intentionally slowing the naturalization process as well as other immigration benefits, such as legal permanent residency.

Four other pieces of immigration legislation that have been passed since the 1980s have contributed to rising naturalization rates. The 1986 IRCA included an amnesty provision in which 2.7 million undocumented residents were granted legal resident status. The first of the now legalized residents were able to apply for naturalization in 1994; Latinos constituted more than two-thirds of those eligible. Secondly, the **Illegal Immigration Reform and Immigrant Responsibility Act of 1996** (IIRIRA) included stipulations to bolster the monitoring of the US border and set up measures to remove criminal and other deportable aliens. This law also provided increased protection for legal workers through worksite enforcement. As a result, the "negative" elements of the IIRIRA created incentives for immigrants to gain greater protections and rights through naturalization.

The 1996 **Personal Responsibility and Work Opportunity Reconciliation Act** (PRWORA) severely limited immigrants' access to public benefits, especially social service programs. The Welfare Act restricted the eligibility of legal immigrants for means-tested public assistance, widened prohibitions against public benefits for undocumented immigrants, and mandated the INS to verify immigration status in order to determine which immigrants would receive public benefits. Part of the requirement for immigrant sponsorship included sponsors assuming financial responsibility for immigrants if they were unable to sustain themselves. The PRWORA made the affidavit of support legally binding. In 1996, the **Antiterrorism and Effective Death Penalty Act** (ATEDPA) greatly facilitated procedures for the removal of "alien terrorists," authorizing state and local law enforcement officials to arrest and detain certain undocumented persons and providing access to confidential INS files through court order. The overall effect of the 1996 legislation was to produce a more negative environment for immigrants, and naturalization became a protective and defensive response.

The post-9/11 period in the United States resulted in broader discretion regarding detainment and limited civil and legal rights for immigrants. Some noteworthy developments since 9/11 have been heightened border enforcement with increases in the numbers of Border Patrol personnel, use of National Guardsmen to intensify border monitoring, construction of more than nine hundred miles of fencing and other structural deterrents, continuation of **Immigration and Customs Enforcement** (ICE) workplace raids, formal deportation processing and hearings for apprehended undocumented persons, and governmental agreements with local law enforcement agencies to assist in identification and processing of undocumented persons. Overall, the tenor of immigration policy considerations is heavily laden with the stringent requirement of securing the border from the crossing of drugs, contraband, and people, limiting any broader discussion of the many other aspects of immigration policy reform.

Since the advent of the Trump administration, changes, attempted changes, and proposed changes have had a direct bearing on the pathways for legal status, converting legal permanent aliens to citizenship, and maintaining one's naturalization. That is, visa bans on persons from Venezuela and several Muslim countries stop a pool of potential permanent resident aliens. The immigration process is made slower by requiring in-face interviews, denying or dismissing applications due to missing information or errors, expanding the definition of public benefits to deny applicants, closing twenty-one USCIS offices overseas, adding an immigration surcharge, ending the diversity lottery, making health insurance mandatory for green card approval, and reducing the family reunification basis for legal admission (Pierce, Bolter, and Selee 2018). The overall policy rationale is to make citizenship more difficult by affecting the flow of immigrants, applying greater economic prerequisites, lengthening the wait times, and expanding discretion by USCIS personnel for approval or dismissal of applicants (Shear, Jordan, and Dickerson 2019).

The National Association of Latino Elected and Appointed Officials (NALEO) has pursued an educational and promotional program to encourage more Latino immigrants to pursue naturalization since the mid-1980s. Materials and informational hotlines were established to facilitate interested Latino immigrants' pursuit of citizenship. In addition, NALEO began working with the INS to streamline processing (long wait periods were developing in many offices) and to reach the intended population. Also, NALEO made use of public service announcements featuring well-known Latino personalities. The increased number of applicants produced bottlenecks within the INS organization. By 1998, the average processing time for applications was twenty-seven months (Singer and Gilbertson 2000), but there was a lot of variation depending on the specific USCIS office. A new report shows a national backlog of more than 700,000 applications as of September 17, 2019. Wait times across the agency field offices ranged from an average of ten to eighteen months, which is in excess of the six months required by statute (Colorado State Advisory Committee to the US Commission on Civil Rights 2019). Even as more Latino resident aliens are currently applying for citizenship, long delays slow the increased pool of prospective voters and may discourage other Latino immigrants from entering the naturalization process.

A more recent development using technology to increase access to legal assistance and reduce language, geographic, and economic barriers for low- and moderate-income immigrant communities is Citizenshipworks 2.0, which was developed by New Americans Campaign partners Pro Bono Net and Immigration Advocates Network, in collaboration with the Immigrant Legal Resource Center. It allows lawful permanent residents to verify their eligibility and complete their naturalization forms on their own or, if needed, connect to nonprofit legal providers in their area. "Research shows that large numbers of young people who are eligible to naturalize are not taking the final step to become US citizens. We are excited by the opportunity to partner with Voto Latino to develop effective digital strategies to reach young immigrants and their families, and help them take advantage of the benefits of citizenship, including the right to vote," said Mark O'Brien, cofounder and executive director of Pro Bono Net (Guest Blog 2020).

The Latino electorate is being boosted by the conversion of a growing Latino immigrant segment into citizens. A study by Bass and Casper (1999) examined the differences in registration and voting behavior between naturalized and native-born Americans. They found that naturalized citizens, who were more likely to be registered and to vote, tended to have more education and higher income levels, be employed, own a home, have lived for a longer period at their current residence, be female, be older, have professional status, and be married (Levin 2013; DeSipio 2006; Street 2017). When researchers controlled for length of time in the United States and region of origin (e.g., Latin America), Latino naturalized citizens' voting and registration rates did not differ significantly from those of native-born Latinos. Abascal (2017) found that Latino naturalization is enhanced if those eligible live in areas with a concentration of naturalized co-ethnics who provide more knowledge and a perceived sense of belonging.

The Political Nature and Involvement of Latino Immigrants

There has been growing research literature on Latino noncitizens and their political engagements. The general characterization has been one of limited involvement and interest in the American political system. Jones-Correa's (1998) book on Latino immigrants in the New York metropolitan region portrays Dominicans, Colombians, and other Latino immigrants as being in political limbo. They did not actively engage in the political process by pursuing citizenship, nor are they involved in political parties or other political organizations. Part of the explanation lies with the "myth" of eventual return to their homeland and a lack of encouragement from political organizations and leaders to participate politically. Research conducted a decade and half earlier by García and de la Garza (1985) found a similar pattern of limited organizational involvement by Mexican-origin immigrants in their respective communities. If they belonged to any organization, it was likely to be a religiously based one, and these Mexican immigrants were less likely to be politically involved.

> **BOX 9.4 Noncitizen Veterans and Trying to Realize Established Pathways toward Citizenship**
>
> Overall, the number of service members who apply to become naturalized citizens is a fraction of the civilian applications, but both pools have shrunk between 2017 and 2019. In the first quarter of the Trump administration, January to March 2017, there were 3,069 foreign-born members of the military who applied to become naturalized citizens. That same quarter, 286,892 foreign-born civilians applied. In the first quarter of fiscal year 2019, USCIS reported it received only 648 military applications for citizenship, a 79 percent drop. For comparison, the agency received 189,410 civilian applications, a 34 percent drop. In 2020 the Trump administration announced that it would make it harder for children born to US service members serving abroad to claim US citizenship. More important than this change was how the new policy fit a trend in which the Trump administration sought to limit both legal and illegal immigration

generally. It tried to make it harder to gain US citizenship by serving in the military, which was a sharp break from the past.

According to the most recent USCIS data available, the agency denied 16.6 percent of military applications for citizenship, compared to an 11.2 percent civilian denial rate in the first quarter of fiscal year 2019, a period that covers October to December 2018. The fiscal year 2019 data is the eighth quarterly report of military naturalization rates since Trump took office. In six of the last eight reports, civilians had a higher rate of approval for citizenship than military applicants did, reversing the previous trend.

For decades, a path toward citizenship was service in the military. Service in the military for at least one year (in peacetime) and service during US military wars/conflicts or since 2001 led to filing for citizenship. The requisites included honorable military service; being a lawful resident; being able to read/write and speak English; knowledge of US history; good moral character; and attachment to the Constitution. This route also lessened residency requirements and waived naturalization fees.

In his recently published book, *Reform Without Justice: Latino Migrant Politics and the Homeland Security State*, Alfonso Gonzales opens with the story of Bernardo Gonzales, a deported veteran now living in Mexico City. Bernardo recounted that at the age of one, he and his family migrated from Cancun to the United States. He eventually joined the US military and was deployed to the Persian Gulf during the 1991 war. In 1993, soon after leaving the military, Bernardo made the mistake of drinking three beers before driving and was arrested in California for driving under the influence (DUI). Seventeen years later, US Immigration and Customs Enforcement (ICE) detained him while raiding the mattress factory where he worked and found out about his DUI conviction. Under California law, such a transgression is a misdemeanor, but under federal law, for a noncitizen, it is an aggravated felony, thus making Bernardo subject to deportation. After six months in detention, the Department of Homeland Security (DHS) "removed" Bernardo, despite his having US-citizen children to support. There are many similar stories in the book and studies by immigrant rights organizations.

Immigrants serving in the US military are being denied citizenship at a higher rate than foreign-born civilians, according to new government data that has revealed the impact of stricter Trump administration immigration policies on service members. "The fall in military naturalization applications is likely attributable in significant part to the Department of Defense's decision not to renew the Military Accessions Vital to the National Interest [MAVNI] program after its expiration at the end of FY17" (Vakili, Pasquarella, and Marcano 2016).

The ACLU report "Discharged, Then Discarded" found that veterans returning home from service were subject to drastic immigration laws that reclassified many minor offenses as deportable crimes, which effectively banished some from this country. "By requiring deportation and stripping immigration courts of the power to consider military service, the United States government abandons these veterans by expelling them to foreign countries at the moment when they most

BOX 9.4 (continued)

need the government's help to rehabilitate their lives after service," said Bardis Vakili, a senior staff attorney with the ACLU of California (Vakili, Pasquarella, and Marcano 2016). Changes in US law in 1996 greatly expanded the number of deportable offenses, while eliminating the ability of judges to exercise any discretion in most cases. From 2013 to 2018, ICE failed to follow its own policies requiring agents to consider a veteran's military record before beginning the process of removal from the country, according to the report. Time in service, awards, and deployments are all among factors that are supposed to be weighed when making a deportation decision.

Congress has been holding hearings on the Veteran Deportation Prevention and Reform Act of 2019 (H.R. 4890). If passed, the bill would bring eligible deported veterans back to the United States and improve tracking by the Department of Homeland Security of noncitizen veterans who wind up in immigration hearings. It would also offer a pathway of citizenship for spouses and children of members of the Armed Services. Hector Barajas, a retired US Army paratrooper once deported to Mexico, testified at the congressional hearings. He'd been deported along with dozens of other honorably discharged US military veterans. At the time, Barajas was running a shelter for deported vets nicknamed "the Bunker," where he offered deported veterans legal and immigration services. Barajas documented more than three hundred veterans who had been deported under a policy dating to Bill Clinton's administration. That law triggers deportation when any immigrant, even a military veteran, commits what's known as an "aggravated felony." That broad term includes a wide array of crimes, including offenses such as failure to show in court, entering the country illegally, and drug possession. Governor Jerry Brown pardoned three deported veterans, including Hector Barajas. Barajas returned to the country he served and was formally sworn in as a citizen in March 2018. The Government Accountability Office investigating the deportation of immigrant veterans found ICE didn't "consistently follow its (own) policies involving veterans" of incorporating their military service during deportation hearings (Vakili, Pasquarella, and Marcano 2016).

The ACLU report made several recommendations for fairer and equitable pathways for deported noncitizen veterans toward citizenship. The judicial and administrative recommendations included the following: 1) restoring judicial discretion to allow judges to consider factors such as military service in cases involving deportation; 2) requiring ICE to adopt an agency-wide moratorium on and/or presumption against removal of any active-duty US service member or honorably discharged veteran; 3) reopening those naturalization applications that were denied or abandoned because an individual was unable to follow through on the naturalization process as a result of their military service; and 4) providing legal representation to active-duty US service members and veterans who are in removal proceedings.

The Texas Civil Rights Project has also researched the Trump administration's policy changes and has made similar recommendations as the ACLU. Since 2017, the Trump administration directed the Department of Defense to implement new barriers restricting the ability of immigrants to serve in the military and to use that service as a path to citizenship. As a result, service members have been filing far fewer applications for naturalization. What's more, service members are now less likely than civilians to have their applications approved. The Defense Department shut down naturalization offices at some of its basic training locations, citing the new policy. But the Trump administration intensified efforts to separate military service from citizenship. The Immigrant Legal Resource Center advised in 2018 that "it may now be faster for [lawful permanent residents] seeking citizenship to remain civilians" (Best et al. 2019).

Immigrants are confronting policies that are designed to be punitive, restrictive, and exclusionary to certain groups. Not only are Latinos being negatively affected, but so are Muslims and others from the Middle East and the rest of Africa.

California's Proposition 187, Arizona's SB 1070, and the 2006 immigrant protests of the Sensenbrenner bill motivated Latino noncitizens to express their views and engage in political activities. These policies were driven by anti-immigrant fear and concern about a negative impact on the economy, jobs, social services, schools, crime, and the social/moral fabric of America. This process of mobilization through threat was documented in earlier chapters, noting that immigration policy in particular has led to major movements of electoral engagement among Latinos. The undocumented population, especially Latinos, found themselves being blamed for states' economic woes, crime, overcrowded schools, and crowded housing. The significance of these actions accented the recurring themes of xenophobia and nativism that have existed throughout American history. In the 1970s, estimates of the undocumented population ranged from one to twelve million. The debate regarding the undocumented resident population usually included emotionalism as well as estimates of cost/benefit assessments. The tension following these events resulted in a loud response from Latinos and immigration advocacy organizations challenging new immigration policies' constitutionality and compliance with civil rights law. Latino political engagement cuts across all segments of this community and has included protests and mass demonstrations, legal challenges, and voter-registration drives (Martinez 2005; Pantoja et al. 2001; O'Leary 2009). Such developments have heightened politicization of the Latino community and elevated immigration reform as the top issue for congressional action.

With increased political involvement by Latino immigrants, a very positive attachment to the United States in terms of loyalty has been exhibited, extolling the opportunities afforded by living in America and support for political institutions (Pachón and DeSipio 1994; García 1997; de la Garza et al. 1993). They displayed participatory attitudes of political support and belief in core American values (de la Garza, Falcón, and García 1996) but have not always followed through with concomitant political activities. Given the national origin of some Latino immigrants (those coming from repressive and nondemocratic regimes), it has been posited that these political cultures do not reinforce, or provide experiences, that lead to democratic participation. In 2001, Espenshade and Ramakrishnan found that coming from a repressive Latin American regime does not affect voting and registration, while anti-immigrant sentiment serves as a catalyst for participation.

Again, we see immigration policies and public response to immigration being linked directly to the political world of Latino immigrants. During the latter part of the 1990s, naturalization rose significantly. For example, more than 1.2 million people naturalized in 1998 alone, which was more than twice the previous year's number. The Clinton administration initiated efforts in 1999 to reduce the backlog of naturalization applications (Pan 1999). Overall, wait periods were cut almost in half; in offices in San Francisco and Houston, the wait period was shortened from thirty-two to nineteen months. Similarly, the thirty-three-month wait period for a green card was reduced to twenty-four months. Ironically, there was a drop in naturalization applications the following year by almost half (McDonnell 2001). These developments are a stark contrast to the current policies.

Since the early 2000s, more systematic research has been performed with respect to the political world of foreign-born Latinos, beyond just the act of naturalization. Works by Barreto and Muñoz (2003) and Barreto et al. (2009) demonstrate that this group's level of political interest, awareness, civic engagement, and political involvement are not disparate from those of native-born Latinos. In addition, examining the Latino immigrant sector has brought the role of Spanish-language media, especially radio, into the politicization process. Works by Portes, Escobar, and Radford (2007), García (2013b), and Escala-Rabadán et al. (2006) have helped to link transnational activities and connections with civic and political engagement in the United States. Even though activities and connectedness with homeland issues are included in transnational networks, organized groups have also become involved in local and domestic issues. Transnationalism among immigrant communities is not disjointed from interest and involvement in US-based politics. For example, a salient interest in educational politics and policy is quite evident among Salvadorans and other Central Americans.

O'Connor (1998) found that when their children's schools were inadequate or facing serious issues, Latino parents raised their concerns about the quality and effectiveness of the schooling their children received. This finding was supported by the Latino National Survey (Fraga et al. 2006a) regarding Latino involvement in school-related matters for both native- and foreign-born Latinos (Fraga et al. 2009). Latinos' interest in education was also reflected in their support for Proposition BB in California, which increased bond funding for schools. Latinos supported the proposition by 82 percent compared to 67 percent for Anglos and 76 percent for African Americans. The second most frequently mentioned area of concern was related to language difficulties and poverty. Other concerns centered on immigrant human and civil rights and access to social services.

The 1990s witnessed concrete signs of Latino immigrant political involvement, especially at the local level, through jobs and unionization. Labor has shown greater interest in, and recognition of, immigrant workers in traditional sectors—agriculture, manufacturing, construction—and, more importantly, in the service sectors. Immigrant workers in the restaurant and hotel industries, janitorial services, and child and elder care have been subject to unionizing activities and strikes. Janitorial worker strikes in Chicago and Los Angeles in 2000 marked significant involvement of immigrant workers (both documented and undocumented) in leadership roles as well as on the picket lines (Guarnizo 1994; Figueroa 1996; Milkman 2000). The labor issues, in addition to wages and benefits, focus on opportunities for legal entry into the United States, access to public services, increased regulation of labor, health, and safety standards, and limited voting rights for noncitizens in school board elections (Milkman 2000).

David Broder (2001) discussed the awakening of the Latino immigrant communities, which included the dishwashers, chambermaids, painters, and bellhops who helped to form the **Organization of Los Angeles Workers** (OLAW). The Service Employees International Union and the Hotel Employees and Restaurant Employees Union were an integral part of OLAW and political-mobilization activities in the city. OLAW was able to recruit more than six hundred canvassers and distribute more than eighty thousand registration cards and forms. Similar organizational efforts were evident in Miami with the Hispanic Coalition. With more than 130,000 immigrants naturalizing in Florida, the coalition helped register new citizens, and the partisan effect was a five-to-one Democratic advantage (Booth 1996). This was due to anxiety among immigrants and anti-immigrant sentiments associated with many Republican leaders and policy initiatives.

Contemporary accounts of the political world of Latino immigrants will not only portray a wide range of political engagement, but also place emphasis on the socialization effects of immigrant youths on immigrant parents (García-Castañon 2011; Cruz 2010; Calderon 2012). Latino noncitizen political participation has taken multiple forms of engagement, including protests, information gathering and political education, organizational affiliations, and leadership roles (Calderon 2012; Félix 2008). There have been rising numbers of naturalization applications, but eventual citizenship among Latinos has slowed due to less supportive actions by the USCIS (Chishti and Bolter 2019; Pierce et al. 2018). Latino immigrants are not insulated from governmental policies, national movements, and Latino organizational activities. Local governments, media, community organizations, political leaders, and hostile policy initiatives have contributed to naturalization increases among Latinos, but hesitancy still exists to become citizens. Jones-Correa's (1998) study of New York City Latino immigrants reinforces the important role that encouragement plays in their political involvement or lack of it. He found that immigrant participation was stymied by both the lack of support to participate and the requirement to renounce former citizenship, which raised the fear of never being able to return to the country of origin. In addition, Barreto and Muñoz (2003) found non-Latinos to be as engaged in nonelectoral activities as their Latino native-born counterparts. Their research demonstrated that traditional socioeconomic variables are important, along with language fluency, percentage of one's time in the United States, and attitudes toward opportunities in America, all contributing to the predictive capacity of models regarding Mexican and other Latino immigrants.

Conclusion

The awakening and greater political involvement of Latino immigrants is attributed, in part, to heightened nativism, xenophobia, and political elites, especially from the Trump administration and its emphasis on immigration policies. These policies are more restrictive and punitive, designed to serve as deterrents to immigrants, and more selective and targeted as to which groups are preferred or considered acceptable to join American society. These policy emphases tend to preclude most Latinos' access and permission to enter and stay in the United States. While events at the end of the late 1990s and early 2000s made immigration more salient and impactful on Latinos, the contemporary climate and present public policies affecting Latinos has heightened the consequences for the broader Latino community. The challenge remains for Latino organizations and leadership to build on the political capital of efforts of the early twenty-first century.

A good example of the political engagement of foreign-born and naturalized Latinos was Salvador Espino, who was seeking political office as a city council member in Fort Worth, Texas. This thirty-three-year-old, Mexican-born, naturalized citizen saw his candidacy as an opportunity to show that the Latino community has a stake in what occurs in city hall (Tórrez and Jackson 2001). Other Latinos in this city are also seeking political opportunities at the city and county levels and transferring their work and business experiences into political organizing and mobilization. We have touched only slightly on the political world of Latino immigrants and the dynamics of activating this segment of the Latino community. Much research is being directed toward gaining a better understanding of the political integration of Latino immigrants; for example, what a sense of belonging means to citizenship and political engagement (Ocampo 2018; Ocampo et al. 2018). Clearly, this is an important aspect of this demographic and political segment of the Latino community.

NALEO recognized the political potential of Latino immigrants more than forty years ago. It was the first Latino organization to target permanent resident aliens for naturalization drives and education. In 2011, more Latino organizations and leaders, as well as the American labor movement and religious institutions, began directing their attention to them. A recurring theme in this book involves the continual development of the dynamics of Latino politics. We are seeing closer political ties between Latino immigrants (i.e., foreign-born) and the second-generation and beyond Latinos, including the undocumented segment. Polls by Latino Decisions demonstrate the direct linkages between the "segments" through familial, friendship, work, and residential connections. The external immigration climate, rhetoric, and punitive policies have affected more of the Latino community and raised this policy area as one of the most salient. In addition, there is greater emphasis on appropriate immigration policy reform centering on normalizing immigrant families' lives with legalization, pathways to citizenship, and assurances of basic rights and freedoms in a democratic society. Clearly, an examination of the immigration arena has ramifications in other realms of Latino political life.

The current volatility of the immigration policy arena also accents the role of emotions and levels of accurate information about immigrants and policy proposals (Gutierrez et al. 2019; Alesina et al. 2019). The pervasiveness of immigration politics traverses the political and socioeconomic world of Latinos and the American political system. If anything, the current climate surrounding immigration politics and policy will only get more divisive and contentious. For example, in response to a growing public health threat associated with the coronavirus, President Trump tied this health issue to his goal of tighter border enforcement by stating that "border security is also health security" (Office of the White House 2020). These statements will only continue to create an environment where Latinos will feel as though they are under siege.

Discussion Questions

1. Most recent polls on Latinos reveal comprehensive immigration reform as this community's most salient issue. What would a comprehensive immigration policy include from a Latino perspective, and what would be required to implement this?
2. Immigration and America's development have gone hand in hand since before the formation of the United States. Discuss the historical bases for US immigration policies until the latter half of the twentieth century.
3. While immigration is the domain of the federal government, since the 1990s many states and some local governments have formulated laws and ordinances targeting the undocumented immigrant. What have been the contributing factors for such developments, the role of public opinion, and the responses of the Latino community?
4. Since 2005, the undocumented community has "come out of the shadows" and taken to the streets to protest restrictive and punitive immigration policies. How would you characterize the political activism of the undocumented Latino community and its effects on the larger Latino community?
5. The 1990s and early 2000s saw a rash of immigration laws as well as executive orders regarding immigration and border security. How would you depict the basic foci and objectives of these policies?
6. In a hostile political and partisan environment, what are strategies that Latinos can pursue to move their immigration policy preferences forward?

Notes

1. The US Supreme Court reasoned that the principle of the identity of the husband and wife was a reasonable requirement in making foreign policy. The Cable Act of 1922 repealed automatic loss of female citizenship but did not include females who married alien men ineligible for citizenship. They continued to lose their citizenship upon marriage until 1931, when Congress repealed the 1907 law.

2. In this case, mixed-status families can consist of parents or children, some of whom may be undocumented, others legal permanent residents, and some native-born.

3. See the following report: https://usipc.ucsd.edu/publications/usipc-working-paper-1.pdf.

4. https://latinodecisions.com/blog/healthcare-in-the-shadows.

5. The goal is to monitor and keep record of activities and sites used. This information could influence applications for citizenship as well as maintenance of their legal status. If the immigrant has successfully secured citizenship, they are no longer monitored, but a history of their social media interactions is kept on file.

6. A green card is a form of identification administered by the Immigration and Naturalization Service that certifies an individual as a legal permanent resident alien (PRA) in the United States. Originally, the green card was the vehicle for identification, and bearers had to register annually to maintain their legal residence. PRAs can be required to produce their green cards at any time. Even though the identification is no longer a physical green card, it is still referred to as such.

CHAPTER 10

Education, Health, and Voting Rights Policy

Adquirir conocimiento, profundizar la sabiduría y proteger nuestros derechos humanos comienzan con la formación académica que sostiene nuestro afán por aprender. Lo usamos para afirmar nuestro auto concepto y vivir con dignidad.

Acquiring knowledge, deepening our wisdom, and protecting our human and civil rights begins with an education that sustains our desire to learn. We use that knowledge to affirm our own self-esteem and to live with dignity.

IN 2016, CALIFORNIA'S SCHOOL SYSTEM remained one of the most segregated in the country for Latinos. The UCLA Civil Rights Project (Orfield et al. 2014) reported that the average Latino student was likely to attend a school that was 84 percent nonwhite (or minority), with high rates of concentrated poverty. In terms of representation in higher education, only 20 percent of Latino students taking the SAT were deemed college-ready, compared to 41 percent of students statewide. Since the US Civil Rights Commission Studies of 1971–1972 first examined the state of education for this population in the Southwest, the themes of isolation, segregation, poorer quality schools and instructional staff, economic resources, and the treatment of cultural values and practices as educational liabilities served to describe California's educational record.

On the other hand, a report by the Pew Hispanic Center (Lopez and Fry 2013) announced that the Hispanic overall population showed gains in its participation in higher education. Hispanic students comprised 16.7 percent of full-time college students (both undergraduate and graduate) in 2011, an increase of 10 percent from 2006 (Hispanics comprised 16 percent of the nation's total population). Women continued their majority status, comprising 55 percent of undergraduates and 60 percent of graduate students. Additional highlights included the following: 53 percent of Hispanic four-year-olds were enrolled in nursery school, up from 43 percent in 1997 and 21 percent in 1987; 27 percent of the population age three and older were enrolled in classes, from nursery school to graduate studies. More than half (59 percent) of all four-year-olds and 39 percent of three-year-olds were enrolled in nursery school. Students in grades one through twelve made up 64 percent of those age three and older enrolled in school. Students age thirty-five and older comprised 15 percent of people enrolled in college; they made up 7 percent of full-time college students and 36 percent of those attending part-time (Davis and Bauman 2008).

Although Latinos continue to demonstrate improvement in their educational achievement, other groups in the nation are improving as well. African and Asian Americans have made similar or greater gains in educational attainment. For example, while the percentage of Latinos aged twenty-five and older who had completed high school in 2015 was nearly 67 percent, the percentage of Asian Americans exceeded 89 percent, and it was 88 percent for whites. This chapter examines three critical policy areas for Latinos: education or schooling, health, and political representation. In the case of the latter, the origins and continued policy implementation of the Voting Rights Act seek to align minority communities' candidate preferences with election outcomes. That is, representation should reflect the community to which the elected official is responsible.

Education: A Continual Latino Priority

The intent of chapter 9 was to examine the nature of the American public policy process and to assess the resources and strategies Latinos must pursue to secure their preferred policy outcomes and ensure their successful implementation. For more than forty-five years, the Mexican American community and other Latino groups have focused their attention and activities on the educational system. Insufficient resources, segregation, exclusion from decision making, lack of representation in the teaching and administrative ranks, poor facilities, mismatched curricular needs, and the absence of bilingual programs represent a major portion of the educational issues facing Latino communities. In 1970, the US Commission on Civil Rights published the six-volume *Mexican American Education Project*. This report outlined the major problems confronting Mexican American children and their parents. The thrust of the report (looking at the five southwestern states) documented the extensive problems Mexican Americans encountered in the educational system, which resulted in low educational achievement, high dropout rates, and thwarted aspirations.

Nearly thirty years later, a 1999 report, *Our Nation on the Fault Line*, by the **President's Advisory Commission on Educational Excellence for Hispanic Americans**, reported that the educational achievement gap between Latinos and non-Latinos persists and recurring problems have not changed. The magnitude of the crisis is unparalleled, according to the commission. An examination of conventional educational indicators reveals that Hispanic Americans are making progress at alarmingly slow rates from preschool through elementary, middle, and high school, on to higher education. The cumulative effect of such neglect is obviously detrimental not only to Hispanics, but also to the nation (President's Advisory Commission 1999, 1).

The particulars of Latino educational well-being indicators identified by the commission included the following:

- Less than 15 percent of all Latinos participate in preschool programs.
- More than twice as many Latinos as non-Latinos are enrolled below grade level (are older than the age associated with the grade level).
- Latinos drop out earlier and at unacceptably high rates.

- The total proportion of bachelor's degrees for Latinos rose only 1.4 percent from 1985 to 1993, even though Latino college enrollment increased by 3.2 percent.
- Illiteracy for Latino adults has remained high compared to other groups.
- Latino students are segregated in schools that are resource poor. (President's Advisory Commission 1999, 3–4)

To compound poor Latino educational achievement, inadequate school funding, treatment of bilingualism as a liability, and a lack of representation on educational policy-making boards are additional obstacles that need to be overcome in order to improve Latinos' educational experiences and outcomes. This long-standing pattern was reflected in a 1972 US Commission on Civil Rights report that characterized the Mexican American educational experience as one of neglect, isolation, discrimination, inadequate resources, and linguistic ostracism. So, while documentation of the substance and scope of Latinos and the educational system has produced repetitive and consistent findings, the range of recommendations has also carried prescriptions similar to those recommended by previous federal commissions. This President's Advisory Commission generated an extensive set of recommendations to try to alleviate the educational neglect of Latinos:

- Model effective programs and intervention strategies in preschool education, dropout prevention, bilingual education, and student motivation.
- End segregation of Latinos.
- Oppose the prevention and termination of educational opportunities for immigrant children.
- Train teachers to deal effectively with multicultural children.
- Ensure adequate funding for bilingual education programs, Title VII of the Improving American Schools Act, and Goals 2000.
- Increase four-year-college access for Latino high school graduates and community college transfer students, especially via financial support initiatives. (President's Advisory Commission 1999, 4–6)

In 2010, President Obama signed a new executive order to establish the **White House Initiative on Educational Excellence for Hispanics**. Some of the focal areas for this initiative include:

- promoting early-learning opportunities (i.e., preschool enrollment and experiences, a comprehensive zero-to-five plan, a Challenge Fund for states to establish model systems of early learning and to fund and implement pathways that will improve access to high-quality programs);
- improving teaching (i.e., Race to the Top awards where forty-six states plus the District of Columbia applied to compete for a Race to the Top award, including more than thirty states that made significant changes in laws or policies to promote education reforms);
- preparing Latino students for college and careers (i.e., increasing college enrollments by improving access to rigorous standards that prepare students for college and a career);
- utilizing assessments that accurately measure student learning growth;

- ensuring that all students, including our neediest, are taught by excellent teachers in schools led by effective leaders;
- ensuring better data and information to follow student learning and to inform teachers, and implementing strategies to transform and improve those schools that have been persistently low performing;
- providing federal financial aid that puts students first by shifting the nation's student aid system to the Direct Loans Program and stabilizing funding for America's Pell Grant recipients;
- providing more affordable student loans to ensure that Americans can better manage their student loan payments and have more choices as to how they will repay their loans;
- improving college affordability and access;
- building American skills through community colleges (i.e., innovations and reforms for the nation's community colleges to raise graduation rates, build industry partnerships, expand course offerings, and improve career and educational pathways);
- strengthening Hispanic serving institutions (HSIs) (the Health Care and Education Reconciliation Act of 2010 will invest more than $2.55 billion in these institutions over the next decade, including $1 billion in America's HSIs).

Each presidential administration now has an established policy response to focus on the educational status of Latinos and produce recommendations with a list of solutions. Yet, our focus on public policy needs to extend beyond a listing of the problems and possible solutions. The educational system must extend beyond professional educators. Administrators and policy makers, like parents, communities, and Latino organizations, play a vital role in defining the policy agenda and impacting legislation. The Latino community has been trying to impact the educational system for decades and continues its struggle. One difficulty of this policy area lies in the multilayered nature of education (i.e., local school boards, state departments of education, federal agencies, etc.).

Structure of the Educational Political "System"

Historically and politically, the crux of educational decision making takes place at the local level. Local school boards and superintendents make policy decisions, and educational professionals are major participants in the decision-making process. At the same time, state governments play a major role in financing with their ability to raise tax revenues for local school districts. More recently, state governments have also gotten involved in standardizing testing of student performance and exit exams for graduation, and the federal government, with its significant revenues, provides intergovernmental aid, especially for desegregation programs, compensatory education programs, and bilingual education funding. Thus, the educational decision-making process involves several policy arenas, political jurisdictions, and key actors. The multiple points of access allow Latinos to develop many different strategies and pressure points to effect change.

A persistent theme resulting from social surveys over the past forty years is the importance of education among Latinos. Originally, surveys were conducted with

Mexican Americans in the Southwest and nationally (Arce 1982), later with Mexicans, Cubans, and Puerto Ricans (de la Garza et al. 1993), and finally with Latinos in the 2006 Latino National Survey (Fraga et al. 2006a). In every case, when asked to identify key issues and concerns, Latinos consistently ranked education among the top three. Even in an era where immigration policy has emerged as a dominant domestic policy issue, education when combined with the cost of higher education was identified as the most important issue to voters in the 2016 Latino Decisions Election Eve survey among 20 percent of the sample, keeping education among the top five most salient issues for Latinos.

Ironically, a popular notion about the poor educational track record among Latinos is that the lack of commitment and value placed on education is the fault of Latinos themselves. The Census Bureau (Ryan and Bauman 2016), Pew Hispanic Center (Fry and Lopez 2012), and Latino Decisions (2014, 2015) have augmented Latinos' education data banks that reinforce the saliency of education to Latinos, the high value Latino families place on education, and the continual shortcomings of current educational policies. Again, the cultural dimension of being Latino comes into play; many have used it as a possible explanation for poor educational attainment. The Latino response has centered on examining the structural dimensions and policy biases instead of blaming the deficiencies within the Latino community. The high salience of education to Latinos is largely the result of Latinos' high levels of concentration in the nation's public school system (see figure 10.1).

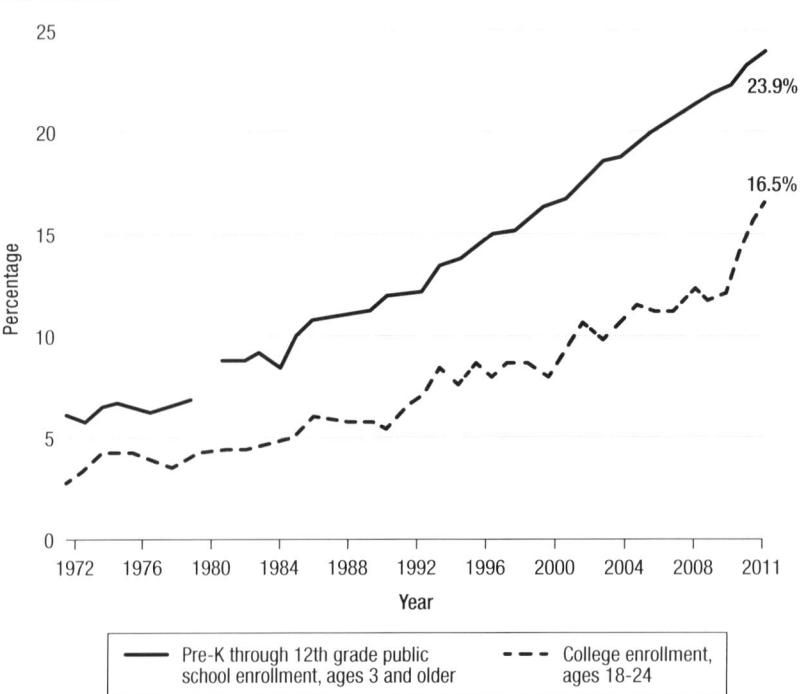

FIGURE 10.1 Proportion of Latino Pre-K through 12th Grade and College Enrollment

Source: Adapted from Pew Hispanic Center analysis of the October Current Population Survey (CPS), Pew Research Center, 2012.

As is consistent with our theme of policy emanating from cultural and situational conditions, the policy area of education entails both. The persistence of Spanish-language use has meant that a significant segment of Latino children begins the school experience with limited or no English-language facility. With learning and understanding based on an English curriculum, the role of language impacts progress through grades K–12 and beyond. For many Latinos, grade repetition, placement in remedial classes, poor standardized test performance, lower participation in college-preparatory classes, and greater incidences of disciplinary actions are common (Duran 1983; Carter and Segura 1979; Meier and Stewart 1991).

Many Mexican Americans still attend **de facto segregated schools** (schools that, due to residential segregation and school-attendance zones, are highly segregated by race, ethnicity, and class). Until the mid-twentieth century, de jure segregation (legally mandated segregation of students based on race and ethnic background) was evident in California and Texas. Two court cases, *Westminster v. Mendez* and *Bastrop I.S.D. v. Gonzalez*, challenged the segregation of Mexican American students. Part of the rationale for the segregation was based on educational or pedagogical needs. School administrators used Latinos' cultural "distinctiveness" as the basis for separating them from the rest of the students in order to educate them properly, while taking nothing away from the educational progress of other students (see figure 10.2).

Another policy question affecting Latinos arose in the 1970s and 1980s regarding desegregation plans for many southern and southwestern communities. It was brought to a head in the cases of *Nichols v. Houston I.S.D.* and *Keyes v. Denver I.S.D.*

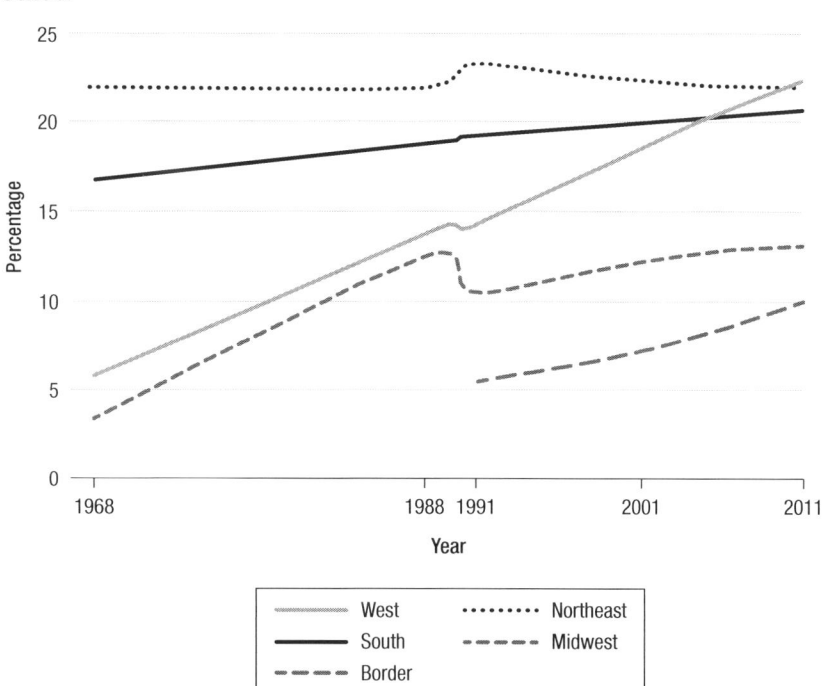

FIGURE 10.2 Percentage of Latino Students Enrolled in 90 Percent+ Minority School

Source: Adapted from the Civil Rights Project, UCLA.

In both situations, the school districts' original desegregation plans involved pairing or reassigning Latino children with African American students. In this manner, the school district would satisfy the racial-mix targets without impacting many Anglo students. The courts ruled that for purposes of desegregation plans, Mexican Americans and other Latinos constituted a separate "ethnic group" and introduced a tri-ethnic formula to determine how desegregation plans would be designed. Establishing Latinos as an official part of the desegregation mix opened the legal door to questions of educational quality and equity. Latinos were concerned about the educational curriculum, bilingual educational programs (or their absence), and overall quality of education, in addition to racial/ethnic isolation.

Even though these cases and others prohibited de jure segregation, the 1990s saw increasing numbers of Latinos being concentrated in ethnically segregated schools and school districts. The youthfulness of Latino populations, mentioned in previous chapters, is reflected in their growing numbers in school districts throughout the country. In many major school districts (e.g., Los Angeles, Houston, Tucson, New York City, Denver), Latinos comprise the majority group, and their percentages will continue to increase in the future. Thus, a condition associated with rising numbers of Latino students is their location in resource-poor districts in terms of tax base, expenditure levels, facilities, teacher salaries, and so on.

In the 1970s and 1980s, these resource disparities were raised in *Serrano v. Priest* and *Rodriguez v. San Antonio I.S.D.* Relying on property taxes to underwrite most school funding disadvantages poorer communities. Much higher tax rates have to be instituted to generate revenues comparable to those collected in more affluent communities. Underlying the legal arguments for the plaintiffs was the matter of educational equity and access to a quality education as a fundamental right. Subsequently, state governments were brought into the policy area of school financing, with court orders to equalize school financing statewide. Over time, greater significance has been given to the importance of educational achievement for all students in order to lead productive and economically rewarding lives. The association of successful completion and achievement in schooling with employability, earnings, overall quality of life, economic mobility, and improved social status emphasizes the centrality of educational success in the modern American society. While the courts did not completely embrace the fundamental-right arguments, states had to address the significant resource disparities across school districts and heavy reliance on property taxes. As a result, most state legislatures dealt with school equalization at the statewide level. State expenditures have increased in providing school financing. Yet, some forty years later, successful implementation of school equalization remains a significant problem.

Alexander Astin (1982, 1985) advanced the idea of an educational pipeline in which identifiable "leaks" illuminate problem areas for students. Normally, the example began with a cohort of one hundred students entering kindergarten and counted the number who progressed to high school graduation. In the case of Latinos, more than half (approximately fifty-five) of the original students did not make it to high school graduation. The list of explanations ranged from lack of preschooling to English-language "deficiency," lack of bilingual or English as a second language programs, grade repetition, poor facilities and resources, segregation in poorer school districts, discriminatory disciplinary actions, tracking into vocational programs or into the general curriculum, inadequate support systems, underrepresentation on school boards and among administrators and teachers, and insensitive and culturally inappropriate standardized testing and assessment (Meier and Stewart 1991; Orfield 1991; Orfield and Ashkinaze 1991). A major point of "leakage" was the loss of many Latinos in the middle school years. For example, 40 percent of sixteen- to twenty-four-year-old Latino dropouts left school with less than a ninth-grade education, compared to 13 percent of non-Latino white dropouts and 11 percent of African American dropouts.

So far, we have catalogued a long list of poor educational outcomes and the need for Latinos to inject themselves into the education policy process. With the primary assumption of successful educational progress being connected to better jobs, earning potential, and quality of life, why are there differential outcomes based on race, ethnicity, gender, and class? Are Latinos, as a group, less able, less motivated, less supportive of educational attainment or culturally limited to succeed in education? Does the educational establishment operate in a way that creates obstacles, and is it designed so that Latinos will consistently do poorly? These questions, while polarizing in nature, can serve to sort through the policy perspectives and alternatives that come from Latinos and other interested parties.

The first perspective points to the primary source of the problem as emanating from Latinos themselves. Poor educational progress and performance can result from a lack of supportive educational values and efforts by families and their community. The cultural dimension for Latinos also comes into play, negatively affecting their educational progress. Persistent Spanish-language use and linguistic isolation reinforce many Latinos' lack of receptivity to an English-language curriculum. In addition, purported cultural values of traditionalism, superstition, machismo, and fatalism are attributed to Latinos (Carter and Segura 1979). Latinos' cultural values and beliefs are viewed as inappropriate to the American educational system. For example, people with a more traditional set of values and outlook assume that Latino students will have less interest in and ability to deal with science and mathematics. The segregation of Mexican Americans in their own schools or in separate classrooms is justified on pedagogical grounds. This policy to isolate Mexican American children aims to teach them separately in light of their cultural "drawbacks," as well as to avoid inhibiting the learning of non-Latino children.

Language has been central in the analysis of the poor educational performance of Latino children. In the 1960s, advocates for bilingual education began to pursue federal legislation to support such a curriculum. It was felt that learning of both content and subject matter, as well as honing of English skills (not just verbal, but syntactic, writing, etc.), would be enhanced with the use of the student's home language. Given this broader view of English-language mastery, the bilingual curriculum would cover a number of grades or periods. In 1968, the Bilingual Education Act was passed with the congressional leadership of Texas senator Ralph Yarborough (Crawford 1992b).

There is substantial evidence that supports bilingual education (Ovando 2003), yet there continues to be resistance and hostility. Ovando has suggested that strong objections to most forms of bilingual education, rooted in "nativistic and melting pot ideologies" (Ovando 2003, 14), tend to politicize the "other." Bilingual education has become more than a pedagogical tool; it has become a societal aggravation that involves a complex set of issues of cultural identity, social class status, and language politics. Is language diversity a problem? Is it a resource? Is it a right?

These issues seem quite remote from the day-to-day realities of bilingual classrooms across the United States, but they are the basis on which bilingual education is either loved or hated (Ovando 1990). Bilingual education, an ideological lightning rod, tends to attract groups with a variety of pedagogical agendas; language-minority educators are armed with solid evidence and become active participants in language policy debates. To hold their ground in the debate, however, Latino advocates need to have a clearly articulated strategy for addressing language issues within a political context to multiple publics (Crawford 2000). Crawford suggests that "educators must learn to participate more effectively in the policy debate, not by distorting research evidence or by denouncing their opponents as racists, but by explaining bilingual pedagogies in a credible way, that is, in a political context that members of the public can understand and endorse" (Crawford 2000, 124). In many respects, policy discussions may require re-embedded bilingual education in the larger frameworks of quality education and access for language-minority communities, promoting bilingualism for all.

At the same time, Latino educational activists and organizations like the National Association of Bilingual Educators lobbied diligently to get federal status and funding. By 1973, the federal government was spending $45 million a year to support bilingual education in twenty-six languages. The early expert witnesses, mostly Latinos, were linguists, psychologists, state legislators, curriculum specialists, school administrators and teachers, and labor and business leaders (Crawford 1992b). Part of the rationale for bilingual education has centered on the psychological effects of a monolingual English curriculum on non-English- or limited-English-speaking children.

A. Bruce Gaarder, head of modern language programs for the US Office of Education, stated in subcommittee testimony, "Language is the most important exteriorization or manifestation of the self, of the human personality. If the school, the all-powerful school, rejects the mother tongue of an entire group of children, it can be expected to affect seriously and adversely those children's concept of their parents, their homes, and . . . themselves" (Crawford 1992a, 78). Thus, the policy debates about bilingual education encompass many issues, concerns, values, and controversies, including:

- the continuance of non-English languages and the extent of assimilation and integration into American life;
- the persistence of "foreign" cultural practices and norms;
- cultural and linguistic balkanization;
- the association of learning and intelligence with language use;
- the appropriateness of bi- or multilingualism in America;
- the state's involvement in promoting other cultures and languages; and
- the meaning of "educational opportunities for all."

In the final analysis, bilingual education is about the growing political empowerment of Latinos in the United States. While bilingual education focuses on curricular methodologies and approaches for children with limited English proficiency, the long-standing problems those Latino children have encountered in school reflect a disempowered position in policy-making bodies. For Mexican Americans, school walkouts in the 1960s and 1970s raised awareness of bilingual education needs and generated teacher and administrator recruitment, cultural studies courses, availability of ethnic foods in the cafeteria, review of disciplinary policies, access to extracurricular activities, and desegregation of schools. The underlying theme was recognition and direct involvement in the educational decision-making process. Similarly, school decentralization efforts in New York City (Gittell and Fantini 1970), especially in the Ocean Hill–Brownsville areas, reflected some major initiatives by Latinos and other minorities to have a greater impact on education.

The push for bilingual education is intermeshed with an overall move by Latinos for greater empowerment in all relevant realms pertaining to Latino educational needs and concerns. One lightning rod for bilingual education and the entire corollary of Latino concerns was Proposition 227 in California, officially titled the English Language Education for Immigrant Children initiative, or the Unz initiative, which Californians voted on in June 1998. The goal of Proposition 227 was to teach English to children in public schools as rapidly as possible. Most instruction would be in English, and limited-English-proficiency students would be placed in English-immersion classes for a year, then "mainstreamed" into regular classes. The legislature would appropriate $50 million annually for ten years to subsidize English classes for adults who agreed to tutor English learners. Early polls indicated strong support for Proposition 227 across all racial and ethnic groups and partisans. The *Los Angeles Times* reported that almost two-thirds of Latino voters indicated support for Proposition 227 (Alvarez 1999).

During the campaign, political mobilization by both established Latino organizations (National Association of Bilingual Educators, Mexican American Political Association [MAPA], League of United Latin American Citizens, etc.) and ad hoc groups pushed for Latinos to oppose Proposition 227. The basis for the opposition ranged from the misrepresentation of what bilingual education entailed to the limited benefits of English immersion for non-English-speaking students. The proposition was viewed as a general attack on the Latino community in California and the overall educational status of Latinos in the United States. While the early pre-election polls indicated strong support across all groups, on Election Day Latinos voted 63 to 37 percent against Proposition 227. Overall, the proposition passed 60.9 percent (for) to 39.1 percent (against). Only two counties voted against the proposition (San Francisco and Alameda), and a majority of whites (67 percent), African Americans (57 percent), and Asian Americans (52 percent) voted for it.

Interestingly, some of the exploratory items in the *Los Angeles Times* exit poll revealed real differences between Latinos and non-Latinos. For instance, 12 percent of Latinos were first-time voters, compared to 4 percent for all voters. Also, 39 percent of Latino voters indicated that they were motivated to vote because of Proposition 227 compared to 27 percent for all voters. Fully 49 percent of pro-Unz voters indicated that all persons should speak English (as a reason to vote for Proposition 227), in contrast to 24 percent of Latino voters (Lopez and Taylor 1994a). On the other hand, 36 percent of Latinos versus 16 percent of non-Latinos indicated that they were motivated to vote on Proposition 227 because they felt that it discriminated against non-English-speaking persons. As the campaign progressed, Latinos became more opposed to and invested in fighting the proposition.

It has been posited (Crawford 2000) that as individuals became more informed about the issues and many of the particulars of the bilingual education curriculum, they were less likely to support it. Part of the underlying issue was a continued activation within the Latino community in California in response to "negatively" targeted initiatives. Opponents of Proposition 227 connected the Unz initiative to several statewide referenda (discontinuing state affirmative action programs, denying immigrants social and educational services, and limiting union contributions to political campaigns) that placed undue burdens on Latinos. The activation of Californian Latinos, due in part to the rise of hostile propositions, stimulated not only greater participation in ballot propositions, but also the election of more Latino legislators and local officials. There is a strong tendency among Latinos to maintain their culture, which includes the Spanish language, and to be bilingual. Thus, while Proposition 227 eliminated bilingual programs, the issue area was not just a pedagogical one. Bilingualism and the perpetuation of a bi- or multilingual American society were also at stake for Latinos. In addition, Official English initiatives at the state and congressional levels have been ongoing since the 1990s.

A survey of Hispanics between 1999 and 2009 asked respondents to indicate the more pressing issues facing the Latino community. The policy area with the greatest concern and attention was education (Pew Hispanic Center 1999–2009; *Washington Post* 1999). Surveys in the 1960s and 1970s reflect the same prioritization in which the education policy area was the most salient. Although education continues to be a high priority among Latinos, some issues persist while others take on new forms. For example, the issue of bilingual education in the 1960s and 1970s addressed its implementation and funding. Once federal legislation was adopted, the focus turned to expanding the number of programs in place and generating broader inclusion of limited-English-speaking students. Only in the 1990s was an organized "backlash" directed toward the bilingual education curriculum. At the same time, matters of overcrowded schools, more racially and ethnically segregated schools and school districts, racially targeted disciplinary actions, social promotion, continued poor standardized test performance, and lack of political and administrative representation on school boards came to fill the Latino educational agenda.

Since the 2000s an additional issue has been identified and examined that can be described as second-generation educational discrimination (Meier et al. 2004). Latinos and other minority students are disproportionately "sorted" into lower academic groups and subjected to harsher and more frequently assessed disciplinary practices. Often white students have better access to gifted classes, are less likely to drop out of school, and are more likely to graduate (Meier et al. 2004). Studies (Fraga, Meier, and England 1986) indicate that greater and harsher use of disciplinary actions does not have a deterrent effect on behavioral problems and has more of a discriminatory effect on Latino students. Leal and Meier (2011) have demonstrated that there is a positive relationship between Latino representation on school boards and effective public policy outputs that benefit Latino students. Some indicators reveal a higher proportion of teachers and administrators who are also Latino, enhanced educational environment, higher graduation rates, and a higher number of students who go on to college.

The commitment to educational attainment and progress and their importance for social and economic mobility form a strong motivation for Latinos to invest in the educational policy arenas. In the span of this modest section on education and Latinos, we have tried to capture the underlying issues and policy directions that Latinos have pursued for decades. At the same time, more recent research has been directed toward the impact of immigrant parents and their children on the educational system. The reauthorization of federal No Child Left Behind legislation has raised many questions regarding attempts to standardize educational progress with state-mandated testing and provisions for improving poorly performing schools and their impact on Latino children. There was an ongoing battle between the Obama administration and the Republican-controlled Congress, with President Obama trying to restructure the No Child Left Behind testing standards with the creation of a Common Core curriculum (National Governors Association 2016). Perspectives of too much testing and instructional planning to the test have been criticized as undermining critical learning skills and skill development for higher education and the workplace. There has been a diversity of perspectives about whether the No Child Left Behind Act has been beneficial (Rocha 2007; Sierra et al. 2006; Rodríguez 2006).

Common Core State Standards established clear, consistent guidelines for what every student should know and be able to do in math and English language arts from kindergarten through twelfth grade. The standards were drafted by experts and teachers from across the country and were designed to ensure that students were prepared for today's entry-level careers, freshman-level college courses, and workforce training programs. The Common Core focuses on developing the critical-thinking, problem-solving, and analytical skills students need to be successful. Opponents sought to have states opt out of the national Common Core Standards and develop their own criteria for educational learning based upon the perceived needs of their own state's children.

Finally, there has been a national movement focused on expanding access to early childhood education programs to a wider segment of the population, with mounting evidence indicating that the earlier children are able to participate in pre-K programs, the better their long-term educational performance will be. For example, economists including James Heckman, a Nobel Laureate, has found that there are high economic returns associated with investment in these programs, and that increasing enrollment of minority students can dramatically reduce educational and income inequalities driven by race over time (Heckman 2017). Unfortunately, Latino students (and African American students as well) are less likely to be enrolled in early childhood education programs across the country, particularly those that have the highest rating levels (Gillispie 2019). This inequality in access to high-quality early childhood programs is critical, as research has suggested that this puts Latino students behind their peers who participate in these programs, before they even begin the formal education process at kindergarten.

Our continuing theme of forming and operating as a community of common cultures and/or interests is quite applicable in this policy area. While there is no absolute consensus on every policy dimension associated with education, Latinos exhibit more of an active, working community in this area. The priority among Latinos to continue to improve educational experiences and outcomes finds them involved in many different policy arenas and playing an increasing role as policy makers.

Health Care, Health Policy, and Latinos

Many barriers in access to health care and the low levels of health insurance have negatively impacted the health status of the Latino community, making health care a high priority for Latino communities. For example, Latinos experience higher mortality rates from diabetes, homicide, chronic liver disease, and HIV infection when compared to the total population and whites (Zambrana and Carter-Pokras 2001).

FIGURE 10.3 Most Important Issues Facing Latino Community That Politicians Should Address in the 2018 Election?

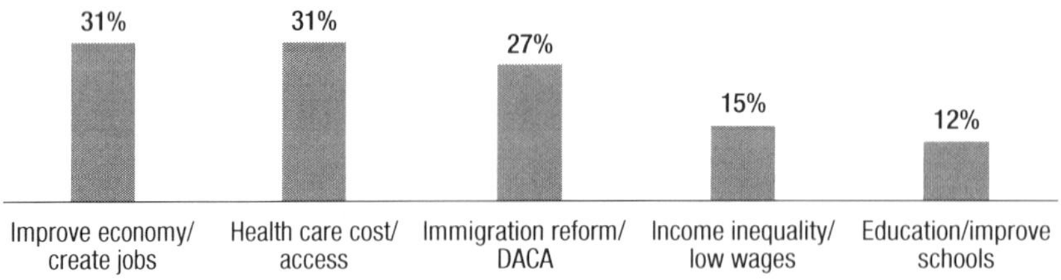

- Improve economy/create jobs: 31%
- Health care cost/access: 31%
- Immigration reform/DACA: 27%
- Income inequality/low wages: 15%
- Education/improve schools: 12%

Source: Latino Decisions 2018 Election Eve Survey.

Also, Latinos have higher rates of stomach cancer, childhood asthma, and obesity when compared to non-Hispanic whites (Zambrana and Carter-Pokras 2001; Escarce, Morales, and Rumbaut 2006). Moreover, Latinas experience alarmingly high rates of cervical cancer, with incidence rates that are double those of white women (Ramirez and Suarez, 2001).

The disparity in health care access the Latino community faces clearly has a negative impact on their health status, and it helps explain why health care has been a political priority for Latinos. In fact, if we look at the Latino Decisions Election Eve Poll from 2018, we see in figure 10.3 that when asked which was the most important issue that Congress and the president should address, health care was the most identified. In fact, across the past three presidential elections, health care was among the top three priorities identified by Latino voters. The salience of health care, as well as the importance of the Affordable Care Act (ACA) over this period, warrants a closer look at Latinos' relationship with the law that has arguably been more impactful on Latinos than any other racial or ethnic group in the United States.

The Important Relationship between the Affordable Care Act and Latinos

For a number of reasons, the Latino population was key in the overall discussion of the success and sustainability of the Affordable Care Act. In particular, the demographic profile of the Latino population in the United States, younger and heavily uninsured, had Latinos occupying a "sweet spot" for those making projections regarding the potential impact of the ACA. For example, Latinos lacked health insurance at the highest rates of any minority group in the nation prior to the passage of the reform law. In 2010, 30.7 percent of the Hispanic population was not covered by health insurance, compared to 11.7 percent of the non-Hispanic white population. In fact, even though their employment rate was similar to that of other racial and ethnic groups, Latinos disproportionately lacked employer-based insurance, and Latinos' access to employer-based insurance declined from the late 1990s to late 2000s (Cooper and Schone 1997). Factors such as citizenship requirements, educational attainment, and socioeconomic status helped to explain why Latinos disproportionately lacked employer-based insurance compared to other racial and ethnic groups (Carrillo et al. 2001). Furthermore, Latinos are more likely to work in industries that do not provide health benefits, such as the agriculture, service, mining, domestic, and construction industries (Carrillo et al. 2001).

FIGURE 10.4 Proportion of Individuals Supporting Expansion of Health Care Coverage

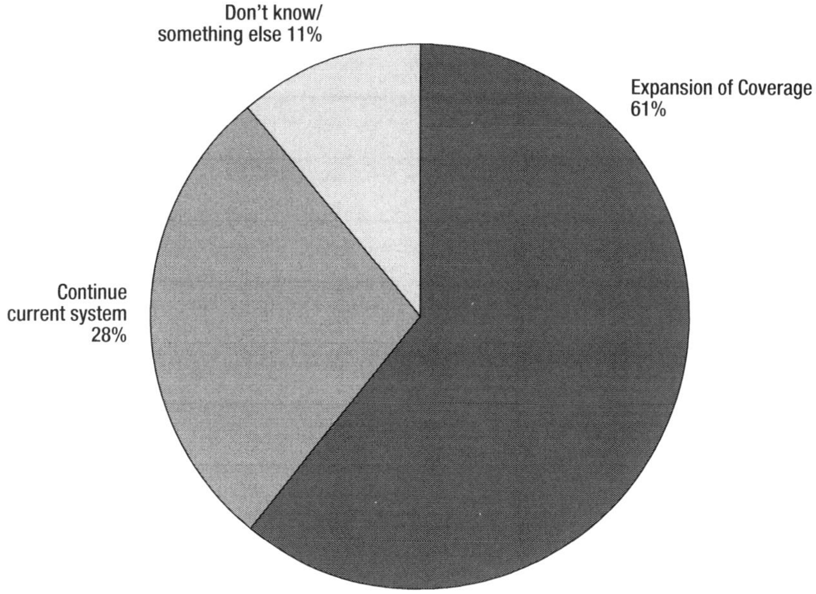

- Don't know/something else 11%
- Expansion of Coverage 61%
- Continue current system 28%

Source: Latino Decisions Poll, November 2009.

Beyond lacking health insurance, there are other barriers to Latinos gaining access to health care. These include language barriers, a lack of interpreter services, and a lack of Latino/a doctors in the United States (Carrillo et al 2001; Pitkin Derose, Escarce, and Lurie 2007; Weinack and Kraus 2000; Fiscella et al. 2002). All of these barriers have led to less health care, less utilization of health services, and policies that are poorly suited for the needs of the Latino community (Carrillo et al. 2001; Pitkin Derose, Escarce, and Lurie 2007).

With the low rates of insurance coverage among Latinos being so pronounced, the ability of President Obama to pass the major reform legislation, as well as the ultimate success of the law, hinged largely on the Latino community. A Latino Decisions/Robert Wood Johnson Foundation Center for Health Policy at the University of New Mexico poll of one thousand Latino registered voters in November 2009 provided the ability to gauge Latino views toward various health policy proposals prior to the passage of the ACA. The survey revealed that Latinos were supportive of expansion of health coverage, as a strong majority (61 percent) of Latinos believed that the federal government should ensure that all people have health insurance, even if it means raising taxes. As reflected in figure 10.4, this was higher than support for universal coverage among the general US population at the time. The survey was valuable to policy makers during this critical period in the history of health care reform, as reports generated by Latino Decisions using this data were viewed by West Wing staff and cited by Sen. Henry Reid.

Despite strong support for expansion of coverage, the November 2009 survey revealed that a large segment (44 percent) of the Latino population felt that public officials did not take into account their health care needs "much" or "at all" during the national health care debate. This survey provided some insights to this question.

For example, the poll also revealed that Latinos appeared to have a broader definition of *universal* health coverage than President Obama and Congress, as a majority (67 percent) of Latinos believed that anyone living in the United States should be eligible to buy or receive health care regardless of citizenship status, contradictory to the law that restricted coverage to American citizens. The tension associated with inclusion of undocumented immigrants in the reform law was on full display when President Obama was interrupted during a presidential address to the nation by a Republican member of Congress who called him a "liar" for suggesting in that address that undocumented immigrants would not be included in the ACA.

Despite this important limitation of the law, many studies have examined the impact of the ACA on Latinos' access to health coverage, with many finding that Latinos have benefited tremendously from the passage of the law (USDHHS 2016; Chen et al. 2016). In fact, multiple studies have shown that Latinos have experienced greater increases in health coverage pre-/post-ACA implementation than any other ethnoracial group compared to white Americans (Sommers et al. 2015; Buchmueller et al. 2016).

The ACA has undoubtedly benefited the Latino community, and recent public opinion data suggests that Latinos are conscious of the importance of the law, despite tremendous opposition to the law among Republicans in Congress and President Trump. As reflected in figure 10.5 below, when asked whether the law should be repealed in the 2018 Latino Decisions Election Eve survey, 67 percent of Latinos responded that the ACA should be expanded and not repealed, compared to only 20 percent who reported it should be repealed. This figure identifies that while Latino support for expanding the ACA is higher than the national average, it is slightly lower than support for the ACA among African Americans and the Asian American and Pacific Islander populations. This may be due to the restriction of ACA tools to documented Americans.

The support for the ACA among Latinos cannot overshadow the implications of the decision of President Obama to not include the undocumented population in the law. Unauthorised immigrants are explicitly excluded from purchasing health insurance

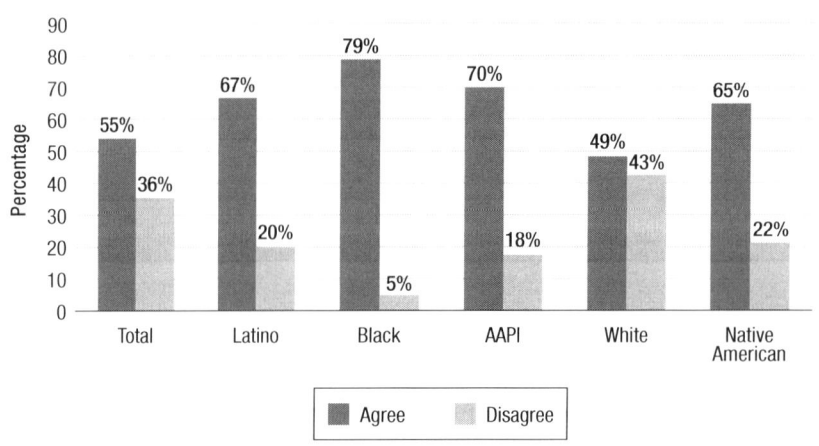

FIGURE 10.5 Access to Affordable Health Care

Source: Latino Decisions 2019a.

coverage through health exchanges and also from Medicaid, Medicare, and the Child Health Insurance Programme (Stephens and Artiga 2013; Joseph and Marrow 2017; Wallace et al. 2013). Consequently, the gap in access to insurance among Latinos based on immigration status and nativity has widened in the ACA years (Sanchez et al. 2017). Among the overall Latino population, the US Department of Health and Human Services (2016) reported that the uninsured rate was 30.5 percent in 2016, down from 41.8 percent before the passage of the ACA. However, once disaggregated by nativity status, the numbers looked quite different. Doty et al. (2016) found that in 2013, foreign-born Latinos had an uninsured rate of 47 percent compared to 24 percent for US-born Latinos. By 2016, the uninsured rate for the foreign born only decreased by 3 percent, whereas the decrease for the US born was 10 percent (Doty et al. 2016). This discussion of Latino access to health insurance underscores the need to look at internal variation among Latinos, as the undocumented population has seen their health care access get worse at a time when the trends look much improved among the documented Latino population.

Our discourse on Latino health must include a summary of the growing research documenting the negative impact the anti-immigrant climate, present in the United States over the past decade, has had on Latino health. As we discussed in more detail in chapter 9, there has been a significant increase in punitive immigration policies at multiple levels of government over the past decade. Also discussed earlier in this chapter, this has included the restriction of access to the tools in the ACA based on citizenship status. However, research has also found that there is an indirect effect of punitive immigration policies and Latino health outcomes (see Vargas, Sanchez, and Juárez 2017; Wallace et al. 2013). This research has indicated that the anti-immigrant political climate that has characterized the nation since 2016 has been so powerful that having undocumented immigrants in your personal network can negatively impact self-rated health among Latinos.

Voting Rights, the Voting Rights Act, and Barriers to Voting for Latinos

In addition to education and health care and the challenges that Latinos continue to face in achieving educational excellence and equity, another policy area of long-standing priority is representation and access to office-holding and political decision making. This section explores the role of voting rights and the laws that have restricted and increased access to the ballot box and political representation for Latinos over time in the United States. This discussion requires reviewing and analyzing the Voting Rights Act (VRA), arguably the law with the greatest impact on Latino political influence.

It has been more than half a century since the enactment of the Voting Rights Act of 1965, which marked a major policy initiative to deal with long-standing practices that had excluded African Americans and other minorities from the electoral process. Such persistent problems had included annual registration systems, literacy tests, hostile election poll locations, economic and physical intimidation of minority-group members, and limited registration locations and hours. These practices had a direct bearing on the relatively low levels of voter registration, absence of minority elected officials, and the resulting lack of policy responsiveness at all levels of government.

While the major impetus behind the VRA was the state of African Americans in the South, subsequent amendments focused on Latinos and other linguistic minorities in other parts of the United States. Basically, the VRA extended federal authority over matters related to all aspects of elections. For the most part, elections were administered by the states. A major factor was the rise of the civil rights movement, which pressured Congress and the White House to deal with civil and voting rights, housing, public accommodations, and employment discrimination.

Even though the Fourteenth and Fifteenth Amendments to the US Constitution were designed specifically to guarantee African Americans the right to vote, implementation was far less than effective. For example, the Fifteenth Amendment forbids both the state and federal government from denying American citizens the right to vote on "account of race, color, creed, or previous condition of servitude." In addition, the **Enforcement Act of 1870** specifically prohibited denial of the right to vote in state and local elections. The **Force Act of 1871** gave federal-court-appointed supervisors the power to oversee registration and election processes upon the request of two citizens. Later in the 1800s, Congress repealed the Enforcement and Force acts, and protective voting rights legislation was virtually nonexistent until the 1950s. At that time a series of legislative enactments (the Civil Rights Acts of 1957, 1960, and 1964) attempted to provide protection, but the remedy was to enable individuals to sue in federal court for voting rights violations. This case-by-case character did not lend itself to any systematic or complete design (Cottrell 1986).

In the summer of 1965, all the inadequacies of previous federal attempts to address basic voting rights and protections were brought to a "policy head." The VRA passed the House by a vote of 328–74 and the Senate by 79–18. The involvement of many civil rights organizations and the civil rights movement played a major role in pressuring Congress to act. The major provisions of this historic piece of legislation included both nationwide applications and special provisions that applied only to certain states and political subdivisions or covered jurisdictions (the VRA applied to political jurisdictions in which registration and turnout were less than 50 percent of the potential electorate). For the most part, states in the South, including Texas and Arizona, were part of the covered jurisdictions. In addition, specific counties in states throughout the country[1] were also included in the VRA's coverage. The previous use of discriminatory tests, devices, and practices in the electoral process was a key determinant in which states, counties, and towns were brought under the VRA.

Essentially, the federal government took an active role in monitoring state and local jurisdictional practices ensuring the availability of open and fair access to all residents. Section 2 of the VRA determined the basis on which voting requirements would be evaluated in terms of their effects on minority populations.[2] Section 5 of the VRA required covered jurisdictions to submit any election-related changes to the Department of Justice for preclearance. Preclearance involved the voting rights section of the Justice Department, which reviewed proposed election changes (different election dates, changed poll locations, election materials, annexations, etc.) in order to assess their impact on minority-group representation and possible voter dilution. The change could not result in minority-voter dilution or negatively impact the equal protection provisions for all citizens.

Additional concerns that were being examined were changes in electoral boundaries resulting from reapportionment: changes in the method of election; changes in the composition of the electorate resulting from annexations, consolidations, or incorporations; provisions establishing voter-registration requirements and candidate qualifications; changes in the form of government; and provisions that set bilingual election procedures and assistance (Cottrell 1986). Amendments to the VRA in 1972 and 1977 expanded coverage to include more jurisdictions in the Southwest and were applicable to Native American and Latino populations.

For the most part, if groups could show that election changes or existing election provisions "harmed" the minority community electorally, then the Justice Department or the courts would deny the proposals or require placement of more neutral election procedures and practices. With the 1982 amendments to the VRA, the results test was included for litigation that challenged the discriminatory effects of election systems and other voting practices. An earlier Supreme Court decision in *Mobile v. Bolden*[3] had placed the burden on the plaintiffs to prove a purpose or intent to discriminate on the part of state or local officials, instead of relying on the effects of the disputed election practices. The 1982 VRA amendment revised the requirements of proof to center on the results of discrimination rather than intent. With that change, the plaintiffs did not face the highly difficult task of proving concrete (or direct) racial design or purpose. The VRA also made use of federal observers to oversee elections and ensure access to the electoral process for minority voters. Local organizations could request that federal examiners observe local elections.

The greater significance of the VRA for Latinos came with the 1975 amendments (section 203), which extended coverage to linguistic minorities and broadened coverage to fourteen states. The minority language groups included Asian Americans, Alaska Natives, various linguistic groups among American Indians, and persons of Spanish heritage. As a result, these affected political jurisdictions had to provide all election materials in the language of the covered language minority group(s). This included registration materials, election notices, and the ballot. Until 1992, the linguistic minority had to comprise the equivalent of 5 percent of the covered jurisdiction's population to require production of bi- or multilingual materials. This was determined through the decennial census and the questions related to language use and abilities. For persons who spoke a language other than English, their responses as to their inability to understand English determined the threshold for VRA coverage. With the 1992 amendments, the minimum language threshold was set at ten thousand for each political jurisdiction.

Congress enacted major amendments to the act in 1970, 1975, 1982, 1992, and 2006. Each amendment coincided with an impending expiration of some or all of the act's special provisions. Originally the act was set to expire by 1970; Congress repeatedly reauthorized the special provisions in recognition of continuing voting discrimination. Congress extended the coverage formula and special provisions tied to it, such as the Section 5 preclearance requirement, for five years in 1970, seven years in 1975, and twenty-five years in both 1982 and 2006. In 1970 and 1975, Congress also expanded the reach of the coverage formula by supplementing it with new 1968 and 1972 trigger dates. Coverage was further enlarged in 1975 when Congress expanded the meaning of "tests or devices" to encompass any jurisdiction that provided English-only election information, such as ballots. These expansions brought numerous jurisdictions outside the South into coverage. Congress liberalized the "bailout procedure" in 1982 by allowing jurisdictions to escape coverage by complying with the act and affirmatively acting to expand minority political participation.

Congress amended and added several provisions to the VRA. For example, Congress expanded the original ban on "tests or devices" to apply nationwide in 1970, and in 1975 Congress made the ban permanent. Originally Section 203 was set to expire after ten years, but Congress reauthorized the section in 1982 for seven years, expanded and reauthorized it in 1992 for fifteen years, and again reauthorized it in 2006 for twenty-five years. The bilingual election requirements have been controversial; Latino advocates contend that bilingual assistance is necessary to enable recently naturalized citizens to vote, while opponents argue that the bilingual election requirement is a costly unfunded mandate and, as an American, one should be able to participate electorally in English.

In 2006, Congress amended the act to overturn two Supreme Court cases: *Reno v. Bossier Parish School Board* (2000), which interpreted the Section 5 preclearance requirement to prohibit only voting changes that were enacted or maintained for a "retrogressive" discriminatory purpose instead of any discriminatory purpose, and *Georgia v. Ashcroft* (2003), which established a broader test for determining whether a redistricting plan had a negative effect under Section 5 than assessing only whether a minority group could elect its preferred candidates. In 2014, the Voting Rights Amendments Act was introduced in Congress to create a new coverage formula and amend various other provisions in response to the Supreme Court case *Shelby County v. Holder* (2013), which struck down the coverage formula as unconstitutional. It was referred to the Constitution and Civil Justice congressional subcommittee on February 11, 2015, but no action has been taken on it.

On June 25, 2013, the Supreme Court held that the coverage formula in Section 4 of the VRA, established in the 1965 act, was unconstitutional (Liptak 2013). Section 4 decided which states have to get clearance from the Justice Department/federal court before making changes to voting protocols such as voter identification laws or redrawing legislative districts. This law applied to nine states (Alabama, Alaska, Arizona, Georgia, Louisiana, Mississippi, South Carolina, Texas, and Virginia) and several counties and municipalities. With a five-to-four vote, the dissenters made note of practices such as "second generation barriers" like **racial gerrymandering**, at-large elections, or voter identification requirements that can have negative effects on minority communities. Interestingly, Texas announced that its voter identification law (previously blocked) would go into effect immediately and its redistricting maps would no longer require federal approval. It would be beneficial if interested readers would further explore the ramifications of this decision and its effects on possible congressional actions and other related parts of the VRA (i.e., neutralization of Section 5, updating criteria for coverage, etc.). These updates lead into how Latinos have engaged with the VRA both historically and with the present changes.

The VRA and Latino Politics

Federal involvement in electoral systems at the state and local levels was designed to remove a legacy of exclusionary practices that impeded the participation of minority citizens. Our knowledge about levels of minority-voter participation has also been enhanced by following the results that have occurred due to the VRA. The law stipulated that the US Census Bureau biannually collect data on voter registration and turnout. In the bureau's 1972 survey, only 46 and 52.7 percent of Mexican Americans and Puerto Ricans, respectively, were registered to vote. Since then, there have been modest gains in the percentage of registered Latinos. Yet, as noted in the discussion of Latino electoral participation in chapter 7, these electoral levels have not changed dramatically.

In addition to opening the electoral process for Latino voters, the VRA provided the opportunity to elect more Latino officials. Increased numbers of Latino voters, the opening of the political process, and continued nonresponsiveness by existing officeholders are connected with greater efforts to elect more Latino officials. As Latinos got more involved electorally, descriptive representation,[4] referring to the population's racial and ethnic makeup and the characteristics of political representatives, became more possible. In descriptive representation, the background characteristics of elected officials mirror the population percentages of racial and ethnic groups. According to records of Latino elected officials kept in the late 1960s and early 1970s (García 1986a), fewer than six hundred Latino elected officials held office at any level of government. Since the passage of the VRA, there has been a marked increase in Latino elected officials. In 2014, the number of Latino elected officials exceeded six thousand (NALEO 2014). At the same time, the distribution of Latino elected officials is heavily concentrated at the local governmental level. More Latinos now serve on school boards, city councils, and county boards of supervisors than at the state or federal levels. At the federal level, the total of three US senators and twenty-eight congresspersons illustrates the slow rate of growth, which is similar at the state legislative level.

Studies by the US Commission on Civil Rights and the Joint Center for Political Studies have documented significant gains among African American elected officials since the passage of the VRA. The rate of change for Latinos since 1970 has been much slower. A number of explanations have been offered for the pace of Latino representation. One factor is the existence of effective Latino organizations to capitalize on the VRA and convert nonregistered Latinos into registered voters. Organizations like the Southwest Voter Registration and Education Project (SVREP), the Mexican American Legal Defense and Education Fund (MALDEF), and the Puerto Rican Legal Defense and Education Fund have focused much of their energy on voter registration drives and educating more Latinos about the electoral process. At times, these organizations encounter reluctance among Latinos to register, and the hesitancy includes distrust of the political system, lack of familiarity with American government and elections, fear of being called for jury duty, and disinterest.

Limited resources (education, income, and life cycle status) also come into play regarding Latinos' electoral participation. These types of factors suggest that Latinos have limited social capital and weaker participatory orientations to be as active electorally. The concept of social capital focuses on the connections that exist among members of civil and political society that serve as a glue connecting citizens to form a community. It is characterized as a set of horizontal associations between people, such as social networks and common norms that affect productivity and collective endeavors for a recognized community. According to Putnam (2000), the accumulation of social capital is the "lubricant" for the working of a democratic society. Therefore, the short-term opportunities afforded through the VRA have had limited returns for registration and turnout levels. At the same time, it has been argued that the absence of any voting rights legislation would have made the situation worse.

A legacy of exclusion and informal practices has discouraged participation. Despite significant gains in the South for African Americans, economic intimidation and physical threats continued after the VRA. Similarly, in areas of the Southwest such as the Rio Grande Valley, powerlessness, economic intimidation, and very limited social capital made it difficult to improve the level of Latinos' representation in the 1970s. Yet, mobilization efforts, active political and social organizations, and leadership resulted in significant gains in the 1980s and beyond. One area of VRA coverage deals with the reapportionment process. Any plans for states under VRA jurisdiction must undergo preclearance. As a result, redistricting, since the 1980s, has helped produce legislative districts (congressional, state, and local) that are more conducive to attracting and electing Latinos to public office.

The structural and historical conditions of many communities with a Latino presence help provide a contextual basis to understand how Latinos have participated or not (Montejano 1987). Latino participation depends not solely on the individual and collective actions of Latinos but also on political and social institutions and legal provisions that can impede, prohibit, or facilitate political involvement. These legacies and continuing practices can mitigate individual initiatives and motivations to get involved politically. Also, hostile environments and biased "rules of the game" can make it quite difficult for Latino organizations to be effective politically. The VRA provisions recognized the role of social and political structures and historical legacies and attempted to remove these particular obstacles. It was hoped that underrepresented group members would be able to enter the electoral arenas more easily.

Political maturation and development have taken place within the Latino community. Since Latinos as a group have had lower levels of electoral involvement, it has been suggested that they have not understood the American political system well enough to be more competitive. With the passage of the VRA and its subsequent extensions and amendments, Latino organizations and their leadership had to design their strategies and actions more effectively regarding voter registration, educational campaigns, and developing a cadre of Latinos to run for elected office. For example, earlier efforts at voter registration were timed many months prior to an election, and newly registered voters did not follow through with using their vote. Door-to-door campaigns, more than just trying to convince Latinos to register and vote, also discussed concerns and issues. The timing of voter registration campaigns was moved closer to election dates. Talking to potential Latino registrants about issues and concerns during the registration campaigns helped identify both important issues and community leaders who could be encouraged to seek elected office.

Recent research on Latino voting and representation has demonstrated the positive effects on Latino constituents. Having more Latino candidates seek elective office is an important first step. Juenke (2014) examines state legislative races in which Latino candidates are uncommon. Once Latinos begin to contest for offices, successive attempts (whether the same candidates or others) substantially increase the probabilities for Latino officeholders. Sanchez and Morin (2011) found meaningful relationships between Latino constituents in four specific outcomes: perception of political alienation, efficacy, political commonality, and linked fate. These constituents are more engaged in the political process and see the political system as potentially more responsive. Similar findings by Pantoja and Segura (2003a) demonstrated a lower degree of political alienation among Latinos with descriptive representation at the state legislature and congressional levels. Finally, García et al. (2008) found that Latina elected officials are more engaged in constituent outreach, especially to the Latinos in their districts, and submit and promote legislation in line with Latino policy priorities.

Two major contributors to the increase in the number of Latino elected representatives have been associated with the VRA (García 1986a): (1) the changeover of **at-large election systems** to **single-member districts**, and (2) reapportionment and redistricting. In the case of the former, litigation initiated by MALDEF and SVREP has challenged the discriminatory effects of the at-large election system. Under this system, candidates did not run and were not elected from any specific part of the community.

The plaintiffs in this litigation showed the exclusionary effects for Latinos under this system by demonstrating the following patterns: a history of exclusion in many facets of local life (schools, housing, representation, public access, etc.), unsuccessful attempts by Latino candidates to win elected office, evidence of voter polarization such that nonminority voters seldom voted for any Latino candidates, evidence of racially biased campaigns, and identifiable preference among Latino voters for Latino candidates. Once the litigants demonstrated these patterns, the defendants (municipalities, counties, school districts, etc.) had to show that they were not the result of discriminatory actions.

These successful litigation attempts resulted in mandating single-member districts, which improved opportunities for Latino candidates. In single-member districts, voters in a specific area of the city or county nominate and elect their representative. Thus, persons in other sections of the community elect representatives who live in their area. When the proposed districts were drawn up, specific attention was given to their racial and ethnic makeup. The preclearance process tied to the VRA approved districts with substantial and/or majority Latino constituencies, thereby opening up access to Latino representation. Subsequently, **alternative voting systems**, such as cumulative voting and **limited voting**, have been utilized to create structurally and procedurally better opportunities for minority candidates. The impact of the 2013 Supreme Court decision has the possibility of affecting litigation options or legislative protection in future redistricting plans. Latino organizational adaptability and creativity will be needed to continue progress in increasing Latino political representation.

During the Reagan administration, the Department of Justice shifted the burden of proof to plaintiffs, who had to not only demonstrate patterns of exclusion but prove discriminatory intent on behalf of the political jurisdiction. When the VRA was extended in 1982, Congress "reinstated" the "results" so that plaintiffs needed to prove that the results of election systems, practices, and so on diluted Latino voter participation and impact, but they no longer had to prove intent. Again, the political jurisdiction would then have to show that the results were not due to discriminatory practices. Over the next fifteen years, the federal courts in particular established the guiding principles used to determine whether the voting rights of Latinos or other covered groups had been violated.

A critical court case that set the standard for creating majority-minority districts was ***Thornburg v. Gingles*** (106 S. Ct. 2752 [1986]). Majority-minority districts are political jurisdictions with primarily minority residents (more than 50 percent of the population). The VRA has specifically protected against election measures and actions that result in minority-voter dilution. In *Gingles*, the courts upheld the constitutionality of creating majority-minority districts when their voting strength had been submerged in multimember districts with white majorities. The courts recognized a state's compelling interest to rectify a pattern of exclusion. The remedy of majority-minority districts is appropriate when racially polarized voting has minimized or canceled out the potential for minority voters to elect candidates of their choice from their own community (Grofman 1995). In addition, if it can be shown that the minority community is sufficiently large, politically cohesive, and geographically concentrated, and that the majority, when voting as a bloc, customarily defeats the minority community's preferred candidate, then a district can be drawn (Pinderhughes 1995). Thus, majority-minority districts became viable alternatives for Latinos and other minority communities to improve the chances that their political representatives would come from their community.

In the early 1990s, a number of lawsuits challenged the creation and existence of majority-minority districts. These suits originated in Texas (*Vera v. Richards*), Louisiana (*Hays v. Louisiana*), North Carolina (*Shaw v. Reno*), Georgia (*Miller v. Johnson*), New York, Illinois, and Florida. Congresspersons Luis Gutierrez (D-IL) and Nydia Velázquez (D-NY) were affected by litigation challenging their district boundaries. In each case, the plaintiffs challenged the predominance of race as the guiding force in the design of legislative or congressional districts, resulting in peculiarly shaped districts. The term "racial gerrymandering" was used to describe majority-minority districts. While the courts have supported the guidelines as compactness, contiguousness, and maintenance of community of interests, the shape of proposed districts triggered concerns among critics of voting rights redistricting (Grofman 1995). The plaintiffs objected to what they saw as racially motivated districting that was taking on the appearance of a system of proportional representation.

Shaw v. Reno brought majority-minority districts into question. The state of North Carolina submitted its redistricting plan to the Department of Justice preclearance division for review. One of its twelve congressional districts was a majority-minority district, but the Justice Department rejected the plan, stating that it had demonstrated neither the purpose nor the effect of preventing a dilution of minority-voting strength (Grofman 1995). At the same time, the Justice Department suggested that a second African American majority district could be drawn in the southeastern part of the state. The state legislature responded with a new plan, although the second majority-minority district was drawn elsewhere in the state, which resulted in an elongated and snakelike twelfth district. This plan was challenged; its shape was deemed bizarre in the extreme.

Eventually, the case went to the Supreme Court. The majority did not rule that the redistricting scheme violated white voter rights by unfairly diluting or canceling out their votes because white voters were not underrepresented with ten of twelve districts having white majorities (Grofman 1995). The majority of the court asserted that equal protection could be betrayed if redistricting legislation "is so extremely irregular on its face that it rationally can be viewed only as an effort to segregate the races for purposes of voting, without regard for traditional districting principles and without sufficiently compelling state justification" (*Shaw v. Reno* 1993). Clearly this ruling brought the issue of the shape of legislative districts into question. Justice Sandra Day O'Connor pointed out that placing into one district African American voters "who are otherwise widely separated by geographic and political boundaries, and who have little in common with one another, but the color of their skin" (*Shaw v. Reno* 1993) raised the level of satisfying a compelling state interest.

Thus, the courts placed some real limitations on race-conscious decision making while, at the same time, not ruling that it was unconstitutional. There is still debate regarding the vagueness of the new equal protection test laid down in *Shaw v. Reno* (for future challenges).[5] At the same time, court decisions in 2000 and 2001 upheld majority-minority districts with "irregular shapes" due to the state's compelling interest to remedy past exclusionary practices. In addition, the courts have not indicated any violation of group rights as a basis for ruling against the North Carolina redistricting and subsequent cases. How can the equal protection clause have been violated when no group's rights have been violated? While this case does not hold race-conscious districting as prima facie unconstitutional, it does indicate that the court has placed some parameters on a "race-conscious remedy." In *Georgia v. Ashcroft* (2003), the court argued that the state of Georgia did not retrogress and violate the VRA when minority voters were spread across several districts rather than being "packed" into a few urban districts. Although the Georgia plan reduced the number of African American voters in a district below a majority, there was support among African American leaders and organizations. This decision solidified the notion of the influential district in which minority voters constitute a sizable proportion (25 to 40 percent) and the courts' changing views about the necessity of majority-minority districts.

A challenge confronting Latinos and other minority communities lies with the possible review of any state's redistricting plan. The process of setting electoral districts, "partisan gerrymandering," is a practice that attempts to establish a political advantage for a particular party or group by manipulating district boundaries to create partisan-advantaged districts. With more state legislatures in Republican control and the disproportionate Latino Democratic Party partisan affiliation and preference, partisan gerrymandering has been a justifiable issue but may be held unconstitutional if it has a sufficiently discriminatory effect. However, what circumstances warrant a finding of unconstitutionality remains to be seen.

While the VRA provides monitoring and opportunities for legal challenges to election systems and procedures, the increased difficulty of race-conscious redistricting plans is particularly important for Latinos and increased representation. While the US Constitution requires Congress to be reapportioned after each decennial census, the Supreme Court cases of *Baker v. Carr* and *Westberry v. Sanders* have similar effects for state legislatures and local governments. As a partial result, the more noticeable gains for Latino representation have come after reapportionment (García 1986a, 1992). Latino gains have been in districts or redrawn districts with more Latinos. As a result, Latino plurality districts are closely associated with an increased number of Latino candidates and elected officials. For example, after the 1970 congressional reapportionment, Latinos in Congress increased from five to nine. During the 1980s and 1990s, the number of Latinos in Congress increased to twenty-one. The reapportionment process is also potentially beneficial to Latinos in the future because of their geographical location in states such as California, Arizona, Texas, Florida, and Colorado, which will receive additional congressional seats due to population growth. Again, the future of Latino representation gains is less certain as partisan gerrymandering becomes more prominent and permissible.

The release of 2010 population counts by states had an important effect on 2011 reapportionment. The new US population figure was 309,183,463 persons, representing a 9.6 percent increase. The regions of the South and West were the fastest-growing areas (14.3 and 13.8 percent, respectively). In addition, states with sizable Latino populations that experienced higher-than-average growth were Nevada (35.1 percent), Arizona (24.6 percent), Texas (20.6 percent), Florida (17.6 percent), and New Mexico (13.2 percent). The following states have added more congressional seats: Texas (+4), Florida (+2), Arizona (+1), Georgia (+1), and Utah (+1). In contrast, Illinois, Iowa, Massachusetts, Michigan, Missouri, New Jersey, and Pennsylvania lost a seat, and both New York and Ohio lost two seats.

While the increasing population growth for Latinos has contributed to the faster-growing states gaining seats in Congress, they still represent a sizable population in those states losing a seat, and it is unclear how Latinos will benefit from future rounds of reapportionment. The noncitizen component, the partisan plan of the party controlling the legislature (particularly in the Republican Party), the courts' disposition to protecting majority-minority districts, and Latino activism in the reapportionment process will determine whether Latinos receive gains in competitive congressional districts similar to their contribution to gains in the states' population growth.

The salience of immigration to American politics in the current era is reflected in some of the more controversial issues in this area regarding the 2020 census. Litigation was introduced to count only eligible voters in creating "equal size" districts. As a result, noncitizens would not figure into that population count. Given the significant noncitizen population among Latinos (similarly applicable to Asian Americans), areas in which Latinos are more concentrated would play a lesser role in shaping legislative districts. This development reinforces the dynamic nature of reapportionment politics and partisan interests that can supersede notions of representation for the entire population rather than only a segment of the general community. Finally, as we have discussed in other areas of this book, the desire of the Trump administration to include citizenship status on the 2020 census led many political experts and pundits to suggest that this was largely motivated by a desire to decrease Latino participation in the census in order to provide the GOP with numerical advantages in the post-census reapportionment process. In fact, a sharp rise in ICE raids in sanctuary cities and states early in 2020 has raised significant concerns among Latino activists and community organizations that this increase in detention and deportation will lead to a Latino undercount (Dickerson and Kanno-Youngs 2020). This is an amazing contrast to the cooperative relationship between ICE and the other federal agencies, who worked together to decrease raids and deportations prior to the 2010 census in an attempt to reduce fear of participating among Latino and immigrant communities.

As suggested in other areas of this book, population growth alone does not guarantee immediate representational gains for Latinos, but it does create many opportunities. Concentration in key states, regions, and urban areas is an asset, in combination with effective leadership and organization and an expanded voting base.

Safe Districts and Voter Participation

While the VRA, with its preclearance and coverage provisions, has contributed to gains in Latino registration and voting, there is concern about unintended consequences for Latino districts. Researchers such as de la Garza and DeSipio (1993, 1996) have raised some concerns about declining voter participation in Latino districts stemming from the creation of majority Latino districts, although this has also contributed to an increase in Latino elected officials. The issue in these districts is that with a Latino representative less in question, voter turnout levels in the district decline, especially for Latino voters. De la Garza and DeSipio have argued that Latino voters should take more interest and participate in elections with Latino elected officials. These **safe districts** establish a Latino in a given elected office almost indefinitely (absent term limits).

The idea of a safe district generally suggests that the incumbent and his or her party are firmly entrenched in the elected office. A safe district can be secure for a particular political party, member of a racial/ethnic group, and/or incumbent. Thus, the debate centers on the responsiveness of Latino elected officials to their constituencies and the voter turnout level. If Latino turnout declines, that means Latino voters are less involved, and officials do not need to pay much attention to their constituencies (Wolfinger 1993; Cain and Kiewiet 1992).

The interplay of representation, participation, responsiveness, and accountability brings together a wide range of considerations and indicators. The criticism of Latino majority districts and declining voter turnout is characteristic of most safe districts, regardless of the racial/ethnic background of the representative and the constituency. Linking voter turnout and policy responsiveness is but one of several ways for constituents to influence their representatives and the policy agenda. Political scientists have examined the meaning of low turnout in terms of apathy, satisfaction, cynicism, disinterest, and representative-constituent issue congruence. To a significant degree, all of these dimensions operate in the constituent-representative relationship. Participation and representation are broader than voter turnout. The networks between the Latino representative and local groups and leadership, issue and policy congruence, constituent evaluation of the representative, and the representative's voting record provide a more comprehensive picture of the relationship between Latinos and Latino elected officials.

It is estimated that in most congressional House elections, less than 10 percent of seats are competitive, and more than 90 percent of incumbents are reelected (Tate 1993; Browning, Marshall, and Tabb 1984). While the number of Latino elected officials has been increasing steadily, work by Barreto (2007) indicates that there are real benefits for Latino constituents in Latino majority-minority districts. His research shows that Latinos have greater interest, higher levels of turnout, and more satisfaction with their representatives in majority-minority districts. Latino support for co-ethnic candidates is a major factor in Latino voter choice. At the same time, there is a decline in turnout among non-Latinos in the district. In effect, Barreto's work substantiates the arguments for majority-minority districts, and the effect is multiplied if the majority-minority districts are congressional, state legislative, or even municipal. That is, living in political jurisdictions where they are the majority enhances Latinos' "political ownership" in American politics.

While the creation of new majority-minority districts may be likely, the creation of **impact or influence districts** and/or multiracial/multiethnic districts is even more likely. Impact or influence districts represent areas in which the Latino community (the principle can be applied to other minority groups or defined interests) constitutes a significant portion of the population and electorate. In this manner, the creation of districts with a sizable proportion of Latinos (30 to 40 percent) establishes a critical mass. Presumably, representatives will be more responsive, and Latinos can exert pressure more effectively. They also develop a closer proximity of Latino neighborhoods to other communities of color (i.e., African Americans and Asian Americans). Further, there is a greater mix of Latino subgroups (Salvadorans, Dominicans, Puerto Ricans, Mexican Americans, etc.) in urban areas such as Los Angeles, Miami, and New York City. This greater racial/ethnic mix of communities of color in political jurisdictions (i.e., congressional and legislative districts) affords an opportunity for inter-minority-group coalitions, such as those in Boston and Los Angeles (Jennings 1992; Sonenshein 1990) to work to create cohesive and coordinated electoral redistricting strategies. The number of racially and ethnically diverse districts will be substantial after the next round of redistricting. The ways in which Latinos pursue coalitional partners in the redistricting process can produce increased Latino representation, in both the short and long term. The more common issue facing multiple minority groups living in the same district is what the elected official's racial background will be. While this is a significant consideration, policy and issue congruence with the majority of the constituents is even more critical.

The VRA has also had a direct effect on the installation of alternative voting systems as a remedy for minority-voter dilution. Alternative voting systems are alternatives to the conventional plurality (i.e., winner-takes-all) or majority system, which is the common mode in American elections. They range from cumulative voting to limited voting, to single-transferable-vote and proportional voting schemes. In several small communities in Texas and North Carolina (García and Branton 2000), the result of voting rights litigation (initiated by SVREP) changed the at-large election system to a **cumulative voting system**, which enabled voters to distribute their votes (the amount being equivalent to the number of positions available). For instance, if five city council seats are available, voters can give one candidate all five of their votes, or split their votes among two candidates, or divide them according to some other combination. Both this election system and limited voting allow cohesive interests (racial/ethnic groups, issue organizations, minority political parties, etc.) to direct their votes to their preferred candidate(s). In limited voting, each voter has fewer votes than the total number of seats or positions up for election. For a five-seat election, the voter has between one and four votes to cast. This method allows voters to target their support to a particular candidate or smaller subset of candidates. Studies by Engstrom (1994) and Engstrom, Taebel, and Cole (1997) in the South and Southwest have demonstrated noticeable gains among minority groups, especially for African Americans.

Engstrom, Taebel, and Cole (1997) and Brischetto and Engstrom (1997) indicated that more minority candidates ran for office with cumulative or limited voting systems than under the prevailing system and enjoyed greater success in winning office. But there are also differences. African Americans have been more active in fielding candidates and winning than Latinos. Somewhat recently, Texas and North Carolina (García and Branton 2000) passed legislation that allowed local governments the option to change to either cumulative (Texas) or limited (North Carolina) voting systems. In May 2000, the Amarillo, Texas, school district held its first cumulative election in which a Latina and an African American were elected to the school board. As voting rights litigation continues to be filed on behalf of Latinos, especially during the next rounds of redistricting, alternative voting systems will be more carefully evaluated and promoted.

While the VRA was enacted in 1965, it has undergone numerous extensions and amendments. The inclusion of linguistic minorities and bilingual-materials provisions served as major opportunities for Latinos to enhance their electoral participation. Over the subsequent extensions and congressional hearings associated with the VRA, efforts have been made to eliminate the bilingual-materials provisions, allow covered jurisdictions to be removed from preclearance review, and provide stricter tests for minority plaintiffs to prove minority-voter dilution and exclusionary practices. The VRA was extended for another twenty-five years in 2006. The role of Latino organizations, Latino leaders, and Latino members of Congress, as well as of other civil rights communities, was pivotal both in extending the VRA and determining whether its provisions considered recent court rulings on redistricting.

Modern Voter Suppression Approaches That Impact Latinos

Voter suppression in America has evolved from physical violence and legalistic barriers into different forms of disenfranchisement that undermine the legitimacy of elections (Stringer 2007). While the VRA has had a marked impact on the presence of these overt suppression efforts, new, more subtle suppression approaches are being implemented across the country. There has been wide suggestion by legal scholars that recent voter identification laws are "Jim Crow 2.0." For many, these laws represent an effort to prevent minority groups from voting just as other forms of voter suppression attempted to do the same in the past (Bentele and O'Brien 2013; Groth 2009; Sobel and Smith 2009).

Recently, for example, extensive analysis by Herron and Smith (2012, 2013) found that efforts to curb early voting in Florida disproportionately affected blacks and Latinos. Research has also suggested that Latinos are more likely to face long wait times on voting day. However, the most highly contested practice among current approaches to revise voting systems are laws that require voters to provide election officials with a current and valid form of ID that includes a photograph. These **Voter ID laws** have been passed by an increasing number of states, with nearly all being contested in the courts by plaintiffs who claim that these laws are in violation of the VRA.

Voter identification requirements range in their restrictiveness by state. The strictest laws require that individuals present an unexpired, state-issued photo identification where the name on the ID must match that on voter rolls (National Conference of State Legislators 2017). Other states, like Wisconsin, allow for the ID to be expired, but voters must also provide proof of residence.

Proponents of Voter ID laws see heightened regulation as necessary for protecting the integrity of elections, while opponents see it as voter suppression targeted at the poor and racial and ethnic minorities (Ellis 2014). Most social scientists who have analyzed the impact of these laws on voters conclude that the addition of voter registration requirements has a negative effect on participation, which is heightened among racial/ethnic minority communities and communities with lower socioeconomic status (SES) (see Barreto, Nuño, and Sanchez 2009; Hajnal, Lajevardi, and Nielson 2017). This is the result of photo-ID laws increasing costs associated with voting, which can outweigh any perceived benefits to voting for many Americans. Contrast of costs and benefits has been the foundation for political behavior research interested in understanding differences in political participation for several decades (see Downs 1957; Verba, Scholzman, and Brady 1995).

Meeting the requirements of these laws often costs time and money, since states levee a fee to issue an ID, and offices that issue IDs are often inaccessible to those who need it most (Gaskins and Iyer 2012). Access to granting agencies can also be challenging. A report by the American Civil Liberties Union (ACLU) pointed to Alabama as a particularly egregious example of how voter IDs can be used to disenfranchise minorities. Soon after Alabama passed voter ID laws, the state closed thirty-one out of sixty-seven Department of Motor Vehicle locations, with most located in counties with large black populations or large concentrations of the poor (Mock 2015). According to a report compiled by the Brennan Center for Justice, 35 percent of the citizen voting-age population in Mississippi lived more than ten miles from a state ID issuing office, and 33 percent did not have access to a vehicle. In Wisconsin, where individuals must present a photo ID with matching name and proof of residence, 30 percent of the citizen voting-age population lived more than ten miles from a state office, and 18 percent did not have access to a car (Gaskins and Iyer 2012).

Leveraging six datasets collected between 2008 and 2014, Barreto and colleagues (2018) measured access to an ID given the laws in each state, and to coincide with the period when the laws were in place but legally contested. As reflected in figure 10.6 below, when the results of those aggregated surveys are broken down by race, nearly 91 percent of white eligible voters possess the required ID for their state, while only 83.7 percent of Latinos are in possession of that ID. Their analysis found that not only do racial and ethnic minorities have lower rates of ID possession at the bivariate level, but those inequalities persist even after controlling for several other factors that could explain differences in possession rates. Their analysis, therefore, makes evident that there is a specific racial disparity in access rates that is not just the product of differences in possession due to socioeconomic factors. Similarly, using a difference-in-difference approach, Dropp (2013) finds voter ID laws disproportionately demobilize the poor, young adults, renters, and African Americans. Social science research has also found disparities in possession rates of the underlying documents required to

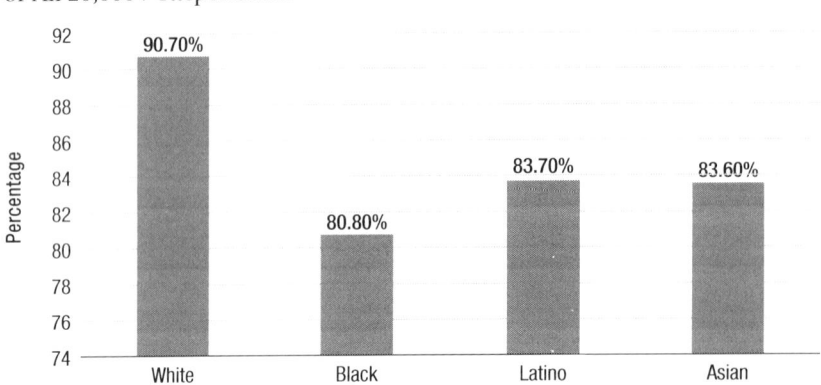

FIGURE 10.6 Possession of State-Issued Photo ID by Race/Ethnicity Aggregation of All 20,000+ Respondents

Source: Barreto and Sanchez 2012.

obtain a photo ID (Ansolabehere 2009; Barreto, Nuño, and Sanchez 2009; Barreto and Sanchez 2014; Nickerson 2015).

Not having the required ID requires otherwise eligible voters to incur additional costs to obtain the underlying documents required to vote. Furthermore, minority voters have been found to be less knowledgeable of the laws in their states (Barreto and Sanchez 2012), which can lead to greater costs for voters who actually have the required identification needed but who have to leave the voting booth when they learn of the law and return with those documents to vote. This increased cost may be too high for many otherwise eligible voters given the relatively low benefits of voting.

Conclusion

Chapter 9 and this chapter have focused on three key policy areas that are salient for Latinos: education, immigration, and voting rights. Policy areas within education include quality of education, bilingual education and curricula to meet the needs of Latino children, equitable funding for education, quality of school facilities, representation in decision-making bodies and among school personnel, disciplinary policies and enforcement, and greater local control and involvement. To a significant extent, the educational issues confronting Latino communities are much the same as those outlined and discussed by the US Commission on Civil Rights more than two generations ago.

The ebb and flow of immigration to the United States and the state of the American economy are closely connected to public policy debates and legislation regarding more restrictive immigration. For the most part, issues surrounding immigration, especially undocumented immigration, have been directed largely toward Latino immigrants and Latino communities. As a result, Latino core concerns include matters of immigration admission policies and processing times, militarization of the US-Mexican border, protection of civil and economic rights, participation in social service programs, more efficient naturalization processing, and seeking political refugee status for Central Americans. The current policy dialogues have centered on fortifying the southern border with an "impenetrable wall" and law enforcement personnel, denial of birthright citizenship, increased apprehension among border-crossers and undocumented residents (including family units), and deportations. These restrictive, punitive policies are in marked contrast with the emphasis that Latino activists and organizations have placed on human and legal rights, normalization of immigration status, and pathways toward citizenship.

A brief history of the Voting Rights Act and its impact on Latino representation and electoral participation shows that it has the political representation and policy responsiveness for Latinos. The provisions of the VRA, especially preclearance and coverage status, have enabled Latino organizations, especially litigation-oriented ones, to challenge voting systems and practices. The introduction of bilingual materials was part of the amendment process that focused on linguistic minorities. Court decisions in the 1990s placed much tighter restrictions on the use of majority-minority districts as remedies for minority-voter dilution. The number of local Latino representatives has increased dramatically, with less dramatic gains at the state and federal levels. The Voting Rights Act, particularly in the past five years, has been challenged as to its continued need and utility in a "post-racial society," and more emphasis has been placed on latitude for states to tailor their election system with constitutional protections for overt forms of discrimination.

What constitutes important policy areas for Latinos extends beyond those discussed here. In many respects, issues and conditions that impact Latinos directly can fall under the Latino policy agenda. For example, if Latinos are concentrated residentially in certain parts of a city and lack basic urban amenities (paved streets, drainage, lighting, etc.), then basic services are a Latino policy issue. In a similar manner, crime, housing, the environment (Pardo 1998), and the like impact Latinos and motivate the community to engage politically. The effectiveness of such involvement can rest on Latinos working by themselves or in concert with other groups that share similar concerns or are impacted significantly. The latter approach, joining in cooperative ventures with other segments of the American political scene, serves as the focus of the next chapter.

Discussion Questions

1. For decades, one of the top issues for Latinos has been education. Why does this salient issue continue to stay at the top of the Latino agenda? Have the subissues changed over time?
2. It seems that each of the past five or so presidential administrations has set up a commission to identify problems for Latinos in the educational system and make possible recommendations. Why make this kind of effort? What difference have such efforts made to Latinos' educational advancement?
3. While bilingual educational programs have been in existence for almost fifty years, how have the politics of bilingual education changed, if at all, over this period?
4. Both the US Constitution (i.e., the mandate for reapportionment) and the Voting Rights Act were integral to the 2011 round of legislative reapportionment. Discuss the political processes and institutions involved, the "interested parties," and the strategies that Latinos have pursued in this reapportionment round.
5. It has been a common practice for political parties to draw districts that enhance a partisan registration advantage. As a result, we have safe districts in which the incumbent is in a secure position. How do safe districts for Latino elected officials affect Latino constituents in terms of representation, responsiveness, and access?

Notes

1. Particular counties and towns are covered by special provisions in Connecticut, California, Colorado, Florida, Hawaii, Idaho, Massachusetts, Michigan, New Hampshire, New York, North Carolina, South Dakota, and Wyoming.

2. The language in section 2 included the following: "(a) no voting qualification or prerequisite for voting or standard, practice or procedure shall be imposed or applied by any State in a manner which results in a denial or abridgement of the right of any citizen . . . to vote on account of race or color, or in contravention of the guarantees set forth in section 1973b(f)(2) of this title, as provided in subsection (b) of this section; and (b) a violation of subsection (a) of this section is established if, based on the totality of circumstances, it is shown that the political

processes are not equally open to participation by members of a class of citizens protected by subsection (a) ... in that its members have less opportunity than other members of the electorate to participate in the political process and to elect representatives of their choice."

3. The plaintiffs challenged that the at-large election system in the city and county of Mobile, Alabama, served as a major obstacle for African American candidates and, subsequently, denied the local African American community opportunities to win elected office. Racial voter polarization, high campaign costs, and racialized campaigning were associated with this election system.

4. For example, the US House of Representatives includes 435 congresspersons. If Latinos comprised about 11 percent of the population, then descriptive representation would constitute approximately 48 representatives.

5. The test's lack of grounding lay in the absence of established criteria. For example, if two districts are drawn on similarly race-based principles, how does the court determine the injurious effect of either plan by virtue of its snakelike design? How does the court conclude any differential racial impact?

CHAPTER 11

Building Political Alliances

Nos damos cuenta que no dejamos de preguntarnos ¿cuál es el verdadero significado de "comunidad" y a quien consideramos nuestro pueblo? Reconocemos la relación que tenemos con nuestro propio pueblo o con otras personas cuya cultura y tradiciones son como las nuestras. O quizás hasta buscamos otras comunidades para explorar y con quien unirnos.

We realize we have not finished answering the question, What is the real meaning of "community" and who do we consider to be our people? We recognize the relationship that we have with our own people and with other people whose culture and traditions are similar to our own. Or perhaps more answers will come when we seek out other communities to understand and with whom to unite.

ONE OF THE PRIMARY THEMES in this book is the concept of community and how it is present, in varying degrees and in different situations, in the Latino community. We have portrayed Latinos as sharing salient issues that impact most segments of the Latino communities. In addition, we have identified and discussed the rise and adjustment of specific Latino organizations and leaders to extend beyond national-origin-group interests only. We have explored the development of group identity and the rise of a pan-ethnic identity and consciousness. While there may be some debate as to the cohesiveness and significant viability of a Latino political community, our position is that real and everyday linkages and interactions do occur among Latinos throughout the United States. Fraga et al. (2010) have contended that "Latino" is an American identity whose origin and meaning are specific to American sociopolitical life.

Moreover, the recognition and cultivation of "Latino-ness" by the mass media, political parties, and national leadership serve to establish even more community links. This chapter further explores the theme of community building and linkages and how they are present among Latinos. The chapter title uses the word "alliances" to discuss both the coming together of individuals of different "Latino" national origin (or intracoalitional behavior) and intergroup associations between Latinos and other groups in American politics (i.e., African Americans, Asian Americans, whites, etc.). It would be a mistake to assume that persons of Mexican origin (or any other

Latino subgroup) always automatically come together with other Latinos. Community is forged by interactions, commonalities, familiarity, trust, and mutual interests (Alvarado and Jaret 2009). This discussion of expanding community will include Latinos' working coalitions or alliances "with and within" other communities in American society.

We began this book by introducing the notion of communities based on culture and interests. The common cultural base extends itself when individuals are closely connected by their participation in a common system of understanding of how culture intersects public life. This understanding of connection can lead to ongoing patterns of customary interactions and behaviors across national "boundaries" (Cornell 1985). Latinos' common cultural traditions include language, religion and religious practices, familial networks, celebrations and holidays, folklore and customs, and the arts. Community of interests exists when Latinos are united by a common set of economic and political concerns and societal impact due in part to their concentration in certain industries or occupational domains, residential segregation (Denton and Massey 1988; Bean and Tienda 1987), or political disenfranchisement (Smith 1990; Acuña 1996). Common conditions and interests can lead to the development of a shared sense of group identity, perceived common conditions, the focus upon the contributing structural factors (discrimination, institutional racism, exclusionary practices, etc.), and the development of common policy agenda (García 2000). In many ways, this chapter extends this line of inquiry to consider whether Latinos see themselves having a broader sense of collective identity with other racial and ethnic communities.

Latino Community Formation: Basis for Partnerships

We will try to expand on the notion of a shared Latino culture and interests by identifying concrete indicators that forge an active Latino community. In previous editions, this book relied on the data derived from the Latino National Survey (LNS) (Fraga et al. 2006a). One benefit of the survey's results had been the range of questions that provided good indicators of commonalities. The LNS included Latinos from all the Latino national-origin groups with a sample of 8,634 respondents. Mexican-origin individuals, Puerto Ricans, and Cubans were well represented, as was the notable increase of Central and South Americans from other social science surveys, allowing for the portrayal of a complete picture of the dynamic Latino community. The indicators used in previous editions included: (1) Latino group identity, (2) interactions among Latinos, (3) perceptions of Latino group discrimination, (4) Latinos' affinity across groups and their home countries, (5) perceived common cultural practices and political or economic interests, and (6) perceptions of linked fate among Latinos, not only with their own national origin and pan-ethnic group, but with other minorities as well.

We are now fortunate to avail ourselves of the data sources of the Latino Decisions organization and the team of researchers who initiated the Collaborative Multiracial Post-Election Survey (CMPS). Founded by Professor Gary Segura and Dr. Matt Barreto (both at UCLA), Latino Decisions has become a leader in Latino political opinion research. Its cadre of highly qualified scholars has leveraged their analytical expertise and cultural competencies to generate polls that examine information about Latino political attitudes, experiences, and engagement. The CMPS group has conducted national surveys subsequent to presidential elections since 2008, with voters and nonvoters alike, on political and social issues. Since 2016, the CMPS has been conducting their surveys via the internet and has collected information from more than 10,000 non-Hispanic whites, Latinos, African Americans, and Asian Americans. Our discussion about political alliances will draw on the more contemporary data from these two sources.

Latino Identity, Affinities, and Connectedness

To explore the connections among Latinos across a broad range of circumstances (national origin, gender, nativity, etc.), we will assess the range of linkages within the Latino community. The extent of group consciousness and linked fate have been important concepts for Latino research, as well as group behavior and identities (Sanchez 2006a, 2006b; Sanchez and Vargas 2016; Sanchez and Masuoka 2010; Sanchez, Masuoka, and Abrams 2019). A sense of connection and affinity in group terms can serve as a conduit for collective behaviors and attitudes. The concept of group consciousness includes a positive group affiliation and an inclination to engage in collective actions (Sanchez 2006a, 2006b; Sanchez and Masuoka 2010). Utilizing the CMPS, we begin our exploration of potential alliances by seeing how important it is for Latino respondents to see themselves connected to other Latinos. Research focused on Latino intergroup connectivity has shown that Latinos who have a heightened sense of pan-ethnic group identity are more likely to see connections with outside groups, including higher levels of perceptions of commonality with African Americans (Sanchez 2006a).

BOX 11.1 The Collaborative Multiracial Post-Election Survey (CMPS)

In a previous edition, we talked about the *Washington Post* collaborative work with the Pew Research Center and Kaiser Family Foundation in 1999 to conduct a national survey of Latinos. Since then numerous organizations, research centers, and collaborative effort by teams of researchers have surveyed Latinos and other minority groups, at the state, local, and national level. A major source for this fourth edition has been the CMPS. **The Collaborative Multiracial Post-Election Survey** is a national survey of voters and nonvoters on political and social issues conducted post-election. The first survey was conducted in 2008, and beginning in 2016, the CMPS is conducted via the internet. It is one of the few surveys that includes sufficient numbers of respondents across racial group analysis to do intergroup analyses. The CMPS is currently housed at UCLA.

The 2008 Collaborative Multiracial Post-Election Survey (CMPS) is a national telephone survey of registered voters, with comparably large samples of African Americans, Asian Americans, Latinos, and whites. The telephone survey was conducted between November 9, 2008, and January 5, 2009. The 2008 CMPS contains 4,563 respondents who registered to vote in the November 2008 presidential election and who self-identified as Asian, Black, Latino, and White. The survey was available in English, Spanish, Mandarin, Cantonese, Korean, and Vietnamese, and respondents were offered the opportunity to interview in their language of choice. Some states were oversampled across the four major racial groups, and supplemental states were added to ensure samples of each group were represented. The November 2008 CMPS provides estimates of the registered voter population by race, age, gender, and education level, which was applied to the sample by racial group, so that the distributions match those of the census on these important demographic categories, There are twenty-one items that capture demographic information, including: age, ancestry, birthplace, education, ethnicity, marital status, number in the household, religiosity, gender, media usage, and residential context.

The CMPS 2012 is comprised of 2,616 registered voters who self-identified as Black, Latino, or White (n = 878). The GfK Group conducted the survey with pretests of the survey conducted November 8–19, 2012, in both English and Spanish. The main survey was conducted November 16–26, 2012. The survey examined individuals' experiences with voting and attitudes about social and economic issues prominent in the 2012 election. Panel members are recruited through national random samples (both by telephone and mail). Households are provided with access to the internet and a netbook computer, if needed. Otherwise, participants are rewarded with incentive points that are redeemable for cash. The median completion time of the survey was twenty minutes, and the completion rate was 56.3 percent. Respondents were considered qualified if they did not refuse to answer more than four of the first seven questions in the survey. Those who refused to answer four or more of the first seven questions were terminated from the survey. The qualification rate was 99.8 percent. The CMPS includes thirty-seven items dealing with sociopolitical attitudes, mobilization political activity, advertising exposure, and neighborhood context as well as three embedded survey experiments with another fifteen items that capture demographic information, including: age, ancestry, birthplace, education, ethnicity, Latin American racial descriptors, skin color, marital status, number in the household, religiosity, gender, sexual orientation, internet usage, and residential context.

The 2016 CMPS included a total of 10,145 completed interviews that were collected online in a respondent self-administered format from December 3, 2016, to February 15, 2017. The survey was available to respondents in English, Spanish, Chinese (simplified), Chinese (traditional), Korean, and Vietnamese. Because of the primary interest in the 2016 election, the project started with a large sample of registered voters; to provide large sample size for analyses, however, nonvoters are also included. The 2016 CMPS invited other researchers to participate in the content of the survey instrument. The survey's main focus is on attitudes about the 2016 election and candidates, debates over immigration, policing, and racial equality, and experiences with racial discrimination across many facets of American life. The full survey contained 394 questions and had a median completion time of 43.2 minutes.

The 2020 CMPS had an expanded overall sample size of approximately 20,000 respondents—4,000 Latino, 4,000 African American, 4,000 Asian American, 2,000 White, 1,000 Muslim American, 1,000 Black Caribbean immigrant, 1,000 Black African immigrant, 1,000 Native American, 1,000

> **BOX 11.1 (continued)**
>
> Native Hawaiian, and 1,000 LGBTQ. It included a panel study group as it did in 2015. The survey focused on a subset of issues important to the study of race, ethnicity, and politics in the United States over time. Appendixes included aggregate-level contextual data, congressional district data, police/criminal justice data, immigration/ICE data, and Facebook, Twitter, and other social media data.
>
> The 2020 CMPS included registered and nonregistered voters, including noncitizens. Respondents used a self-administered format following the 2020 presidential election. The survey (and invitation) was available to respondents in English, Spanish, Chinese (simplified and traditional), Korean, Vietnamese, Arabic, and possibly other languages. An online platform was used in combination with web-based random sampling directly from the voter registration rolls. The CMPS continues to be a good example of active researchers designing the sampling and content and targeting the broad range of racial and ethnic groups in America.

The CMPS asked three separate questions to try to assess the degree of connection within segments of the Latino community. They began by asking, "How much is being of Latino ancestry or origin an important part of how you see yourself?" The CMPS then follows up with a measure of linked fate, a concept we have discussed at length in earlier chapters. The specific question asked in the CMPS is: "Do you think that what happens generally to Latino people in this country will have something to do with what happens in your life?" If the respondent answered affirmatively to the second question, they were asked to choose between "a lot, some, or not very much." The final question is a measure of collective or pan-ethnic-based linked fate: "Do you think that what happens generally to any Latino community in the US will have something to do with what happens to all Latino communities in the US?" Our theme of an identifiable community is reflected by the widespread presence of Latino/Hispanic choices that coexist with the retention of a national origin. The researchers involved with the Latino National Survey did demonstrate that identifying as Latino is grounded in an American identity (Fraga et al. 2010).

Previous work by Jones-Correa and Leal (1996) used the idea of primary or secondary identification, which placed pan-ethnicity within a constellation of multiple identities. Latinos born in the United States, as well as those with families here for several generations, were more likely to select a pan-ethnic identification, particularly the Mexican-origin respondents. Jones-Correa and Leal (1996) suggested that pan-ethnicity has been socially constructed over time, contributing to increases in pan-ethnic identification among Latinos. It seems clear that members of Latino national-origin groups are recognized by the larger society as Latinos (more so than by any specific Latino subgroup), and awareness is growing among Latinos to describe themselves consciously as a pan-ethnic group. In the book *Latino Lives in America: Making It Home* (Fraga et al. 2010), focus group participants freely identified themselves

TABLE 11.1 Extent of Affinity and Identification among Latinos in the CMPS

	Items Tapping Extent of Latinos Seeing Themselves Connected to Other Latinos			
Degree of Importance on Latino Affinities[a]	Being Latino Is Important to How You See Yourself	Generally, What Happens to Latinos Has Something to Do with Your Life	How Much Will It Affect You?[b]	What Happens to ANY Latino Has Something to Do with ALL Latinos[c]
Very important	1,582 (55.3%)	28.2%	540 (31.1%)	779 (25.9)
Somewhat important	904 (29.2%)	50.3%	1,022 (58.9%)	1,545 (51.5%)
Not very important	350 (11.4%)	16.5%		485 (16.2%)
Not at all important	166 (5.2%)	6.3%	173 (10.0%)	193 (6.4%)
Yes		1,735		
No		1,267		

Source: Data for this table generated from analysis of the 2016 Collaborative Multi-Racial Post-Election Survey (CMPS).

Note: The Collaborative Multiracial Post-Election Survey (CMPS) is a national survey of voters and nonvoters on political and social issues conducted post-election. Since 2016, the CMPS is conducted via the internet, and it is one of the few surveys that includes enough respondents to do across racial group analysis. The CMPS is currently housed at UCLA.

[a] The number of respondents is reflected by a split sample protocol.
[b] The response categories for how much this will affect you are: a lot, some, and not at all.
[c] Slight variation from "very important" sequence to that of a lot, some, not much, not at all.

as Latinos or Hispanics, regardless of nativity or extent of time in the United States. With this pattern, how strong or salient is this identity, and what are the underlying bases for this sense of a broader pan-ethnic community?

Table 11.1 shows how CMPS respondents replied to the selected questions outlined in text above. When asked how important being Latino is in how they see themselves, a majority (55.3 percent) indicated it was very important. Add to that those who said it was somewhat important, and this positive connection covered over four-fifths of all Latinos. The second question portrayed a similar picture. That is, 57.8 percent of the CMPS respondents indicated that what happens to Latinos overall has something to do with what happens in the respondent's life. For those who said it would affect their lives, 90 percent said it would affect them "a lot" or "some." This is indicative of a high sense of linked or common fate among Latinos. Finally, for the third question, asking whether there was a perceived link between "any" and "all" communities, one-fourth of the CMPS respondents indicated it would affect them a lot, and another 51.5 percent said it would have some effect. One observation is that Latino identity is clearly reflected in these responses, and both personal and general connections are evident. Secondly, the idea of being Latino has social meaning in the United States and represents recognition of being American while maintaining a sense of culture and ancestry. These results reinforce what we covered earlier in the book about group consciousness and linked fate.

TABLE 11.2 Sense of Feeling Positive or Not about One's Racial/Ethnic Group among CMPS Respondents

Feeling Positive or Not about Link to One's Racial/Ethnic Group	Latinos				
	Country of Origin			Gender	
	Born in US	Born outside US	Born in Puerto Rico	Female	Male
Feel positive	1,037 (48.7%)	363 (50.3%)	68 (45.3%)	977 (48.0%)	489 (50.9%)
Feel negative	179 (8.4%)	58 (8.0%)	11 (7.3%)	143 (7.0%)	105 (10.9%)
Feel neither positive nor negative	915 (42.9%)	300 (41.6%)	71 (47.3%)	916 (45.0%)	367 (38.2%)

Source: Data for this table generated from analysis of the 2016 Collaborative Multi-Racial Post-Election Survey (CMPS).
Note: The Collaborative Multiracial Post-Election Survey (CMPS) is a national survey of voters and nonvoters on political and social issues conducted post-election. Since 2016, the CMPS is conducted via the internet, and it is one of the few surveys that includes enough respondents to do across racial group analysis. The CMPS is currently housed at UCLA.

The CMPS also examined whether the attachment an individual may have to their race and/or ethnicity is perceived to be negative or positive. The question asked was, "Some people feel positively about the link they have with their racial or ethnic group members, while others feel negatively about the idea that their lives may be influenced by how well the larger group is doing. Which comes closer to your feelings?" The available responses to this question were positive, negative, or neither positive nor negative (table 11.2). For our analysis, we compared responses by gender and nativity, which are key distinctions that cut across Latino subgroups. As for gender, there was little difference among Latino/as in feeling positive about their race/ethnicity (48.0 percent and 50.9 percent, respectively). Latinas are slightly more neutral about whether having a linked or connected fate to other Latinos is good or bad for them. A similar pattern occurred when questioned about nativity (including those born in Puerto Rico). A majority of both US-born (48.7 percent) and foreign-born Latinos (50.3 percent) felt positive, while a slightly lower percentage was recorded for Puerto Ricans. The percentage of respondents in the neutral category raises a challenge as to the possible shift for the future. Our earlier discussions about mobilization and messages that encourage collective actions have a direct bearing on the "neutral" respondents, since an important aspect of community building is the degree and composition of interpersonal networks that exist among Latinos.

A central foundation of this book's study of Latino politics and their base for political engagement is the community of culture and interests. Within the CMPS, two items addressed these considerations. They are, "Do you agree or disagree that: even though we speak the same language and share certain cultural aspects, there are many fundamental differences between persons from Latino-origin countries and other Latinos?" and "Do you agree or disagree that even though we come from different countries, Latinos share many fundamental interests that unite us?" In this split sample set of questions, the responses ranged from strongly agree to strongly disagree (see table 11.3). The perception that common interests cut across national-origin countries is strong. That is, almost one-half (48.7 percent) answered that they strongly

TABLE 11.3 Extent of Agreement or Not among CMPS Respondents Regarding Spanish Language and Interests

Extent of Agreement about Latino Commonalities: Language and Interests[a]	Even Speak Same Languages and Similar Cultures, Have Fundamental Differences	Come from Different Countries, Latinos Share Fundamental Interests to Unite
Strongly agree	585 (39.1%)	734 (48.7%)
Somewhat agree	693 (46.4%)	654 (43.4%)
Somewhat disagree	165 (11.0%)	86 (5.7%)
Strongly disagree	52 (3.5%)	33 (2.2%)

Source: Data for this table generated from analysis of the 2016 Collaborative Multi-Racial Post-Election Survey (CMPS).

Note: The Collaborative Multiracial Post-Election Survey (CMPS) is a national survey of voters and nonvoters on political and social issues conducted post-election. Since 2016, the CMPS is conducted via the internet, and it is one of the few surveys that includes enough respondents to do across racial group analysis. The CMPS is currently housed at UCLA.

[a] Numbers of respondents tied to a split sample design.

agree, while 43.4 percent indicated they somewhat agree. In comparison, almost two-fifths (39.1 percent) agreed strongly and another 46.4 percent somewhat agreed. If we combine these two response categories, common interests reach 92.1 percent in comparison to 85.5 percent for the common culture indicator. We feel there is evidence that these two linkages can be bases for political engagement.

Prospects of Alliances or Coalitions among Latinos and Other Groups

Our interest in the potential for building alliances with the various Latino subgroups includes linkages across other social groups in America. Previous works on coalitions across racial and ethnic lines have shown that affinities and perceived common circumstances, along with interactions and respect, can go a long way toward building cooperative behaviors (Barreto and Sanchez 2014; Barreto et al. 2013; Barreto et al. 2010). Table 11.4 highlights Latinos' sense of linked fate (Sanchez and Medeiros 2016; Sanchez and Vargas 2016) specifically with three groups: immigrants, racial and ethnic minorities, and African Americans. Because of Latinos' saliency with immigration policy, higher rates of foreign-born among their community, and close ties with immigrants (via family and/or neighborhood), there is some indication of perceived linked fate with immigrants; a combined 46.2 percent of Latino respondents see commonality with immigrants. On the other hand, one-fifth (21.9 percent) see no linkage at all. The linkage with other racial and ethnic communities is stronger; a combined 52.7 percent see commonality with other minority communities.

The link to African Americans is the lowest among this group, with a combined percentage of 27 percent among Latino respondents; however, there is a growing emphasis on "black-brown" coalitions and the prospects for successful partnerships (Barreto et al. 2010; Sanchez 2008; García 2000), which we will discuss in a later section of this chapter. Nevertheless, all of these groups are potential allies on specific policy issues and in specific arenas. The underlying basis for exploring possible linkages is due to the marginalized status of each of these groups and a common goal of equity, justice, and empowerment.

TABLE 11.4 Extent of Commonality (Affinity) among Latinos toward Immigrants, Minorities, and African Americans among CMPS Respondents

Extent of Commonality or Affinity Latinos Have with Other Groups	What Happens Generally to Immigrants Will Have Something to Do with What Happens in My Life	What Happens to Racial/Ethnic Minorities Will Have Something to Do with What Happens in My Life	How Much Does Latinos Doing Well Depend on African Americans Doing Well?
A lot	461 (17.2%)	551 (18.2%)	297 (9.9%)
Some	926 (30.4%)	1,031 (33.4%)	815 (28.1%)
Not much	699 (22.6%)	663 (23.6%)	926 (30.8%)
Not at all	656 (22.3%)	489 (16.3%)	554 (17.5%)
Don't know	260 (9.1%)	268 (10.6%)	410 (13.7%)

Source: Data for this table generated from analysis of the 2016 Collaborative Multi-Racial Post-Election Survey (CMPS).
Note: The Collaborative Multiracial Post-Election Survey (CMPS) is a national survey of voters and nonvoters on political and social issues conducted post-election. Since 2016, the CMPS is conducted via the internet, and it is one of the few surveys that includes enough respondents to do across racial group analysis. The CMPS is currently housed at UCLA.

BOX 11.2 Racial/Ethnic Coalitions in Los Angeles?

Research on Los Angeles (Waldinger and Bozorgmehr 1996; Yu and Chang 1995; Ong, Bonacich, and Cheng 1994) introduced the factor of the growing Asian American community and some corresponding political developments. The unsuccessful mayoral campaign of Michael Wu to succeed Tom Bradley included the strategy of forging a multiethnic/multiracial coalition. Interminority electoral coalitions elected Tom Bradley in Los Angeles, David Dinkins in New York, Federico Peña and Wellington Webb in Denver, and Harold Washington in Chicago. In essence, being a global city afforded Los Angeles, with its diverse ethnic/racial mix, greater opportunities and accumulated experience to build on working relationships. After Bradley decided not to run for mayor again, there were numerous discussions among African Americans, Latinos, Asian Americans, and white liberals (Sonenshein 1994) to reach an accord on a common candidate to support. Michael Wu, a longtime member of the city council and a close ally of the Bradley coalition, emerged as the coalition's bearer. The level of support and voting strength that Bradley had developed did not transfer to the Wu candidacy. While the strength of the rainbow-like Los Angeles coalition was not the sole factor in his defeat, it did play an important role.

Another dimension of interethnic relations in Los Angeles is the recent gains in political representation among Asian Americans and Latinos. This development has altered political alignments and networks in Los Angeles local politics, in some ways challenging political positions and networks in the African American community, as well as between them and white liberal networks. In addition, gains among Latinos in the California State Assembly, particularly in leadership positions, were achieved by creating working coalitions. The combination of changing demographics, continued growth, and political development (representation, organizational resources and skills, raised political capital, etc.) among minority groups, especially Latinos and Asian Americans, and broader networks across activists and organized groups makes both cooperative and competitive activities take place more frequently.

Since each minority community had developed its own base of power and influence, they had created opportunities and challenges to interact with one another as potentially significant partners or adversaries in the Los Angeles political arena. As a result, members of different groups weigh overlapping interests and calculate the cost-benefit ratios of cooperation versus competition for enhancing their individual group's benefits (Henry and Muñoz 1991). By their very nature, these interracial coalitions tend to be short-lived and sustained by specific, identifiable goals and interpersonal connections and respect.

Exploring Latinos' possible linkages with these three groups by gender and nativity provides some additional analysis (tables 11.5 and 11.6). If there are some differences by such categories, the insight could prove useful for outreach and mobilization messages and efforts. When it comes to gender, Latino/as exhibit similar patterns; slightly less than one-half of them see a lot or some connection with immigrants, while about one-fifth did not think there was any link at all. We included assessments by African Americans and Asian Americans to explore the relevance of "rainbow coalitions" (Barreto et al. 2013). Interestingly, Asian Americans displayed higher levels of common linkage with immigrants at the "some level" response category (37.6 percent female and 42.5 percent male). Gender-specific differences do not appear to be pronounced, and their overall immigrant link is present but not overwhelming. The gender pattern toward other minority groups demonstrates a stronger relationship. That is, most males and females (in the combined categories of "a lot" and "some") indicate a connection with other minority communities. This pattern is more prevalent among African American males and females than the other two groups. The underlying minority group status these parties share lends credence to research the conditions and issues under which rainbow coalitions might operate.

Table 11.6 examines the connections with immigrant groups and minorities by nativity. Somewhat surprisingly, there was not a big difference between native-born and foreign-born Latinos. Although foreign-born Latinos are immigrants themselves and therefore closer to the immigrant experience and status, they only had a 5.9 percent higher response for the "a lot" category. Combining the two categories of a positive link are comparable for the three nativity measures for Latinos. There was a marked difference between native and foreign-born African Americans, as the foreign-born were 12 percent higher in the combined positive categories. The nativity groups among Asians were more similar (49.4 percent and 52.3 percent, respectively). Researchers (Viruell-Fuentes, Miranda, and Abdulrahim 2012; Zepeda-Millán 2017; Yarbrough 2010) have outlined the racialization processes in the United States and how immigrants have fallen under the same dynamics of racial attribution that has applied to African Americans and Latinos. Continuation of such developments could increase the perceived linkages among immigrants and minority groups.

TABLE 11.5 Extent of Connections with Immigrant and Minority Groups by Gender and Racial/Ethnic Group among CMPS Respondents

Connections with	Latinos		African Americans		Asian Americans	
	Female	Male	Female	Male	Female	Male
Immigrants*						
A Lot	320 (15.7%)	141 (14.75%)	327 (15.3%)	135 (14.1%)	235 (13.1%)	124 (10.3%)
Some	610 (30.0%)	314 (32.7%)	620 (28.9%)	303 (31.7%)	674 (37.6%)	512 (42.5%)
Not Much	458 (22.5%)	241 (25.1%)	494 (23.1%)	235 (24.6%)	483 (26.9%)	353 (29.3%)
Not at All	453 (22.2%)	203 (21.1%)	399 (18.6%)	176 (18.4%)	199 (11.1%)	104 (8.6%)
Don't Know	195 (9.6%)	62 (6.5%)	303 (14.1%)	107 (11.2%)	202 (11.3%)	113 (9.4%)
Other Minority Groups*						
A Lot	377 (18.5%)	173 (18.0%)	755 (35.2%)	306 (32.0%)	302 (16.8%)	164 (13.6%)
Some	700 (34.4%)	330 (34.3%)	724 (33.8%)	338 (35.4%)	738 (41.2%)	503 (41.7%)
Not Much	427 (21.0%)	236 (24.6%)	268 (12.5%)	163 (17.1%)	415 (23.1%)	345 (28.6%)
Not at All	333 (16.3%)	156 (16.2%)	160 (7.5%)	67 (7.0%)	134 (7.5%)	78 (6.5%)
Don't Know	199 (9.8%)	66 (6.9%)	236 (11.0%)	82 (8.6%)	204 (11.4%)	116 (9.6%)

Source: Data for this table generated from analysis of the 2016 Collaborative Multi-Racial Post-Election Survey (CMPS).

Note: The Collaborative Multiracial Post-Election Survey (CMPS) is a national survey of voters and nonvoters on political and social issues conducted post-election. Since 2016, the CMPS is conducted via the internet, and it is one of the few surveys that includes enough respondents to do across racial group analysis. The CMPS is currently housed at UCLA.

* Significant at <.05 level.

TABLE 11.6 Connections with Immigrant and Minority Groups among CMPS Latinos, African Americans, and Asian Americans among CMPS Respondents

Connections with	Latinos			African Americans		Asian Americans	
	US Born	Born Outside US	Born in Puerto Rico	US Born	Born Outside US	US Born	Born Outside US
Immigrants*							
A Lot	300 (14.1%)	144 (20.0%)	17 (11.3%)	412 (14.7%)	51 (25.9%)	192 (12.1%)	168 (12.3%)
Some	645 (30.3%)	235 (32.6%)	46 (30.7%)	862 (30.7%)	61 (31.0%)	617 (38.9%)	570 (41.6%)
Not Much	523 (24.5%)	146 (20.2%)	30 (20.0%)	592 (21.1%)	37 (18.7%)	476 (30.0%)	362 (26.4%)
Not at All	469 (22.0%)	146 (20.2%)	41 (27.3%)	548 (19.5%)	28 (14.2%)	178 (11.2%)	126 (9.2%)
Don't Know	194 (9.1%)	50 (6.9%)	16 (10.7%)	390 (13.9%)	20 (10.%2)	122 (7.7%)	145 (10.6%)
Other Minority Groups*							
A Lot	390 (18.3%)	127 (17.6%)	34 (22.7%)	996 (34.3%)	66 (33.5%)	286 (17.5%)	183 (13.0%)
Some	743 (34.9%)	243 (33.7%)	45 (30.0%)	999 (34.4%)	63 (32.0%)	660 (40.4%)	582 (41.2%)
Not Much	465 (21.8%)	169 (23.4%)	29 (19.3%)	399 (13.7%)	32 (16.2%)	410 (25.1%)	392 (27.8%)
Not at All	331 (15.5%)	129 (17.9%)	29 (19.3%)	207 (7.1%)	21 (10.7%)	121 (7.4%)	91 (6.4%)
Don't Know	202 (9.5%)	53 (7.4%)	13 (8.7%)	304 (10.5%)	15 (7.6%)	158 (9.7%)	163 (11.6%)

Source: Data for this table generated from analysis of the 2016 Collaborative Multi-Racial Post-Election Survey (CMPS).

Note: The Collaborative Multiracial Post-Election Survey (CMPS) is a national survey of voters and nonvoters on political and social issues conducted post-election. Since 2016, the CMPS is conducted via the internet, and it is one of the few surveys that includes enough respondents to do across racial group analysis. The CMPS is currently housed at UCLA.

* Significant at the <.05 level.

Discrimination as a Motivating Factor for Alliances across Groups

A key criterion that characterizes minority-group status, in addition to a sense of group identity, is differential treatment. As we covered in more detail earlier in the book, discriminatory practices directed toward Latinos can serve to enhance group solidarity (i.e., in- versus out-group distinction) and a sense of linked fate and group consciousness. While the direct experience of discrimination has an important effect on individuals (de la Garza et al. 1993), individual perceptions of group-based discrimination are equally important. Similar conditions, perceptions, and experiences can serve to establish the sense of community when that population feels threatened or marginalized in society (Sanchez, Masuoka, and Abrams 2019). The recent series of more aggressive immigration enforcement actions by ICE, the Border Patrol, and Homeland Security has raised issues about the criminalization and racialization of immigrants, primarily Latinos (Romero 2006; Vázquez 2015; Maldonado 2014). Our earlier examination of perceived linkages of Latinos with immigrants is also tied to experiences of discrimination. The perception of Latinos as immigrants, especially as unauthorized immigrants, can provide the basis for discriminatory behavior. In fact, a growing body of literature has found a link between punitive immigration policies and Latino collective identity (see Vargas, Sanchez, and Valdez 2017). For example, Douglas Massey and Magaly Sánchez (2010) illustrate through in-depth interviews that immigrants from Latin America formulate a Latino identity almost immediately after arriving to the United States largely due to a hostile environment that includes punitive policies. This is supported by the work of Wiley, Figueroa, and Taylor (2014), who find that Latino immigrants have become aware of their perceived unrecognized place in society by the large number of deportations and punitive laws.

So, we are suggesting that experiences of discrimination by Latinos serve as connecting experiences both with other Latinos as well as with other marginalized groups in the United States. Figure 11.1 details the extent that Latinos have experienced discrimination and other unfair treatments. Overall, 38 percent of all Latinos interviewed had faced differential treatment, with higher levels among second generation and the foreign-born. The discriminatory experiences included being criticized for speaking Spanish in public, being called offensive names, and being told to return to their home country. These results, taken from a larger Pew Hispanic Center (Lopez et al. 2018) report, document Latinos feeling more vulnerable and uncomfortable living in the United States. At the same time, Latinos exposed to such actions received countervailing support from their friends and family. There is some evidence that those of Mexican origin experience a greater amount of discrimination than other Latino subgroup members (Vargas et al. 2018). In fact, being mistaken as Mexican, even if they are of a different Latino ancestry, increases the probability of experiencing discrimination (Vargas et al. 2018).

It is interesting to compare perceptions of discrimination directed toward one's own group and how group members view unfair treatment of others. The CMPS asked about the perception of discrimination for non-Hispanic whites, Latinos, African Americans and Asian Americans (see table 11.7). Whites received the lowest response for facing discrimination while each of the remaining groups were rated as having higher degrees of discriminatory experiences. The three minority groups indicated

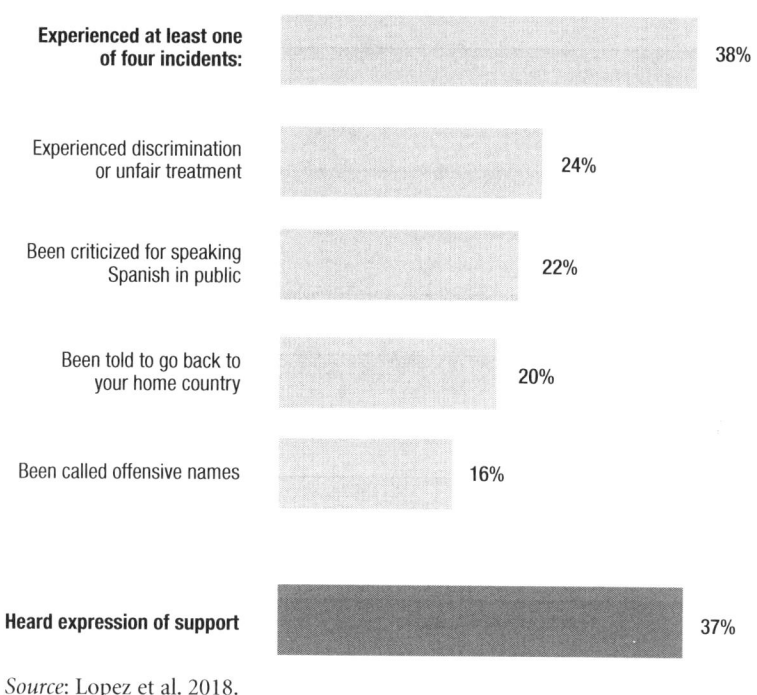

FIGURE 11.1 Incidence of Discrimination and Support Experienced by Latinos by Generation

Source: Lopez et al. 2018.

that 4.4 percent to 6.0 percent of non-Hispanic whites faced a lot of discrimination. On the other hand, all groups rated African Americans as facing a lot of discrimination (African Americans themselves responded at the 70 percent level). Minority groups members expressed higher levels of discrimination than their non-Hispanic counterparts (51.2 percent Latinos, 37.4 percent Asian Americans, and 29.5 percent non-Hispanic whites).

Latinos and African Americans indicated similar response levels of perceived discrimination; the "a lot" response was 35.6 percent and 36.2 percent, respectively. Asian Americans and non-Hispanic whites reported 19.3 percent and 19.9 percent, respectively. For the most part, perception of the extent of Asian American discriminatory experiences was very similar to non-Hispanic whites; they recorded the lowest at 7.1 percent, with African Americans recording the highest at 14.4 percent. When including the immigrant category, we found paired similarities between non-Hispanic whites and Asian Americans (37.7 percent and 34.2 percent, respectively) compared to Latinos (59.2 percent) and African Americans (56.2 percent). With a significant portion of the Asian American community being foreign-born, the perception of the experiences of Asian and Latino immigrants could be viewed quite differently. We were unable to differentiate the extent of Latino subgroup members' experiences with discrimination; however, Vargas et al. (2018) indicated a higher discriminatory cost of being Mexican than other Latino nationalities.

TABLE 11.7 Perceived Extent of Discrimination for Racial and Ethnic Groups by CMPS Respondents

Extent of Discrimination for Racial, Ethnic, and Immigrant Groups	White/Non-Hispanic	Latino	African American	Asian American	Total
Whites*					
A lot	110 (10.6%)	161 (5.4%)	186 (6.0%)	133 (4.4%)	590
Some	259 (25.0%)	340 (11.3%)	342 (11.0%)	368 (12.2%)	1,309
A little	311 (30.1%)	769 (25.6%)	763 (24.6%)	784 (26.1%)	2,627
None at all	277 (26.8%)	1,518 (50.6%)	1,544 (49.8%)	1,386 (46.1%)	4,725
Don't know	77 (7.4%)	214 (7.1%)	267 (8.6%)	335 (11.1%)	893
African Americans*					
A lot	305 (29.5%)	1,536 (51.2%)	2,172 (70.0%)	1,125 (37.4%)	5,138
Some	442 (42.7%)	859 (28.6%)	603 (19.4%)	1,011 (33.6%)	2,915
A little	184 (17.8%)	370 (12.3%)	128 (4.1%)	488 (16.2%)	1,170
None at all	48 (4.6%)	87 (2.9%)	57 (1.8%)	131 (4.4%)	323
Don't know	55 (5.3%)	150 (5.0%)	142 (4.6%)	251 (8.3%)	598
Asian Americans*					
A Lot	73 (7.1%)	306 (10.2%)	448 (14.4%)	359 (11.2%)	1,186
Some	373 (36.1%)	931 (30.9%)	1,154 (37.2%)	1,342 (41.9%)	3,800
A little	368 (35.6%)	998 (33.1%)	812 (26.2%)	873 (27.2%)	3,041
None at all	128 (12.4%)	460 (15.3%)	317 (10.2%)	371 (11.6%)	1,276
Don't know	92 (8.9%)	317 (10.5%)	371 (12.0%)	261 (8.1%)	1,041
Immigrants*					
A lot	390 (37.7%)	1,778 (59.2%)	1,742 (56.2%)	1,027 (34.2%)	4,937
Some	365 (35.3%)	677 (22.6%)	802 (25.9%)	1,183 (39.4%)	3,027
A Little	162 (15.7%)	313 (10.4%)	239 (7.7%)	437 (14.5%)	1,151
None at all	45 (4.4%)	84 (2.8%)	90 (2.9%)	124 (4.1%)	343
Don't know	72 (7.0%)	150 (5.0%)	229 (7.4%)	235 (7.8%)	686
Latinos*					
A lot	200 (19.3%)	1,068 (35.6%)	1,124 (36.2%)	597 (19.9%)	2,989
Some	448 (43.3%)	1,176 (39.2%)	1,197 (38.6%)	1,254 (41.7%)	4,075
A little	260 (25.1%)	501 (16.7%)	421 (13.6%)	640 (21.3%)	1,822
None at all	53 (5.1%)	96 (3.2%)	109 (3.5%)	183 (6.1%)	441
Don't know	73 (7.1%)	161 (5.4%)	251 (8.1%)	332 (11.0%)	817

Source: Data for this table generated from analysis of the 2016 Collaborative Multi-Racial Post-Election Survey (CMPS).
Note: The Collaborative Multiracial Post-Election Survey (CMPS) is a national survey of voters and nonvoters on political and social issues conducted post-election. Since 2016, the CMPS is conducted via the internet, and it is one of the few surveys that includes enough respondents to do across racial group analysis. The CMPS is currently housed at UCLA.
* Significant at the <.05 level.

Our focus on the discriminatory experiences of different groups also contributes to the potentially common encounters for these group members. This type of commonality can serve as a basis to examine why discriminatory experience is felt more by minority groups. Matters of prejudices, racism, power differentials, and institutional practices and biases may direct social change efforts by each of these communities and/

TABLE 11.8 Latinos Respond to Factors Contributing to Discriminatory Treatment

Perceived Factors Affecting Discriminatory Treatment	White Non-Hispanic	Latino	African American	Asian American	Total
Racial background or ethnicity	169 (3.6%)	1,359 (28.7%)	1,887 (39.9)	1,315 (27.8%)	4,730
Skin color	160 (4.2%)	936 (24.3%)	1,870 (48.6%)	884 (23.0%)	3,850
Gender, gender identity, sexuality	218 (10.2%)	587 (27.5%)	818 (38.3%)	510 (23.9%)	2,133
Immigration status	15 (1.9%)	327 (40.5%)	151 (18.7%)	314 (38.9%)	807
Religion	132 (13.1%)	349 (34.7%)	288 (28.6%)	238 (23.6%)	1,007
Accent	75 (4.7%)	625 (39.5%)	329 (20.8%)	555 (35.0%)	1,584

Source: Data for this table generated from analysis of the 2016 Collaborative Multi-Racial Post-Election Survey (CMPS).
Note: Numbers represent those respondents who answered yes to experiencing discriminatory treatment.

or by uniting resources and leadership to combat discrimination. The policy arenas could be residential segregation and redlining, educational segregation, biases in the criminal justice system, and other social welfare policy domains. Pertaining to this book specifically, what are the costs of "being Latino" and how much is race/ethnicity driving such differential treatment?

Within the CMPS questionnaire, respondents were asked if they experienced unfair treatment and what they believed was the cause for such behaviors. The causes of discriminatory behaviors included: racial background or ethnicity; skin color; gender, gender identity, sexuality; immigration status; religion; and accent. Table 11.8 presents the response of the four groups represented in the CMPS. For non-Hispanic whites, the gender array had the highest number of responses, followed by skin color and racial background. For African Americans, the modal response categories were racial background and skin color. For Asian Americans, it was racial background, followed by skin color. However, for Latinos, the responses were distributed more widely across the categories. The order of responses was: (1) racial/ethnic background, (2) skin color, (3) accent, (4) gender array, (5) religion, and (6) immigration status. The fact that no one reason predominated may validate the concept of triple oppression and intersectionality (Hochreiter 2014; Nabors et al. 2001). That is, concepts of race, class, and gender can have multiple effects on those "possessing" these characteristics. Hochreiter (2014) also incorporated queer theory as another contributor to the multiple "conditions" of social marginality. For example, a Latino who is an immigrant, speaks with an accent, is dark-skinned, and is transgender may encounter different bases for discriminatory behavior over the course of any given day. These cross-cutting characteristics can serve to organize and aggregate multiple communities that traverse national origin or nativity. At the same time, expressions of support among fellow co-ethnics who have experienced discrimination are a critical factor nurturing group affinity and solidarity. In figure 11.2, almost two-fifths of Latinos express words of support to fellow discriminated Latinos. There is a drop-off among the third generation and beyond. As Latinos continue to experience discriminatory attitudes and behaviors, the sense of group commonality is an important ingredient for political engagement.

FIGURE 11.2 Incidence of Discrimination and Support Experienced by Latinos in the Past Year

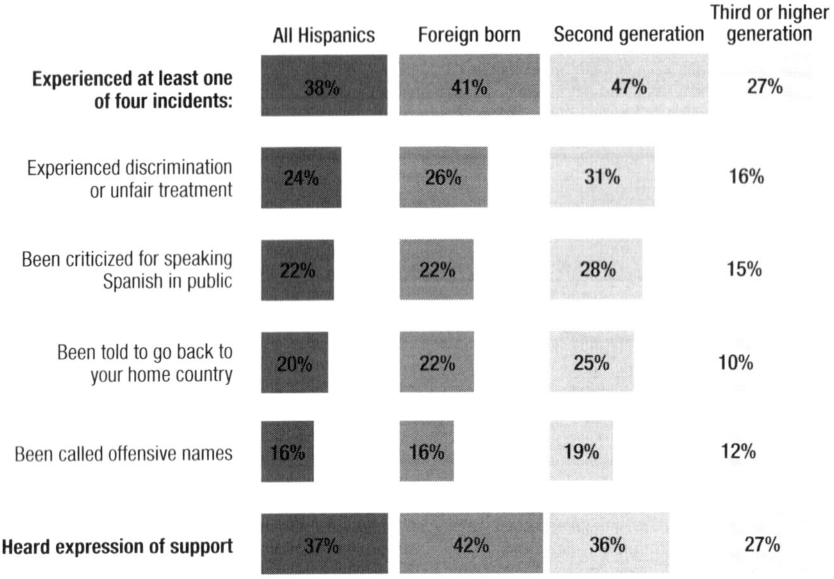

	All Hispanics	Foreign born	Second generation	Third or higher generation
Experienced at least one of four incidents:	38%	41%	47%	27%
Experienced discrimination or unfair treatment	24%	26%	31%	16%
Been criticized for speaking Spanish in public	22%	22%	28%	15%
Been told to go back to your home country	20%	22%	25%	10%
Been called offensive names	16%	16%	19%	12%
Heard expression of support	37%	42%	36%	27%

Source: Lopez et al. 2018.

Although discrimination is clearly a driving factor for both intragroup and intergroup relationships involving Latinos, research has suggested that this is a complex phenomenon. One of the limitations of this area of research is the assumption that when discrimination occurs among Latinos the perpetrator of that negative experience was white. Lavariega Monforti and Sanchez (2010) used data from the Pew Hispanic Research Center to identify that a majority of Latinos felt that Latinos discriminating against other Latinos was a major problem in American society, an indicator that the assumption that whites are the only source of discrimination for Latinos does not hold. More recently, scholars associated with the CMPS have asked respondents who reported that they have faced discrimination what the race of the person who discriminated against them was in their most recent experience. A sizable segment of all racial and ethnic groups in the sample report that they were discriminated against by someone who was not white. Although discrimination from whites was the highest category for all groups, 12 percent of Latinos were discriminated against by another Latino, which is similar to the 11 percent of African Americans who were discriminated against by someone from their own group. This variation has important implications for identity formation among Latinos, as scholars have found that while discrimination from whites and African Americans increases a sense of linked fate among Latinos, as the theory implies, Latinos who reported discrimination from co-ethnics report lower levels of linked fate (Sanchez and Rodriguez Espinosa 2016). This evidence suggests that internal discrimination suppresses a sense of pan-ethnic identity among Latinos. Future research should employ a similar research design to explore whether discrimination from other minority groups influences Latino's attitudes toward those groups, including support for coalition formation.

FIGURE 11.3 Rate of Discrimination Based on Skin Tone

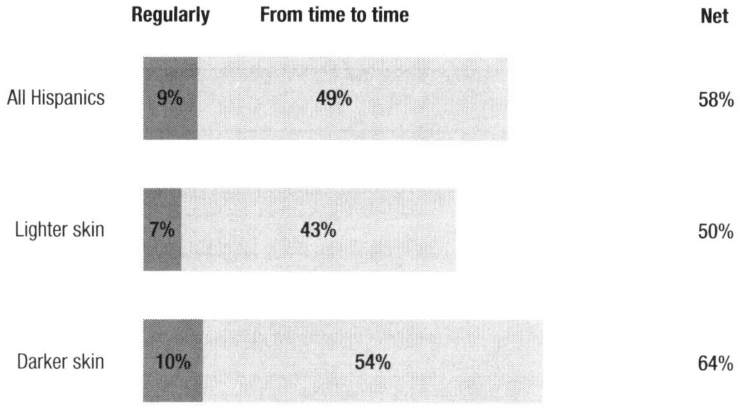

	Regularly	From time to time	Net
All Hispanics	9%	49%	58%
Lighter skin	7%	43%	50%
Darker skin	10%	54%	64%

Source: Lopez et al. 2018.

Let's look at another source of discrimination; discriminatory behavior based upon a person's skin color, the lightness or darkness of one's skin. This bias is usually discussed under the concept of colorism, which includes skin tone and other phenotypical features (Hunter 2007; Norwood 2013; Quiros and Dawson 2013). For Latinos and Asian Americans, discrimination based upon skin color was the second most cited response and was the top response for African Americans based on the CMPS data. Earlier, we introduced some results from the Pew Hispanic Center (Lopez et al. 2018) that illustrated the significance of skin tone discrimination. Figure 11.3 compares the percentage of Latinos who had experienced discrimination with the difference between those with lighter and darker skin. Overall, 58 percent of Latinos had experienced discrimination daily or from time to time. Based on skin tone,[1] 14 percent more dark-skinned Latinos had experienced discrimination, particularly in the "from time to time" category. The same survey presented several other types of discriminatory occurrences and how those incidences varied by one's skin tone. Responses indicated darker-skinned Latinos were viewed as not being smart, were more subject to slurs, feared for their personal safety, were unfairly stopped by police, and were discriminated against in the employment sector (i.e., hiring, pay, and promotion). In all incidences, darker-skinned Latinos had higher rates of discrimination than their lighter counterparts.

There is additional systematic research that confirms the significant role that one's skin tone plays in everyday experiences, affecting opportunities and accomplishments. In the context of potential alliances, recent works by Wilkinson and Earle (2013) and Wilkinson, Garand, and Dunaway (2015) found that self-reported skin tone substantially explained Latinos' attitudes toward whites and blacks; light-skinned Latinos sensed greater commonality with whites and less with blacks than dark-skinned Latinos. In addition, they also found that skin tone moderated the relationship between linked fate with Latinos and closeness with whites, as well as the relationship between social contact and closeness with blacks and whites. In the research of Wilkinson, Garand, and Dunaway (2015), skin tone had an effect only on blacks' perceptions of Hispanics. Light-skinned blacks were less likely to perceive commonality and more likely to perceive employment competition with Latinos, relative to blacks with darker skin tones. Some evidence suggests that the effect of skin tone on blacks' perceptions of commonality with Latinos is moderated by educational levels.

Clearly, the recent research on both experiences with, and perception of, discrimination directed toward Latinos (Lavariega Monforti and Sanchez 2010; Sanchez 2006b) demonstrates its effects on sociomobility, identity, and political consciousness. There is evidence that discrimination aimed at Latinos cuts across the various Latino subgroups. This connection with discrimination, as an assessment of Latinos' status in the United States, binds people together through a sense of common circumstances. A sense of some degree of "out-group" status is not uncommon for many Latinos. What is less clear is how these experiences are interpreted and internalized within and across the different Latino subcommunities. Other dimensions that can influence intergroup coalitions and cooperation are the perceptions of common economic, social, and political positions in American society.

Social Contact and Group Competition/Threat Theories

Aside from experiences with discrimination, the perceptions of commonalities along the lines of similar social and economic status have been viewed as strong linkages to engaging in cooperative actions (Sanchez and Espinosa 2016; Wilkinson 2015; Glasford and Calcagno 2012). The common circumstances of marginalization and having less than enough political resources serve as the basis for racial minorities potentially working together in specific policy areas (Mohamed 2017). At the same time, there is research (Vaca 2004; Kaufman 2003) that indicates that competition between minority groups over resources, recognition, and limited political returns produces more competition than cooperation.

This includes the group competition theory, which posits that marginalized groups often become competitive for scarce economic resources. Research referencing this theory finds that groups are likely to perceive each other as economic and political competitors (Gay 2006; Vaca 2004). This research includes work that is focused on economic threat specifically, noting that individual level views about out-groups can be cued or heightened by underlying competition for jobs (Barrett and Roediger 1997; Bobo and Hutchings 1996).

Research looking at intergroup attitudes also relies on social context or social contact theory developed by Blalock (1967). This theory suggests that the size of an out-group that lives in proximity to an individual is an important predictor of perceptions of threat and competition with members of outside groups. Scholars, for example, have found that negative attitudes toward Latinos increase with higher concentrations of Latinos in the neighborhoods in which black respondents live, particularly when blacks are disadvantaged economically relative to Latinos (Cain, Citrin, and Wong 2000; Morris 2000; Gay 2004; Barreto, Sanchez, and Morín 2010; Barreto, Gonzalez, and Sanchez 2013; Mindiola, Niemann, and Rodriguez 2002). This includes work that has shown perceptions of competition among Latinos with African Americans increases until the population size of each group in a geographical area becomes equal, at which point competitive attitudes level off or may actually decrease (Barreto, Sanchez, and Morín 2010; Barreto, Gonzalez, and Sanchez 2013).

Although not enough of this work investigates the power of structural racism across society to influence the intergroup relationships we discuss in this chapter, some studies do argue that intergroup competition between blacks and Latinos occurs due to their similar economic and political conditions being at the bottom of the social structure (Bobo and Hutchings 1996; Borjas 2001; Gimpel and Morris 2007). This class inequality common between Latinos and Africans could be the basis for both electoral and policy coalitions, but the constant struggle to "fight over crumbs" created by structures biased toward racial and ethnic minorities creates a severe obstacle. For example, studies have found that blacks and Latinos perceive each other as competitors for multiple resources, including low-income housing and jobs, as well as health care and education; these perceptions of competition culminate in interracial tensions between African Americans and Latinos (Cravey 1997; Hackenberg and Kukulka 1995; Hamermesh and Bean 1998; Millard and Chapa 2004; Kandel and Parrado 2005).

Although much of the work that draws on social context suggests that interactions with out-groups can motivate tension of competition, there is also more positive framed research that utilizes the principles associated with Blalock's (1967) social context framework. For example, **social contact theory** suggests that positive contact or interactions with out-groups fosters positive views of those groups and can motivate more collaborative behavior than the group competition theory suggests (Pettigrew 1998; Allport 1954; McClain et al. 2006; Wallsten and Nteta 2011; Wallsten and Nteta 2017).

Oliver and Wong (2003), for example, find that negative stereotypes and perceptions of competition among both blacks and Latinos decrease as their neighborhoods become more racially and ethnically diverse, resulting in greater tolerance among ethno-racial groups. Similarly, Wilkinson and colleagues have found that several factors such as skin tone, linked fate, sense of power, and quality of resources in communities can motivate greater Latino perceptions of commonality with both whites and blacks (Wilkinson 2015; Wilkinson 2014; Wilkinson, Garand, and Dunaway 2015; Wilkinson and Earle 2013).

This is typically measured with geographic measures from the US census but can also be captured more directly through friendships and other positive individual-level interactions measured through surveys. Social networks theory is closely tied to social contact, as work in this vein suggests that more extended contact with out-groups in one's social network can yield positive attitudes (Wright et al. 1997). Providing support for a deeper dive into social networks, the literature has found that friendships with people of different racial and ethnic backgrounds can temper more general perceptions of competition with those groups, as well as increase perceptions of commonality (Wilner et al. 1955; Cook 1963; Jackman and Crane 1986; Ellison and Powers 1994; Sigelman and Welch 1993; Alvarez and Widener 2008; Wilkinson and Earle 2013; Wilkinson 2014). This work complements the rich literature about a person's social networks and how these interactions affect political attitudes and behaviors (Zuckerman 2005; Passy and Monsch 2014; Sokhey and Djupe 2011).

The importance of social networks and friendships identified in the literature motivates analysis of what Latino social networks and friendships looks like. Briefly, drawing on the LNS, which included a series of questions about the composition of respondents' friendship networks and workplace settings, the results indicated that Latinos have a lot of contact with fellow Latinos as well as with a mixture of non-Latinos (tables 11.7 and 11.8). Specifically, table 11.9 lists the race/ethnicity of friendship networks for first-generation Latinos (i.e., naturalized citizens and foreign

TABLE 11.9 Race/Ethnicity of Friendship Network by Generation and Citizenship

		First Generation			2nd + Generation citizens	Grand Total
Response	Frequency	Non-Citizen	Citizens	Total for 1st Generation		
Mix of all of the above	Frequency	841	674	1,515	907	2,422
	Row %	55.5%	44.5%	62.6%	37.5%	100%
	Column %	21.8%	34.4%	26.1%	33.7%	28.5%
Mostly Latino/ Hispanic	Frequency	1,918	600	2,518	628	3,146
	Row %	76.2%	23.8%	80.0%	20.0%	100%
	Column %	49.8%	30.6%	43.3%	23.4%	37.0%
Mostly White	Frequency	124	106	250	225	455
	Row %	53.9%	46.1%	50.6%	49.5%	100%
	Column %	3.2%	5.4%	4.0%	8.4%	5.4%
Mixed (Latino/ Hispanic and White)	Frequency	817	442	1,259	661	1,920
	Row %	64.9%	35.1%	65.6%	34.4%	100%
	Column %	21.2%	22.5%	21.7%	24.6%	22.6%
Mostly Black	Frequency	11	8	19	42	61
	Row %	57.9%	41.1%	31.2%	68.9%	100%
	Column %	.3%	.4%	.3%	1.6%	.7%
Mixed (Latino/ Hispanic and Black)	Frequency	119	113	232	186	418
	Row %	28.5%	27.0%	55.5%	44.5%	100%
	Column %	3.1%	5.8%	4.0%	6.9%	4.9%
Other	Frequency	23	18	41	40	81
	Row %	56.1%	43.9%	50.6%	49.4%	100%
	Column %	.6%	.9%	.7%	1.5%	.95%
Total	Frequency	3,853	1,961	5,814	2,689	8,503
	Row %	66.3%	33.7%	68.4%	31.6%	100%
	Column %	100%	100%	100%	100%	100%

Question wording: "How would you describe your friends?"
Table tests of independence: 1st and 2nd generation: One way (6 d.f.) 80.37 (P = 0.00), Citizen/non-citizen (1st generation only): One way (6 d.f.) 37.31 (P = 0.00).
Source: Fraga et al. 2006a.
Notes: The categories for "Mostly Asian" and "Mixed Asian/Latino" have been eliminated from this table as they are only residents of California, Texas, New York, and Illinois. Island-born Puerto Ricans are coded as 1st generation.

nationals) and members of the second generation and beyond. Almost half (49.78 percent) of Latino immigrants reported that the majority of those in their friendship network were other Latinos. In contrast, 30.6 percent of naturalized Latinos had mostly Latinos as friends, while the drop was greater among members of the second generation and beyond (23.4 percent). The second-largest friendship network consisted of a mix of friends from a wide variety of backgrounds (for foreign-born, 26.1

percent; for native-born, 33.73 percent). The third-largest category comprised a mix of Latinos and white people. It was not possible to identify the specific Latino subgroups the respondents interacted with or the percentage of each of the specific group types. Latinos serve as the anchor or core of Latino networks (primarily other family members and neighbors), but non-Latino friends were introduced into the network through intermarriage, residential location, and social activities.

While having friendships across racial groups appears to be correlated with positive attitudes toward out-groups, scholars have found that high levels of social interaction across racial groups in other contexts, including within the workplace, heightens perceptions of competition due to this type of social interaction being more naturally competitive (Fletcher, Major, and Davis 2008; Chen, Zhu, and Zhou 2015). For example, through a qualitative analysis, Stuesse's (2009) work supports these findings in the South, where most Hispanics do not see much in common with their African American coworkers, often perceiving blacks to be privileged within the employment hierarchy and themselves and other Latinos to be exploited in the workforce. These studies highlight important differences between Latino and African American relationships when it comes to friendships and professional interactions.

In the work setting, there is greater incidence of contact with non-Latino coworkers; this could represent the labor market sectors in which Latinos are located. That is, perhaps the service and agricultural sectors are more immigrant dominated, whereas the construction and manufacturing sectors may be more mixed. In table 11.10, among the first generation, or noncitizens, the modal category is mostly Latino coworkers (43.6 percent), followed by two categories of a general mix of all backgrounds (20.5 percent), and a mix of Latinos and whites (22.1 percent). In contrast, the second generation had 21.9 percent mostly Latino coworkers, which was comparable to the other categories of friendship "types"—mix of all groups (26.1 percent), mostly white (22 percent), and mix of Latinos and whites (19.9 percent).

While the Latinos in the LNS are not totally "ethnically" immersed in dense Latino social networks, there is clear indication that fellow Latinos are a substantial part of their networks. At the same time, their friends and coworkers represent a more racially/ethnically diverse world, indicating that they are not living in isolation. This has ramifications regarding knowledge and understanding of American society (especially for the first generation); diverse contacts can affect comparisons of Latinos' status and circumstances in the United States relative to those of non-Latinos. Obviously, the whole area of the composition of Latinos' social networks is complemented by the content and subjects related to these interactions and their political consequences.

We have argued throughout the book that context matters, and the same holds true for intergroup relationships. Regional variation is a good example of this larger point, with several scholars noting the unique social environment within the American South that has resulted in enhanced competition between Latinos and African Americans. The structural conditions of the South, including a significant increase in Latino immigrants in a short period of time, have marked impacts on relationships. This includes the preexisting severe economic gap between blacks and whites, particularly in the rural South, that has led to greater levels of both perceived and real competition between blacks and Latinos in this region (Dunn, Aragonés, and Shivers 2005; Rich and Miranda 2005; Marrow 2009; McClain et al. 2009; Winders and Smith 2012). Research on the American South has found that because blacks have suffered from

TABLE 11.10 Race/Ethnicity of Coworkers by Generation and Citizenship

Response	Frequency	First Generation			2nd + Generation citizens	Grand Total
		Non-Citizen	Citizens	Total for 1st Generation		
Mix of all of the above	Frequency	699	520	1,219	613	1,832
	Row %	57.3%	42.7%	66.5%	33.5%	100%
	Column %	20.5%	30.4%	23.8%	26.1%	24.5%
Mostly Latino/ Hispanic	Frequency	1,487	434	1,921	513	2,434
	Row %	77.4%	22.6%	78.9%	21.1%	100%
	Column %	43.6%	25.4%	37.5%	21.9%	32.6%
Mostly White	Frequency	288	262	550	516	1,066
	Row %	52.4%	47.6%	51.6%	48.4%	100%
	Column %	8.4%	15.3%	10.7%	22.0%	14.3%
Mixed (Latino/ Hispanic and White)	Frequency	755	345	1,100	467	1,567
	Row %	68.6%	31.4%	70.2%	29.8%	100%
	Column %	22.1%	20.2%	21.5%	19.9%	21.0%
Mostly Black	Frequency	32	23	55	54	109
	Row %	58.2%	41.8%	50.5%	49.5%	100%
	Column %	.94%	1.3%	1.1%	2.3%	1.5%
Mixed (Latino/ Hispanic and Black)	Frequency	88	76	164	102	266
	Row %	53.7%	46.3%	61.7%	38.3%	100%
	Column %	2.6%	4.4%	3.2%	4.3%	3.6%
Other	Frequency	64	50	114	80	194
	Row %	56.1%	43.9%	58.8%	41.2%	100%
	Column %	1.9%	2.9%	2.2%	3.4%	2.6%
Total	Frequency	3,413	1,710	5,123	2,345	7,468
	Row %	66.6%	33.4%	68.6%	31.4%	100%
	Column %	100%	100%	100%	100%	100%

Question wording: "How would you describe your coworkers?"
Table tests of independence: 1st and 2nd generation: One way (6 d.f.) 62.59 (P = 0.00); Citizen/non-citizen (1st generation only): One way (6 d.f.) 32.27 (P = 0.00).
Source: Fraga et al. 2006a.
Notes: The categories for "Mostly Asian" and "Mixed Asian/Latino" have been eliminated from this table as they are only residents of California, Texas, New York, and Illinois. Island-born Puerto Ricans are coded as 1st generation.

living in an area where they have been subjugated by economic inequalities for multiple generations, the threat associated with Latinos who are new to this landscape can lead to greater levels of intergroup discrimination (Kasinitz, Mollenkopf, and Waters 2008; Marrow 2009; Winders and Smith 2012).

Coalitional Affinities: Discrimination and Social Distance

We now look at a sense of linked fate by adding connections with other groups in society. LNS respondents were asked, "How much does [national origin group's] 'doing well' depend on African Americans also doing well?" (with response choices being a lot, some, a little, or not at all). Interestingly, almost four-fifths of the first-generation Latinos indicated a high degree of linked fate with African Americans. While promising for collation-formation prospects, there is a drop-off in linked fate with African Americans among Latinos of the second generation and beyond. Therefore, while overall, more than three-fifths of all Latinos indicated some or a lot of linked fate with African Americans, the apparent drop in these positive attitudes as Latinos assimilate into American society is an important factor to consider when looking for opportunities to build alliances among the nation's two largest racial and ethnic minority groups. While there has been much emphasis on the growth of the Latino community, especially in the past decade, there has also been much discussion about the political influence achieved by the African American community (Walton 1997; Dawson 1994).

Works by McClain and Karnig (1990) and McClain and Stewart (1999) have established the prospects and limitations of an interracial/interethnic coalition between Latinos and African Americans. Competitive forces have been the primary area of emphasis between these two groups. As a result, coalitions are made tenuous (due to competition for municipal employment positions, business contracts, elected positions, etc.). At the same time, some more recent research (García 2000; Jennings 1994; Jaynes 2000) outlined possible inducements and/or situations for working together. Growing research literature on the causes and consequences of Latino/African American competition and the results of possible coalition (Telles et al. 2011; Mindiola et al. 2002; Rodríguez 2012; McClain et al. 2011) is being examined more systematically.

Our discussion of inter-racial coalitions attempts to measure the receptivity of Latinos and African Americans for a collective endeavor. The significant migration of Latinos into the southern region has been the focus of research in reaching conclusions about coalition formation. Work by McClain et al. (2006) examined the propensity of Latinos and African Americans in southern communities to pursue coalitional activities. The competitive consideration of potential Latino gains is viewed as coming at the expense of African Americans. Because the levels of trust between these two groups are not high, engaging in possible coalitions was not seen as a viable option. Work by Meier et al. (2004) examined multiracial relationships between Latinos and African Americans in 194 school districts. There were instances of both cooperation and competition between the two groups regarding school district policies. Scarcity of resources (i.e., hiring teachers and administrators) aroused competition (viewed as a zero-sum game), while, if scarcity such as overall school performance initiatives were not factored in, then cooperation was more the mode. Recent work by Jones-Correa, Wallace, and Zepeda-Millán (2015) explored Latinos' participation in the 2006 immigrant protest in terms of those participants being more likely to see commonalities with other "marginalized" groups. They found that participants exhibited a heightened sense of in-group identity that was associated with a greater sense of commonality with African Americans. This sense of stronger pan-ethnic identification as well as a shared sense of perceived discrimination is a positive contributor for inclination to join coalitions (Kaufmann 2003). Works by Wilkinson (2015) and Kaufmann (2003) show how perception of economic threat by one group will discourage possible cooperative ventures.

The critical factors of one's own group identification and positive interactions with other groups (including trust, familiarity, and common circumstances) are essential ingredients for successful coalitions. Alvarado and Jaret (2009) examined "black/brown" coalitions in the Southeast. These groups encountered each other in work settings, at school, in neighborhoods, and at other public places. When members of each group shared linked common obstacles in dealing with employment mobility, housing discrimination, poor schools, police harassment, and so on, possibilities for collaboration, starting dialogues, and seeking mutual solutions came into play. Alvarado and Jaret (2009) also found that some of these collective endeavors were laden with misunderstandings, competition, suspicion, hostility, and conflict. In most cases, the role of leadership was pivotal in working through these areas of tension and conflict. Establishing networks and joint resources benefit from pooling talents and mutual assistance on collective actions.

This discussion treats coalitions as being purposeful, situationally specific, and temporary. A discrimination model of coalition formation (Uhlaner 1991; García 2000), along with collective group orientations (sense of empowerment, efficacy, and consciousness) and socioeconomic status, can work interactively to determine areas of cooperation and obtain resources to be effective. This type of model suggests that both Latinos and African Americans experience discriminatory practices in the United States, which creates a common link or bond.

Connection through discriminatory experiences can produce a heightened sense of a group identity (such as Latinos, African Americans), with each seeing the other as experiencing common obstacles and barriers, which can motivate people to get involved politically on behalf of common concerns. For example, a pan-ethnic identification among Latinos serves as a predictor to engage in coalitional behavior with African Americans (Kaufman 2003). The expression of in-group identification and solidarity can serve as a marker of collectivist political orientations (Segura 2011) and seeing common issues across group boundaries. Similar findings were presented by Sanchez and Espinosa (2016).

Socioeconomic status helps provide the political resources to be effective in political arenas. Works such as Browning, Marshall, and Tabb (1990) looked at local politics in the San Francisco Bay area to illustrate that minority coalitions could include white liberals for effective policy outcomes. In California, Jackson and Preston (1991) and Sonenshein (1994) examined electoral efforts that connected the Latino and African American communities, especially in Los Angeles. Also, Gilliam (1996) found that if governing coalitions in Los Angeles supported minority empowerment and access existed, then blacks and Latinos were more likely to be politically engaged.

The basis for the **discrimination-plus model** (García 2000) depends on common experiences, issue priorities, and values among minority-group members for them to be receptive to joint political activities and collective efforts. Even if individuals make these kinds of connections, minority organizations and leadership play a critical role in implementing strategies and developing plans to act on these common goals and issue concerns. Organizations and their leadership function to outline specific political strategies, activities, communication links to the community, and motivational cues to stimulate action. Carmichael and Hamilton (1967) identified necessary requisites for any coalition to form, which include: (1) recognition of each party's self-interests, (2) recognition that each party's self-interest is benefited by an alliance, (3) each party's having an independent base of support, and (4) the coalition's effort focusing on specific and identifiable goals. The continual political empowerment of Latinos strengthens their partnership contribution to any coalition effort. The link is the discrimination experience perceived by Latinos and African Americans.

Earlier work by Uhlaner (1991) suggested that recognition of differential treatment can lead minority groups to feel sympathetic across groups, feel more disadvantaged than others, or be inclined to protect their own group more. Experiences with discrimination also affect individuals; they are more likely to possess a strong sense of racial and/or ethnic identity and support for specific group issues or problems (Uhlaner 1991). The key for Latino/African American coalitions lies with each assessing its disadvantaged status, seeing the inter-connectedness, and having a "common target" (i.e., specific officials, political institution, etc.). McClain and Karnig (1990) demonstrated that in American cities with a critical mass of both Latinos and African Americans, political coalitions were viable if both minority groups saw themselves as combating the "white power structure." When they shared a common target in vying for elective office, Latino and African American officials could make gains at the expense of current nonminority officeholders. At the same time, some level of trust between the two groups was essential for any degree of success. Oliver and Johnson (1984) showed that a low level of trust between Latinos and African Americans does exist in Los Angeles. Similarly, Barreto, Gonzalez, and Sanchez (2014) showed that most Latinos do not view blacks with suspicion or as competitors, but as potential partners. One cautionary note: The prospect for collective efforts is dependent on many local circumstances and the prior history of intergroup relations, as well as the particulars of the political issue at hand.

A second aspect of commonalities across groups concerns the extent of commonality between Latinos' political situation (i.e., representation, empowerment, government jobs, etc.) and that of African Americans. That is, three-fifths of native-born Latinos perceive political commonalities with African Americans. Across the different Latino subgroups, a high percentage sees political commonalities with African Americans. This proclivity could be due to greater geographical contact with African Americans (more so for Dominicans, Puerto Ricans, and Colombians) and a longer history of interaction (especially for Puerto Ricans). Also, the results suggest that an ample proportion of Latinos see their lives as interwoven, to a noticeable degree, with those of African Americans. As our focus lies with politics and political activities, this perceived level of commonality with other groups is intended to serve as the entry point for discussion and exploration of ways in which Latinos can work with other groups for common objectives.

BOX 11.3 Latinos, across National Origin, Respond to Hurricane Maria and the 2020 Earthquakes

Hurricane Maria (2017) devastated many Caribbean Island countries, and Puerto Rico was hit very hard. In late 2019 and early 2020, Puerto Rico experienced multiple earthquakes and aftershocks that resulted in more damage to the island infrastructure and the daily lives of its residents. There has been dissatisfaction among Puerto Ricans in the United States, Puerto Rican officials, and mainland Puerto Ricans about the extent and effectiveness of FEMA, other US agencies, and congressional and presidential leadership. At the same time,

BOX 11.3 (continued)

Latinos and their organizations and leadership responded to the needs of Puerto Rico through charitable projects, donations, and by pushing for a more responsive American government. We have illustrated these responses with examples of efforts and advocating for Puerto Ricans.

UnidosUS

Hurricane Maria brought shocking and unprecedented devastation to Puerto Rico, the effects of which will be felt for years to come. In response, the Hispanic Federation (HF) launched the Unidos program, by pushing for with grassroots organizations, individuals, businesses, and foundations to address the multiple long-term needs of the island's residents. HF mobilized swiftly to reach Puerto Rico's seventy-eight municipalities, transporting emergency first responders and providing 7.4 million pounds of food, water, and essentials in the critical days and weeks after the storm hit. Today, HF is proud to be among the largest institutional contributors to Puerto Rico's relief and recovery efforts.

The scale of disaster in Puerto Rico requires all of us to support islanders and displaced families in what is unquestionably a long journey toward a just recovery. HF believes that nonprofit agencies, local organizations, and community-based partnerships are in the best position to steer the recovery and rebuilding of Puerto Rico. HF has committed $30 million to support more than 110 local groups and initiatives across the island that are delivering ground-up, innovative projects—all built around long-term recovery, resiliency, sustainability, and increased self-sufficiency and community empowerment. We have seen unprecedented support for the island's recovery from individuals, corporations, and foundations on the mainland.

LatinoJusticePRLDEF Ayuda Legal Huracán María (ALHM)

This group helped create a Puerto Rico–led disaster relief legal response initiative called ALHM to assist thousands of Puerto Ricans affected by Hurricane Maria in seeking Federal Emergency Management Agency (FEMA) assistance, housing assistance, resettlement and relocation assistance, and other aid. It supports legal efforts on Puerto Rico, and in Florida and other states, it is working with Puerto Ricans displaced by the hurricane.

Massachusetts United for Puerto Rico Fund

In partnership with the Latino Legacy Fund, the Boston Foundation has agreed to champion this effort free of charge. The money raised will be invested in three areas: disaster relief, sustainable rebuilding, and capacity building for NGOs in Massachusetts, as a substantial migration of Puerto Ricans to Boston and throughout the commonwealth is expected. Up to one-third will be immediately distributed for relief efforts, and another third will be deployed over two years to support reconstruction and economic recovery projects that are sustainable in the long term. The final third will support resettlement efforts in Massachusetts.

Puerto Rico Hurricane Relief Fund at Heart of Florida United Way

Puerto Rico Hurricane Relief Fund at Heart of Florida United Way will assist with emergency assistance and basic needs of those affected. One hundred percent of every dollar raised will go toward alleviating immediate storm-related needs in Puerto Rico, long-term community recovery, and displacement assistance for families in Central Florida. The organization has been in contact with Fondos Unidos de Puerto Rico, the United Way that serves the entire island, in order to assess the immediate needs of their community. In an area still recovering from Hurricane Maria's carnage, the damage is formidable. While the federal government approved a major disaster declaration that will release more funds to the island and permit FEMA to offer further assistance, relief will take time—time that the residents of Puerto Rico just cannot spare.

Governor's Advisory Commission on Latino Affairs (GACLA) (Pennsylvania)

According to Dr. Damary Bonilla-Rodriguez of the Governor's Advisory Commission on Latino Affairs (PA), "There could be some shock related to what's happening. People are still rebuilding, and then this happens [the earthquake], but because of what happened during Hurricane Maria, we know that the people are emotionally drained, the infrastructure is not sturdy, and there is still a lack of resources and funding, compounded by what just happened. There's almost a greater need right now" (Wolf 2017). But throughout Monroe County and Pennsylvania, individuals, nonprofit groups, and government commissions are coming together to make a difference.

"The Governor's Commission actually hosted a state-wide call today," Bonilla-Rodriguez said. "We had faith-based organizations, nonprofit organizations, businesses, local, state and federal agencies, and it was an opportunity for everyone to provide an update about what they are doing to allow the commissioners to know what efforts are going on" (Wolf 2017).

Bonilla-Rodriguez said that GACLA and other groups are compiling contact information to keep track of relief efforts and contributions, which will allow them to more efficiently direct assistance. They are also looking into possible partners to help provide necessary items, such as major pharmaceutical companies from Pennsylvania that could provide valuable medical supplies. Residents in Pennsylvania may wonder how they can go about helping in such a situation. Michele Baehr, executive director of American Red Cross of the Pocono

BOX 11.3 (continued)

Mountains, said that the answer is actually quite simple: donate some cash. Not only is it easy to send and applicable to just about any need, but it can help to stimulate the local economy.

The Delaware Hispanic Commission

This group has created the Delaware for Puerto Rico Task Force Subcommittee. This committee is focused on working with existing local nonprofit organizations, state agencies, and federal entities in providing additional support and resources for those directly affected in Puerto Rico by Hurricane Maria. As the task force subcommittee continues to cement goals and a cohesive plan of action, they will provide updates and resources that can assist and support those most in need in Puerto Rico.

Due to the rising challenges of shipping and distribution of donated items, the organization recommends monetary donations, as those funds will go directly toward immediate assistance.

League of United Latin American Citizens (LULAC)

The oldest and largest US Hispanic advocacy organization addressed the impact of Hurricane Maria on the island during its ninetieth annual convention, held in Milwaukee on July 11, 2019. During the convention, Puerto Rican leaders shared the harsh reality still facing the island: "Even though almost two years have passed, the people of Puerto Rico are struggling to recover from a natural disaster that no other generation on the Island has ever seen before," said Carmelo Rios, Puerto Rico Senate majority leader and NHCSL (National Hispanic Caucus of State Legislators) president. "The recovery process from the US government has not been sufficient, but as part of our efforts, we are promoting Puerto Rico as a tourist destination that will help revamp our economy. We look forward to showing the world everything that Puerto Rico has to offer."

LULAC continues to offer strong support to fellow US citizens who reside in Puerto Rico regarding their legitimate right as US citizens vote in presidential elections, as well as for their corresponding voting members of Congress. The organization is also committed to continuing to push government officials to provide equal opportunities and treatment to the three million US citizens residing on the island.

The converse of commonality would be if Latinos saw themselves more in competition with African Americans. In the LNS, the Latino respondents were asked, "Some have suggested that Latinos or Hispanics are in competition with African Americans." The areas of potential competition included jobs, education, government, and elected offices. In the case of competition for jobs, there is a tendency to see little or no competition. A similar pattern existed when the potential competitive arena was education and quality schools, governmental jobs, and holding elected office. It would be unrealistic, in any given area of the country, to expect no competition in these areas between Latinos and other groups in the community. At the same time, the modal responses would indicate that competition may not be a salient point of contention, or it may be one in which some resolution is more possible than not.

Some literature suggests that rising Latino immigration in communities with other minority populations, especially African Americans, could accentuate competition in domains such as jobs, social services, and so forth (Rocha 2007; Meier et al. 2004; McClain et al. 2009). The competition for economic resources, attention from the major political parties, and educational resources can pit the interests of each group against the other. At the same time, research by Rodrígues and Segura (2007) indicates that intergroup relations operate at both the elite and mass levels. They argue that one needs to observe and understand both sets of dynamics. The specific situation, personalities of the leadership, and historical patterns of minority treatment and empowerment all come into play as to how different groups respond to sociopolitical issues and events. In addition, Wallsten and Nteta (2017) note that elites promoting intergroup cooperation do not necessarily generate the desired outcome of elites.

For example, evidence from mass attitudes can point to salient issues leading toward cooperation as well as perceived social distance. We would suggest that elite leadership can be a critical component in contact and communication with other groups, but other considerations like established channels of communication across groups, extent of mutual trust, and any prior cooperative experiences need to be factored in as well. Kaufman (2003) found pan-ethnic identification to be associated with Latinos' positive perceptions of African Americans. Understanding the underlying bases of perceived linked fate and commonalities with other groups serves as the fulcrum for collective endeavors.

While the "intra-coalitional" possibilities across the various Latino national-origin groups have become more established over the past twenty years or so, there are clear indicators of the growing pervasiveness of pan-ethnic identification, inter-Latino group contacts, and organizations that advocate for and represent broader-based Latino interests at work. At the same time, national-origin-based organizations still exist and are active on behalf of their respective communities. Mexican-origin, Dominican, Cuban, Puerto Rican, Salvadoran, and other communities have organizations that focus on their salient issues. Specific Latino national-origin groups confront very specific issues; on other occasions, there is overlap with other Latino communities, and collaborative or umbrella Latino organizations become engaged. It was suggested, in the first edition of this book, that the future of Latino politics would involve Latino national-origin groups concentrating on their own group's needs and issues, with occasional joint efforts with other Latino national-origin groups. A second scenario involved a more sustained pan-ethnic politics whereby national Latino pan-ethnic organizations would advance Latino interests. The two scenarios can operate in concert. Thus, this chapter's focus on alliances can treat Latinos of different national-origin backgrounds as coming together for collective purposes.

Our additional examination of intergroup alliances with the African American community is driven by the commonality of negative differential treatment (discrimination), which can serve as a bridge to join cooperative ventures. Given this preliminary examination, Uhlaner's 1991 work, and Garcia's (2000), the preconditions for successful alliances or coalitions would include each group's having independent bases of leadership, resources, and well-defined goals. Agreeing on a common target and well-defined objectives increases the possibilities for cooperative efforts. In addition, trust, interpersonal contact, and familiarity with other group members can facilitate collaborated efforts. While there are some marked group differences, the added information from the LNS reinforces the role of common interests enabling Latinos to coalesce, not only with other minority groups, but possibly with non-minorities. Clearly, policy concerns and priorities are a real bridge for collective action.

Research literature on political participation and mobilization indicates there has been an increase of Latino candidates. While Latino voters take a greater interest in elections in which Latinos are candidates, they also tend to vote for co-ethnic candidates when they get a chance to do so (McConnaughy et al. 2010; Barreto and Nuño 2011). In addition, the increase of Latino candidates is more evident among Latinas (Hardy-Fanta et al. 2007). One of the impacts of Latina legislators is that they place greater emphasis on representing the interests of multiple minority groups, promote conflict resolution, and build consensus both in the legislature as a whole and within the Latino caucus (Fraga et al. 2006a). Latinas are also more likely than Latino representatives to introduce and successfully pass legislation important to Latino constituents. One of the implications of more co-ethnic candidates and heightened Latino voter interest is that issues and ideology are central factors affecting their vote choice (Abrajano and Alvarez 2010). Even though co-ethnic candidates enjoy Latino support, voters will scrutinize all candidates to see if their issue positions and ideological orientation are most closely aligned with their own, and that becomes the deciding factor of voter choice (James 2011; Abrajano and Alvarez 2010). So electorally, as more districts are comprised of multiple minority communities, possible electoral coalitions become one of the options. Clearly more opportunities and challenges will present themselves or will be initiated by Latino and African American leadership and organizations, as well as other groups. Physical proximity, such as sharing common residential and commercial areas, can also increase interactions. At the same time, undercurrents of greater competition for limited political and economic gains highlight the zero-sum calculation: that working together may incur unequal costs and benefits to one's own group. The politics of alliances depends on several situational conditions and circumstances, as well as having the political resources to act. This growth area for research extends beyond other racial/ethnic partners into labor, issue advocacy groups, and social justice movements.

Finally, just as we have noted that the current sociopolitical environment which is viewed by many Latinos to be hostile toward their community has enhanced Latino pan-ethnic identity, there is evidence that this environment has provided opportunities for cross-group collaboration. The most salient example of this opportunity is a common concern across racial groups regarding the rise in racial tensions associated with the Trump campaign and policies of his administration. Drawing from the 2018 Latino Decisions Election Eve study, the figure below illustrates that nonwhite voters in 2018 had severe concerns about the president's words and actions (see figure 11.4). This anger and fear could be transformed into not only an electoral coalition in 2020, but also into more broad policy coalitions focused on common policy concerns, including criminal justice reform and police violence.

FIGURE 11.4 Has Trump Made You Feel Angry or Disrespected by Something He Has Said or Done?

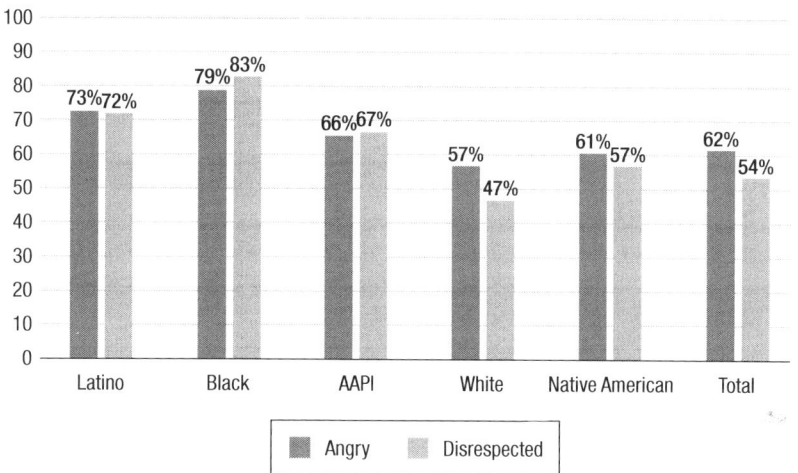

Source: 2016 Collaborative Multi-Racial Post-Election Survey.

Conclusion: A Pan-Ethnic Community and Broader Partnerships

Considering the examination of community building, what is the extent of a working community among Latinos? Community building and working together, as presented in this chapter, are based on common status (cultural, political, and minority) and positive affinities toward one another. The data suggest that a major solidification of a pan-ethnic community now has more promise and increased optimism. There is clear evidence that the Latino communities are aware of one another and connected in a variety of ways (geographic proximity, common issues, organizational activities and leadership, and pan-ethnic identification). The maintenance of a sense of national-origin identity does not impede the acquisition of and attachment to a pan-ethnic identification as well. As a matter of fact, within the LNS and CMPS battery on key identities, it is quite possible for a respondent to identify himself or herself as a Peruvian, a Latino/a, and an American. External events, social movements, and treatment by interest groups, politicians, and parties can serve to unite Latinos as an identifiable and working community. In addition, the density of Latino/African American networks has increased (along with other groups and organizations) and lines of communication and mutual awareness are more evident.

The activities directed toward Latinos in the 2016 and 2018 elections increased the value of building a more active Latino community and have attracted the attention of the major political parties (to a greater extent the Democratic Party), the media, and leadership in the socioeconomic sectors of America. While there was strong support among Latino voters for Barack Obama's elections, and Hilary Clinton in 2016, one consequence has been a greater partisan divide among Latinos than for the general electorate. Our attempt to identify the building blocks for alliances, pan-ethnic identification, intergroup contact, the extent of discrimination, and perceived commonalities along socioeconomic status points to conducive conditions for alliances or coalitions to occur. We would suggest that cooperative endeavors can be temporal and specific to incidents or events. This temporal element can be illustrated by differentiating between coalitions and alliances. Coalitions can refer to partners coming together around a need to achieve a certain goal. These partners operate autonomously and are not usually connected to each other. When the actions are completed, the coalitions dissolve and go back to their own work. The concept of an alliance reaches a deeper level of commitment that is longer standing, deeper, and built upon a more trusting interpersonal relationship. Allies are viewed as people who are struggling together on several fronts, not only over a single issue. An alliance is an ongoing and a long-term arrangement. Whether Latinos engage in coalitions and/or alliances, the community is trying to improve its circumstances and positions of influence in American society.

As we move to chapter 12, we will be presenting four scenarios about the future of Latino communities and the political system. The Latino community will continue to be a dynamic force both within its own subcommunities and in the larger aggregation of a national Latino community. Dynamism within the Latino community involves the process of defining itself further (its cultural and group boundaries, interests, and organizational landscape) and establishing itself as an active political participant whose goals, interests, and impact will become more identifiable in the political and economic life of the United States. How this manifests itself will be deliberated in the scenarios we have generated.

Discussion Questions

1. When we discuss alliances or coalitions, intergroup relations are the primary focus. At the same time, the Latino community comprises more than twenty national-origin groups. How do the concepts of community of interests, community of common cultures, linked fate, discrimination, and pan-ethnic identity come into play in the formation of intracommunity alliances?
2. Focusing on intracommunity alliances, discuss the experiences and interactions between the Latino foreign- and native-born segments in terms of collective behaviors.
3. Shared minority status would suggest that issues of empowerment, representation, access, and policy responsiveness can serve as a bridge to unite different minority groups. Discuss the positives and obstacles for Latinos in forming coalitions with other minority communities, especially the African American community.
4. Coalition formation is usually based on common interests and policy agendas. If this is the case, are there any limitations for Latinos to form alliances with whites (Anglos) as well as with, or in addition to, other minority communities?
5. We have introduced the concept of social contact as an important component of intergroup relations. How do social contact and social networks influence Latinos' relationships with other racial and ethnic groups?

Note

1. The Pew Hispanic Center survey asked black and Hispanic respondents to identify the skin tone that best resembles their own using a modified version of the Massey-Martin scale. Respondents were shown five skin tones that ranged from fair to dark.

CHAPTER 12

The Latino Community
Going Beyond Recognition Politics

Hicimos nuestra peregrinación y nos preguntamos—¿Dónde esta nuestra comunidad y cuales son los elementos más importantes que sostienen nuestra comunidad? La verdad es que somos muchas diferentes comunidades que a la vez nos desarrollamos hasta alcanzar otro nivel como comunidad. Tenemos que insistir en preguntarnos ¿Dónde está nuestra comunidad?

We have made our pilgrimage, and we have asked ourselves, Where is our community, and which are the most important elements that sustain it? The truth is that we are many different communities simultaneously evolving toward a higher level of community. We have to persist in asking ourselves, Where is our community?

WE BEGAN THIS BOOK BY exploring the nature and extent of the community that exists within the various Latino subcommunities in the United States. Using the concepts of community, common cultures, and community of interests, we constructed guidelines and analytical narratives to explore what kind of "political shape" the Latino community was in. We focused on political resource development among Latinos, their organizations, leadership, and the responses of the US political system. In addition to their striking population growth, particularly over the past forty-five years, are Latinos increasing their political capital? Are they making significant gains in education, income, and occupational status, in increased numbers of naturalized citizens and elected officials at all levels, and in operating more cohesive and effective organizations? And finally, will Latino ethnic identity fade as a greater share of Latinos move further away from the immigrant experience? As we approach these key questions, we will briefly summarize the ground we have covered across the book that can help you come up with your own conclusions regarding the future of "Latino politics" in the United States.

We have suggested that community-building among the twenty-plus Latino national-origin groups can provide greater resources, visibility, and political-economic leverage in the American political system. At the same time, the cost and energy required to establish the degree of community necessary for the inclusion of all Latino subgroups remains a significant challenge. This chapter will develop some possible and quite probable scenarios to characterize the politics of the Latino community as we move through the middle part of this new millennium. We will introduce some major political issues that will continue to challenge Latinos to impact the political system in the *future*.

Basic Community Facts: Continued Latino Growth and Diversity

Before we begin to discuss those issues that will challenge Latinos in the future, it is important to examine the key advances and developments that have already occurred within Latino communities and in the American political system. The first "fact" lies with Latinos' projected population growth. While much has been made of the rapid and continuous growth of the "largest minority," this pattern will be reinforced in the future. US Census Bureau (2020) population decennial counts and future projections into midcentury continue to show the Latino growth rate exceeding that of all other populations. It is estimated that by 2050, Latinos will make up one-fourth of the US population; in 2011, they constituted one-seventh. One of the noteworthy consequences is the continued growth of the Latino electorate both by increases in native-born Latinos and expected naturalizations. Figure 12.1 reflects the expected significant growth of Latinos in the American electorate.

The other major development in this continued population growth is the geographic dispersion of Latinos throughout all regions of the United States. In 1990, approximately 90 percent of all Latinos lived in ten states. According to the 2009 American Community Survey, 78.7 percent of all Latinos were in these same ten states. However, in 2012, there were twenty-two states in which Latinos were the largest

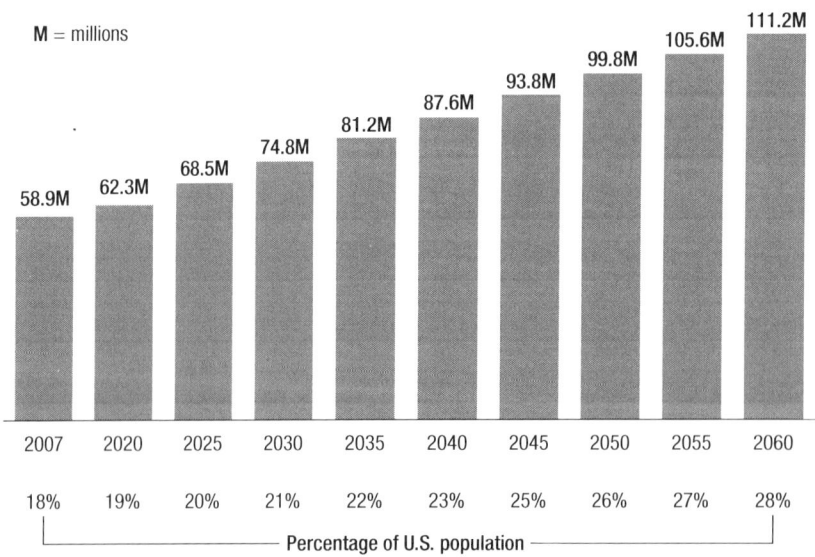

FIGURE 12.1 Hispanic Population to Reach 111 Million by 2060

Source: United States Census Bureau 2020.

minority group, meaning that areas of traditional concentration continue to grow, but new areas, primarily in the South, Northwest, and Midwest, are experiencing dramatic growth. By 2018, there were twenty-seven states in which Latinos were the largest minority group (Maciag 2019).

The influx of Latinos into less "traditional" areas is becoming more evident. For example, during a Christmas-season Protestant service in suburban Portland, Oregon, a call went out to congregational members to give clothing, books, and other practical gifts to needy individuals. The organizer said that the first twenty-eight of the seventy-five households on the list were Spanish speakers, so there was a need for people who could speak Spanish to help deliver the gifts. Other indicators of the increase in the Latino population in Portland include Spanish-language signs posted throughout the Oregon Museum of Science and Industry, as well as Spanish signs and voice recordings on the MAX (the light-rail system). In terms of growth rates, the fastest-growing Latino populations are in states located in the Midwest and South, with North Dakota, Kentucky, and Louisiana leading the way (Stepler and Lopez 2016) (see figure 12.2).

An earlier edition of this book described the Latino transformation in Dalton, Georgia (in the northwestern part of the state), where mostly Mexicans moved to the "carpet capital of the world." In 2000, Latinos constituted a near majority (51.4 percent) of the students in the public schools in this town of twenty-three thousand (Roedemeier 2000). Across northern Georgia, an influx of mostly Latino immigrants began arriving to work in the poultry-processing plants and carpet mills. Since then, Latinos have worked hard to integrate themselves in Dalton and exercise influence and sustained participation.

FIGURE 12.2 The South Has Seen the Nation's Biggest Latino Population Growth since 2008

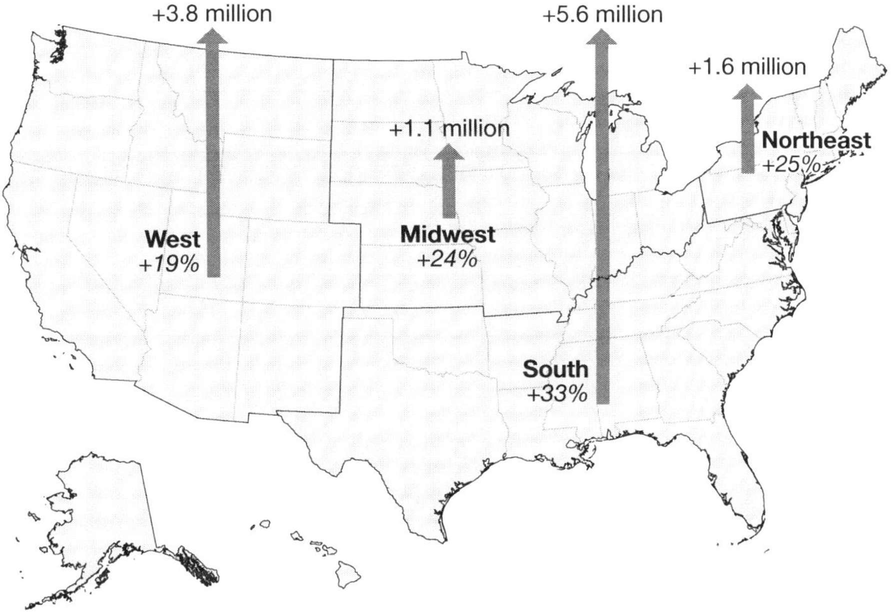

Source: Pew Research Center analysis of US intercensal population estimates for 2008 and US Census Bureau Vintage 2018 estimates.

For example, the **Coalition of Latino Leaders (CLILA)** has become the "anchor organization" in Whitfield County, providing English classes, civics classes, civic participation education, legal services, and afterschool programs. CLILA has also led the local community in advocacy and organizing by participating in and testifying in front of the board of regents to provide undocumented students access to Dalton State College, hosting town hall meetings to discuss legislation, advocating for DACA, and joining local, state, and national efforts for inclusion of Latino voices and contributions in decision making. Truly a community center, CLILA provides one-on-one assistance to individuals and families, hosts gatherings, designs cultural events such as "Festival Del Sabor," which had an attendance of approximately four thousand in 2016, and conducts meetings with law enforcement agencies. CLILA has served as a liaison with law enforcement officials regarding the use of roadblocks in Latino communities and challenging Georgia's recent more restrictive immigrant laws. These actions have improved community relationships. Members of the college and greater Dalton communities gathered on campus recently to celebrate Dalton State's status as a Hispanic Serving Institution, the first in the state of Georgia and one of the first in the southeastern United States. This scenario can be recounted in many other communities throughout the South, the Rocky Mountain regions, America's heartland, New England, and the suburban Northeast.

As we discussed earlier in the book, the explosion of the Latino population (mostly immigrants) across the South has led to some challenges for Latinos who are finding their space in an area where race is defined from a white/black paradigm. Something to watch for into the future is how race relations will evolve as the children of predominately immigrant families age and potentially stay in these new destination states and establish more long-term roots. Also, the fastest-growing states for Latinos are outside the traditional areas of "settlement" (see figure 12.3).

Another growth factor in the US Latino population is the burgeoning growth of Central and South Americans within the Latino community. While persons of Mexican origin continue to maintain high growth rates (in terms of both birthrates and immigration), the numbers of Latinos from El Salvador, Guatemala, and Honduras as well as Venezuela, Colombia, Peru, and the Dominican Republic are growing faster and becoming more geographically important. Latinos from Central and South America have settled, for the most part, in areas where people of Mexican origin, Cubans, and Puerto Ricans are located. While contributing to overall Latino growth, this pattern also represents a broader mix of Latino interests and potential resource building. These expanded areas would include pressing for Central American political refugee recognition (especially adolescents and unaccompanied minors), and restoring TPS protective status for all covered before the Trump termination of TPS. At the same time, the asylum policies, humane treatment of unaccompanied children, limited detention centers, "incarceration," eliminating harsh treatment, and "normalizing" the status of DACA and DAPA registrants would broaden the scope of Latinos' immigration policy agenda.

Another example of the changing world for Latinos can be seen with the Dominican population in New York City. In 1980, the Dominican population was 125,380. That number grew to 332,713 by 1990, and by 2017 it reached 872,504. Such growth represents policy interests and demands on the New York City educational system, housing, employment, and basic city services. The growing Dominican community has created its own organizations and seeks to enhance its political and economic

FIGURE 12.3 States with Fastest-Growing Latino Populations, 2000–2014

	2014 Latino population	2000 Latino population	% change 2000-2014
South Dakota	29,000	10,000	190
Tennessee	322,000	117,000	176
South Carolina	258,000	95,000	172
Alabama	190,000	72,000	164
Kentucky	145,000	57,000	154
Arkansas	205,000	85,000	141
North Dakota	18,000	7,000	141
Maryland	556,000	231,000	141
North Carolina	890,000	377,000	136
Virginia	732,000	333,000	120

Source: Stepler and Lopez 2016.

influence in the city overall, as well as in relation to Puerto Rican and other Latino communities.

El Salvadorans have now moved into the top five national-origin groups. At a recent redistricting conference in Los Angeles (sponsored by the **Southwest Voter Registration and Education Project**), activists from the Los Angeles Salvadoran community attended and became involved in providing their perspectives and interests in the strategy sessions, proposing boundaries for legislative and congressional districts. For the future, the continual significant growth of Central American– and South American–origin Latinos will help shape the nature of Latino politics in terms of issues, leadership, and challenges for collective efforts and cooperation. Nora Torres (CA), Debbie Mucarsel-Powell (FL), and Hilda Solis (CA) are examples of congressional representatives from Guatemala, Ecuador, and Nicaragua, respectively.

The expansion of Latinos into metropolitan areas and regions of the country where they had been less evident serves several developmental political and social purposes. First, the continuing growth (with more varied geographical settlement patterns) provides Latinos with an even greater national presence. In some regions, particularly in the South, Northwest, and upper Midwest, public awareness of and experience with Latinos had been virtually nonexistent. At the same time, the expansion of Latinos into more locales has produced positive and negative consequences. The above-mentioned Latino movement to Dalton, Georgia, helped to meet the demand for jobs and workers; however, the rapid Latino transformation also resulted in intergroup tensions and anti-immigrant sentiments from "native" Georgians. In box 12.1 we describe the impact of Latino migrants on rural America, an area of the country that is decreasing in population density across the country, which is leading to major divisions regarding policy priorities and preferences.

BOX 12.1 Immigrants and Latinos Bring Population Growth to Rural Communities

Parts of rural America suffer from stagnant or shrinking population numbers due to an aging population. This "brain drain" which saw young people leave their hometowns by being attracted to opportunities in urban areas was depleting rural America's economic and population futures. Kenneth Johnson, a demographer who studies rural America, has found that one in three US counties are "dying."

Immigrants are helping to avert the losses. Recent US census data used by Johnson showed that where there is growth in rural areas, minorities account for 83 percent. The Hispanic population in nonmetropolitan areas grew at the fastest rate of any racial or ethnic group during the 1990s and post-2000. Johnson describes the dynamic in rural communities this way: "Young people leave, and older adults stay in place and age. Unless something dramatic changes—for instance, new developments such as a meatpacking plant to attract young Hispanics—these areas are likely to have more and more natural decrease" (quoted in Hanson 2016).

Immigration has slowed or even overcome population decline on the county level across the central United States since 1990. Latino foreign-born population growth has countered native-born loss to slow overall population loss. One consequence is that incoming Latinos have created net growth in overall county population. Much of this change has taken place in rural counties across the nation's midsection, stretching from Texas to the Dakotas.

The Center for Rural Affairs' Rural Enterprise Assistance Project (REAP) and University of Nebraska (UNL) join forces to provide entrepreneurs many services, including financial assistance, business training, technical assistance, and continuous education. They offer educational courses for current business owners and entrepreneurs. Workshops offered in both English and Spanish have included business plan basics, online marketing, and even industry-specific classes, such as "Cleaning Academy" and "Emerging Small Construction Start-Ups."

In 2016, REAP and UNL began their partnership to help Latino-owned businesses, and today they assist 123 businesses all over Nebraska. Ninety of those businesses are in Grand Island and include restaurants, travel agencies, tattoo parlors, nail salons, and more. Approximately 80 percent of those businesses have received financing or loans through REAP. More than 60 percent of the businesses belong to women. Sixty-seven workshops or training events were offered collaboratively by REAP and UNL in 2018. The impact of Latinos in rural America has had socioeconomic benefits and is serving as a basis for mutual intergroup integration efforts.

Obviously, part of the future of Latino politics is the process of community building within the Latino community, as well as joining with existing community interests and institutions in more recently settled areas. Continued growth exceeding the national average and movement into areas populated with fewer Latinos are the basic characteristics of the future profile of Latinos in the United States. They represent both challenges and opportunities for Latinos to establish their roots in the community and develop the resource base and interest to influence local policy makers and employers.

Latino Pan-Ethnicity and Its Viability

The second basic factor that bears relevance to the future of Latino politics is the existence of a pan-ethnic community. Our examination reveals that a high level of pan-ethnic identification and acknowledgment exists among Latinos. Established organizations continue to represent and advocate on behalf of Latinos, and many newer organizations have been formed. They have organized around issues of civil and political rights and salient policy areas (immigration, language policies, housing, education, voting rights, etc.), as well as work-related groups and culture- and neighborhood-based interests. Political and economic elites have established networks and, at times, cooperative activities that cut across specific Latino subgroups (Cubans, Dominicans, Salvadorans, etc.). At the same time, a 2015 Pew Hispanic Center poll found that almost 50 percent of Latinos used their national origin as their primary identity, and one-fourth used Latino or Hispanic. Our position has been that the integration of one's Hispanic ancestry is an integral part of one's Latino identity (see figure 12.4). A substantial proportion of Latinos, from the first through the third generation, see themselves as Latino or Hispanic.

The dispersion of Latinos across different regions of the country has put a more diverse mix of Latinos into contact where previously only one group predominated.

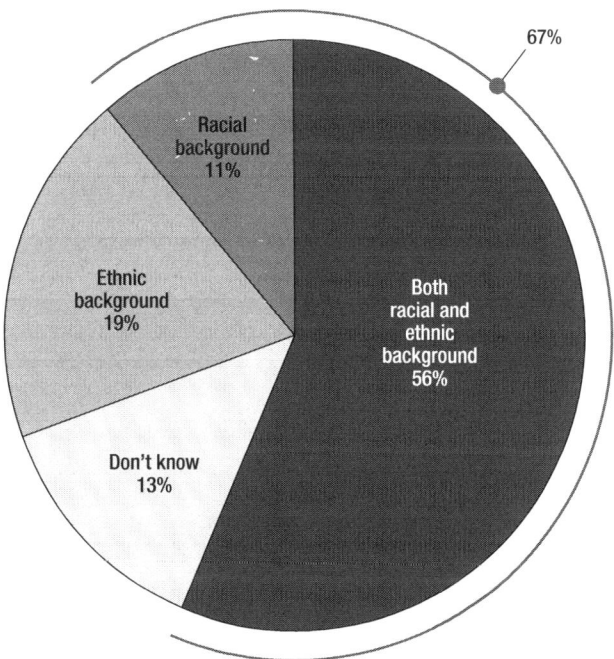

FIGURE 12.4 Two-Thirds of Hispanic Adults Say Being Hispanic Is Part of Their Racial Background

Source: Pew Research Center Survey, February 6–April 6, 2015 (n = 2,438 sampled Hispanic adults).

For example, the Latino mix in the Miami metropolitan area has changed; a majority of Latinos are now non-Cubans. While inter-Latino group interactions may vary by group and some can be more competitive than cooperative in nature (vying for scarce public and private resources, political resources, etc.), the changed Latino landscape has created pressures and incentives to come together as a broader community. These developments, in conjunction with the media's attention, have continued to reinforce the expansion and activities of Latinos throughout the country and serve to influence Latino community building. We have suggested that community can come together as a result of both internal efforts by Latinos themselves and how the "larger" society, its institutions and key elites, perceive and act in recognition of their presence.

A central question for Latinos regarding pan-ethnicity is who is defining Latinos and the Latino community and for what purpose does it exist? The development and advancement of organizations and leadership have been addressing the nature of Latino interests while obtaining public recognition. Over time, there have been more extensive interactions and contact across the different Latino subgroups, creating a robust Latino community. While we have pondered throughout this book about the existence of a Latino community, our answer is in the affirmative. The next stage is the implementation of a functioning and effective Latino community with an impact on political, economic, and social matters at the various levels of government and the economy.

The Latino Vessel Has Arrived

The mid-1990s firmly established the real political capital of Latinos in American politics. Soundbites about "invisibility," "a sleeping giant," and Latinos "soon to have their place in the sun" have been used for decades, especially in reference to the Mexican-origin population. Since the mid-1990s, the mass media, political and economic leaders, activists, and organizational leaders from the different Latino communities have sounded similar themes of potentiality and the conversion of a significant, growing population into a major political, economic, and cultural force. Now there is even greater evidence that the "Latino vessel has arrived" on the American political and social shores.

Another important development has been the expansion of Spanish-language media. A 2005 survey on ethnic media by Bendixen and Amandi (2006) reported that almost nine-tenths (87 percent) of all Latinos watched Spanish-language television, listened to Spanish radio stations, or read Spanish-language newspapers on a regular basis. They also noted that Latino users of these media had increased significantly, with one-fifth of Latino adults preferring Spanish-language newspapers to their English-language counterparts. Cubans were the greatest users of Spanish-language media (television), while South Americans had a higher percentage of Spanish-language newspaper readers (Bendixen and Amandi 2015). Radio stations and their disc jockeys played a major role in communicating with the Latino community at the onset of and throughout the 2006 immigrant protest demonstrations (Bada, Fox, and Selee 2006). The use of Spanish-language media for political mobilization (Abrajano and Panagopoulos 2011) boosted Latino turnout. English-language appeals were effective "across the board," whereas Spanish-language outreach was effective only with low-propensity Spanish-speaking voters.

Spanish-language news media tend to more closely cover issues of importance to their audience, such as immigration (Branton and Dunaway 2008). Furthermore, the ways in which Spanish-language media cover issues that are important to Latinos in the United States are different from English-language media approaches. A recent ethnographic content analysis found that in news segments about Latino migrants and immigrants on Fox News, MSNBC, and Univision, Fox News portrayed Latino immigrants in a generally neutral or negative tone, MSNBC in a neutral or positive tone, and Univision in a positive tone. Fox's stories often referred to Latino immigrants as a "problem to be solved," while Univision framed immigration as a problem of global, neoliberal capitalism that creates a need for mass migration and defines activism and social change as a solution. Spanish and bilingual speakers might choose to watch Spanish-language media to bolster their ethnic social identity (Harwood 1999) and as a means of protecting their own self-identity (Abrams and Giles 2007). In one study, as consumption by Spanish and bilingual speakers of English-language content increased, so did general perceptions of prejudice, discrimination, and legitimacy of treatment (Ortiz and Behm-Morawitz 2015). Some research points to a correlation between civic engagement and local Spanish-language news coverage. For example, researchers Felix Oberholzer-Gee and Joel Waldfogel (2006) found a larger voter turnout (5 to 10 percent increase) of Latinos in communities with a dedicated local Spanish-language TV news source. We should see a continuing and expanding role of the use of Spanish language in the public and political life of Latinos (Subervi-Velez 2008).

A visible political front is the rise of Latino elected officials at the state and federal levels. The 2017 NALEO Directory of Latino Elected Officials reported nearly 6,600 Latinos serving in elected office nationwide. This is up from the 6,011 in 2013, an increase of nearly 10 percent. The four states with the largest number of Latino elected officials are Texas, California, New Mexico, and Arizona. A noticeable growth in the number of Latina elected officials found 2,401 Latinas serving in elected office, comprising 36 percent of the total number of Latino elected officials nationwide, a 17 percent increase from 2013.

The state of California serves as one of the better examples, with Cruz Bustamante as lieutenant governor and Richard Polanco as California Senate majority leader. Significant gains in the California state legislature have marked a breakthrough for Latinos in that state. California has had the greatest number of Latinos, primarily of Mexican origin, for several decades, yet electoral representation has not been manifested in similar proportions. In 2014, for the first time in California history, the state senate and assembly were headed by Mexican Americans. Latinos accounted for 20 percent of the 120 state senators and assemblypersons. In a 2000 study, twenty-nine of the fifty-two congressional districts had a Latino population of one hundred thousand or more.

In the elections of 2016, Catherine Cortez-Masto of Nevada was elected as the nation's first Latina US senator, a significant milestone for the Latino community. Senator Cortez-Masto joined Latino US senators Ted Cruz (R-TX), Robert Menendez (D-NJ), and Marco Rubio (R-FL) in the 115th Congress. Twelve Latinos currently serve in statewide executive offices, including two Latinos as governors (Sandoval-R and Lujan-Grisham-D). The number of Latinos in state legislatures reached a new record in 2017, as there are 321 Latinos serving in the state legislatures of thirty-eight states, with 77 serving in state senates and 244 serving in state lower houses.

Latinos serving in state senates include 66 Democrats and 11 Republicans; both parties added two Latino state senators. The states that gained Latino elected officials were Arizona (+ 3 state senators), Florida (+1), Illinois (+1), Nebraska (+1), and West Virginia (+1). In state lower houses, there are 194 Latino Democrats and 50 Republicans serving in elected office. Finally, in the US House of Representatives, Latino representation increased by seven in the 115th Congress, for a total of 34; this group represented the largest class of Latinos serving in the US House of Representatives in history. The partisan composition among Latinos in the US House of Representatives shifted from 22 Democrats and 7 Republicans in the 114th Congress to 27 Democrats and 7 Republicans in the 115th.

While growth among Latinos in federal and state legislatures has been steady, Latinos holding statewide offices remain a major challenge; however, increasing numbers of Latino candidates, whether successful or not, will play an important role in engaging Latinos in the electoral process (Juenke 2014). The combination of factors that include more widespread and effective voter-registration campaigns, activism regarding state propositions, anti-immigrant legislation and initiatives, and increased numbers of Latino candidates will help more Latinos engage in the electoral process (Barreto 2010). The opportunity to compete for elective offices due to term limits, greater Latino organizational effectiveness and cooperation, more visible and active local community efforts (labor movements, service-delivery issues, police matters, etc.), and higher rates of naturalization have effectively contributed to the growth of the Latino electorate.

More than half a million more Latinos voted in the 1998 congressional elections than in 1994, increasing their presence at the polls from 3.5 million to 4.1 million (Day and Gaither 2000b). The number of Latinos of voting age increased from 10.4 million to 12.4 million in 1998. These changes occurred at a time when other groups (particularly whites) were evidencing a decline in voter registration. (See table 12.1) Projections beyond 2010 indicate that states with the largest number of voting-age Latinos will be California (7 million), Texas (4 million), New York (1.8 million), and Florida (1.8 million) (Day and Gaither 2000a; Barreto 2010). Figure 12.5 shows that the Latino percentage share of the electorate has almost doubled since 2000 (7.4 to 13.3 percent).

In the 2008 elections, Latino voter turnout was higher in twenty-six states than in the 2004 elections, especially in Georgia, Florida, and North Carolina. Minorities, as a proportion of the electorate, increased, with Latinos constituting 8.5 percent, African Americans 12 percent, Asian Americans 3 percent, and non-Hispanic whites

TABLE 12.1 Age and Citizen Voting-Eligible Latinos, 2012–2030 (millions)

	2012	2030 (projected)	Share of Growth (%)
All	215	256	100
Hispanic	24	40	40
White	154	163	23
Black	27	35	21
Asian	9	16	15

Source: Adapted from Pew Hispanic Center tabulations of the August 2012 Current Population Survey and Pew Research Center projections, 2012.
Notes: White, black, and Asian data include only the non-Hispanic figures of those populations. American Indian/Alaska Native data are not shown. Share data are calculated before rounding.

FIGURE 12.5 Latino Share of US Electorate, 2020

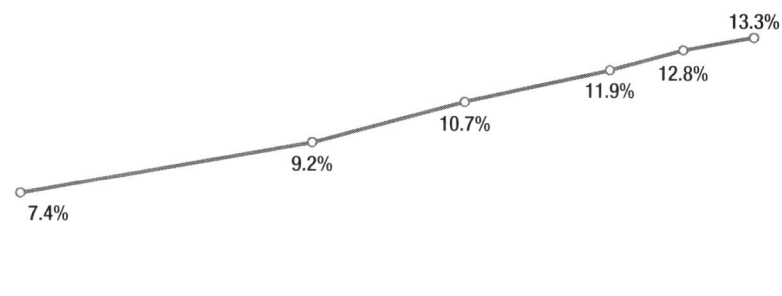

Source: Pew Research Center analysis of 2018, 2016, 2012, and 2008 American Community Survey and 2000 decennial census (IPUMS). Pew Research Center projections for 2020 based on the US Census Bureau 2017 population projections.

74 percent. The 2018 midterm elections saw a record turnout for Latinos and other minority group members. Latinos had a 13 percent increase from the 2014 midterm elections. The heightened polarizing rhetoric of political parties and divisive issues like immigration, wages, and unions stimulated both interest and engagement among Latinos for the 2020 elections (see figure 12.6).

FIGURE 12.6 Voter Turnout Rates, 1990–2018

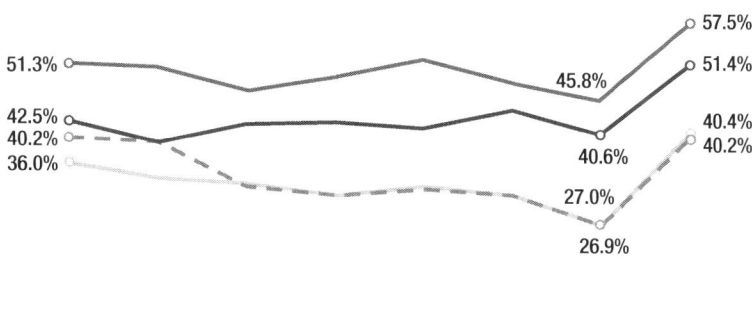
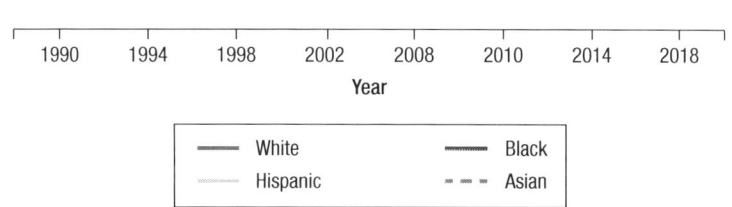

Source: Pew Research Center analysis of the Current Population Survey, November Supplements, 1990–2018.

In Figure 12.5, the trend lines demonstrate the significant gains in the number of Latino eligible voters, which increased by 15 percent over a span of seven years. The gains made by both naturalized voters and second-generation Latino citizens increased by 21.1 percent. The latter group represents sons and daughters of Latino immigrants who may or may not have become naturalized citizens. It is noteworthy that in a relatively short period of time (i.e., seven years), the increase in any category of eligible voters was in double-digit figures.

Socioeconomic developments among Latinos have contributed to a more concrete reality and impact for Latinos. That is, a portion of the growing population represents a greater percentage of younger Latinos reaching eighteen years of age. The continuing percentage of Latinos attaining voting age and/or becoming naturalized citizens has reached a critical mass, meaning that gains in numbers of voter registrants will be steeper than during the previous fifteen years. This development is also reflected in the increasing numbers of Latinos who are registered and make up a larger proportion of the electorate (Jamieson, Shinn, and Day 2002; Taylor et al. 2012a).

In updating some socioeconomic gains among Latinos since the last edition of this book, the Latino community accounted for a combined $2.13 trillion in economic spending activity in 2015. Latinos are projected to account for nearly a quarter of the total US GDP growth by 2020. US-born Latinos own 600,000 businesses, accounting for $26 billion in business income, while non-US-born Latinos own 1.2 million businesses, accounting for $36.5 billion. Latinos make up a large share of the employment in the construction, agriculture, and leisure and hospitality industries and are credited with a significant portion of the total workforce's increase in the first half of this decade. Household income for Latinos reached $50,486 but is still well below the current national average of $61,372. Disparities in employment and earnings and changes to retirement accounts all contribute to the fact that many Latinos are not as prepared for retirement. Between 2013 and 2016, the median net worth for Latino households grew by more than 45 percent, but the overall net worth for Latino households still lags well behind white households.

Education attainment and enrollment among Latinos continues an upward trend, as Latinos have seen large education-related gains over the last decade, including a sharp decline in dropout rates and increases in both four- and two-year college enrollment. In 2015, 36 percent of Latinos between the age of eighteen and twenty-four were enrolled in college (either a four-year or two-year program), a 10 percent increase from the previous five years. In 2017, there were more than eleven million Latina women in the labor force, and that participation rate is only expected to increase, reaching nearly fourteen million by 2024. This trend will contribute to the Latino community being a larger portion of the labor force and population.

When socioeconomic improvement occurs among Latinos, it reinforces the social capital accumulation, individually and collectively, as a viable community. The results of the 2000 census showed a growing middle class among Latinos. More than 2.5 million Latino households earned between $40,000 and $140,000; from 1979 to 1999, the Latino middle class grew by 71.2 percent (Pimentel 2002). These households had a total purchasing power of $278 billion annually. With the addition of Latino households earning more than $140,000, the figure rose to $333 billion. With an expanding middle class, as well as a larger percentage of the population older than eighteen years of age, the political resource base for the Latino community will continue to provide opportunities for empowerment.

Similar developments are evident in other parts of the country. The Cuban community continues to expand its political presence in Florida, especially southern Florida. Mayors and city council members in many southern Florida cities (Miami, Hialeah, Coral Gables, etc.) are well represented by members of the Cuban community as well as administrators and public employees. Likewise, Cubans, both from southern Florida and other parts of the state (Tampa, St. Petersburg), serve in the state legislature. With the political redistricting in 2001, Cubans continued to expand their political representation at the local, state, and federal levels. In 2010, Marco Rubio was elected to the US Senate from Florida, and in 2015 he declared his candidacy for the Republican nomination for president. Eventually he withdrew from the race in the spring of 2016.

Latino organizations and other labor- and minority-driven groups have placed greater emphasis and taken more "independent" initiatives to advance the empowerment of Latino communities and their more salient issues. Poll results from Latino Decisions over the last three election cycles have shown that Latinos' major reason for political engagement is to advance their communities and is only secondarily partisanship. It has been a challenge to operate in a polarized partisan environment with less responsiveness and attention from the Republican Party. As a result, victories at the state and local levels could yield more concrete policy change. The national political arena remains a real challenge for sustained and continuous change and progress. The 2020 elections may provide more evidence as to how far Latinos have come in the American political system.

Latino Politics and the New Millennium: Some Possible Scenarios

Community constitutes ongoing links between leaders and the general Latino public as well as interactions on a variety of issues (housing, work, organizational life, and public policy). However, community does not require complete consensus and uniformity of thought. Our discussion of Latinos and politics characterizes community as an interconnected and interacting set of members who share basic goals and visions and can work together regularly to advance their objectives. This type of community is pragmatic and goal-oriented rather than ideologically "pure." Do significant gains in political participation and representation constitute a short-term pattern for Latinos, or do they indicate a more active political and economic future? In the upcoming pages, we have developed four possible scenarios for the future of Latino politics.

Scenario 1: Continual Latino Political Development

The following are five major contributing factors in the contemporary political development of Latinos: (1) activation of a greater segment of the Latino community in various forms of political involvement (local community involvement, organizational affiliation, political awareness, campaigning, voting, etc.); (2) external actions and developments that serve as catalysts for political involvement (anti-immigrant and English-only initiatives, concerns about cultural balkanization, attention from national political parties and leaders, etc.); (3) an increase of individual social capital among Latinos (gains in educational attainment and income, expanding adult populations and citizens, occupational mobility, etc.); (4) expanding organizational networks across Latino subgroup lines and collaborative efforts; and (5) heightened local political activities in communities throughout the United States.

This scenario portrays the future of Latino politics as one of continued progress in political capital and effectiveness. For this progress to continue, the intersection of leadership, organizations, and Latino publics must be expanded and made more integrative and cooperative. It is essential to build on the momentum established in the late 1990s and early 2000s. Maintaining political involvement and communication on the part of leaders and with the general Latino public serves to delineate more clearly the Latino policy agenda and its priorities and helps to pursue change on a continual basis. Latinos have positioned themselves in formal political institutions and operate in established organizational vehicles of advocacy and influence, and they constitute an expanding electorate.

Also included in this scenario are specific areas in which Latino political development can build. One is the accelerated conversion of Latinos as political actors by becoming more politically engaged. Organizational and local community efforts continue to encourage eligible Latino permanent resident aliens to naturalize. Such activities not only educate Latino immigrants and activate them to file for citizenship, but they also pressure the United States Citizenship and Information Services (USCIS) to be a more efficient and receptive agency to the Latino community and all immigrants. Under the current administration's practices, supportive actions are much less likely without a significant change in leadership, and the 2020 election becomes a benchmark of altering present-day punitive and restrictive immigration-related policies. The recent increases in Latino immigrant naturalization may slow due to the rising fees for filing for citizenship and additional "public charge" protocols for acquiring green cards.

It is critical to note that expansion of Latino political empowerment in the future will heavily depend on the extent to which Latinos are mobilized by external actors, including the parties, candidates, and interest groups. While we were able to show a good example of how effective and early mobilization proved valuable in 2018, we also demonstrated that far too many Latinos remain left out of the mobilization process. This must change for Latinos to be more powerful politically. The reality is unfortunately that this is somewhat of a vicious cycle, as the likelihood of mobilization agents increasing resources invested in the Latino community will depend on Latino turnout in 2020 and 2022, as these agents want to see a return on their investment.

Latino organizations and leaders are faced with designing immigration-related reform policies that not only serve the Latino "immigrant" community but enhance further Latino political development. Latino organizations are finding it more difficult to work with and/or pressure the **Department of Homeland Security** (DHS) to generate facilitating practices for shortening the time between filing for naturalization and final swearing in. Agency actions to maintain civil rights protections (due process for deportation hearings, access to higher education for undocumented students, workplace protection, etc.) are part of a changed policy agenda for Latinos. In the case of the latter, more systematic prosecutions of apprehended undocumented immigrants have resulted in family separations, formal deportation hearings and sentencing, incarcerations, and more restrictive and punitive legislation affecting immigrants. As a result, the primary importance of immigration reform has cut across virtually all segments of the Latino community. Operating in a hostile environment with less-responsive political institutions presents tactical and power-related challenges to devising schemes and broadening coalition efforts for political impact.

Under the Trump administration, immigration policy was very much at the national forefront. The tone and level of rancor polarized this policy area even more than in the past. A recent Latino Decisions poll indicated that Latinos would disproportionately blame the Republican Party if immigration reform were not enacted. In contrast, during the presidential elections of 2008 and 2012, immigration was downplayed or rarely mentioned. Latinos have always been the focal point of immigration policy as Latino immigrants (and at times, all Latinos) have been viewed as contributors to the negative side of immigration, especially the undocumented. This "hostile" environment has drawn more Latinos into the policy debate, through both the stigmatization of foreigners and the growing connectedness among Latinos with family, friends, and coworker networks in the undocumented community (Latino Decisions 2014). Figure 12.7 shows the overall disapproval of Latinos for President Trump and dissatisfaction with the direction of the country. Yet there is some variation based on the partisan affiliation of Latinos, such that Latino Republicans are less disapproving and dissatisfied.

The absence of policy progress at the national level has caused partisan distance from the traditionally supported Democratic Party and a greater divide with the Republican Party. Political development for Latinos would require more concrete policy action that is more in concert with the Latino policy immigration preferences (stabilizing residence, pathway to citizenship, decriminalizing undocumented entry, civil rights and protections) (Latino Decisions 2014). At best, the current policy initiatives, with their more stringent immigration guidelines and penalties, are reminiscent of the Immigration Reform and Control Act of 1986, a sort of déjà vu experience. Stopgap efforts are necessary, but Latinos need to continue to push for actual reform and to form alliances with those of similar interests in order to gain the power necessary to challenge those representatives bent on obstructing (or hindering) Latino policy proposals.

Political partisanship among Latinos is reaching a critical juncture. Although Latinos support the Democratic Party and its candidates, that support has been waning, and the relationship between Latinos and the Democratic Party is soft. This was

FIGURE 12.7 Hispanic Voters' Disapproval of President Trump and Dissatisfaction with the Nation's Direction

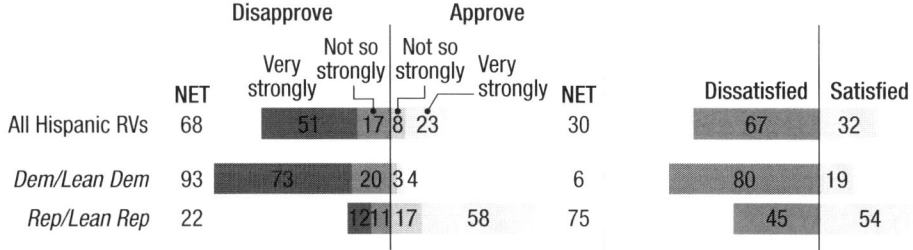

Source: National Survey of Latinos conducted December 3–23, 2019.

recently demonstrated by Morín, Macías Mejía, and Sanchez (2020), who have found that ethnic identity has become just as, and arguably more, powerful in driving Latino voting behavior than partisanship over the past several elections. However, the Republican Party is not benefiting from this partisan shift either; movement is directed more toward the independent category (Lopez, Gonzalez-Barrera, and Krogstad 2014). Although not exclusive, immigration is a central component of Latinos' assessment of both political parties. In pursuing partisan strategies, a clear challenge is the relatively low responsiveness and decision-making position of Latinos within the Democratic Party and the unwelcoming, and even hostile, tone of many of the Republican leaders (see figure 12.8). The long-standing issue has been party responsiveness and active participation in the party's actions and policy emphasis. Data from Latino Decisions has consistently noted that while the current climate surrounding immigration has posed significant challenges for the GOP to maintain strong relationships with this important voting bloc, there is a path for the GOP to repair relationships with Latinos if they are willing to change their language and position surrounding immigration.

While there is a tendency to portray politics in national terms, attention to local issues and politics is critical for greater Latino political development. Local issues such as housing, jobs, crime and law enforcement, social services, gentrification, schools and educational services, and access to decision makers are primary concerns and conditions that many Latinos face daily. By focusing on the most pertinent and visible issues, Latinos continue to expand political skills and accumulate experience from which to learn for future political involvement. The "politics is local" dictum involves getting people engaged in matters affecting their daily lives, thus affording

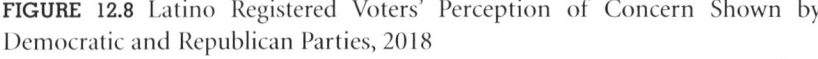

FIGURE 12.8 Latino Registered Voters' Perception of Concern Shown by Democratic and Republican Parties, 2018

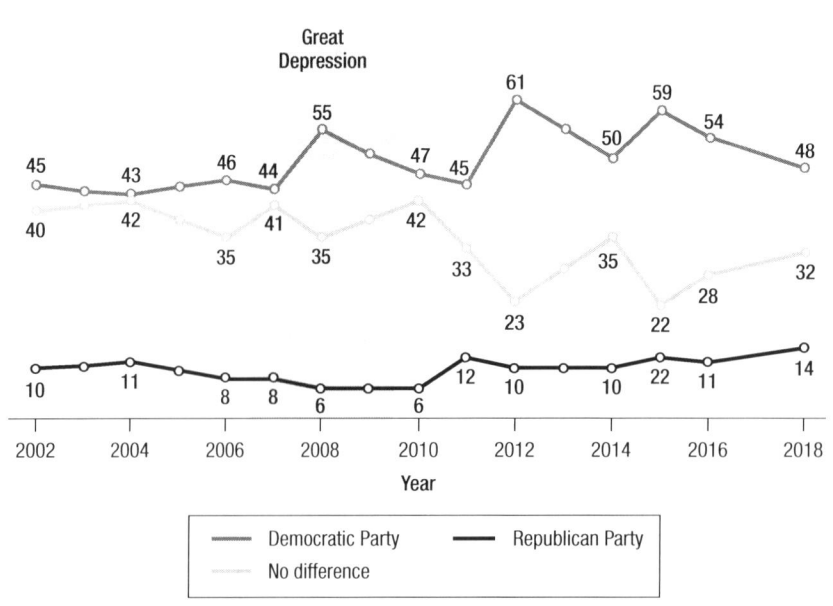

Source: Lopez et al. 2018.

the opportunity to interact, use skills, gain greater political awareness and knowledge, accumulate valuable civic experiences, and be mobilized by organizations advocating Latino interests. Many state and local governments have initiated ordinances and laws affecting undocumented immigrants in a variety of settings (employment, housing, health services, court standing, etc.). The direct effect has been the activation of a broad spectrum of the Latino community. Many Latino organizations have legally challenged state and local laws and have campaigned against incumbents who have pushed for punitive immigration laws. Another consequence has been Latino organizations being actively involved and working jointly with immigration advocacy organizations and labor unions. In the future, more of these policy-driven issues will provide opportunities for Latinos to establish ongoing networks of political alliances, not only on immigration, but with the **United States Mexico Canada Agreement (USMCA),** health-care reform, minimum wage changes, social welfare policies, and other common policy areas of concern.

A second area requiring attention is the greater degree of interaction across the multitude of Latino subgroups. How do Latinos of many different national origins interact and come together in a variety of social and economic situations? The regional concentration of Latino subgroups is less rigidly defined with greater residential and labor market overlap (living and working in the same areas), affording Latinos greater opportunities to establish a broader sense of community. However, as we've discussed, increased interactions do not guarantee harmonious and cooperative ventures, so the roles of leadership and the framing of common issues and visions become important elements in this equation. The litany of Latino organizations that meet annually (**National Hispana Leadership Institute** [NHLI], UnidosUS, **Hispanic Association of Colleges and Universities** [HACU], National Association of Latino Elected and Appointed Officials [NALEO], etc.) serve as examples of bringing together all Latinos for common concerns, actions, and community building.

In the first edition of this book, the discussions of Latinos and politics revolved largely around the Mexican-origin community, Cubans, and Puerto Ricans. As a contemporary portrayal of the changing Latino community indicates, the inclusion and involvement of Central and South Americans, as well as Dominicans, is essential. Together they form an integral part of the Latino political-development scenario. These other Latino subgroups are becoming more actively engaged in issues particular to their respective communities. In many respects, issues about immigration status and adjustment, refugee policies (especially for Central Americans), basic services, employment training and opportunities, educational quality, and language assistance are very similar issues of importance to Mexican-origin people, Puerto Ricans, and Cubans.

While the relative proportion of the Mexican-origin community remains at slightly more than three-fifths of all Latinos, the growth of Central and South Americans and Dominicans has been dramatic. More recently the growth of South American immigrants are additional mixes to the Latino community.

Each Latino subgroup has been developing its own political capital (political resources, organizations, leadership base, political knowledge, and experience with its own political and economic institutions). As they do so, issues, interests, and the utility of collaborative efforts with other Latino subgroups become clearer. An emphasis on lines of communication and mutual discussions across Latino subgroups can further collective political empowerment and political-economic agendas. There is evidence that such linkages in the 1990s and continuation of these developments will enhance Latino political development.

The **Congressional Hispanic Caucus Institute** (CHCI), United States Hispanic Leadership Institute (USHLI), and National Hispanic Leadership Agenda (NHLA) are good examples of organizational efforts to bring Latinos together around policy issues, political education, and leadership development. The CHCI provides leadership development programs and educational services to students and young emerging Latino leaders. USHLI tries to fulfill the promises and principles of democracy by promoting education, research, and leadership development and by empowering Latinos and similarly disenfranchised groups by maximizing their civic awareness, engagement, and participation. The NHLA annual conference produces a Hispanic Policy Agenda, which is a comprehensive document that addresses prime policy issues facing Hispanics in eight main issue areas: education, civil rights, immigration, economic security and improvement, health, government accountability, environment and energy, and criminal justice. These are organizations that are interconnected and use a pan-ethnic policy agenda to facilitate open lines of communication and collective efforts, even with partisan and ideological differences. Although there is a history of shared concerns about social welfare policies, immigration and refugee adjustments, language-focused legislation, expanding Latino political influence, and numerous other issues, it would be less than realistic to expect complete consensus across all members of any caucus all the time.

The third area of consideration in furthering Latino political development is an extension of the first. We have already discussed mobilizing more Latinos to become politically involved in their communities, better informed politically, and more experienced in civic affairs, and in the first area of examination, converting the significant, growing population. This third area focuses on expanding economic resources from which Latino political endeavors would benefit. Studies such as the CMPS (2016) provide additional documentation and assessment of the sociopolitical world of Latinos and areas of strength, gains, and remaining challenges.

Economic resources come from both individuals and the business sector. Recent Latino political and economic advancement, the persistence of salient issues, and economic mobility and growth among Latino professionals and entrepreneurs serve as identifiable economic resources for the Latino community. Obviously, the linkage assessing their needs, interests, and affinities with the activities of Latino organizations and groups is a necessary condition. While many may see this type of focus directed toward more nationally visible Latino-based organizations, the act of directing money toward a variety of efforts (charities, neighborhood activities, specific projects, local organizations, etc.) not only benefits specific recipients but also further establishes the need for, and impact of, greater economic resources derived from Latinos to address common concerns and issues. Related to this point is the potential for Latinos to "flex their consumer muscles" more effectively to use their economic buying power as a leverage point to advance the causes they feel are important.

Given recent Supreme Court decisions, our final, but important, discussion is the future of the Voting Rights Act. The "removal" of Section 4 of the VRA neutralized the preclearance section, which many Latino communities had used to change election voting systems, redistricting boundaries, and voter identification laws (Sanchez and

Morin 2011). Section 3 still enables actions of election-related changes for jurisdictions that have a history of racial/ethnic exclusion, but the evidentiary burden will be steep. In addition, challenges to the differential effects of voter identification laws, current challenges to the drawing of legislative districts based only on eligible voters (rather than the total population), and the removal of birthright citizenship to children of undocumented residents all have direct bearing on the Latino electorate and their potential to have greater electoral import. The drawing of districts based upon eligible voters has direct implications on Latino political power. The CVAP (Citizen Voter Age Population) has been drawn by Republican strategists to neutralize the growing minority population by not recognizing persons younger than age eighteen and noncitizens as part of the redistricting population base. The post-census 2020 counts, and how reapportionment files will be used, whether based upon decennial census counts of the total population as opposed to CVAP, have a bearing on Latino representation in the future, if this argument is judicially successful.

Scenario 2: A Symbolic Pan-Ethnic Community and Independent Actions

Our second scenario regarding the future of Latino politics reaffirms the existence of some level of a pan-ethnic community among the various Latino subgroups, but with a more symbolic tone. "Community" connotes identifying and associating with perceived similar people, as well as maintaining a level of awareness and public recognition of Latinos as a social category. Thus, our second scenario suggests that the Latino umbrella takes on a more symbolic, intermittent connection for public presentation. The advent of Latinos as a group is the result, in part, of governmental policies that combined, or "merged," the various Latino subgroups into a larger grouping. The mass media chooses to characterize persons and nationalities of Spanish origin under the general category of Latinos or Hispanics. This can also reinforce general awareness of a symbolic community.

This scenario posits a limited basis for the idea of a broader Latino community, which is motivated by pragmatic collaboration, but, for the most part, each Latino subgroup pursues its own political agenda. Therefore, the similarities or cultural connections that may exist among the various Latino subgroups are not enough to form an ongoing, working community. This pan-ethnic Latino community is more likely to consist of loose networks and connections, operating as a loosely fitting collection of different Latino subgroups, that may use the term "Latino," but are referring primarily to their own national-origin group. The concept of **loose coupling** has some relevance here as it is an approach of interconnecting components in a system or network, so that those components (also called elements) depend on each other to the least extent practicable. For example, a Latino-based group presenting before a Tucson city council meeting may describe their interests as Latinos' even though the group is comprised exclusively of Mexican-origin members.

Another recent example of this "loose coupling" pan-ethnic community can be seen in Cuba's attempts to dismantle Castro's communist regime while maintaining trade embargoes and expanding refugee admissions. The policy objectives have been more salient for the Cuban community than the rest of the Latino subgroups. The actions by the Obama administration to normalize relations between Cuba and the United States reflected a greater support among non-Cuban Latino leaders, as well as a shift among the general Cuban population, toward a change in past policies. The contemporary Cubans have become more diverse, demographically and in their political perspectives. Just as we have suggested that the wider mix of Latino subgroups is affecting intergroup dynamics, issues, and interactions, it would seem these dynamics will affect Latino subgroups internally. The Cuban American political leadership still pursues policies that continue to pressure the Cuban government to open the political system and institute more democratic changes. Actions such as opposing the nomination of the ambassador to Cuba, funding an embassy in Cuba, and continued trade embargoes would change if certain political accommodations are made by Cuba.

Legalizing the immigration status of Central Americans, especially Salvadorans, Guatemalans, and Hondurans, by recognizing political refugee status may be more salient among the affected groups—Salvadorans, Guatemalans, and Nicaraguans—than among Puerto Ricans or Cubans. Continued political violence, drug cartels, domestic abuse, and other destabilizing conditions have seen more Mexican nationals seeking asylum. At the same time, US-Mexico agreements on immigration (border enforcement, providing asylum and asylee assistance) have placed Mexico between US policies and Central Americans' interests. Recognizing political refugee status is an area of US immigration policy that could be incorporated within a broader set of reforms supported by the entire Latino community or by some of the Latino subgroups. The currently stepped-up "campaigns" of ICE to deport immigrants, especially Central American children (unaccompanied or not) and parents, as well as eliminating TPS for northern triangle Central Americans, might result in a joint effort across the Latino communities.

The political status of Puerto Rico (statehood, independence, commonwealth) and the immediate closing of the Vieques site for bomb testing have been of great concern for the Puerto Rican community. More recently, the current financial crisis in Puerto Rico that could possibly bankrupt the commonwealth has been an even greater concern among Puerto Ricans and their leadership. Congressmen Velasquez (NY) and Gutierrez (IL), along with the governor of Puerto Rico, have made impassioned requests for Congress to pass legislation that could alleviate the debt crisis. Partisan lines indicate unwillingness by the Republican Party to initiate any legislation; the Democratic Party leadership has presented a bill to place a temporary stay on Puerto Rico's creditors until Congress acts, a bill that is not expected to be successful. In 2019, political dissent was largely responsible for the resignation of Puerto Rican governor Ricardo Rossello, whose obscenity-laced online messages with eleven other men in his administration about women infuriated Puerto Ricans who were already frustrated with corruption, mismanagement, economic crisis, and the sluggish recovery from Hurricane Maria nearly two years earlier. Hurricane Maria and earthquakes in early 2020 strengthened the connections between mainland and island Puerto Ricans. Even though more Puerto Ricans live on the US mainland, political and personal interests run high among both; other Latinos have also been involved in relief and support efforts for island residents.

The focus and perspective on very specific issues by each Latino subgroup may be limited to their respective communities or may occupy a lower priority for other Latino subgroups. This scenario would reinforce the decision of each Latino subgroup to pursue its own interests, consistent with its own salient issues, through its own organizations and activities, portraying more of an either/or contingency. However, our scenarios are not mutually exclusive, and the "intermittent" involvement is related to pan-ethnic identification and networks. Dominicans in New York City may be seeking redress for poor educational quality (poor facilities, lack of curricular offerings, need for bilingual programs, etc.) in their neighborhood schools. In their public actions and public discourse, especially with the media, Dominican leaders may refer to these specific problems or concerns as Latino issues. Doing so can afford other Latino subgroups the opportunity to support their efforts, as well as to piggyback in addressing their specific issues to the same political institutions.

Another factor that may influence the preference and reality of individual Latino subgroups going their own way is the assessment that each is in competition with the other. Again, referring to the Dominican community in the New York City area, Dominican political and economic issues and concerns are viewed as vying for recognition and policy responsiveness with those of Puerto Ricans, Colombians, and other Latino subgroups. Advancement can be viewed as a potential zero-sum game, in which the political system pits one group against the other for limited resources. Thus, Latino politics becomes a competition among various subgroups for political recognition, policies, and rewards. Specific Latino groups that have accumulated political resources and positions will try to maintain their power position, while the other Latino subgroups may view the established groups as impeding their own progress.

In Florida, there exists some inter-Latino tension, especially in southern Florida, between the Cuban community, several Central and South American groups (Panamanians, Nicaraguans, Venezuelans, Colombians, etc.), and Puerto Ricans. This competition centers, in part, on access, influence, and power in southern Florida and statewide. The noticeable influx of Puerto Ricans in the Orlando metropolitan area adds to the wider mix of Latino subgroups. Competition over economic policies that affect non-Cuban Latinos and concerns over political representation and access may be directed more toward the Cuban political leadership and organizations, as they are the established Latino political community.

The presence of a Latino/a presidential candidate or other national level leader may provide an opportunity to explore whether this scenario will play out in the future. Two contemporary examples provide support for this scenario. The historic nomination of Justice Sotomayor to the Supreme Court of the United States provided an opportunity to examine how this major event for the Latino community was viewed by the community. Analysis of Google search data suggested that the greatest interest in this event was in New York City and other areas with high Puerto Rican population. This led the research to conclude that Puerto Rican identity may have triggered the most pronounced attention to the event, indicative of the enduring salience and attachments to particularized national-origin groups.[1] Furthermore, analysis of available survey data for recent Latino presidential candidates suggests that these potential leaders have had a difficult time gaining traction with Latino voters outside of their specific region and national-origin group. Until a prominent Latino leader can capture the hearts and minds of Latinos across all national-origin groups and regions of the nation, there may remain speculation that this scenario is the dominant model for Latino pan-ethnic identity.

The competitive nature of relations among Latino subgroups tends to accentuate intergroup differences rather than commonalties. As a result, maintaining any competitive advantage restricts cooperative and collaborative ventures. Within this scenario, a broader representation of Latino politics can be advanced, despite the competitive tensions, if each Latino subgroup can portray a more public depiction of cooperativeness and unity while dealing with differences more directly in private forums. The analogy of keeping family matters and disparities *en la casa* while showing a unified public face outside the home fits this scenario of Latino politics. Thus, this approach requires looking at Latino communities as a confederation of overlapping interests where, under certain conditions, the communities may come together.

Scenario 3: A Latino Community with One or More "Outliers"

This scenario represents a limited community membership in which some Latino subgroups engage in collaborative and cooperative activities or regular joint relations. This limited form of Latino political community refers to broad-based organizations that are inclusive (in terms of constituencies, staffing, and agenda) of the various Latino subgroups. Thus, our theme of communities of common interests and cultures brings together most of the Latino subgroups to function as a political community, and it implies that Latino subgroups or coalitions may join forces outside the Latino communities. We have discussed the broadening of alliances and coalitions outside the Latino community in chapter 11, and these activities are certainly part of scenarios 1 and 3.

The outlier component of this scenario suggests that one or more Latino subgroups will pursue their own agenda rather than negotiate or compromise with other Latino subgroups on their public policy agenda (policies in force or proposed alternatives) by identifying their own issue priorities. In addition, each Latino subgroup uses its own political resources, base, and accumulated experiences of effectiveness to continue its own path. Intragroup solidarity with established lines of political and economic communication and influence, clarity of political objectives, and relative unanimity among its leaders are factors that may encourage an "outlier" to operate in the American political system without active membership in the broader Latino community.

The Cuban community provides an example of an outlier community in which their central political objectives have distanced them, somewhat, from the larger Latino community. Its long-standing, defined, and active involvement in shaping US foreign policy regarding Castro's Cuba remains a central core of the Cuban policy agenda because of the primacy of this issue. Since 2005 there have been different sets of policy orientations (normalizing relations, removing the trade embargo, adjusting Cuban refugee admission) on the part of other Latino activists and politicians. Some of these actions have contributed to Cubans' distancing themselves (policy-wise) from the larger Latino community. The extended political battle over Elian González[2] and the fervency and sustained effort within the Cuban community in addressing it has not been mirrored to the same degree by other Latino communities and leaders. The amount of expended political capital and mass media portrayal of the Cuban community served, in part, to accentuate policy divergence and tensions between Cubans and other Latinos. A possible mediating force within the Cuban community is the growing segment of native-born (second-generation) Cubans whose political preferences and foci can differ noticeably from those of their parents' generation. Clearly, more recent polls indicate that second-generation Cubans' political views are different from those of their parents' generation.

A possible benefit for the Cuban community when exploring this outlier model is their close ties, not shared by most other Latino subgroups, to the Republican Party. This relatively long-standing pattern heightens intergroup competitiveness as the Republican Party seeks to make greater inroads with other Latinos and to highlight differences in policy preferences. The regional concentration of Cubans (nearly 90 percent live in Florida, especially southern Florida) makes them a political base with greater socioeconomic status and resources than other Latinos. Their strong group politicization operates as an independent basis of action and encourages them to follow their own path. Contributing strongly to the outlier strategy or position of Cubans in the United States is the strength of their organizations, their relative success in penetrating political institutions, their economic resources and entrepreneurial activities, and their commitment to a clearly defined agenda. More recently, the presidential candidacies of Marco Rubio and Ted Cruz have attracted the Tea Party and other conservative segments' endorsement and support. Yet, their ideological and policy positions do not align very well with Latino political opinion and policy preferences. Similar ties have been evident among Latino evangelicals and politically conservative action groups. In a very significant way, these examples outline a tension between a co-ethnic leadership and the ideological and policy preferences of the Latino constituency. While being a co-ethnic can dispose Latinos or specific national-origin group members to be supportive, it is not enough to solidify their vote.

Does a Latino subgroup operate as an outlier for an indefinite period? Even if the outlier scenario continues, there are symbolic and public perceptions of linkages between Cubans and other Latino communities. In addition, this scenario does not preclude interaction, dialogue, and joint support between the outlier and the rest of the Latino community. For example, on matters of economic development initiatives, sampling adjustments for Census 2000, affirmative action, benefits and services to immigrants, language policies, and voting rights (National Council of La Raza 1999), Cuban members of the US House of Representatives voted in accord with the other Latino representatives. Therefore, this approach lays out an independent direction and control of the agenda, strategies, and priorities within a specific Latino subgroup. A major element of our scenarios is the extent of collective activities across Latino subgroups and the frequency of such collaborations.

An outlier Latino subgroup does not function in isolation. Other Latino subgroups might move in the same direction if good working relations do not exist within the broader Latino community or if their agendas and priorities do not receive adequate attention and support. An assessment of group resources and strengths may indicate that pursuing an independent path might be an effective approach. This third scenario shows how the concept of community can organize itself in a way that some semblance of community exists while functioning more meaningfully within the various subcommunities.

Scenario 4: Weakening Ethnic Attachments and Identity Leads to a Diminished Latino Community in the Future

One of the most thought-provoking trends we identified in the data focused on the apparent drop in ethnic attachment and identity among two specific subgroups of the Latino population, the more socially acculturated and the youngest cohort of Latinos. In chapter 5 we discussed findings from a recent Pew Hispanic Research Center report that found pan-ethnic identity to be lowest among Americans with Spanish-origin ancestry four generations or more removed from the immigration experience (Lopez, Gonzalez-Barrera, and Lopez 2017). For review, in that chapter we noted that while 97 percent of foreign-born respondents who have Latino ancestry define themselves as Latino or Hispanic, that number falls to only 50 percent among those who are fourth generation or greater! When asked why this is the case in an open-ended follow-up question in their study, the single most common response (27 percent) was that their Hispanic ancestry was too far back, or their background is mixed, which led to not thinking of themselves as Latino or Hispanic. This report raises an important question of how strong or meaningful Latino identity will be in the future as the Latino population continues to evolve through both intermarriage and slowed external migration (see Figure 12.9).

Reinforcing this finding was the work we discussed in that chapter that suggests that linked fate among Latinos is greater among Latino immigrants and decreases significantly with further distance from the immigrant experience in subsequent generations. In fact, the authors of one study cited in that chapter combined language use and nativity to show the stark difference in linked-fate levels among Latinos who are foreign-born and Spanish dominant and who had the highest levels of linked fate, from those who are English dominant and US born and who had much lower levels of linked fate. The role of language in this research is key, as research discussed early in the book suggested that Spanish-language usage and skills were highly correlated with age, with younger Latinos being less likely to speak Spanish.

FIGURE 12.9 Identification among Americans with Hispanic Ancestry as Hispanic or Latino across Immigrant Generations

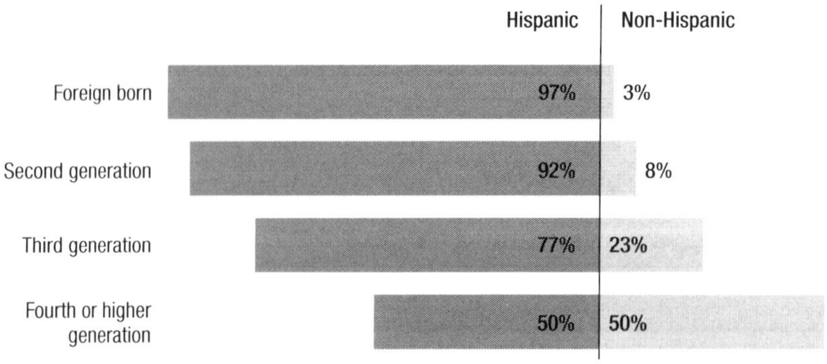

	Hispanic	Non-Hispanic
Foreign born	97%	3%
Second generation	92%	8%
Third generation	77%	23%
Fourth or higher generation	50%	50%

Source: Pew Research Center 2015 National Survey of Latinos (October 21–November 30, 2015) and survey of self-identified non-Hispanics with Hispanic ancestry or heritage only (November 11, 2015–February 7, 2016).

Given that the demographic projections we discussed early in the book indicated that Latino population growth has shifted from being predominately driven by external migration to growth in the US-born population, these findings related to acculturation and identity are very interesting and important. Will Latinos become less attached to their ethnic identity as they become less attached to the immigrant experience and more likely to speak Spanish? If so, what consequences will this have for Latino politics given the strong relationship linked fate and group consciousness have on all aspects of Latino political behavior?

Although this is an important question that must be monitored closely, we temper speculation of a weakening or diminished Latino community due to decreased ethnic identity among Latinos. Our perspective is based on the research on racial and ethnic identity, which has identified discrimination to be the most prominent driver of identity formation for all racial and ethnic minorities, including Latinos. Latino Decisions begins all their surveys with a basic question of what are the most important issues facing your community that the president and Congress should address? While issue areas including immigration, health care, and education consistently rank among the most salient issues identified by respondents, a growing percentage of Latinos are indicating that stopping or addressing anti-Latino racism is one of their top two priorities.

This is a recent phenomenon, as prior to 2016 this was not an issue that had more than a handful of mentions but is now consistently in the top 5 priorities. If discrimination continues to be a major concern for Latinos, this will be a driver for linked fate and other forms of Latino identity to remain strong and maybe even increase. Finally, although it is true that external migration from Latin America has slowed, this is not set in stone. As we discuss in detail in this book, migration patterns wax and wane, driven by a host of push and pull factors. If the global economy shifts alongside revisions to our national and state-level immigration policies that are more welcoming to immigrants, there is no reason to believe that Latin American migration patterns will not increase to be more similar to the trends witnessed in the 1990s and early 2000s. If so, not only will ethnic identity be influenced by the direct effects associated with more immigrants who have strong ethnic attachments across the population, but also by the indirect effects on US-born Latinos, whose relationships with their family and friends will include more immigrants. In many ways, the future of Latino politics may depend more on the outcome of this scenario than any other.

Conclusion: Latinos, Community, and Politics— A Dynamic Process

In this book, the concept of community is developed as a series of interacting links among persons of Spanish origin and their experiences in the United States to form the basis of a political community. The concepts of community of common cultures and community of interests have served as the organizing theme for the discussion of Latinos and their involvement in American politics. Given the diversity of national origins captured by the general description of Latinos or Hispanics, an immediate challenge lies in portraying and integrating important characteristics and experiences among twenty-plus national-origin groups. Demographic profiles, historical developments and experiences, and issue concerns provide some evidence of Latino community dynamics. Clearly the political development of Latino subgroups and Latinos as a broader community have evolved and will continue to do so. Over time, the dynamisms of internal changes inside the Latino communities, and the external developments of public opinion, political climate, partisan response, and the like will drive and define Latino politics in the future.

Political actors, institutions, and parties, the mass media, public opinion, and the general social climate recognize that Latinos are not only altering the demographic landscape but also affecting political processes, agendas, and decision-making institutions. The theme of potentiality and promise, which has characterized discussions of Latinos for generations, has moved dramatically beyond speculation since the mid-1990s. We have explored those developments as well as the issues and challenges that still confront greater Latino political effectiveness and more widespread political involvement. At the same time, political progress has not been linear; seeking political power is usually accompanied by countering moves to create obstacles and/or reestablish another group's political advantage.

Future analysis, interpretation, and discussion of Latinos and their politics and impact must be placed within a dynamic context. The internal forces of Latino activists, their ideas and perspectives, and their strategy assessments will affect the development and continued shaping of Latino politics and their intergroup dialogues.

As mentioned previously, the external climate and actions taken by political institutions, actors, and interest groups create political scenarios that are played out at many political levels (state, local, national, and even global). Continued attention to improving intergroup communication and cooperation is part of future Latino political development. Further expansion of political resources (active participants, financial resources, positive participatory orientations, organizational infrastructures and resources) serves to enhance the growing political capital of Latinos and define their direction and purpose. Our examination of Latino politics has both a historical context and a dynamic nature, revealing an evolving sense of community and how it can work in the American political system. In a very real sense, the ongoing discussion of these developments and important contributors precludes any formal ending to the fourth edition of this book.

The whole expanse of intergroup relations outside the Latino community will play an even greater role as Latinos reach enough partnership status to warrant serious working collaborations with other political communities. An additional evolving component is the role of partisanship and the major political parties. Both parties have become very polarized and serve to divide the Latino communities along the lines of religious fervor and evangelical affiliations, possibly class, and generation. The last category represents Latinos who are three and four generations removed from their immigrant ancestors. It appears that the Democratic Party is trying to broaden its Latino base, seemingly more engaged in integrating Latinos into the core of their organizations and decision-making structures, while a possible Republican Party strategy is to target either specific Latino subgroups or segments within, as we just described above. For Democrats, maintaining their competitive advantage is a primary factor, but Latinos are more critical and conditional as to how the party needs to respond to them. The Republican Party could be served by sorting out a policy and ideological map that has appeal to segments of the Latino community. Electorally, if the Republican candidates can penetrate 25 to 35 percent of Latino voters, they can provide a critical supplement to their primary base.

As for Latino political aspirants, somewhat regardless of party affiliation, pathways to elected office may depend on a knowledgeable and activated Latino base that is supportive of Latino candidates that address their community's interests. The relevance and intrigue of Latino politics lies with its dynamic nature and the many paths toward greater empowerment and influence in the American political system. Hopefully this discussion indicates curiosity, evaluation, and closer contact with American politics for readers.

Discussion Questions

1. We have suggested that Latinos' political capital and influence in American politics is still on an upward trajectory. Yet, promise and potential have been long-standing themes in Latino politics. What concrete indicators and developments would support this positive assessment of Latino political development?
2. While we have presented four scenarios to project the future of Latino politics, can other scenarios be developed and substantiated?
3. An ongoing issue for Latinos is how they will participate in partisan politics. Despite a long-standing preference for the Democratic Party, some have argued that the returns for such loyalty have been quite limited. What would you suggest as effective partisan strategies for Latinos?
4. Demographically, one could characterize the Latino community as more diverse (in terms of size and number of national-origin groups, especially Central and South Americans); the proportion that is of Mexican origin, however, continues to dominate the Latino landscape. How does the mix of Latino subgroups affect the political development of the overall Latino community?

Notes

1. https://latinodecisions.com/blog/the-sotomayor-nomination-evidence-of-panethnic-political-interest.
2. Elian González was a six-year-old Cuban émigré whose mother and her significant other attempted to cross the Caribbean Sea in the spring of 2000. They took Elian with them. Both adults died at sea, and young Elian was rescued by the Coast Guard and taken to a hospital in Miami. Subsequently, an uncle in Miami sought to secure asylum for him, which began a major national debate and a political incident involving the Cuban government, Fidel Castro, the INS, the Department of Justice, the Cuban community and leadership, and eventually the Office of the President. Through a protracted legal battle, and despite rulings by the INS and the federal courts for the return of Elian González to his father in Cuba, the Cuban family, supported by the Cuban community, refused to surrender him to the authorities. Eventually an early morning INS "raid" secured Elian from the Miami relatives, and ultimately, he was reunited with his father.

CHAPTER 13

COVID Pandemic and Racial Justice Movements

THE COVID-19 PUBLIC HEALTH PANDEMIC that was declared a national emergency in the United States in March of 2020 has fundamentally shifted ALL aspects of American life, creating the need for our book to include a brief summary of how this virus has impacted the Latino community. Our discussion below draws on the best data available at the time of publication to identify how Latinos have fared in regard to COVID-19 infection and casualty rates, financial stress caused by the severe virus-driven recession, employment status, housing, politicization dimensions tied to election 2020, and the challenges Latino families have faced attempting to homeschool their children as schools moved away from in-person schooling due to fears of spreading the virus.

In short, COVID-19 has illuminated the large inequalities that Latinos face in the United Sates. This includes income inequality, educational quality and achievement, access to health-care coverage and governmental support programs, and so on. As more and higher-quality data becomes available on infection and death rates associated with COVID-19, there is no debating that Latinos have been disproportionately impacted. Data compiled by Dr. Rogelio Saenz for the forty-six states where data were available shows that Latinos are disproportionately overrepresented among people infected by the virus in forty-five states and are overrepresented among the deceased in sixteen.[1] The Centers for Disease Control (CDC) data we pulled from August 2020 showed that Latinos nationally were 2.8 times more likely to test positive for COVID-19, 4.8 times more likely than whites to be hospitalized, and 1.1 times more likely to die from the virus than whites. The *New York Times* (July 10, 2020) also reported on racial/ethnic disparities, relying primarily on CDC reports. They stated that Latinos were three times more likely to contract COVID and twice as likely to die from the virus.

Our mention of existing COVID-related data has raised some questions of quality and specificity of data to delineate possible differential effects of the pandemic among racial and ethnic groups. Clearly the extant data does show Latinos are experiencing higher rates of infection, hospitalization, and death. At the same time, in the United States overall, approximately 39 percent of the COVID cases did not have race or ethnicity identifiers, and the same is true for 10 percent of the death cases. In Texas, a much higher 91 percent of cases and 77 percent of deaths did not have a race and ethnicity identification (Sáenz 2020). By summer 2020, the spike in COVID cases was occurring more so in the southern and western United States. There is a considerable overlap of these geographic regions and significant numbers of Latino residents. It would be expected that COVID reporting with more complete race and ethnicity information would reinforce the racial/ethnic disparities.

Socioeconomic gaps with whites and being more vulnerable to economic downturns are contributing factors for Latinos. Surveys by Latino Decisions over the summer and fall of 2020 should help clarify the extent of COVID cases, hospitalizations, deaths, and the full range of impact on Latinos.

The disparity in COVID-19 outcomes between Latinos and whites is the result of a number of factors, including Latinos being over-represented among essential employees. The SOMOS Latino Decisions COVID-19 survey, for example, reports that 36 percent of Latinos nationally are still working outside of their homes, with 64 percent of that group of respondents worried that their working conditions are going to make them sick because employers are not fully implementing CDC mitigation guidelines as well as not taking the necessary precautions, such as requiring hand washing, wearing of masks or gloves, or providing them with the proper equipment to protect them.

In the case of meat- and poultry-processing-plant workers, even with additional protocols and equipment, the nature of their work makes it very difficult to establish social distancing. Similarly, agricultural workers (over-represented by Latinos) are most vulnerable to COVID and less able to meet the mitigation protocols (protected equipment, social distancing, etc.). Many Latinos live in multigenerational households, and quarantining is very difficult in small quarters, and many are trying to avoid losing workdays and the accompanying pay. Another contributing factor is the prevalence of preexisting conditions such as diabetes, obesity, high blood pressure, and asthma, for which Latinos have higher rates of occurrence. Essential Latino workers in the "food chain" face external pressure from government and elected officials to minimally disrupt food production while subjecting themselves to higher COVID risk. Similarly, many essential health-care workers (including janitors, responders, aides, etc.) are Latino.

In addition to increased exposure to the virus through work obligations, Professor Sanchez and his colleagues identified the powerful role of structural racism in COVID-19 rates (Sanchez, Sayuri-Dominguez, and Vargas 2020). This includes living in segregated neighborhoods with high population density and poor air quality and having less access to health care. These authors also identified that Latinos and other communities of color were not responsible for their higher rates of COVID-19 infection, as they were more likely to make changes in their personal behavior to limit the spread of the virus. This includes wearing a mask or scarf in public.

Sanchez et al.'s article reinforces the existence of systematic inequities, as Latinos who try to implement COVID precautions can be limited by their living preconditions and location in the workforce. For example, President Trump signed a bill that would give workers two weeks of paid sick leave at 100 percent of the person's normal salary up to $511 per day. It would also provide up to twelve weeks of paid family and medical leave at 67 percent of a person's normal pay, up to $200 per day. In a worst-case scenario, 12 percent of the nation's 159 million workers could be left without any sick leave pay at all (Long 2020). Our current limited discussion of public policies aimed at assisting workers and families warrants future policy analysis of the coverage and benefits to Latinos.

As a result of layoffs and job loss, approximately 40 percent of Latino households are facing food insecurity compared to 20 percent of white households. The end of supplemental federal unemployment insurance payments and some protection from eviction at the end of July 2020 should have a more negative impact on the Latino community.

Latino Decisions data also identified that the economic impact of COVID-19 on Latino families across the country has been severe. Their National COVID-19 Family Survey conducted in June 2020 revealed that 29 percent of Latino families had someone in their household lose their job, and 33 percent had their business either closed completely or experienced a significant drop in revenue due to COVID-19. The rise in unemployment among Latinos has also generated a decrease in insurance coverage among families, as 37 percent of respondents indicated that they or someone in their household had lost their employer-provided insurance benefits. Among those who lost insurance, 54 percent reported that their children lost their insurance as well. Earlier research by Gómez-Aguiñaga et al. (2017) documents the lower rates of health insurance, and corresponding health-care utilization and access, that in a time of a pandemic makes Latinos (particularly Latino immigrants) even more vulnerable. This could unfortunately mean that the significant improvements in health coverage for Latino families through the implementation of the Affordable Care Act discussed in this book could be ultimately wiped out by the recession caused by COVID-19. As we write this chapter, the Supreme Court of the United States is considering the fate of the Affordable Care Act, with early indications from the court suggesting that they would reject requests by the Trump administration to kill the law altogether, though the individual mandate might be struck down as unconstitutional.

COVID, Latinos, and Schools

As the pandemic spread and a significant rise in cases occurred in March and the succeeding months, there were school closings and a move to distance learning for millions of children. Again, Latino Decisions, on behalf of Abriendo Puertas/ Opening Doors (June 19, 2020), conducted a national survey of Latino parents and grandparents who had children age eighteen or younger. The focus was on children's educational status and progress considering the spring school closings. Not unlike all parents, Latino families reported that 85 percent provided home schooling during the pandemic. Much national debate is occurring about the reopening of our schools in the fall of 2020. The Trump administration has been "pushing" for schools to reopen in a "normal" mode, while the current summer COVID resurgence has substantial percentages of parents and public health scientists expressing severe caution from a public health perspective. The administration's rationale is continued need to stimulate the economy, loss of educational time for students, and undue burden for parents to continue to homeschool. The results we are presenting offer survey data on where Latino parents and grandparents stand on school reopenings. Also, the survey results provide a clear "picture" of the impact of the spring closings on Latino households and what they prioritize for a successful reopening of schools.

How did Latino parents deal with the spring school closings, their challenges, and desires for changes in school for the fall? Two main challenges identified in the survey for Latino parents were access to high-speed internet for distancing learning and difficulty understanding the content of their children's lesson plans. In the case of the latter, math (59 percent), writing (49 percent), and science (47 percent) were the subjects they felt limited in when helping their children. The command of the subject was more acutely felt by Latinos living in rural areas, parents with less than a high school education, and predominantly Spanish speakers (Sanchez, Pedraza, and Vargas 2020).

With the possibility of schools reopening in fall 2020, Latino parents are very concerned about access to online tools and having the necessary computers. When asked what were the most important educational issues that government should address, assistance with online education (43 percent), more information on good school operation practices (36 percent), access to quality childcare for afterschool time (27 percent), better access to internet (26 percent), and access to early learning and day care (19 percent) were the top concerns. For Latino households with multiple children in school, no laptops or tablets or too many children for the number of laptops/tablets available were everyday realities (see figure 13.1).

Latino parents and grandparents in this Latino Decisions survey had serious concerns about what changes were necessary for schools to implement for opening in the fall. The major theme for a successful return centered on a safe and protective school environment. In figure 13.2, Latino parents and grandparents wanted to make sure classrooms were extensively cleaned and masks were required (87 percent). Given the politicization

FIGURE 13.1 Most Important Educational Issues Government Should Address

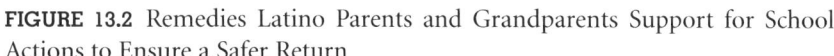

Source: Latino Decisions, 2020.

FIGURE 13.2 Remedies Latino Parents and Grandparents Support for School Actions to Ensure a Safer Return

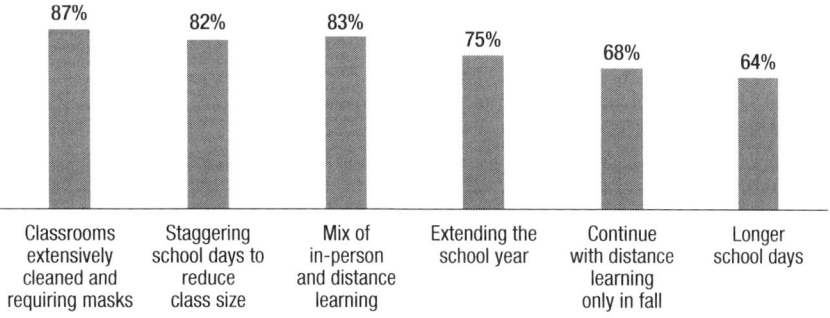

Source: Latino Decisions, 2020.

of wearing and requiring masks, Latinos were much more supportive of wearing masks as part of the COVID protocols. Adjustments to the school schedule (i.e., staggering days to reduce class size, hybrid of in-person and distance learning, extending the school year, etc.) reflect Latinos' strong preference for getting their children's educational experiences closer to normal, but not at the expense of greater risk of COVID for their children and the teachers who work with them. Absent the announcement of formal school distance opening protocols, already 58 percent of Latino parents/grandparents and caregivers were considering not sending their children in the fall.

At the same time, Latino parents were very worried about their children's educational progress or their children falling behind as a result of the pandemic. They suggested solutions that included availability of one-to-one tutoring and more in-person/virtual time with their children's teachers. This sentiment was more accentuated among immigrant parents. Finally, the survey results indicate a strong desire for regular communication with the school in direct personal or virtual participation. We had noted in chapter 10 the continual struggle for Latinos to achieve educational equity and quality. In a time of COVID, such goals add to their struggles and will ensure that education remains a salient issue for Latinos well into the future.

Amid a COVID Pandemic: Movement for Racial Justice and Police Abuse

We have demonstrated the differential impact of COVID, as well as how the pandemic has shed light on the structural inequalities Latinos face across a wide range of issues, such as health-care access and utilization, housing, labor market participation and equity, economic vulnerability, and governmental support and responsiveness. We close with a discussion of the national movement regarding police brutality that took place during the same period in response to police-related fatalities involving African Americans in several of our nation's cities.

While police abuse, excessive force, and fatal incidents with police have been a long-standing reality for the African American community and activists, the murder of George Floyd on May 25, 2020, by members of the Minneapolis police force resulted in almost unprecedented protests and calls for major structural reforms to combat institutional racism. Prior to George Floyd's death, cases involving Breonna Taylor, Ahmaud Arbery, and numerous other African American victims coincided with the police shootings of Andres Guardado (Gardenia, CA) and Carlos Ingram Lopez (Tucson, while in custody).

In our chapter on political alliances outside the Latino community, we noted the proclivity for and actual cooperative activities between Latinos and African Americans, in addition to other communities of color. Racial discrimination and socioeconomic and political disparities have been areas of common experiences and circumstances. The video footage of George Floyd being killed by the police and resultant nationwide protest resonated in the Latino community.

Again, the Latino Decisions survey on Latino families included items on racial discrimination, structural racism, and police violence. While data on police-involved shooting has been harder to track by race and ethnicity, it is clear that Latinos are more likely than whites to be killed by police. The survey indicated that 72 percent of Latino children had seen footage of the police officer placing his knee on George Floyd's neck.

FIGURE 13.3 Latinos Who Have Experienced Incidents of Excessive Force by Law Enforcement

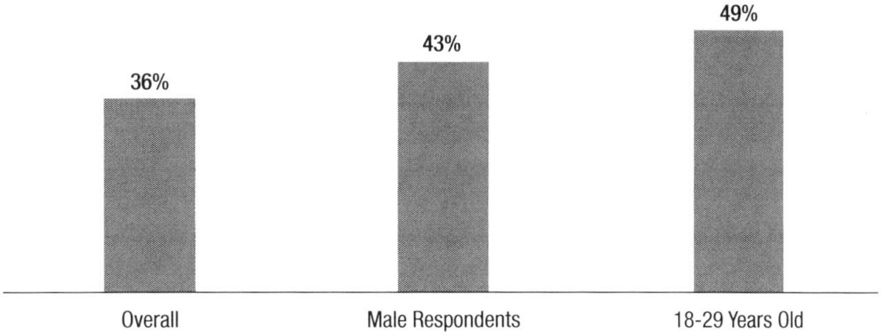

- Overall: 36%
- Male Respondents: 43%
- 18-29 Years Old: 49%

Source: Latino Decisions, 2020.

Fifty-six percent of Latino respondents reported watching this incident together as a family. Such exposure was followed by a robust 89 percent of these family watchers who made it an opportunity to discuss racial inequality and bias. For Latino families, this awareness highlighted a high level of fear about their children's dealings with law enforcement.

The survey also made clear that Latinos are concerned about police brutality and excessive force. A significant 81 percent of Latino respondents (including 91 percent of Spanish speakers) are worried that their children may encounter excessive force by the police. Part of that concern stems from personal experiences with law enforcement. As reflected in figure 13.3, 36 percent of the respondents or members of their household had an incidence of excessive force by the police. This percentage was higher for males (43 percent) and younger Latino/as in the eighteen to twenty-nine age range (49 percent). These shared experiences of Latinos and African Americans lead to a causal sense of solidarity based on police brutality and structural racism. Nearly 88 percent of Latino/a respondents said they understood the pain and frustration the black community feels as Latinos face a similar situation. While the racial justice movement continues, and there have been some policy changes and proposals, Latino politics is affected.

A central feature of Latino politics is the dynamic nature of Latino activism and engagement. While we are still in the midst of this worldwide pandemic, Latino political lives operate in a dynamic world. We suspect that many studies will be conducted on the widespread effects of COVID on the Latino community. The politicization of this pandemic, especially by the Trump administration, in addition to policy needs and poor policy responsiveness, to date, add to the motivations and issues that can affect Latino political mobilization and participation in the 2020 election. For example, efforts to expand vote by mail, in part driven by safeguarding voters from COVID, have become a battle. That is, using the theme of voter fraud and election integrity, President Trump and his supporters have opposed efforts to extend mail ballots, while proponents see their efforts as voter suppression disproportionately impacting minority communities.

President Trump's continued efforts to remove US residents who are suspected of being undocumented from the census population count for reapportionment have a direct bearing on the Latino community. We were encouraged by our publisher, Rowman & Littlefield, to add some discussion and analysis of the COVID pandemic and its impact on the Latino community. In doing so, we try to reinforce some common themes and understandings about the nature of Latino politics, already presented in this fourth edition. Issues of racial justice and discrimination, structural racism, and equality are central to Latino politics and their efforts to effect change.

Note

1. See the following for the full analysis: https://latinodecisions.com/blog/the-covid-19-rising-toll-on-latinos-a-look-at-the-beginning-of-july-2020.

Glossary

287(g) Program, one of ICE's top partnership initiatives, allows state and local law enforcement entities to enter into a partnership with ICE under a joint memorandum of agreement. The state or local entity receives delegated authority for immigration enforcement within its jurisdiction.

alternative voting systems are options that differ from the conventional plurality (winner-takes-all) or majority system used in American elections. They range from cumulative voting to limited voting, single transferable votes, and proportional voting schemes.

Antiterrorism and Effective Death Penalty Act of 1996 (ATEDPA) greatly facilitated procedures for the removal of "alien terrorists" and authorized state and local enforcement officials to arrest and detain certain undocumented persons and to provide access to confidential INS files through court order.

Arizona Senate Bill (SB) 1070, or the "Support Our Law Enforcement and Safe Neighborhoods Act," is a broad and strict anti–illegal immigration measure adopted in Arizona. US federal law requires certain aliens to register with the government and to keep registration documents in their possession at all times. SB 1070 makes it a state misdemeanor for an alien to be in Arizona without carrying the required documents, bars state and local officials and agencies from restricting enforcement of federal immigration laws, and penalizes those who shelter, hire, or transport "illegal aliens."

Senate Bill 1070, as amended by House Bill 2162:

1. prohibits state and local law enforcement from restricting the enforcement of federal immigration laws;
2. requires law enforcement, in making a lawful stop, detention, or arrest for another law, to make a reasonable attempt to determine the person's immigration status where reasonable suspicion exists that the person is not lawfully present in the country;
3. creates a new misdemeanor offense for the willful failure to complete or carry an immigrant registration document under certain circumstances;

4. authorizes a peace officer involved in enforcement related to human smuggling to lawfully stop anyone in a motor vehicle on reasonable suspicion that the person is violating a civil traffic law;
5. creates misdemeanor offenses, in certain circumstances, for (a) stopping to hire and pick up passengers for work while blocking traffic, (b) getting hired in such a fashion, and (c) applying for or soliciting work while unlawfully present in the country;
6. creates misdemeanor offenses (or felonies if ten or more illegal immigrants are involved) for unlawfully transporting or concealing an illegal immigrant or encouraging one to enter or remain in the country illegally;
7. authorizes a peace officer to arrest a person without a warrant on probable cause that the person has committed a public offense that makes the person removable from the country;
8. requires employers to keep employee eligibility records for three years or the duration of employment, whichever is longer;
9. allows employers to raise an affirmative defense of entrapment to a charge of knowingly or intentionally employing unauthorized immigrants;
10. adds to the list of reasons a peace officer must remove and either immobilize or impound a vehicle.

at-large election system is a process whereby candidates do not run or get elected from a specific part of the community but compete city- or countywide.

birthright citizenship is a legal right to citizenship for all children born in a country's territory, regardless of parentage.

Border Patrol was established in 1924, and in 1933 the Bureaus of Immigration and Naturalization were merged into the INS, whose primary mission is to detect and prevent the smuggling and unlawful entry of undocumented aliens into the United States and to apprehend individuals in violation of US immigration laws.

Boricua is a Puerto Rican, especially one living in the United States. This identification term is often used to signal an indigenous identity or precolonialism identity among Puerto Rican individuals.

civic life is the public life of the citizen concerned with the affairs of the community and nation as contrasted with private or personal life, which is devoted to the pursuit of private and personal interests. It also involves developing the combination of knowledge, skills, values, and motivation to make that difference. Many align civic life with civic engagement.

Coalition of Latino Leaders (CLILA) is a Latino community-based organization located in Whitfield County, Georgia. They provide English classes, civics classes, civic participation education, legal services, and afterschool programs. CLILA has also led the local community in advocacy and organizing by participating in and testifying in front of the board of regents to provide undocumented students access to Dalton State College, hosting town hall meetings to discuss legislation, advocating for DACA, and joining local, state, and national efforts for inclusion of Latino voices and contributions in decision making.

co-ethnic is a person of the same ethnicity. It implies a shared relationship based on ethnicity. For example, if an elected official or political candidate is referenced as a co-ethnic for Latino constituents or voters, this means that there is a shared Latino ethnicity between the candidate and the voter.

community emerged as a group of people with distinctive characteristics who are linked by social ties, share common perspectives, and engage in joint action in geographical locations or settings. The participants differed in the emphasis they placed on particular elements of the community.

community of common or similar cultures exists when individuals are linked closely by their participation in a common system of meaning with concomitant patterns of customary interactions of culture (language, customs, art, etc.).

community of interests refers to the conditions, statuses, and experiences that Latinos share with members of other Latino subgroups.

Congressional Hispanic Caucus Institute (CHCI) is a nonprofit and nonpartisan 501(c)(3) organization providing leadership development programs and educational services to students and young emerging Latino leaders.

cumulative voting systems enable voters to distribute their votes (one for each position available) in whatever manner they desire. For example, if three offices are to be decided, voters can cast their votes in any combination (all three votes to one candidate, two for one and one for another, etc.).

Customs and Border Protection (CBP) is one of the world's largest law enforcement organizations and is charged with keeping terrorists and their weapons out of the United States while facilitating lawful international travel and trade. It has more than 60,000 employees. According to CBP, they take a comprehensive approach to border management and control, combining customs, immigration, border security, and agricultural protection into one coordinated and supportive activity.

Deferred Action for Childhood Arrivals (DACA) is an American immigration policy that allows certain undocumented immigrants who entered the country before their sixteenth birthday and before June 2007 to receive a renewable two-year work permit and exemption from deportation.

Deferred Action for Parents of Americans (DAPA) was a US immigration policy to grant deferred action status to certain illegal immigrants who have lived in the United States since 2010 and have children who are either American citizens or lawful permanent residents. Deferred action would not be legal status but would come with a three-year renewable work permit and exemption from deportation. DAPA was a presidential executive action, not a law passed by Congress.

de facto segregated schools are those that, due to residential segregation and school-attendance zones, are highly segregated by race, ethnicity, and class.

Denaturalization is the revocation of citizenship of a naturalized immigrant by the US government. By law, denaturalization can only occur by a judicial order either through civil proceedings or a criminal conviction for naturalization fraud.

Department of Homeland Security (DHS) oversees efforts to counter terrorism and enhance security, secure and manage our borders while facilitating trade and travel, enforce and administer our immigration laws, safeguard and secure cyberspace, build resilience to disasters, and provide essential support for national and economic security in coordination with federal, state, local, international, and private-sector partners.

descriptive representation refers to the population's racial and ethnic makeup and the characteristics of political representatives. The population percentages of racial and ethnic groups mirror the background characteristics of their elected officials.

detainer orders are ICE written requests that a local jail or other law enforcement agency detain an individual for an additional forty-eight hours after his or her release date in order to provide ICE agents extra time to decide whether to take the individual into federal custody for removal purposes.

Development, Relief, and Education for Alien Minors Act (DREAM) is a legislative proposal introduced in the Senate on August 1, 2001, and reintroduced there and in the House on March 26, 2009. As yet unpassed, this bill provides conditional permanent residency to certain illegal and deportable alien students who are of good moral character, have graduated from US high schools, arrived in the United States illegally as minors, and have been in the country continuously for at least five years prior to the bill's enactment. If they complete two years in the military or at a four-year institution of higher learning, they will obtain temporary residency for a six-year period. Within that period, a qualified student must have "acquired a degree from an institution of higher education in the United States or [have] completed at least 2 years, in good standing, in a program for a bachelor's degree or higher degree in the U.S." or have "served in the armed services for at least 2 years and, if discharged, [have] received an honorable discharge."

discrimination-plus model characterizes coalition formation as influenced by minority-group members' common experiences, issue priorities, and values, which make them receptive to joint political activities and collective efforts.

DREAMers. *See* Development, Relief, and Education for Alien Minors Act (DREAM)

Enforcement Act of 1870 specifically prohibited denial of the right to vote in state and local elections.

English-only initiatives establish English as the official language of a state and require that all official business and activities be conducted only in English. Similar efforts have focused on the US Congress for national legislation.

ethnic groups are social groups or categories of the population that, in a larger society, are set apart and bound together by common ties of race, language, nationality, or culture.

ethnic identity is a set of self-ideas about one's ethnic group membership, which includes knowledge, feelings, and preferences about one's ethnicity. It includes a sense of self as a member of an ethnic group.

ethnicity can be defined as a collectivity within the larger society having a real or putative common ancestry, memories of a shared historical past, and a cultural focus on one or more symbolic elements defined as the epitome of peoplehood. Also, ethnicity is seen as a web of sentiments, beliefs, worldviews, and practices that individuals hold in common.

Force Act of 1871 gave federal-court-appointed supervisors the power to oversee registration and election processes when two citizens make that request. Later in the 1800s, Congress repealed the Enforcement and Force acts, and protective-voting-rights legislation was virtually nonexistent until the 1950s.

Hispanic Association of Colleges and Universities (HACU) represents more than 450 colleges and universities committed to Hispanic higher-education success in the United States, Puerto Rico, Latin America, and Spain. Founded in 1986, HACU is a national association representing existing and emerging Hispanic-Serving

Institutions (HSIs). Many young Latinos benefit from HACU internships, scholarships, college retention and advancement programs, precollegiate support, and career development opportunities and programs.

Hispanicity refers to the community formed by the people and countries that share a common Hispanic heritage and cultural pattern. Twenty-two nations are included in the Spanish-speaking countries.

Hotel Employees and Restaurant Employees Union (HERE) is a US labor union, formed in 1891, representing workers in the hospitality industry. In 2004, HERE merged with the Union of Needle Trades, Industrial and Textile Employees (UNITE) to form UNITE HERE. Major employers contracted with this union include several large casinos and hotel chains. UNITE HERE was affiliated with the AFL-CIO until September 2005, when UNITE HERE voted to leave the AFL-CIO and join the Change to Win coalition.

human capital is concept that is found in economics literature. As individuals motivated to obtain more education, greater degrees of training, and more experience invest in their human resource "portfolio," they are poised to reap greater returns in the job market via earnings. The idea is that acquiring greater human resources produces economic returns. Human capital also can be thought of as political capital: Individuals with greater skills, knowledge, and interest in the political process can act more effectively.

Illegal Immigration Reform and Immigrant Responsibility Act of 1996 (IIRIRA) had stipulations to bolster the monitoring of the US border and set up measures to remove criminal and other deportable aliens. In addition, this law provided increased protection for legal workers through worksite enforcement.

Immigration and Customs Enforcement (ICE) is the principal investigative arm of the US Department of Homeland Security and the second-largest investigative agency in the federal government. Created in 2003 through a merger of the investigative and interior enforcement elements of the US Customs Service and the Immigration and Naturalization Service, ICE now has more than twenty thousand employees in offices in all fifty states and forty-eight foreign countries.

Immigration Reform and Control Act of 1986 (IRCA) was a major reform bill that sought multiple policy goals. It attempted to restrict legal immigration by establishing more fixed annual admission ceilings; increasing border enforcement and staffing to interrupt the flow of undocumented migration; establishing criteria for an amnesty program for residing undocumented persons (agricultural workers and other workers/families); sanctioning employers and monitoring the hiring of undocumented workers; and requiring proof of legal status for employment.

impact or influence districts represent areas in which the Latino community (the principle can be applied to other minority groups or defined interests) constitutes a significant portion of the population and electorate. Usually a population threshold of 30 percent is viewed as a sizable demographic presence to which officials are responsive.

latinidad is a Spanish-language term that refers to the various attributes shared by Latin American people and their descendants without reducing those similarities to any single essential trait. As a social construct, *latinidad* references "a particular geopolitical experience but it also contains within it the complexities and contradictions of immigration, (post)(neo)colonialism, race, color, legal status, class, nation, language and the politics of location" (https://en.wikipedia.org/wiki/Latinidad#cite_note-3).Theoretically, *latinidad* can be a useful way to discuss consolidations of Latin American cultures and communities outside of any singular national frame. *Latinidad* can be the result of forging a shared cultural identity out of disparate elements in order to wield political and social power through pan-Latino/a solidarity.

Latinization of America can include that the speaking of Spanish will only strengthen, not disappear, and that the culture and values of Hispanics' countries of origin will continue to permeate American society. In addition, Latinos are going through a paced and successful process of Americanization and integration. The United States is a nation shaped by many different Hispanic heritages.

Latino National Political Survey, conducted from 1989 to 1990, was the first national probability survey of adults of Mexican, Cuban, and Puerto Rican origin. It focused on political attitudes and behavior, group identity, policy preferences, and other aspects of political life.

Latino National Survey is a probability survey that was conducted from 2005 to 2006 of 8,634 Latino adults in fifteen states and metropolitan Washington, DC. It covers subjects such as political and civic engagement, identity, transnationalism, public policy preferences, demographic characteristics, attitudes, partisanship, and voting.

Latinx is a gender-neutral neologism, used instead of Latino or Latina to refer to people of Latin American cultural or ethnic identity. The term was first seen around 2004, predominantly online, among intersectional advocacy groups combining the identity politics of race, class, and gender.

limited voting is a system in which the voter has fewer votes than the total number of positions up for election. For example, if three seats are to be decided, the voter has only one or two votes to cast. No uniform practice determines the number of votes allowed, other than there must be at least one fewer than the number of elected positions being contested.

linked fate suggests that given the centrality of racial stratification in the United States, minority political beliefs and their actions as individuals are related to their perceptions of racial group interests.

loose coupling is an approach to interconnecting the components in a system or network so that those components, or elements, depend on each other to the least extent practicable. Coupling refers to the degree of direct knowledge that one element has of another.

majority-minority districts are political jurisdictions in which residents are primarily minority (more than 50 percent of the population).

minority status refers to a category of people who experience relative disadvantage as compared to members of a dominant social group. Minority group membership is based on differences in observable characteristics or practices, such as: ethnicity (ethnic minority), race (racial minority), religion (religious minority), sexual orientation (sexual minority), or disability. The framework of intersectionality recognizes that an individual may simultaneously hold membership in multiple minority groups (e.g., both a racial and religious minority). This term often occurs with the discourse of civil rights and collective rights, as members of minority groups are prone to differential treatment in the countries and societies in which they live. Minority group members often face discrimination in multiple areas of social life.

mobilization is the process by which political candidates, political parties, activists, and groups try to induce other people to participate and get involved. Participation involves three key ingredients: resources, psychological orientations, and recruitment.

NALEO Educational Fund is a 501(c)(3) non-profit, non-partisan organization that facilitates full Latino participation in the American political process, from citizenship to public service. Founded in 1981, NALEO Educational Fund approaches its mission through integrated strategies that include increasing the effectiveness of Latino policymakers, mobilizing the Latino community to engage in civic life, and promoting policies that advance Latino political engagement.

National Association of Bilingual Educators (NABE) is a professional organization at the national level wholly devoted to representing both the interests of language-minority students and the bilingual education professionals who serve them.

National Hispana Leadership Institute (NHLI) is a national organization for Latinas that selects twenty-two leaders from the public and private sectors to participate in its Executive Leadership Program (ELP). The ELP is held in conjunction with the J. F. Kennedy School of Government (Harvard University) and the Center for Creative Leadership. The program consists of a four-week training curriculum that spans nine months. The learning experience addresses skills development and cultural application through a female and a Hispanic cultural lens. ELP training includes cross-cultural communication, strategic management, public policy, leadership skills building, mentoring, and implementation of a leadership project. Upon graduation, each participant mentors two young Latinas and completes a project in her community that impacts at least twenty-five Hispanics. NHLI's programs are designed to develop Hispanic women as ethical leaders for positions of national and international influence and public policy impact and as contributors to the advancement of the Latino community.

National Origins Act of 1924 set a ceiling on the number of immigrants admitted annually. A formula was based on 2 percent of the national-origin group registered in the 1890 census. The implementation of the act heavily favored natives of northern and western Europe. Japanese persons and citizens of the Asiatic zone were excluded.

No Child Left Behind Act of 2001 (NCLB) is an act of Congress concerning the education of children in public schools. Passed during the administration of George W. Bush, it was guided through the Senate by Sen. Ted Kennedy and received strong bipartisan support. President Bush signed it into law on January 8, 2002. NCLB includes standards-based education reform, setting high standards and establishing measurable goals that can improve individual outcomes in education. The act requires states hoping to receive federal funding for schools to develop assessments in basic skills to be given to all students in certain grades.

Northern Triangle refers to the three Central American countries of Guatemala, Honduras, and El Salvador. The term is used with respect to the countries' economic integration and their shared challenges, including widespread poverty, violence, and corruption, which have prompted many to become refugees fleeing the three nations.

Organization of Los Angeles Workers (OLAW) promotes workers' rights. It worked diligently for the mayoral campaign of Antonio Villaraigosa. The Service Employees International Union and the Hotel Employees and Restaurant Employees Union were an integral part of OLAW and political-mobilization activities in the city. OLAW was able to recruit more than six hundred canvassers and distribute more than eighty thousand registration cards and forms.

pan-ethnicity refers to a sense of group affinity and identification that transcends one's own national-origin group. Thus, a pan-ethnic identity does not necessarily replace one's national-origin affinity but encompasses a broader configuration to define the group; for instance, the terms *Latino* and *Hispanic* include several national origins. Pan-ethnicity can also apply to a sociopolitical collectivity made up of people of several different national origins.

partisan gerrymandering is a practice that attempts to establish a political advantage for a particular party or group by manipulating district boundaries to create partisan-advantaged districts.

Personal Responsibility and Work Opportunity Reconciliation Act of 1996 (PRWORA) restricted the eligibility of legal immigrants for means-tested public assistance, widened prohibitions on public benefits for undocumented immigrants, and mandated the INS to verify immigration status before immigrants could receive public benefits. Immigrant sponsorship required the sponsor to assume financial responsibility for an immigrant who was unable to sustain himself. The PRWORA made the affidavit of support legally binding.

political incorporation focuses on how persons learn about and involve themselves with the American political system. It generally focuses on newcomers to the political system (young persons assuming adult status or immigrants) and "marginalized" populations such as minority-group members. For our purposes, political incorporation is the process by which group interests are represented in the policy-making process.

political participation involves the process of influencing the distribution of social goods and values. The critical factors for involvement are resources, time, opportunities, beliefs, values, ideology, and participatory political attitudes. In addition, participation is affected by organizations, leaders, and political parties, which strategically choose to activate specific individuals and/or groups.

power relations focus on political resources, agenda setting, organizational development, leadership and mobilization, authority, influence, and legitimacy. Power is distributed among individuals and groups in society, and power relationships deal with the use of power and interactions between groups and individuals.

preclearance involves the voting rights section of the Justice Department, which reviews proposed election changes (affecting election dates, poll locations, election materials, annexations, etc.) in covered jurisdictions in order to assess their impact on minority-group representation and possible voter dilution. A change may not result in minority-voter dilution or negatively impact the equal protection provisions for all citizens. The voting rights division clears or rejects any proposed changes.

President's Advisory Commission on Educational Excellence for Hispanic Americans produced a report titled *Our Nation on the Fault Line.* President Bill Clinton created this presidential commission to examine the state of Hispanics and the educational system.

Proposition 187, or the Save Our State Proposition, was passed by the California electorate in 1994. This law barred undocumented immigrants from public education as well as other social services provided by the state (welfare and health care).

Proposition 227, officially titled the English-Language Initiative for Immigrant Children (Unz initiative), was designed to eliminate bilingual education programs. Limited-English-proficiency children would take a one-year English-immersion program and then be mainstreamed into the regular English-language curriculum.

racial gerrymandering is used to describe majority-minority districts. The courts have supported redistricting guidelines of compactness, contiguousness, and maintenance of community of interests. In the case of the latter, racial and other minorities (i.e., Latinos, Native Americans, Asian Americans) have been considered factors in maintaining community of interests.

redistricting is a decennial process by which political jurisdictions reconfigure their electoral districts to meet standards of equal size, compactness, and contiguity, as well as to maintain communities of interest. The redistricting plan can be implemented by the state legislature, a local governmental body, the courts, or an independent redistricting commission.

representation is the act of representing; standing in for someone or some group and speaking with authority on their behalf. It is also the state of serving as an official and authorized delegate or agent.

safe districts are generally those in which the incumbent and her party are firmly entrenched in an elected office. Thus, a safe district can be secure for a particular political party, member of a racial/ethnic group, and/or current incumbent.

Service Employees International Union (SEIU) is a labor union representing about 1.8 million workers in more than one hundred occupations in the United States, Canada, and Puerto Rico. SEIU has focused on organizing workers in three sectors: health care (including hospital, home-care, and nursing home workers); public services (local and state government employees); and property services (including janitors, security officers, and food-service workers).

single-member districts are specific areas of a city or county in which voters nominate and elect their representatives.

social construct refers to any occurrence or phenomenon invented or constructed by a society focusing on contingent variables of our social selves rather than any inherent or innate quality it possesses.

social construct of race usually refers to a group of persons who define themselves as distinct due to perceived common physical characteristics. The sense or categorization of race is the result of self-identification, institutional definitions of racial categories, and organized segments that develop or construct ideas about elements of racial membership.

social contact theory is also known as the inter-group contact theory. This refers to the hypothesis that people-to-people contact may be a good way to resolve conflict and develop better understanding between groups.

Southwest Voter Registration and Education Project (SVREP) was founded in 1974 and serves as the largest and oldest nonpartisan Latino voter participation organization in the United States. Founded by William C. Velasquez Jr., SVREP has registered 2.6 million Latino voters, trained 150,000 leaders, and encouraged thousands of individuals to volunteer in their communities.

structural factors have to do with the rules of the game and how political institutions function, especially focusing on access, individual or group legal standing, rights and protections, and the formal requirements for participation.

tamalada is primarily a traditional Mexican event where groups of family and friends get together to assemble tamales. Tamale making *can* be labor intensive, but it's not difficult, so a **tamalada** can help spread the load. The rewards include everyone taking home tamales and creating wonderful memories.

targeted mobilization involves the identification of persons who, when contacted, are more likely to respond to calls for involvement.

Thornburg v. Gingles (106 S. Ct. 2752 [1986]) is a Supreme Court ruling upholding the constitutionality of creating majority-minority districts when minority voting strength has been submerged in multimember districts with white majorities. The courts recognized a state's compelling interest in rectifying a pattern of exclusion. The remedy of majority-minority districts is appropriate when racially polarized voting has minimized or canceled out the potential for minority voters to elect candidates of their choice from their own community.

Treaty of Guadalupe Hidalgo, officially entitled the Treaty of Peace, Friendship, Limits and Settlement between the United States of America and the Mexican Republic, was signed on February 2, 1848, in the Villa de Guadalupe Hidalgo and ended the Mexican-American War (1846–1848). The treaty called for the United States to pay $15 million to Mexico and to pay off the claims of American citizens against Mexico up to $3.25 million. It gave the United States the Rio Grande as a boundary for Texas as well as ownership of California and a large area comprising roughly half of New Mexico, most of Arizona, Nevada, Utah, and parts of Wyoming and Colorado. Mexicans in those annexed areas had the choice of relocating to within Mexico's new boundaries or receiving American citizenship with full civil rights.

undocumented person is one who is residing in the United States who is a foreign national ignoring US immigration laws by either entering the country without government permission (i.e., a visa) or once lawfully entering, remaining within the country beyond the termination date of a temporary visa.

UnidosUS—formerly known as NCLR—is a nonpartisan voice for Latinos serving the Latino community through research, policy analysis, and state and national advocacy efforts, as well as program work in communities nationwide. With a network of nearly three hundred affiliates across the country, it works in the areas of civic engagement, civil rights and immigration, education, workforce and the economy, health, and housing.

United States Mexico Canada Agreement (USMCA) is an updated version of the decades-old, trillion-dollar North American Free Trade Agreement (NAFTA). It includes major changes on cars and new policies on labor and environmental standards, intellectual property protections, and some digital trade provisions.

Voter ID laws require a person to provide some form of official identification before they are permitted to register to vote, receive a ballot for an election, or actually vote in elections in the United States. Debate has included the extent of voter fraud that is the basis for Voter ID laws and the impact on voter participation among low-income and/or minority populations.

Voting Rights Act of 1965 (VRA) was a major policy initiative addressing long-standing practices that had served to exclude African Americans and other minorities from the electoral process, including annual registration systems, literacy tests, hostile election poll locations, economic and physical intimidation of minority-group members, and limited registration locations and hours. Consequently, suspension of literacy tests, use of federal monitors, review of election-related changes, the right for local persons or groups to mount legal challenges, and standards for voter dilution were key elements of the legislation.

White House Initiative on Educational Excellence for Hispanics was originally launched by President George H. W. Bush and was expanded by President Barack Obama to improve educational opportunities for Hispanic students at every level. The order includes an enhanced interagency working group and a thirty-member presidential advisory commission.

References

Abascal, Maria. 2017. "Tu Casa, Mi Casa: Naturalization and Belonging among Latino Immigrants." *International Migration Review* 51, no. 2 (June): 291–322.

———. 2010b. *Campaigning to the New American Electorate: Advertising to Latino Voters*. Redwood City, CA: Stanford University Press.

Abrajano, Marisa, and Costas Panagopoulos. 2011. "Does Language Matter? The Impact of Spanish Versus English-Language GOTV Efforts on Latino Turnout." *American Politics Research* 39 (July): 643–63.

Abrajano, Marisa A., and R. Michael Alvarez. 2005. "Natural Experiment of Race-Based and Issue Voting: The 2001 City of Los Angeles Elections." *Political Research Quarterly* 58 (June): 203–18.

———. 2009. "Assessing the Causes and Effects of Political Trust among U.S. Latinos." *American Politics Research* 38, no. 1: 110–41.

Abrajano, M. A., and R. M. Alvarez. 2010. *New Faces, New Voices: The Hispanic Electorate in America*. Princeton, NJ: Princeton University Press.

Abrams, J. R., and H. Giles. 2007. "Ethnic Identity Gratifications Selection and Avoidance by African Americans: A Group Vitality and Social Identity Gratifications Perspective." *Media Psychology* 9, no. 1: 115–34.

Acuña, Rodolfo. 1976. *Occupied America: A History of Chicanos*. 2nd ed. New York: Harper & Row.

———. 1981. *Occupied America: A History of Chicanos*. 3rd ed. New York: Harper & Row.

———. 1988. *Occupied America: A History of Chicanos*. 4th ed. New York: Harper & Row.

———. 1996. *Anything but Mexican: Chicanos in Contemporary Los Angeles*. New York: Verso.

———. 1998. *Sometimes There Is No Other Side: Chicanos and the Myth of Equality*. Notre Dame, IN: University of Notre Dame Press.

Adams, Greg D. 1996. "Legislative Effects of Single-Member vs. Multi-Member Districts." *American Journal of Political Science* 40 (February): 129–44.

Alesina, Alberto, Armando Miano, and Stefanie Stantcheva. 2019. "Immigration and Redistribution." Working Paper No. 24733. National Bureau of Economic Research.

Alinsky, Saul. 1971. *Rules for Radicals: A Practical Primer for Realistic Radicals*. New York: Vintage.

Allport, Gordon W. 1954. *The Nature of Prejudice*. Rutherford, NJ: Addison Publishing.

Allsup, Carl. 1982. *The American GI Forum: Origins and Evolution*. Austin: University of Texas Press.

Almond, Gabriel, and Sidney Verba. 1963. *The Civic Culture*. Princeton, NJ: Princeton University Press.

Alvarado, Joel, and Charles Jaret. 2009. "Building Black-Brown Coalitions in the Southeast: Four African American–Latino Collaborations." Atlanta: Southern Regional Council.

Alvarez, L., and D. Widener. 2008. "A History of Black and Brown: Chicana/o–African American Cultural and Political Relations." *Aztlán: A Journal of Chicano Studies* 33, no. 1: 143–54.

Alvarez, R. Michael. 1999. "Why Did Proposition 227 Pass?" Division of the Humanities and Social Sciences, California Institute of Technology, Pasadena, CA. Social Science Working Paper 1062, April.

Alvarez, R. Michael, and Tara L. Butterfield. 2000. "The Resurgence of Nativism in California? The Case of Proposition 187 and Illegal Immigration." *Social Science Quarterly* 81, no. 1 (March): 167–79.

Alvarez-Lopez, Luis, Sherrie Baver, Jean Weisman, Ramona Hernandez, and Nancy Lopez. 1997. *Dominican Studies: Resources and Research Questions*. New York: CUNY Academic Works.

Amnesty International. 2010. *Invisible Victims: Migrants on the Move in Mexico*. London: Amnesty International Publications.

Ansolabehere, Stephen. 2009. "Effects of Identification Requirements on Voting: Evidence from the Experience of Voters on Election Day." *PS: Political Science and Politics* 42, no. 1 (January): 127–30.

Antecol, Heather, Deborah A. Cobb-Clark, and Stephen J. Trejo. 2003. "Immigration Policy and the Skills of Immigrants to Australia, Canada, and the United States." *Journal of Human Resources* 38, no. 1 (Winter): 192–218.

Arce, Carlos. 1982. "A Reconsideration of Chicano Culture and Identification." *Daedalus* 110, no. 2: 177–91.

Arizona State Legislature v. Arizona Independent Redistricting Commission. 2015. No. 13-1314. Washington, DC: US Supreme Court.

Armbruster, Ralph, Kim Geron, and Edna Bonacich. 1995. "The Assault on California Immigrants: The Politics of Proposition 187." *International Journal of Urban and Regional Research* 19 (December): 655–64.

Astin, Alexander. 1982. *Minorities in Higher Education*. San Francisco: Jossey-Bass.

———. 1985. *Achieving Academic Excellence*. San Francisco: Jossey-Bass.

Auclair, Gregory, and Jeanne Batalova. 2013. *Naturalization Trends in the United States*. Washington, DC: Migration Policy Institute.

Ayala, Christine. 2015. "Congressional Hispanic Caucus Fears 55 Percent of Latinos Would Be Impacted If Texas Loses 'One Person, One Vote' Case." *Dallas Morning News*, December 8.

Bada, Xochitl, Jonathan Fox, and Andrew Selee, eds. 2006. "Invisible No More: Mexican Migrant Civic Participation in the United States." Washington, DC: Woodrow Wilson Center Mexico Institute.

Baker, Susan G. 1997. "The 'Amnesty' Aftermath: Current Policy Issues Stemming from the Legalization Programs of the 1986 Immigration Reform and Control Act." *International Migration Review* 31, no. 1: 5–27.

Barajas-Gonzalez, R. Gabriela, Cecilia Ayón, and Franco Torres. 2018. "Applying a Community Violence Framework to Understand the Impact of Immigration Enforcement Threat on Latino Children." *Society for Research Child Development* 31, no. 3 (Fall): 1–24.

Barrera, Mario. 1979. *Race and Class in the Southwest: A Theory of Race and Class Inequality*. Notre Dame, IN: University of Notre Dame Press.

———. 1988. *Beyond Aztlan: Ethnic Autonomy in Comparative Perspectives*. New York: Praeger.

Barrera, Mario, Charles Ornelas, and Carlos Muñoz. 1972. "The Barrio as an Internal Colony." In *People and Politics in Urban Society*, edited by H. Hahn, 465–98. Los Angeles: Sage.

Barreto, Matt A. 2003. "National Origin (Mis)Identification among Latinos in the 2000 Census: The Growth of the 'Other Hispanic or Latino' Category." *Harvard Journal of Hispanic Policy* 15 (June): 39–63.

———. 2007. "Sí Se Puede! Latino Candidates and the Mobilization of Latino Voters." *American Political Science Review* 101 (August): 425–41.

———. 2010. *Ethnic Cues: The Role of Shared Ethnicity in Latino Political Participation*. Ann Arbor: University of Michigan Press.

———. 2013. "The Prop 187 Effect: How the California GOP Lost Their Way and Implications for 2014 and Beyond." *Latino Decisions*, https://latinodecisions.com/blog/prop187effect/.

———. 2019. "Would Booker and Castro Be in Tonight's Debate If Polls Counted People of Color Accurately?" *MonkeyCage*, https://www.washingtonpost.com/politics/2019/12/19/would-booker-castro-be-tonights-debate-if-polls-counted-people-color-accurately/.

Barreto, Matt A., Loren Colingwood, and Silvia Manzano. 2010. "A New Measure of Group Influence in Presidential Elections: Assessing Latino Influence in 2008." *Political Research Quarterly* 63, no. 4 (December): 908–21.

Barreto, Matt A., Victoria DeFrancesco, and Jennifer Merolla. 2011. "Multiple Dimensions of Mobilization: The Impact of Direct Contact and Political Ads on Latino Turnout in the 2000 Presidential Election." *Journal of Political Marketing* 10, no. 4 (October): 303–27.

Barreto, Matt A., Benjamin F. Gonzalez, and Gabriel R. Sanchez. 2013. "An Examination of Inter-group Attitudes among Multiple Populations: The Role of Neighborhood Context and Group-Based Threat." Western Political Science Association Meeting, Los Angeles.

———. 2014. "Rainbow Coalition in the Golden State? Exposing Myths, Uncovering New Realities in Latino Attitudes toward Blacks." In *Black and Brown in Los Angeles: Beyond Conflict and Coalition*, eds. Josh Kun and Laura Pulido, 203–32. Berkeley: University of California Press.

Barreto, Matt A., Sylvia Manzano, Ricardo Ramírez, and Kathy Rim. 2009. "Mobilization, Participation, and Solidaridad: Latino Participation in the 2006 Immigration Protest Rallies." *Urban Affairs Review* 44, no. 5: 736–64.

Barreto, Matt A., and José Muñoz. 2003. "Reexamining the 'Politics of In-Between': Political Participation among Mexican Immigrants in the United States." *Hispanic Journal of Behavioral Sciences* 25 (November): 427–47.

Barreto, Matt A., and Stephen A. Nuño. 2011. "The Effectiveness of Co-Ethnic Contact on Latino Political Recruitment." *Political Research Quarterly* 64 (June): 448–59.

Barreto, Matt A., Stephen A. Nuño, and Gabriel R. Sanchez. 2007. "Voter ID Requirements and the Disenfranchisements of Latino, Black and Asian Voters." In annual meeting of the American Political Science Association, Chicago, August.

———. 2009. "The Disproportionate Impact of Voter-ID Requirements on the Electorate: New Evidence from Indiana." *Political Science and Politics* 42, no. 1: 111–16.

Barreto, Matt A., Stephen Nuño, Gabriel R. Sanchez, and Hannah L. Walker. 2018. "The Racial Implications of Voter Identification Laws in America." *American Politics Research* 47, no. 2: 238–49.

Barreto, Matt A., Ricardo Ramirez, and Nathan D. Woods. 2005. "Are Naturalized Voters Driving the California Latino Electorate? Measuring the Effect of IRCA Citizens on Latino Voting." *Social Science Quarterly* 86, no. 4 (December): 792–811.

Barreto, Matt A., and Gabriel R. Sanchez. 2012. "Rates of Possession of Accepted Photo Identification, among Different Subgroups in the Eligible Voter Population, Milwaukee County, Wisconsin." Expert Report Submitted on Behalf of Plaintiffs.

———. 2014. "A 'Southern Exception' in Black-Latino Attitudes? Perceptions of Competition with African Americans and Other Latinos." In *Latino Politics in Ciencia Politica: The*

Search for Latino Identity and Racial Consciousness, eds. Tony Affigne, Evelyn Hu-Dehart, and Marion Orr, 206–27. New York: New York University Press.

Barreto, Matt A., Gabriel R. Sanchez, and Jason Morín. 2010. "Perceptions of Competition between Latinos and Blacks: The Development of a Relative Measure of Inter-Group Competition." In *Black-Brown Relations*, eds. Edward Telles, Gaspar Rivera-Salgado, and Sylvia Zamora. New York: Russell Sage.

Barreto, Matt A., Gary M. Segura, and Nathan D. Woods. 2004. "The Mobilizing Effect of Majority Minority Districts on Latino Turnout." *American Political Science Review* 98: 65–75.

Barrett, J. R., and D. Roediger. 1997. "Inbetween Peoples: Race, Nationality and the New Immigrant Working Class." In *American Exceptionalism?*, 181–220. London: Palgrave Macmillan.

Barrett, Martyn, and Ian Brunton-Smith. 2014. "Political and Civic Engagement and Participation: Towards an Integrative Perspective." *Journal of Civil Society* 10, no. 1: 5–28.

Barvosa, Edwina. 1999. "Multiple Identities and Coalition Building: How Identity Differences within Us Enable Radical Alliances among Us." *Contemporary Justice Review* 2, no. 2: 111–26.

———. 2008. *Wealth of Selves: Multiple Identities, Mestiza Consciousness, and the Subject of Politics*. College Station: Texas A&M University Press.

Bass, Loretta, and Lynne Casper. 1999. "Are There Differences in Registration and Voting Behavior between Naturalized and Native-Born Americans?" Population Division Working Paper 28. Washington, DC: US Census Bureau.

Batalova, Jeanne, and Jie Zong. 2017. "Cuban Immigrants in the United States." Washington, DC: Migration Policy Institute.

Baum, M., B. Dietrich, R. Goldstein, and M. Sen. 2019. "Estimating the Effect of Asking about Citizenship on the US Census: Results from a Randomized Controlled Trial." J. F. Kennedy School of Government, Harvard University.

Bean, Frank, and Marta Tienda. 1987. *The Hispanic Population of the United States*. New York: Russell Sage Foundation.

Bejarano, C. E. 2016. "New Directions at the Intersection of Race, Ethnicity and Gender." *The Political Psychology of Women in US Politics*, 111–28.

Beltrán, Cristina. 2010. *The Trouble with Unity: Latino Politics and the Creation of Identity*. New York: Oxford University Press.

Bendixen, Sergio. 2006. National Study of Young Hispanics (Ages 16–29). Miami: Bendixen and Amandi Associates.

———. 2011. *The Emerging Hispanic Electorate: The Young Giant Awakens*. Miami: Bendixen and Amandi Associates.

Bendixen, Sergio, and Fernand Amandi. 2015. "National Survey of Cuban Americans." Miami, FL: Bendixen and Amandi Associates.

Benitez, Christina. 2007. *Latinization: How Latino Culture Is Transforming the United States*. Ithaca, NY: Paramount Market.

Bentele, Keith Gunnar, and Erin E. O'Brien. 2013. "Jim Crow 2.0? Why States Consider and Adopt Restrictive Voter Access Policies." *Perspectives on Politics* 11, no. 4: 1088–1116.

Bernal, Martha, and Phylis Martinelli, eds. 1993. *Mexican American Identity*. Encino, CA: Floricanto Press.

Best, Rebecca, Kyleanne Hunter, Theresa Schroeder, and Jeremy Teigen. 2019. "Military Service Was Once a Fast Track to U.S. Citizenship. The Trump Administration Keeps Narrowing That Possibility." *Washington Post*, September 6.

Bialik, Kristen. 2019. "For the Fifth Time in a Row, the New Congress Is the Most Racially and Ethnically Diverse Ever." *Pew Research Center*, February 8, https://www.pewresearch.org/fact-tank/2019/02/08/for-the-fifth-time-in-a-row-the-new-congress-is-the-most-racially-and-ethnically-diverse-ever/.

Bishin, Benjamin G., and Casey A. Klofstad. 2012. "The Political Incorporation of Cuban Americans: Why Won't Little Havana Turn Blue?" *Political Research Quarterly* 65, no. 3: 586–99.

Bishin, Benjamin, Daniel Stevens, and Christian Wilson. 2005. "Truth or Consequences? Character and Swing Voters in the 2000 Election." *Public Integrity* 7: 129–46.

Blalock, Hubert M. 1967. *Toward a Theory of Minority-Group Relations*. New York: Wiley Publishers.

Bloemraad, Irene. 2006. *Becoming a Citizen: Incorporating Immigrants and Refugees in the United States and Canada*. Berkeley: University of California Press.

Bloemraad, Irene, Anna Korteweg, and Gökçe Yurdakul. 2008. "Citizenship and Immigration: Multiculturalism, Assimilation, and Challenges to the Nation-State." *Annual Review of Sociology* 34: 153–79.

Bloemraad, Irene, and Christine Trost. 2008. "It's a Family Affair: Intergenerational Mobilization in the Spring 2006 Protests." *American Behavioral Scientist* 52, no. 4: 507–32.

Bobo, Lawrence, and Vincent Hutchings. 1996. "Perceptions of Racial Group Competition: Extending Blumer's Theory of Group Position to a Multiracial Social Context." *American Sociological Review* 61, no. 6: 951–72.

Bonilla, Frank, and Rebecca Morales. 1998. *Borderless Borders: Latinos, Latin Americans, and Paradox of Interdependence*. Philadelphia: Temple University Press.

Bonilla-Silva, Eduardo. 2013. *Racism without Racists: Color-Blind Racism and the Persistence of Racial Inequality in America*. 4th ed. Lanham, MD: Rowman & Littlefield.

Booth, William. 1996. "In a Rush: New Citizens Register Their Political Interest as Mexican Immigrants Become Naturalized." *Washington Post*, September 26.

Borjas, George. 2001. *Heaven's Door: Immigration Policy and the American Economy*. Princeton, NJ: Princeton University Press.

Bosniak, Linda S. 1996. "Opposing Prop. 187: Undocumented Immigrants and the National Imagination." *Connecticut Law Review* 28: 555.

Boswell, Thomas. 1994. "A Demographic Profile of Cuban Americans." Miami: Cuban American National Planning Council.

Boswell, Thomas, and J. R. Curtis. 1984. *The Cuban American Experience: Culture, Images, and Perspectives*. Totowa, NJ: Rowman & Allanheld.

Boushey, Graeme, and Adam Luedtke. 2011. "Immigrants across the U.S. Federal Laboratory: Explaining State-Level Innovation in Immigration Policy." *State Politics & Policy Quarterly* 11, no. 4: 390–414.

Brady, Henry, Sidney Verba, and Kay Scholzman. 1995. "Beyond SES: A Resource Model of Political Participation." *American Political Science Review* 89 (June): 271–94.

Branton, Regina, and Johanna Dunaway. 2008. "English- and Spanish-Language Media Coverage of Immigration: A Comparative Analysis." *Social Science Quarterly* 89, no. 4: 1006–22.

Briegal, Kaye. 1970. "The Development of Mexican American Organizations." In *Mexican Americans: An Awakening Minority*, edited by Manuel Servin, 160–78. Beverly Hills, CA: Glencoe.

———. 1974. "Alianza Hispano Americano and Some Civil Rights Cases in the 1950s." In *Mexican Americans: An Awakening Minority*, edited by Manuel Servin, 174–87, 2nd ed. Beverly Hills: Glencoe.

Brischetto, Robert, and Rodolfo de la Garza. 1983. *The Mexican American Electorate: Political Participation and Ideology*. Austin: Center for Mexican American Studies, University of Texas.

———. 1985. *The Mexican American Electorate: Political Opinions and Behavior across Cultures in San Antonio*. Austin: Center for Mexican American Studies, University of Texas.

Brischetto, Robert, and Richard L. Engstrom. 1997. "Cumulative Voting and Latino Representation: Exit Surveys in Fifteen Texas Communities." *Social Science Quarterly* 78, no. 4: 973–1000.

Broder, David. 2001. "Awakening of the Latino Community Will Change the Political Map." *Washington Post*, May 23.

Brown, Anna, Gustavo López, and Mark Hugo Lopez. 2016. "Digital Divide Narrows for Latinos as More Spanish Speaking and Immigrants Go Online: Broadband Little Change in Recent Years among Hispanics." Washington, DC: Pew Hispanic Research Center.

Browning, Rufus, D. Marshall, and D. Tabb. 1984. *Protest Is Not Enough: The Struggle of Blacks and Hispanics for Equality in Urban Politics*. Berkeley: University of California Press.

———. 1990. *Racial Politics in American Cities*. New York: Longman.

Buchmueller, Thomas C., Z. M. Levinson, H. G. Levy, and B. L. Wolfe. 2016. "Effect of the Affordable Care Act on Racial and Ethnic Disparities in Health Insurance Coverage." *American Journal of Public Health* 106, no. 8: 1416–21.

Budiman, Abby. 2020. "Key Findings about U.S. Immigrants." Washington, DC: Pew Hispanic Center.

Budryk, Zack. 2018. "Deportations Lower under Trump Administration Than Obama: Report." *The Hill*, November 18.

Cain, Bruce, Jack Citrin, and Cara Wong. 2000. *Ethnic Context, Race Relations, and California Politics*. San Francisco: Public Policy Institute of California.

Cain, Bruce, and D. Roderick Kiewiet. 1992. *Minorities in California*. New York: Seaver Foundation.

Cain, Bruce E., D. Roderick Kiewiet, and Carole Jean Uhlaner. 1991 "The Acquisition of Partisanship by Latinos and Asian-Americans." *American Journal of Political Science* 35 (May): 390–422.

Calderon, Shanilinin M. 2012. "The Extent of Political Participation in the United States among Latino Non-Citizens and Citizens." *McNair Scholars Research Journal* 5, no. 1: 4.

Campbell, A., P. E. Converse, W. E. Miller, and D. E. Stokes. 1960. *The American Voter*. New York: John Wiley.

Candelaria, Cordelia. 1980. "Six Reference Works on Mexican-American Women: A Review Essay." *Frontiers: A Journal of Women's Studies* 5, no. 2 (Summer): 75–80.

Cano, Gustavo. 2004. "Organizing Immigrant Communities in American Cities: Is This Transnationalism, or What?" *Center for Comparative Immigration Studies* Working Paper #103. San Diego: University of California.

———. 2008. "Political Mobilization of Latino Immigrants in American Cities and the U.S. Immigration Debate." Paper delivered at the 2008 Annual Meeting of the American Political Science Association, August 28–31.

Carey, Tony E., Jr., Regina P. Branton, and Valerie Martinez-Ebers. 2014. "The Influence of Social Protests on Issue Salience among Latinos." *Political Research Quarterly* 67, no. 3 (September): 615–27.

Carmichael, Stokely, and Charles Hamilton. 1967. *Black Power: Politics of Liberation in America*. New York: Vintage.

Carrillo, J. Emilio, Fernando M. Trevino, Joseph R. Betancourt, and Alberto Coutasse. 2001. "Latino Access to Health Care: The Role of Insurance, Managed Care, and Institutional Barriers." In *Health Issues in the Latino Community*, ed. M. Aquirre-Molina, 55–73. San Francisco: Josey-Bass.

Carroll, Linda. 2019. "Anti-Immigrant Rhetoric May Put Health of U.S. Latinos at Risk." Reuters, November 1.

Carter, Thomas, and Roberto Segura. 1979. *Mexican Americans in School: A Decade of Change*. New York: College Entrance Examination Board.

Casellas, J. P., and D. L. Leal. 2013. "Partisanship or Population? House and Senate Immigration Votes in the 109th and 110th Congresses." *Politics, Groups, and Identities* 1, no. 1: 48–65.

Casellas, Jason. 2007. "Latino Representation in Congress: To What Extent Are Latinos Substantively Represented." In *Latino Politics: Identity, Mobilization and Representation*, eds. Rodolfo Espino, David Leal, and Ken Meier, 219–31. Charlottesville: University of Virginia.

———. 2011. *Latino Representation in State Houses and Congress*. New York: Cambridge University Press.

Casper, Lynne, and Loretta Bass. 1998. "Voting and Registration in the Election of 1996. Current Population Reports P20-523RV." Washington, DC: US Census Bureau.

Castro, Joaquin. 2019. "Congressional Hispanic Caucus Statement on Shooting in El Paso." CHC Statement, August 3.

Channing, Mavrellis. 2017. "Transnational Crime and the Developing World." Washington, DC: Global Financial Integrity, March 27.

Chapa, Jorge. 1995. "Mexican American Class Structure and Political Participation." *New England Journal of Public Policy* 11, no. 1, Article 12.

Chavez, Jorge M., and Doris Marie Provine. 2009. "Race and the Response of State Legislatures to Unauthorized Immigrants." *Annals of the American Academy of Political and Social Science* 623 (May): 78–92.

Chavez, Leo, Belinda Campo, Karina Corona, Daina Sanchez, and Catherine Belyeu Ruiz. 2019. "Words Hurt: Political Rhetoric, Emotions/Affect, and Psychological Well-Being among Mexican-Origin Youth." *Social Science & Medicine* 228 (May): 240–51.

Chen, Jie, Arturo Vargas-Bustamante, Karoline Mortensen, and Alexander N. Ortega. 2016. "Racial and Ethnic Disparities in Health Care Access and Utilization under the Affordable Care Act." *Medical Care* 54, no 2: 140–46.

Chen, Ming H. 2016. "Trust in Immigration Enforcement: State Noncooperation and Sanctuary Cities after Secure Communities." *Chi.-Kent L. Rev.* 91, no. 13.

Chen, Zhijun, Jing Zhu, and Mingjian Zhou. 2015. "How Does a Servant Leader Fuel the Service Fire? A Multilevel Model of Servant Leadership, Individual Self Identity, Group Competition Climate, and Customer Service Performance." *Journal of Applied Psychology* 100, no. 2: 511.

Chicano/Mexican American Digital History Project. 2012. *Proposition 227—The Anti Bilingual Education Initiative of 1996*. Sacramento, CA: Institute for Democracy and Education.

Chishti, Muzaffar, and Jessica Bolter. 2019. "'Merit-Based' Immigration: Trump Proposal Would Dramatically Revamp Immigrant Selection Criteria, but with Modest Effects on Numbers." Washington, DC: Migration Policy Institute, May 30.

Cohn, D'vera, Jeffrey Passel, and Kristen Bialik. 2019. "Many Immigrants with Temporary Protected Status Face Uncertain Future in U.S." Washington, DC: Pew Hispanic Research Center, November 27.

Coleman, Mathew, and Austin Kocher. 2011. "Detention, Deportation, Devolution and Immigrant Incapacitation in the US, Post 9/11." *The Geographical Journal* 177, no. 3: 228–37.

Colorado State Advisory Committee to the US Commission on Civil Rights. 2019. "Citizenship Delayed: Civil Rights and Voting Rights Implications of the Backlog in Citizenship and Naturalization Applications." Boulder, CO: United States Commission on Civil Rights.

Common Education Data Standards (CEDS). Washington, DC: Council of Chief State School Officers, http://www.ccsso.org.

Cook, Stuart W. 1963. "Desegregation: A Psychological Analysis." In *Readings in the Social Psychology of Education*, eds. W. W. Charters Jr. and N. L. Gage. Boston: Allyn and Bacon.

Cooper, Philip F., and Barbara Steinberg Schone. 1997. "More Offers, Fewer Takers for Employment-Based Health Insurance: 1987 and 1996." *Health Affairs* 16, no. 6: 142–49.

Copp, Tara. 2020. "Military Personnel Getting US Citizenship on the Rise for the First Time in Years," Washington DC: McClatchy News Bureau, July 23.

Cordova, Teresa, John A. Garcia, and Juan Garcia, eds. 1986. *Chicana Voices: Intersections of Class, Race, and Gender*. Austin: Center for Mexican American Studies Publications, University of Texas.

Cornell, Stephen. 1985. "The Variable Ties That Bind: Context and Governance in Ethnic Processes." *Ethnic and Racial Studies* 13: 368–88.

———. 1988. *The Return of the Native*. New York: Oxford University Press.

Cornell, Stephen, and Douglas Hartman. 1998. *Ethnicity and Race: Making Identities in a Changing World*. Thousand Oaks, CA: Pine Forge.

Cortés, Ernesto. 1996. "Solving the New Inequality: What about Organizing?" *Boston Review* 21, no. 6 (December 1).

Cottrell, Charles. 1986. "Introduction: Assessing the Effects of the U.S. Voting Rights Act." *Publius* 16, no. 4: 5–17.

Cowan, Gloria, Livier Martinez, and Stephanie Mendiola. 1997. "Predictors of Attitudes toward Illegal Immigrants." *Hispanic Journal of Behavioral Sciences* 19, no. 4: 403–17.

Cravey, Altha J. 1997. "Latino Labor and Poultry Production in Rural North Carolina." *Southeast Geography* 37, no. 2: 295–300.

Crawford, James. 1992a. *Hold Your Tongue: Bilingualism and the Politics of "English Only."* Menlo Park, CA: Addison-Wesley.

———. 1992b. *Language Loyalties: A Sourcebook on the Official English Controversy*. Chicago: University of Chicago Press.

———. 2000. *At War with Diversity: U.S. Language Policy in an Age of Anxiety*. Buffalo, NY: Multilingual Matters.

Croucher, Sheila. 1997. *Imagining Miami: Ethnic Politics in a Postmodern World*. Charlottesville: University of Virginia Press.

Cruz, Jose. 1998. *Identity and Power: Puerto Rican Politics and Challenges of Ethnicity*. Philadelphia: Temple University Press.

Cruz, Vanessa. 2010. "Tucking in the Sleeping Giant: Political Socialization as It Relates to the Incorporation and Family Dynamics of Latino Families." Paper presented at the annual meeting of the Midwest Political Science Association, Chicago.

Cruz-Nichols, Vanessa, A. LeBron, and F. Pedraza. 2014. "Living in the Shadows: The Political Engagement and Disengagement of U.S.-Born and Foreign-Born Latinos." Paper presented at Coalition for Interdisciplinary Research of Latina/o Issues (CIRLI), University of Michigan–Ann Arbor.

Cuello, José. 1996. *Latinos and Hispanics: A Primer on Terminology*. Detroit: Wayne State University Press.

Davis, Jessica W., and Kurt J. Bauman. 2008. "School Enrollment in the United States: 2006. Current Population Reports P20-559." Washington, DC: US Bureau of the Census.

Dawson, Michael. 1994. *Behind the Mule: Race and Class in African American Politics*. Princeton, NJ: Princeton University Press.

Dawson, Michael, Ronald Brown, and James S. Jackson. 1993. "National Black Politics Study." ICPSR02018-v2. Ann Arbor, MI: Inter-university Consortium for Political and Social Research, 2008-12-03. doi: 10.3886/ICPSR02018.

Day, Jennifer. 1998. "Hispanic Population Shows Gains in Educational Attainment." *Census Bureau Reports* CB98-107. Washington, DC: US Census Bureau.

Day, Jennifer, and Avalaura Gaither. 2000a. "California, Texas, and Florida Will Show Biggest Increases in Voting Age Populations in November 2000." *Census Bureau Reports* CB00-125. Washington, DC: US Census Bureau.

———. 2000b. "Voting and Registration in the Election of November 1998." *Current Population Reports* P20-523RV. Washington, DC: Department of Commerce.

de la Garza, Rodolfo O., and Louis DeSipio. 1992. *From Rhetoric to Reality: Latino Politics in the 1988 Elections*. Boulder, CO: Westview.

———. 1993. "Save the Baby, Change the Bath Water, Get a New Tub: Latino Electoral Participation after Seventeen Years of Voting Rights Coverage." *University of Texas Law Review* 71: 1029–42.

———. 1996. *Ethnic Ironies: Latino Politics in the 1992 Elections*. Boulder, CO: Westview.

de la Garza, Rodolfo O., Louis DeSipio, F. Chris García, John A. García, and Angelo Falcón. 1993. *Latino Voices: Mexican, Puerto Rican, and Cuban Perspectives on American Politics*. Boulder, CO: Westview.

de la Garza, Rodolfo O., Angelo Falcón, and F. Chris García. 1996. "Will the Real Americans Please Stand Up: A Comparison of Anglo and Mexican American Support for Core American Values." *American Journal of Political Science* 40, no. 2: 335–51.

de la Garza, Rodolfo O., A. Falcón, F. Chris García, and John A. García. 1994. "Mexican Immigrants, Mexican Americans, and American Political Culture." In *Immigration and Ethnicity: The Integration of America's Newest Arrivals*, eds. Barry Edmondston and J. Passel, 227–50. Washington, DC: Urban Institute Press.

de la Garza, Rodolfo O., Z. Anthony Kruszewski, and Tomas A. Arciniega, eds. 1973. *Chicanos and Native Americans: The Territorial Minorities*. Englewood Cliffs, NJ: Prentice Hall.

de la Garza, Rodolfo O., Martha Menchaca, and Louis DeSipio. 1994. "Barrio Ballots: Latino Politics in the 1992 Elections." Boulder, CO: Westview.

de la Garza, Rodolfo O., and David Vaughn. 1984. "The Political Socialization of Chicano Elites: A Generational Approach." *Social Science Quarterly* 65, no. 2 (June): 290–307.

de la Garza, Rodolfo O., and Alan Yang. 2015. "Language Dominance, Bilingualism, and Latino Political Participation in the United States." *Political Science Quarterly* 130, no. 4: 655–99.

del Olmo, Frank. 1998. "Giant Is Awake and Is a Force in California: Latino Voters' Pivotal Role in the Elections Puts All Politicians on Notice." *Los Angeles Times*, June 7.

———. 2001. "Bush Is Reaching Out to Latinos beyond the Beltway." *Los Angeles Times*, April 22.

del Pinal, Jorge, Elyn Martin, Claudette Bennett, and Art Cresce. 2007. *Overview of the Results of New Race and Hispanic Origin Questions in Census 2000*. Research Report Series, Survey Methodology #2007-05. Washington, DC: US Census Bureau.

del Real, Jose A. 2018. "Who Are We Talking about When We Talk about Latino Voters?" *New York Times*, October 24.

DeNavas-Walt, Carmen, and Bernadette D. Proctor. 2014. "Income and Poverty in the United States: 2013." Current Population Reports P60-249. Washington, DC: US Bureau of the Census (September).

Denton, Nancy, and Douglas Massey. 1988. "Residential Segregation of Blacks, Hispanics, and Asian Americans by Socioeconomic Status and Generation." *Social Science Quarterly* 69: 797–817.

———. 1989. "Racial Identity among Caribbean Hispanics: The Effects of Double Minority Status on Residential Segregation." *American Sociological Review* 54, no. 5: 790–809.

Department of Homeland Security. 2013. "The Costs and Benefits of Border Security." Washington, DC: Department of Homeland Security, https://www.usimmigration.com/cost-benefits-border-security.html.

———. 2016. "Budget-in-Brief Fiscal Year 2016." Washington, DC: Department of Homeland Security.

DeSipio, Louis. 1996. *Counting the Latino Vote: Latinos as a New Electorate*. Charlottesville: University of Virginia Press.

———. 2006. "Latino Civic and Political Participation." In *Hispanics and the Future of America*, edited by Marta Tienda and Faith Mitchell, 447–79. Washington, DC: National Academies Press.

DeSipio, Louis, and Rodolfo O. de la Garza. 1998. *Making Americans and Remaking Americans: Immigration and Immigrant Policy*. Boulder, CO: Westview.

———. 2002. "Forever Seen as New: Latino Participation in American Elections." In *Latinos: Remaking America*, edited by Marcelo M. Suárez-Orozco and Mariela M. Páez, 398–409. Berkeley: University of California Press.

DeSipio, Louis, and Carole Jean Uhlaner. 2007. "Immigrant and Native: Mexican American 2004 Presidential Vote Choice across Immigrant Generations." *American Politics Research* 35, no. 2 (March): 176–201.

Díaz-Briquets, Sergio. 1990. "The Central American Demographic Situation: Trends and Implications." In *Mexican and Central American Population in U.S. Immigration Policy*, edited by Frank Bean, J. Schmandt, and S. Weintraub. Austin: University of Texas Press.

DiBranco, Alex. 2010. "DHS Analysis Finds That 287(g) Program Is a Big, Fat Flop." ImmigrationChange.org, April 7, http://immigration.change.org/blog/view/dhs_analysis_finds_that_287g_program_is_a_big_fat_flop.

Dickerson, Caitlin, and Zolan Kanno-Youngs. 2020. "Border Patrol Will Deploy Elite Tactical Agents to Sanctuary Cities." *New York Times*, February 14, https://www.nytimes.com/2020/02/14/us/Border-Patrol-ICE-Sanctuary-Cities.html.

Dill, Bonnie Thornton, and Ruth Zambrana, eds. 2009. *Emerging Intersections: Race, Class, and Gender in Theory, Policy, and Practice*. New Brunswick, NJ: Rutgers University Press.

Doctors Without Borders. 2020. "No Way Out: The Humanitarian Crisis for Migrants and Asylum Seekers Trapped between the United States, Mexico and the Northern Triangle of Central America." New York: Doctors Without Borders.

Doty, Michelle M., Munira Z. Gunja, Sara R. Collins, and Sophie Beutel. 2016. "Latinos and Blacks Have Made Major Gains under the Affordable Care Act, but Inequalities Remain." *The Commonwealth Fund*, August 18.

Dovi, Suzanne. 2007. *The Good Representative*. New York: Wiley-Blackwell Publishing.

Downs, Anthony. 1957. "An Economic Theory of Political Action in a Democracy." *Journal of Political Economy* 65, no. 2: 135–50.

Dropp, Kyle. 2013. "Voter Identification Laws and Voter Turnout." Unpublished manuscript.

Dunn, T. J., A. M. Aragonés, and G. Shivers. 2005. "Recent Mexican Migration in the Rural Delmarva Peninsula: Human Rights Versus Citizenship Rights in a Local Context." In *New Destinations: Mexican Immigration in the United States*, edited by Víctor Zúñiga and Rubén Hernández-León, 155–83. New York: Russell Sage Foundation.

Duran, Richard. 1983. *Hispanics' Education and Background: Predictors of College Achievement*. New York: College Entrance Examination Board.

Dye, Thomas R. 1992. *Understanding Public Policy*. 7th ed. Englewood Cliffs, NJ: Prentice Hall.

Ellis, A. R. 2014. "A Price Too High: Efficiencies, Voter Suppression, and the Redefining of Citizenship." *Southwestern University Law Review* 43, no. 2015-1.

Ellis, Atiba R. 2009. "The Cost of the Vote: Poll Taxes, Voter Identification Laws, and the Price of Democracy." *Denver University Law Review* 86: 1023, 1068.

Ellis, Basia D., Roberto G. Gonzales, and Sarah A. Rendón García. 2019. "The Power of Inclusion: Theorizing 'Abjectivity' and Agency under DACA." Cultural Studies. *Critical Methodologies* 19, no. 3: 161–72.

Ellison, Christopher G., and Daniel A. Powers. 1994. "The Contact Hypothesis and Racial Attitudes among Black Americans." *Social Science Quarterly* 75, no. 2: 385–99.

Elliston, Jon. 1995. "The Myth of the Miami Monolith." *NACLA Report on the Americas* 29, no. 2: 40–42.

Enchautegui, María E. 2013. "Broken Immigration Policy: Broken Families." Washington, DC: Urban Institute.

Enders, Walter, and Todd Sandler. 2005. "After 9/11: Is It All Different Now?" *Journal of Conflict Resolution* 49, no. 2: 259–77.

Engstrom, Richard L. 1992. "Modified Multi-Seat Election Systems as Remedies for Minority Vote Dilution." *Stetson Law Review* 21: 743–70.

———. 1994. "The Voting Rights Act: Disenfranchisement, Dilution, and Alternative Election Systems." *PS: Political Science and Politics* 27, no. 4: 685–88.

Engstrom, Richard L., Delbert A. Taebel, and Richard L. Cole. 1997. "Cumulative Voting as a Remedy for Minority Vote Dilution: The Case of Alamogordo, New Mexico." *Journal of Law and Politics* 5: 469–97.

Ennis, Sharon R., Merarys Rios-Vargas, and Nora G. Albert. 2011. "The Hispanic Population: 2010." *U.S. Census Briefs*. Washington, DC: US Census Bureau.

Epps, Garrett. 2019. "Is the Citizen Question Dead?" *The Atlantic*, June 27.

Escala-Rabadán, Luis, Xóchitl Bada, and Gaspar Rivera-Salgado. 2006. "Mexican Migrant Civic and Political Participation in the US: The Case of Hometown Associations in Los Angeles and Chicago." *Norteamérica. Revista Académica del CISAN-UNAM* 1, no. 2: 127–72.

Escarce, Jose, Leo S. Morales, Ruben G. Rumbaut. 2006. "The Health Status and Health Behaviors of Hispanics." In *Hispanics and the Future of America*, eds. Marta Tienda and Faith Mitchell, 362–409. Washington, DC: National Academies Press.

Esman, Milton. 1985. "Two Dimensions of Ethnic Politics: A Defense of Homeland and Immigrant Rights." *Ethnic and Racial Studies* 8: 438–50.

———. 1995. *Ethnic Politics*. Ithaca, NY: Cornell University Press.

Espenshade, Thomas, and S. Karthick Ramakrishnan. 2001. "Immigrant Incorporation and Political Participation." *International Migration Review* 35, no. 3 (Autumn): 870–909.

Espiritu, Yen Lee. 1992. *Asian American Pan Ethnicity: Bonding Institutions and Identities*. Philadelphia: Temple University Press.

———. 1996. "Colonial Expression, Labour Importation, and Group Formation: Filipinos in the United States." *Ethnic and Racial Studies* 19: 28–48.

———. 1997. *Asian American Women and Men: Labor, Laws, and Love*. Thousand Oaks, CA: Sage.

Eveland, William P., Jr., and Myiah Hutchens Hively. 2009. "Political Discussion Frequency, Network Size, and Heterogeneity of Discussion as Predictors of Political Knowledge and Participation." *Journal of Communication* 59, no. 2: 205–24.

Eviatar, Daphne. 2009. "Immigration Program Expands, Despite Abuse Record." *Washington Independent*, July 23, http://washingtonindependent.com/52197/immigrationprogram-expands-despite-abuse-record.

Faiola, Anthony, and Nick Miroff. 2018. "As Trump Tightens Asylum Rules, Thousands of Venezuelans Find a Warm Welcome in Miami." *Washington Post*, May 18.

Falcón, Angelo. 1988. "Black and Latino Politics in New York City." In *Latinos and the Political System*, ed. F. Chris García. Notre Dame, IN: University of Notre Dame Press.

———. 1992. "Time to Rethink the Voting Rights Act." *Social Policy* (Fall–Winter): 17–23.

———. 1995. "Puerto Ricans and the Politics of Racial Identity." In *Racial and Ethnic Identity: Psychological Development and Creative Expression*, edited by Ezra Griffith, Howard Blue, and Herbert Harris, 193–207. New York: Routledge & Kegan Paul.

Falcón, Angelo, and John Santiago, eds. 1993. "Race, Ethnicity, and Redistricting in New York City: The Gartner Report and Its Critics." IPR Policy Forums Proceedings. New York: Institute for Puerto Rican Policy.

Farley, Reynolds. 1996. *The New American Reality: Who We Are, How We Got There, Where We Are Going*. New York: Sage.

Feagin, Joseph, and Clarice Feagin. 1996. *Race and Ethnic Relations*. 5th ed. Englewood Cliffs, NJ: Prentice Hall.

Félix, Adrián. 2008. "New Americans or Diasporic Nationalists? Mexican Migrant Responses to Naturalization and Implications for Political Participation." *American Quarterly* 60, no. 3 (September): 601–24.

Feriss, Susan. 2019. "Number of Detainees with No Criminal Record Rises Sharply, Defying Rhetoric." Washington, DC: Center for Public Integrity, June 25.

Fernández, Edward. 1985. "Persons of Spanish Origin in the United States, March 1982, Series P-20, no. 396." Washington, DC: US Government Printing Office.

Fernández, Maria Elena. 1999. "Prop. 187 Backers Pushing New Initiatives." *Los Angeles Times*, December 3.

Figueroa, Hector. 1996. "The Growing Force of Latino Labor." *NACLA Report on the Americas* 30 (November–December): 19–24.

File, Thom. 2013. "The Diversifying Electorate: Voting Rates by Race and Hispanic Origin in 2012 (and Other Recent Elections)." Washington, DC: US Census Bureau.

———. 2015. "Who Votes? Congressional Elections and the American Electorate: 1978–2014." Washington, DC: US Census Bureau.

———. 2018. "Characteristics of Voters in the Presidential Election of 2016." United States Census Bureau, https://www.census.gov/content/dam/Census/library/publications/2018/demo/P20-582.pdf.

File, Thom, and Sarah Crissey. 2010. "Voting and Registration in the Election of 2008." *Current Population Reports P20-562*. Washington, DC: US Census Bureau.

Fiscella, Kevin, Peter Franks, Mark P. Doescher, and Barry G. Saver. 2002. "Disparities in Health Care by Race, Ethnicity, and Language among the Insured: Findings from a National Sample." *Medical Care* 40, no. 1 (January): 52–59.

Fitzgerald, Joseph. 1971. *Puerto Rican Americans: The Meaning of Migration to the Mainland*. Englewood Cliffs, NJ: Prentice Hall.

Fitzpatrick, Joseph P., and Lourdes Travieso Parker. 1981. "Hispanic Americans in the Eastern U.S." *Annals of the American Academy of Political and Social Sciences* 454: 98–110.

Fix, Janet. 2001. "The Changing Face of Unions." *Detroit Free Press*, April 30.

Fletcher, Thomas D., Debra A. Major, and Donald D. Davis. 2008. "The Interactive Relationship of Competitive Climate and Trait Competitiveness with Workplace Attitudes, Stress, and Performance." *Journal of Organizational Behavior* 29, no. 7: 899–922.

Flores, Antonio, and Mark Hugo Lopez. 2018a. "Key Facts about Latinos in 2018 Midterms." Pew Research Center, https://www.pewresearch.org/fact-tank/2018/10/15/key-facts-about-latinos-in-the-2018-midterm-elections/.

———. 2018b. "Among U.S. Latinos the Internet Now Rivals Television as a Source of News." Washington, DC: Pew Hispanic Research Center (January).

Flores, William V. 2003. "New Citizens, New Rights: Undocumented Immigrants and Latino Cultural Citizenship." *Latin American Perspectives* 30, no. 2 (March): 87–100.

Foley, Douglas. 1988. *From Peones to Politicos: Class and Ethnicity in a South Texas Town*. Austin: University of Texas Press.

Foley, Elise. 2010. "Kyl Pushes for Expansion of Operation Streamline." *Washington Independent*, July 23, http://washingtonindependent.com/92374/kyl-pushes-for-expansion-of-operation-streamline.

Fontenot, Albert E., Jr. 2018. "Using Two Separate Questions for Race and Ethnicity in 2018 End-to-End Census Test and 2020 Census." US Bureau of the Census, 2020 Census Program Memorandum Series, Washington, DC, January 26.

Forgey, Quint. 2019. "Trump Claims He'll Strike Deal for Dreamers with Dems If SCOTUS Overturns DACA." *Politico*, November 12.

Fox, Geoffrey. 1997. *Hispanic Nation: Culture, Politics, and Construction of Identity*. Tucson: University of Arizona Press.

Fox, Jonathan A. 2006. "Invisible No More: Mexican Migrant Civic Participation in the United States." Santa Cruz, CA: Center for Global, International, and Regional Studies.

Fraga, Luis R. 2009. "Education and Latinos: Civic Engagement in School-Related Matters, Results from the Latino National Survey." Paper presented at the annual meeting of the Midwest Political Science Association, Chicago, April.

Fraga, Luis R., John A. García, Rodney Hero, Michael Jones-Correa, Valerie Martinez-Ebers, and Gary M. Segura. 2006a. Latino National Survey (LNS). ICPSR20862-v4. Ann Arbor, MI: Inter-University Consortium for Political and Social Research, 2010-05-26. doi: 10.3886/ICPSR20862.

———. 2006b. "Su Casa Es Nuestra Casa: Latino Politics Research and the Development of American Political Science." *American Political Science Review* 100, no. 4 (November): 515–22.

———. 2010. *Latino Lives in America: Making It Home*. Philadelphia: Temple University Press.

———. 2012. *Latinos in the New Millennium: An Almanac of Opinion, Behavior, and Policy Preferences*. New York: Cambridge University Press.

Fraga, Luis R., Linda Lopez, Valerie Martinez-Ebers, and Ricardo Ramírez. 2006. "Gender and Ethnicity: Patterns of Electoral Success and Legislative Advocacy among Latina and Latino State Officials in Four States." *Journal of Women, Politics and Policy* 28, no. 3–4: 121–45.

Fraga, Luis R., Kenneth J. Meier, and Robert E. England. 1986. "Hispanic Americans and Educational Policy: Limits to Equal Access." *Journal of Politics* 48, no. 4: 850–76.

Fraga, Luis R., and Gary Segura. 2006. "Culture Clash? Contesting Notions of American Identity and the Effects of Latin American Immigration." *PS: Political Science and Politics* 4, no. 2 (June): 279.

Franco, Celinda. 2009. "Federal Domestic Illegal Drug Enforcement Efforts: Are They Working?" *CRS-5700*. Washington, DC: Congressional Research Service.

Frankenberg, Erica, and Gary Orfield, eds. 2012. *The Resegregation of Suburban Schools: A Hidden Crisis in American Education*. Cambridge, MA: Harvard University Press.

Fry, Richard, and Mark Lopez. 2012. *Hispanic Student Enrollments Reaches New High in 2011*. Washington, DC: Pew Hispanic Center.

Fuchs, Lawrence. 1990. *The American Kaleidoscope: Race, Ethnicity, and the Civic Culture*. Middletown, CT: Wesleyan University Press.

Gaertner, Samuel L., Mary C. Rust, John F. Dovidio, Betty A. Bachman, and Phyllis A. Anastasio. 1994. "The Contact Hypothesis: The Role of a Common Ingroup Identity on Reducing Intergroup Bias." *Small Group Research* 25, no. 2: 224–49.

Galston, William A. 2001. "Political Knowledge, Political Engagement, and Civic Education." *Annual Review of Political Science* 4, no. 1: 217–34.

Gambino, L. 2018. "Latino Turnout Up 174% in 2018 Midterms Elections, Democrats Say." *The Guardian*, https://www.theguardian.com/us-news/2018/nov/14/latino-turnout-up-174-in-2018-midterms-elections-democrats-say.

Gamboa, Suzanne. 2010. "At Least $800M Spent for Boeing's 53-Mile Border Fence." *Seattle Times*, June 17, http://seattletimes.nwsource.com/html/politics/2012140924_apusborders ecurityvirtualfence.html.

———. 2015. "Island Fiscal Crisis Shifts Puerto Rican Power from NY to Florida." *NBC News*, October 8.

Gamboa, Suzanne, and Asma Khalid. 2015. "As Florida's Puerto Rican Population Booms, Political Parties Move." *NPR*, December 6.

Gandara, Patricia, and Frances Contreras. 2010. *The Latino Education Crisis: The Consequences of Failed Social Policies*. Boston: Harvard University Press.

García, F. Chris, ed. 1974. *La Causa Politica: A Chicano Politics Reader*. Notre Dame, IN: University of Notre Dame Press.

———. 1988. *Latinos and the Political System*. Notre Dame, IN: University of Notre Dame Press.

———. 1997. *Pursuing Power: Latino Politics*. Notre Dame, IN: University of Notre Dame Press.

Garcia, John. 2019. "Yes, I Marked 'Some Other Race.' So What Does That Mean about Race and Latinos?" Arizona State University; Raul Yzaguirre Lecture Series, November.

García, John A. 1977. "Chicano Voting Patterns in School Board Elections: Bloc Voting and Internal Lines of Support for Chicano Candidates." *Atisbos* (Winter): 1–14.

———. 1981a. "The Political Integration of Mexican Immigrants: Explorations into the Naturalization Process." *International Migration Review* 15: 608–25.

———. 1981b. "Yo Soy Chicano: Self-Identification and Sociodemographic Correlates." *Social Science Quarterly* 62: 88–98.

———. 1981c. "Political Integration and Mexican Immigrants: A Preliminary Report." In *U.S. Immigration Policy and the National Interest*, ed. US Commission on Immigration Reform. Washington, DC: US Government Printing Office.

———. 1982. "Ethnic Identification, Consciousness, Identity: Explanations of Measurement and Inter-Relationships." *Hispanic Journal of Behavioral Sciences* (September): 295–313.

———. 1986a. "The Voting Rights Act and Hispanic Political Representation." *Publius* 16: 49–66.

———. 1986b. "Caribbean Migration to the Mainland: A Review of Adaptive Experiences." *Annals of the American Academy of Political and Social Science* 487 (September): 114–26.

———. 1987. "Political Orientations of Mexican Immigrants: Examining Some Political Orientations." *International Migration Review* 21: 377–89.

———. 1989. "Chicano Electoral Behavior and Orientations." In *Curriculum Resources in Chicano Studies*, ed. Gary Keller, 174–82. New York: Bilingual Review Press.

———. 1992. "Hispanic Americans in the Mainstream of American Politics." *Public Perspective* 3, no. 5: 19–23.

———. 1995. "A Multi-Cultural America: Living in a Sea of Diversity." In *Multi-Culturalism at the Margins: Non-Dominant Voices on Differences and Diversity*, ed. D. Harris, 29–38. Westport, CT: Bergen & Garvey.

———. 1996. "The Chicano Movement: Its Legacy for Politics and Policy." In *Chicana/os at the Crossroads: Social, Economic, and Political*, ed. David Maciel and Isidro Ortiz, 83–107. Tucson: University of Arizona Press.

———. 1997. "Hispanic Political Participation and Demographic Correlates." In *Pursuing Political Power: Latinos and the Political System*, ed. F. Chris García, 44–71. Notre Dame, IN: University of Notre Dame Press.

———. 2000. "The Latino and African American Communities: Bases for Coalition Formation and Political Action." In *Immigration and Race: New Challenges for American Democracy*, ed. Gerald Jaynes, 255–76. New Haven, CT: Yale University Press.

———. 2009. "Latino Public Opinion: Exploring Political Community and Policy Preferences." In *Understanding Public Opinion*, 3rd ed., ed. Barbara Norrander and Clyde Wilcox, 25–42. Washington, DC: Congressional Quarterly Press.

———. 2013a. "A Holistic Alternative to Current Survey Research Approaches to Race." In *Mapping "Race": A Critical Reader on Health Disparities*, ed. Laura Gómez and Nancy Lopez. New Brunswick, NJ: Rutgers University Press.

———. 2013b. "Latino Immigrants: Transnationalism and Patterns of Multiple Citizenship Patterns." In *Immigration and the Border: Politics and Policy in the New Latino Century*, eds. David Leal and Jose Limon. Notre Dame, IN: University of Notre Dame Press.

———. 2014. "The Obama Factor and Pan-Minority Coalitions?" *Politics, Groups and Identity* 2, no. 3: 491–99.
García, John A., and Carlos Arce. 1988. "Political Orientations and Behavior of Chicanos." In *Latinos and the Political System*, ed. F. Chris García. Notre Dame, IN: University of Notre Dame Press.
García, John A., and Regina Branton. 2000. "Alternative Voting Systems: Explorations into Cumulative and Limited Voting and Minority Representation and Participation." Paper presented at the annual meeting of the American Political Science Association, Washington, D.C., September.
García, John A., and Rodolfo O. de la Garza. 1985. "Mobilizing the Mexican Immigrant: The Role of Mexican American Organizations." *Western Political Quarterly* 38: 551–64.
García, John A., Rodolfo O. de la Garza, F. Chris García, and Angelo Falcón. 1994. "Ethnicity and National Origin Status: Patterns of Identities among Latinos in the U.S." Paper presented at the annual meeting of the American Political Science Association, Washington, D.C., September.
García, John A., and Sylvia Pedraza-Bailey. 1990. "Hispanicity and the Phenomenon of Communities of Interest and Culture among Latinos." Paper presented at the annual meeting of the American Political Science Association, Washington, DC.
García, John A., and Gabriel Sanchez. 2004. "Electoral Politics." In *Latino Americans and Participation of Latinos*, ed. Sharon A. Navarro and Armando Xavier Mejia, 121–72. Santa Barbara, CA: ABC-CLIO.
García, Juan R. 1980. *Operation Wetback: The Mass Deportation of Mexican Undocumented Workers in 1954*. Westport, CT: Greenwood.
———. 1995. *Mexican American Women: Changing Images*. Tucson, AZ: Mexican American Studies and Research Center.
García, Mario. 1989. *Mexicans and Americans: Leadership, Ideology, and Identity*. New Haven, CT: Yale University Press.
García, Sonia R., Valerie Martinez-Ebers, Irasema Coronado, Sharon A. Navarro, and Patricia A. Jaramillo. 2008. *Políticas: Latina Public Officials in Texas*. Austin: University of Texas Press.
García Bedolla, Lisa, and Melissa R. Michelson. 2012. *Mobilizing Inclusion: Transforming the Electorate through Get-Out-the-Vote Campaigns*. New Haven, CT: Yale University Press.
García-Castañon, Marcela. 2010. "Politica and Politics: The Role of Country of Origin Political Participation in the Political Socialization Process of Immigrants." Paper presented at the annual meeting of the Midwest Political Science Association, Chicago.
———. 2011. "Parents, Politics and Political Socialization: The Role of Family in White and Latino Political Socialization." Western Political Science Association 2011 Annual Meeting Paper, https://ssrn.com/abstract=1767230.
Gaskins, Keesha, and Sundeep Iyer. 2012. *The Challenge of Obtaining Voter Identification*. New York: Brennan Center for Justice, New York University School of Law.
Gay, Claudine. 2004. "Putting Race in Context: Identifying the Environmental Determinants of Black Racial Attitudes." *American Political Science Review* 98, no. 4: 547–62.
———. 2006. "Seeing Difference: The Effect of Economic Disparity on Black Attitudes toward Latinos." *American Journal of Political Science* 50, no. 4: 982–97.
Gershon, Sarah Allen, Celeste Montoya, Christina Bejarano, and Nadia Brown. 2019. "Intersectional Linked Fate and Political Representation." *Politics, Groups, and Identities* 7, no. 3: 642–53.
Gershon, Sarah Allen, and Adrian D. Pantoja. 2008. "Political Orientations and Latino Immigrant Incorporation." In *Latinas/os in the United States: Changing the Face of America*, ed. Havidán Rodríguez, Rogelio Sáenz, and Cecilia Menjívar, 340–51. Boston: Springer.

Gerstle, Gary, and John Mollenkopf, eds. 2001. *E Pluribus Unum? Contemporary and Historical Perspectives on Immigrant Political Incorporation*. New York: Russell Sage Foundation.

Gibson, Campbell, and Kay Jung. 2006. "Historical Census Statistics on the Foreign-Born Population in the United States: 1850 to 2000." Population Division Working Paper no. 81. Washington, DC: US Census Bureau. http://www.census.gov/population/www/techpap.html.

Gilliam, Frank D., Jr. 1996. "Exploring Minority Empowerment: Symbolic Politics, Governing Coalitions and Traces of Political Style in Los Angeles." *American Journal of Political Science* 40, no. 1 (February): 56–81.

Gillispie, Carrie. 2019. "Young Learners, Missed Opportunities." The Education Trust, https://edtrust.org/the-equity-line/young-learners-missed-opportunities/.

Gimpel, James G., and Frank Morris. 2007. *Immigration, Intergroup Conflict, and the Erosion of African-American Political Power in the 21st Century*. Washington, DC: Center for Immigration Studies.

Ginorio, Angela, and Michelle Huston. 2000. *Si, Se Puede! Yes, We Can: Latinas in School*. Washington, DC: American Association of University Women.

Gittell, Marilyn, and Mario Fantini. 1970. *Community Control and the Urban School*. New York: Praeger.

Glasford, Demis, and Justine Calcagno. 2012. "The Conflict of Harmony: Intergroup Contact, Commonality and Political Solidarity between Minority Groups." *Journal of Experimental Social Psychology* 48, no. 1, doi: 10.1016/j.jesp.2011.10.001.

Glassman, Brian. 2019. *Puerto Rico Outmigration Increases. Poverty Declines*. US Census Bureau Report. October 10.

Gómez, Laura. 1992. "The Birth of the Hispanic Generation: Attitudes of Mexican American Political Elites toward the Hispanic Label." *Latin American Perspectives* 19, no. 4 (February): 45–59.

Gómez, Laura E. 2018. *Manifest Destinies: The Making of the Mexican American Race*. 2nd ed. New York: New York University Press.

Gómez-Aguiñaga, Bárbara. 2020. "One Group, Two Worlds? Latino Perceptions of Policy Salience among Mainstream and Spanish-Language News Consumers." *Social Science Quarterly*. doi: 10.1111/ssqu.12884.

Gómez-Aguiñaga, Bárbara, Melina D. Juárez, Francisco I. Pedraza, and Gabriel R. Sanchez. 2017. "Nativity and Citizenship Status Affect Latinos' Health Insurance Coverage under the ACA." *Journal of Ethnic and Migration Studies* 43, no. 12: 1–18.

Gómez-Quiñones, Juan. 1990. *Chicano Politics: Realities and Promise*. Albuquerque: University of New Mexico Press.

Gonzales, Roberto G., and Leo R. Chavez. 2012. "Awakening to a Nightmare: Abjectivity and Illegality in the Lives of Undocumented 1.5 Generation Latino Immigrants in the United States." *Current Anthropology* 53, no 3.

Gonzales, Roberto G. 2008. "Left Out but Not Shut Down: Political Activism and the Undocumented Student Movement." *Northwestern Journal of Law & Social Policy* 3, no. 2: 219.

Gonzalez, R. G., and Bautista-Chavez, A. M. 2014. *Two Years and Counting: Assessing the Power of DACA*. Washington, DC: American Immigration Council.

Gonzales, Roberto G., Veronica Terriquez, and Stephen Ruszczyk. 2014. "Becoming DACAmented: Assessing the Short-Term Benefits of Deferred Action for Childhood Arrivals (DACA)." *American Behavioral Scientist* 58, no. 14: 1852–72.

Gonzalez O'Brien, Benjamin, Loren Collingwood, and Stephen Omar El-Khatib. 2017. "The Politics of Refuge: Sanctuary Cities, Crime, and Undocumented Immigration." *Urban Affairs Review* 55, no. 1: 3–40.

Gordon, M. M. 1964. *Assimilation in American Life: The Role of Race, Religion, and National Origins*. Oxford: Oxford University Press on Demand.

Grenier, Guillermo J., and Hugh Gladwin. 2014. *2014 FIU Cuban Poll: How Cuban Americans in Miami View U.S. Policies toward Cuba.* Miami: Cuban Research Institute Florida International University.

Griswold del Castillo, R., and R. A. Garcia. 1995. "Cesar Chavez: A Triumph of Spirit." The Oklahoma Western Biographies (USA). Norman: University of Oklahoma Press.

Grofman, B., L. Handley, and R. G. Niemi. 1992. *Minority Representation and the Quest for Voting Equality.* New York: Cambridge University Press.

Grofman, Bernard. 1995. "*Shaw v. Reno* and the Future of Voting Rights." *PS: Political Science and Politics* 28 (March): 25–26.

Grofman, Bernard, and Chandler Davidson. 2011. *Controversies in Minority Voting: The Voting Rights Act in Perspective.* Washington, DC: Brookings Institution.

Gross, J. H., and I. Cuevas-Molina. 2020. "Latino Influence and the 2016 Presidential Election: Beyond All or Nothing." *The Latino Vote in the 2016 Election*, ed. G. Sanchez, R. Ramirez, and L. Fraga. East Lansing: Michigan State University Press.

Groth, William R. 2009. "Litigating the Indiana Photo ID Law: Lessons in Judicial Dissonance and Abdication." *PS: Political Science and Politics* 42, no. 1: 97–101.

Guarnizo, Luis. 1994. "Los Dominicanyorks: The Making of a Bi-National Society." *Annals of the American Academy of Political and Social Science* 533: 70–86.

Guest Blog. 2020. "Citizenshipworks: Virtual Review Pioneer." New York: Pro Bono Net, September 18.

Gutierrez, Angela, Angela X. Ocampo, Matt A. Barreto, and Gary Segura. 2019. "Somos Más: How Racial Threat and Anger Mobilized Latino Voters in the Trump Era." *Political Research Quarterly* 72, no. 4: 960–75.

Gutiérrez, David G. 1995. *Walls and Mirrors: Mexican Americans, Mexican Immigrants, and the Politics of Ethnicity.* Berkeley: University of California Press.

Gutierrez, A., and H. Hirsch. 1973. "The Militant Challenge to the American Ethos: 'Chicanos' and 'Mexican Americans.'" *Social Science Quarterly* 830–45.

Guzman, Gloria. 2019. "New Data Show Income Increased in 14 States in 10 of the Largest Metros." US Census Bureau, https://www.census.gov/library/stories/2019/09/us-medianhousehold-income-up-in-2018-from-2017.html (accessed May 1, 2020).

Hackenberg, Robert A., and Gary Kukulka. 1995. "Industries, Immigrants, and Illness in the New Midwest." In *Any Way You Cut It: Meat Processing and Small-Town America*, ed. Donald D. Stull, Michael J. Broadway, and David Griffith, 187–211. Lawrence: University of Kansas Press.

Hajnal, Zoltan, Nazita Lajevardi, and Lindsay Nielson. 2017. "Voter Identification Laws and the Suppression of Minority Votes." *The Journal of Politics* 79, no. 2: 363–79.

Hamermesh, Daniel S., and Frank D. Bean. 1998. *Help or Hindrance? The Economic Implications of Immigration for African Americans.* New York: Russell Sage Foundation.

Hanson, Brian. 2016. "Part 1: Immigrants and Latinos Bring Population Growth to Rural Communities." Center for Rural Affairs, June 22.

Hardy-Fanta, Carol, Pei-te Lien, Dianne Pinderhughes, and Christine Marie Sierra. 2016. *Contested Transformation: Race, Gender, and Political Leadership in 21st Century.* New York: Cambridge University Press.

———. 2007. "Gender, Race, and Descriptive Representation in the United States: Findings from the Gender and Multicultural Leadership Project." *Journal of Women, Politics & Policy* 28: 7–40.

Hartman, Jean M., Samuel D. Bradley, and Julian Bond. 2016. *Double Exposure: Poverty and Race in America.* London: Routledge.

Harwood, J. 1999. "Age Identification, Social Identity Gratifications, and Television Viewing." *Journal of Broadcasting & Electronic Media* 43: 123–36.

Hayduk, Ron, and Marcela García-Castañon. 2018. "Xenophobia, Belonging and Agency: Citizenship in Immigrant America." *New Political Science* 40, no. 2: 309–16.

Hayes-Bautista, David E. 1980. "Identifying 'Hispanic' Populations: The Influence of Research Methodology upon Public Policy." *American Journal of Public Health* 70, no. 4: 353–56.

Heckman, James J. 2017. "Research Summary: The Lifecycle Benefits of an Influential Early Childhood Program." The Heckman Equation, https://heckmanequation.org/resource/research-summary-lifecycle-benefits-influential-early-childhood-program.

Henry, Charles, and Carlos Muñoz. 1991. "Ideology and Interest Linkage to California's Rainbow Coalition." In *Race and Ethnic Politics in California*, edited by B. Jackson and M. Preston. Berkeley: Institute for Governmental Research, University of California.

Hernandez, J., L. Estrada, and D. Alvirez. 1973. "Census Data and the Problem of Conceptually Defining the Mexican American Population." *Social Science Quarterly*: 671–87.

Hernández, Ramona, and A. Stevens-Acevedo. 2011. "Dominican Immigrants." In *Multicultural America: An Encyclopedia of the Newest American*, ed. Ronald H. Bayor, volume 4, 471–532. Santa Barbara, CA: Greenwood.

Hero, R. 1992. *Latinos and the US Political System*. Philadelphia: Temple University Press.

Hero, Rodney, and Caroline Tolbert. 1995. "Latinos and Substantive Representation in the U.S. House of Representatives: Direct, Indirect, or Nonexistent?" *American Journal of Political Science* 39, no. 3: 640–52.

Herron, Michael, and Daniel A. Smith. 2012. "Souls to the Polls: Early Voting in Florida in the Shadow of House Bill 1355." *Election Law Journal* 11, no. 3: 331–47.

———. 2013. "House Bill 1355 and Voter Registration in Florida." *State Politics and Policy Quarterly* 13, no. 3: 279–305.

Hilbert, Emma. 2018. "Land of the Free, No Home to the Brave: A Report on the Social, Economic, and Moral Cost of Deporting Veterans." Austin: Texas Civil Rights Project.

Hill, Kevin, and Dario Moreno. 1996. "Second-Generation Cubans." *Hispanic Journal of Behavioral Sciences* 18, no. 2: 175–93.

Hirsch, H. 1974. "Ethnic Identity and Students' Perceptions of a Community Controlled School." *Social Science Quarterly* 425–38.

Hochreiter, Susanne. 2014. "Race, Class, Gender? Intersectionality Troubles." *Journal of Research in Gender Studies* 4, no. 2: 401–8.

Hoffman, Abraham. 1979. *Unwanted Mexican Americans in the Great Depression: Repatriation Pressures, 1929–1939*. Tucson: University of Arizona Press.

Hood, M. V., III, and Irwin L. Morris. 1997. "Amigo or Enemigo? Context, Attitudes, and Anglo Public Opinion toward Immigration." *Social Science Quarterly* 78, no. 32 (June): 309–24.

Hood, M. V., III, Irwin L. Morris, and Kurt Shirkey. 1997b. "Quedete or Vete: Unraveling the Determinants of Hispanic Public Opinion toward Immigration." *Political Research Quarterly* 50: 627–47.

Hopkins, Daniel J. 2011. "Translating into Votes: The Electoral Impacts of Spanish-Language Ballots." *American Journal of Political Science* 55, no. 4 (October): 813–29.

Hritzuk, Natasha, and David Park. 2000. "The Question of Latino Participation: From an SES to a Social Structural Explanation" *Social Science Quarterly* 8, no. 1: 151–66.

Hufstedler, Shirley. 1999. "The Final Report of the Commission on Immigration Reform." Statement before the US House of Representatives Subcommittee on Immigration and Claims, Washington, DC.

Human Rights Watch. 2020. "Deported to Danger: United States Deportation Policies Expose Salvadorans to Death and Abuse." New York: Human Rights Watch.

Humes, Karen, Nicholas Jones, and Roberto Ramirez. 2011. "Overview of Race and Hispanic Origin." *Current Population Reports: C2011Ba-02*. Washington, DC: US Census Bureau.

Hunter, Margaret. 2007. "The Persistent Problem of Colorism: Skin Tone, Status, and Inequality." *Sociology Compass* 1, no. 1: 237–54.
Hurtado, Aida, and Patricia Gurin. 2004. *Chicana/o Identity in a Changing US Society: Quien Soy? Quienes Somos.* Tucson: University of Arizona Press.
Ibe, Peniel, and Johnson, Kathryn. 2020. "Trump Has Ended Temporary Protected Status for Hundreds of Thousands of Immigrants. Here's What You Need to Know." *News & Commentary*, January 8.
Igielink, Ruth. 2019. "Men and Women in the U.S. Continue to Differ in Voter Turnout Rate, Party Identification." Washington, DC: Pew Hispanic Research Center, August 18.
Immigration Law Resource Center. 2018. "Changes to the Expedited Naturalization Process for Military Service Members: October 2017 Department of Defense Policies Impacting Lawful Permanent Residents and Other Non-U.S. Citizens Serving in the Military." San Francisco, CA: Immigration Law Resource Center.
Immigration and Naturalization Service. 1996. *1996 Statistical Yearbook of the Immigration and Naturalization Service*. Washington, DC: US Government Printing Office.
———. 1997. "Annual Report on Legal Immigration: Fiscal Year 1997." Washington, DC: US Government Printing Office.
———. 2000. *1998 Statistical Yearbook of the INS*. Washington, DC: US Government Printing Office.
Jackman, Mary R., and Marie Crane. 1986. "Some of My Best Friends Are Black: Interracial Friendships and Whites' Racial Attitudes." *Public Option Quarterly* 50, no. 4: 459–86.
Jackson, Bryon, Elizabeth R. Gerber, and Bruce E. Cain. 1994. "Coalitional Perspectives in a Multi-Racial Society: African American Attitudes toward Others." *Political Research Quarterly* 47, no. 2: 277–94.
Jackson, Bryon, and Michael Preston, eds. 1991. *Racial and Ethnic Politics in California*. Berkeley: University of California Press.
Jackson, James S., Vincent L. Hutchings, Ronald Brown, and Cara Wong. 2004. National Politics Study. ICPSR24483-v1. Ann Arbor, MI: Inter-University Consortium for Political and Social Research, 2009-03-23. doi: 10.3886/ICPSR24483.
Jacobs, Jacob, and Rachel Marks. 2020. "Collecting and Tabulating Ethnicity and Race Responses for the 2020 Census." Washington, DC: US Bureau of the Census, Population Division, February 13.
James, Michael Rabinder. 2011. "The Priority of Racial Constituency over Descriptive Representation." *Journal of Politics* 73, no. 3 (July): 899–914.
Jamieson, Amie, Hyon Shinn, and Jennifer Day. 2002. "Voting and Registration in the Election of November 2000." *Current Population Reports P20-542*. Washington, DC: Department of Commerce.
Jaynes, Gerald, ed. 2000. *Immigration and Race: New Challenge for American Democracy*. New Haven, CT: Yale University Press.
Jennings, James. 1977. *Puerto Rican Politics in New York City*. Washington, DC: University Press of America.
———. 1992. *The Politics of Black Empowerment: Transformation of Black Activism in Urban America*. Detroit: Wayne State University Press.
———. 1994. *Blacks, Latinos, and Asians in Urban America*. Westport, CT: Greenwood.
Jennings, James, and Monte Rivera. 1984. *Puerto Rican Politics in Urban America*. Westport, CT: Greenwood.
Johnson, Hans, Belinda Reyes, Laura Mameesh, and Elisa Barber. 1999. *Taking the Oath: An Analysis of Naturalization in California and the United States*. San Francisco: Public Policy Institute of California.
Jones-Correa, Michael. 1998. *Between Two Nations: The Political Predicament of Latinos in New York City*. Ithaca, NY: Cornell University Press.

———. 2001a. "Under Two Flags: Dual Nationality in Latin America and Its Consequences for Naturalization in the United States." *International Migration Review* 35, no. 4: 997–1029.

———. 2001b. "Institutional and Contextual Factors in Immigrant Naturalization and Voting." *Citizenship Studies* 5, no. 1: 41–56.

———. 2009. "Coming to America: Latinos and the Adoption of Identity." Paper presented at the annual meeting of the Midwest Political Science Association, Chicago, April 12–15.

Jones-Correa, Michael, and Els de Graauw. 2013. "The Illegality Trap: The Politics of Immigration and the Lens of Illegality." *Daedalus* 142, no. 3: 185–98.

Jones-Correa, Michael, and Katherine Fennelly. 2009. "Immigration Enforcement and Its Effects on Latino Lives in Two Rural North Carolina Communities." Paper presented at the Undocumented Hispanic Migration: On the Margins of a Dream Conference, Connecticut College, New London, CT, October 16–18.

Jones-Correa, Michael, and David Leal. 1996. "Becoming Hispanic: Secondary Pan-Ethnic Identity among Latin American Origin Population in the U.S." *Hispanic Journal of Behavioral Sciences* 18, no. 2 (May): 214–54.

Jones-Correa, Michael, Sophia J. Wallace, and Chris Zepeda-Millán. 2015. "The Impact of Large-Scale Collective Action on Latino Perceptions of Commonality and Competition with African-Americans." *Social Science Quarterly* 96, no. 4.

Jordan, Barbara. 1994. *U.S. Immigration Policy: Restoring Credibility*. Washington, DC: US Government Printing Office.

Jordan, Howard. 1995. "Immigrant Rights: A Puerto Rican Issue." *NACLA Report on the Americas* 29, no. 3: 35–39.

Joseph, Tiffany D., and Helen B. Marrow. 2017. "Health Care, Immigrants, and Minorities: Lessons from the Affordable Care Act in the U.S." *Journal of Ethnic and Migration Studies* 43, no. 12: 1965–84.

Juárez, Melina. 2018. "Queering Latinidad: Latinx Politics beyond Nativity." PhD diss., University of New Mexico.

Juenke, Eric Gonzalez. 2014. "Ignorance Is Bias: The Effect of Latino Losers on Models of Latino Representation." *American Journal of Political Science* 58, no. 3 (July): 593–603.

Kalmoe, Nathan P. 2014. "Fueling the Fire: Violent Metaphors, Trait Aggression, and Support for Political Violence." *Political Communication* 31, no. 4: 545–63.

Kamasaki, Charles. 1988. "Testimony on Segregation and Housing Discrimination in the Hispanic Community." National Council of La Raza.

Kandel, William, and Emilio Parrado. 2005. "Hispanic Population Growth, Age Structure, and Public School Response in New Immigrant Destinations." In *The New South: Latinos and the Transformation of Place*, ed. Heather Smith and Owen Furuseth, 111–34. Aldershot, UK: Ashgate.

Kaplan, Ethan, and Sharun Mukand. 2011. *The Persistence of Political Partisanship: Evidence from 9/11*. Working Paper, University of Maryland.

Kasarda, John D. 1985. "Urban Change and Minority Opportunities." In *The New Urban Reality*, ed. Paul Peterson, 33–68. Washington, DC: Brookings Institute.

———. 1989. "Urban Industrial Transformation and the Underclass." *Annals of the Academy of Political Science and Sociology* 501 (January): 26–47.

Kasinitz, Philip, John Mollenkopf, and Mary Waters. 2008. *Inheriting the City: The Children of Immigrants Come of Age*. New York: Russell Sage Foundation.

Kaufmann, Karen M. 2003. "Cracks in the Rainbow: Group Commonality as a Basis for Latino and African-American Coalitions." *Political Research Quarterly* 56 (June): 199–210.

Keefe, Susan, and Amado Padilla. 1989. *Chicano Ethnicity*. Albuquerque: University of New Mexico Press.

Kelly, Daryl. 1997. "Illegal Immigrants Remain a Concern Despite Economy." *Los Angeles Times*, November 2.

Kennedy, Merrit. 2019. "FBI Opens Domestic Terrorism Investigation into Garlic Festival Shooting." NPR, August 6.

Kerevel, Y. P. 2011. "The Influence of Spanish-Language Media on Latino Public Opinion and Group Consciousness." *Social Science Quarterly* 92: 509–34.

Kerlikowske, R. Gil. 2015. "America's Heroin Epidemic at the Border: Local, State, and Federal Law Enforcement Efforts to Combat Illicit Narcotic Trafficking." Written testimony of CBP Commissioner for a Senate Committee on Homeland Security and Governmental Affairs hearing, Phoenix, Arizona, November 23.

Kerr, Brinck, and Will Miller. 1997. "Latino Representation, It's Direct and Indirect." *American Journal of Political Science* 41, no. 3: 1066–71.

Kopan, Tal. 2018. "DHS Ends Protections for Nearly 90,000 Central Americans." CNN, May 6.

Krantz, Colleen. 2001. "Responses Are Mixed to Latino Immigrants." *Des Moines Register*, March 18.

Krogstad, Jens Manuel. 2014. "After Decades of GOP Support, Cubans Shifting Toward the Democratic Party." Pew Research Center Brief, June, 24, https://www.pewresearch.org/fact-tank/2014/06/24/after-decades-of-gop-support-cubans-shifting-toward-the-democratic-party/.

Krogstad, Jens Manuel, and Gustavo Lopez. 2016. "Roughly Half of Hispanics Have Experienced Discrimination." Washington, DC: Pew Hispanic Center.

Krogstad, Jens, Mark Hugo Lopez, Gustavo Lopez, Jeffrey Passel, and Eileen Patten. 2016. *Millennials Make Up Almost Half of Latino Eligible Voters*. Washington, DC: Pew Hispanic Center.

Krogstad, Jens Manuel, Luis Noe-Bustamante, and Antonio Flores. 2019. "Historic Highs in 2018 Voter Turnout Extended across Racial and Ethnic Groups." Washington, DC: Pew Hispanic Center.

Kunerth, Jeff, and Sherri Owens. 2001. "Hispanics Reshape Civil Rights Agenda." *Orlando Sentinel*, July 1.

Landis, Michael Todd. 2018. "How the Know Nothing Party Turned Nativism into a Political Strategy in the 1840's and 50's, Secretive Anti-Immigrant Societies Played on National Fears Fed by the Spread of Slavery." What It Means to Be an American, A National Conversation Hosted by the Smithsonian Institution and Arizona State University, July 12, https://whatitmeanstobeanAmerican.org.

Latino Decisions. 2010. "Latino Election Eve Poll Results: November 2, 2010." November 2, http://latinodecisions.wordpress.com/2010/11/02/latino-election-eve-poll-results-november-2-2010.

———. 2014. "Latino Election Eve Poll Results: November 4, 2014." https://latinodecisions.com/polls-and-research/2014-election-eve-poll.

———. 2018. "Nearly 1 in 4 Latino Registered Voters View Protecting Immigrant Rights as Top Issue in Election 2018." Seattle, WA: Latino Decisions, October 9.

———. 2019. "Latinos Will Play a Decisive Role in 2020 Elections." Seattle, WA: Latino Decisions, November 14.

———. 2019a. "DOJ Attack on Obamacare Has Big Implications for Latinos." Seattle, WA: Latino Decisions, March 28.

Latino Decisions/Center for American Progress Action Fund. 2014. "Immigration Poll—Executive Actions and Its Political Effects." Seattle: Latino Decisions.

Latino Decisions/NALEO. 2010. "National Survey of Latinos and the 2010 Census." Seattle: Latino Decisions.

Latino Decisions/Presente. 2013. *What Latinos Voters Really Want to See in Immigration Reform*. Seattle: Latino Decisions.

Latino Decisions/University of New Mexico RWJF Center for Health Policy. 2015. "National Latino Health and Immigration Survey." Seattle: Latino Decisions.

Lavariega Monforti, Jessica, and Gabriel R. Sanchez. 2010. "The Politics of Perception: An Investigation of the Presence and Source of Perceived Discrimination among Latinos." *Social Science Quarterly* 91, no. 1 (March): 245–65.

Leal, David L. 2002. "Political Participation by Latino Non-Citizens in the United States." *British Journal of Political Science* 32, no. 2: 353–70.

Leal, David L., Valerie Martinez-Ebers, and Kenneth J. Meier. 2004. "The Politics of Latino Education: The Biases of At-Large Elections." *Journal of Politics* 66, no. 4: 1224–44.

Leal, David L., and Kenneth J. Meier, eds. 2011. *The Politics of Latino Education*. New York: College Teachers Press.

Lee, James, and Katie Foreman. 2014. "U.S. Naturalizations: 2013." Washington, DC: Office of Immigration Statistics Policy Directorate, Department of Homeland Security.

Leighley, Jan E. 2001. *Strength in Numbers: The Political Mobilization of Racial and Ethnic Minorities*. Princeton, NJ: Princeton University Press.

Leighley, Jan E., and Arnold Vedlitz. 1999. "Race, Ethnicity, and Political Participation: Competing Models and Contrasting Explanations." *Journal of Politics* 61, no. 4 (November): 1092–114.

Levin, Ines. 2013. "Political Inclusion of Latino Immigrants: Becoming a Citizen and Political Participation." *American Politics Research* 41, no. 4: 535–68.

Liebler, Carolyn, Sonya Rastogi, Leticia E. Fernandez, James M. Noon, and Sharon R. Ennis. 2014. "America's Churning Races: Race and Ethnic Response Changes between Census 2000 and the 2010 Census." CARRA Working Paper Series, Working Paper #2014-09, Center for Administrative Records Research and Applications. Washington, DC: US Census Bureau, Paper Issued August 4.

Lindholm, Kathryn, and Amado Padilla. 1981. "Socialization Communication: Language Interaction Patterns Used by Hispanic Mothers and Children in Mastery Skill Communication." In *Latino Language and Communicative Behavior*, ed. Richard Duran. Norwood, NJ: ABLEX.

Liptak, Adam. 2013. "Supreme Court Invalidates Key Part of Voting Rights Act." *New York Times*, June 25.

———. 2019. "Supreme Court Leaves Census Question on Citizenship in Doubt." *New York Times*, June 27.

Livaudais, Maria, Edward D. Vargas, and Gabriel Sanchez. 2020. "Did Latino Millennial Voters Turnout in 2016?" *Latinos and the 2016 Election: Latino Resistance and the Election of Donald Trump*, ed. Gabriel R. Sanchez, Luis Fraga, and Ricardo Ramirez, 71–86. East Lansing: Michigan State University Press.

Long, Heather. 2020. "Paid Sick Leave: Who Gets It during the Coronavirus Outbreak." *Washington Post*, March 17.

Lopez, David, and Yen Espiritu. 1990. "Panethnicity in the United States: A Theoretical Framework." *Ethnic and Racial Studies* 13, no. 32: 198–223.

Lopez, Gustavo. 2015. *Hispanics of Salvadoran Origin in the United States, 2013*. Washington, DC: Pew Hispanic Center.

Lopez, Mark Hugo, and Richard Fry. 2013. *Among Recent High School Grads, Hispanic College Enrollment Rate Surpasses That of Whites*. Washington, DC: Pew Hispanic Center.

Lopez, Mark Hugo, Ana Gonzalez-Barrera, and Danielle Cuddington. 2013. *Diverse Origins: The Nation's 14 Largest Hispanic-Origin Groups*. Washington, DC: Pew Hispanic Center.

Lopez, Mark Hugo, Ana Gonzalez-Barrera, and Jens Manuel Krogstad. 2014. *Latino Support for Democrats Falls, but Democratic Advantage Remains: Immigration Not a Deal-Breaker Issue for Half of Latino Voters*. Washington, DC: Pew Research Center.

———. 2018. "More Latinos Have Serious Concerns about Their Place in America under Trump." Washington, DC: Pew Hispanic Center.

Lopez, Mark Hugo, Ana Gonzalez-Barrera, Jens Manual Krogstad, and Gustavo López. 2016a. "Latinos and the American Political Parties." *Pew Research Center*, https://www.pewresearch.org/hispanic/2016/10/11/latinos-and-the-political-parties.

———. 2016b. "Democrats Maintain Edge as Party 'More Concerned' for Latinos, but Views Similar to 2012." Pew Research Center, http://www.pewhispanic.org.

Lopez, Mark Hugo, Gretchen Livingston, and Rakesh Kochhar. 2009. *Hispanics and the Economic Downturn: Housing Woes and Remittance Cuts*. Washington, DC: Pew Hispanic Center.

Lopez, Mark Hugo, Ana Gonzalez-Barrera, and Gustavo Lopez. 2017. "Hispanic Identity Fades across Generations as Immigrant Connections Fall Away: 11% of American Adults with Hispanic Ancestry Do Not Identify as Hispanic." Washington, DC: Pew Hispanic Center.

Lopez, Mark Hugo, and Paul Taylor. 2012. *Latino Voters in the 2012 Election*. Washington, DC: Pew Hispanic Center.

———. 1994a. "Study No. 413 Exit Poll: California Primary Election." *Los Angeles Times*, June 2.

———. 1994b. "The Post-Election Study." *Los Angeles Times*, June 7.

López, Nancy, Edward Vargas, Melina Juárez, Lisa Cacari-Stone, and Sonia Benitez. 2018. "What's Your 'Street Race'? Leveraging Multidimensional Measures of Race and Intersectionality for Examining Physical and Mental Health Status among Latinxs." *Sociology of Race and Ethnicity* 4, no. 1: 49–66.

Lublin, David. 1997. *The Paradox of Representation: Racial Gerrymandering and Minority Interests in Congress*. Princeton, NJ: Princeton University Press.

Lydgate, Joanna. 2010. "Assembly-Line Justice: A Review of Operation Streamline." *Policy Brief*. Berkeley: Berkeley Law School, University of California.

Maciag, Michael. 2019. "State Population by Race, Ethnicity Data: Census Statistics for Hispanics, Whites, Blacks, and Asians for Each State." Governing.com, March 1.

Macias Mejia, Yoshira. 2019. *Racial Identity among Latino Millennials: A Determining Factor for Political Behavior*. Dissertation, Department of Political Science, University of New Mexico.

Magaña, Lisa, and Erik Lee. 2013. *Latino Politics and Arizona's Immigration Law SB 1070*. New York: Springer.

Makinen, Gail. 2002. "The Economic Effects of 9/11: A Retrospective Assessment." *Library of Congress*. Washington, DC: Congressional Research Service.

Maldonado, Marta Maria. 2014. "Latino Incorporation and Racialized Border Politics in the Heartland: Interior Enforcement and Policeability in an English-Only State." *American Behavioral Scientist* 58, no. 14: 1927–45.

Mansbridge, Jane. 1999. "Should Blacks Represent Blacks and Women Represent Women? A Contingent 'Yes.'" *Journal of Politics* 61, no. 3 (August): 628–57.

Manzano, Sylvia, Matt A. Barreto, Ricardo Ramirez, and Kathy Rim. 2009. "Mobilization, Participation, and Solidaridad: Latino Participation in the 2006 Immigration Protest Rallies." *Urban Affairs Review* 44, no. 5: 736–64.

Manzano, Sylvia, Ricardo Ramírez, and Kathy Rim. 2009. "Solidaridad and Politics by Other Means: Latino Participation in the 2006 Immigration Protest Rallies." *Urban Affairs Review* 44, no. 5 (May): 736–64.

Manzano, Sylvia, and Gabriel R. Sanchez. 2010. "Take One for The Team: Ethnic Identity, Candidate Qualification and Co-Ethnic Voting." *Political Research Quarterly* 63, no. 3: 568–80.

Márquez, Benjamin. 1985. *Power and Politics in a Chicano Barrio: A Study of Mobilization Efforts and Community Power in El Paso*. Lanham, MD: University Press of America.

———. 1988. "The Politics of Racial Assimilation: League of United Latin American Citizens." *Western Political Quarterly* 42, no 2: 355–77.

———. 1993. "The Industrial Areas Foundation and the Mexican American in Texas: The Politics of Mobilization." In *Minority Group Influence: Agenda Setting, Formation, and Public Policy*, ed. Paula McClain, 127–46. Westport, CT: Greenwood.

Marquez, Timothy, and Scot Schraufnagel. 2013. "Hispanic Population Growth and State Immigration Policy: An Analysis of Restriction (2008–2012)." *Publius: The Journal of Federalism* 43, no. 3: 347–67.

Marrow, Helen. 2009. "New Immigration Destinations and the American Colour Line." *Racial and Ethnic Studies* 32, no. 6: 1037–57.

Martin, Philip, and E. Midgley. 1996. *Immigration to the United States*. Washington, DC: Population Reference Bureau Publications.

Martinez, Lisa M. 2005. "Yes, We Can: Latino Participation in Unconventional Politics." *Social Forces* 84, no. 1 (September): 135–55.

Martinez, Omar, Elwin Wu, Theo Sandfort, Brian Dodge, Alex Carballo-Dieguez, Rogeiro Pinto, Scott D. Rhodes, Eva Moya, and Silvia Chavez-Baray. 2015. "Evaluating the Impact of Immigration Policies on Health Status among Undocumented Immigrants: A Systematic Review." *Journal of Immigrant and Minority Health* 17, no. 3 (June): 947–70.

Martinez-Ebers, Valerie, Luis Ricardo Fraga, Linda Lopez, and Arturo Vargas. 2000. "Latino Interests in Education, Health, and Criminal Justice Policy." *PS: Political Science and Politics* 33, no. 3 (September): 547–54.

Mascaro, Lisa. 2016. "New Data Suggest GOP 2016 Nominee Will Need to Win Nearly Half of Latino Vote." *Los Angeles Times*, https://www.latimes.com/nation/la-na-latino-gop-20150717-story.html.

Massey, D. S. 1989. "International Migration Today, Vol. 1: Trends and Prospects; Vol. 2: Emerging Issues." *Population and Development Review* 15, no. 3: 568–69.

Massey, D. S., and M. Sánchez. 2010. *Brokered Boundaries: Immigrant Identity in Anti-Immigrant Times*. New York: Russell Sage Foundation.

Massey, Douglas. 1979. "Effects of Socioeconomic Status Factors on Residential Segregation of Blacks and Spanish Americans in United States Urbanized Areas." *American Sociological Review* 44, no. 6 (December): 1015–22.

———. 1981. "Hispanic Residential Segregation: A Comparison of Mexicans, Cubans, and Puerto Ricans." *Sociology and Social Research* 65 (April): 311–22.

Massey, Douglas, and Nancy Denton. 1993. *American Apartheid: Segregation and the Making of an Underclass*. Cambridge, MA: Harvard University Press.

Masuoka, Natalie. 2006. "Together They Become One: Examining the Predictors of Panethnic Group Consciousness among Asian Americans and Latinos." *Social Science Quarterly* 87, no. 5 (December): 993–1011.

———. 2008. "Political Attitudes and Ideologies of Multiracial Americans: The Implications of Mixed Race in the United States." *Political Research Quarterly* 61, no. 2: 253–67.

Matsubayashi, Tetsuya, and Rene R. Rocha. 2012. "Racial Diversity and Public Policy in the States." *Political Research Quarterly* 65, no. 3: 600–614.

May, Channing. 2017. *Transnational Crime and the Developing World*. Washington, DC: Global Financial Integrity.

McClain, Paula. 2006. "Racial Intergroup Relations in a Set of Cities: A Twenty-Year Perspective." *Journal of Politics* 68, no. 4 (November): 757–70.

McClain, Paula, Jessica D. Johnson Carew, Eugene Walton Jr., and Candis S. Watts. 2009. "Group Membership, Group Identity, and Group Consciousness: Measures of Racial Identity in American Politics?" *Annual Review of Political Science* 12: 471–85.

McClain, Paula, Niambi M. Carter, Victoria M. DeFrancesco Soto, Monique L. Lyle, Jeffrey D. Grynaviski, Shayla C. Nunnally, Thomas J. Scotto, J. Alan Kendrick, Gerald F. Lackey, and Kendra Davenport Cotton. 2006. "Racial Distancing in a Southern City: Latino Immigrants' Views of Black Americans." *Journal of Politics* 68, no. 3 (August): 571–84.

McClain, Paula, and Albert Karnig. 1990. "Black and Hispanic Socioeconomic Status and Political Competition." *American Political Science Review* 84, no. 2 (June): 535–45.

McClain, Paula, and Joseph Stewart. 1999. *"Can We All Get Along?": Racial and Ethnic Minorities in American Politics*. Boulder, CO: Westview.

McClain, Paula D., Gerald F. Lackey, Efren O. Pérez, Niambi M. Carter, Jessica Johnson Carew, Eugene Walton Jr., Candis Watts Smith, Monique L. Lyle, and Shayla C. Nunnally. 2011. "Intergroup Relations in Three Southern Cities." In *Just Neighbors? Research on African American and Latino Relations in the United States*, ed. Edward Telles, Mark Sawyer, and Gaspar Rivera-Salgado, 201–41. New York: Russell Sage Foundation.

McConnaughy, Corrine, Ismail White, David L. Leal, and Jason P. Casellas. 2010. "A Latino on the Ballot: Explaining Co-Ethnic Voting among Latinos and the Response of White Americans." *Journal of Politics* 72, no. 4 (October): 1199–1211.

McConnell, Eileen Diaz. 2008. "The US Destinations of Contemporary Mexican Immigrants." *International Migration Review* 42, no. 4 (Winter): 767–802.

McDonnell, Patrick. 2001. "Citizenship Process Is Streamlined, but Applications Decline." *Los Angeles Times*, July 4.

Meier, Ken, and J. Stewart. 1991. *The Politics of Hispanic Education*. Albany: State University of New York Press.

Meier, Kenneth J., Joseph Stewart, and Robert E. England. 1989. *Race, Class, and Education: The Politics of Second-Generation Discrimination*. Madison: University of Wisconsin Press.

Meier, Kenneth J., Paula D. McClain, Jerry L. Polinard, and Robert D. Wrinkle. 2004. "Divided or Together? Conflict and Cooperation between African-Americans and Latinos." *Political Research Quarterly* 57, no. 3: 399–410.

Menjívar, Cecilia, and Cynthia Bejarano. 2004. "Latino Immigrants' Perceptions of Crime and Police Authorities in the United States: A Case Study from the Phoenix Metropolitan Area." *Ethnic and Racial Studies* 27, no. 1: 120–48.

Meyer, David, and Sidney Tarrow, eds. 1997. *The Social Movement Society: Politics for a New Century*. Boulder, CO: Rowman & Littlefield.

Mi Familia Voto. 2018. "The Importance of the Latino Millennial Vote." Phoenix: Mi Familia Voto, May 28.

Michelson, Melissa R. 2003a. "The Corrosive Effect of Acculturation: How Mexican Americans Lose Political Trust." *Social Science Quarterly* 84: 918–33.

———. 2003b. "Getting Out the Latino Vote: How Door-to-Door Canvassing Influences Voter Turnout in Rural Central California." *Political Behavior* 25, no. 3: 247–63.

———. 2005. "Does Ethnicity Trump Party? Competing Vote Cues and Latino Voting Behavior." *Journal of Political Marketing* 4, no. 4 (December): 1–25.

———. 2006. "Mobilizing the Latino Youth Vote: Some Experimental Results." *Social Science Quarterly* 87, no. 1: 1188–1206.

Michelson, Melissa R., Lisa García Bedolla, and Margaret A. McConnell. 2009. "Heeding the Call: The Effect of Targeted Two-Round Phone Banks on Voter Turnout." *Journal of Politics* 71, no. 4 (October): 1549–63.

Michelson, Melissa R., and Amalia Pallares. 2001. "The Politicization of Chicago Mexican Americans: Naturalization, the Vote, and Perceptions of Discrimination." *Aztlán* 26, no. 2: 63–86.

Milbank, Dana. 2000. "The Year of the Latino Voter? Only in Campaign Rhetoric." *Washington Post*, May 21.

Milbrath, Lester, and M. L. Hoel. 1977. *Political Participation*. 2nd ed. Skokie, IL: Rand McNally.

Milkman, Ruth. 2000. *Organizing Immigrants: The Challenge for Unions in California*. Ithaca, NY: Cornell University Press.

———. 2011. "Immigrant Workers, Precarious Work, and the US Labor Movement." *Globalizations* 8, no. 3: 361–72.
Millard, Ann V., and Jorge Chapa. 2004. *Apple Pie and Enchiladas: Latino Newcomers in the Rural Midwest*. Austin: University of Texas Press.
Miller, Arthur, Patricia Gurin, Gerry Gurin, and Oksana Malanchuk. 1981. "Group Consciousness and Political Participation." *American Journal of Political Science* 25, no. 3 (August): 494–511.
Mindiola, Tatcho, Yolanda Flores Niemann, and Nestor Rodriguez. 2002. *Black-Brown Relations and Stereotypes*. Austin: University of Texas Press.
Minta, Michael D. 2011. *Oversight: Representing Black and Latino Interests in Congress*. Princeton, NJ: Princeton University Press.
Miroff, N. 2018. "Trump's Zero Tolerance at the Border Is Causing Child Shelters to Fill Up Fast." *Washington Post*, May 29.
———. 2019. "DHS Extends Protections for Immigrants with Temporary Status, Complying with Courts." *Washington Post*, February 29.
Mock, Brentin. 2015. "Will Closing Alabama DMV Offices Affect Black Voters? Even with Its Strict Voter-ID Law, More Than 30 Offices in the State Are Set to Close." *The Atlantic*, October 12.
Mohamed, Heather Silber. 2013. "Can Protests Make Latinos 'American'? Identity, Immigration Politics, and the 2006 Marches." *American Politics Research* 41, no. 2: 298–327.
———. 2017. *The New Americans? Immigration, Protest, and the Politics of Latino Identity*. Lawrence: University Press of Kansas.
Monogan, James E., III. 2013. "Immigration Policy in the Fifty U.S. States, 2005–2011." *Journal of Public Policy* 33, no. 1: 35–64.
Montejano, David. 1987. *Anglos and Mexicans in the Making of Texas, 1836–1986*. Austin: University of Texas Press.
Montoya, Lisa, Carol Hardy-Fanta, and Sonia García. 2000. "Latina Politics: Gender, Participation, and Leadership." *PS: Political Science and Politics* 33: 555–61.
Moore, Joan, and Raquel Pinderhughes, eds. 1993. *In the Barrios: Latinos and the Underclass Debate*. New York: Russell Sage Foundation.
Mora, Cristina. 2009. "De Muchos, Uno: The Institutionalization of Latino Panethnicity, 1960–1990." Doctoral Dissertation in Sociology, Princeton University.
Morales, Rebecca, and Frank Bonilla, eds. 1993. *Latinos in a Changing U.S. Economy: Perspectives in Growing Inequality*. Newbury, CA: Russell Sage Foundation.
Moreno, Dario, and Christopher Warren. 1992. "The Conservative Enclave: Cubans in Florida." In *From Rhetoric to Reality: Latinos and the 1988 Elections*, edited by Rodolfo de la Garza and Louis DeSipio. Boulder, CO: Westview.
Morín, J. L., Y. Macías Mejía, and G. R. Sanchez. Forthcoming. "Is the Bridge Broken? Increasing Ethnic Attachments and Declining Party Influence among Latino Voters." *Political Research Quarterly*, https://doi.org/10.1177/1065912919888577.
Morris, Irwin L. 2000. "African American Voting on Proposition 187." *Political Research Quarterly* 53 (March): 77–98.
Morse, Ann. 2016. "In-State Tuition and Unauthorized Immigrant Students." In *Immigration and America's Cities: A Handbook on Evolving Services*, ed. Joaquin J. Gonzalez III and Roger L. Kemp, 160–64. Jefferson, NC: McFarland & Co.
Motomura, Hiroshi. 2012. "Making Legal: The Dream Act, Birthright Citizenship, and Broad-Scale Legalization." *Lewis & Clark Law Review* 16, no. 4 (Winter): 1127–48.
Muñoz, Carlos. 1989. *Youth, Identity, and Power: The Chicano Movement*. London: Verso.
Murillo, Enrique G., Jr., Sofia Villenas, Ruth Trinidad Galván, Juan Sánchez Muñoz, Corinne Martínez, and Margarita Machado-Casas, eds. 2009. *Handbook of Latinos and Education: Theory, Research, and Practice*. UK: Routledge.

Nabors, Nina A., Ruth L. Hall, Marie L. Miville, Reginald Nettles, Monique L. Pauling, and Brian L. Ragsdale. 2001. "Multiple Minority Group Oppression: Divided We Stand?" *Journal of the Gay and Lesbian Medical Association* 5, no. 3: 101–5.

Nagel, Joanne. 1996. *American Indian Renewal: Red Power and Resurgence of Identity and Culture.* New York: Oxford University Press.

Narea, Natalie. 2019. "The Battle over DACA Comes to the Supreme Court." *Vox*, November 11.

National Association of Latino Elected and Appointed Officials (NALEO) Educational Fund. 2011. *The Latino Vote.* Washington, DC: NALEO Publications.

———. 2014. *Latino Elected Officials in America.* Washington, DC: NALEO Publications.

———. 2016. "Voting, Victories and Viewpoints: A Look at the Top Races and Issues for Latinos in Election 2016." Washington, DC: NALEO, October 18.

National Conference of State Legislatures. 2013. "2012 Immigration-Related Laws and Resolutions in the States (January 1–December 31, 2012)." http://www.ncsl.org/research/immigration/2012-immigrationrelated- laws-jan-december-2012.aspx.

———. 2017. "Voter ID History: History of Voter ID." Washington, DC: National Conference of State Legislatures, May 31.

National Council of La Raza (NCLR). 1999. *Legislative Update.* Washington, DC: NCLR.

National Governors Association (NGA) and the Council of Chief State School Officers (CCSSO). 2016. *Common Core State Standards Initiatives.* Washington, DC: NGA and CCSSO.

National Hispanic Leadership Agenda (NHLA). 1998. *Congressional Scorecard, 105th Congress.* Washington, DC: NHLA.

———. 2000. *Congressional Scorecard, 106th Congress.* Washington, DC: NHLA.

NBC News. 2015. "Puerto Ricans Rally on Capitol Hill: We're American Citizens." December 2.

Negro-Chin, Maria Pia. 2016. "Why Paterson, New Jersey, Is Famous in Lima, Peru: Thousands of Peruvian Emigrants Have Turned a City of 150,000 into the Unofficial Capital of Their Home Country's Diaspora." *The Atlantic*, May 18.

Nelson, Candice, and Marta Tienda. 1985. "The Structuring of Hispanic Ethnicity: Historical and Contemporary Perspectives." *Ethnic and Racial Studies* 8, no. 1 (January): 49–74.

Nelson, Dale C. 1979. "Ethnicity and Socioeconomic Status as Sources of Participation: The Case for Ethnic Political Culture." *American Political Science Review* 73, no. 4: 1024–38.

Nelson, William E., Jr., and Jessica Lavariega, eds. 2006. *Black and Latino/a Politics: Issues in Political Development in the United States.* Miami: Barnhardt and Ashe Publishing.

New York Times Editorial Board. 2020. "The Data on COVID-19's Racial and Ethnic Gap Tells a Painfully Familiar Story." *New York Times*, July 10.

Ngai, Mae M. 2007. "Birthright Citizenship and the Alien Citizen." *Fordham Law Review* 75, no. 5: 2521–30.

Nicholson, S. P., A. Pantoja, and G. M. Segura. 2006. "Political Knowledge and Issue Voting among the Latino Electorate." *Political Research Quarterly* 59, no. 2: 259–71.

Nicholson-Crotty, Jill, and Sean Nicholson-Crotty. 2011. "Industry Strength and Immigrant Policy in the American States." *Political Research Quarterly* 64, no. 3: 612–24.

Nickerson, David. 2015. "Do Voter Registration Drives Increase Participation? For Whom and When?" *The Journal of Politics* 77: 1, 88101.

Nie, Norman, Jane Junn, and Kenneth Stehlik-Barry. 1996. *Education and Democratic Citizenship in America.* Chicago: University of Chicago Press.

Nielsen. 2016. "The Latino Listener: How Do Hispanics Tune in to the Radio?" *Media and Entertainment*. New York: Nielsen.

Noe-Bustamante, Luis, Antonio Flores, and Sono Shah. 2019. *Facts on Hispanics of Honduran Origin in the United States, 2017.* Washington, DC: Pew Hispanic Center.

———. 2019. *Facts on Hispanics of Guatemalan Origin in the United States, 2017.* Washington, DC: Pew Hispanic Center.

———. 2019. *Facts on Hispanics of Mexican Origin in the United States, 2017*. Washington, DC: Pew Hispanic Center.

———. 2019. *Facts on Hispanics of Puerto Rican Origin in the United States, 2017*. Washington, DC: Pew Hispanic Center.

———. 2019. *Facts on Hispanics of Salvadoran Origin in the United States, 2017*. Washington, DC: Pew Hispanic Center.

———. 2019. *Facts on Hispanics of Cuban Origin in the United States, 2017*. Washington, DC: Pew Hispanic Center.

Norwood, Kimberly Jade, ed. 2013. *Color Matters: Skin Tone Bias and the Myth of a Post Racial America*. UK: Routledge.

Nteta, T. M., and K. J. Wallsten. 2012. "Preaching to the Choir? Religious Leaders and American Opinion on Immigration Reform." *Social Science Quarterly* 93: 891–910, https://doi.org/10.1111/j.1540-6237.2012.00865.x.

Oberholzer-Gee, F., and J. Waldfogel. 2006. "Does Local News en Español Raise Hispanic Voter Turnout?" Working paper 12317. Cambridge: National Bureau of Economic Research (NBER).

Oboler, Suzanne. 1995. *Ethnic Labels, Latino Lives: Identity and the Politics of (Re)Presentation in the United States*. Minneapolis: University of Minnesota Press.

O'Brien, Matt. 2011. "Salvadorans Now Fourth Largest Latino Group in U.S." *Contra Costa Times*, May 26.

Ocampo, Angela X., Karam Dana, and Matt A. Barreto. 2018. "The American Muslim Voter: Community Belonging and Political Participation." *Social Science Research* 72 (May): 84–99.

Ocampo, Angela Ximena. 2018. "The Politics of Inclusion: A Sense of Belonging to US Society and Latino Political Participation." PhD diss., UCLA.

O'Connor, Allison, Jeanne Batalova, and Jessica Bolter. 2019. "Central American Immigrants in the United States." Washington, DC: Migration Policy Institute.

O'Connor, Ann Marie. 1998. "School Is Top Issue for Two Immigrant Groups." *Los Angeles Times*, March 19.

Office of Immigration Statistics. 2014. *2013 Yearbook of Immigration Statistics*. Washington, DC: Department of Homeland Security.

Office of the White House. 2020. "Proclamation on Suspension of Entry as Immigrants and Nonimmigrants of Certain Additional Persons Who Pose a Risk of Transmitting Novel Coronavirus (Immigration)." Statement by President Trump, May 24.

O'Leary, Anna Ochoa. 2009. "Arizona's Legislative-Imposed Injunctions: Implications for Immigrant Civic and Political Participation." Mexico, Institute-Woodrow Wilson Center for Scholars, January (Research Paper Series on Latino Immigrant Civic and Political Participation, no. 2).

Oliver, J. Eric, and Janelle Wong. 2003. "Inter-Group Prejudice in Multiethnic Settings." *American Journal of Political Science* 47, no. 4: 567–82.

Oliver, Melvin, and Charles Johnson. 1984. "Inter-Ethnic Conflict in an Urban Ghetto: The Case of Blacks and Latinos in Los Angeles." *Social Movement, Conflict, and Change* 6: 57–94.

Omi, Michael, and Howard Winant. 1994. *Racial Transformation in the U.S.: From the 1960s to 1980s*. New York: Routledge & Kegan Paul.

Ong, Paul, Edna Bonacich, and Lucie Cheng. 1994. *The New Asian Immigration in Los Angeles and Global Restructuring*. Philadelphia: Temple University Press.

Orfield, Gary. 1991. *Status of School Desegregation, 1968–1986: Segregation, Integration, and Public Policy—National, State and Metro Trends*. Alexandria, VA: National School Board Association.

Orfield, Gary, and Carole Ashkinaze. 1991. *The Closing Door: Conservative Policy and Black Opportunity*. Chicago: University of Chicago Press.

Orfield, Gary, and Erica Frankenberg, with Jongyeon Ee and John Kuscera. 2014. "Brown at 60: Great Progress, a Long Retreat and an Uncertain Future." UCLA Civil Rights Project, May 15.

Orr, Marion, and Domingo Morel, eds. 2018. *Latino Mayors: Political Change in the Postindustrial City*. Philadelphia: Temple University Press.

Ortiz, Michelle, and Elizabeth Behm-Morawitz. 2015. "Latinos' Perceptions of Intergroup Relations in the United States: The Cultivation of Group-Based Attitudes and Beliefs from English- and Spanish-Language Television." *Journal of Social Issues* 71, no. 1.

Ortiz, Vilma, and Edward Telles. 2012. "Racial Identity and Racial Treatment of Mexican Americans." *Race and Social Problems* 4, no. 1 (April): 1–22.

Ortman. Jennifer M., and Hyon B. Shin. 2011. "Language Projections: 2010 to 2020." Population Division US Census Bureau Social, Economic, and Housing Statistics Division, US Census Bureau. Presented at the annual meetings of the American Sociological Association, Las Vegas, Nevada, August 20–23.

Ostfeld, Mara. 2013. "*'Nuestro Idioma': Effects of Spanish-Language News Media on Latino Public Opinion*." Ann Arbor, MI: Coalition for Interdisciplinary Research on Latino/a Issues.

O'Toole, Molly. 2019. "Venezuela, Now a Top Source of US Asylum Claims, Poses a Challenge for Trump." *Los Angeles Times*, June 5.

Ovando, Carlos. 1990. "Essay Reviews: Politics and Pedagogy—The Case of Bilingual Education." *Harvard Educational Review* 60, no. 3: 341–57.

———. 2003. "Bilingual Education in the United States: Historical Development and Current Issues." *Bilingual Research Journal* 27, no. 1: 1–24.

Pachón, Harry. 1987. "An Overview of Citizenship: Naturalization in the Hispanic Community." *International Migration Review* 21, no. 2 (Summer): 199–210.

Pachón, Harry, and Louis DeSipio. 1990. "Future Research on Latino Immigrants and the Political Process." Paper presented at the Inter-University Program for Latino Research, Pomona, CA.

———. 1994. *New Americans by Choice: Political Perspectives of Latino Immigrants*. Boulder, CO: Westview.

Padilla, Amado. 1974. "The Study of Bilingual Language Acquisition." Report to the National Science Foundation GY 411534. Spanish-Speaking Mental Health Center No. 1191. Los Angeles: UCLA.

Padilla, Felix. 1986. *Latino Ethnic Consciousness: Case of Mexican Americans and Puerto Ricans*. Notre Dame, IN: University of Notre Dame Press.

Padilla, Steve. 2010. "Questions and Answers on SB 1070—A Guide to Arizona's New Immigration Law." *Los Angeles Times*, July 23, http://latimesblogs.latimes.com/washington/2010/07/arizona-immigration-law.html.

Pan, Phillip. 1999. "INS Says Citizenship Backlog Cut." *Washington Post*, October 29.

Pantoja, Adrian D. 2005. "Transnational Ties and Immigrant Political Incorporation: The Case of Dominicans in Washington Heights, New York." *International Migration* 43, no. 4 (October): 123–44.

———. 2013. *What Latino Voters Really Want to See in Immigration Reform*. Seattle: Latino Decisions.

———. 2015. "Dominican Americans in Northeast Growing Political Power." Seattle: Latino Decisions.

———. 2020."Addressing Racism and Discrimination Has Become a Top Priority for Latinos." Seattle: Latino Decisions.

Pantoja, Adrian D., and Sarah Allen Gershon. 2006. "Political Orientations and Naturalization among Latino and Latina Immigrants." *Social Science Quarterly* 87, no. 1: 1171–87.

Pantoja, Adrian D., Cecilia Menjívar, and Lisa Magaña. 2008. "The Spring Marches of 2006: Latinos, Immigration, and Political Mobilization in the 21st Century." *American Behavioral Scientist* 52, no. 4: 499–506.

Pantoja, Adrian D., Ricardo Ramirez, and Gary M. Segura. 2001. "Citizens by Choice, Voters by Necessity: Patterns in Political Mobilization by Naturalized Latinos." *Political Research Quarterly* 54, no. 4: 729–50.

Pantoja, Adrian D., and Gary M. Segura. 2003a. "Does Ethnicity Matter? Descriptive Representation in Legislatures and Political Alienation among Latinos." *Social Science Quarterly* 84, no. 2: 441–60.

———. 2003b. "Fear and Loathing in California: Contextual Threat and Political Sophistication among Latino Voters." *Political Behavior* 25, no. 3: 265–86.

Pardo, Mary. 1998. *Mexican American Women Activists: Identity and Resistance in Two Los Angeles Communities*. Philadelphia: Temple University Press.

Parker, Kim, Rich Morin, Juliana Menasce Horowitz, Mark Hugo Lopez, and Molly Rohal. 2015. "Multiracial in America Proud, Diverse and Growing in Numbers." Washington, DC: Pew Hispanic Center.

Passel, Jeffrey, and Paul Taylor. 2010. *Unauthorized Immigrants and Their U.S. Born Children*. Washington, DC: Pew Hispanic Center.

Passel, Jeffrey S., and D'Vera Cohn. 2009. *A Portrait of Unauthorized Immigrants in the United States*. Washington, DC: Pew Hispanic Center.

Passy, Florence, and Gian-Andrea Monsch. 2014. "Do Social Networks Really Matter in Contentious Politics?" *Social Movement Studies* 13, no. 1: 22–47.

Pastor, Manuel, Justin Scoggins, and Magaly N. López. 2016. *Rock the (Naturalized) Vote II: The Size and Location of the Recently Naturalized Voting Age Citizen*. Population Center for the Study of Immigrant Integration (CSII), University of Southern California, September.

Patterson, Orlando. 1975. "Context and Choice in Ethnic Allegiance: A Theoretical Framework and Caribbean Case Study." In *Ethnicity, Theory, and Experience*, eds. Nathan Glazer and Daniel Moynihan, 305–49. Cambridge, MA: Harvard University Press.

———. 2001. "Race by the Numbers." *New York Times*, May 8.

Payne, Richard J. 1998. *Getting Beyond Race*. Boulder, CO: Westview.

Pearson-Merkowitz, Shanna. 2012. "Aqui No Hay Oportunidades: Latino Segregation and the Keys to Political Participation." *Politics and Policy* 40, no. 2: 258–95.

Pedraza, Francisco, and Eduardo Vargas. 2015. *National Health and Immigration Survey*. Albuquerque: Robert Wood Johnson Center for Health Policy, University of New Mexico.

Pedraza-Bailey, Sylvia. 1985. *Political and Economic Migrants in America: Cubans and Mexicans*. Austin: University of Texas Press.

Pedraza-Bailey, Sylvia, and Ruben Rumbault, eds. 1995. *Origin and Destinies: Immigration, Race, and Ethnicity*. Belmont, CA: Wadsworth.

Peña, Devon. 1998. *Chicano Culture, Ecology, and Politics: Subversive Kin*. Tucson: University of Arizona Press.

Pérez, Efrén O. 2015. "Xenophobic Rhetoric and Its Political Effects on Immigrants and Their Co-Ethnics." *American Journal of Political Science* 59, no. 3: 549–64.

Pérez, Lisandro. 1985. "The Cuban Population of the United States: Results from the 1980 Census of Population." *Cuban Studies* 15, no. 2: 1–18.

———. 1986. "Immigrant Economic Adjustment and Family Organization: The Cuban Success Story Reexamined." *International Migration Review* 20, no. 1 (Spring): 4–20.

Petersen, Mark. 1995. "Leading Cuban American Entrepreneurs: The Process of Developing Motives, Abilities, and Resources." *Human Relations* 48 (October): 1193–1216.

Pettigrew, Thomas F. 1998. "Intergroup Contact Theory." *Annual Review of Psychology* 49, no. 1: 65–85.

Pew Hispanic Center. 1999–2009. "Publications List of Latino Surveys." Washington, DC: Pew Hispanic Center, https://www.pewresearch.org/publications/?programs=global-migration-and-demography.

———. 2009. *Latinos and Education: Explaining the Attainment Gap*. Washington, DC: Pew Hispanic Center, http://pewhispanic.org/data.

———. 2014. *2012 National Survey of Latinos*. Washington, DC: Pew Hispanic Center.

Pierce, Sarah, Jesse Bolter, and Andrew Selee. 2018. "U.S. Immigration Policy under Trump: Deep Changes and Lasting Impacts." Washington, DC: TransAtlantic Council on Immigration (MPI).

Pimentel, O. Ricardo. 2002. "Hispanic Middle Class Growing Fast." *Tucson Citizen*, January 10.

Pinderhughes, Dianne. 1995. "The Voting Rights Act: Whither History." *PS: Political Science and Politics* 28, no. 2: 55–56.

Pitkin Derose, Kathryn, José J. Escarce, and Nicole Lurie. 2007. "Immigrants and Health Care: Sources of Vulnerability." *Health Affairs* 26, no. 5: 1258–68.

Pitt, Leonard. 1966. "The Decline of the Californios: A Social and Political History of Spanish-Speaking California." Berkeley: University of California Press.

Piven, Frances, and Richard Cloward. 1979. *Poor People's Movements: Why They Succeed, How They Fail*. New York: Random House.

———. 1988. *Why Americans Do Not Vote*. New York: Pantheon.

———. 1993. *Regulating the Poor: The Functions of Public Welfare*. New York: Vintage.

———. 2000. *Why Americans Still Don't Vote and Why Politicians Want It That Way*. Boston: Beacon.

Popke, Jeff. 2011. "Latino Migration and Neoliberalism in the US South: Notes Toward a Rural Cosmopolitanism." *Southeastern Geographer* 51, no. 2: 242–59.

Portes, Alejandro. 1984. "The Rise of Ethnicity and Determinants of Ethnic Perspectives of U.S. Society among Cuban Exiles." *American Sociological Review* 49: 383–497.

———. 1985. "The Political Adaptation Process of Cubans and Other Ethnic Minorities in the United States: A Preliminary Analysis." *International Migration Review* 19: 35–63.

———. 1998. "Morning in Miami: A New Era for Cuban-American Politics." *American Prospect* 9, no. 38 (May–June): 28–33.

Portes, Alejandro, Cristina Escobar, and Renelinda Arana. 2008. "Bridging the Gap: Transnational and Ethnic Organizations in the Political Incorporation of Immigrants in the United States." *Ethnic and Racial Studies* 31, no. 6: 1056–90.

Portes, Alejandro, Cristina Escobar, and Alexandria Walton Radford. 2007. "Immigrant Transnational Organizations and Development: A Comparative Study." *International Migration Review* 41, no. 1 (Spring): 242–81.

Portes, Alejandro, and Dag MacLeod. 1996. "Educational Progress of Children of Immigrants: The Roles of Class, Ethnicity, and School Context." *Sociology of Education* 69, no. 4 (October): 255–75.

Portes, Alejandro, and R. Mozo. 1985. "The Political Adaptation Process of Cubans and Other Ethnic Minorities in the United States: A Preliminary Analysis." *International Migration Review* 19: 35–63.

Portes, Alejandro, and Rubén Rumbaut. 1990. *Immigrant America*. Berkeley: University of California Press.

Portes, Alejandro, and A. Stepnick. 1993. *City on the Edge: The Transformation of Miami*. Berkeley: University of California Press.

Portes, Pedro R., Spencer Salas, Patricia Baquedano-López, and Paula J. Mellom, eds. 2014. *US Latinos and Education Policy: Research-Based Directions for Change*. UK: Routledge.

President's Advisory Commission on Educational Excellence for Hispanic Americans. 1999. *Our Nation on the Fault Line*. Washington, DC: US Government Printing Office.

Preston, Julia, and Lizette Alvarez. 2016. "Florida's Changing Latino Population Veers from G.O.P." *New York Times*, October 3.

Price, Patricia, Christopher Lukinbeal, Richard Gioioso, Daniel Arreola, Damian Fernandez, Timothy Ready, and Maria de la Angeles Torres. 2011. "Placing Latino Civic Engagement." *Urban Geography* 32, no. 2: 170–207.

Public Policy Institute of California. 2000. "The Changing Social and Political Landscape of California." Research Brief. San Francisco: Public Policy Institute of California (PPIC), April.

Pulído, Laura. 1996. *Environmental Racism and Economic Justice*. Tucson: University of Arizona Press.

Putnam, Robert. 2000. *Bowling Alone: The Collapse and Revival of American Democracy*. New York: Simon & Schuster.

Quiros, Laura, and Beverly Araujo Dawson. 2013. "The Color Paradigm: The Impact of Colorism on the Racial Identity and Identification of Latinas." *Journal of Human Behavior in the Social Environment* 23, no. 3: 287–97.

Radford, J. 2019. "Key Findings about U.S. Immigrants." Pew Research Center, https://www.pewresearch.org/fact-tank/2019/06/17/key-findings-about-u-s-immigrants/.

Ramakrishnan, S. Karthick, and Thomas J. Espenshade. 2001. "Immigrant Incorporation and Political Participation in the United States." *International Migration Review* 35, no. 3: 870–909.

Ramirez, Amelie G., and Lucina Suarez. 2001. "The Impact of Cancer on Latino Populations." In *Health Issues in the Latino Community*, ed. Marilyn Aguirre-Molina, Carlos W. Molina, and Ruth Enid Zambrana, 211–44. San Francisco: Jossey-Bass.

Ramirez, Quixmen. 2019. "Ted Cruz Says El Paso Mass Shooting Is 'Heinous Act of Terrorism and White Supremacy.'" News 4, San Antonio, August 4.

Ramírez, Ricardo. 2005. "Giving Voice to Latino Voters: A Field Experiment on the Effectiveness of a National Nonpartisan Mobilization Effort." *Annals of the American Academy of Political and Social Science* 601, no. 1 (September): 66–84.

———. 2007. "Segmented Mobilization: Latino Non-Partisan Get Out the Vote Efforts in the 2000 General Election." *American Politics Research* 35, no. 2: 155–75.

———. 2013. *Mobilizing Opportunities: The Evolving Latino Electorate and the Future of American Politics*. Charlottesville: University of Virginia Press.

Ramírez, Roberto. 1999. "The Hispanic Population in the United States: Population Characteristics." *Current Population Reports P20-527*. Washington, DC: US Census Bureau.

Raphelson, Samantha. 2017. "Central American Immigrants Brace for End of Temporary Protected Status Program." National Public Radio, November 10.

Reed, John. 1997. "The Hispanic Population in the United States: March 1995." *Current Population Reports P20-501*. Washington, DC: US Census Bureau.

———. 1998. "Hispanic Population Nears 30 Million." *Census Bureau Reports CB 98-137*. Washington, DC: US Census Bureau.

Reed, John, and Roberto Ramirez. 1998. "The Hispanic Population in the United States, March 1997." Washington, DC: US Census Bureau.

Renshon, Stanley A. 2009. *Non-Citizen Voting and American Democracy*. Denver, CO: Rowman & Littlefield.

Resnick, Brian. 2014. "Why 90,000 Children Flooding Our Border Is Not an Immigration Story." *National Journal*, June 16.

Reyes, Corinna A. 2006. "Awakening the Sleeping Giant: 21st Century Latino Political Mobilization." Paper presented at the Midwest Political Science Association's Annual Conference, Chicago, April 14.

Reza, H. G. 1998. "Group Stirs Outrage with Billboard Deploring Illegal Immigration." *Los Angeles Times*, May 6.

Rich, Brian L., and Marta Miranda. 2005. "The Sociopolitical Dynamics of Mexican Immigration in Lexington, Kentucky, 1977 to 2002: An Ambivalent Community Responds." In *New Destinations: Mexican Immigration to the United States*, ed. Victor Zúñiga and Rubén Hernández León, 187–219. New York: Russell Sage Foundation.

Rim, Kathy H. 2009. "Latino and Asian American Mobilization in the 2006 Immigration Protests." *Social Science Quarterly* 90, no. 3: 703–21.

Rivero, Daniel. 2019. "Cuban Immigrants Were Given a Haven in the US; Now They're Being Deported." *National Public Radio*, May 11.

Rocha, Rene. 2007. "Black-Brown Coalitions in Local School Board Elections." *Political Research Quarterly* 60, no. 2: 315–27.

Rocha, Rene, and Rodolfo Espino. 2010. "Segregation, Immigrations and Latino Participation in Ethnic Politics." *American Political Research* 38: 614–35.

Rocha, Rene R., Caroline J. Tolbert, Daniel C. Bowen, and Christopher J. Clark. 2010. "Race and Turnout: Does Descriptive Representation in State Legislatures Increase Minority Voting?" *Political Research Quarterly* 63, no. 4: 890–907.

Rodrígues, Helena A., and Gary M. Segura. 2007. "A Place at the Lunch Counter: Latinos, African-Americans, and the Dynamics of American Race Politics." In *Latino Politics: Identity, Mobilization, and Representation*, ed. Kenneth Meier, Rodolfo Espino, and David Leal, 142–60. Charlottesville: University of Virginia Press.

Rodríguez, Clara. 1998. *Puerto Ricans: Born in the USA*. Boston: Unwin Hyman.

———. 2000. *Changing Race: Latinos, the Census, and the History of Ethnicity in the United States*. New York: New York University Press.

Rodríguez, Gregory. 1996. "The Browning of California: Proposition 187 Backfires." *New Republic*, September 18–28.

———. 1998. "Latino Voters Are Finally Awakening to Their Political Power: But Will Cultural Attitudes Reduce Their Effect?" *Los Angeles Times*, January 11.

Rodriguez, Havidán, Rogelio Sáenz, and Cecilia Menjívar, eds. 2008. *Latinas/os in the United States: Changing the Face of América*. New York: Springer.

Rodríguez, Lori. 2000. "Top Candidates Court Latino Vote in Key Primaries." *Houston Chronicle*, February 26.

———. 2001. "Latino Mix Becomes More Diverse." *Houston Chronicle*, May 23.

———. 2006. "Melting Pot: If No Child Is to Be Left Behind, Texas Must Do a Better Job of Classifying Its Students." *Houston Chronicle*, August 21.

Rodríguez, Nestor. 2012. "New Southern Neighbors: Latino Immigration and Prospects for Intergroup Relations between African-Americans and Latinos in the South." *Latino Studies* 10, no. 1: 18–40.

Rodriguez, Robert M., Jesus R. Torres, Jennifer Sun, Harrison Alter, Carolina Ornelas, Mayra Cruz, Leah Fraimow-Wong, Alexis Aleman, Luis M. Lovato, Angela Wong, and Breena Taira. 2019. "Declared Impact of the US President's Statements and Campaign Statements on Latino Populations' Perceptions of Safety and Emergency Care Access." *PLoS One* 14, no. 10: e0222837.

Roedemeier, Chad. 2000. "Hispanic Transformation: Immigrants Stream into North Georgia for Jobs, Changing the Social Fabric of Town and Schools." Associated Press.

Romero, Mary. 2006. "Racial Profiling and Immigration Law Enforcement: Rounding Up of Usual Suspects in the Latino Community." *Critical Sociology* 32, no. 2–3: 447–73.

Romero, Mindy S. 2018. "The Strength of the Latina Vote: Gender Differences in Latino Voting Participation." Washington, DC: UNIDOSUS Policy Brief Special Series: Issue Three, October.

Rosenstone, Steve, and Mark Hansen. 1993. *Mobilization, Participation, and Democracy in the U.S.* New York: Macmillan.

Russell, Mark, and Martha Russell. 1989. "Chicago's Hispanics." *American Demographics* (September): 58–60.

Ryan, Camille L., and Kurt Bauman. 2016. "Educational Attainment in the United States: 2015." *Report no. P20-578*. Washington, DC: US Census Bureau.

Sáenz, Rogelio. 2012. "Engine of U.S. Population Growth: Latinos and the Changing of America." Paper presented at the 2012 Applied Demography Conference, San Antonio, TX, January 9.

———. 2020. "The COVID-19 Rising Toll on Latinos, a Look at the Beginning of July 2020" (Blog). Latino Decisions, July 14.

Saito, Leonard. 1998. *Race and Politics: Asian Americans, Latinos, and Whites in a Los Angeles Suburb*. Urbana: University of Illinois Press.

San Jose Mercury News. 1998. "Vote Turnout Was a Record for Latinos." June 7.

San Miguel, Guadalupe. 1987. *Let Them All Take Heed: Mexican Americans and the Campaign for Educational Equality*. Albuquerque: University of New Mexico Press.

San Miguel, Guadalupe, Jr., and Rubén Donato. 2009. "Latino Education in Twentieth-Century America: A Brief History." In *Handbook of Latinos and Education*, ed. Enrique G. Murillo, Sofia A. Villenas, Ruth Trinidad Galván, Juán Sánchez Muñoz, Corinne Martínez, and Margarita Machado-Casas, 53–88. UK: Routledge.

Sanchez, Gabriel. 2006a. "Latino Group Consciousness and Perceptions of Commonality with African Americans." *Social Science Quarterly* 89, no. 2: 428–44.

———. 2006b. "The Role of Group Consciousness in Latino Public Opinion." *Political Research Quarterly* 59: 433–46.

———. 2012. *Taking a Closer Look at Latino Pan-Ethnic Identity*. Seattle: Latino Decisions.

Sanchez, Gabriel, Adrian Pedraza, and Edward D. Vargas. 2020. "Latino Families Have Personal Connections to the Pain of the Black Community Due to Similar Experiences with Police Brutality." Latino Decisions, July 22.

———. 2020. "The Impact of COVID-19 on Latino Families Views about Returning to School in the Fall: Results from the 2020 National Latino Family Survey." Latino Decisions, July.

Sanchez, Gabriel R., and Bárbara Gómez-Aguiñaga. 2017. "Latino Rejection of the Trump Campaign: How Trump's Racialized Rhetoric Mobilized the Latino Electorate as Never Before." *Aztlán: A Journal of Chicano Studies* 42, no. 2 (Fall): 165–81.

Sanchez, Gabriel R., and Natalie Masuoka. 2010. "Brown Utility Heuristic? The Presence and Contributing Factors of Latino Linked Fate." *The Hispanic Journal of Behavioral Sciences* 32, no. 4: 519–31.

Sanchez, Gabriel, Natalie Masuoka, and Brooke Abrams. 2019. "Revisiting the Brown-Utility Heuristic: A Comparison of Latino Linked Fate in 2006 and 2016." *Politics, Groups, and Identities* 7, no. 3: 673–83.

Sanchez, Gabriel R., and Jillian Medeiros. 2016. "Linked Fate and Latino Attitudes Regarding Health Care Reform Policy." *Social Science Quarterly* 97, no. 3: 525–39.

Sanchez, Gabriel R., and Jason L. Morin. 2011. "The Effect of Descriptive Representation on Latinos' Views of Government and of Themselves." *Social Science Quarterly* 92, no. 2 (June): 483–508.

Sanchez, Gabriel R., and Patricia Rodriguez Espinosa. 2016. "Revisiting Discrimination Theory: The Relationship between Co-Ethnic Discrimination and Linked Fate among Latinos in the United States." *Sociology of Race and Ethnicity* 2, no. 4: 531–47.

Sanchez, Gabriel R., Melanie Sayuri-Dominguez, and Edward D. Vargas. 2020. "Structural Inequalities and Not Behavior Explain COVID-19 Racial Disparities." Latino Decisions, April.

Sanchez, Gabriel R., and Eduardo Vargas. 2016. "Taking a Closer Look at Group Identity: The Link between Theory and Measurement of Group Consciousness and Linked Fate." *Political Research Quarterly* 69, no. 1: 160–74.

Sanchez, Gabriel R., Edward D. Vargas, Melina D. Juárez, Bárbara Gómez-Aguiñaga, and Francisco I. Pedraza. 2017. "Nativity and Citizenship Status Affect Latinos' Health Insurance Coverage under the ACA." *Journal of Ethnic and Migration Studies* 43, no. 12: 2037–54, doi: 10.1080/1369183X.2017.1323450.

Sanchez, Gabriel R., Edward D. Vargas, Hannah L. Walker, and Vickie D. Ybarra. 2015. "Stuck between a Rock and a Hard Place: The Relationship between Latino/a's Personal Connections to Immigrants and Issue Salience and Presidential Approval." *Politics, Groups, and Identities* 3, no. 3: 454–68.

Sanchez, Lisa. 2016. "Latino Ideology, Congressional Polarization, and Racial Threat: An Analysis of the Influence of Latinos on Congressional Politics." PhD diss., Albuquerque: University of New Mexico.

Sanchez Korrol, Virginia. 1994. *From Colonia to Community: The History of Puerto Ricans in New York City.* Berkeley: University of California Press.

Santillán, Richard. 1985. "The Latino Community and State and Congressional Redistricting, 1961–1985." *Journal of Hispanic Policy* 1: 52–66.

Saperstein, Aliya. 2013. "Representing the Multi-Dimensionality of Race in Survey Research." In *Mapping "Race": Critical Approaches to Health Disparities Research,* ed. Laura E. Gómez and Nancy Lopez, 167–87. New Brunswick, NJ: Rutgers University Press.

Sassen-Koob, Saskia. 1979. "Formal and Informal Associations: Dominicans and Colombians in New York." *International Migration Review* 13, no. 2: 314–29.

———. 1985. "The Changing Composition and Labor Market Location of Hispanic Immigrants in New York City." In *Hispanics and the U.S. Economy,* ed. Marta Tienda and George Borjas. Orlando, FL: Academic.

———. 1988. *The Mobility of Labor and Capital: A Study in International Investment Flow.* New York: Cambridge University Press.

Schermerhorn, R. A. 1970. *Comparative Ethnic Relations: A Framework for Theory and Research.* New York: Random House.

Schildkraut, Deborah J. 2005. "The Rise and Fall of Political Engagement among Latinos: The Role of Identity and Perceptions of Discrimination." *Political Behavior* 27, no. 3: 285–312.

Schleifer, Theodore. 2015. "Donald Trump Launches First Attacks against Ted Cruz." CNN, December 12.

———. 2016. "McConnell Worries Trump Could Have Goldwater Effect on Latino Voters." CNN, June 13.

Schlossberg, Jeremy. 1989. "Hispanic Hot Seat: Hispanics Who Live in New York City." *American Demographics* 10 (August): 49–52.

Schwartz, Seth J., Hilda Pantin, Summer Sullivan, Guillermo Prado, and José Szapocznik. 2006. "Nativity and Years in the Receiving Culture as Markers of Acculturation in Ethnic Enclaves." *Journal of Cross-Cultural Psychology* 37, no. 3: 345–53.

Scutti, Susan. 2019. "Festival Shooter Santini Legan Wore Tactical Gear, Sunglasses and a Ballcap. He Seemed Confident in His Use of the Gun." CNN, July 30.

Segura, Denise. 1984. "Chicanas and Triple Oppression in the Labor Force." Paper presented at the National Association for Chicano and Chicana Studies Annual Conference, Austin, Texas.

Segura, Gary M. 2007. "Transnational Linkages, Generational Change, and Latino Political Engagement." Paper presented at the annual meeting of the Midwest Political Science Association, Chicago, May.

———. 2011. "In-Group Identification and Out-Group Attitudes: Latinidad and Relations with Whites and African Americans." Paper presented at the annual meeting of the Southern Political Science Association, New Orleans, January 6–8.

Segura, Gary M., and Adrian D. Pantoja. 2003. "Fear and Loathing in California: Contextual Threat and Political Sophistication among Latino Voters." *Political Behavior* 25, no. 3: 265–86.

Segura, Gary, and Wayne Santoro. 2004. "Assimilation, Incorporation, and Ethnic Identity in Understanding Latino Electoral and Non-electoral Political Participation." Paper presented at the annual meeting of the Midwest Political Science Association, Chicago, April 15–18.

Semana. 2001. "Colombians Are Fastest Growing Latino Group in the U.S." May 14.

Shaw v. Reno. 1993. 509 U.S. 630; 113 S. Ct. 2816.

Shear, Michael D., Miriam Jordan, and Caitlin Dickerson. 2019. "Trump's Policy Could Alter the Face of the American Immigrant." *New York Times*, August 14.

Shelby County, Alabama, Petitioner v. Eric H. Holder, JR., Attorney General, et al. 2013. No. 12-96. Supreme Court of the United States on Petition for a Writ of Certiorari to the United States Court of Appeals for the District of Columbia Circuit.

Sheridan, Mary Beth. 2019. "Cubans Were Once Privileged Migrants to the United States. Now They're Stuck at the Border, Like Everyone Else." *Washington Post*, November 5.

Shockley, John S. 1974. *Chicano Revolt in a Texas Town*. Notre Dame, IN: University of Notre Dame Press.

Sierra, Christine. 1987. *Latinos and the New Immigration: Response for the Mexican American Community*. Renato Rosaldo Lecture Series Monograph 3. Tucson, AZ: Mexican American Studies and Research Center.

———. 1991. "Latino Organizational Strategies on Immigration Reform: Success and Limits of Public Policy-Making." In *Latinos and Political Coalitions: Political Empowerment for the 90s*, ed. Roberto E. Villareal and Norma G. Hernandez. New York: Greenwood.

Sierra, Christine, Teresa Carrillo, Louis DeSipio, and Michael Jones-Correa. 2000. "Latino Immigration and Citizenship." *PS: Political Science and Politics* 33, no. 3: 535–40.

Sierra, Christine, Carol Hardy-Fanta, Pei-te Lien, and Dianne Pinderhughes. 2006. "Gender, Race and Descriptive Representation in the United States: Findings from the Gender and Multicultural Leadership Project." *Journal of Women, Politics and Policy* 28, no. 3/4: 7–41.

Sigelman, Lee, and Susan Welch. 1993. "The Contact Hypothesis Revisited: Black-White Interaction and Positive Racial Attitudes." *Social Forces* 71, no. 3: 781–95.

Singer, Audrey. 2014. "U.S. Immigration Demographics and Immigrant Integration." The Brookings Institution–National Convening on Immigrant Integration, the White House, July 16.

Singer, Audrey, and Greta Gilbertson. 1996. "Naturalization among Latin American Immigrants." Paper presented at the annual meeting of the American Sociological Association, New York, August.

———. 2000. "Naturalization in the Wake of Anti-Immigrant Legislation: Dominicans in New York City." Working Paper 10. Washington, DC: Carnegie Endowment for International Peace.

Singer, Audrey, and Nicole Prchal Svajlenka. 2013. "Immigration Facts: Deferred Action for Childhood Arrivals (DACA)." Washington, DC: The Brookings Institution.

Skerry, Peter. 1993. *Mexican Americans: The Ambivalent Minority*. Boston: Free Press.

Smith, Anthony. 1981. *The Ethnic Renewal in the Modern World*. Cambridge: Cambridge University Press.

Smith, Candice. 2015. "Donald Trump Deletes Tweet about Jeb Bush's Wife." ABC News, July 6.

Smith, James P., and Barry Edmondston. 1998. *The Immigration Debate: Studies in the Economic, Demographic, and Fiscal Impacts of Immigration*. Washington, DC: National Academy Press.

Smith, Tom. 1990. "Ethnic Survey: The General Social Survey." *Technical Report 19*. Chicago: National Opinion Research Center, University of Chicago.

Sobel, Richard, and Robert Ellis Smith. 2009. "Voter ID Laws Discourage Participation, Particularly among Minorities, and Trigger a Constitutional Remedy in Lost Representation." *PS: Political Science and Politics* 42, no. 1: 107–10.

Sokhey, Anand E., and Paul A. Djupe. 2011. "Interpersonal Networks and Democratic Politics." *PS: Political Science & Politics* 44, no. 1: 55–59.

Sommers, Ben D., M. Z. Gunja, K. Finegold, and T. Musco. 2015. "Changes in Self-Reported Insurance Coverage, Access to Care, and Health under the Affordable Care Act." *JAMA* 314, no. 4: 366–74.

Sonenshein, Raphael. 1990. "Bi-Racial Coalitions Politics in Los Angeles." In *Racial Politics in American Cities*, eds. Rufus P. Browning, Dale Rogers Marshall, and David H. Tabb. New York: Longman.

———. 1994. *Politics in Black and White*. Princeton, NJ: Princeton University Press.

———. 2006. *The City at Stake: Secession, Reform, and the Battle for Los Angeles*. Princeton, NJ: Princeton University Press.

Sonenshein, Raphael, and Susan H. Pinkus. 2002. "The Dynamics of Latino Political Incorporation: The 2001 Los Angeles Mayoral Election as Seen in 'Los Angeles Times' Exit Polls." *PS: Political Science and Politics* 35, no. 1: 67–74.

Southern Poverty Law Center. 2012. "Alabama's Anti-Immigrant Law a Cautionary Tale for Other States." Montgomery, AL: Southern Poverty Law Center.

State of Georgia v. John Ashcroft et al. 539 U.S. 461 123 S. Ct. 2498; 156 L. Ed. 2d 428; 2003 U.S. LEXIS 5012; 71 U.S.L.W. 4545; 2003 Cal. Daily Op. Service 5549; 2003 Daily Journal DAR 7001; 16 Fla. L. Weekly Fed. S 448.

Stavans, Ilan. 1996. *The Hispanic Condition: Reflections on Culture and Identity in America*. New York: Harper.

Steinhauer, Jennifer, Jonathan Martin, and David M. Herszenhorn. 2016. "Paul Ryan Calls Donald Trump's Attack on Judge 'Racist,' but Still Backs Him." *New York Times*, June 7.

Stephens, Jessica, and Samantha Artiga. 2013. "Key Facts on Health Coverage for Low-Income Immigrants Today and under the Affordable Care Act." Kaiser Family Foundation Report.

Stepler, Renee, and Mark Hugo Lopez. 2016. "U.S. Latino Population Growth and Dispersion Has Slowed since Onset of the Great Recession." Washington, DC: Pew Hispanic Center.

Stevens, Jeff. 2001. "Hispanics Next in Line for Power." *Odessa American*, May 17.

Stokes-Brown, Atiya Kai. 2006. "Racial Identity and Latino Vote Choice." *American Politics Research* 34, no. 5 (September): 627–52.

Street, Alex. 2017. "The Political Effects of Immigrant Naturalization." *International Migration Review* 51, no. 2: 323–43.

Stringer, J. T. 2007. "Criminalizing Voter Suppression: The Necessity of Restoring Legitimacy in Federal Elections and Reversing Disillusionment in Minority Communities." *Emory Law Journal* 57: 1011.

Stuesse, Angela. 2009. "Race, Migration, and Labor Control: Neoliberal Challenges to Organizing Mississippi's Poultry Workers." In *Latino Immigrants and the Transformation of the U.S. South*, eds. Mary E. Odem and Elaine Lacy, 91–111. Athens: University of Georgia Press.

Stumpf, Juliet P. 2007. "States of Confusion: The Rise of State and Local Power over Immigration." *NCL rev.* 86: 1557.

Subervi-Velez, Federico. 2008. *The Mass Media and Latino Politics: Studies of U.S. Media Content, Campaign Strategies and Survey Research: 1984–2004*. New York: Routledge.

Tarrow, Sidney. 1998. *Power in Movement: Social Movements and Contentious Politics*. New York: Cambridge University Press.

Tate, Kathleen. 1993. *From Protest to Politics: The New Black Voters in American Elections*. Princeton, NJ: Princeton University Press.

Taylor, Paul, Ana Gonzalez-Barrera, Jeffrey S. Passel, and Mark Hugo Lopez. 2012a. *An Awakened Giant: The Hispanic Electorate Is Likely to Double by 2030*. Washington, DC: Pew Hispanic Center.

Taylor, Paul, Mark Hugo Lopez, Jessica Martínez, and Gabriel Velasco. 2012b. *When Labels Don't Fit: Hispanics and Their Views of Identity*. Washington, DC: Pew Hispanic Center.

Telles, Edward. 2018. "Latinos, Race, and the US Census." *The ANNALS of the American Academy of Political and Social Science* 677, no. 1: 153–64.

Telles, Edward, Mark Sawyer, and Gaspar Rivera-Salgado. 2011. *Just Neighbors? Research on African American and Latino Relations in the United States*. New York: Russell Sage Foundation.

Tienda, Marta, and Faith Mitchell, eds. 2006. "Hispanics and the Future of America National Research Council (US) Panel on Hispanics in the United States." Washington, DC: National Academies Press (US).

Tilly, Charles. 1978. *From Mobilization to Revolution*. Reading, MA: Addison-Wesley.

Timberg, Craig, and R. H. Melton. 2001. "GOP Designs Mostly Latino N. VA. District." *Washington Post*, April 11.

Tirado, Miguel. 1970. "The Mexican American Minority's Participation in Voluntary Political Associations." PhD diss., Claremont Graduate School (the Claremont Colleges).

Tobar, Hector. 1998. "Water Bill Triggers Off a Revolt from a Tiny Garage in Maywood, California." *Los Angeles Times*, July 24.

Tolbert, Caroline J., and Rodney E. Hero. 1996. "Race/Ethnicity and Direct Democracy: An Analysis of California's Illegal Immigration Initiative." *Journal of Politics* 58, no. 3: 806–18.

Tolbert, Caroline J., Ramona S. McNeal, and Daniel A. Smith. 2003. "Enhancing Civic Engagement: The Effect of Direct Democracy on Political Participation and Knowledge." *State Politics & Policy Quarterly* 3, no. 1: 23–41.

Torres-Saillant, Silvio. 1998. "The Tribulations in Blackness: States in Dominican Racial Identity." *Latin American Perspectives* 25 (May): 126–46.

———. 2015. *The Dominican Americans (The New Americans)*. 2nd ed. Westport, CT: Greenwood.

Torres-Saillant, Silvio, and Ramona Hernández. 1998. *The Dominican Americans*. Westport, CT: Greenwood.

Tórrez, Adrianna, and Bechetta Jackson. 2001. "Hispanics Planning to Run for Council: Leaders Emerging, Latinos Say." *Ft. Worth Star Telegram*, April 22.

Totenberg, Nina. 2016. "Who Is Judge Gonzalo Curiel, the Man Trump Attacked for His Mexican Ancestry?" NPR, June 7.

Tran, Van C. 2017. "Beyond the Ballot Box: Age-at-Arrival, Civic Institutions and Political Participation among Latinos." *Journal of Ethnic and Migration Studies* 43, no. 5: 766–90.

Tucker, Clyde, and Brian Kojetin. 1996. "Testing Racial and Ethnic Origin Questions in the CPS Supplement." *Monthly Labor Review* 119: 3.

Ture, Kwame, and Charles Hamilton. 1992. *Black Power: The Politics of Liberation*. New York: Vintage.

Uhlaner, Carole. 1991. "Perceived Prejudiced and Coalitional Prospects among Blacks, Latinos, and Asian Americans." In *Ethnic and Racial Politics in California*, ed. Byron Jackson and Michael Preston, 339–71. Berkeley, CA: Institute for Governmental Studies.

Uhlaner, Carole, B. Cain, and R. Kiewiet. 1989. "Ethnic Minorities in the 1990s." *Political Behavior* 11: 195–231.

Umaña-Taylor, Adriana J., and Mark A. Fine. 2004. "Examining Ethnic Identity among Mexican-Origin Adolescents Living in the United States." *Hispanic Journal of Behavioral Sciences* 26, no. 1: 36–59.

Umaña-Taylor, Adriana J., and Amy B. Guimond. 2010. "A Longitudinal Examination of Parenting Behaviors and Perceived Discrimination Predicting Latino Adolescents' Ethnic Identity." *Developmental Psychology* 46, no. 3: 636–50.

United States Census Bureau. 1993. *We the Americans . . . Hispanics.* Washington, DC: Department of Commerce.

———. 2002. "The Hispanic Population of the United States: Population Characteristics." *Current Population Reports P20-527.* Washington, DC: Department of Commerce.

———. 2020. 2017 National Population Projections Tables. Washington, DC: Department of Commerce.

United States Civil Rights Commission. 1972. "The Unfinished Education: Outcomes of Minorities in Five Southwestern States." *The Mexican American Education Project.* Washington, DC: US Government Printing Office.

———. 1974. "Toward Quality Education for Mexican Americans." *The Mexican American Education Project.* Washington, DC: US Government Printing Office.

———. 2001. *Voting Irregularities in Florida during the 2000 Presidential Elections.* Washington, DC: US Government Printing Office.

UNODC. 2018. "Global Study on Smuggling of Migrants." New York: United Nations Office of Drugs and Crime, No. E.18.IV9.

US Commission on Immigration Reform. 1995. *Legal Immigration: Setting Priorities.* Washington, DC: US Commission on Immigration Reform.

———. 1997. *Becoming an American: Immigration and Immigrant Policy.* Washington, DC: US Commission on Immigration Reform.

USDHHS (United States Department of Health and Human Services). 2016. "The ACA Is Working for the Latino Community." USDHHS, July 21.

Vaca, Nicolas C. 2004. *The Presumed Alliance: The Unspoken Conflict Between Latinos and Blacks and What It Means for America.* New York: Rayo.

Vakili, Bardis, Jennie Pasquarella, and Tony Marcano. 2016. "Discharged, Then Discarded: How U.S. Veterans Are Banished by the Country They Swore to Protect." ACLU of California (San Diego and Imperial counties).

Valenzuela, A., and Michelson, M. 2016. "Turnout, Status, and Identity: Mobilizing Latinos to Vote and Group Appeals." *American Political Science Review* 110, no. 4: 615–30.

Vallejo, Jody Agius. 2016. "The Effect Racist Rhetoric Has on Young Latinos, and Why All Americans Should Care." *The Conversation*, April 26.

Van Sant, Shannon. 2019. "Trump Administration Revising U.S. Citizenship Test." National Public Radio, July 20.

Vargas, Edward D., Melina Juárez, Gabriel R. Sanchez, and Maria Livaudais. 2018. "Latinos' Connections to Immigrants: How Knowing a Deportee Impacts Latino Health." *Journal of Ethnic and Migration Studies* 45, no. 15: 2971–88.

Vargas, Edward D., Melina Juarez, Lisa Cacari Stone, and Nancy Lopez. 2021. "Critical 'Street Race' Praxis: Advancing the Measurement of Racial Discrimination among Diverse Latinx Communities in the U.S." *Critical Public Health.*

Vargas, Eduardo, Gabriel R. Sanchez, and Juan A. Valdez Jr. 2017. "Immigration Politics and Group Identity: How Immigrant Laws Affect Linked Fate among U.S. Latino Populations." *The Journal of Race, Ethnicity, and Politics* 2, no. 1: 35–62.

Vargas, Edward D., Gabriel R. Sanchez, and Melina Juárez. 2017. "Fear by Association: Perceptions of Anti-Immigrant Policy and Health Outcomes." *Journal of Health Politics, Policy and Law* 42, no. 3 (2017): 459–83.

Vargas, Eduardo, Nadia Winston, John García, and Gabriel Sanchez. 2016. "Latina/o or Mexicana/o?: The Relationship between Socially Assigned Race and Experiences with Discrimination." *Sociology of Race and Ethnicity* 2, no. 4: 498–515.

Vázquez, Yolanda. 2015. "Constructing Crimmigration: Latino Subordination in a Post-Racial World." *Immigration. & Nationality L. Rev.* 36: 713.

Verba, Sidney, and Jae-on Kim. 1978. *Participation and Political Equality*. New York: Cambridge University Press.

Verba, Sidney, and Norman Nie. 1972. *Participation in America: Political Democracy and Social Equality*. New York: Harper & Row.

Verba, Sidney, Kay Scholzman, and Henry Brady. 1995. *Voice and Equality: Civic Voluntarism in American Politics*. Cambridge, MA: Harvard University Press.

Verba, Sidney, Kay Scholzman, Henry Brady, and Norman Nie. 1992. "Race, Ethnicity, and the Resources for Political Participation: The Role of Religion." Paper presented at the annual meeting of the American Political Science Association, Chicago, September 3–6.

Viruell-Fuentes, Edna A., Patricia Y. Miranda, and Sawsan Abdulrahim. 2012. "More Than Culture: Structural Racism, Intersectionality Theory, and Immigrant Health." *Social Science & Medicine* 75, no. 12: 2099–2106.

Viruell-Fuentes, Edna A., Jeffrey D. Morenoff, David R. Williams, and James S. House. 2013. "Contextualizing Nativity Status, Latino Social Ties, and Ethnic Enclaves: An Examination of the 'Immigrant Social Ties Hypothesis.'" *Ethnicity & Health* 18, no. 6: 586–609.

Voto Latino. 2017. "Citizenshipworks Partners with Voto Latino to Promote U.S. Naturalization through Technology."

Vourvoulias, Sabrina. 2019. "Latinx and Reeling from the Shooting in El Paso? These Philly Organizations Have Your Back." *Generocity*, August 7.

Waldinger, Roger. 1989. "Immigration and Urban Change." *Annual Review of Sociology* 15: 359–85.

Waldinger, Roger, and Mehdi Bozorgmehr. 1996. *Ethnic Los Angeles*. New York: Sage.

Wallace, Sophia J. 2014. "Representing Latinos: Examining Descriptive and Substantive Representation in Congress." *Political Research Quarterly* 67, no. 4: 917–29.

Wallace, Steven P., Jacqueline Torres, Tabashir Sadegh-Nobari, Nadereh Pourat, and E. Richard Brown. 2013. "Undocumented Immigrants and Health Care Reform." UCLA Center for Health Policy Research, August 31.

Wallsten, Kevin, and Tatishe M. Nteta. 2017. "Race, Partisanship, and Perceptions of Interminority Commonality." *Politics, Groups, and Identities* 5, no. 2: 298–320.

Walton, Hanes. 1997. *African American Power and Politics: The Political Context Variable*. New York: Columbia University Press.

Warren, Mark. 1996. "Creating a Multi-Racial Democratic Community: A Case Study of the Texas Industrial Areas Foundation." Paper presented at the Conference on Social Welfare and Urban Poverty, Russell Sage Foundation, New York.

Washington Post. 1999. "Survey Portrays Hispanic Poverty: In Alexandria, a Stark Picture of Growing Group." December 9.

Washington Post Staff. 2015. "Full Text: Donald Trump Announces a Presidential Bid." *Washington Post*, June 16.

Watanabe, Teresa, and Hector Becerra. 2006. "How DJ's Put 50,000 Marchers in Motion." *Los Angeles Times*, March 28.

Weekend Edition (NPR). 2019. "Representative Veronica Escobar on El Paso Shooting." NPR, August 4.

Weinack, Robin M., and Nancy A. Kraus. 2000. "Racial/Ethnic Differences in Children's Access to Care." *American Journal of Public Health* 90, no. 11 (November): 1771–74.

Welch, Susan, and John Hibbing. 1984. "Hispanic Representation in the U.S. Congress." *Social Science Quarterly* 65: 328–35.

West, Cornel. 1994. *Race Matters*. New York: Vintage.

White House, The. 2019. "Remarks by President Trump on the Mass Shootings in Texas and Ohio." *Law and Justice*, August 5.

Wilcox-Archuleta, Bryan. 2018. "Latino Origins: Context, Group Identity and the Politics of Place." *Political Research Quarterly* 71, no. 4: 906–74.

Wiley, Shaun, Jessica Figueroa, and Lauricella Taylor. 2014. "When Does Dual Identity Predict Protest? The Moderating Roles of Anti-Immigrant Policies and Opinion-Based Group Identity." *European Journal of Social Psychology* 44: 209–15.

Wilkinson, Betina. 2015. *Partners or Rivals? Power and Latino, Black, and White Relations in the Twenty-First Century*. Charlottesville: University of Virginia Press.

Wilkinson, Betina Cutaia. 2014. "Perceptions of Commonality and Latino–Black, Latino–White Relations in a Multiethnic United States." *Political Research Quarterly* 67, no. 4: 905–16.

Wilkinson, Betina Cutaia, and Emily Earle. 2013. "Taking a New Perspective to Latino Racial Attitudes: Examining the Impact of Skin Tone on Latino Perceptions of Commonality with Whites and Blacks." *American Politics Research* 41, no. 5: 783–818.

Wilkinson, Betina Cutaia, James C. Garand, and Johanna Dunaway. 2015. "Skin Tone and Individuals' Perceptions of Commonality and Competition with Other Racial and Ethnic Groups." *Race and Social Problems* 7, no. 3: 181–97.

Wilson, Paul. 1977. *Immigration and Politics*. Amistral: Australian National University Press.

Wilner, D. N., R. P. Walkley, and S. W. Cook. 1955. *Human Relations in Interracial Housing*. Minneapolis: University of Minnesota Press.

Wilson, Walter. 2010. "Descriptive Representation and Latino Interest Bill Sponsorship in Congress." *Social Sciences Quarterly* 91, no. 4: 1043–62.

Winders, Jamie, and Barbara E. Smith. 2012. "Excepting/Accepting the South: New Geographies of Latino Migration, New Directions in Latino Studies." *Latino Studies* 10, no. 1: 220–45.

Wolf, Tom. 2017. "Governor Wolf Announces More Aid to Puerto Rico, Calls for Swifter Federal Action to Help Americans" and "Governor Wolf Announces Resource Guide to Help Evacuees from Puerto Rico and Other Devastated Areas." Pennsylvania Governor's Commission on Latino Affairs, News Announcements, September and December.

Wolfinger, Raymond. 1993. "Improving Voter Participation." In *What to Do: Improving the Electoral Process*, eds. P. Frank and W. Mayer. Boston: Northeastern University Press.

Wolfinger, Raymond, and Steven Rosenstone. 1980. *Who Votes?* New Haven, CT: Yale University Press.

Wong, Janelle. 2000. "The Effects of Age and Political Exposure on the Development of Party Identification among Asian Americans and Latino Immigrants in the United States." *Political Behavior* 22, no. 4 (December): 341–71.

———. 2006. *Democracy's Promise: Immigrants and American Civic Institutions*. Ann Arbor: University of Michigan Press.

Wong, Tom. 2017. "The Effect of Sanctuary Policies on Crime and the Economy." Washington, DC: Center for American Progress.

Wong, Tom K., K. Shklyan, A. Isorena, and S. Peng, 2019. "The Impact of Interior Immigration Enforcement on the Day-to-Day Behaviors of Undocumented Immigrants." Working Paper 1. La Jolla, CA: US Immigration Policy Center.

Wray-Lake, Laura, Rachel Wells, Lauren Alvis, Sandra Delgado, Amy K. Syvertsen, and Aaron Metzger. 2018. "Being a Latinx Adolescent under a Trump Presidency: Analysis of Latinx Youth's Reactions to Immigration Politics." *Children and Youth Services Review* 87: 192–204.

Wright, Stephen C., Arthur Aron, Tracy McLaughlin-Volpe, and Stacy Ropp. 1997. "The Extended Contact Effect: Knowledge of Cross-Group Friendships and Prejudice." *Journal of Personality and Social Psychology* 73, no. 1: 73–90.

Yanez, Salvador. 2018. "The Giant Is Awake: The Political Influence of the Hispanic Millennial." Hispanic Heritage Foundation, April 30.

Yarbrough, Robert A. 2010. "Becoming 'Hispanic' in the 'New South': Central American Immigrants' Racialization Experiences in Atlanta, GA, USA." *GeoJournal* 75, no. 3: 249–60.

Ybarra, Vickie D., Lisa M. Sanchez, and Gabriel R. Sanchez. 2016. "Anti-Immigrant Anxieties in State Policy: The Great Recession and Punitive Immigration Policy in the American States, 2005–2012." *State Politics and Policy Quarterly* 16, no. 3: 313–39.

Ye Hee Lee, Michelle. 2015. "Donald Trump's False Comments Connecting Mexican Immigrants and Crime." *Washington Post*, July 15.

Yu, Eu, and Edward Chang. 1995. "Minorities Talking Coalition Building in Los Angeles." A two-day symposium.

Zambrana, Ruth Enid. 2011. *Latinos in American Society: Families and Communities in Transition*. Ithaca, NY: Cornell University Press.

Zambrana, Ruth E., and Olivia Carter-Pokras. 2001. "Health Data Issues for Hispanics: Implications for Public Health Research." *Journal of Health Care for the Poor and Underserved* 12, no. 1: 20–34. doi:10.1353/hpu.2010.0547.

Zambrana, Ruth Enid, and Sylvia Hurtado. 2015. *The Magic Key: The Educational Journey of Mexican Americans from K–12 to College and Beyond*. Austin: University of Texas Press.

Zepeda-Millán, Chris. 2017. *Latino Mass Mobilization: Immigration, Racialization, and Activism*. Cambridge, England: Cambridge University Press.

Zingher, Joshua. 2014. "The Ideological and Electoral Determinants of Laws Targeting Undocumented Migrants in the U.S. States." *State Politics & Policy Quarterly* 14, no. 1: 90–117.

Zlolniski, Christian. 2008. "Political Mobilization and Activism among Latinos/as in the United States." In *Latinas/os in the United States: Changing the Face of America*, ed. Havidán Rodriguez, Rogelio Sáenz, and Cecilia Menjívar, 352–68. New York: Springer.

Zong, Jie, and Jeanne Batalova. 2018. "Mexican Immigrants in the United States." Washington, DC: Migration Policy Institute.

Zuberi, Tukufu. 2001. *Thicker Than Blood: How Racial Statistics Lie*. Minneapolis: University of Minnesota Press.

Zuckerman, Alan S., ed. 2005. *The Social Logic of Politics: Personal Networks as Contexts for Political Behavior*. Philadelphia: Temple University Press.

Index

Note: Italicized page numbers indicate illustrations or tables.

Abbott, Greg, 2
ACA. *See* Affordable Care Act
acculturation, *152*
ACLU. *See* American Civil Liberties Union
activists, identity formation and, 92–95
Affordable Care Act (ACA): relationship with, 232–35; support for, 234, *234*; lack of ACA coverage for undocumented immigrants and, 234–35
AFL-CIO, 172, 173
African Americans: alliances with, 276–77; American South and, 273–74; civic engagement and, *111*; class bifurcation and, 16–17; CMPS political activities assessment of, *112*, 112–14, *113*, *115*, 116; competition and, 271, 275, 280–81; Congress diversity and, *163*; coworkers and, 273–74, *274*; discrimination, contributing factors, 267, *267*; discrimination, perception of, and, 264–65, *266*; discrimination, perpetrators of, 268; discrimination, skin tone, *269*, 269–70, 284n1; discrimination model applied to, 276–77; fertility patterns, 48–49, *49*; friendship network and, *272*; gender and, 261, *262*; grandfather clause and, 13, 22n8; immigration reform and, *207*, 207–8; interest in politics among, 109–10, *110*; internet/social networking and, 116, *117*, 118; linked fate of, 16–17, 259, *260*, 275; Los Angeles alliances with, *260*; *Mobile v. Bolden* and, 237, 251n3; police abuse of, 316–17; political commonalities with, 277; VRA and, 235–36
Alabama House Bill 56, 198
ALHM. *See* Ayuda Legal Huracán María
La Alianza HispanoAmericano, 166, 180
Alinsky, Saul, 178, 179–80
alliances: ALHM, *278*; black/brown, 276–77; CMPS on, 259, *260*, 261, *262*; coalitional affinities and, 274–77, 280–82; conclusions, 283–84; Delaware Hispanic Commission and, *280*; discrimination model of, 276–77; discrimination motivating, 264–70, *265*, *266*, *267*, *268*, *269*; GACLA, *279*; gender and, 261, *262*; Latino Legacy Fund, *278*; among Latinos and other groups, 259, *260*, 261, *262*; linked fate and, 259, *260*, 261, *262*; loose coupling and, 303–4; in Los Angeles, *260*; LULAC, *280*; national-origin groups, 281; political commonalities and, 277; political development and, 301; politics of, 282; preconditions for successful, 281–82; Puerto Rican disasters and, *277*; requisites for, 276; social contact and, 270–74, *272*, *274*; Trump and, 282, *283*; UnidosUS program, *278*; United Way, *279*; white power structure and, 277; women and, 282
alternative voting system, 246–47
American Civil Liberties Union (ACLU), 213, 248
Andrade, Miguel, 3

372

Antiterrorism and Effective Death Penalty Act (ATEDPA), 210
arenas of participation, 112, 155n1
Arizona Proposition 200, 149–50
Arizona Senate Bill 1070, 126; Alabama House Bill 56 and, 198; federal government and, 99–100; ICE and, *186*; provisions, *187*
Arizona Senate Bill 2281, *186*
Asian Americans: civic engagement and, *111*; CMPS political activities assessment of, *112*, 112–14, *113*, *115*, 116; Congress diversity and, *163*; discrimination, contributing factors, 267, *267*; discrimination, perception of, and, 264–65, *266*; gender and, 261, *262*; immigration reform and, *207*, 207–8; interest in politics among, 109–10, *110*; internet/social networking and, 116, *117*, 118; Los Angeles alliances with, *260*
Asociación Communal de Dominicanos Progresistas, 83
Aspira v. New York Board of Education, 168
Astin, Alexander, 226
asylum: detention centers and, 202; immigration policies, US, 201–8; protection qualifications, 203; UAC and, 201–2
at-large election system, 241, 246, 251n3
ATEDPA. *See* Antiterrorism and Effective Death Penalty Act
Ayuda Legal Huracán María (ALHM), *278*

Baker v. Carr, 243
Balaguer, Joaquín, 83, 86n4
ballot propositions, 126; Proposition 187, 67, 128n7, 142, 209, 215; Proposition 200, 149–50; Proposition 209, 67, 128n7; Proposition 227, 150, 229–30; Proposition 237, 67; Proposition BB, 216; Wilson and, 50
Barajas, Hector, *214*
Barajas-Gonzalez, R., 6
Barreto, Matt, *8*, 9
Bastrop I.S.D. v. Gonzalez, 225
Biden, Joe: mass shootings and, 2; polarization and, 144; voting behavior toward, 139, *140*
bilingual education, 171–72, 183n5, 227–30
birthright citizenship, 198, 249, 303, 320
Bonilla-Rodriguez, Damary, *279*

Booker, Cory, 2
Border Patrol, 192–93, 194–95, 202, 210
Boricuas, 71
Bradley, Tom, *260*
Brown Berets, 95–96
Bush, George W.: CANF and, 170; voting behavior toward, 139, *140*
business organizations, 172–73

CAFÉ. *See* Cuban Americans for Engagement
California: elected officials rise in, 293–94; Los Angeles, 217, *260*, 289; migration to, 66–67; Proposition 187, 67, 128n7, 142, 209, 215; Proposition 209, 67, 128n7; Proposition 227, 150, 229–30; school segregation and, 220
Callegari-Balarezo, Guillermo, *80*
Cambio Cubano, 170
CANC. *See* Cuban American National Council
CANF. *See* Cuban American National Foundation
Castro, Fidel, 74
Castro, Joaquin, 3
Castro, Julian, 2, 143
Castro, Raúl, 75
CBDG. *See* Community Block Development Grant
CBP. *See* Customs and Border Protection
CCD. *See* Committee for Cuban Democracy
CDC. *See* Center for Disease Control
census: citizenship status question and, 7–9, *8*, 11; combined-question format, 10; fertility patterns, 48–49, *49*; Latino trust in, 7, 22n4; multiple-response option, 10–11; NALEO and, 177, 183n10; 1970, 42; 1980, 92; population measurement, 9–11; race and ethnicity in, 9–11, 22n6; racial categories in, 40n2; rural communities and, *290*; short and long forms of, 26, 40n1; "some other race" question on, 12–13, 35, *35*, *37*, 89; 2000, 183n10; 2010, 18, 35, *35*; 2020 decennial, 7–10, *8*, 12–13, 18, 45; US decennial, 40n1
Center for Disease Control (CDC), 312
Center for Rural Affairs, *290*
Central America: Northern Triangle and, 77–80, 81–82; political development and, 301; political refugee status and, 304; population and, 288–89. *See also specific countries*

CHCI. *See* Congressional Hispanic Caucus Institute
Chicago, 67, 95
citizenship: husband and wife, 192, 219n1; immigration reform and, *207*, 207–8; naturalization and immigration, 208–12, *209*; naturalization rates, 53–54; obstacles to seeking, 208–9; reasons for attaining, 208; status question, 7–9, *8*, 11; surge in, 209–10; veterans and, *212*. *See also* League of United Latin American Citizens; non-citizen immigrants
Citizenshipworks 2.0, 211
citizen voting age population (CVAP), 8–9
civic engagement: CMPS on, 110–12, *111*; mobilization and, 141–43; mobilizing factors of, 129; news media and, 293; social science research, 129, 155n2
civic life, 103, 125, 208, 320
civil rights: organizations, 168–69; Texas Civil Rights Project, *214*; topics addressed, 20. *See also* racial justice
class bifurcation: African Americans and, 16–17; Latinos and, 17
CLILA. *See* Coalition of Latino Leaders
Clinton, Hillary, 139, *140*
Clinton, William J.: CANF and, 170; Sotomayor and, 176
Clinton administration, 216
CMPS. *See* Collaborative Multiracial Post-Election Survey
Coalition of Latino Leaders (CLILA), 288
coalitions. *See* alliances
co-ethnic, 118, 127, 143
Collaborative Multiracial Post-Election Survey (CMPS), 29; on alliances, 259, *260*, 261, *262*; civic engagement and, 110–12, *111*; on culture and communities of interest, 258–59, *259*; electoral participation factors and, 140; gender and nativity and, 114, *115*, 116, 261, *262*; on identity, affinities, and connectiveness, 254, 256–59, *257*, *258*, *259*; importance of political activities assessed in, *113*, 113–14; interest in politics measured in, 109–10, *110*; internet/social networking and, 116, *117*, 118; on language, 258–59, *259*; number of political activities engaged in, 112–13, *113*; origins of, 253–54; overview about, 109, 128n3, 254–55; political activities and, *112*, 112–14, *113*, *115*, 116;

political orientations in, 109–10, *110*; range of political activities assessed in, 114, *115*, 116; 2008–2009, 254–55; 2012, 255; 2016, 255; 2020, 255–56
Colombians: community involvement of, 84; demographic profile of, 46, 47, 48
Committee for Cuban Democracy (CCD), 76
Common Core State Standards, 231
communities of interest: CMPS on, 258–59, *259*; conclusions, 59–60, 253; education and, 54, *55*, 56; immigration and, 17–18; labor and, 56–57, *57*, 62n5
community: arrival of Latino vessel of, 292–97; characterization of, 297; of common cultures, 17, 53, 60, 62n7, 253; common purpose and, 30–32; conclusions about, 309–11; identity, affinities, and connectiveness, 254, 256–59, *257*, *258*, *259*; language and, 27–28, 292–93; mass interactions and, 19, 22n9; nativity and, 27, 28–29; organizations, 178–80; potential of, 292; public policy linked with, 189–91; rhetoric used toward, 2–4, *5*, 7; Spanish-language media and, 292–93. *See also* pan-ethnic community
Community Block Development Grant (CBDG), 179
community building: conclusions, 101–2; language and, 27–28; mobilization of, 97–101; nativity and, 27, 28–29; partnerships and, 253–54. *See also* alliances
Community Organized for Public Services (COPS), 178–79
Community Services Organization (CSO), 178
competition, group: African Americans and, 271, 275, 280–81; American South and, 273–74; areas of, 280–81; in Florida, 305; independent actions and, 305–6; labor and, 273–74, *274*; social contact and, 270–74, *272*, *274*; theory of, 270
Congress: descriptive representation in, 158, *159*, 163; diversity growing in, *163*
Congressional Hispanic Caucus Institute (CHCI), 175–76, 302
COPS. *See* Community Organized for Public Services
Cortés, Ernesto, Jr., 179
Cortez-Masto, Catherine, 293
COVID-19 Pandemic: economic impact, 314; education and, 314–16, *315*; factors

contributing to infection, 313; inequalities revealed by, 312–13; police abuse related to, 316–18, *317*; racial justice movements and, 312–18; reporting issues, 312–13
Crawford, James, 228
crime, sanctuary cities and, 199–200
Crusius, Patrick, 1–2
Cruz, Ted, 307; El Paso shooting and, 2; Trump and, 143
CSO. *See* Community Services Organization
Cuban American National Council (CANC), 170
Cuban American National Foundation (CANF), 74, 75, 169–70
Cuban Americans for Engagement (CAFÉ), 76
Cuban Committee for Democracy, 170
Cuban Liberty and Solidarity Act, 77, 86n3
Cubans, 15, 16, 32, 33; demographic profile of, *46*, 47, 48; as entrepreneurs, 76–77; as exile community, 73–77; exile organizations of, 169–71; Florida and, 296; foreign-born, 29; foreign-born status of, 49–50, *50*, *51*, 53; geographic distribution, 63–64, *64*; González, Elian, and, 306, 311n2; Hispanic ancestries of, *36*; loose coupling and, 303–4; as outlying community, 306–7; political development and, 301; as refugees, 25; regional concentration of, 24, 25; Republican Party and, 307; second-generation, 75–76; Spanish-language media and, 292; wet foot, dry foot policy and, 169–70
culture: acculturation and, *152*; CMPS on, 258–59, *259*; commonality of, 30–32; community of common, 17; demographics and, 50–54; educational political system and, 227; language and nativity related to, 53; political participation and, 150–52; politics of, 20
cumulative voting system, 246
Curiel, Gonzalo, 99
Current Population Survey, 140
Customs and Border Protection (CBP), 194–95
CVAP. *See* citizen voting age population

DACA. *See* Deferred Action for Childhood Arrivals
Dalton, Georgia, 45, 287–88, 289

DANR. *See* Dominican American National Roundtable
DAPA. *See* Deferred Action for Parents of Americans
de facto segregated schools, 225, 321
Deferred Action for Childhood Arrivals (DACA), 105, 189, 195, 200–201, *201*
Deferred Action for Parents of Americans (DAPA), 189, 195, 200–201, *201*
Delaware Hispanic Commission, *280*
Democrat Party: movement toward, 139, *140*; perception of concern shown by, 300, *300*; soft support of, 299–300; 2014 midterm elections and, *137*; 2018 election and, 142–43
demographics: age, 58–59, *60*; conclusions, 59–60; culture and, 50–54; educational attainment, 54, *55*, 56; English proficiency, 50–52, *52*, 61n3; household income and, 56–57, *57*; labor, 56–57, *57*, 62n5; Latino population across US, 42–45, *43*, *44*; Millennials, 118; of national-origin groups, 45–48, *46*; overview, 41–42; poverty rates, 58, *59*; sociodemographic maps, 15–16; trends fueling population growth, 48–50, *49*, *50*, *51*
Department of Homeland Security, 185, 204, 213, 214, 298, 321
deportation: immigration policies, US, 201–8; TPS preventing, *204*; Trump and, 75; of veterans, 213
descriptive representation: defined, 158; diversity and, 162, *163*; rise of elected officials and, 158, *159*, 162–64; VRA and, 239, 250n4
detention centers, 202
detainer orders, 199, 322
"Discharged, Then Discarded" (ACLU report), *213*
discrimination: African Americans and, 264–65, *266*, 267, *267*, 269, 269–70, 276–77, 284n1; alliances and, 264–70, *265*, *266*, *267*, *268*, *269*, 276–77; Asian Americans and, 264–65, *266*, 267, *267*; factors contributing to, 267, *267*; identity and, 29–30; immigration and, 126, 264–65, *266*; incidence of, 264, *265*; minority status and, 31; news media and, 293; pan-ethnic community and, 30; perception of, 264–65, *266*; perpetrators of, 268;

skin tone and, *269*, 269–70, 284n1; social distance and, 274–77, 280–82; voting rights and, 148–51. *See also* racial gerrymandering; racial justice; racism

discrimination-plus model, 276, 322

domestic terrorism: El Paso shootings, 1–4; Gilroy shootings, 1, 4; Latinos as foreigners and, 4

Dominican American National Roundtable (DANR), 83, *178*

Dominicans: demographic profile of, *46*, 47–48; foreign-born status of, 49, *50*, *51*; geographic distribution, 63–64, *64*; Hispanic ancestries of, *36*; migration of, 82–84; in New York City, 288–89, 305; political development and, 301; political interest of, 83–84; population growth of, 82

Dream and Promise Act, *205*, *207*, 207–8

DREAMers, 105, 195, 200

earthquakes, *277*

economics: COVID-19 Pandemic and, 314; organizations, 172–73; political development and, 302; TPS and, *204*

Ecuadorans, foreign-born status of, 49–50, *50*

education: Arizona Senate Bill 2281 and, *186*; *Aspira v. New York Board of Education*, 168; attainment of, 54, *55*, 56; California and, 220; COVID-19 Pandemic and, 314–16, *315*; denial of, *187*; gains in, 296; IAF and, 179; increased participation in, 220–21; isolation and, 58, 62n6; Latino interest in, 216; LULAC and, 167; MALDEF, 20, 149, 165, 168–69; Mexican American Education Project, 221; MWVREP and SVREP, 177; NABE and, 171–72, 183n5; Obama and, 222–23; online, 315, *315*; *Our Nation on the Fault Line* report, 221–22; parental involvement in, 123–24; political participation and, 105, 123–24; pre-K through college enrollment, *224*; as priority, 221–23; PRLDEF, 149, 168–69, *278*; racial justice and, 314–16; segregation in, 220, *225*, 225–26; SVREP, 177; value of, 223–24, *224*; White House Initiative on Educational Excellence for Hispanics, 222–23

educational political system: arenas of, 223; bilingual education and, 227–30; Common Core State Standards and, 231; conclusions, 230–31; cultural and situational conditions, 225; cultural values and, 227; desegregation plans and, 225–26; dropouts and, 226–27; early childhood education and, 231; financial equalization in, 226; No Child Left Behind and, 230–31; Proposition 227 and, 229–30; segregation and, *225*, 225–26; sorting of students and, 230; structure of, 223–31

elected officials: female, 293; rise of, 158, *159*, 162–64, 293–94; State Senates, 294

elections: co-ethnic candidates and, 143–44; future and, 153; gender gap and, 135; grandfather clause and, 13, 22n8; Latino electorate growth and, 131–32, *132*; Latino import in, 5; Latino influence in, 133; Latinos as determinant of, 131–34; Latino share of electorate, 294, *295*; local, 130; LULAC and, 131; midterm turnouts, *135*, 135–36, *137*; mobilization and, 103, 141–43; participation critical factors, 140–41; partisanship and, 144–45; scenario setting, 130; topics addressed on, 129–30; Trump Bump and, 142; 2014 midterm, *137*; 2016, 141–42; 2018, 142–44; 2020, 103, 142, 144; of women, 144. *See also* Collaborative Multiracial Post-Election Survey (CMPS); Latino Decisions; National Association of Latino Elected and Appointed Officials; voting

elites, Latino: identity formation and, 92–95; mobilization and, 97–101; pan-ethnicity and, 26–27

El Paso shooting: Crusius and, 1–2; Latino electorate response to, 3–4; Latinos as foreigners and, 4; public officials' response to, 2–3; response to, 2–4

Enforcement Act of 1870, 236

engagement, 103

English-only initiatives, 17, 20, 50, 74, 297, 322

Escobar, Veronica, 3

Esman, Milton, 190

Espino, Salvador, 218

ethnic group: common descent and, 12; discrimination motivating, 264–70, *265*, *266*, *267*, *268*, *269*; Latinos as racial or, 34–38, *35*, *36*; national-origin groups and, 27, 40n3; partisanship and, 145; positive/negative feelings about, 258, *258*

ethnic identity, 11, 13, 22n7, 23, 24, 25, 27, 28, 29, 52, 88, 89, 94, 97, 98, 130, 143, 145, 158, 277, 285, 300, 309, 322
ethnicity: associations with, 26; census and, 9–11, 22n6; daily routines shaping, 16; discrimination and, 29–30; group identity and, 11; identity and, 11–14; pan-ethnicity, 11, 22n7; race and, 9–14; Schermerhorn defining, 12; situational, 24; "some other race" question and, 12–13, 89
exile organizations, 169–71

family: labor and, 57–58; mixed-status households, 195, 219n2
fertility patterns, 48–49, *49*
Fifteenth Amendment, 236
Florida, 76, 296; competition in, 305; González, Elian, and, 306, 311n2
Floyd, George, 316
Force Act of 1871, 236
foreign-born persons, 29, 40n4; immigration and, 49–50, *50, 51*, 52–53, 62n4; native-born and, 131; resident alien status of, 125, 128n5; US categorizations of, 128n5
Fraga, Louise R., 97, 256–57
friendship network, 271–73, *272*
future: arrival of Latino community, 292–97; conclusions about, 309–11; elections and, 153; media and, 292–93; outlier subgroups and, 306–7; pan-ethnicity viability in, *291*, 291–92; political development, 297–303; population growth projections, *286*, 286–87, *287*; scenarios, 297–309; symbolic pan-ethnic community, 303–6; topics addressed, 20–21; weakening attachments and identity, 308–9

Gaarder, A. Bruce, 228
GACLA. *See* Governor's Advisory Commission on Latino Affairs
Garcia, Alfredo, *81*
gender: alliances and, 261, *262*; CMPS and, 114, *115*, 116, 261, *262*; discrimination, contributing factors, 267, *267*; elections and, 135; gap, 146–47; political participation and, 123, 146–47
Georgia v. Ashcroft, 238, 243
Gilroy shooting, 1, 4
Global Financial Integrity, 194–95

Gómez-Aguiñaga, Barbara, 6
Gonzales, Alfonso, *213*
Gonzales, Bernardo, *213*
González, Elian, 306, 311n2
Governor's Advisory Commission on Latino Affairs (GACLA), *279*
Graham, Lindsey, *137*
great replacement theory, 2
green card, 219n6
group consciousness: conclusions about, 38–39; mobilization and, 100–101; pan-ethnic community and, 32–34
"Growth and Opportunity Project" (RNC), *137*
Guatemalans: demographic profile of, 46, 47; foreign-born status of, 49, *50, 51*, 53; Hispanic ancestries of, *36*; political refugee status and, 304; UAC from, 202. *See also* Northern Triangle
Gutiérrez, Ana Maria Sol, 164
Gutierrez, Luis, 304

Harris, Kamala, 2
health care: ACA and, 232–35; barriers to, 232–33; expansion of coverage for, 233, *233*; insurance and, 232; as priority, 231–32, *232*
Helms, Jesse, 170
Hispanic Federation (HF), *278*
Hispanic label. *See* Latino-Hispanic label
Hispanics: ancestries, *36*; coworkers and, *274*; Delaware Hispanic Commission, *280*; friendship network and, *272*; growth projections for, *286*, 286–87, *287*; identification among Latinos and, 308, *308*; identification terminology and, 88–92, *90, 91, 93*; NHLA and, 302; Pew Hispanic Center, 173, 220; racial background and, *291*; self-description by, *90, 91*; skin tone and, *269*, 269–70, 284n1; White House Initiative on Educational Excellence for Hispanics, 222–23
Hispanicity, 26, 27, 34, 323
Hofeller, Thomas, 9
Hondurans: political refugee status and, 304; TPS and, *204*. *See also* Northern Triangle
Honduras, UAC and, 202
Horne, Tom, *186*
Hufstedler, Shirley, 198
human capital, 145–46, 156n3
Hurricane Maria, 46, *277*

IAF. *See* Industrial Areas Foundation
ICE. *See* Immigration and Customs Enforcement
identity: affinities and connectiveness related to, 254, 256–59, *257*, *258*, *259*; common purpose and, 30–32; conclusions about, 38–39; daily routines shaping, 16; discrimination and, 29–30; ethnicity and, 11–14; ethnic or racial group, 34–38, *35*, *36*; Latino-Hispanic label and, 32–34; Latino political elites and, 92–95; mobilization and, 98–99; Padilla and, 94; pan-ethnic community and, 32, 33, 126–27, 254, 256–59, *257*, *258*, *259*; partisanship and, 145; race and ethnicity related to, 11–14; social, 32, 33; terminology preferences and, 88–92, *90*, *91*; topics addressed, 11, 87–88; triple oppression and, 33; vignettes, 95–97, *97*; weakening, 308–9. *See also* pan-ethnic community
Illegal Immigration Reform and Immigrant Responsibility Act (IIRIRA), 210
immigration: ACA and, 234–35; birth certificate and education denial, *187*; Citizenshipworks 2.0 and, 211; Democrat Party and, 299; discrimination and, 126, 264–65, *266*; educational attainment and, 54, *55*, 56; exile organizations and, 169–71; foreign-born status and, 49–50, *50*, *51*, 52–53, 62n4; impact of enforcement threats, 6; Latino Decisions Election Eve Poll and, *138*; laws hindering, 130; LULAC and, 167; mobilization and, 99–100, 205–6, *206*; NALEO and, 177; Operation Streamline and, *186*; partisanship and, 144–45; police collaboration programs and, *185*; political incorporation and, 150–51; political participation and, 126; political refugee status and, 304; population growth in US, *195*, 195–96; protest marches and, 7, 107, *180*; public policy and community life, 189–91; reform, 191, 197, *207*, 207–8, 210, 298–99; rural communities and, *290*; Sensenbrenner immigration bill, 107; social movements and, *180*; source countries, 196, *196*; state and local legislation, *188*; topics addressed, 184–85; Trump administration and, *185*, 185–89, 197, 205–7, *207*, 219n5; US as conflicted about, 184; US border militarization and, *186*; US panorama of, 185–91; voting and, *138*, 205–6, *206*, *207*. *See also* non-citizen immigrants
Immigration and Customs Enforcement (ICE), *185*, *186*, 199, 210
Immigration and Nationality Act (INA), 193
Immigration and Naturalization Service (INS), 192
immigration policies, US: admission categories, 197; Alabama House Bill 56, 198; Arizona Senate Bill 1070 and, 99–100, 126, *186*, *187*, 198; Arizona Senate Bill 2281 and, *186*; asylum and deportations, 201–8; Border Patrol, 192–93; CBP and, 194–95; conclusions, 217–18; contemporary patterns, *195*, 195–98, *196*; DAPA and DACA, 200–201, *201*; detention centers, 202; economically driven, 197; 1876–1924, 192; employment-based preference, 197; historical overview, 191–94; husband and wife citizenship, 192, 219n1; INS, 192; legislation, 210; mixed-status households, 195, 219n2; National Origins Act, 192; naturalization and, 208–12, *209*; 9/11 shifting, 194–95; 1924–present, 192–94; other, 205–6, 219n5; post-9/11, 210–11; preference categories in, 193–94; protection qualifications in, 203; protective state, 199; punitive state, 198–99; reform desired for, *207*, 207–8; saliency for Latinos of, 205–6, *206*; sanctuary cities and, 199–200; 1790–1875, 191–92; skills selection criteria, 197; social media and, 205, 219n5; state and local, 198–201; TPS and, *204*; 2005–present, *185*; UAC, 201–2; war and, 193
Immigration Reform and Control Act (IRCA), 191, 197
impact or influence districts, 245–46
INA. *See* Immigration and Nationality Act
Industrial Areas Foundation (IAF), 178, 179–80
INS. *See* Immigration and Naturalization Service
insurance, health, 232
intergroup cooperation, 281. *See also* alliances
internet: CMPS and, 116, *117*, 118; social movements and, *181*

IRCA. *See* Immigration Reform and Control Act

Johnson, Kenneth, *290*
Jones-Correa, Michael, 256

Kennedy, John F., 131
Keyes v. Denver I.S.D., 225–26
Kushner, Jared, 197

labor: AFL-CIO and, 172, 173; competition, group, and, 273–74, *274*; COVID-19 Pandemic and, 313; coworkers and, 273–74, *274*; Cubans and, 76–77; demographics, 56–57, *57*, 62n5; family values and, 57–58; household income and, 56–57, *57*; as immigration category, 197; location and, 56; non-citizen immigrants and, 216–17; Northern Triangle and, 78; occupational clusters within, 56; organizations, 172–73; participation rates, *55*, 56, 62n5; poverty rates, 58, *59*; TPS and, *204*; unionization rates, 173, *174, 175*
Labor Council for Latin American Advancement (LCLAA), 172
LADO. *See* Latin American Defense Organization
language: bilingual education and, 171–72, 183n5, 227–30; CMPS on, 258–59, *259*; community and, 27–28, 292–93; community building and, 27–28; English proficiency and, 50–52, *52*, 61n3; Gaarder on, 228; media and, 292–93; mobilization and, 98; NABE and, 171–72, 183n5; nativity and, 53; trends in, 28; Trump use of, 282, *283*
Lara, Perla Y., 3
Latin American Defense Organization (LADO), 95–96
Latinas. *See* women
Latinidad, 13
Latinization, in US, 4, 33
Latino Decisions: CMPS and, 253–54; election polls, 4, 6, 29, *138*; issues facing Latinos, 232, *232*; as research organization, 173–74; on saliency of immigration, 205–6, *206*; Trump language and, 282, *283*; undocumented status and, 200
Latino-Hispanic label: identification terminology and, 88–92, *90, 91*; LNS and, 34; pan-ethnic dimension and, 32–34; preference within, 90, *91*; subgroups choices related to, 90, *90*; as viable identity, 32
Latino Justice, 168–69
Latino Legacy Fund, *278*
Latino Lives in America (Fraga), 256–57
Latino National Political Survey (LNPS), 34
Latino National Survey (LNS): contact with public officials assessed in, 120, *121*, 122; education and, 123–24; focus group vignette and, 96–97, *97*; identity and labeling explored in, 34; indicators used in, 253; Latino-Hispanic label and, 34; social science data and, 129, 155n2
Latino Policy Forum, 2–3
Latinos Lives in America (Fraga), 97
Latinx, 14, 22n3, 38
LCLAA. *See* Labor Council for Latin American Advancement
leadership: conclusions, 182; in Congress, 158, *159, 163*; IAF and, 179; LULAC and, 167; NHLA, 302; state and local, 162–64, *163*; topics addressed, 19, 157–58
League of United Latin American Citizens (LULAC): overview of, 167; Puerto Rican relief from, *280*; swing vote and, 131
Leal, David, 256
legal permanent resident (LPR), 208, 219n6
Legan, William, 1
limited voting, 13, 217
linked fate, 16–17, 23, 28, 30, 38, 87, 100, 256, 259, *260, 262*, 275
LNS. *See* Latino National Survey
local level activism, 19–20
loose coupling, 303–4
Los Angeles: alliances in, *260*; OLAW in, 217; Salvadorans in, 289
LPR. *See* legal permanent resident
Lujan-Grisham, Michelle, 144
LULAC. *See* League of United Latin American Citizens

majority-minority districts, 241–42, 245
MALDEF. *See* Mexican American Legal Defense and Education Fund
Manhattan, *69*, 69–73
Mariel flotilla, 74
Martinez, Susana, 144, 163
Massachusetts, *278*
McCarran-Walter Act. *See* Immigration and Nationality Act

media: news, 293; pan-ethnicity and, 26–27; social movements and, *181*; Spanish-language, 292–93; Spanish- versus English-language, 293; transnationalism and, 216. *See also* social media
Mexican American Education Project, 221
Mexican American Legal Defense and Education Fund (MALDEF), 20, 149, 165, 168–69
Mexican Americans, 31; attachment to Mexico, 65, 86n1; Border Patrol and, 192–93; demographic profile of, 45–46, *46*; foreign-born status of, 50, *50*, *51*; geographic distribution, 63–64, *64*; Hispanic ancestries of, *36*; labels and, 93–94; LULAC and, 167; organizations historical origins and, 165–67, *166*; political development and, 301; regional concentration of, 24, 25; rhetoric and, 6; unionization rates, 173, *174*, *175*; US growth of communities of, 65–69, *68*
Mexicans: political refugee status and, 304; UAC from, 202
middle class, 296–97
Midwest Voter Registration and Education Project (MWVREP), 177
Millennials: demographics related to, 118; generations distribution in voting and, 119, *119*; ideologies of, 119–20; interests of, 118–19; political participation of, 118–20, *119*, *120*; share of racial and ethnic groups, 119, *120*
minority status, 31
mixed-status households, 195, 219n2
Mobile v. Bolden, 237, 251n3
mobilization: African Americans and, 16–17; anti-immigrant fear increasing, 215; of civic engagement, 129, 141–43; co-ethnic candidates and, 143–44; of community building, 97–101; conclusions, 101–2; defined, 97–98; elections and, 103, 141–43; group consciousness and, 100–101; identification process and, 106; identity and, 98–99; immigration and, 99–100, 205–6, *206*; political development and, 297; political participation and, 106; power relations and, 15; Proposition 187 and, 142; protest marches and, 107; reactive, 142; saliency of immigration fostering, 205–6, *206*; social movements and, *180*; Spanish-language media and, 292; targeted, 98, 106; Trump Bump and, 142; 2016 election and, 141–42; 2018 election and, 142–43; 2020 election and, 103, 142; women and, 100–101
MWVREP. *See* Midwest Voter Registration and Education Project

NABE. *See* National Association of Bilingual Educators
NALEO. *See* National Association of Latino Elected and Appointed Officials
National Association of Bilingual Educators (NABE), 171–72, 183n5
National Association of Latino Elected and Appointed Officials (NALEO): census and, 177, 183n10; immigrant potential recognized by, 218; naturalization focus of, 53–54, 132, 176–77, 211; 2016 election and, 163
National Council of La Raza (NCLR), 67. *See also* UnidosUS
National Hispanic Leadership Agenda (NHLA), 302
national-origin groups: alliances and, 281; demographics of, 45–48, *46*; ethnic group and, 27, 40n3; pan-ethnic community and, 25–26. *See also specific groups*
National Origins Act (1924), 192, 210
nativity: CMPS and, 114, *115*, 116; community building and, 27, 28–29; political participation and, 123
naturalization: Citizenshipworks 2.0 and, 211; Clinton administration and, 216; electorate growth and, 131–32; Espino and, 218; foreign-born persons and, 131; immigration policies and, 208–12, *209*; INS, 192; legislation fostering, 210; NALEO and, 53–54, 132, 176–77, 211; non-citizen veterans and, *212*; reasons for and against, *134*, 134–35; requirements, 208; surge in, 209–10; Trump administration slowing, 210; voting and registration rates related to, 212; voting turnout rates and, 131–32, *132*
NCLR. *See* National Council of La Raza; UnidosUS
Neumann-Ortiz, Christine, 3
Nevada, 293
New Mexico, 66

New York City: Dominicans in, 288–89, 305; Manhattan, *69*, 69–73; Sotomayor and, 305

NHLA. *See* National Hispanic Leadership Agenda

Nicaraguans: foreign-born status of, 49, *50*; political refugee status and, 304; TPS and, *204*

Nichols v. Houston I.S.D., 225–26

9/11, 194–95

No Child Left Behind, 230–31

non-citizen immigrants: anti-immigrant fear motivating, 215; apathy toward politics of, 212; contemporary accounts of, 217; labor and, 216–17; loyalty of, 215; OLAW and, 217; political nature and involvement of, 212–17; transnationalism and, 216; veterans, *212*

Northern Triangle: of Central America, 77–80, 81–82; geographic distribution from, 78–79; inflow to US from, 196–97; labor migration and, 78; political refugee status and, 81–82; UAC from, 202

Obama, Barack, 75, 76, 77; CANF and, 170; education initiative signed by, 222–23; mixed record of, 98–99; No Child Left Behind and, 231; Sotomayor and, 175–76; voting behavior toward, 139, *140*; young voters and, 125

Obama administration: Cuba and, 303–4; DAPA/DACA and, 200–201, *201*

Ocasio-Cortez, Alexandria, 144

O'Connor, Sandra Day, 242–43

Office of Management and Budget (OMB), 9–10

OLAW. *See* Organization of Los Angeles Workers

OMB. *See* Office of Management and Budget

Operation Streamline, *186*

Orden de los Hijos de America, 166, 180

Organization of Los Angeles Workers (OLAW), 217

organizations: business, 172–73; civil rights and litigation, 168–69; community-based, 178–80; conclusions, 182; Cuban, 169–71; dimensions and aspects of, 166, *166*; economics, 172–73; exile, 169–71; grass roots, 178–80; historical origins of, 165–67, *166*; within political institutions, 174–77; professional, 171–74; research, 173–74; social movements, *180*; topics addressed, 157–58; types of, 165; unionization rates, 173, *174*, *175*. *See also specific organizations*

Our Nation on the Fault Line (President's Advisory Commission on Educational Excellence for Hispanic Americans), 221–22

outlier subgroups, 306–7

Padilla, F.: identity and, 94; Latino consciousness idea of, 32

pandemic. *See* COVID-19 Pandemic

pan-ethnic community, 4; broader partnerships and, 283–84; conclusions about, 38–39; discrimination and, 30; group consciousness and, 32–34; identity, affinities, and connectiveness, 254, 256–59, *257*, *258*, *259*; independent actions and, 303–6; Latino elites and media related to, 26–27; Latino/Hispanic as viable identity and, 32; Latino-Hispanic label and, 32–34; linked fate and, 256; loose coupling and, 303–4; national-origin groups and, 25–26; political participation and, 126–27; social identity and, 32, 33; symbolic, 303–6; targeted mobilization and, 98; topics addressed, 18, 23–24; viability of, *291*, 291–92

pan-ethnicity: benefits of identification with, 14; defined, 11, 22n7, 86n2

partisan gerrymandering, 243–44

partisanship: elections and, 144–45; ethnic identity and, 145; 2020 election, 144

partnerships, 253–54

Paterson, New Jersey, *80*

Pence, Mike, 2

Personal Responsibility and Work Opportunity Reconciliation Act (PRWORA), 210

Peruvians: demographic profile of, *46*, 47; foreign-born status of, 49–50, *50*; in US, *80*

Pew Hispanic Center, 173, 220

police: abuse, 316–18, *317*; collaboration programs, *185*

political development: alliances and, 301; continuing, 297–303; economic resources for, 302; engagement in, 297; factors contributing to, 297–98; future of, 297–303; immigration reform and, 298–99;

local issues and, 300–301; mobilization and, 297; partisanship and, 299–300; subgroups and, 301–2; VRA and, 302–3
political incorporation: culture and, 150–52; immigrants and, 150–51; organizational affiliation and, 151–52; political participation and, 147–48; three-step process of, 150
political participation: acculturation and, *152*; analysis of contributors to, 124–27; assets of Latino, 125–26; ballot propositions and, 126, 128n7; co-ethnic candidates and, 143–44; conclusions, 108, 127, 153–55; contact with public officials as, 120, *121*, 122; critical mass in, 44, 61n1; culture and, 150–52; education and, 105, 123–24; engagement and, 103; evolution of process of, 105–8; factors influencing, 103, 105; forms of, 107–8; future, 153; gender/nativity and, 123, 146–47; identification process for, 106; immigration laws and, 126; information gathering and, 120, *121*; interest in politics and, 122; Latino, 108–18, 125–26; liabilities of Latino, 125; limited and sporadic, 106; of Millennials, 118–20, *119*, *120*; mobilization and, 106; national origin and, 150–52; other dimensions of, 120–24, *121*; pan-ethnic identity and, 126–27; political incorporation and, 147–48; population growth/distribution impacting, 126; protest marches and, 107; resident alien status and, 125; residential areas, 126; as right, 104; roles and, 148–50; rules of game and, 104, 128n1; skills and, 106, 128n2; socialization and, 105; social science research, 129, 155n2; social structures and, 148–50; socioeconomic status and, 145–47; survey sources on, 108–9; themes, 129; topics addressed, 18–19, 104–5; voting rights and, 148–51, 156n4; youth and, 105, 125. *See also* Collaborative Multiracial Post-Election Survey; elected officials; elections; Millennials; voting
political refugee status, 81–82, 304
politics, Latino. *See specific topics*
population: census measurement of, 9–11; Central and South American migration and, 288, 289; Current Population Survey, 140; CVAP, 8–9; Dalton and, 287–88; Dominican growth in, 82; Dominicans in New York City, 288–89; fastest growing, *289*; foreign- versus native-born persons and, 131; geographic dispersion of, 286–87, *287*; growth of US immigrant, *195*, 195–96; growth projections, *286*, 286–87, *287*; Portland and, 287; rural communities and, *290*; trends fueling growth in, 48–50, *49*, *50*, *51*; across US, 42–45, *43*, *44*; US states with concentrated Latino, 126, 128n6
Portland, Oregon, 287
poverty rates, 58, *59*
power relations, 15
preclearance, 148, 150, 236–238, 240–42, 244, 247, 249, 302
President's Advisory Commission on Educational Excellence for Hispanic Americans, 221
PRLDEF. *See* Puerto Rican Legal Defense and Education Fund
propositions. *See* ballot propositions
Proposition 187, 142, 149, 209, 215
Proposition 227, 150, 229, 230
protest marches, 107
PRWORA. *See* Personal Responsibility and Work Opportunity Reconciliation Act
public policy: community life linked with, 189–91; Esman and, 190; factors influencing, 190–91; immigration and, 189–91; organizations focused on, 171–74; topics addressed, 20
Puerto Rican Legal Defense and Education Fund (PRLDEF), 149; ALHM and, *278*; as civil rights organization, 168–69
Puerto Ricans, 16, 33; big three and, 15; census and, 10; demographic profile of, 46, *46*, 48; foreign-born status of, 49, *50*, *51*, 53; geographic distribution, 63–64, *64*; Hispanic ancestries of, *36*; political development and, 301; political strategies, 69; regional concentration of, 24, 25; Sotomayor and, 305
Puerto Rico: Delaware Hispanic Commission and, *280*; disasters in, *277*; financial crisis in, 71–72; GACLA and, *279*; LULAC relief for, *280*; Manhattan or, 69, 69–73; Massachusetts and, *278*; political status of, 69, 70–71, 304; race and, 72; UnidosUS program and, *278*; United Way relief for, *279*

race: associations with, 26; as binary, 37; biology and, 11–12; census and, 9–11, 22n6; census categories of, 40n2; ethnicity and, 9–14; Hispanics background, *291*; identity and, 11–14; Millennials and, 119, *120*; positive/negative feelings about, 258, *258*; Puerto Rico and, 72; social construct of, 11–12, 37; "some other race" question, 12–13, 35, *35*, *37*, 89. *See also* Collaborative Multiracial Post-Election Survey
racial gerrymandering, 238, 242
racial group, Latinos as ethnic or, 34–38, *35*, *36*
racial justice: COVID Pandemic and, 312–18; education and, 314–16; police abuse and, 316–18, *317*
racism: Latino Decisions poll and, 4; police abuse and, 316–18, *317*; Trump and, 99
rainbow coalitions, *260*, 261
REAP. *See* Rural Enterprise Assistance Project
redistricting, 15–16, 149, 168, 238, 240, 242–43
Reform Without Justice (Gonzales, Alfonso), *213*
refugee, 25, 81–82, 304
Refugee Act of 1980, 193
Reno v. Bossier Parish School Board, 238
representation: in Congress, 158, *159*, *163*; descriptive, 158, *159*, 162–64, 239, 250n4; state and local, 162–64, *163*; substantive, 164
Republican National Committee (RNC), *137*
Republican Party: Cubans ties with and, 307; disaffection with, *299*, *299*; immigration reform and, 207, *207*; partisanship and, 300; perception of concern shown by, 300, *300*; 2014 midterm elections and, *137*
resident alien status, 125, 128n5
rhetoric: hostile, *5*; Mexican Americans and, 6; response to negative, *5*; of Trump, 2–4, *5*, 7
Richardson, Bill, 143
Rios, Carmelo, *280*
RNC. *See* Republican National Committee
Roberts, John G., Jr., 9
Rodríguez, Clara, 72
Rodríguez, Lori, 68
Rodriguez, Robert, 6

Rodriquez v. San Antonio I.S.D., 226
Romero, Regina, 144, 164, 199
Romney, Mitt, 139, *140*
Rossello, Ricardo, 304
Rubio, Marco, 143, 307
rules of the game, 104, 128n1
Rural Enterprise Assistance Project (REAP), *290*
Ryan, Paul, 99

Saenz, Rogelio, 312
safe districts, 244–45
Salvadorans: demographic profile of, *46*, 46–47; foreign-born status of, 49, *50*, *51*, 53; geographic distribution, 63–64, *64*; Hispanic ancestries of, *36*; in Los Angeles, 289; political refugee status and, 304; TPS and, *204*. *See also* Northern Triangle
sanctuary cities, crime and, 199–200
Schermerhorn, R. A., 12
segregation, 220, *225*, 225–26
SEIU. *See* Service Employees International Union
Sensenbrenner Bill, *180*
Sensenbrenner immigration bill, 107
Serrano v. Priest, 226
Service Employees International Union (SEIU), 172
Shaw v. Reno, 242–43, 251n5
Shelby County v. Holder, 238
SIGs. *See* special interest groups
skin tone, *269*, 269–70, 284n1
social construct 11, 37, 42
social contact: friendship network and, 271–73, *272*; group competition and, 270–74, *272*, *274*; social network and, 271; theory of, 270, 271
social media: CMPS and, 116, *117*, 118; immigration policy and, 205, 219n5; information gathering and, 120, *121*
social networking, 116, *117*, 118, 271
sociodemographic maps, 15–16
socioeconomic status: educational attainment and, 54, *55*, 56; gains in, 296; household income and, 56–57, *57*; human capital and, 145–46, 156n3; labor and, 56–57, *57*, 62n5; resources, voting and, 145–47; social capital reinforced by, 296–97
Sotomayor, Sonia, 175–76, 305
South America. *See specific countries*

South Americans: growth rates and, 288, 289; political development and, 301; Spanish-language media and, 292
Southwest Voter Registration and Education Project (SVREP), 177
special interest groups (SIGs), 171–72, 183n5
structural factors, 18, 87, 130, 145, 147–48, 153, 155, 253
subcommunities, Latino: common purpose and, 31–32; mass interactions and, 19, 22n9; topics addressed, 18
subgroups, Latino: Colombians, *84*; conclusions, 85; Cubans, 73–77; Dominicans, 82–84, 85; geographic distribution, 63–65, *64*; independent actions of, 303–6; label choice among, 90, *90*; Mexican-origin, 65–69, *68*; Northern Triangle of Central America, 77–80, 81–82; outlier, 306–7; overview, 64–65; Peruvians, *80*; political development and, 301–2; Puerto Ricans, 69, 69–73; socioeconomic status of, 85; symbolic pan-ethnic community and, 303–6. *See also specific groups*
substantive representation, 164
Supreme Court, US, 8, 9. *See also specific cases*
SVREP. *See* Southwest Voter Registration and Education Project

targeted mobilization, 98, 106
Temporary Protected Status (TPS), *204*
Texas, 66, 68
Texas Civil Rights Project, *214*
Thornburg v. Gingles, 241–42
TPS. *See* Temporary Protected Status
Treaty of Guadalupe Hidalgo, 65
triple oppression, 33
Trump, Donald, 144; alliances and, 282, *283*; Cruz and, 143; deportations and, 75; disapproval of, 299, *299*; El Paso shooting response of, 2; Latino Decisions Election Eve Poll and, 6; Latino Policy Forum and, 2–3; negative rhetoric of, 2–4, *5*, 7; racialization by, 99; voting behavior toward, 139, *140*
Trump administration: asylum protection qualifications and, 203; citizenship status question and, 7–9, *8*; COVID-19 Pandemic and, 314; DACA terminated by, 201; immigration and, *185*, 185–89, 197, 205–7, *207*, 219n5; immigration policies, 2005–present, *185*; immigration reform and, 207, *207*; naturalization slowed by, 210; other immigration policies of, 205–6, 219n5; point system of, 197; sanctuary cities and, 199–200; TPS and, *204*; veterans' path to citizenship and, *214*
Trump Bump, 142
287(g) Program, *185*
Tyler v. Phloe, 168

UAC. *See* unaccompanied alien children
UFW. *See* United Farm Workers of America
unaccompanied alien children (UAC), 201–2
undocumented persons: ACA and, 234–35; Latino Decisions and, 200; percentage of Latinos knowing, *203*; 2006 immigrant protest marches and, 7
UnidosUS: evolution of, 165–66; Puerto Rico and, *278*
United Farm Workers of America (UFW), 172, 173
United States Mexico Canada Agreement (see USMCA), 301
United Service Workers Union, 172–73
United States (US): American South, 273–74; border militarization, *186*; fertility patterns, 48–49, *49*; foreign-born people in, 29, 40n4; as immigrant nation, 184; immigration panorama in, 185–91; Latinization in, 4, 33; Latino population across, 42–45, *43*, *44*; mass shootings and, 2; national-origin groups demographic profiles, 45–48, *46*; naturalization in, 53–54; Peruvians in, *80*; population and, 42–45, *43*, *44*, *126*, 128n6, *195*, 195–96; Refugee Act of 1980, 193; Supreme Court, 8, 9. *See also* immigration policies, US; *specific cities and states*
United Way, *279*
University of Nebraska (UNL), *290*
US. *See* United States
US Hispanic Chamber of Commerce (USHCC), 172

VAP. *See* voting age population
Vargas, Arturo, 163
Velázquez, Nydia, 304
Venezuelans: demographic profile of, *46*, 47; foreign-born status of, 49–50, *50*
VEP. *See* voting eligible population

Veteran Deportation Prevention and Reform Act, *214*
veterans, *212, 213, 214*
Voces de la Frontera, 3
Voter ID laws, 247–49, *248*
voting: age and eligibility for, 294, *294*; bloc, 130; conclusions, 153–55, 249–50; culture and, 150–52; democratic candidates and, 139, *140*; eligibility to, 132–33, *133*, 136, 294, *294, 295*, 296; gender gap and, 146–47; generations distribution in, 119, *119*; human capital and, 145–46, 156n3; ideology and, 282; immigration, saliency of, for, 205–6, *206*; immigration and, *138*, 205–6, *206, 207*; immigration reform and, *207*; Latino Decisions Election Eve Poll and, *138*; national origin and, 150–52; naturalization related to, 212; naturalized citizens turnout rates, 131–32, *132*; photo-identification requirements, 149; political incorporation and, 147–48; politics of alliances and, 282; psychological/political attitudes and, 147–48; registration and turnout, 134–39, *137*; rights, 148–51, 156n4; social structures and, 148–50; socioeconomic status and, 145–47; SVREP, 177; swing, 131; turnout, 128n4, 131–32, *132*, 294–95, *295*; 2014 party affect and, *138*; VAP and VEP related to, 136
voting age population (VAP), 136
voting eligible population (VEP), 136
voting rights: political participation and, 148–51, 156n4; topics addressed, 20, 235
Voting Rights Act (VRA), 13; African Americans and, 235–36; alternative voting system and, 241, 246–47; amendments to, 237–38; at-large election systems and, 241; conclusions, 249; cumulative voting system and, 246; descriptive representation and, 239, 250n4; *Georgia v. Ashcroft* and, 243; ID laws and, 247–49, *248*; impact or influence districts and, 245–46; Latino politics and, 238–44; limited returns of, 239–40; majority-minority districts and, 241–42, 245; *Mobile v. Bolden* and, 237, 251n3; partisan gerrymandering and, 243–44; passage of, 236; preclearance section of, 302–3; problems addressed in, 235; provisions of, 236; rise of elected officials and, 239, 241; safe districts and, 244–45; Section 2 of, 236, 250n2; Section 4 of, 238; Section 5 of, 236, 238; *Shaw v. Reno* and, 242–43, 251n5; *Thornburg v. Gingles* and, 241–42; voter suppression and, 247–49, *248*
VRA. *See* Voting Rights Act

Westberry v. Sanders, 243
Westminster v. Mendez, 225
wet foot, dry foot policy, 169–70
White House Initiative on Educational Excellence for Hispanics, 222–23
Wilson, Pete, 50
women: alliances and, 282; CMPS and, 114, *115*, 116; elected officials who are, 293; mobilization and, 100–101; 2018 election and, 144
Wu, Michael, *260*

youth: political participation and, 105, 125; political socialization of, 125. *See also* Millennials